W9-AXA-539

Plans, Pointers, Reasons and Resources
7th Edition

Theodore E. Wade, Jr., *General Author and Editor*

Authors of special chapters

Virginia Birt Baker
Sandra Ballard
Ruth Beechick
Kathy Babbitt
Laura Coker
Inga Dubay
Donna Faturos
Kevin Ferreira
Carol Sue Fromboluti
Barbara Getty
Sandra Gogel
Meg Johnson
Christopher J. Klicka
Kay Kuzma
David D. & Laurie Lanier
Jonathan Lindvall
Edwin Myers
Brian D. Ray
Marilyn Rockett
Margaret Savage
Cindy L. Short
J. Wesley Taylor, V
Mark B. Thogmartin
Sue Welch
Jackie Wellwood
Velma Woodruff

Other contributing authors

Debra A. Deffinbaugh
Cathy Duffy
Michael P. Farris
Lyn A. Gatling
Gayle Graham
Gregg Harris
Lorinda Lasher
Raymond & Dorothy Moore
Karl Reed
Monroe Morford
Kathryn Perkinson
J. Michael Smith
Kim Solga
Judy Stark
Karen Wade
Jon Wartes

Artists

Lishi Laurance, Buck Jones (text illustrations); Laurie Barrows, Jonathan Wade (cover)

Gazelle Publications
Excellence in education since 1976

Gazelle Publications

11580 Red Bud Trail, Berrien Springs, MI 49103
(616) 471-4717 or for sales information (800) 650-5076

Online catalog at www.hoofprint.com E-mail kivu@juno.com or
tedw@andrews.edu or check website for current e-mail address

Printed in the United States of America.

Library of Congress Catalog Card Number: 97-71346
International Standard Book Number: 0-930192-36-2

For parents
who sense a responsibility
for guiding their children
to wholesome development
in every area of life.

Contents

Principles of Home Education

Areas of Learning

Theory Into Practice

Appendices — Resource Information

Forms for Keeping Records

1

The Starting Line

My colleagues and I have written about purposes, methods and rewards for parents who teach their own children instead of sending them off to school. A glance at the table of contents will reveal the broad scope of topics, from planning, to teaching methods, to finding help, to making it all work for your own situation. After all, your real purpose centers in your children. We trust that their experience will become richer.

Whether novice or veteran, you'll find here a warehouse filled with ideas to help make your teaching better and more enjoyable. Although I have arranged the chapters in a logical order, they should also make sense independently.

This 7th edition is really the 9th. The first appeared in 1980 with a different title, *School at Home*, and there were two 6th editions (the second a minor revision). During this time, home schooling has become much more popular and better understood. Legislatures have made laws dealing specifically with home teaching. Numerous programs, products, newsletters, and support groups have been set into motion by people who have seen a need and filled it.

We have updated, clarified, and expanded many of the chapters from the previous edition of this book. The appendix section has been expanded and is better organized. The reviews, incidentally, are good for more than ideas about what to buy. They help you form concepts about what sorts of things lead to good learning, and they sometimes offer teaching ideas. So when you are thinking about what to teach in a certain subject, read the chapters involved and browse through the corresponding appendix section.

Information such as we have shown about supporting organizations, and laws will change in time, but having access to these resources is worth the trouble of a few invalid entries.

I should note particularly Appendix H, "Ideas That Work." It's worth reading through carefully as if it were a chapter.

Choosing What to Read In This Book

At the end of this brief introduction, you will be invited to join one of several guided tours of the book. The tours direct you to recommended chapters depending on your particular interest. Of course you can leave your tour at any time to visit other chapters. And after you have begun teaching, you will want to return to read new material or to reread from the new perspective of experience.

For a one-minute lesson in how to home teach, see the side bar on page 19.

The more I learn about learning, the more I see the principles of true life preparation illuminated in God's ancient book. Of course we have written for all parents who love their kids. Here and there we mention a Bible principle, but we have tried to minimize elaboration, leaving you to draw your own conclusions.

Let's pull together

To a certain degree, those of us involved in home schooling have tended to pull apart in the way we organize ourselves. It's a coin with two sides. Some feel the importance of fellowship on common spiritual interests while others work for openness and the rights of all parents to teach their own children. Of course, we really need both unity based on common interests, and diversity to profit from each other's strengths. Whenever possible, let's work together while respecting the right of assembly for those with common beliefs. After all, most social groups feel the importance of outreach as well as of internal unity.

About the authors

This book's wide range of strength I owe to the team of contributing authors. Although they come from different religious backgrounds, they bring a unity of conviction about the importance of quality in home education. All of them are well prepared to write on their particular topics. You will find notes about them with the chapters they have written or have contributed to.

My wife, Karen, has helped set the direction for our little publishing company since its beginning in 1976. She is a CPA by profession and now works for a Christian university. Her name appears on the title page for contributing several book reviews.

In addition to what you read in the biographical note on the back cover, it might interest you to know that Karen's and my children are adults now. The youngest, Melvin, is principal of a Christian school in Niles, Michigan. His wife is Lois. Our daughter, Dorothea, is a registered dietitian. Her husband is a physical therapist. They, too, live in the Niles area. Our older son, Tim, is a computer programmer living north of Elkhart, Indiana with his wife, Charilyn, who is a nurse. In all, we have five young grandsons. God has been good.

Guided tours

Since people who open this book will have somewhat different objectives, I have prepared lists of suggested chapters. Of course if you want specific information such as the address of a certain supplier, you can use the table of contents or the index for direction. The tours are for groups of people with different general interests, as noted. *The lighter chapter numbers indicate lower priority reading. Also, note only parts of chapters are recommended in a few cases.*

TOUR A

For those investigating the idea of home schooling.

And browse other chapters.

TOUR B

For the education of young or preschool children.

TOUR C

For people who are new to home schooling and are planning elementary school teaching.

TOUR D

For parents with a year or more experience who are continuing at the elementary school level.

TOUR E

For those interested in high school at home.

Plus more from section I if new to home education.

TOUR F

For teachers of children with handicaps.

TOUR G

For teaching gifted children

Read the chapter, "Teaching Gifted Children," then 18, 19, 20, 51 and others you feel might apply.

From all of us

In writing out our thoughts, we have enjoyed thinking how you would study our words and put some of the ideas to work in your own home school. Let us know how we can improve. Responsible home teaching calls for purpose and effort – for guiding your children to wholesome development in every area of life. In the process, you are building a relationship to enjoy now and for the years to come. We wish you the best of success with what will probably be one of the most important jobs you will ever do – teaching your own children.

Theodore E. Wade, Jr. (Ted)

Principles of Home Education

SECTION ONE

2

The Home School Alternative

As parents you are fundamentally responsible for the development of your children. Any school is only an extension of the home. Education always begins at home, even when parents don't care about their children and have no plan for guiding them. Most parents, however, do care, at least to a degree, how their children develop. And this concern doesn't stop when the children are sent off to school. As a rule teachers, too, want good education for the children sent to them, and they work for it.

Then why do some parents teach their children at home? Maralee Mayberry did a research study to determine why Oregon home schooling families had opted against classroom schools.[1] Essentially all the parents in her study wanted to protect family unity, to guard against unwanted ideologies or influences, and to avoid control by public schools. But four motivating factors tended to classify them into groups. The proportions of parents in each group appear in the pie chart on this page.

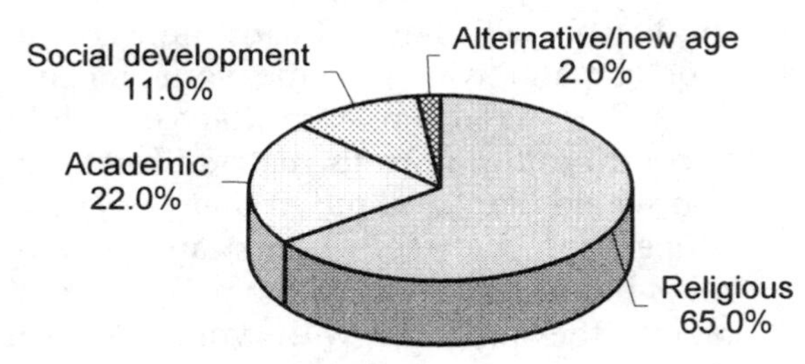

Questions to answer

You no doubt already have particular reasons for feeling that the popular system of education is unsuitable for your children. We won't take much paper and ink trying to convince you about what you already believe. But is school at home really your ideal solution or might another alternative be better? Are you qualified to teach? What all is involved in a good home school program? Can legal problems be avoided? When and how should home education begin?

In this book, my co-authors and I will help you answer these questions for your own family. Then if you choose home education, we'll provide nuts and bolts for getting started plus advanced ideas to help you lead your children on to excellence.

Even before home schooling became well publicized, people were teaching their own children. Most of these, however, chose the alternative because they were too far from a school or because exceptional needs of a child prevented success in the classroom; while a few braved tradition to teach at home just because they realized they could do it better.

The great majority of home schooling parents now enjoy the full cooperation or the tacit approval of the public school authorities, fulfilling a responsibility they consider to be their own - raising their children. A few have had to stand up for their rights - and yours.

Facing a school problem

To help you as a parent think through the question of whether or not you should teach your own children, we will first assume that you see a problem with the school situation they would otherwise face.

Conflicts or problems are often developed by differences in philosophy. Everyone has a philosophy. You have one, too. Your philosophy is the way you feel you should relate to the world around you. It's what you consider to be truth - how you decide what is right and wrong. As a parent, you train your children based on your philosophy or understanding of truth.

Before you plant your flag pole for a home school, let's consider some other options for solving a school problem:

➢ Reform the school. This is in somewhat the same category as moving mountains but there are ways to go about it if your philosophy is in harmony with that of a significant number of other parents.

➢ Help the teacher see your need. This is certainly worth considering if the issue centers around the teacher. You could run into a brick wall here, but more than likely you will be surprised to learn that the teacher will have already noticed the problem and will welcome your suggestions. You may even learn that your child is contributing more to the problem than you would like to admit. In that case, solid cooperation between home and school may be wiser than running away and taking the problem with you. We will discuss this more in Chapter 4.

➢ Talk with the principal if you have not been able to work out a satisfactory understanding with the teacher. Keep your mind open to the possibility that you may have misinterpreted the situation. It may be possible to have your child assigned to a different teacher.

➢ Consider private school enrollment. Ask about the school's philosophy of education. Visit the school. If it's a junior or senior high, it will likely have a school paper. Ask to see copies. Look through some of the textbooks. Study the school catalog. If you find a reasonable match with your own ideals, including what you consider to be a proper balance between moral, intellectual, and physical education, this could be your solution.

➢ Hire a teacher and establish a private school. Due to past struggles for religious liberty, private schools are more or less free to teach what they want, usually with uncertified teachers.

➢ Consider a home school. Probably you already have, since that's what this book is all about. Home schools are operated in a variety of ways from being closely tied to a classroom to being entirely independent. I'll list the general categories in that order.

Home school organizational options
arranged in the order of increasing independence.

➢ Ask a public or private classroom school to enroll your child as an extension student. This may be called independent study. Most any school can enroll your child as a home student. They routinely supervise home study for those who are sick and unable to come to school. However, the school principal, if not in sympathy with home schools, may refuse because even once-a-week visits mean more teacher time and increased expense. This and other options are discussed further in the chapter, "Developing an Educational Framework."

➢ Join or establish a cooperative school. This plan uses the abilities of several families. It could include some study in individual homes. The extra transportation and administrative time needed compared to the one-family school may offset some of the saving in teaching time, but for many homes there could be significant advantages. More on this in the chapters, "Planning for Teaching," and "Teenagers Taught at Home."

➢ Arrange for a supervising teacher. In-home guidance by a certified teacher is generally a legal option. You may be able to arrange for your teacher through a controlling organization. You still do most of the teaching, but you have help a certain number of hours each week.

➢ Establish a home school using correspondence courses. Several schools offer home study programs (See Appendix A). At the elementary level, the parent or tutor teaches from lesson plans and materials furnished by the school. Secondary level students follow a study guide for each course which coordinates their study from books and other materials; lessons are sent in for grading, and supervised examinations are taken at regular intervals.

➢ Choose a curriculum package. A number of programs are available which provide basic materials for practically a whole learning program for the elementary grades. This option is similar to correspondence school enrollment, except that textbooks and workbooks are replaced by materials created by the organization. As a rule, you buy the package without ongoing guidance. This category includes work-texts where the student progresses through one booklet after another.

The fact that these programs are designed for home teaching is an advantage, but they have the potential danger of not having the breadth characteristic of traditional textbooks. Textbooks do generally have more material than you may need or want, but they are designed as tools. Choosing what seems best or most interesting while skipping other parts is often appropriate. Please understand that I am not offering this as a blanket criticism, but as a possibility that you might want to be alert to.[2] You may find the package still the best for your needs. You can add enrichment, as appropriate, considering your child's interests.

➢ Enroll your child with a home schooling guidance center. This may also be called a school services organization or an umbrella school. You carry the primary responsibility for your school. The center may provide such services as helping you decide what to teach and selling you some or all of the materials. It may provide standardized tests and keep your records on file. You would be expected to ask for counsel whenever you need it. Your home school may be considered a branch of the supporting organization.

➢ Establish an independent home

How to set up a home school

A one-minute lesson

The process isn't really difficult. You don't need to know everything professional teachers should know.

- ❑ *Think about what you believe education should do for your kids. Discuss the idea with your family.*
- ❑ *Pray for wisdom.*
- ❑ *Read the essential chapters in this book and browse through the rest. Read other books on the topic.*
- ❑ *Ask your state or area organization for a basic information packet.*
- ❑ *Choose an organizational approach.*
- ❑ *Find a support group and pick up ideas from people who have already been home teaching.*
- ❑ *Purchase the essential materials you will need and sketch out your overall plan.*
- ❑ *Arrange to satisfy legal requirements.*
- ❑ *Make friends with families who have similar interests.*
- ❑ *Expect to modify your program as you discover what works best for your situation.*

school where you do the planning as well as the teaching. This is a good choice at the preschool level for parents who have chosen to delay their child's entrance into formal learning. Also, parents who feel that learning should have relatively little formal structure would likely choose this option. Although the independent home school which follows the typical school curriculum requires more preparation, it is possible for most parents at the elementary level. In secondary school, it might be a little more difficult to do a good job without subject matter and/or teaching expertise.

The topic of establishing various types of home schools is discussed throughout this book.

Advantages of school at home

Teaching your own children at home is a serious commitment, not a decision you can easily change from day to day like subscribing to a newspaper. You can weigh the pros and cons for your own family as you read through the pages of this book. To start your thinking, here are some points to consider. Some may not apply in your situation, and you may want to add others.

- *In a home school you can educate your children according to your own convictions.* For example, if you believe God inspired the Scriptures as a guide for living, you will certainly want the Bible to be a key source in the education of your children.

Your child cannot live around other children who think constantly about sex and drugs, and who lie, cheat, steal, and use obscenities without being influenced. If you are tempted to think that your kids know better, that they will turn out all right in spite of their surroundings, beware! Mistakes here are for keeps. You will never be able to turn back the years to do your job over again.

Many parents object to strategies of modern public schools. In the chapter on teaching social studies, we will examine the educational practices known as "values clarification" and "moral development." In the chapter, "Developing an Educational Framework," we discuss outcome-based education, a current concern of home schooling leaders.

- *The competitive nature of classroom schools hurts both winners and losers.* Games and grades are generally dealt with in modern schools to minimize competition, but the media and Barbie dolls still teach children the wrong goals. Competitive sports still teach youth to hate their enemies, and pairing off as couples begins in elementary school. Children who have developed a degree of maturity can handle mild competition without taking it personally, but school is the major occupation for children and youth. It counts big. In a home school, the child can focus attention on achieving goals rather than on trying to be better than the rest or worrying about being a loser.

- *A home environment enhances social development.* Home schools have a more restricted social atmosphere. This most obvious distinction is often considered a disadvantage. The question deserves attention. In our chapter on early education you will see that, for the social development of small children, home is far better than school. Older children and youth are naturally more peer-oriented and certainly need to know how to relate.

Home school parents should assure that they, and even the younger children, can be around friends. However, the most important society even for high school youth is the family unit. This association should provide the principle elements for social development: love, security, discipline, interdependence and responsibility. Friends outside the family are important, but they don't have to be present every day for the formation of socially well-developed individuals. In the chapter on social development, I have quoted a letter describing the Woodruff family home school. Their children were obviously not socially impaired even though taught at home through high school.

▪ *School at home encourages what we might call "self-propelled" learning.* In a classroom it's easy to drift along with the crowd depending on the calendar to get through the year. Studying alone, the learner soon realizes that progress is a direct result of effort.

The self-directed student selects and independently pursues objectives and projects – under supervision, of course. The greater motivation leads to more achievement. Although home school doesn't automatically result in self-directed learning, the one-to-one relationship gives more opportunity to provide for it.

▪ *Home schools educate children and youth who live too far away to attend the public school or to attend a private school with a compatible philosophy.* Often even when school bus service is available, the ride to and from school takes too much time and provides too much poorly supervised association. For parents who travel extensively and for those in foreign countries, distance is an obvious reason to choose home school; authorities don't generally question it under these circumstances.

▪ *School at home is often an advantage for children with problems which threaten their opportunity to achieve.* Self-confidence and self-control are easily crushed in a competitive classroom environment. Children can't concentrate on school assignments, and they begin to fail. At the same time, their behavior problems generally increase. They can't get along with other students. Sometimes they withdraw. They view themselves as abnormal and unable, and everyone else sees them in that same light.

Removed from the damaging atmosphere for a year or so and given patient encouragement, the child can begin to achieve. Success builds self-confidence, and restores the normal independent psychological function of the individual.

Some children with serious physical or mental handicaps are often better off in a special environment outside of regular schools. Attendance laws provide for this type of exception, although specially trained teachers may be required.

▪ *Individualized instruction may keep efforts directed toward specific learning needs.*

▪ *Flexibility allows convenient scheduling of family trips and other activities.* Special trips or activities may be planned around the father's available time. Unusual learning opportunities may require being able to attend an event when classroom schools would be in session.

▪ *Relief from tuition expense.* If Mom works, private-school tuition for one child may be cheaper than her staying home to teach. But when there are several or when the mother's presence at home is valued for the sake of a preschooler, home school becomes the better economic choice.

▪ *School at home brings parents a sense of satisfaction.* It's not easy, but rewarding accomplishments seldom are. You can develop a much fuller relationship with your children if you teach them yourself. And as a bonus, you will sharpen your own knowledge and skills in the subjects they are learning.

Disadvantages

On the other side of the coin, what difficulties might home school parents face?

▪ *Conflicts with school authorities.* This concern may cause those considering home school the greatest hesitation. Actually, only a small number of home schools are challenged and some of them would not have been if they had taken more care to establish good legal footing. There are ways to deal with the problem. We discuss them in Chapter 5, "Keeping Peace With School Authorities."

▪ *Time.* Although you will probably spend less time than a classroom teacher would, you cannot just give your child a book and go off to town. Quality home teaching takes time. We discuss this more later.

▪ *Risk from a poor home environment.* Not many parents in an unsatisfactory home even consider teaching their own children. When they do, the children at greatest risk are sometimes ones whose parents are least apt to admit their own weaknesses. The biggest question to ask is, How are my children being influenced by attitudes and habits of others in the household? Let's continue this discussion in the next chapter.

Public Schools

One of the strongest motivators for choosing to teach kids at home is the feeling that classroom schools of any kind are categorically bad, public schools are worse, and US public schools are the very worst. My wife and I chose not send our kids to public school when schools were much better now. But as you and I consider all the things we hear and read, let's remember an interesting phenomenon that tends to distort our reasoning. It can happen in any group that arises from the perceived inferiority of birds of a different feather. I'm talking about the them–and–us attitude. We see it, for example, between political groups and between religious groups. It is enhanced by fostering a spirit of competition. When leaders arise to expose the evils of a group we do not identify ourselves with, we tend to gobble up the bad news as fast as they dish it out. Somehow we tend to feel superior because of real or perceived weaknesses in those we compare ourselves with. Most of us don't intend unreasonable attitudes. They just develop naturally. Politicians seek support by making people feel they would be saved from terrible opposing candidates.

Now let's think about schools. When US President Bush was pushing his ideas about educational reform (or being pressured to push them), he needed some facts. He apparently wanted to be the brave knight who saved the beautiful maiden. So Sandia National Laboratories took ten million dollars to look at public schools. Why didn't people hear about what they found? Likely because things weren't as bad as Bush had hoped.

Here are some of the Sandia study results:[4] ❧ IQ scores of students are seven points above those of their parents and 14 points ahead compared to their grandparents. ❧ Since 1975, Scholastic Aptitude Test scores had been increasing for individual groups (whites, blacks, Asians, etc.). Part of the apparent decline before was because more of the less able students were being included in the research studies. In other words, the lower score averages didn't mean the students were worse. ❧ The US had the highest rate of earned bachelor degrees in the world. And it is best for women and minorities. ❧ Our per–pupil costs were less than those of Japan, Austria, Denmark, West Germany, Canada, and several other industrialized nations. ❧ Our dropout rate was the best in the world; 85% of our high school students graduate.

In 1995 another major study confirmed the picture. It was conducted by the Rand Corporation which specializes in educational research. ☙ They found that test scores on the National Assessment of Educational Progress have been rising slowly over the past 20 years. This is the only testing which takes a reliable cross-section of the nation's students. Minorities had been improving. Also the report found that 87% of those entering college, graduated, while only 57% did in 1957.[4]

Of course, there's bad news, too. And it's not getting any better. Plenty of other people have already told you about it. I have mentioned some positive things simply to remind you (and me) to think clearly and act responsibly. We should note one negative point that gives a little different perspective from what you may have heard: Many educators interviewed for the Sandia report expressed the feeling that with more working parents, society is expecting the schools to engineer social change by meeting more nonacademic needs. Here's more unpleasant news:

☙ The Third International Mathematics and Science Study (1997) ranked the US near the bottom in the list of participating nations for 12th graders (with 4th graders slightly above average.) Numbers for science literacy, also measured by the study, were better but still 2 percentage points less then the average of the 32 nations[5] . Numbers like this are fuel for school criticism, but. . . .

☙ Set this information against reading literacy comparisons reported in 1990. In the largest such study up to its time (and perhaps since), the US ranked second among 32 countries. Both the US and New Zealand showed well in spite of their whole language emphasis.[6]

☙ One more point of interest relates to reading ability. Our frequent return to the old ways of teaching, is partly based on the idea that the old methods were better. Then-and-now studies are difficult because standardized testing and record keeping have not been prevalent until more recent years. But the twenty some studies comparing spans between 1845 and 1976 point mostly to improvement over time. None give evidence of declines in reading ability. [7]

While achievement, so far, looks good in US schools, guns come to school even in more prosperous neighborhoods. In the lower socio-economic areas, police patrol the halls and kids are screened by metal detectors. Often the kids essentially control the schools. I write from personal know-ledge about schools not far from where I live in Southwest Michigan. The attitude toward sex taught on TV pervades the schools and is followed with plagues of disease and suffering. I don't see this situation getting any better. It will likely affect overall academic success, too. So listen with both ears and read with both eyes.

Transfer to a conventional school

Parents are sometimes concerned about whether children from home education programs can easily transfer to classroom schools. This doesn't qualify as a "disad-vantage," but it's appropriate to discuss in this context. Transfer seldom presents any serious difficulty. Tests may be given if the school personnel doubt your judgment about grade placement. Faithfully taught home school students generally show up very well. The fact that your home school was unofficial or that you were uncertified is not likely to cause a problem. Most administrators would include other factors in their consideration. Accreditation would not affect elementary grades. Achievement tests and evidence of course work could validate secondary credits.

Being placed in the wrong grade is unlikely. Deciding the proper grade should depend on more than test results. Repeat-ing a grade may be wise, but if your child only missed studying South America and a minor math concept which the others were exposed to, and if studying extra to catch up is a realistic expectation, he or she could avoid the discouragement of being a grade behind. Of course pushing ahead when seriously lacking preparation will very likely compound the problem. You might ask for a trial period or seek wider counsel. And in any case, resist letting parental pride make the decision.

Whenever students make a transition from one type of school to another, a certain degree of adjustment in learning style is necessary. Home schooled students coming into a classroom situation sometimes have to learn: (1) to get more information from lectures, (2) to move more with the class, performing particular learning tasks at stipulated times, (3) to move ahead in a study task without someone standing by to prompt each step, (4) not to leave their seats at liberty, and (5) that they don't "know it all."

These minor adjustments may be a little more difficult than changes students make in the transition from one school to another, but you can prepare your child by: expecting self-direction, planning opportunities for learning from lectures, and by arranging for group interaction.

How well does home schooling work academically?

By Jon Wartes

In the interest of precision, I would propose breaking the question into three parts: (1) Does home schooling work? (2) Do homeschoolers do better than conventionally educated students? (3) Is home schooling a superior educational method compared to conventional schooling?

1. Does home schooling work? The answer is "yes." There is a wealth of anecdotal information in the home schooling literature showing positive examples of home schooling. Also, virtually all existing tabulations of test score data from homeschooler groups around the nation have produced mean scores in the average to above average range.

2. Do homeschoolers do better than conventionally educated students? The present evidence is inconclusive. The best studies so far (those having the least sources of potential bias and the largest sample size) have frequently shown above average scores for home schooled children, but not always strongly so. The primary problem with all of these studies is that test scores from a significant proportion of homeschoolers are not available to the researcher. There is a belief that parents of the lower scoring students would be less likely to have the child tested or to report the scores compared to parents of higher scoring children. Because homeschoolers tend to be an independent lot, obtaining a systematic sampling remains a difficult challenge to home school researchers.

3. Is home schooling an academically superior educational method compared to conventional schooling? There is virtually no empirical evidence available on this topic. While homeschoolers commonly do well, the proper research design would need to show that any difference is not due to other factors. For example, it is commonly acknowledged that the homeschoolers have parents who are more dedicated and supportive than usual. Is the academic outcome a result of the home schooling or of having supportive parents? It is commonly observed that conventionally educated children who have supportive parents also tend to do well.

Jon Wartes

Evidence of success

Do children taught at home really learn as well as they would in a traditional classroom school? I've told you they can, but how do you know I'm right? Other authors have described their success with home education, but you have to ask whether or not their cases are typical. Parents whose home schooling experience failed would not likely write a book about it.

Research studies provide reliable indications of the validity of home schooling if care is taken not to overgeneralize from the findings. Evidence from the success of home schooled students, contrary to how it appears, does not clearly prove the superiority of studying at home. Children of parents who care that much usually do better anyway. Still, research helps us understand. Of course, in particular situations home education may clearly be an academic advantage. And we would not want to forget that the strongest reasons for home schooling do not depend on test scores.

I asked project leader Jon Wartes for his observations on what research really tells us about the achievement of home educated students. His reply is in a side bar.

Findings

Many researchers have studied home schooling. I'll describe the largest study, one conducted by Brian Ray for the Home School Legal Defense Association.[8] During the 1994–'95 and the '95–'96 school years, nearly 6000 survey forms were distributed to a cross section of home school families and to home schooling groups for their members. 1,657 were returned. Researchers never get 100% returns on a large population sample like this, but 28% is lower than ideal. The results may be considered fairly dependable, however, because results of several factors in this survey are similar to those of Ray's 1990 study which had a good 70% return rate.[9] I'll comment on some of the significant results.

Number of children home schooled The estimate for the fall of 1996 is 1.23 million! The number has been growing at about 10% per year.

Achievement In '95–'95 test scores in language, math, science, social studies, and study skills were at the 85th percentile for the basic battery (set of tests) and 87% for the complete battery. By definition, the national average is the 50th percentile.

Effect of teacher certification Students with one parent who had been certified at some time achieved only 3 percentile points more than those with both never-certified parents.

Effect of educational level of parents Achievement is affected very little by their parents' attainments. A mother without having completed high school may expect nearly the same success as one with a college degree (5 percential points less). For public schools students, there is a big difference.[10]

Minority achievement I was pleased to see that reading scores of minority students were the same as for whites and math scores were only 5 points lower.

Cost per student compared to public school Home school families pay on an average of $546 per child where public education costs nearly ten times that amount. Of course if all the public school teachers and administrators worked for free and they paid nothing for their buildings, then the comparison might be different.

Effect of government regulation The degree of sate control over home education makes no significant difference in how well the children do.

Curriculum types in use Most parents (71%) were found to design their own curriculum, hand picking their materials. Nearly 24% used a curriculum package. Libraries are visited once or twice a month by over half of the families. Another 38% visit 3 to 5 times.

Use of computers 84% of families use a computer for learning.

Socialization An amazing 98% of kids are involved in 2 or more social activities. 94% watch TV less than 3 hours per week compared to 38% of public school students.

Ages of students 20% are high school age.

❈

In the chapter, "Social Development," we look at evidence that home schooling does more for children socially than giving them an "equal opportunity." Some of the best help in deciding whether or not to teach your children at home can come from others who are doing it. Talk to several families including one who has been home teaching for several years. Talk with the kids, too.

As you evaluate the possibility of school at home for your family, many factors must figure into your consideration. Some parents have to reject the idea, but the overall advantages are greater than many people realize.

Endnotes

1. "Why Home Schooling? A Profile of Four Categories of Home Schoolers" by Maralee Mayberry, in *Home School Researcher*, Sept., 1988. Published by the National Home Education Research Institute. (See appendix C.)

2. Mary McCarthy of Lakewood, New Jersey told me: "Something that I would like to see addressed is the burnout that comes with packaged curriculums. An awful lot of new home schoolers feel very overburdened by the regimen and "must-do" of them. They end up squabbling with the kids because the lessons aren't getting done about 6 months into it. There's that temptation to buy everything you see without regard to actually using it. . . . We need to address the idea that we're not all Colfaxes and expectations shouldn't be quite so high. New home schoolers feel like failures when they can't keep up and that's not right" (personal correspondence, 4/12/1993).

3. Ken Schroeder, "In Brief," *Education Digest*, April, 1993, p. 72, reporting on a 1991 study. Also *Phi Delta Kappan*, pp. 718–721, May, 1993.

4. The Rand Corporation, *Student Achievement and the American Family*, 1995, Discussed in *Practioner*, Dec., 1996 in an article by James Haas.

5. *U.S. Showing in Twelfth-Grade International Math Study Unacceptable, But Not Unexpected.* News release from National Council of Teachers of Mathematics reported by PR Newswire, Feb. 24, 1998.

6. Robert Rothman, "U.S. Ranks High In International Study of Reading," in *Education Week*, Sept. 30, 1992. The article compares this good news to the ratings in math and science.

7. "Today's Students Read Better Than Yesterday's: Here's Proof," *Education Digest*, Jan., 1994, from *Journal of Reading*, Sept., 1993, 28–40.

8. Brian D. Ray, *Home Education Across the United States*, 1997. Available from the National Home Education Research Institute, P.O. Box 13939, Salem, OR 97309; (503) 364-1490; http:/www.nheri.org or from Home School Legal Defense Association. $5 with postage to US addresses.

9. Brian D. Ray, *A Nationwide Study of Home Education: Family Characteristics, Legal Matters, and Student Achievement*, 1990, pp. 46, 47.

10. Similar results found by Jennie Rakestraw and Jon Wartes were reported in the Dec., 1988 issue of *The Home School Researcher*. Rakestraw found no relationship between the parents' educational level and student standardized achievement test scores. It is interesting to note that, in Wartes' research, a small positive relationship did emerge between the parent's educational level and student test scores, but it disappeared after two years of home schooling.

We appreciate the information ***Jon Wartes*** *has shared for this chapter, about the success of home education. He is Project Leader for the Washington Homeschool Research Project. Mr. Wartes is also Head Counselor at Bothell Senior High, and his own children are taught at home.*

Brian Ray *has also been helpful. I'll tell you about him in the note with his chapter on teaching science.*

3

Parents and Education

Teaching is as natural for parents as learning is for children. Loving is sharing, and sharing – when it involves ideas – is teaching. You teach as you communicate with your children, as you take care of them, and as you play with them. To a young child the world is new, interesting, and sometimes frightening. You as a parent are the interpreter. Your child's natural curiosities, fears, needs and wants are your cues.

Because you love your child you want him or her to be happy and to learn. So you teach. And as your child develops and acquires new needs and interests, your teaching naturally adapts. At a certain stage it is such fun to get love and attention from Mommy and Daddy through the teaching-learning process that the child seems to make up the questions like a perpetual quiz show. You may not know every answer in detail but details are not important at this age anyway.

This process of learning and expanding horizons is moving along at top speed when, according to popular thinking, the parents suddenly become "inadequate." When most children are five or six, professionally trained educators take over a giant part of the teaching.

This pattern is especially alarming when you consider that the most important things you can teach your child are not facts and skills, but values – your philosophy, or your knowledge of God. Sending your child off to school suddenly interferes with this essential character-building education. At the typical school entrance age, children do what you tell them because they want to please, not because they have an internal sense of right and wrong. Conscience is developed later.

If you love your children and have the skills and knowledge of a normal literate adult, of course you can teach them. You will have to spend time. You will need to find materials. And you should sometimes get counsel. But you can do it.

Parents as teachers, four stages

I'm not suggesting that you will want to try to teach your children everything they ever learn in life. Your ability to teach obviously depends on their level of learning.

As children mature, the teacher role of their parents goes through four general stages: *should, can, might,* and *can't.* At the beginning, responsible parents *should* teach their children. During the earliest years they are, by nature, the best teachers. Later, they *can* do a perfectly adequate job but so can someone else. As the young scholars mature, parents *might* be able to teach them the total normal school program. At this stage providing an adequate education is difficult. Finally, if the children continue the pursuit of knowledge, their learning needs definitely pass beyond the competence of any one or two people. Their parents *can't* teach what they need to know.

Unfortunately, the common thinking of most people, educators and parents included, allows for only two of these stages. Usually it is a very short *can* followed by *can't* (or a *prefer not to).* More fortunate children come from homes where the early teaching attitude is *should* instead of *can,* but even for most of these, *can't* begins around age six.

As you continue reading the pages of this book, think about your own situation. Do you see a *can* or a *should* extending past the typical school entrance age and a *might* for a few years after that?

Another question to keep in mind is where to draw the lines between these stages. Of course, a final decision has to wait. It depends on the development and changing needs of your child as well as on your own obligations and resources.

What is teaching?

To get a better idea of if and when you should establish a home school, let's look briefly at what teaching is. Seeing what teachers do and what skills they need will help clarify what it will take for you to teach.

For state certification, teachers are required to study various aspects of education including philosophy, psychology, and methodology; they must practice teaching under supervision; and they must have a solid general background for the subject areas they will be teaching. In addition, they need whatever other courses are required for a college degree. It is understandable, then, to question how a parent without this preparation and often without any college training, could successfully conduct a home school.

A tailor produces a suit from cloth. A baker uses flour to bake bread. A hairdresser makes a change in a person's appearance. By applying their skills to raw materials, these people produce the desired results. But a teacher does not, in the same sense, cause learning. Learning is very much the job of the individual who learns. Until that person feels the need to learn, receives the information, assimilates it, and is willing to apply it, we can't say that successful learning has occurred.

I am not making a case for the elimination of teachers. Nor do I feel that the teacher's responsibility is unimportant. Teachers certainly help learning happen even though they don't create it.

Most people (and even some teachers) think of teaching primarily as lecturing, although they realize that making assignments, giving tests, and grading papers are also part of the job. This very narrow concept of teaching overlooks the more important ways of presenting information, and it totally ignores the essential task of shaping the student's environment to make the desired learning possible.

In helping students learn, teachers have basically two functions. They assure that conditions are right for the learner to receive the instruction, and they present or make available the information, skills, and attitudes to be learned. Now let's examine these two functions in more detail to give you a general idea of what teaching involves. In later chapters you will find more specific suggestions on how to do it.

Controlling learning conditions

Teaching is like painting an old house. Choosing the right color of paint and spreading it evenly is important, but the job involves much more than applying paint. If your experience has been like mine, you have found that most of the work lies in getting the surface ready. So in teaching, making sure that conditions are favorable – that the learner is as nearly ready as possible to receive instruction – is the groundwork of the educator's responsibility. A good learning environment depends on several factors.

☺ The student must, first of all, be physically ready to learn. He or she must have a clear, alert mind. This preparation includes such taken-for-granted health practices as good nutrition, ample rest, physical exercise, and freedom from the use of stimulating or depressing substances of all kinds (including some sold as food).

☺ The environment where the student comes to learn also has an effect on learning efficiency. Proper light, fresh air, and a comfortable temperature as well as the absence of distracting sights and sounds are obviously important.

☺ An individual's emotional condition has a profound effect on learning. In homes where parents are fighting or have recently separated, children are almost sure to have difficulty learning. The stimulation of sports competition upsets the calm interest important for serious study. The isolation and hurt that children feel from being shut out of a social circle or from being a loser on the playfield or in the classroom can block learning entirely. The trauma of boyfriend-girlfriend interaction which is inevitable and necessary as young people look forward to marriage, often creates an obstacle to learning even in the elementary school.

☺ A large part of the teacher's responsibility in controlling the emotional environment at school is in maintaining good discipline. A calm command of the situation along with an interesting learning program and a sincere demonstration of appreciation for good work is what it takes. The goal of good discipline is to develop self-discipline.

☺ One of the most elusive, hard-to-analyze teaching skills is fostering motivation. The amount of learning that occurs depends directly on the individual's desire to learn.

One possible approach to assuring motivation is to teach only what the student indicates an interest in wanting to know. This obviously risks omitting certain fundamental concepts naturally uninteresting to the child, but which he or she would, as an adult, regret having missed. The other extreme would be to present a structured body of knowledge, insensitive to student interest. Good teaching seems to lie somewhere in the middle. To a limited degree, students should be able to choose what they want to study, but the framework and most learning activities are usually prearranged.

Good teachers are careful to build interest in a topic as the first step in presenting it for learning. Interest is developed by helping the student see purpose and importance in what he or she is expected to know.

Several things make people want to learn. The ideal motivation is interest in the subject itself. Mature scholars view the end result to which the learning will finally be applied as sufficient reason to persevere, but this is a rather remote objective for children. Grades are important mostly to good students who are also easily motivated by a more direct interest in the subject. Certain other

specially arranged rewards for learning sometimes help and may be worth experimenting with.

Appropriate praise is no doubt the most successful motivator. Not praise which nourishes self-centeredness, but sincere appreciation focused on work well done. Even students who are naturally interested in the topic to be studied generally perform their learning tasks to please the teacher and sometimes for their peers. Imagine how most students would feel if, after completing a test or turning in their homework, the teacher announced that this was their lucky day. Everyone would get an A. Then without being read, the whole stack of papers were dropped directly into the trash. All of us like to be appreciated and have someone notice what we do. Students who work hard on a written assignment are disappointed if the teacher doesn't read it. A few words of appropriate encouragement and praise make most of us eager to perform nearly any reasonable task. (More on motivation later.)

☺ Another condition for learning is having the background knowledge necessary to understand what is presented. We acquire any new concept by breaking it down and relating its components to prior learning. Thus before learning to add fractions a person must be able to find lowest common denominators along with a host of other number skills, not to mention vocabulary and writing abilities. In order to learn the reasons for changes in the prime interest rate, a person must first understand how banks operate by borrowing and lending money.

Seeing that the student has the necessary background understanding is not as difficult a task for the perceptive teacher as it might seem. First, a carefully planned curriculum builds the structure in a logical order. Frequent reviews and a variety of approaches not only reinforce learning but provide repeated opportunities for those who might not have caught on at first. Textbook authors generally plan their materials for this repetition of key concepts.

> **Preparation for Learning**
>
> ❄ *A clear mind*
>
> ❄ *A good physical environment*
>
> ❄ *Calm emotions*
>
> ❄ *An atmosphere of order*
>
> ❄ *Encouragement to learn*
>
> ❄ *Background knowledge*
>
> ❄ *Appropriate maturity*

Even with the best materials and well-prepared teachers, students sometimes come to new learning goals with gaps in their backgrounds. Although patience and individual attention are needed, it usually isn't too difficult to analyze where a student got left behind and to help him or her catch up. The teacher breaks down the new concept with the student into the elements necessary to understand it. Then either the student suddenly gets all the pieces together, or else the missing foundation block becomes apparent.

☺ Finally, the readiness of young learners depends on their maturity. As children grow into adolescents and then into adults, their natural interest and aptitudes go through many complex changes. Understanding how children develop physically, socially, mentally and morally helps the teacher evaluate their readiness for particular learning tasks. All too often pressures from eager parents, school entrance laws and the typical curriculum push children into school study tasks before they are ready. This problem is discussed in another chapter.

Presentation of ideas to be learned

We have explored the principles of assuring that the student is ready to receive instruction. Now we will discuss delivering it. Even if you delegate most of the planning to a curriculum-providing organization, you will still have a part in presenting the ideas. A quick look at the more general job of teaching will help you understand your part better.

The process is sometimes as simple as handing the individual a book or turning on the television. However, to make learning efficient and to achieve specific desirable results, the instructional process requires considerable thought and usually a good deal of effort.

The first step in making learning available to the receptive student is choosing goals and objectives. Teachers have a limited general influence on the goals or purposes of the educational system. They have a little more to say about the objectives of what is taught in their school. But they are largely responsible for the interpretation of these objectives into specific learning outcomes in their classrooms.

As a parent you have a responsibility to know and to care about what your children are learning and why. Most people don't often question where modern schools are leading their children. They figure if everyone is following along, it must be to a good destination. But if you view the school as an extension of the home – as a service to help you educate your children – you will care very much what happens there.

For a home school, the process of choosing desired outcomes is much simpler than it sounds. We'll discuss it more in Chapter 9. My point here is that good teaching begins with a sense of direction. When you know where you are headed, it is time to select textbooks and other learning materials to help achieve your goals and objectives.

Textbooks or their equivalent will probably be your most important materials purchases. Schools also use other teaching aids such as filmstrips, sound recordings, laboratory equipment, video equipment, computers and library books.

After selecting materials comes planning. A teacher who doesn't plan well typically plods along in the textbook having students read and answer questions from it until the school year comes to an end. Using good materials is never a substitute for planning. Even if the plan is to adopt a preplanned plan, the teacher must know the objectives and have a clear, functional idea of how they can be achieved. The general plan for the school year is laid out according to the goals set for the grade or class. Then each day or week during the course of the year more precise plans are prepared. The plans are modified constantly as students' needs become evident.

With students ready to learn, directions set, materials chosen, and plans made, the stage is set for the learner's reception of the desired concepts. Communicating these understandings, skills, and values, or making them available and attractive to the student is what we think of in the narrow sense as "teaching."

When considering how to teach, most people think first of lecturing. But because the brain seems to remember best what it is actively involved in acquiring, teacher talk should be limited. Concepts are learned from books and other materials, from experimentation, from other people including teachers and, in brief, from the total environment.

A good teacher knows best how to communicate ideas by focusing on the learner – by being constantly perceptive to his or her needs and achievements. Teaching is like guiding travelers across an unfamiliar wilderness. The instructor must know not only the destination and how to get to it, but must also watch and direct the travelers. Can you imagine the guide saying, "If you are smart, you will follow me," then proceeding to cross the wilderness with great speed and skill, never looking back?

Tests or examinations stimulate learning in several ways. Most importantly, they provide a short-range reason for study. Also, during the time of the examination the mind is usually very alert. Reinforcement occurs, and, when ideas are to be combined in new ways, original learning often occurs.

Evaluation is the final step in the teaching process as well as a continuous part of it. Students, parents and teachers must know how well learning objectives are being met in order to modify teaching and learning strategies and to set new goals. Examinations and written assignments provide only a part of the information for evaluation. Observation and counseling are also important.

Grades are a convenient, condensed expression of evaluation. Unfortunately, when grades are used to compare individuals, they too often build pride for some and create poor self-images for others. Descriptive evaluation reports help learners focus more on the achievement of objectives and less on competition with other students.

Instructing

- Choosing goals
- Selecting materials
- Planning
- Communicating
- Evaluating

The total process

Although I have divided the teaching responsibility into categories to describe it clearly, most of these activities go on simultaneously, and all blend into the teaching process.

I have outlined what teachers need to achieve, but have said little in practical terms about how it might be accomplished. My purpose here has been to analyze what teaching basically is, whether for a classroom in Africa, for the school down the street, or for a tutor working with an individual. Specific suggestions for operating a home school appear later in this book.

Perfection is impossible. No one can be absolutely sure that every student is completely ready and that instruction is given in a way which will be perfectly understood and assimilated. An attempt to perfect one area would risk not getting around to the others. Good teachers know how to balance their efforts to achieve the best results. The human mind is amazingly adaptable and often learns even with imperfect teaching.

Can parents play the role of school teacher?

Teaching is a natural result of communication. Parents teach even without planning to. But as we have seen, teaching with a purpose is complex. Should parents without formal training in the field of education try it?

Consider first the general area of making sure that conditions are right for learning to occur. This is the real art of teaching — helping students be ready to receive instruction. As a parent you have a distinct advantage here. Much of what we have discussed as controlling learning conditions, good parents do anyway. You probably know well how to assure a good physical and emotional environment. You may not feel as skilled in motivation but, with practice, the art of appropriate encouragement can be steadily improved. Being sure that background learning has occurred may seem like more of a challenge to you, but if you progress carefully through a well planned program and patiently analyze reasons for lack of success when it occurs, you should have no difficulty. Missing prerequisite understanding is much less of a problem in one-to-one teaching than it is in a classroom because the direct contact with a single student allows for the kind of communication which tends to identify deficiencies immediately and precisely.

Parents who have spent time learning to understand their children – which is usually the case for those who want a home school – tend to achieve most of the right learning conditions naturally. A good home atmosphere is generally also a good learning atmosphere.

Presenting ideas to be learned – the other teaching skills area – is greatly simplified by using the services of a guidance center or enrolling your child in a correspondence school. (See Appendix A.) Even parents who set up their own independent home schools find help from most student textbooks and from guidelines provided in teachers' editions. A supervising teacher, who visits the home from time to time, can help the parent keep on target particularly in setting up the scurriculum and in evaluation.

Operating a home school requires time and effort, but most parents can do it very well.

Sample Beliefs and Goals

The statements below were established by Georgians for Freedom in Education. We list them here as a source of ideas. For their address, see Appendix D.

We Believe:

◆ That our children do not belong to the state; that it is the responsibility of *parents* to properly direct the needs of their children mentally, emotionally, spiritually, socially, and physically.

◆ That parents have the constitutional right to choose the best method of providing for each of these needs, including the child's formal education.

◆ That the learning process begins at home from the moment of birth, and parents *are* the prime educators of their children.

◆ That conscientious parents can provide in the home a very adequate and often superior comprehensive program for their children's education.

◆ That home schools offer the very best method of teaching: *one-to-one tutoring.*

◆ That a child's educational needs can be met on a more individual basis in a home environment; that the flexible nature of a home school program allows each child to progress at his own ideal pace in every subject, without stressful competition or pressure.

◆ That the home school atmosphere encourages an intensive adventure into learning through natural self-discovery; this builds self-confidence and individual thinking rather than peer dependence.

◆ That home education encourages valuable social interaction with people of *all* ages, in the home and in the community. This helps the child learn to relate well to people outside his own peer group.

◆ That the *family* is the basic link in the structure of any society, and that America has seen a definite weakening of the family unit in recent years. Home schoolers have found that the relaxed, intimate interaction between parent and child in the home school serves to strengthen family unity as well as providing the best possible alternative for education.

Our Goals Are:

◆ To support and encourage parents desiring to educate their children at home.

◆ To provide helpful information in every way possible to parents who choose home education.

◆ To promote legislation in support of the parents' primary and constitutionally guaranteed rights in education.

◆ To promote public awareness of the parents' right to choose the educational environment for their children, and awareness of the alternative to educate them at home.

◆ To support the highest standards possible for education of children in every school situation, in public and private schools as well as home schools.

◆ To support minimal govern- mental control and maximum local and family control of education.

4

When Not to Try Home Schooling

In the preceding chapter we examined the teaching-learning process and concluded that parents can generally succeed as teachers for their own children. Applying the principles of good education at home does not require the same level of professional training and competence as does teaching in a classroom. It's easier to monitor the needs of a single individual than it is to intelligently teach a whole classroom of students guided by feedback from a few vocal ones. For the individual, learning difficulties can be cleared quickly, keeping anxiety to a minimum.

Most parents who care enough about their children to want to teach them at home have the necessary qualifications. Still for various reasons, home school beyond the preschool years is not for every family.

Teaching is full time work

The amount of time needed will vary from much to very much, depending to a degree on your skill, the needs of your child, and the assistance you get from a guidance center or correspondence course. Even if you are a trained teacher and purchase a well prepared materials package, holding a regular outside job would make responsible home schooling almost impossible. It might work, however, if another person could carry a big part of the instructional contact.

First graders take the greatest amount of time because they learn mostly from you and from your direct guidance. You obviously can't send them off to read and follow printed instructions. Also they have short attention spans and need very brief learning tasks. As children mature they become more able to concentrate on serious learning goals and require less of your direct attention. You can expect no sense of self-directed learning from children starting school unless you have delayed beginning their formal study until well past the typical school entrance age of six.

High school students, even on a correspondence program, still require your time. But your major responsibilities then are encouragement, occasional help, and often gentle pushing. Difficult learning tasks may appear to the young learner as insurmountable obstacles. The help you give is valuable not because you are more skilled at the subject involved but because you lend courage and stability to the struggler.

Teaching requires good discipline

Parents who are seriously concerned about their children's training generally have good home discipline. If your home doesn't, they will probably be better off in a classroom school where a more significant part of their direction and development can come from people outside the home.

In most homes children are occasionally ill-tempered and exhibit unpleasant behavior. Normal parents slip once in a while, too, and act unwisely. But when a tense parent-child relationship is the rule rather than the exception, home school is not a good idea. Children in these cases need the influence of other adults. People can't learn well in an atmosphere of high anxiety.

I'm not suggesting that sending your children off to school will solve a serious home discipline problem. There are things you can and should do, especially if your children are still quite young. But until the situation is under control, a home school is probably not your best option.

Teaching requires commitment and organization

Most parents find that setting up school and teaching at home is a very interesting idea. But unlike a hobby that can be put aside when it ceases to be fun, your school program requires steady rain–or–shine commitment. If you aren't in the habit of following through on long projects, or if you anticipate frequent periods of time during the school year when "more urgent" tasks are apt to "unexpectedly" take you away from your teaching, you had better send your child away to a conventional school to begin with.

Of course you can build your school schedule around necessary trips and special projects. Vacations are important too. You will be successful in getting through your school program as long as you have a plan that is not apt to be interrupted whenever you hear of a good sale, or when someone asks you to help arrange a wedding, or when you have a hard time finding help to pick your peach orchard, or when the house needs painting or when hundreds of other very worthy tasks demand your attention. I'm not saying never, never stop to pick peaches, but weigh the value to your children. Then if it seems worthy and it doesn't interfere with meeting your objectives, change your plan to allow for it.

Organization is related to commit–ment. Do you tend to plan your time and follow through on your plan? Do you see the tasks you want to do as having various degrees of importance? And do you sometimes put aside low priority activities for what you consider more important? Do you plan your shopping to avoid frequent trips? Are you master of the TV and the telephone, or do they dictate what else you accomplish and when?

Organization can be improved with effort. But if you seldom accomplish a great deal in a day, your school program could suffer. You could plod along for twelve months and still not complete what should have taken nine. If you have a serious organization problem, don't try home school until you have made some giant steps toward improvement.

See the endnote for feedback to all this advice.*

Teaching requires knowledge

As already explained, you should know something about how to guide learning and control the learning environment. Hopefully this book can help. You also need to have some basic knowledge in the areas you are teaching, although not much more than you plan to teach. To some extent you can learn along with your child, but don't try home school without certain minimum understandings and abilities. First of all, you need basic reading skills. Speed reading ability isn't necessary, but being a very poor reader would be a handicap in all your teaching.

In math, you should be able to handle with ease (and without a calculator) the basic operations of addition, subtraction, multiplication, and division. For middle grades and beyond you should have a simple understanding of fractions. Refinements of these math skills and additional concepts such as percents and metric units can be sharpened up as you go.

Finally, you should be able to use standard English. Your child's ability to communicate as an adult depends on the quality of language heard all day every day as well as on the skill with which his or her written and spoken language is corrected. I would not argue that different dialects are bad, and I am not referring to accent, but if an individual can't use standard English when it is expedient to do so, his or her future opportunities are certain to be limited.

Of course, knowing more than these minimum elements is better, as long as you are patient and don't lose your feel for the young learner just beginning to grapple with what you think should be obvious.

Running away might teach the wrong lesson

Although most parents who withdraw their children from a regular school to teach them at home are giving them a greater future, a few are encouraging negative character traits instead.

Consider your motivation. What led to your idea that home school is better? If your mother-hen instinct got all fluffed up because your little chick wasn't assigned to the advanced reading group; or because, without asking your opinion, your early adolescent boy was counseled about being too familiar with a certain girl; or because your young cherub lost points because the *teacher* thought she was cheating when *you* know she would never do such a thing, beware! You may be teaching your child that anything that crosses the ego should be squashed or escaped. You could be gaining better reading opportunities at the expense of a calm, unselfish character.

Rules needed for keeping the classroom in order seem quite restrictive to the child used to getting his way at home. Rebellion then surfaces naturally. Efforts to help him overcome the problem are sometimes thwarted by his parents' defense of the behavior. They have always given him free reign hardly realizing the strength of his self-will, and they take any suggestion of his wrongdoing as a personal affront. After all, he does it at home, and its being "wrong" at school challenges their judgment. If the child is taken out of school at this point to be taught at home, you can see what happens to character development.

The parents' mistaken attitude is sometimes camouflaged when the teacher hasn't handled the situation prudently. He or she may have misjudged, or maybe the rule wasn't really that important. Also, the child's own bias in explaining what happened might have distorted the facts. Even if the teacher is wrong, the child is seldom entirely innocent. A "win" for the parents may settle things well between them and the teacher, but the child loses!

While we are on the topic, we should also point out that parents' opposite overreaction to school discipline by denouncing and harshly punishing the child at home can equally sow seeds of bitterness and rebellion.

I'm not saying that conflicts in opinion should always be ignored, or that an unpleasant situation should never prompt a change in the school environment. Just try to find a solution in a spirit of respect and cooperation. Your own attitude teaches more valuable lessons than can ever come from math or science or reading.

Some children have special learning needs

If your child seems to be having more than the expected difficulty in learning, you must be alert to the idea that special help may be needed. You want to avoid both ignoring a possible disability, and imagining grave defects whenever a little problem surfaces. Neglect may result in tardy identification of a special need which might have been helped by early intervention. At the same time, I can understand reluctance to ask for state assistance which could take over some of your own decision making. Dr. & Mrs. Lanier discuss this in their chapter, "Home Schooling the Special Needs Child."

As mentioned elsewhere in this book,

scholastic achievement depends much more on simple attitudes and preparation than it does on inherited intelligence. If you suspect a learning problem consider first the possibility of a defect in the child's environment. Read the chapters "Helping Your Child Learn" and "Inspiring Motivation." Then read about learning disabilities (or about physical handicaps, if they are the issue). Appendix C has a section on organizations, and Appendix I lists books. If you might need it, seek professional counsel.

In considering a home school remember that, because challenged individuals are different, they tend to be sidetracked by society and miss much of the normal interaction with other people needed for social development. On the other hand, although home school means associating with fewer people, it may be a necessity for your situation. Or it may be highly desirable for part of your child's learning program. In principle, however, life is already abnormal for your handicapped child. You will want to do all you can to help him or her feel like an important part of the big world. That may mean the regular classroom for a portion of formal education. Plan to encourage a positive self-image in your child. This will no doubt be a greater asset than success in school subjects.

As you may already know, state education funds often pay an extension teacher from the local school system to visit homes of children who cannot easily fit into the school system. Also special regulations may govern how handicapped children are taught.

Home schooling needs a balanced approach

Parents who are interested in school at home are not usually run-of-the-mill people. They have distinctive opinions, and when decisions are to be made, they don't often look around first to be sure all their friends approve of what they are about to do.

Acting on principle instead of on popularity is commendable. Occasionally, however, independent thinkers specialize in a single idea. They write, talk, plan, and dream about it. The risk I see for them is not in teaching the idea to their children. Parents have a responsibility to pass on what they consider valuable information and right principles. The danger is that learning that is essential to success in life might be neglected. The children's future is at stake.

A course of study could differ from what is normally taught in the public schools and still prepare the student for a successful life, but in my opinion, it could not be satisfactory while ignoring the essentials of the major subjects most schools try to teach. See Appendix G, For a listing of what is typically taught in each grade.

If you are not ready to provide your child the essential array of skills and knowledge in sufficient depth to function efficiently and effectively as an adult, you should let a more traditional school do the job. You can teach your special idea at home after school hours.

But

If you are naturally timid, don't be too quick to conclude from this chapter that you can't teach. I've described important qualities for the home teacher, but I believe that most people who want to teach their own children and who are concerned enough to read this book have what it takes. Look back over the qualifications. If you are really bad in one or more areas, OK, throw in the towel. But if you see some weaknesses that aren't clearly problems, go have a heart-to-heart chat with someone who knows you and is sympathetic to the home school idea (or call a contact person from a home schooling group in your area). Maybe you are underselling yourself. All of us have stronger and weaker areas.

If your final decision is to give it a try, then pick up your courage and go for it!

Endnote

* Mary McCarthy of Lakewood, NJ wrote (3/15/1993): "I saw your letter in HEM. You must have known we were discussing *The Home School Manual* on the [Prodigy, computer] bulletin board! . . . thought you'd enjoy [some of] our comments. . . .

"My only suggestion would be not to try and discourage home schoolers quite so much. It's a tough decision, and if we're going to have to take into account our housekeeping skills - well there wouldn't be many of us left."

One lady on the bulletin board had quoted the whole section on organization from this chapter. She got some interesting responses (that tended to induce a little humility for me). Here's part of one from Janet Latham of Chewsville, MD:

"QUICK, lose that book!!! Or your Messies card may be forfeited! We started home educating years ago and it sounds like nonsense to me! And it is written by a MAN! Sorry guys. But I have not met a man yet who was home educating although some do support duty. We are 'muddle' of the roaders in structure favoring unit studies and . . . a Unit is where you find it - maybe the furnace today, the space shuttle in the back yard tomorrow. . . . With 9s and unders most of the curriculum can be learning to love reading and math and science together with a dose of our world thrown in for geography and social studies. For the 9s and up we recommend doing some goal setting with gradually more and more of the responsibility being the student's."

My advice would be a little different, but these ideas (except for losing the book) are worth thinking about. Maybe my critics didn't read to the end of the chapter. Anyway, I'm really glad now to have a good chapter on *how* to be organized and another one on self-discipline. And please note, gals: they're both by women!

5

Keeping Peace With School Authorities

We don't need to look back past very many yesterdays to see the time when few children had any significant amount of schooling. Here in the United States, before the Civil War, a typical child whose parents saw the importance of education might have attended school for a few months out of the year when his or her time couldn't have been more "profitably" spent working.

The Massachusetts legislature passed a compulsory school attendance law in 1852. Other states began to follow the example after the Civil War. The Massachusetts law required children between eight and fourteen years of age to attend school for at least twelve weeks every school year. Parents unable to afford the tuition were exempted from the fine set for violation. Now, every state requires attendance for certain ages.

As early as 1642 a colonial Massachusetts law required parents to teach their children how to read. But only gradually and many years later when education became tax-supported and compulsory, and when laws restricted child labor, did school become a standard and significant part of American childhood. As recently as 1898, for example, the average school year was 143 days compared to our present 170 or 180. But the average days of attendance for those who were enrolled as pupils was only 98.

Now, let's come a little closer to the question of why educators today might question your teaching your own children at home instead of sending them to a classroom school. Several factors influence them.

Most school leaders like to do their jobs well. They are people who entered the field of education because they like young people and enjoy helping them learn. Anyone who, through years of study and experience, has gained expertise in a particular profession, might naturally take a dim view of novices who claim to have a better way.

Attendance in public schools is threatened by more than parents wanting to teach their own children. Truancy is increasing; many of the better students attend private schools; a few parents are delaying starting their children until after the mandatory entrance age; and some people even argue that attendance laws should be abolished altogether. (After all, couldn't nonscholastic individuals prepare for life better outside the typical school environment? and good scholars would attend anyway.) Thus some educators fear that to allow greater freedom in the establishment of home schools would only accelerate the erosion of control over school attendance.

Maybe policy makers really are concerned that home schooled children might miss something, but I am increasingly convinced that the bigger reason for defending school attendance in most cases has nothing to do with what's good for kids. Instead, it seems to me that many teachers, through their unions, want to protect their job security, and I expect they would also like to keep more of the kids that make teaching enjoyable.

Caution

In discussing legal situations, please understand: Nothing in this book is intended as legal advice. Suggestions for one situation in one place may not apply to someone else's problem elsewhere.

The law and home schools

You probably want to know simply whether the law will permit you to teach your children at home. Under the right (and sometimes unreasonable) circumstances, yes. Laws differ from state to state, and in Canada provincial laws vary, too.

Often the superintendent or board of the local school district authorizes or screens home schools. The plan of local authority is reasonable. Sometimes, however the local decision makers are not. Each year, laws and regulations relating to home schools are better defined. But interpretations still often seem prejudiced, and sometimes the school boards succeed in frightening home school parents into submission by get-tough tactics.

Legal requirements in various areas

The perspective of this chapter is obviously for the United States. From what I understand, legal situations in other countries represented in Appendices E and F are somewhat similar. The best advice, even for the U.S. is from legal matters firms specializing in home education and from major, active home schooling organizations in your political jurisdiction. This chapter can give you some general ideas.

As we have noted, statutes differ and they change – usually for the better, although we can't count on it. Regulations based on those laws also differ and change. Case law (or the body of precedents of interpretation that are being established by the courts and which are used as the basis of future decisions) is expanding and changing.

For a summary of the legal situation in various of the states in the US before press time, see the beginning of Appendix D. Otherwise, for specific current information for your state, province, or country: (1) Contact a home school organization (Appendix D, E, or F). (2) Get precise information (for the U.S. or Canada) from a report by HSLDA or by the Rutherford Institute (Appendix C). (3) Your public library might have a section of state statutes. Look under school attendance laws and under regulations pertaining to home schools or private schools.

Religious liberty

Parents' religious convictions that public schools have a bad influence on their children may be the reason for starting most home schools. Private church-operated schools would be a satisfactory solution for some of these families, but often they feel unable to afford it or no suitable school is close enough.

The First Amendment to the United States Constitution states that "Congress shall make no law respecting an establishment of religion, or prohibiting the free exercise thereof. . . ." A number of Supreme Court rulings based on this amendment relate to education. Among them is the decision supporting the right of parents to send their children to nonpublic schools.[1]

Of recent interest is the April, 1990 United States Supreme Court decision which severely restricts religious freedom in general but which strengthens it as it relates to home schooling. Christopher Klicka discusses the ruling in the next chapter.

Many other religious liberty decisions of interest to home school parents have come from lower courts. Of course rulings in one state or province do not have the force of law outside the jurisdictions where they were made, but the precedents set help establish parallel rights in other places. Several other rulings are discussed later in this chapter.

Applying for approval

Some states pass the responsibility for approval down to local superintendents or boards of education who determine some of their own policies. If you live in an "approval" state, contact home school leaders in your area before approaching your school district office about approval. Ask them for suggestions or guidelines so you can check the strength of your own situation.

Learning about policies in advance gives you time to look for alternatives or to consider your defense before getting accused of truancy.

Fortunately, school authorities in most areas do deal fairly with parents wanting to teach their own children and recognize home schooling as a viable alternative to the more traditional educational systems.

In applying for approval, you may need to provide a considerable amount of information about your goals and curriculum plan, about methods and equipment you expect to use, about your schedule, and about your own qualifications; or you may be asked only to declare that you are teaching certain standard subjects for a minimum number of days per year.

Often parents and educational administrators each view the other group as adversaries. Parents are frightened when they hear about school people who seem to want to control the situation. And educators who misunderstand school at home, or confuse parents wanting to educate their own children with those who don't care, often feel an obligation to be tough. Communication reduces misunderstanding, and a demonstration of good faith and cooperation eases restrictions. Many home school parents across North America consider training their own children to be a fundamental right and responsibility.

Reducing the possibility of trouble

Most home school parents don't want a

confrontation with the law even if they feel they are doing the right thing and that they could win in court. Here are several suggestions that may help keep you out of trouble:

♦ Know the statutes for your area that apply to school attendance and teaching children at home. Learn what you can about court cases where these statutes have been tested and interpretations established. This helps you know where you stand and gives you a background for intelligent discussion of your position.

♦ Do your job well. Intelligent, well-adjusted students constitute a powerful argument for your educational program whether you are called into court or whether you need to convince your relatives that you aren't ruining your children.

♦ Accumulate a portfolio of your child's progress. A daily log in a teacher's plan book would be excellent evidence of a serious educational plan. Keep samples of school work. Keep good teaching materials, especially any you make. Keep any records you have from a previously attended school.

♦ If responsibility or teaching ability is the issue, you might begin teaching during the summer. Then before fall enrollment time have your child tested. If results are good, they could strengthen your case. Get some advice first about what difference this might make.

♦ Cooperate in every way you can. Cooperation disarms prejudice and reduces unnecessary differences. If you should be called into court, your case will be much easier to defend if it involves interpretation of the law rather than a rationale for disobedience. For example, private or home schools are often required by law to file certain reports. Should your school status be challenged, having submitted the reports would show that you were complying with the law as you interpreted it. Of course I'm not suggesting you do something that violates your conscience and casts doubt on your sincerity.

♦ Consider joining a legal defense group. The directors of the Home School Legal Defense Association in their brochure, state their belief that "God imposes a responsibility on all parents to train their children in a manner pleasing to Him," and that "home schooling, when it is responsibly done, is legally protected by the Constitution. . . ." For information, see Appendix C.

♦ If your competence to teach might be an issue, and if classroom teachers (and not home teachers) in your area are required to pass a general abilities exam, consider taking it yourself. It will probably cover major school subjects at the eighth-grade level. You could brush up on weak areas. An acceptable test score would certainly be evidence of ability. The school authorities would probably not know the test results if you don't reveal them. Ask your nearest university teachers' college for information.

When you are told, "Send them to school or else!"

Attorney J. Michael Smith, in addressing a home schooling conference and later in personal letters, has outlined a typical approach that school authorities might take in an effort to get your children enrolled in "school," and he has suggested how you might react.

The ideas here apply most directly where the legal situation is not entirely clear and where you feel you have a right to teach your children. As time passes, laws address the home schooling issue more specifically. Each situation is obviously different and your responses should depend on the particular circumstances. The following could happen:

*The contributions of **J. Michael Smith** for this chapter are greatly appreciated. He is vice president of Home School Legal Defense Association.*

☼ The superintendent's office gets a call, perhaps from a local school principal who learned that your children have not returned to school after being enrolled the previous year or when a neighbor complains. You are contacted by personal letter, by telephone or by a visit from a truancy officer to let you know that your children must be enrolled within a certain few days.

I'll add a few comments here to expand on Attorney Smith's first point. Some parents who have no intentions of teaching at home just don't bother to enroll their children. They need some kind of push to get their kids into school before Christmas, so the intent of the contact isn't always bad.

If you get your neighbors on your side of

the question before they get the wrong ideas, you might never receive a letter from the superintendent's office. After you have gotten acquainted, let them know what you are doing and what a good opportunity it is for your children. Anticipating questions that might come to their minds, show that your children are learning better than they would in school and how their social contacts are helping them develop. Have the kids do some special things for the neighbors.

☼ Many times the mother is the one contacted. If the father lives with the family, she should obtain the school official's name and phone number promising that the father will respond promptly. This gives time to prepare an intelligent response after consulting with others, and it puts the husband in his God-given responsibility as the family protector and covering.

If you are told at the door or on the phone, certain things about what you must do, ask for statements in writing and suggest that the caller check with an attorney due to the possibility of civil rights violation.[2] If you feel it is appropriate, state that the U.S. Supreme Court decision, Wisconsin v. Yoder[1] gives parents a prior right to educate their children and supersedes any State law or decision to the contrary. You could refer to the Smith decision. (See the next chapter.)

☼ Either contact an attorney capable of handling a possible attendance problem or talk to someone who understands home schooling. If your children are part of an umbrella school or guidance center, contact the organization.

☼ You may be asked to come to a hearing. In California, the group is called a Student Attendance Review Board. If the request is by letter, you should probably accept the "invitation." Legal consultation is critical at this point. If you receive a court subpoena, attendance is mandatory. In either case, if you can, arrange for counsel to represent your views. Please remember, your statements can be used against you in court.

☼ If you expect a serious confrontation, prepare a declaration under penalty of perjury stating your reasons for home schooling. If any of the reasons are based on religious conviction, biblical references would be appropriate. Become familiar with pertinent decisions from the U.S. Supreme Court and from your state courts. Use these decisions, as appropriate, to support your position for home teaching. Use wording from the decisions as it applies to your situation, and give the references.

The declaration should be typed, signed by both parents and notarized. It could be presented to the truant officer at the first contact. It will become the cornerstone for the entire confrontation.

☼ Normally, unless you have convinced the authorities that what you are doing is all right, the next step is being ordered to appear in court. The school district, not the state office of education, takes this responsibility. If you haven't already gotten legal counsel, be sure to do so now.

☼ Your legal adviser will want to give information to the school superintendent or to the judge that will help them see that they should drop the case.

☼ The best approach in dealing with an unfair school law may be to challenge its constitutionality. If your attorney takes this route, he will want to do so before entering a plea. Failure to do so in some states waives the right to attack the constitutionality of the statute involved.

☼ If you face the judge, your carefully kept records and fidelity to the law as you had interpreted it will greatly improve your chance of success. If your reasons for home schooling are religious, be sure you can explain them clearly. You will show that your children are being well educated and that you are being a responsible parent according to your sincere religious convictions.

Additional suggestions for defending your rights

A relatively small number of home school parents are accused of violating attendance laws, and of that group only a fraction are tried in court. In addition to doing your best to minimize the possibility of confrontation, and responding intelligently in the scenario Attorney Smith outlined, here are several more suggestions to consider if your home school is threatened:

⌗ Ask for all communications from school officials to be in be in writing. Keep copies of all their responses.

⌗ You may be contacted by a school attendance officer who is not really hostile but is fulfilling his responsibility to investigate your situation following a complaint.

⌗ If you should have made a formal application or declaration for a home school, get counsel about the advisability of conforming with the requirement.

⌗ I have already mentioned the importance of keeping careful records. If you feel that you may be called into court, records from a school previously attended could be valuable for establishing that your child is currently making good progress.

⌗ If keeping your child out of the regular school is a religious conviction, seek help on that basis. Some religious organizations have policies on religious rights and employ personnel who specialize in providing help.

⌗ Consult an attorney. As with a physician, you may have to pay a fee for a visit, but you are still free to refuse to go ahead with the expensive "operation." Contact your attorney as early as you can when you see a problem coming. It's always nicer to avoid trouble than it is trying to get untangled from a confrontation.

Any attorney can help you, but one familiar with school attendance problems will have the advantage of experience and will require less time in study. You can find an attorney by checking your phone book for an attorney referral service. I would talk with several lawyers, asking about their experience and their fees. Several organizations specialize in home schooling and similar legal affairs. See Appendix C.

⌗ Any school that wanted to, could probably enroll your child as an extension student or home student, but they usually require that the child be unable to attend.

⌗ Sometimes families who see no other reasonable solution to the legal restrictions threatening their home teaching plans, move away.

Significant legal decisions and opinions

Significant decisions from the past few years are discussed by Christopher Klicka in the next chapter.

Statutes and regulations as various states and provinces have decided them and opinions from court cases help clarify the home school position with respect to the law. The most fundamental legal backbone is the Constitution itself with amendments defining basic rights. Several key U.S. Supreme Court decisions have been briefly mentioned and are cited in the endnotes for this chapter. To be thoroughly prepared to defend a serious case, your attorney would want to be familiar with them and with subsequent cases which have considered their results applicable or not applicable. The four quotations which appear in the following paragraphs are of general significance, but are not intended to be comprehensive.

On requiring college degrees for private school teachers

From the partially dissenting opinion of Judge C. J. Krivosha in the Nebraska State Supreme Court decision, *State* v. *Faith Baptist Church*, 1981. The Nebraska statutes have since changed. This issue is less of an issue today, but the concepts are worth thinking about.

I find nothing either in our statutes or in logic which compels a conclusion that one may not teach in a private school without a baccalaureate degree if the children are to be properly educated. Under our holding today, Eric Hoffer could not teach philosophy in a grade school, public or private; Julia Child could not teach cooking; and Thomas Edison could not teach the theories of electricity. While none of them could teach in the primary or secondary grades, all of them could teach in college. I have some difficulty with a law which results in requiring that those who teach must have a baccalaureate degree, but those who teach those who teach need not. The logic of it escapes me. The experience of time has failed to establish that requiring all teachers to earn a baccalaureate degree from anywhere results in providing children with a better education.

While it may be appropriate for a state to set such requirements in a public school where state funds are expended and, in effect, the state is the employer, I find no basis in law or fact for imposing a similar requirement in a private school. .

In my view, attempting to strike a balance

between the various interests of the parties herein does not justify requiring that all persons teaching in appellants' school can qualify as a teacher only by holding a baccalaureate degree.

. . .

I believe there are other reasonable regulations which can be adopted for private schools that would permit these schools to continue, thereby striking the necessary balance between the two competing interests. I would have so held.

On local school board authority in regulating home schools

Quoting from Utah Assistant Attorney General Opinion (83-20):

> The Home instruction exemption to the compulsory attendance law [in the state of Utah] . . . attempts to balance three important interests: parent, public, and student. *Wisconsin* v. *Yoder*, 408 U.S. 205 (1972).
>
> The parents of the school child have a fundamental interest in directing the upbringing and education of their child. Pierce v. Society of Sisters, 268 U.S. 510 (1925). While this interest finds protection in the constitutional concepts of privacy and liberty, it is not absolute or unlimited. Generally, parents can act in good faith to accomplish the proper education of their own child through their own efforts at home; but the public, through the school officials, can set reasonable standards to see that the child is well educated. Prince v. Massachusetts, 321 U.S. 158 (1944).
>
> The public has a compelling interest to assure that every child is educated in the branches prescribed by law; but it cannot require every child to attend public school exclusively. The public can set reasonable, minimal education and academic standards to accomplish the prescribed education of the child in the appropriate branches.
>
> The student's interest is to become reasonably well educated. He is entitled to become capable, responsible and self-sufficient enough that he can participate in a politically and civilly responsible manner within his ability. At the same time he should not be so independent as to be unable to function in society.
>
> Thus, there arises a juxtaposition of three interests: parent, public and student; a balance hopefully pursued in a cooperative manner to accomplish a common goal with no one interest being overwhelmed by another. . . . With the school district setting standards for instruction and the parents selecting the time, place and manner of instruction, it is imperative that there be a close cooperation and trust between school officials and parents to accomplish the common goal of properly educating the child. The child is benefited by an education reasonably equivalent to that acquired by children in public school, but the school district cannot require the individual child to become "identical" to the children in the public schools. . . .

A question sometimes arises regarding aid to students in private schools based on the establishment clause of the United States Constitution. The objection is that government aid seems to promote or entangle religion, but it has been clearly held that a school district can furnish texts to promote the interests of the individual student, and that such aid is not a significant support to or entanglement with religion. *Board of Education* v. *Allen*, 392 U.S. 236 (1968). However, the question of religious entanglement should not even arise in our situation because under Utah law a private school is clearly different than home instruction and a home instruction program receiving district support is clearly in the interest of a child and would not be questioned under the establishment clause.

Not every home school case is decided in favor of the parents, but most seem to be, so in the unlikely event that your right to teach your children is challenged, you should not be discouraged. And while the legal wheels are turning, you may be allowed to follow your convictions. If you do your job well, you may be able to clear your own record and be instrumental in setting precedents that will help other families.

Endnotes

1. *Pierce* v. *The Society of Sisters*, 268 U.S. 510 (1925); *Wisconsin* v. *Yoder*, 406, U.S. 205 (1972).
2. Civil rights act, (42 U.S.C. 1983).

6

Battle for the Right to Home School

Christopher Klicka

Every now and then I wonder how the right sto teach our own children, one of the most basic of all rights, could be in jeopardy in a free country such as ours. I don't want to believe it is really happening. As I travel around defending home school families in court, speaking at conferences, and testifying before legislatures, I sense the crucial war waging over the control of our children. Families trying diligently to teach their own children are being harassed and intimidated by local public school authorities.

Some families have been charged with truancy or child neglect for following God's call to take a personal interest in educating their own children. Others are even threatened with having their children taken away.

Although the number of parents fighting on the front lines for their First Amendment freedoms is actually quite small compared to the mass of home schooling families, their battle is for all of us. If they lose, Christian schools lose, and ultimately the family will lose. We dare not take this conflict lightly.

The issue

It is becoming increasingly apparent that the issue is not whether the children are being educated, because in virtually every case in which the Home School Legal Defense Association (HSLDA) has ever been involved, the children have performed above average on standardized test scores. The real issue involves who has the authority to dictate how the children are educated: their parents or the public school authorities. This issue can be further divided into two underlying themes: control and money.

In talking with public school teachers, administrators and superintendents, I have found that they often believe that only the system that they (and the National Education Association) represent is capable of educating children. Time and again superintendents have told me that parents who have not had at least seven years of higher education cannot possibly provide their children with an adequate education. Some superintendents have personally asserted that no form of home schooling is adequate. They have refused to allow home schools to operate in their districts.

> ***Christopher J. Klicka** is Senior Counsel at the Home School Legal Defense Association, and author of* The Right Choice . . . Home Schooling.

Other superintendents have denied home schoolers the right to exist claiming that the children, not being with others their age, will not be properly socialized. One outrageous argument was raised by the prosecutor in a home school trial in North Dakota. He stated that home schooling was inadequate because the children did not have the educational advantage of being pushed around by a school bully! In other words, it is harmful for the child to be sheltered from bullies because he would miss an important social experience which would prepare him for life. Of course, this is the exact type of "negative" socialization which home schoolers want to avoid and replace with godly standards and church involvement.

The crux of the matter that I see is that many of the school administrators actually believe that both the authority and the responsibility to teach the children resides in the state. They believe that they are the "guardians" of the children and that their authority surpasses that of the children's parents. They reason that the education of the children should be left to the professionals who have teaching certificates and are specially trained. Therefore, many superintendents operate on the assumption that they have virtually unlimited authority to control the home school program. Resistance from the home schooling family often damages their pride.

Vested interest

This country's largest union, the National Education Association, nurtures the mentality that demands control over home schools. The NEA recommends that its members push for laws in accordance with its resolution concerning home schooling. At its 1992 convention in New Orleans, the NEA passed a resolution stating that it "believes that home schooling programs cannot provide the child with a comprehensive education experience." The resolution goes on to say that,

> . . . if parental preference home schooling study occurs, students enrolled must meet all state requirements. Instruction should be by persons who are licensed by the appropriate state education licensure agency, and a curriculum approved by the state department of education should be used.[1]

In every legislative battle over home schooling, the proponents of greater regulation have always been supported by the NEA. They need the tight controls in order to achieve their agenda. They would like to create home schools into small public schools. In fact, I have personally talked with dozens of public school superintendents who have claimed that home schools are "extensions of the public school" thus justifying restrictive standards and tight monitoring. The pervading philosophy held by the public school administrators is that home schooling is a privilege not a right.

The other issue, besides the philosophy of control, involves money. Your child is worth some $4,000 to $5,000 in tax money which will be designated to the school district if he or she is enrolled in the public schools. It is to the advantage of public school officials to deny a home schooler the right to exist in order to get the child back in public school. The more lenient the laws and policies, the more likely larger numbers of students will leave the public schools. The survival of public schools and the NEA teachers union depends on the number of children in the system. Home schooling is competing with their vested interest in public education.

In several states, superintendents receive state aid for home schoolers. They insist on strict monitoring procedures because they feel they have to provide a service to justify the per pupil state aid they are receiving. This incentive for collecting state aid needs to be cut off because it interferes with the home schooler's right to due process.

One of the elements of due process is the individual's right to have a neutral decision maker preside over whether or not they can exercise a certain privilege–in this case, teaching their children at home. The neutral decision maker must be available at the first instance. Thus a superintendent or school board with a vested financial interest is not neutral and must not be allowed to determine whether or not a home school may operate.

A case restricting religious freedom but reinforcing parental rights

A recent United States supreme Court decision which upholds the right of parents,[2] involved two American Indians who were fired from a private drug rehabilitation organization because they ingested "peyote," a hallucinogenic drug, as part of their religious belief. When they sought unemployment compensation, they were denied because they had been discharged for "misconduct.")

The Indians appealed to the Oregon Court of Appeals who reversed on the grounds that they had the right to freely exercise their religious beliefs by taking drugs. As expected, the U.S. Supreme Court reversed the case again finding that the First Amendment did not protect drug use. So what does the case have to do with parental rights?

After the Court ruled against the Indians, it then analyzed the application of the First Amendment's Free Exercise Clause generally. The Court wrongly decided to throw out the Free Exercise Clause as a defense to any "neutral" law that might violate an individual's religious convictions.[4] In the process of destroying religious freedom, the Court went out of its way to say that the parents' rights to control the education of their children is still a fundamental right. The Court declared that the "compelling interest test"[3] is applicable, not to the Free Exercise Clause by itself, but

> . . . to the Free Exercise Clause in conjunction with other constitutional protections such as . . . the right of parents, acknowledged in *Pierce* v. *Society of Sisters*, 268 U.S. 510 (1925), to direct the education of their children, see *Wisconsin* v. *Yoder*, 406 U.S. 205 (1972) invalidating compulsory-attendance laws as applied to Amish parents who refused on religious grounds to send their children to school.[5]

In other words, under this precedent, the fact that a family is home schooling for religious reasons is not enough to be a defense against a state requirement such as teacher certification. However, since that religious conviction to home school is *combined* with the fundamental right of parents to control the education of their children as guaranteed under the Fourteenth Amendment, the home school family battling the restrictive state regulation still is protected by the "compelling interest test."[6] This means the state must prove, with evidence, that teacher certification is necessary for children to be educated and if so, that only the least restrictive means is being required to assure it.

As a result, a requirement, such as teacher certification, should not prevail over a home school family's religious beliefs, if the state cannot prove *more* than that the teacher certification requirement is "reasonable." The Court in *Smith* quoted its previous case of *Wisconsin* v. *Yoder:*

> *Yoder* said that "The Court's holding in *Pierce* stands as a charter for the rights of parents to teach the religious upbringing of their children. And when the interests of parenthood are combined with a free exercise claim . . . more than merely a reasonable relationship to some purpose within the competency of the State is

required to sustain the validity of the State's requirement under the First Amendment." 406 U.S., at 233.[7]

Instead of merely showing that teacher certification is reasonable, the state must, therefore, reach the higher standard of the "compelling interest test."

Consequently, the constitutional right of a parent to direct the upbringing and education of his child is firmly entrenched in the U.S. Supreme Court case history.

A victory for home education

On May 25, 1993, the Michigan Supreme Court in *People* v. *DeJonge* affirmed the compelling interest test as it applied to the right of parents to educate their children. This is probably the most significant religious freedom decision on behalf of home schoolers that has come down from any State Supreme Court during the last twenty years.

The case involved Mark and Chris DeJonge who were teaching their children at home. They were contacted by their local school district in the state of Michigan and were told they had to use a certified teacher or be certified themselves. Because of their strong religious convictions that God had called them to home school their children and that they believed it was a sin for them to be certified or to be required to use a certified teacher, the family could not comply with the requirement. As a consequence, they were charged and convicted of criminal truancy. After I handled eight long years of litigation on behalf of the DeJonges, the Michigan Supreme Court ruled in a 4-3 decision that the teacher certification requirement in Michigan was unconstitutional. The Court stated:

> In summary, we conclude that the historical underpinnings of the First Amendment to the U.S. Constitution and the case law in support of it, compels the conclusion that the imposition of the certification requirement upon the DeJonges violates the Free Exercise Clause. We so conclude because we find that the certification requirement is not essential to nor is it the least restrictive means of achieving the State's claimed interest. Thus, we reaffirm that sphere of inviolable conscience and belief which is the mark of a free people. We hold that the teacher certification requirement is an unconstitutional violation of the Free Exercise Clause of the First Amendment as applied to families whose religious convictions prohibit the use of certified instructors. Such families, therefore, are exempt from the dictates of the teacher certification requirements.[8]

This case upholds the proper application of the compelling interest test providing protection for families who choose to home school, yet object on religious grounds to certain restrictive requirements. Overnight, Michigan changed from one of the worst states for home schooling to one of the best.

A summary of the legal atmosphere in the fifty states (editorially amended for harmony with the facts in early 1998. A sate-by-state summary of requirements appears at the beginning of Appendix D. *tw*)

A short description of the home school legislation and case precedent will reveal the national trend to limit state controls over private education in favor of expanding parental liberty. Since 1982, the majority of states have changed their compulsory attendance laws and several state boards of education have amended their regulations to specifically allow for home schooling with certain minimal requirements. In addition, two more states, Alaska and Nebraska, amended their private school statutes in 1984, allowing for any private school to opt out of accreditation and certification requirements by asserting sincerely held religious beliefs.[9]

More than thirty states by statute or regulation specifically allow "home instruction" or "home schooling," provided that certain requirements are met.[10]

Several of them require home schoolers to submit an annual notice of intent, verifying that instruction will be given in certain core subjects for the same amount of days as in public schools. In fact, in Missouri, home schoolers even have an option not to notify at all. These states' laws tend to be "model" laws since they are properly based on the "honor system" which protects parental liberty and takes all monitoring power from the state authorities.

Colorado and Georgia have laws similar to the five mentioned above, but parents are required to have the children tested every other year. The best part of these laws is that the test scores do not have to be submitted to the public schools.

Many home school statutes require, in addition, that home schoolers administer an annual standardized achievement test or have an evaluation performed which shows that the child has made adequate progress. Tennessee, for example, requires that home schooled children be tested in grades 2, 3, 6, 8, and 10. Some states specify a minimum test result.

The other of the fifty states have no specific statutes referring to home instruction, although all states allow home schooling under certain conditions. For example, in at least twelve states, home schools may operate as private schools. These states are Alabama, Alaska, California, Delaware, Illinois, Indiana, Kansas, Kentucky, Michigan, Nebraska, Oklahoma, and Texas. In all of these states, home schoolers need only provide instruction in certain core subjects for the same time as public schools do. Although each year, certain school districts challenge the right of home schools to exist as private schools in these states, home schoolers have thus far been successful.

Approval from the local superintendent or school board is required in several states. These approval states have somewhat vague requirements for home schools, leaving each school district to create its own arbitrary interpretations. Great disparity results.

Ultimately, the Home School Legal Defense Association has been successful year after year both in amending legislation to provide greater freedoms for home schoolers and in winning cases involved in striking down excessive regulation. But the battle is fierce. Home schoolers need to join together to protect their rights.

Facing the conflict

From our perspective at HSLDA, we see the battles are intensifying. The spiritual warfare is growing fierce. Around 85 or 90 percent of home schoolers are teaching their own children for religious reasons. They believe God has called them to personally teach their children so they can apply the principles of God's Word to every subject. They want to protect their children from the humanism and from the "negative socialization" – from the drugs, violence and sex – occurring in public schools and in some private schools. They also want their children to have the basic skills enabling them to read God's Word and live in His world. They don't want them to be among the 27 million illiterate children graduating from our nation's public schools.

Please Remember

School laws change. Contact your state organization or a legal service organization such as HSLDA for current information.

The newest attack has been through the child welfare system. People who do not like home schoolers often give social workers an "anonymous tip" fabricating allegations of abuse. We at HSLDA work nearly every week on protecting home school families from investigations by social workers insisting on entering the home and interrogating the children separately. The attack intensifies as the national trend continues to increases the power of the social welfare burearcracy.[11]

Home education – one of our most crucial rights – is guaranteed by the First and Fourteenth Amendments of the U.S. Constitution. I think the enemy sees the danger of this growing movement and is seeking to regulate home schools out of existence or into conformity.

The war has two fronts. First, the spiritual, requiring constant commitment and prayer by God's people. This conflict could result in intimidation or even prosecution

Secondly, it is a legal battle, taking place in the courts and legislatures of this country. The staff of HSLDA needs commitment from its members and from home schoolers in general in support of their ministry. The right to teach our own children, free from unreasonable government restrictions and threats, is too precious to lose.

Endnotes

1. *National Education Association, Resolutions,* 1992. C-34.

2. *Employment Division of Oregon* v. *Smith II. 494 U.S. 872 (1990).*

3. The "compelling interest test" is the legal process of determining whether a state law or regulation may override a fundamental right of an individual. To establish a compelling interest, it must be proved that (1) an individual's right is at risk of being burdened, (2) the state's requirement is essential or necessary to fulfill the more fundamental interest, and (3) the least restrictive means is to be used in meeting the requirement. See the last section of the previous chapter.

4. By God's grace, the negative aspects of this case were reversed in the passage of the Religious Freedom Restoration Act of 1993. The Home School Legal Defense Association helped organize a coalition of religious freedom groups to draft and successfully pass the RFRA thereby restoring religious freedom to all. [The 1993 Act has since been attacked. *ed.*]

5. *Id.*, at p. 881. Bold face emphasis supplied.

6. The U.S. Supreme Court has regularly applied the "compelling interest test" to fundamental rights that arise out of the Liberty Clause of the Fourteenth Amendment. In *Roe* v. *Wade*, 410 U.S. 113, 144 (1973), the Court said: "Where fundamental rights are involved . . . regulation limiting these rights may be justified *only* by a *compelling state interest* . . . ."

7. *Id.*, at p. 881. Bold face emphasis supplied.

8. *People* v. *DeJonge,* 501 N.W. 2d 127, Michigan Supreme Court, May 25, 1993.

9. See Alaska Statutes § 79-1701(2). Home schoolers in these two states can now freely operate under these religious exemptions.

10. See generally, Christopher Klicka, *Home Schooling in the United States: A Legal Analysis.* This publication is updated every August and is published by The Home School Legal Defense Association, P.O. Box 159, Paeonian Springs, VA 22129.

11. See the review of Attorney Klicka's book, *The Right Choice . . . Home Schooling* in Appendix I.

7

Helping Your Child Learn

An earlier chapter pointed out that teachers don't produce learning; students do. But teachers certainly help it happen. In this chapter, I will make some observations about how you can help it happen in your home school.

Being a parent-teacher

As a parent, you have known your child longer than he or she has known you. From birth, you have fed, clothed, disciplined, and loved your child. But this child-parent relationship, important as it is, could cover up the realization that each of us is an individual – young and dependent at first, but still a living being, more valuable than all the gold in the world, with tremendous potential for good or evil.

I would not imply that you and your child are peers. You are not. As a parent you have the responsibility for directing and guiding your young charge. He or she has the responsibility to obey. What you must avoid is the subconscious feeling that the child is your property. Adolescent kids have a way of disillusioning their parents on this point, but it is well to understand it much earlier.

Now you face a new role–teacher. Of course it's new only in a sense. You have been teaching all along, even when you haven't intended to. But your responsibility is now expanding to include intellectual and skill development traditionally committed to "experts" outside the home.

What is the difference between a home school teacher who is obviously still a parent, and a more traditional parent who teaches outside of school hours as a normal part of parenthood? Both have tremendous responsibility. The major distinction is that teaching school must be planned and carried out in a serious way. Of course, education before school years and outside of school time is serious, too, but it can have a more casual stride. Your conscious instruction to your preschool or out-of-school child is given whenever it seems appropriate.

The biggest part of casual teaching is being there, caring, and controlling the environment. As your child matures, however, the educational program must be more carefully planned and diligently pursued. Spontaneous? Yes, as much as possible, but directed. And when there is no spark of interest? Stir the fire! We discuss this more in other chapters.

Qualifications for teaching

To be a good teacher, how much education is enough? Recent research shows that the home schooling parent's own level of education and whether or not she (or he) is a certified teacher makes almost no difference in student achievement.[1] In private schools, students generally do better than their public school counterparts, even though their teachers are less apt to be certified. Of course, they have a stronger base from their home backgrounds.

The home teacher's academic background is still relevant. How much should a teacher know beyond the level taught? Enough to permit some flexibility. Enough for a degree of freedom in answering unexpected questions. Many parents with only a high school education have successfully instructed their elementary children. In fact, most people with even less formal education who are well read, studious, and organized should be able to succeed. Using preplanned home study materials obviously requires fewer years of formal education than are needed for teaching independently.

In addition to knowing subject matter, a good teacher also understands something about how children learn. Here again, formal teacher training isn't necessary for school at home. An intuitive notion of these learning principles may be developed, at least to a degree, by watching children and interacting with them.

A person may successfully teach an idea without having previously learned it in school. True, the teacher who learns just in advance of passing on the knowledge or skill usually lacks the broader understanding helpful in directing the student's spontaneous interests. But teaching new material has an advantage, too. The learning teacher, having just found a way to master the new concept, remembers how it was analyzed, broken down, and made understandable. He or she tends more to see from the learner's viewpoint. This is at least one reason why students often find it easier to understand their peers than their teachers.

I'm not suggesting that teacher training and certification are unimportant. I do maintain, however, that they are unnecessary for the home school.

Your children must like you

Now let's talk about how to teach. I have appreciated a little book by James L. Hymes, Jr. entitled *A Child Development Point of View*. The chapter titles themselves have something important to say: You Are a "Teacher," "Your Youngsters Must Like You," "Your Youngsters Must Like Their Work," "Your Youngsters Must Like Themselves," and "Your Youngsters Can Climb the Highest Peaks."

Approaching our discussion of teaching from the line of thinking in Hymes' book (although with not all the same ideas), let's consider first the importance of your youngsters liking you. Whether child or adult, we all learn from someone else more easily in an atmosphere of confidence than in an adversary relationship. When we trust the one we are with and feel that that person has our best interest at heart, our minds are free to concentrate on the learning task; we can ask questions and test out our ideas in discussion. Children, even more than adults, perform to please their teacher. The better they like the teacher, the more their energy goes into learning.

As a parent who cares, your relationship with your son or daughter is probably not all that bad, but realizing its influence on learning emphasizes the value of improving it. More than good learning performance on school tasks is at stake. Children unconsciously want to be like people they admire. This indirect potential for character development is an even greater reason for working to strengthen the bond.

Children need adult support and affection during all their growing-up years. Your child wants to admire you all the time, but expectations are different during different stages of development. Young children through the early grades especially need physical contact. They need to be "mothered." Take their hand now and then. Give them a little squeeze.

As this period merges into the intermediate elementary years, the ideal for the parent or teacher changes. This is the time they want to see you do the active things they like to do – play games, run, ride a bicycle.

Then at the junior and senior high school level, young people want you to respect them like adults. They aren't entirely grown up yet, and they know it. But they look to you to admit them to your adult world by the way you relate to them.

This pattern of a personal, caring relationship with your children doesn't mean you let them do whatever they please. Notice Hymes' explanation:

> The meaning is clear for every age. Be friendly, sure. Be warm and approachable. Be decent, but be an adult. Children want you to be. They need someone stronger than they are — more aware, more alert — as a prop to their own efforts to do the right thing.
>
> Youngsters don't want rules staring them in the face wherever they turn. They don't want to be picked up on every little thing they do every second of the day. They appreciate a little flexibility. If the same law is broken time and time again, they hope you will take a second look at the rule to see if it really is a good one.
>
> They want some patience on your part. You cannot pass a law and expect children to be letter-perfect on it the very next second. Children need time to learn how to do the right thing, the way it takes them time to learn to read or to do arithmetic. . . . You have to allow time for mistakes in grammar to straighten out. The heavens must not fall every time there is a slip.
>
> Youngsters like it best, too, when you talk things over and keep talking them over, day after day. If you are harsh, you push children away from you. If you are severe, you push them back. If you are tough, you push them off. When you explain, interpret, discuss, then you draw the youngsters in.
>
> If you have a rule, if it is a good rule, stick by it. Your sensible, reasonable rule joins hands with the friendly talking way you uphold the rule. The two together — your rule and your friendliness — develop strength and security in youngsters.[2]

Your children must like their work

People learn better when their motivation comes from inside. When your child picks up a consuming interest in some special topic – it could be growing tomatoes, or amateur radio, or one of a million other things–learning really happens. An external system of rewards and punishment may support a certain degree of learning – just enough to get by. But even when "getting by" is all you want, the ultimate name of the game with only outside motivation is "beat the system."

For children to like what they are doing, the first requirement beyond liking their teacher is having the ability to succeed in what is expected of them. Whether the task is walking, knitting, or working word problems about boats going up- or downstream, success depends on more than trying hard. Until the child has the necessary maturity, the result will be failure, frustration, and a block to learning.

How can you tell when your young student is ready to learn? The calendar won't tell you because each child is different. Maturity is difficult to define and measure, but still, readiness for a specific learning task is clear and obvious. The key is enthusiasm.

Adults can fake it. They can look interested when they are bored. But not kids. When they are ready to learn, you can see it all over them, in their questions, their remarks, their willingness to listen. Of course, you wouldn't interpret an intelligent question about what holds aircraft up in the sky as an indication that your young child is ready to begin flight training. If you attempt more than very simple answers before your child is ready for serious learning, you may be tuned out after the first sentence. Besides enthusiasm, two other indications of readiness are sincer- ity and duration of interest – qualities almost synonymous with maturity.

I am not suggesting that you just sit and

wait for an indication of interest in something, then try to teach it. You and the textbooks provide the material to be interested in. Also, your child will pick up ideas worthy of building into the curriculum.

From a practical standpoint, you may need to push ahead even when your child isn't wild with enthusiasm. But when your boy or girl is obviously not ready, hold off.

At every point of development, a child is ready for some worthwhile learning. As a home school teacher, you have a real advantage. You can observe more closely, and you can alter the curriculum as needed.

> You have to keep searching for children's interests. Once you find them, don't let the youngsters off easy. They don't want you to. They want you to have high standards, just as long as the learning makes sense to them. They want you to hold them to the grindstone, and they respect you and are grateful when you do. They want your expectations to stretch them up to the peak of their growing powers. They count on you to ask the most searching questions, to check them on details, to open up the next step in thinking or doing. Youngsters want to achieve.[3]

Another characteristic of elementary children which affects how well they will like what they are to learn is action. You may enjoy sitting in the summer breeze, watching the world go by. But not kids. They are part of the world that you see going by – at top speed. Learning tasks need to involve physical action, especially for the very young.

Also, for young children, attention spans are very short. Plan activities that are quickly finished. Break longer tasks into short segments. You can easily adjust the length of your assignments and explanations as you teach. Just remember to be sensitive and watch the level of interest.

Your children must like themselves

Much of what we have already discussed about getting your young scholars to like you and to like what they are doing contributes also to the third principle in promoting learning: helping children to like themselves.

If you believe that humanity has a higher object of affection than itself, you have a right to question advice to encourage children's ideas of their own importance. You know how easily children show disrespect to elders and are demeaning to other children. We must differentiate between self-worth and self-centeredness. People who have been hurt and hated often place a low value on themselves and try to push other people around. People who feel good about themselves usually feel good about other people too.

The Christian's self-denial isn't a process of depressing the individual worth (Matt. 11:28, 29). It means trusting God rather than going it alone. In view of Heaven's sacrifice at Calvary, each person is valuable beyond measure.

If you remember that children are people and you realize the price paid for their redemption, you can have the kind of respect for them that will help them feel important in the right way. You are still in charge, but you will look for opportunities to help them use all their potential.

Kids like to work; they want to achieve; and they look to you to help them feel good about it.

Teaching techniques

You may have expected this chapter to tell you what procedures to follow to produce learning in various subject areas. In raising cattle, precise feed formulas and specific treatment of the animals have been figured out to achieve optimum results. Educating people, however, is not that simple. Certainly, vast amounts of research have been done on teaching techniques. And there are good ways to get ideas across. But more basic than teaching methods is the teacher.

This chapter has briefly traced a few ideas that can help you be a good teacher. In order that you not get the idea that techniques are unimportant, that you can just be nice to your kids and they will learn, I should clarify. You do need to follow a consistent teaching program using logical methods. Common sense is usually your best guide.

How to teach is discussed in many parts of this book. Textbooks, teacher's editions, and guidelines with package programs also offer help. As you get into the process of planning and teaching, the great mystery of what to do will shrivel up.

Be sure to read Appendix L, "Ideas That Work." It is more than a directory to be consulted for specific questions. It covers bushels of principles you can use in your teaching.

Endnotes

1. See the discussion of Brian Ray's research near the end of Chapter 2, and the endnote pertaining to it.
2. James L. Hymes, Jr., *A Child Development Point of View*, pp. 43, 44. Original copyright 1955 by Prentice-Hall. Reprinted by permission of Allyn & Bacon, Inc.
3. *Ibid.*, p. 100.

8

Inspiring Motivation

Have you ever tried to build up enthusiasm in a disinterested child, wishing for a "want-to" button you could press? In a broad sense, the previous chapter, "Helping Your Child Learn," told you how to foster motivation. Here I want to share with you what I see as the very bottom line – the causes behind why anyone does anything. Then I'll suggest how you might face a problem with a reluctant learner.

Parents' responsibility

Some would advise just letting children do what they feel like – encouraging them to follow whatever motivation they happen to have, as long as they don't injure anyone. I've oversimplified this theory a little. Advocates do believe in guidance. The basic idea is that the standard for right and wrong develops from within the individual and that, in time, good will emerge. I disagree. First, people just don't get better by following natural inclinations. And second, I believe parents have a responsibility not only to love and provide for their children but also to guide them – to help them develop a sense of right and of priorities.

In this guidance, we must realize that children mature. Activities we proffer should, as far as possible, depend on the child. The successful instructor takes advantage of the learner's readiness or, when appropriate, helps create the circumstances to produce it. Also we would not want to violate the learner's creative interest and individuality by insisting on an inflexible learning program that leaves no room for the adventure of exploring.

No one does anything without a reason. The reason may be selfish and based on misunderstanding or it may be right and sensible, but there is a reason. Even doing nothing is an "action" prompted by a reason because it is a decision to reject opportunity.

So the boy who doesn't want to learn about fractions has a reason for dragging his feet. The girl who gazes off into space while you tell about how boats float, although maybe not aware of it, has a reason, too.

Reasons for not wanting to learn

What reasons might hinder motivation to learn? Here are some possibilities:

- Lessons that don't make sense are boring. Without the maturity to understand or with gaps in prerequisite learning leaving new ideas unclear, the individual may not be motivated to try. Memorizing chemical names, for example, won't likely have much appeal until the uses and behaviors of the substances are discussed and maybe the system for determining chemical names is understood. The more a person can connect new ideas into his or her existing structure of understanding, the clearer and more appealing they become. However, as you can see, some- - thing has to come first. So now and then, learning with only a slight relationship to previous understanding is necessary.

- Certain learning tasks may be seen as contrary to personal goals already established. If a boy wants to be considered "tough" and he thinks an interest in poetry might jeopardize that image, then he will avoid the area as much as he can. Peers often influence what children see as desirable.

- An interesting psychological mechanism tends to protect us from the hurt of failure, and to lead us to "invest" in areas that promise success. Thus it's much safer not to be interested in a topic than it is to face inability to understand it. Peer or teacher intimidation strengthen the tendency. Unfortunately, the avoidance this process produces only makes matters worse. Disinclination and failure through neglect turn to burnout. How important it is then for the parent-teacher to encourage balanced learning and to watch for intentional disinterest in any area.

You have probably read about right-brain and left-brain individuals. Apparently one side of the brain tends to deal with logic and order while the other specializes in feelings or the aesthetic. Our protection mechanism tends to strengthen whichever side is stronger while neglecting the weaker.

Certainly we wouldn't argue that everyone should have the same interests and abilities. For example, we expect men to be logical and women to be sensitive. We like it that way, but how sad to see either essentially devoid of the opposite traits.

- Mental application may be blocked by an unsolved personal problem. This might be a marriage problem between parents, rejection by boyfriend or girlfriend, threat of physical harm, lack of money to meet needs, or guilt.
- Drugs, alcohol, lack of sleep, or similar physical abuses could simply put the mind out of gear.
- Serious physical needs may be unmet. Hunger, cold, inability to see well, or other similar problems could be stopping learning.
- The teacher's intent may be interpreted negatively causing a lack of trust.
- The mind may be overstimulated. The source could be, for example, drama from reading or television, sports, or an improper diet.
- Through spirit possession or hypnosis the mind may have been turned over to another intelligence.

Quest for happiness

We have considered factors that impede interest in learning. What encourages it? Selfishness may appear to achieve happiness, but the end result is always disappointment and misery.

What brings deep, lasting happiness? Would cooking or music or building a dog

house or whatever you usually enjoy be any fun with no one to share the results? Motivation, then, is the lure of personal satisfaction. And, for sincere people, this means the desire to create happiness for someone else. God wants this kind of personal satisfaction for His children and has given them the drive to seek it.

How the motivating force develops with maturity

As an individual matures, his or her ways of seeking happiness expand. In the ideal pattern for development, the source of greatest satisfaction shifts through four levels:

1. ***The personal comfort stage.*** In infancy happiness is enjoying the love and protection of parents and having the physical comforts of being warm, clean, fed and so on.

2. ***The caregiver approval stage.*** The child's focus of affection turns first to the visible sources of authority and comfort – the mother and father and, in the primary grades, the teacher. The comfort desires of the earlier stage expand to include whatever makes life easy and fun.

3. ***The selected friends stage.*** In teen years satisfaction often comes from pleasing peers. The individual's desire to look good to these friends influences choices of activities, material possessions, and values, as well as learning.

A person with a religious orientation or with a more balanced outlook may be less influenced by special friends, but will still see them as important. For the Christian, God is seen as Provider, Protector, and Source of all good things. Accepting Him gives comfort and security.

Most people never pass this level. Their values change as they get older but are still largely determined by friends. Even those who think more independently usually focus their actions on themselves or on certain people who meet their approval. People are valued because they belong to the same race, the same nation, the same church fellowship or the same side in a dispute.

4. ***The unrestricted stage.*** Here love doesn't require being loved first, or even being loved in return. Happiness comes from helping people simply because they need help. Close friends are still selected as people who support similar ideals, but kindness and understanding aren't restricted to them.

For the devoted individual, God becomes a close companion. Pleasing Him at any cost brings deep satisfaction. Following His will is no longer seen as a means to earn salvation or to fulfill expectations of friends. The individual identifies with his Maker's interests and objectives.

As I see it, the shifts from one stage to the next are not abrupt. Also happiness for a person at a certain level may often come from a lower level or occasionally from the next higher level.

Planning for motivation

How, then, can understanding the basics of motivation help you encourage better learning? For example, if your child sees good spelling as a means to achieve happiness, spelling lessons may take on new importance. At the caregiver-approval stage, spelling is desirable for clear communication. When selected friends are important, its appeal may be the achievement of better social acceptance. And for the individual with mature happiness goals, spelling as a part of communication is seen as a tool for helping and loving people.

In planning, we would want to appeal to the highest sources of happiness the individual is capable of understanding. Nothing is wrong with a mature individual's wanting to be warm and dry, but appealing to these desires while neglecting their relationship with higher purposes, would encourage selfishness.

Of course you should talk about how to find greater sources of happiness even to young children. You may not see a response. You may feel that your words are not getting through, but remember to mention it as it seems appropriate. The concepts will crystallize later. Your own example is extremely important in giving the ideas reality and in helping them take root.

Let's not overlook the obvious importance of making learning fun. This means: Show enthusiasm and understanding yourself. Relate learning to established interests. Think of interesting activities. Choose attractive materials and physical surroundings. And give your child a significant role in planning.

Even with high happiness goals established, all learners, especially young ones, also need short-term objectives like preparing for a test, or finishing the chapter before lunch, or even occasionally the promise of a special treat. But these reasons to achieve should be understood as helping reach the genuine end goal.

When interest fizzles

Now let's face reality. Everything doesn't always turn out as we might wish. What do you do when your child shows little interest and just doesn't want to get in and dig for understanding? In the box are some suggestions for approaching the problem of lack of motivation.

In the end, we recognize that only God, who has given to each a measure of faith can, in connection with that faith, give motivation.

Solving a Motivation Problem

- *Search for the reason for not wanting to learn — for refusing opportunity. It may be a delicate issue. Probably even your child won't have identified the problem. Listen more than talk. Care.*
- *Help the learner work it through. This may take time.*
- *Help the individual to internalize the happiness goals to see all appropriate learning as a means of bringing joy to others and to God.*
- *Hold high (and reasonably attainable) expectations, but present them in small steps with short range objectives, especially for younger children.*
- *Show appreciation. If this doesn't come naturally, practice. It's vitally important.*
- *Consider the possible influence of attention deficit disorder or other learning handicaps. (See the chapter on this topic.)*
- *From the Christian viewpoint, exalt Jesus by life and word. He is Heaven's window.*

9

Developing an Educational Framework

Your interest in home schooling may have come from a fairly clear picture of what you *don't* want for your children. Your purpose should be more, however, than keeping them away from a certain school situation or wanting a home environment. A person who sets out on a trip with no particular destination in mind generally arrives at no particular place. To a certain degree education is the same way. You can plan some good activities and study some good books with your child, and certainly some good learning will occur. The question you must face is, in the end, will the young person in your care be fully balanced and prepared to function adequately to his or her full potential? Some of the details of your purposes will develop as you go along, but the general directions and some of the mileposts should be marked out before you start.

You need "goals" and "objectives." Goals are more general. The educational goals you establish tell the broad purposes of your child's learning. They are chosen in harmony with your philosophy. An example of a goal is to handle finances wisely and efficiently.

Objectives are more specific and are developed from the goals. The objective of being able to convert between fractions and decimal numbers, along with many other objectives, leads to the goal of handling finances wisely and efficiently.

Wait. Don't get discouraged at this point. Not even professional educators sit down and, from scratch, write out a detailed chart of goals and objectives. They have help, and you will find that most of your work is already done, too. I suggest a goals list later in this chapter. Your school district office will also have one which you could look at. Objectives may be chosen from lists such as are in Appendix H and you can add your own.

Your job then is first to think of some of the things you really want for your child. Then see to what extent they are covered by the lists you look at.

The next step in making your educational plan is to place priorities on the goals. Priorities are developed naturally from your philosophy. Keeping them straight doesn't take fancy planning. Just stop now and then to consider what you are doing, and whether you are teaching what is most important. If you don't, you could end up with mostly frosting and very little cake.

The final step is determining a sequence for meeting the objectives. Actually, you don't need to worry much about this either, because textbook authors and the curriculum committees which influence them have already planned a good sequence for most of the objectives, and the small details of what comes first often don't matter.

Next let's look more closely at the process of setting goals, then at the matter of sequence and of choosing an educational program.

Considering goals

In the 1989 education summit in Charlottesville, Virginia, President Bush and the state governors agreed on six major goals to be reached by the year 2000:[1]

> ***Readiness for School*** By the year 2000, all children in America will start school ready to learn.
>
> ***High School Completion*** By the year 2000, the high school graduation

rate will increase to at least 90 percent.

Student Achievement and Citizenship By the year 2000, American students will leave grades four, eight, and twelve having demonstrated competency in challenging subject matter including English, mathematics, science, history, and geography; and every school in America will ensure that all students learn to use their minds well, so they may be prepared for responsible citizenship, further learning, and productive employment in our modern economy.

Science and Mathematics By the year 2000, U.S. students will be first in the world in science and mathematics achievement.

Adult Literacy and Lifelong Learning By the year 2000, every adult American will be literate and will possess the knowledge and skills necessary to compete in a global economy and exercise the rights and responsibilities of citizenship.

Safe, Disciplined, and Drug-Free Schools By the year 2000, every school in America will be free of drugs and violence and will offer a disciplined environment conducive to learning.

How nice it would be if our country (and others in the world) could even move in the *direction* of these goals. I'm not very optimistic. Still, I appreciate the goals. Improved schools are important for all of us.

Interest in the good of other people is briefly mentioned in terms of "good citizenship, community service, and personal responsibility," but the greater emphasis seems to be as expressed in the introduction: a preparation for being "internationally competitive" with an "educational performance . . . second to none in the 21st century."

Home Schooling, as we think of it, is not discussed but a couple of encouraging points are worth noting.[2] One of the three objectives listed with the first goal is: "Every parent in America will be a child's first teacher and devote time each day helping his or her preschool child learn; parents will have access to the training and support they need."

In addition to recognizing a need for a restructuring of schools to "focus on results, not on procedures," the new emphasis calls for "providing a way for . . . giving parents more responsibility for their children's education through magnet schools, public school choice, and other strategies."

Outcomes-based education, a current trend

Home schooling proponents have been sounding the alarm about the trend in public schooling toward what is called "outcomes-based education." In simple terms, OBE is an effort to "focus on results" as mentioned in the preceding paragraph. Samuel Blumenfeld calls it "Educational Revolution by Stealth." He writes, "Now that the educationist planners have decided that the traditional educational model . . . cannot meet the demands of the future, they are busily paving over the last 150 years of educational experience with a new concept for the government schools. . . ." Among other concerns Blumenfeld points out that "The emphasis is on performance, not content, on behavior, not knowledge. . . . Curriculum and instruction are geared to 'what we want the kids to demonstrate successfully at the end.'"[3]

Educational critics have long deplored the fact that some students have been passed along from one grade to the next until they hold their high school diploma, hardly able to read what it says. We also hear of studying math without being able to balance a checkbook. Now the education establishment is coming to some of the same conclusions. They are saying that our focus needs to be on final competencies. Do we still disagree, demanding that the emphasis remain on content rather than the behavior that shows the content to mean something useful in real life? We can learn the content without being able to use it, but if we can apply knowledge the content has to have been understood, too.

Inge P. Cannon[4] lists sample OBE goals such as being able to communicate in family and community, and making environmentally sound decisions. She asks how these can possibly be measured objectively. I would ask, Does it matter? Unmeasurable goals are not new. We wish for the goals of the good old days when more patriotism and honesty were taught. In church schools, we teach for the highest of all objectives – eternal salvation. The measurable elements are the least important. We wouldn't want to limit our instruction to them.

When I was taking my doctoral course work, a psychology professor declared that we could measure anything we asked kids to learn. I disagreed, and I expect that many educational planners would, too. (He took teaching neatness as an example. His measure would have been counting the number of pieces of paper any child threw down on the playground.)

Some unmeasurable characteristics we can judge by observation. Good teachers (and certainly parents) have always been able to see, for example, whether their students could resolve interpersonal differences peaceably; and they have aimed for corresponding educational goals. Although we cannot know whether our children will later try to save the whales and the redwoods, we can choose to expose them to reading and viewing material in harmony with such objectives.

The danger

Another goal Inge Cannon mentions involves overcoming prejudice.[6] This is indeed a sensitive area since most of us do not approve of homosexual life-partner choices. When we see something as clearly (Scripturally) wrong, we should not encourage our children to doubt it in a "critical thinking" exercise. Of course, our convictions are not license for prejudice against the wrongdoer as a person (Matt. 18:23-35). Inge Cannon does have a point in that the public school teacher (or the national teachers' union) might change this goal to teach that any choice is okay. In the current atmosphere, however, this is unlikely because objectives are set state-by-state and are often suggestions. Time could change this, of course.

One way in which schools may try to assess attitudes is by personal opinion questionnaires. Teaching could be directed toward predetermined values. As education becomes more nationally controlled, a system like OBE could become a dangerously powerful religio-political tool.

In light of this threat, Cathy Duffy points out another danger: "Many conservatives recommend that private schools back voucher proposals, claiming that they can write them to limit the power of both the public education bureaucracy and the legislatures to regulate private (including home) education. Unfortunately, the history of voucher proposals has demonstrated clearly that there will be a trade off for any voucher plan. Schools that receive voucher funding will have to abide by certain restrictions such as not requiring students to attend chapel or use Christian curriculum. Moreover, testing and standards requirements are likely to be part of the State's efforts to hold private schools 'accountable.' It seems clear that vouchers will ultimately force private schools to adopt the same goals and agenda as public schools."[7]

Another of my memorable experiences in graduate school was to assist Dr. J. Galen Saylor, a recognized authority in the area of curriculum. One of his greatest concerns was that centralized government might try to control what all American schools taught. That was more than twenty years ago. His fears are much closer to being realized now.

In my opinion, outcomes-based education is good in principle. Teaching *must* be directed toward end results. The issue is over who is to control the outcomes.

See my review of the book, America 2000 / Goals 2000, *in Appendix I.*

We must oppose:

↳ A tracking system that would follow every child and prescribe for his or her educational "needs." This opens the door to state control of children, and loss of liberty.

↳ Any government decisions of what moral values should be taught, beyond the general goals of respecting the freedoms of other individuals and being sensitive to their needs. This usurps the responsibility God has given directly to parents.

What do you want for your children?

As you think about your own educational goals, remember that they should focus on the results you expect for the student, not on a list of what you think should be taught. Although you may not sit down and put your goals into words, you should, from time to time, think about the education your children are getting and question whether or not they are being directed in the general way you feel they should go. Lists of goals can help you focus on what you feel is important. In the box are goals I would choose.

Notice that this list does not directly mention specific school subjects, although you can see if you look back over it, that many of the typical subjects lead toward these goals. For example, language arts or English produces communication skills. Math helps conduct personal business,

Educational Goals

Each individual should learn. . . .

To love sincerely. Love and respect for other people grows out of a personal relationship with God and a realization of self-worth. Sensitivity to the values and needs of others, built on a stable, caring home life leads to a happy marriage, to good citizenship, and to successful human relationships in general.

To live healthfully. A healthy mind and body is one of the most important factors in personal happiness and in usefulness to society.

To work responsibly. Time is the essence of life. Each individual should be able to use it efficiently. Each needs salable skills, a sense of dependability, a respect for the property of other people, and an appreciation for the value of all kinds of productive labor.

To communicate clearly. Human relationships and learning depend on skills in listening, speaking, reading and writing.

To enjoy beauty. Beauty is found in the simple as well as in the magnificent. To see it, to receive satisfaction from it, and to share it are part of happiness.

To reason perceptively. Clear understanding, good logic and creative application of knowledge constitute thinking, the highest level of human capability and a necessary element in freedom.

To conduct personal business prudently. Earning responsibly, investing wisely, spending effectively, and planning carefully form the atmosphere for efficient human functioning.

To relate intelligently to the environment. Life is supported and enriched from natural resources. Understanding and using them wisely makes a better life for everyone now and for generations to come.

stimulates thinking, and affects working responsibly. Science leads to the goals about health and the environment. And so on. Some of the goals are not typically achieved through studying school subjects. But this should not be surprising since education is a product of an individual's total environment (whether good or bad) and continues during the entire life span. With a home school you have the opportunity for a few early years to coordinate the total development of your child.

Your own list may be somewhat different from mine. You may want to place major emphasis on some points I have only indirectly assumed. Remember that you are guiding a life that is not your personal property. The effects of your teaching will continue long after you have ceased to be a part of this old world.

I prepared this list of goals to be acceptable to parents with differing philosophies. Those of you who hold a system of priorities similar to what my wife and I believe is important, will want to expand the first goal and emphasize the "personal relationship with God." I'd like to preach a little sermon here, but I'll just urge you to read God's word for its deeper meaning. You might begin with John 17, especially verse 3, and with Luke 10:27.

At the beginning of the school year and at appropriate times thereafter, take a few minutes to talk about the big reasons for education, relating goals to your child's level of understanding. A good way to do this is to have a family discussion looking at lists like the one I have proposed. Input from two families with children at various ages would lend strength and meaning. It would stimulate resolve for excellence.

As you work with your child from day to day, teach for a balanced education. Keep in mind that the subjects and the separate learning tasks are only important as they lead to the final goals. And remember, too, Rome was not built in a day – nor by a single individual

Knowing what to teach and when

As you begin to think of specific objectives, you will realize that a framework is necessary. What do you teach? And when? Actually the problem is much simpler than you might think. If you use a preplanned home study learning package, this is figured out for you. Even if you don't, textbook companies realize that teachers like help in this respect. They prepare "scope and sequence" charts for each series of textbooks in a subject area. These charts describe what is covered in each grade in each of several categories of objectives. The order in which the various concepts are presented in the books is also shown on the charts. In other words, these charts are like outlines for the books. In most cases, following through the textbook assures you of a good scope and sequence, and gives you good objectives as well.

Appendix G shows the subjects and general topics typically taught from kindergarten through the twelfth grade.

Perhaps in giving you the theoretical basis for choosing what to teach, we have left you with the feeling that you need an extra six months for research in order to establish your own special curriculum – to reinvent your own wheel. In practice, it's not so difficult. Your task will tend to be finding sources, approving what you see as desirable, making modifications to include or emphasize what you consider high priorities, and adding special items central to your own philosophy.

Challenging tradition

School reformers Raymond and Dorothy Moore and John Holt along with many others, have made serious contributions in helping parents know how to make the break with tradition.

The Moores believe, through their study of research, that formal book learning should be delayed until a child is around eight years old. See my chapter, "Planning for the Early Years," for more on this topic.

John Holt believed that schools in general are poor places to learn because traditional educators tend to separate teaching from real life; to feel that only they can teach, that schooling makes people better, and that they, not the students, must decide what is to be learned.

In pressing for drastic school reform, Holt insisted that children should learn whenever and however they want to, guided by their own curiosity instead of at someone else's command; that the "fixed" curriculum should be made open and free; that the system of testing and grading, which he viewed as corrupting, impeding, and without useful function in learning, be abolished; and that children should be allowed to learn without being "taught." He argues that "compulsory school attendance no longer serves a useful function, either to schools, teachers or students, and that it should be done away with or greatly modified."[8]

Most home schooling parents are conservative Christians who would not agree with most of Holt's ideas, and would want a little more structure than the Moores seem to advocate.

What to expect from guidance providers

Using the services of a home study guidance system (like many in Appendix A)

In enrolling your children in a correspondence school, you will have more to do than stick on stamps and seal envelopes. You or someone you designate will be responsible for directing the learning day by day at least through most of the elementary years.

If you use a correspondence school program, you can expect the school to set up the curriculum, choose or prepare the learning materials, provide a syllabus of teaching instructions, give counsel and encouragement as needed, and, in most cases, grade tests at several points during the year.

A guidance center or supporting school will not give you as detailed a syllabus, but materials will be provided or suggested with general instructions and probably standardized tests.

The factors which follow can help you decide which school or program can best serve the needs of your family – particularly at the elementary level:

• First, you would expect the philosophy of study materials and methods to not conflict with your own. This problem is not generally serious. In the elementary grades where you will be the teacher, to a large degree you will be left to make your own interpretations. Even Bible classes are designed to teach mostly principles of behavior and attitudes you will appreciate. If this is a concern, you may arrange to make omissions or substitutions as you see fit.

• Obviously, you want a school which provides an effective and efficient program. "Well educated" is difficult to define, but whatever it means to you, that is what you want for your children from the school program. You can get cues about the quality of what a school offers by studying its promotional brochures. Opinions of parents using the program or specific lists of materials and samples may also be helpful.

If you decide to use a preplanned program, you should still plan to add to it any concepts and skills which seem especially important to achieve the education you want for your child.

Working under the guidance of a local school or school system

The educational establishment, both public and private, sometimes views home schooling more as an attempt to circumvent good education than as a serious concept to be studied and encouraged. But this picture is changing.

Leaders in church-operated schools have always recognized the home as the foundation of moral strength. Now they are beginning to see the total educational potential of home schools and to be a little less concerned about the threat to their sometimes small enrollments.

Some private classroom schools now offer supervision services for home schools. In California (and possibly some other states), public schools may also elect to accept enrollments for children studying at home.

Local schools (public or private) can serve cooperating home schools in several ways. They can:

(1) provide legal enrollment with grade and attendance records,

(2) give supervision through a visiting professional teacher,

(3) instruct parents through training sessions,

(4) accept extension students into the classroom for special events or for certain classes,

(5) loan books and school equipment,

(6) evaluate extension students with standardized and other examinations,

(7) provide a smooth transition into the classroom school, and

(8) in general, hold high standards assuring quality education for the few students whose parents may be tempted to become lax.

A school planning to accept extension students will want to set up a plan for administering the "branch" home schools. Obviously the degree of control could vary from only writing down a child's name to holding to a duplication of every learning objective and test set for the corresponding classroom. I believe that any school which agrees to enroll a child must also carry a degree of responsibility for the learning that occurs. At the same time, the goals, resources, and skills of the home teacher call for broad flexibility.

Here are suggestions to consider: The school will need to plan one or several conferences with the parents as part of the registration process. If the parents already have a well-defined plan, one meeting may be enough. If not, a first meeting would serve for exploring options. At the final conference, the general teaching plans for the year would be approved by the sponsoring teacher, and the child's official enrollment would be accepted. Starting the process in June for a fall enrollment would be ideal. General plans would include the school calendar, textbook selection, course outlines, and a list of services expected from the supporting school. Using a structured correspondence course may simplify administration and teaching.

Some schools will want to record letter grades. I would suggest only progress reports with yearly promotions noted. Parents, student, and supporting school need to understand that neglecting to follow through with the teaching responsibility or a serious lack of learning progress would automatically call for a re-evaluation of the plan. A contract can clarify plans, conditions, and responsibilities.

Endnotes

1. *National Goals for Education*, U.S. Department of Education, July 1990.

By way of contrast, here is the list of American goals from the 1955 "White House Conference on Education." (1) The fundamental skills of communication – reading, writing, spelling, as well as other elements of effective oral and written expression; the arithmetical and mathematical skills, including problem solving. . . . (2) Appreciation for our democratic heritage. (3) Civic rights and responsibilities, and knowledge of American institutions. (4) Respect and appreciation for human values and for the beliefs of others. (5) Ability to think and evaluate constructively and creatively. (6) Effective work habits and self-discipline. (7) Social competency as a contributing member of his family and community. (8) Ethical behavior based on a sense of moral and spiritual values. (9) Intellectual curiosity and eagerness for lifelong learning. (10) Aesthetics appreciation and self-expression in the arts. (11) Physical and mental health. (12) Wise use of time, including constructive leisure pursuits. (13) Understanding of the physical world and man's relation to it as represented through basic knowledge of the sciences. (14) An awareness of our relationships with the world community.

2. *Ibid.*, pp. 1, 10.

3. Samuel L. Blumenfeld, *The Blumenfeld Education Letter*, April 1993.

4. Inge P. Cannon, *National Center for Home Education, Special Report*, Dec. 1992.

5. Education Digest, Sept. 1993.

6. The goal she quotes actually reads: "All students relate in writing, speech or other media, the history and nature of various forms of prejudice to current problems facing communities and nations, including the U.S."

7. Cathy Duffy, from *Radical Reforms to Restructure Education Spell Danger for Homeschooling Parents*, Copyright 1994. Statement revised, 1997.

8. John Holt in *The Radcliffe Quarterly*, March 1978; *The Underachieving School*, Dell, 1969. p. 202.

10

Planning for Teaching

So far, we have considered some of the basic principles of home education and have discussed initial decisions important in setting up a scholastic program. This chapter is about getting ready for action. The next chapter deals with effective teaching methods, organizing the teaching responsibilities, and evaluation. Although I write here as if you have chosen the option of an independent home school and will plan as a professional teacher would, much of the discussion will also be valuable for preplanned programs.

Selecting major learning materials

If your enthusiasm about home teaching is not already aglow, it will probably come to life when you begin looking at the great variety of excellent learning materials on the market. Your problem may be more in choosing what you like best than in being able to find something that will work.

Good textbooks don't teach by themselves, but used wisely they certainly carry a heavy part of the load. Even when following an independent unit touching several subject areas, they are important resources. We'll have more to say about units later.

Selecting materials which help you meet your objectives is an important consideration unless you are using a preplanned package such as home study schools offer. Even then you can, to a degree, judge the school by the materials it uses. And you would be wise to consider adding elements you feel are especially important for your children.

Many home schooling families operate under the direction of a guidance center or provider school. Most of these organizations suggest materials depending on your interests and felt needs. You can add and subtract on your own initiative.

To begin learning about materials, look through opinions of reviewers (Appendix X). Descriptions in suppliers' catalogs are also worth studying. And see my reviews in Appendices N through Y.

A nice way to actually see learning materials is to attend a curriculum fair. Major support groups often sponsor them along with meetings. Vendors come and display their wares.

If you have time, you could visit a curriculum library at a university education department or at a school district office. Publishers send them materials knowing that their students will soon be teachers choosing textbooks. You will not only find books and other materials, but also you will get ideas about what is taught in the various subjects and even how it is presented. For more religiously oriented books, you may also want to look at materials in a nearby nonpublic school.

Visiting with a teacher of the grade you are interested in might be another way to get help selecting textbooks. In fact, you may even be able to borrow or buy books from the school. You could get a cool reception, but you are more apt to develop a friendly source of future counsel and support. For classroom textbooks, it's nice to have both student's and teacher's books, although one or the other may be adequate.

Workbooks may be helpful, although they are never necessary unless used as textbooks. Just try to avoid any materials that produce only busywork.

You will be able to order special books for students with learning problems. Catalog descriptions identify books for special use.

The school calendar

Setting up a school calendar and a weekly schedule may seem like a formality important only for the efficient operation of schools involving more than one or two families. Not so. Time planning is important for teaching only one child just as it is for operating a large school system. It is important whether your home school is entirely independent or whether your child is enrolled in a preplanned program.

Your school calendar helps both you and your child to know that, during school time, other activities have to wait. It also shows vacation times when the books can be put on the shelf and temporarily forgotten with a clear conscience. By keeping your educational program moving, a calendar helps you get through the grade without having work to finish during the summer months when young friends are enjoying their "freedom."

State laws require around 180 school days each year for their public schools. Often the minimum applies to home schools, too. If your child masters the concepts slated for the grade before the end of the required number of days, you can plan "supplementary" experiences for the rest of the time. Think of the tremendous range of possibilities for worthwhile learning!

Needs will arise to take off days scheduled for school. Making up the time ahead (when possible) will help your child understand that learning is serious business.

Making a weekly schedule

School laws often call for six hours in the elementary student's day. With half an hour off for lunch, school typically runs from 8:30 to 3:00. First graders normally have a shorter day and kindergarten is conducted for even less time each day, usually only three or four hours.

Ideally, school hours should be planned for the time of day your young person is most alert. From a practical point of view, your schedule is also influenced by the

Evaluating Textbooks

These principles for choosing textbooks are less important for parents who have already adopted a curriculum package or a school that chooses for them.

✎ First of all, check the book to see whether it covers objectives you believe are important. If you have a list of specific objectives before you start looking at texts, it probably will not be a long one. Here you can expand your vision, deciding if what the textbook authors expect, is suitable for your use. Look at the table of contents to get a quick idea of the scope of the book. Textbooks usually cover more than the average class gets through in a year so that, to a certain degree, teachers can choose what they like to teach.

✎ Compare the clarity of the writing style in the books you are looking at. A number of factors such as the length of the sentences and how often long words are used determine what is called the reading level – the grade in which the material can be easily read. This and type size are well controlled by most elementary textbook publishers. For your inspection, just look for nice style and clarity.

✎ See if the exercises or study questions seem useful for the student and easy to check.

✎ Look for review and self-check exercises. Skill-building subjects like math, grammar, and spelling need an ample amount of practice. Pick a specific concept like reducing fractions or capitalization that is introduced at the particular grade level, and compare the books you are looking at to see how much work is available on the topic and whether or not sufficient review reinforces the concept. (The beginning part of most school books in subjects that build on past learning, is a review of the previous year's work, although it is not labeled as such.) You will not use every exercise and question, but a good number should be available to you.

✎ Attractiveness is important. Of course you expect your child to be interested in the basic subject matter, but in reality, nice illustrations and interesting format add a little sparkle to what might be a rather ho-hum school experience from the child's viewpoint.

✎ Verify to see that concepts contrary to your philosophy are not promoted. Depending on your ideas, these might be marginal profanity, portrayals of activities and feelings you would not want imitated, fantasy, humanism (extolling the greatness of humans in and of themselves), evolution, violence, deception, hatred, and so on.

✎ Finally, look at the teacher's edition (when you are sure you, as a home teacher, can get it). Check to see that it will be easy for you to use. The teaching suggestions should be clear and practical for your home setting. Often a teacher's edition will have extra questions and problems that can be used for quizzes.

pattern of family needs and activities. For example, if the father, whose work keeps him away from home during the day, teaches one of the subjects, you may want to have an evening session. A shorter day on Friday can be arranged by lengthening the other days.

Plan for frequent physical activity. Children in the lower grades need two or three 15 to 20 minute recess periods in addition to lunch time. For upper grades, one or two. You can plan one of the recess periods as physical education.

Weekly Schedule

An Example for Middle Grades Classroom

Home schools are generally more flexible although this may provide ideas.

	Monday - Thursday	Friday
8:00 - 8:45	*Opening period (Scriptures)*	*Opening period*
8:45 - 9:30	*Math*	*Math*
9:30 - 10:00	*Language arts (listening, writing, etc.)*	*Language arts*
10:00 - 10:15	Recess	Recess
10:15 - 11:00	*Reading*	*Reading*
11:00 - 11:30	*Social studies*	*Science & health*
11:30 - 12:00	*Supervised study*	*Supervised study*
12:00 - 1:00	Lunch	Lunch
1:00 - 1:15	*Handwriting (Mon., Wed.) Spelling (Tu., Th.)*	*Physical education*
1:15 - 1:45	*Science & health*	*Art*
1:45 - 2:45	*Home skills*	
2:45 - 3:45	*Music including practice*	

Even high school students need breaks for physical activity. In the traditional school program the five minutes for changing classes along with physical education periods provide the refreshing shift from brain concentration to body activity. In the home school where changing classes means reaching for different study materials, be sure to plan for active breaks. A brief run in the fresh air invigorates the body and lifts the spirits. One way to memorize material is to summarize it on cards and learn while walking. The mind is alert with good circulation and fresh air.

The subjects normally included in the first six grades are: math, reading, language arts (grammar, composition, spelling, handwriting, etc.), social studies, science, health, art, music, and physical education. In grades seven and eight, reading and language are modified and become English, handwriting drops out of the picture, and science is more specialized. Often state history or government is required. Appendix G outlines the "typical course of study."

If your philosophy has a Christian orientation, Bible study may be part of the curriculum, and you should consider beginning each day with a devotional period.

An important area to consider adding to your curriculum includes cooking, sewing, mechanics, house maintenance, and gardening. You could plan a period each day for these and call it "home skills" or "practical skills." One or two of the skills would be taught for several weeks or months; then the program would change, depending on the season and available resources. This would be a planned learning program, although jobs that need doing could be part of it.

Other special topics you may think of will probably fit into one of the regular subjects. The environment, for example, would be part of science. Computer language fits into math. Making tiffany lamp shades could come under art, and so on.

The school day normally begins with opening exercises. This short period may be spiritual or secular and could include discussing any special plans for the day, reading from a story book to your child, singing, saluting the flag, and similar activities. The religious opening exercises or devotional period would include prayer.

Most home teachers don't divide the day into short time blocks the way classroom teachers often do, but you may want to. A fifth- or sixth-grade schedule for a 32-hour week with short periods might look like the one shown.

Of course this schedule should be modified according to the subjects you teach and the emphasis you give them. The opening period could lead into a Bible class. You could reduce or eliminate the supervised study period since parts of most classes are usually supervised study. All-day field trips, visits to the library, and other such special activities would make exceptions to the schedule.

Instead of the precise schedule suggested, you may want to plan larger blocks of time for general curriculum areas. The language arts, for example, could be lumped together in your schedule. You could concentrate for several days on a particular subject such as reading, then shift to spelling or writing. You might plan for language arts and math in the mornings and other subjects in the afternoons. (In a more open schedule like this you could capitalize on natural motivations, but balanced learning would be harder to maintain.) You would want to guard against the temptation to neglect areas less appealing to you and your child.

Even if you choose a relatively unstructured approach, you should still plan carefully to meet certain general objectives and add structure to your program as needed. A definite schedule, even if you don't follow it closely, provides a point of reference. Many parent-teachers mark out each day what learning activities are to be done; and when they are completed, that's it. You may succeed without following a close schedule, but don't forget your purposes. An aimless study plan achieves worthwhile goals more or less by chance and teaches your child to drift through life in the same way.

Thoughts on interpreting a schedule

Raymond and Dorothy Moore have prepared "Sample Program" sheets, one for younger children and one for older ones. They suggest that the following daily schedule may be helpful if you need to present plans for approval. Their book, *Home Grown Kids*, explains their recommendations.

Suggested Schedule

9:00	*Bible*
9:40	*Music*
10:00	Recess
10:10	*Language arts*
10:40	*Science*
11:20	Recess
11:30	*Math*
12:00	Lunch
1:00	*Story time & rest*
2:00	*Social studies*
2:30	*Art*

A general note on the sheet "for a child less than 8 or 9 years old" reads: "Adapt and adjust this schedule to your home program and your particular needs. . . . We do not suggest that the child do any reading of books or writing of his own except as he asks to do it or picks it up by himself. Many of the above activities can take place incidentally in connection with your daily household duties, but all may not need to be included in one day."

The following comments offer ideas on how to approach the various subjects for children in this younger age range:

Bible: "Reading or telling Bible stories to the child, finger plays, verses, etc. as in children's Bible School."

Music: "Singing, marching, listening to records or tapes, etc. (Formal music lessons such as piano are not recommended at this age.)"

Language Arts: "This includes reading to your child, playing word games . . . [thinking of words that rhyme or begin with the same sound, etc.] to sharpen hearing skills, and conversation to help him build vocabulary, organize thoughts, etc. Give opportunities for him to tell you a story or an incident. Sometimes let him dictate a story, letter, or incident. A daily diary is good for the parent or older sibling to write."

Science: "Collecting natural things like leaves, rocks, shells, etc., nature stories read or told to the child, a walk in the woods, experimenting with an ant farm, caring for an animal, etc. Simple physiology and anatomy, keeping track of the weather, or stories about such things are also `science.'"

Math: "Measuring in the kitchen or garden, sorting or counting, learning to tell time, learning about money, etc."

Social Studies: "Trips to the market, bakery, post office, library, etc., stories of how people live in other lands, or any kind of simple history or geography stories, or experiences are appropriate."

Art: "Coloring, painting, crafts, etc."

For children beginning at age 8 or older, the Moores suggest a gradual transition "from informal activities to textbook study"– at first 20 or 30 minutes a day, increasing to 60 or 90 minutes with several breaks. "However, all the time you spend in responsive companionship with your child, whether baking bread, or raking leaves is education and can be interpreted in your schedule as `comparable to that of public school.'"

"List any educational aids which you use. There is no limit to the amount of enrichment you can put into a home program, but be sure to put it all in the framework of consistent discipline and character development which is accomplished best in practical work with you in the daily tasks of the home or your vocation."

> ***Raymond Moore and his wife Dorothy*** *helped get feet marching for the quiet movement toward home teaching. Raymond Moore made a study of research into aspects of early academic teaching and recommend not starting it so soon.* (The Moore Foundation, Box 1 Camas, WA 98607)

Notes on the program sheet for older children suggest what might be involved in teaching the different subjects:

Bible: "Continue to read or tell Bible stories to your child, memorize Bible verses, and look up some of these in a large print Bible, repeating enough so the child will learn to do it independently. You and your child or children could role play appropriate stories."

Music: "Continue to sing, march, listen to records or tapes, etc. Formal music lessons such as piano should probably be postponed another year or two."

Language Arts: "Follow a teachers' guide in using reading, writing, spelling and phonics books. Continue to read to your child, play sound word games to strengthen hearing skills, and converse with him to build vocabulary, organize thoughts, etc. Give opportunities for him to tell someone a story or an incident, perhaps on the telephone. Let him write or copy a short story, letter, or incident. Keeping a diary or daily log is good."

Science: "Follow a good elementary science program. Continue to collect and identify natural things, including bird songs and other nature sounds."

Math: "Gradually introduce formal math, following the Teachers' Guide of a good math series."

Social Studies: "Child may draw a floor plan of his house, a map of the neighborhood, learn to be the navigator on trips, etc. Widen his horizons by stories and experiences as much as practical."

Art: "Woodworking, sewing, and practical arts are appropriate here as well as other typical creative arts."

In practice, the Moores view the specific program more as a reference guide than a pronouncement of what would happen each day at certain times.

Here is Mary Hood's schedule from her book, *The Relaxed Home School* (See Appendix I). She considers her map of the whole day as a very flexible guide. Also compare the weekly schedule of Margaret Savage in her chapter, "The Redwooded Headpecker."

8 a.m.	breakfast, Bible story
8:30 until 9:30 or 10	chore time
9:30 or 10 until noon	academic time
noon until 1	lunch, free time
1 until 2	"quiet time"
2 until 5	errands, library, practices, lessons
evening	family or individual activities

The yearly teaching plan

We have discussed planning the school calendar and deciding when to teach each subject. Now we face the question of what to do with the time allocated. Of course you could just plunge right in and see how much book you have left over at the end of the year. Although teachers sometimes do this, planning ahead has the obvious advantage of helping you know how to use school time most efficiently. Also, instead of achieving objectives that just happen along on your voyage through the text, you can work toward them with intelligently directed effort. And if your right to teach your children is being questioned, neat, purposeful plans are evidence that you know what you are doing.

Theoretically, teachers view textbooks only as tools to use as appropriate for meeting particular, independently determined objectives. Often in practice, however, the textbook becomes the principle source for what is to be learned. For the parent-teacher, carefully chosen textbooks are often the curriculum backbone.

The table of contents provides a starting point for laying out the year's study. Look at the suggestions in the teacher's guide indicating how much time might be allotted for the various chapters or units. If you don't find suggestions of this nature, check the number of pages in each chapter for a clue to which ones might require more and less time.

Even though the textbook will probably be your major learning source, plan to use other resources as well. Some of these can be figured into your year's master plan. Others will become apparent as the year unfolds. You can then modify your plans, always keeping an eye on the overall goals.

For lower and middle grades, you will want a day
or two each month for review and for unit tests. By the time seventh and eighth grades come along, I would plan two or three days' review plus a day for examinations four to six times during the year.

Thus your yearly teaching plans can be quite simple. They might be only dates and notes written on your textbook table of contents pages. Or, much better but still simple, a chart divided into thirty-four to thirty-six weeks with columns for various subjects. The margin designating the weeks would show specific dates and would take into account vacations and holidays planned in your calendar. In the blocks you could write topics or objectives, textbook page numbers, and notes about nontextbook learning experiences.

Specific plans

After you have distributed the principle topics of a particular subject over the school year, you can begin to make more specific plans showing what you expect to accomplish each day. Include the objectives you are attempting to achieve, the particular teaching strategies you expect to use (such as discussion, questioning, demonstrating, problem solving, or reading), references to the textbooks and other sources, notes about tests, and other evaluations, and, as appropriate, assignments for independent study.

You will find it best to make these more specific plans in blocks of several days or even weeks. Plan a whole textbook section with accompanying special activities as a continuous unit, leaving the final details for the daily lesson preparation.

Then, while you are polishing up your daily written plan, think through carefully what you expect to do. The plan on paper is to reinforce the more important plan in your head. You will learn much about the subject from reading the textbook itself as you prepare to have your child read it. Don't let this intimidate you. Professional teachers also learn from the textbooks. Modify the plan according to the current progress and needs of your student. And add notes as cues for comments, discussion questions, quizzes, and so on.

As you teach, your plan should be adapted to the dynamics of the situation. Your child's reactions, and needs that become apparent should alter your strategies and determine how you advance.. Incidentally, this shaping of the lesson plans is done in the classroom, too, but there, only a small degree of individualization is possible. Generally, the whole class is pulled ahead or held back to satisfy the most obvious needs.

It isn't necessary to prepare work out plans for all the year's sections at once. In fact, teaching your first topic will give you ideas about how to plan the next ones.

Don't be afraid to let your child help you plan, especially when you see alternative ways of achieving your objectives.

To give you an idea of what daily teaching plans might look like, the side bar shows an example for two subjects.

You could write even less in your plan book, relying on notes and marks in the textbook itself. You will want to write enough so you will have a record of what you did, and thus what to expect from your child.

If you use a correspondence or packaged home study program, much of the planning is done for you. Still, every day you must understand the lesson, and decide how far to go. Also, consider enriching the sometimes bare-bones preplanned program with field trips, supplementary reading, extra problems as needed, or other special learning events. Remember, you are essentially the teacher even if someone else plans the overall program, makes the tests, and gives the grades.

Good planning takes time, although not as much as you might think. Some people tend to drift along with little planning. If you are one of them, you might feel a bit scolded as you read this book. (Sorry about that!) At the other extreme, however, are a few valiant souls who busywork themselves into total inefficiency. Learn to plan quickly. Look for shortcuts in identifying textbook concepts, and find fast ways

Sample Lesson Plans

Math

Percents

Relate percents to fractions.

Tell how word helps explain meaning.

Have him read explanation on p. 138.

Then go through sample problem on board.

Have him try samples from p. 138.

Assignment: All of exercise 17-2, pp. 138, 139.

Have him check with key.

Remind him of test next week.

Spelling

Have him review list on p. 64.

Quiz over p. 64.

Review missed words & quiz again.

Then fill in exercise on p. 65.

to transfer plans to paper. Remember that your written plans are signposts, not a complex surveyor's map of the highway.

Printed forms for planning and record keeping are available from several home school sources. Basic ones may be photocopied from samples just before the index of this book. Forms can simplify your preparation. An assignment book could be used as your central point of reference. Ginny Baker explains how she did this in her chapter, "Fitting School to Four Children."

Planning not only makes your teaching easier, but well-planned, well-organized teaching inspires the same kind of learning. Interest is maintained and behavior problems are minimized.

Unit Studies

In many home schools and even in public schools, the curriculum is partly organized as a unit study. In a unit study, a selected topic is explored over a period of days or weeks, or more commonly, whole school years.

In the briefer plan, wanting to find out about railroads, for example, would lead to reading about the how they got started. That story involves the invention of the steam engine and the physics of how it works. Then one could study the history of the rail system including its impact the economy, how passenger rail service declined, the development of city rail transit systems, and so on. A visit to a museum, a rail switching yard, or even a model train display would reinforce and expand the learning. And think what fun it would be to ride on an old steam train!

With the trains topic we have suggested learning in the areas of science, history and economics. Writing (hence spelling and grammar) is also a definite part of the unit study. Bible, art, literature, and other subjects as well, may often be related to unit topics. You may wish to broaden a suggested topic. Instead of only trains, for example, transportation in general could be studied. Or instead of expanding you may more often need to limit the topic to keep the learning useful and interesting.

So in what ways do unit studies teach better than textbooks?

❉ Learning is more fun when guided by interest. Instead of trying to absorb condensed, summarized knowledge, young scholars learn to help figure out what is important and then search for it.

❉ All your children can work on the same unit with assignments depending on their education levels.

❉ Sharing information with the rest of the team gives immediate purpose to finding it (even when Mom is the only other team member). Friends and relatives or at least Dad could be invited for a final project report.

Units may be scheduled as part of the larger curriculum plan. Math, more than other subjects, requires sequential study and planned practice so needs a regular and separate class time. I would plan a regular time for spiritual study, too, unless it is a key part of the unit. A week or a month is probably a good length of time to plan for a shorter unit, although you would certainly want to be flexible.

You may begin with suggestions from your children and develop ideas for areas to explore within a chosen topic. Your resources are personal observation, the library in your area, knowledgeable people, materials you may purchase, encyclopedias, textbooks, and various other information sources. Before beginning unit studies you may want to spend some time learning about the library.

You will want to keep records to remember what has been covered, especially if you are required to report on your curriculum. Comparing your record with typical learning objectives will give you ideas for other areas you will want to cover. See Appendix G.

To some degree, the scope of the more traditional curriculum is arbitrary. But most of it, in my opinion, you would not want to miss. This need not be a serious constraint for extensive use of units, however. You may want to cover a topic only briefly that the school down the street is spending much more time on. And the other way around, too. Also, you cannot cover all the good things to learn in a lifetime, much less in the few years that society allots to elementary and secondary education.

I suggest a mix of units and traditional textbook study. The ratio would depend on how well important topics are being covered. If you are more comfortable with the textbooks or are following a packaged curriculum, you might want to break only a few times during the year for a unit. As you see success with your units, you could begin spending more time on them. Between units, you may want to teach selected areas covered in the textbooks.

I have written as if you would plan your own study. A number of authors are marketing their own plans for your use. This goes back toward the textbook idea although options are offered on what topics to cover.

Unit studies are less appropriate for high school, but some degree of their key ingredient of flexibility still is. Research projects may delve into specific topics, and some subjects may be treated lightly in order to specialize in chosen directions.

For unit study methods and materials, see Appendix Y.

Organizing for convenient operation

To begin planning your instructional environment, designate a special place for school. Standard school desks and a chalkboard are nice but not necessary. Your children can help plan and keep order in your home classroom. Arrange a specific place for the children's school books and for your records and materials. Arrange for good lighting and ventilation.

A second person may share the teaching responsibility. Most home schools have one teacher – Mother. As a second teacher, Father often makes an ideal team mate. He may teach a subject for which he happens to be better prepared or that is in an area of his special competence. The second teacher may be a retired professional teacher who also supervises the regular home teacher. For art or music, lessons can be arranged outside the home. Sometimes two or three mothers will set up a school for their children and will each cover certain areas of the curriculum.

Unless one of the instructors is a trained teacher and comes to supervise the home school part of the time, a divided teaching responsibility should be on the basis of subjects or grades.

If you know other home school families in your area, consider organizing a joint school once a week or once a month. This will require more planning and coordination, but could be very rewarding. You could divide up the children by grades, each teacher-parent taking a group. Students could prepare special assignments at home. Most children will benefit from the experience of studying for someone other than Mom and of discussing in the presence of peers.

For whatever plans you make, each teacher must be fully committed to the task. No subject of any importance can be taught successfully on a when-I-get-time basis.

Frequently, school at home involves more than one child. With a few organizing techniques and careful planning, as Meg Johnson and others point out, one teacher can probably handle several grades. Also see Marilyn Rockett's chapter, "Organize to Survive."

Except in math and reading which depend heavily on past learning, classes for consecutive grades may be easily taught together. Classes, even in subjects that build on past learning, may be partially combined by studying the same topics but with different assignments. Certainly projects like putting on a play or planning and preparing a meal or making a "museum" can involve your whole school.

In much of your teaching you will want to plan discussion and explanation for one grade while others read or write out assignments. Expect your older students to learn more directly from the textbook without leaning on you unnecessarily, so your explanations can be brief.

Another way to simplify teaching several grades is to ask an older child to help teach a younger one. I'm not suggesting that an older student should take the full responsibility for a subject, although in a special case this might work out. All of your children need time to do their own class work. And responsible teaching takes a degree of maturity. The older child can listen to a younger one read, drill spelling words, help explain math problems, read stories, and so on. The secret of success is good supervision and planning on your part.

11

Techniques for Teaching

Teaching methods are explained or implied all through this book. Chapters in the next section of this book, "Areas of Learning," deal with methods for particular subjects and with school levels like preschool and high school. Here we look at some general teaching tools which you may find useful.

A foundation for new learning

Learning any concept depends on prerequisite knowledge. For example, a cookbook may provide instructions for making a certain dessert. One of the steps may be to blanch almonds. The cookbook author, in teaching you how to make the dessert, assumes you already know how to "blanch," as well as many other things including how to read the instructions. Without a complex array of knowledge you would certainly fail at learning how to make the special dish.

Now take a rather obvious example from math. If a child is absent when the classroom teacher explains long division, he or she could not expect to do other mathematical calculations dependent on the process. Fortunately, instruction is normally planned by textbook authors as well as by teachers so that essential concepts and skills like this are presented more than once. Succeeding presentations, however, come as review and a shy child that misses the initial explanation may fail to ask the right questions when the concept is reviewed.

For several reasons, home school students are less likely to totally miss an essential concept, but if by oversight the idea is not covered or if it is assumed erroneously to have been part of previous learning, a student might be unable to move ahead.

When a new concept seems unusually difficult to grasp, one of the things to do is to ask what is difficult about the new idea. If your child can't explain – which will probably be the case – start asking about all the component ideas.

For example, you may be teaching the science concept of pressure. Suppose the pressure cooker idea is used to help in the explanation. If your child missed the concept that water expands as it changes to steam, the pressure cooker won't make sense, and therefore the concept of pressure won't be learned, unless by another avenue.

When, with a little probing, you uncover the difficulty, remember that the book and your lesson outline are not in charge of the teaching. You are. Tactfully and without undue fuss go back to the idea that got missed and build through to the concept in question.

Of course, remember also that learning blocks often occur for reasons other than lack of prior knowledge. Your child may be mentally, emotionally, or physically unready for what you are trying to teach. Again, patiently talking it over will help you realize the problem, and wisdom will help you know how to modify the educational plan.

Learning styles

For all of us, learning is a skill which depends on personality and habit. How well we learn is affected by the conditions of our environment, the mode in which ideas are presented, and what we do to fix them in our minds. These factors also determine which subjects we learn most easily and what motivates us. The ways of learning math are necessarily quite different from how a musical instrument can be mastered.

We absorb information in a variety of ways and all tend to prefer some of those ways over others. Hence some learning skills are stronger than others. Learners may be simply labeled "visual," "auditory," or "kinesthetic" (because they prefer to learn by seeing, by hearing or by physical activity). A system defined by Keith Golay[1] may be more useful. He divides children's learning styles into four categories: actual-spontaneous, actual-routine, conceptual-specific, and conceptual-global. At the risk of over- simplification, I would describe the "actual" category students as doers, and the "conceptual" students as thinkers. The doers are then characterized as "spontaneous" or "routine," and the thinkers are divided between "specific" (problem solvers) and "global" (social).

For more on this topic, see my review of *Learning in Spite of Labels* in Appendix J, Part 2.

From printed page to understanding

Few people learn thoroughly the explanations they read or hear. Most of the words, as the old cliché puts it, just go in one ear and out the other. For typical students, if a point is emphasized very strongly or somehow captures the imagination, it may stick until the next day. Then if the teacher goes over it again or assigns exercises that use it, or builds more simple ideas on it, long-term learning could occur. Good teachers do emphasize and repeat and reuse ideas, but they also try to help their students become aggressive, active learners.

Of the four major personal characteristics which I see as producing learning achievement, inherited mental ability is for most individuals, the least critical. The other three – time spent, sustained interest in the topic, and study skills – make the big difference. You know what I mean by how to spend time. The second factor, interest (or motivation), we have discussed in two previous chapters. Here we would add guidelines for developing what is probably the most significant mature study skill – learning effectively from printed text. The general principles apply also to learning from lectures. Every point on this list wouldn't be appropriate for every chapter and article or for every student. If you understand and practice them, you will know how and when to introduce your child to them.

➲ Before reading a chapter or starting a book, leaf through it to see how it fits into the overall theme and purpose.

➲ Glance through your chapter or article, touching down here and there to see how the author organized it – to see where he or she is leading. Ideas make more sense when seen as part of a structure.

➲ Then return to the beginning and read carefully. Compare the new thoughts with what you already know. Stop after every few paragraphs to see if you caught what the author said. What were the boiled-down concepts? Often the majority of an author's words are used to convince you that the topic is important, to help you enjoy it, or even to explore side issues just too good to leave out. Looking for the major ideas helps you sift out what you don't need to remember.

Four Types of Learners

Doers (actual)	Spontaneous Routine
Thinkers (conceptual)	Problem Solvers Social

➲ Before going on, underline a few key words that can help you recall these ideas at a later date. You could underline large sections of text just to show you liked it, but you won't then be able to quickly find and review the concepts.

➲ When you come to the end, reconsider the whole chapter or article, asking what big ideas the author tried to get across. If appropriate, write a note by the title stating the thesis and maybe your opinion of it.

➲ Outline the article or chapter if all of it is important and if the relationship among concepts is significant.

➲ Write the ideas you want to learn on a card.

➲ Review. Even well-understood concepts fade unless reviewed. Going over them, say, a day later, a week later, and a month later will make them more permanent.

➲ When preparing for a test, try to guess what the teacher might ask and make up answers for the imaginary questions. Then check your responses and fill in the weak spots.

Learning by memory

Memorizing is easier when the structure of ideas is analyzed. The sequence of thoughts then becomes a logically arranged skeleton for the specific words. And even if some of the words fade from memory, the mind might still call the ideas into service.

For material that does not follow in an obvious logical order, like the names of the planets arranged by their distance from the sun, you can use an easy-to-remember sequence such as the first letters of words in a made-up sentence. Remembering the first eight books of the Bible, for example, would require making up a sentence with words beginning with G E L N D J J R. Memory aids like this are called mnemonics (ne-MON-ics). Also songs may assist the memory as the tunes help recall the words. The downside of mnemonics tricks is that they may tend to be extra bridges to cross to get to what you want to remember. Thinking of logical, related ideas would, in the end, give quicker access to the desired information. For more on memorizing, read item 32 in Appendix H, "Ideas That Work."

Mastery learning

In the typical classroom, some students naturally learn faster and better than others. They apply themselves devotedly and shed big tears over anything less than "A" grades. Others plod along at varying paces and only become serious the night before the test. Still others who have not had successful school experiences actively resist cooperation and learning, seeking their rewards in other ways.

In spite of this wide range of ability and interest, most schools achieve an amazing degree of success. Extra projects are assigned to the enthusiastic, while stragglers are pressured and sometimes given extra help.

The general learning pace is a compromise. Usually only the top students experience thorough, complete understanding. If the teaching process is slowed down and intensified in expectation of total achievement for all but the anti-learners, the top students are bored, and even the poorer students become unhappy because they feel guilty for holding up progress, and because many of them really don't consider good grades worth all the effort anyway.

No matter what methods are used, schooling widens the achievement gap between good and poor students. Mastery learning attempts to minimize the problem. Although a class operated by this technique may meet for some group learning experiences such as lectures, audiovisual presentations, and discussion, students do much independent study. The course is divided into modules with specific learning objectives. When the student feels competent in the objectives designated for a certain module, he or she goes to the teacher or testing center for the module examination.

A nearly perfect test score indicates that the objectives it covers have been adequately mastered, and the student moves on to the next module. If the proper performance level is not attained, the student goes back to study more and returns to take a parallel examination on the same objectives.

With recent talk of more emphasis on objectives and criteria in public schools, and the anticipated misuse of central control of students, mastery learning has come under a bit of sniper fire. As I mention elsewhere, I am definitely concerned about the future of the educational system in the U.S. (and around the globe, too) but the concept of mastery is not bad at home. Maybe we should rename it to avoid misunderstanding.

Mastery learning eliminates the grade competition problem which causes good students to become conceited and low-achieving students to develop poor self-images. It is also efficient, making the best use of student time during the course. However, the most important advantage may be the preparation of a solid base for future learning and future life experiences.

In schools, the mastery concept is not applied as much as it might be because it requires more teaching energy and therefore more expense. Home schools are already geared to the individual student, and applying the principles of mastery learning does not significantly increase the teaching effort. In fact, although the process may at first seem tedious, later learning should require less review and will come easier.

Teaching for mastery doesn't mean you should expect perfect work. Mistakes aren't crimes, and children aren't mature adults. The object is to work patiently and carefully toward short-range goals, clearing up misunderstandings, and building skill.

With a single student you don't really need examinations to have a good idea of whether or not goals have been reached, but you may be wise to use them anyway beginning with the middle grades, depending on the individual child.

Some may feel that mastery learning spoils motivation and freedom. Their concern is important. Learning is certainly more successful when following interest in the topic rather than pursuing a teacher's list of objectives. But thorough learning is important, too. So there are times for unpressured exploring and times for disciplined mastery of external objectives. Of course learning of predefined objectives isn't necessarily boring to the mind disciplined for acting on principle.

Evaluation

Some people believe that giving grades interferes with ideal learning.[2] I would agree that, *if misused*, the traditional system of accumulating points to be converted into grades good enough to pass at the end of the year could tend to set teachers and students against each other. Teachers could say, in effect, "If you don't learn what I tell you, I'll fail you or at least embarrass you properly." Students' battle tactics might include arguing for points, getting the teacher off the subject to avoid a quiz, and cheating.

In spite of the inherent weaknesses of giving grades, most educators agree that abandoning the system entirely would be much worse. Grades are convenient and concise. Their fundamental purpose is to express evaluation. So our interest in grading, whether for school at home or elsewhere, leads us to consider the broader issue – evaluation.

Evaluation (which may or may not include examinations and grades) helps both student and teacher see the results of their efforts. It indicates the extent to which goals and objectives are being reached. It implies directions for continued study. And beyond these purely logistic functions, evaluation is a channel of reward for the fundamental human desire to achieve and to be appreciated.

While tests and schoolwork in general are the most obvious sources for evaluation, students may also be judged by general observation of how they react to instruction. A single student in a home school can be observed more easily than a whole classroom of children. The mother-teacher, faced with the extra effort required for making and grading tests, may be tempted to rely entirely on informal observation for evaluating success.

Importance of testing

Tests would not tell the home teacher much she did not already know about her child's ability, but they are valuable in several ways.

(1) Tests measure achievement. (You already understand this.)
(2) Tests promote learning by stimulating study. They furnish short-range purposes for learning. Tests help keep students on their toes. The home school's lack of stimulation from competition with other students makes this reason for tests more important.
(3) Tests teach. They induce recall which improves remembering, and they may even cause new learning by requiring the student to pull ideas together to solve problems or to form conclusions.
(4) Tests are a vehicle for reward. It's fun to find the right answers and to have someone notice. Also concrete test results show that efforts to learn have succeeded. It's a little like the reward of a paycheck.

The frequency and nature of examinations should depend on the subject and the maturity of the student. Young learners need to be observed, but formal examinations, even oral ones, don't make much sense for six- and seven-year-olds. Plan serious tests for older children every few weeks during the school year clearly explaining ahead of time what they are to cover. Quizzes may come in between. Textbook publishers often offer examination booklets with keys to make your job easier. You can use or adapt them.

Now a few words about tests which originate from outside the home. (If this doesn't apply in your case, you might want to skip down to the next section).

Being naturally eager for their children to look good, home teachers sometimes teach for the test. They look at the examinations prepared by the textbook publisher and make sure their children are capable of responding accurately to all the items.

For two reasons this is usually not a good idea: first, tests, as a rule, only *sample* the student's understanding. An automobile manufacturer could make the reports on new models look very good if he knew which vehicles would be borrowed for the test drives. So an examination measuring only specifically prepared understandings doesn't give an accurate picture of achievement in the broader area. Second, textbooks and printed tests are tools. Good ones have good objectives, but you are the teacher and (if planning your own course) should decide the details of what your children are to learn. Thus you can add or subtract from the publisher's tests or scrap them for your own.

Submission of the examination for grading is a pledge of having followed the instructions for giving it; and the test results for a student who has been specifically coached present a dishonest measure.

Of course, reviewing for the general objectives of a test is honest, responsible preparation. Also, practicing with items similar in format to ones on the test is sometimes a good idea because it can relieve some of the student's anxiety.

Standardized testing is justly opposed when misused, but I fear for home-taught students who do not receive occasional evaluation from outside the home.

Expectations

What is satisfactory achievement for your child? How good is good enough? You may feel a little frustrated by not knowing how your child compares with other children in the same grade. Of course, comparing with goals is much better than comparing with other children. Still, you want to set reasonable expectations. You could ask someone at a regular school to test your child, or if you are associated with a home study guidance center, standardized tests may be available to you. Or your state department of education may require and administer standardized examinations. In any case, as long as the textbook material is fairly well understood, you can feel confident of success.

A special caution is in order relative to the level of achievement you should expect. It's easy to push too hard, especially if your home school situation is threatened. Children need free time to relax. But relaxing now and then doesn't mean low standards. Both learning efficiency and self-worth call for a high degree of success. Also, as we pointed out in an earlier chapter, children want you to expect them to work hard. Just be sure fun time is part of the program.

The most important kind of evaluation is self-evaluation. Talk over with your student what is to be accomplished. When a segment of study is completed, encourage him or her to figure out whether or not objectives have been achieved. With guidance, expectations can be realistic, not too hard, not too easy. Then instead of performing only to satisfy you, learning starts to become your child's responsibility.

Make a conscious effort to expect work to be done completely, done well, and done on time. Work habits can suffer in a home school situation. If you and your child feel that a certain concept is understood, you will be tempted to stop working on it with papers and projects incomplete. Or tasks might be dropped when interest wanes. Of course, there is a time to abandon an unproductive project, but this should be the exception, not the rule. Also, schedules and reasonable deadlines could be easily neglected in the one-student school.

You can help your child build habits of regularity, efficiency, punctuality, dependability, and thoroughness by your own planning and direction of school at home.

Feedback

The kind of feedback you give can tend toward motivation or discouragement. If praised by written and spoken comment for work well done, your child will be ready to reach for the stars for you. Positive reports to others around the house and in letters also encourage good work. Even if the task you are evaluating was a general failure, you can usually find something to praise – perhaps an original idea. If the work was an improvement over past performance, praise the progress.

Praise doesn't mean pretending something is excellent when it's terrible. Kids know when their work is bad. Be warm and sincere. Evaluate in a way that lifts and inspires, rather than crushes. Instead of writing a big red F and saying to your child, "I told you how to do this. You are acting as if you didn't have a brain in your head," your comment would be, "You need a little more practice with this, but you did remember to watch your handwriting this time. It looks nice." Expect good work and don't put up with obvious attempts to circumvent the rules. But be careful not to interpret misunderstanding and inability to perform as naughtiness. Show that you care when something is hard or tedious. Instead of scolding, help your child set goals to improve weaknesses. Don't constantly show an attitude that says, "Not quite good enough – you can do better" or your child will miss the joy of work well done.

And one more suggestion that you might not have thought of: In grading complex work, don't try to point out every failing at once. For example, in a story writing assignment, you might focus on making complete sentences and on verb agreement while only briefly noting other flagrant errors. In fact, if your student knows ahead of time what you will consider most important in grading, he or she can better sharpen those specific skills. This approach saves your child from feeling overwhelmed, and it makes your work a little easier, too.

When your child is old enough, give written assignments. Use points. Write remarks or orally comment. Recognize work well done. Show areas for improvement.

Should you give grades? That is, A, B, C, D and F? It depends somewhat on how you use them. For early grades S and N are better (and are used in classrooms). They mean "satisfactory" and "needs improvement" You could add E for "excellent." U means "unsatisfactory" It's another word for F. Technically it has a place, but can be discouraging.

I'll digress a bit. In my own teaching of mature students, I don't give F grades even for totally bad work as long as the student tries. Sometimes the F is deserved and received. For young students and especially in a home, one-on-one situation, it's better to talk over the problem and not give any grade. Be careful about scolding, too. Depending on the situation, you may want to ease off, then come back with a different assignment to teach the same idea.

Beginning with about grade 4, you might experiment with the ABC grades. And before transfer to a classroom school, they would be a good idea.

With the mastery learning concept you won't need grades. The choice there is to do well or to try again. The "try again" doesn't need to occur often when the student plans to be ready before trying the test in anticipation of moving up to the next level.

Professional Growth for the Home Educator

You may feel that this book already has more in it than you will ever have time to absorb. It just seems to grow with each new edition. Of course, you can pick what seems most important and then come back to look at different chapters in greater detail as you see needs for them. And it's not a bad idea to read other authors.

Participation in a support group provides opportunities to learn from other home school parents and from lectures. (See Cindy Short's chapter on this topic.)

Home schooling periodicals are a particularly important source of continued learning. I would subscribe to at least one — maybe two or three. Reading them regularly can keep you in touch with the legal scene, bring you a fresh flow of teaching ideas and inspire courage as you learn how other families face the home schooling challenge.

Seeing sample copies will help you decide which periodicals you might like best. You'll find a list in Appendix K. Support organizations often have helpful newsletters, too.

Teaching in the home school is a challenge worthy of the effort. You may not do everything perfectly and probably won't follow every idea I have described in this chapter, but children are adaptable and with reasonable effort and common sense you are bound to succeed.

Endnotes

1. *Learning Patterns and Temperament Styles*, by Keith Golay.
2. For example, see John Holt, *What Shall I Do Monday?*, Chapter 27, 1970, or Howard Kirschenbaum, et al, *Wad-ja-get? The Grading Game in American Education*. 1971.

12

Structure for Learning

Why should some adult – or even worse, a distant group of them – decide what, when, how, and where children should learn? Wouldn't a child left free to think and grow naturally, do better?

From my own childhood, I can remember my third-grade teacher passing out duplicated sheets with pictures to be colored. Robert, one of my special friends, liked to find short crayons with the paper peeled off and color his pictures with the crayon flat on the sheet instead of using the end of the crayon. The teacher did NOT approve. I'm still not sure what could have been bad about that. Most likely, it was simply not the way she had said to do it.

And, of course, unnecessary exactions can creep into the major subjects in the curriculum, too. Instead of helping students think for themselves, a few teachers tend to demand that only their own explanations be learned, or mark papers wrong for not parroting the textbook.

In reaction to such situations it's easy to get the idea that all structure is harmful – that it inhibits "real" learning. Perhaps this is why we see an emphasis by some home school writers on a sort of blissful freedom for children to learn if and how and when they feel like it. Of course resources are provided and guidance is offered.

One unschooling mother described a typical learning day. Her boy got interested in an important topic and while reading about it, picked up on another topic and followed that for an hour or so. Then a neighbor boy came in and the two got into a fight. Because learning to settle differences is important part of education, the mother let them fight it out.

You probably have sensed by now my concern that home teaching is sometimes too loosely structured – that decisions and planning should be based on more than what feels good and seems like fun at the moment. Please note also that the opposite extreme – insensitivity to your student's interests, and lack of concern for making learning enjoyable – could be just as bad. The challenge is to help your child achieve full, balanced development in a pleasurable atmosphere. In fact, if schoolwork is bitter medicine, development would certainly be stifled.

Home school parents have many reasons for wanting to teach their own children. The appeal of seeing their children mature with the freedom to develop their own interests under appropriate guidance is certainly one of these reasons. Structure could be seen as working against this natural development. The question is, can we help children develop clear thinking and self-directed, moral behavior — character traits expected from an atmosphere of greater freedom — and still teach them such things as how to follow through after a project loses its initial appeal, how to cooperate when their own ideas aren't adopted by the group, and how to stick to a schedule? I believe we can.

"Natural" learning

You may have read glowing reports of children learning everything from Latin to computers in a relaxed home environment on their own initiative. These homes are said to provide an exhilarating environment of such potential experiences as contact with outstanding people, books, and travel. The children seem so happy and well adjusted. How could anyone think of calling for more structure and "regimentation"?

The reasoning which leads to providing only a good environment and letting children learn as they feel like it is similar to the ideas advocated by the 18th century philosopher Jean Jacques Rousseau. He believed that a child's potential is within himself or herself and may be fully realized only in an environment where self-development is unrestricted – where the child can unfold naturally. Parents who see a Source of wisdom and strength outside of humanity and who believe they have been given the responsibility for guiding their children, obviously take a different view of education. And every parent, from no matter what background, can see the problems of the unlovely traits of character "unfolding naturally" as well as the good traits.

Kathleen McCurdy believes that "the desire for knowledge is built into every living creature, though often we mistakenly suppress it; that skills are best learned through example and encouragement; that all parents instinctively want their children to be equipped to survive in our society; and that they will be successful at home schooling if they will just practice the art of parenting as it has been done for thousands of years."[1] I would see more than she does in the parent-teacher's responsibility, but a basic principle is worth emphasizing: Good parenting is good teaching.

While not all natural learning is good, good learning is, in a sense, natural; and home is where it can blossom and bear fruit. In the chapter that closes this book (and in several book reviews,[2]) I have tried to capture the essence of a successful learning environment. Good teaching is a little like helping your child climb a mountain. You have the trail map and the experience. You must keep the objective alive. At times you should encourage her (or him) to make her own trail – to discover the unusual, and certainly there are times to relax. You should help make the climbing fun. But you must also say No to walking along dangerous precipices. You must keep her hiking, and on the main trail much of the time in order to reach the top and pitch camp before dark.

Structure as part of freedom

I have learned that people need both structure and freedom. Even though these two concepts seem like opposites, they go together. And I don't mean part of the time structure and part of the time freedom, either. To see how the two ideas relate, let's examine what we mean by self-discipline.[3]

Imposed discipline is justified only as it helps develop self-discipline. You already know that discipline is not punishment (although punishment or withholding of privileges may have to come into it). But real discipline goes beyond avoidance of punishment in inhibiting bad behavior. It also leads to *good* behavior. So when we set a goal of self-discipline for our children we try to lead them to do right not because we are watching, but because it is right. And that's where the freedom comes into it. Constructive, helpful, achieving behavior by solid, personal choice. Then the structure is self-imposed, or when working with other people it is voluntarily accepted. No one needs to follow this kind of individual around with a paddle (or with tax audits, for that matter).

Notice that I'm not advocating blind adherence to someone else's thinking as is expected by totalitarian governments, or TV commercials, or even often by labor unions. Freedom? Yes, within chosen or accepted unselfish structure.

How is self-discipline achieved? Little children certainly don't begin life with it. As parents, it is our privilege and responsibility to help mold their characters. Our children depend on us for more than food and clothes. They depend on us to direct their behavior and they naturally feel secure in our guidance. As they get older they start edging toward the driver's seat. And that's good, too. The proper environment for a teenager is not proper for a six-year-old. Parents need the discernment to know how much structure to impose and how much to expect from self-discipline.

A balanced life includes opportunities to dream and relax. But even these times for the really mature individual don't come by the whim of the moment any more than do times for study, work, eating, sleeping, or worship.

What do planning and routine have to do with good discipline? The disciplined, mature individual does not act simply to gratify the feelings and impulses of the moment. He or she sees long range objectives. Lasting happiness for this person comes not from current sensations but from the achievement of happiness for others. And happiness for others means being a caring and productive part of society.

Here is where education comes into the picture. A good education develops useful skills and understandings, and it teaches the individual to be sensitive to the needs and feelings of other people. But beyond knowing, a well balanced education must teach the willingness and internal drive to act. Acting means effective use of time. Many "educated" people in the world who aren't much good either to themselves or to society because they aren't self-structured enough to be productive.

Can time be used responsibly without routine? Not as I see it. Routine doesn't mean nose-to-the-grindstone every minute. It must include time to relax and refresh. When it becomes obvious that a plan needs to be changed, break the routine or revise it. A planned program of activity should be a guide and servant, not a slave master.

What child has learned to play the piano by practicing only by the impulse of the moment? You may be able to think of a few young Mozarts that have avidly developed their musical abilities, but they are rare and they certainly didn't learn by relying on whim. They worked rain or shine for their self-imposed goal. In fact, they may well have needed a little parental direction to bring balance into their lives. For them, outdoor activities and social graces may not have come so naturally.

Incidentally, I'm not suggesting "force feeding" for any subject, least of all music. Help your child internalize worthwhile goals as much as possible. Then as readiness develops for working toward certain components of the goals, lend your support of adult maturity by encouragement and gentle, appropriate pressure.

Along with other home school enthusiasts, I feel that our lawmakers need to take a more reasonable look at compulsory school attendance requirements. But should children and youth old enough for formal learning attend school only when they feel like it? Here I mean either school at home or school at school. A good home under most circumstances is the best place to learn, but whether at home or in the classroom, study must be guided by more than interests of the moment.

You and I as adults – if we want to learn something new that takes more than an hour or so to achieve, whether Spanish or computer programming or how to service automatic transmissions or whatever – we are not apt to be successful unless we plan and follow through. If we go to our teacher or to our book only when we feel like it, we'll soon drop out.

Appropriate structure depends on maturity

You may have read convincing arguments for letting children learn instead of "schooling" them. Other writers object, placing a strong emphasis on structure. To help you make sense out of this dilemma, let me suggest that it may not be so much *which* is right but more *when* – under what circumstances.

As already implied, the degree and type of structure should depend on maturity. Much of the educational program described by casual learning advocates is quite appropriate for early, informal years. However, at around the age of about seven (some say earlier) children begin merging into different ways of thinking. An orderly environment is important from birth, but the kind of structure and how parents should apply it changes as the child develops. Also, with increasing maturity, the source of determination for structure or discipline shifts from the parents to the child. Chapter 19, "Planning for the Early Years," develops these ideas further.

Choosing with reason

We have discussed time structure. Content, or what we teach, also needs structure. Most of us would resist expecting our children to learn something merely because schools teach it. Tradition isn't automatically best, but neither is originality. We need to think through carefully what we want education to do for our children, then be sure we know a better way before abandoning the core of what schools teach. Creativity is good, but creative spelling due to lack of solid study in the subject is a serious handicap. Choosing books to read because they are interesting may be enriching, but a good citizen will, interesting or not, know something of the major forces that have shaped history. Understanding such things as how the Communist world has changed, what got our country into World War II, and what led to the fall of the Roman Empire lead to more responsible participation in seeking solutions to current government problems.

The mama robin knows by instinct what to teach her young, but people parents face a vastly more complex world. God's gift of individual freedom calls for choice based on application of principle. Learning must involve much more than wandering aimlessly here and there exploring experiences that happen to appeal to parent or child. Rather, it's an extremely important preparation for life here and in eternity.

Kids may get the idea that because they are too young to earn a good wage, too young to vote, and too young to get a driver's license, therefore their time isn't valuable – that to do something important, they have to grow up. What a mistake! And often adults, too, think kids' time is cheap – a double mistake!

Some may believe that structure discourages children from thinking for themselves. Maybe this idea comes from a misunderstanding of what good structure is. We aren't talking about a rigid inflexible formality but about a sensible plan. Children can help work out the schedule and even help choose what is to be learned. We don't expect to become slaves to the minute hand on the clock, especially in a home school. But we do need an overall daily and long range guide to the learning program that can be altered whenever a change can better serve the goal. Encourage spontaneous discovery experiences as you would for occasional pauses along the path, for picking flowers. Minor route changes don't need to affect the destination as long as the goal isn't obscured by the daisies.

The primary elements of school structure are: goals, a definite program with suitable materials, a specific time and place to study, and evaluation as appropriate.

Can unstructured learning succeed? For young children with caring parents, yes; and for anyone through brief incidental experiences, yes. But for long-range life skills, not so well. Children in classroom schools learn something good in spite of the teaching rather than because of it. They often do at home, too. But why settle for bits and pieces when you can help your children build a solid foundation? Will they grow up like weeds or as well developed plants?

Were the old ways really better?

My reason for adding this section is prompted by interest in a curriculum structure inspired by the medieval European educational system. Before I go on to tell you what I am going to tell you, I need to explain that some really nice people might disagree with me. In fact, articles I have read contain some good thoughts. You may draw your own conclusions.

In 1947 English writer Dorothy L. Sayers presented a paper entitled "The Lost Tools of Learning."[5] She felt that the concept of mind training, which apparently fostered the upper-class system of education in medieval times, should guide the curriculum structure for modern education.

In those days, the system for becoming recognized as "educated" called for successfully passing through two major steps, first the *trivium* and then the *quadrivium*. The trivium was divided into the *grammar, dialectic* and *rhetoric* stages which emphasized respectively a study of particulars, of systems and of interrelatedness – in that order and each essentially mastered before moving on to the next. The idea of the trivium was to build the tools for superior achievement in preparation for the quadrivium which, translated to our day, would begin at the university level or possibly before. (The quadrivium originally meant music, arithmetic, geometry and astronomy.) Together, the trivium and the quadrivium made up the seven "liberal arts."

The trivium has been adopted by a few well-meaning home school advocates as a structural model for elementary and possibly secondary school. Some of the principal ideas in the adaptation are: (1) Since small children memorize easily, the early years are especially suitable for learning isolated facts. (2) As in other subjects, the facts of history and geography are learned first, then applied to systems, and finally to a whole in the three trivium stages.[6] (3) Classical languages are emphasized, vocabulary first. Latin would begin in early or middle elementary. Greek would be introduced soon after. Then Hebrew or modern languages would follow. The Christian parent might see some value in learning Greek if Biblical Greek were substituted for the classical Greek which is typically studied. (4) Mathematics is studied rigorously. (5) Chemistry and physics are particularly important. (6) Grammar, composition and literature are taught perhaps as they would be in a regular school, except that importance would likely be given to classical literature. (7) Logic and debate, studied near the end of the trivium, are considered good training for thinking skills. (8) Theology was a part of the ancient study system. This would take on a different form in the modern adaptation for a Christian school but would still stress early learning of particulars.

To put these ideas in perspective, we will next see why they aren't being followed in modern educational systems.

Learning to learn

Until as recently as fifty or sixty years ago, a set of formal courses such as Latin,

Greek, and advanced geometry dominated the American high school curriculum. The elementary school had already broken away from a similar pattern, and high school educators were eager to try out new ideas, too. But college entrance requirements dictated most of the curriculum. The strict set of courses was thought to prepare the mind for advanced study. Adventurous educators disagreed, and from this frustration developed what became known as the "Eight-year Study."[7]

Thirty high schools were chosen, and agreed to set their own graduation requirements. Between 1936 and 1939, about 2000 of their students entered colleges and 1475 of these were matched one by one with students having similar backgrounds and abilities but who had graduated from traditional schools. The college success of both groups was carefully checked.

When the massive accumulation of data was finally sorted and tallied, the experimental group from the thirty schools was found to have achieved more in every scholastic area except foreign languages, where the comparison group did a little better. Also, personality and social attributes of the experimental students were rated slightly better. Even in memorization ability, they were 3% ahead of the comparison group.

We must take care in drawing conclusions. College success wasn't shown to be improved by just following natural interests and inclinations in secondary school. The experimental students had challenging graduation requirements to meet. But the results certainly did strip the ivy from the traditional curriculum tower which had been considered so important for building learning competence. The thirty schools taught so their students would be ready for life, and that goal turned out to give them the better preparation for college as well.

Returning to the question of the trivium, even if it did produce better learning, I don't see how it would justify such an austere curriculum with no life science, no health education, no fine arts, and no physical or practical skills education. It's easy to agree to add some of these, but how can you with such a demanding program already? Remember, too, that a balanced education means development of more than the intellect.

Reasoning from particulars to generalities is known as *induction* or inductive reasoning. The opposite, reasoning from accepted general principles to particular outcomes, is called *deduction*. The system we have been discussing seems to imply that practically all precollege learning should develop through induction. It's true that the carpenter learns his particular tools, but in real life, he doesn't learn all of them and master every skill before considering the whole job and seeing which tools need more attention.

Young children do learn by seeing particulars and putting them together to make sense out of their world, but they also develop their reasoning ability by exercises – looking at a general mixture of objects and classifying them into particular groups. The Suzuki music method owes much of its success to a strong emphasis on interrelatedness – actually making music – with learning the particulars to come as the need is felt. The point is that both in learning and in life functions, deduction and induction occur together.

How people learn

In the side bar on the following page, I explain how I understand the process. This pattern describes learning all through life. You can compare with your own experience and with what you have observed in your children.

It doesn't hurt to examine how the medieval upper class were educated. We might pick up some helpful ideas. But, in my opinion, loving God with heart, soul, mind, and strength and loving others as ourselves (Mark 12:30, 31) implies a much broader education and a very different base.

✕✕

So we face two opposite dangers: learning with too little guidance or following strict but wrong directions. Although no teaching is perfect, do what you can to assure its success.

Endnotes

1. Kathleen McCurdy, Family Learning Organization of Washington, personal correspondence, October 1, 1985.
2. *Child's Work* is reviewed in Appendix I, and *Learning All the Time* in Appendix J.
3. Chapter 48 is on self-discipline.
4. See my review of *How to Create Your Own Unit Study* in Appendix J.
5. See *The Teaching Home* June/July, August/September and October/November, 1985 for a discussion of the "lost tools of learning."
6. For my opinions in this area, see the chapter on teaching social studies.
7. Wilford M. Aikin, *The Story of the Eight-year Study*, Harper & Brothers, 1942. And James Hemming, *Teach Them to Live*, Longmans, Green, 1948, 1957.

How People Learn

(1) A need to know is sensed.

(2) If, in trying to understand, certain elements are unclear, the main object is postponed while they are acquired. They include background concepts and necessary communication transmitters, such as word meanings.

(3) The new idea derives meaning as it is related to prior knowledge through both induction and deduction.

4) Final possession of the concept occurs when it is applied and found to work. The process is successive and stops if any step fails.

13

Memorize Quickly and Make it Stick

Kevin Ferreira

Although the author's interest in memorization was developed from his desire to learn Bible passages, the principles of finding ways to remember may be applied to other topics as well.

As a child in a Christian elementary school, I was required to learn a certain number of verses. I can remember being frightened, thinking about having to recite them in front of my teacher, although actually quoting them was enjoyable. For a number of years, I have wanted to memorize more Scripture, but haven't, except for school tests.

***Kevin and Rose Ferreira** are a delightful young couple from South Africa, here in the United States preparing to serve their Lord through the health education ministry. Kevin thanks his wife and, of course his God, for encouragement and ideas on this topic of memorizing.*

Recently my wife, Rose, shared a method that sparked my interest. At first I listened to be polite. Then I saw her use the idea, and I became more curious. She not only got an 'A' in a test for which memory work had been required, but she learned the necessary material in a fraction of the time needed by others in the class! Still, I was skeptical. Would it really work for me, or for anyone else for that matter? I was determined to find out.

Some time later, I tried her idea. I started off with Psalm 1. I had already attempted to memorize this short passage but could never get beyond the third verse. With renewed determination, I looked at the first verse. "Blessed is the man that walks not in the council of the ungodly, nor stands in the way of sinners, nor sits in the seat of the scornful."[1]

I started to sketch out my developing mental image. As I looked back over what I had drawn – the stick men, the pathways, a council table, and a stick man in a chair – the verse slowly came back to me. I then proceeded to draw out the other five verses. After a mere fifteen minutes, the whole chapter had been illustrated by a mixture of sketches and words. Although haltingly at first, I was able to recall the verses without looking at the printed chapter.

To say the least, I was surprised. Previously I couldn't even remember the third verse, after having read the chapter ten times or more. Now in just a few minutes I had memorized all of it! Since this discovery it has been a delight for me to share the method with others and to see that anyone can memorize successfully.

The method

1. Start simple. With your first attempt, don't choose an abstract verse with few nouns. Start with something easily put into visual symbols. The Psalms are generally graphic. For instance I will show you how I depicted Psalm 1:1–3[1]. Of course you might draw the ideas differently.

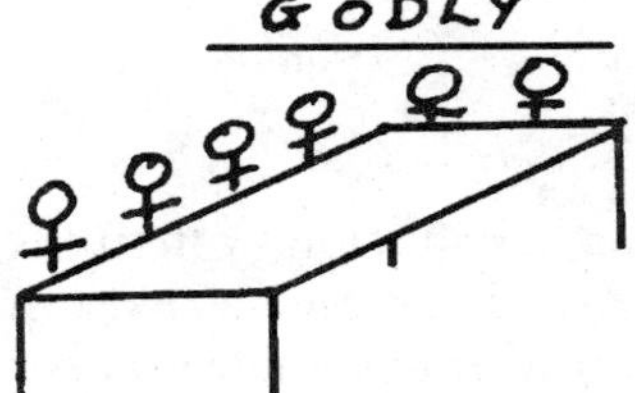

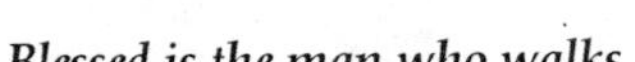

Blessed is the man who walks — Rays of blessing are shown

not — X for "not"

in the counsel of the ungodly, — The counsel (or council) is under the word, godly.

nor stands in the path of sinners,

nor sits in the seat of the scornful;

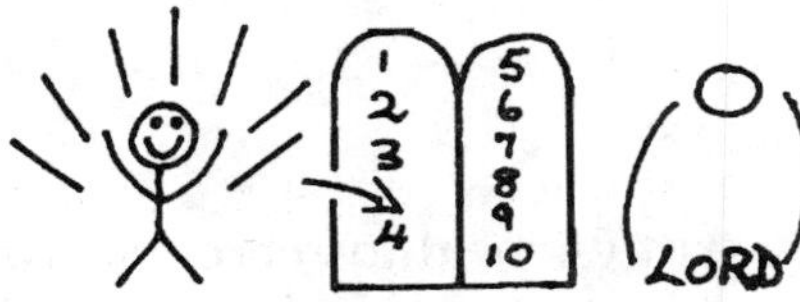

but his delight is in the law *of the Lord*

and in His law *he meditates* *day and night.*

He shall be

like a tree *planted by the rivers of water*
The man is in the tree.

that brings forth its fruit in its season.

whose leaf also *shall not* *wither;* *and* *whatever he does* *shall prosper.*
Arrows show "whatever."

2. Start small. Don't attempt to memorize the whole of Psalm 91 with all of its 16 verses. In my experience it takes quite a while to draw out the whole chapter. Start with one verse at a time. When you see how rapidly you learn, you will be encouraged and want to try more.

3. Use simple drawings. It's not necessary to produce a masterpiece. Use stick men and women and easy-to-understand symbols. For example a gift-wrapped box and a clock can represent a part of a sentence worded, "in the present time."

4. Your own symbols will mean more to you, and you will remember them more easily. My symbol for God is illustrated on the left, but a mountain with a cloud around it (Ex. 19:9, 16–19) might better represent God for you.

5. Be consistent. If, in a certain verse, you used a skirt (or belt) to represent truth (Eph. 6:14), use the same symbol for truth in other verses. Changing symbols could easily confuse you.

6. Don't skimp on size. I have found that if I draw the pictures very small it's harder to recall the symbols. Try making a stick man at least half an inch (13 mm) tall.[2]

7. Lastly, arrange your symbols as works best for you. Using many symbols to make up one large picture might be better for you than using one picture per word or phrase. The choice is yours, but do try both ways.

Here is an example showing the two ways. Psalm 91:1 is illustrated. *"He who dwells in the secret place of the Most High shall abide under the shadow of the Almighty."*

composite

The man in the house shows "dwell in." The heart signifies a secret place, and the hand from nowhere symbolizes the Most High. At the right is a man sitting in the shadow beneath the Almighty.

discrete

Here the arrow pointing into the house shows that the man dwells. The dwelling occurs in the heart of God (His secret place). Using letters in the symbol for God can represent specific names for Him as shown here.

8. Don't be afraid to use a written word now and then. I have found that it doesn't make memorizing more difficult. Some abstract words are hard to find pictures for.

The value of memorization

We remember things better if we see, hear, read and take part in them. In other words, if we use as many senses as we can while we are learning, we're likely to remember better and thus also be able to apply them in a more practical way in our lives. Perhaps this is the reason why television has such a great impact on people.

Critics of visual aids (or multi-sensory presentations like TV) note that, although there are advantages, there are also disadvantages. These include (1) a reduction in the learners' ability to use imagination, (2) less participation in the unfolding of ideas – fostering passive learning, and (3) increased expense and time searching for good visual aids.

With the method of memorization described in this chapter, you can see that none of these drawbacks apply. (1) Imagination is challenged. (2) You are always involved in the learning process, either by drawing or by going through what you have drawn. And (3) pencil and paper are easy to get.

We know that mechanically memorized words from a textbook stand little chance of being retained. If, however, we thoughtfully learn what a passage means, we are far more apt to remember it.[3] Learning is more likely to be permanent if, (1) it is well motivated, (2) its purpose and value are clear, and (3) it is applied.

Simple line drawings have been shown to be more effective as information transmitters than either shaded drawings or real-life photographs. As stimuli for learning, full-realism pictures that flood the viewer with too much visual information are inferior to simplified pictures or drawings.[4]

Memorization is important for more than Scripture. I believe that thinking in picture form is useful for understanding analogies and concepts. It also seems to me that such graphic thinking will tend to make you more creative and dynamic in speaking, because the mind has more than words to work with.

Success with children

A friend of mine, while on vacation, had the opportunity to share this method of memorization with a young girl about 11 years old. They drew out a few verses of Scripture and memorized them. The next day the girl asked, "When are we going to do memorizing again. It was so much fun."

What more could we ask for than to have children learn and for them to enjoy the experience. The method is good for learning. It works.

Additional thoughts by Ted Wade

Ideas for teaching

You can experiment with Rose and Kevin's ideas in your home school. Here are some activities to try after you have explained the method. Have several children or family members individually illustrate the same verse, then compare the results. (2) Ask children to choose and illustrate a verse (or a science principle, etc.) from a certain area you are studying. Everyone will have fun guessing the meaning of the other students' compositions. (3) Divide a passage into phrases and call on different persons to illustrate a phrase as the passage is developed on the chalkboard.

Conceptual memorizing

Another approach to remembering passages is to analyze them, exploring relationships among the ideas.

As an example, here is how we can look at Psalm 1: In the first verse, the happy man (person) does not do three things. The actions are walking, standing, and sitting. This is a logical progression (toward less active) which makes the three easier to remember.

The psalmist may have used these three symbols to introduce the decline of righteousness which the happy man does not experience. To each symbol is attached an environment and a type of evil person: "the counsel of the ungodly," "the path of sinners," and "the seat of the scornful." We can see that each of the conditions leads to the next until one sits in the very place he once recognized as wicked. He has first followed ideas of sinners, then associated with them, and finally become one of them.

Next, let's look at the rest of the chapter without filling in so much detail. The second verse shows the contrast – what the happy man does instead. Next comes a blessing and a curse. And the psalm ends by comparing the ways of the righteous and the ungodly.

Having a structural idea of what the psalm is saying makes the pieces easier to fit together. And, in the process, we have learned much of the deeper meaning.

An example

For remembering the first three verses of Psalm 1.

The blessed (happy) man

Does not do (verse 1)
  walk
    counsel
      ungodly
  stand
    path
      sinners
  sit
    seat
      scornful

But does (verse 2)
  delight in law
  meditate on it
      day & night

Results (verse 3)
  like tree
    by rivers
    fruit in season
    leaf does not wither
    prosperity (spiritual[5])
      in everything

I believe even young scholars can pick up ideas in this way, but I suggest it especially as a delightful challenge for your upper grade and high school students (and yourself). Add sketches to the diagram emphasizing the underlying concepts, fixing them more firmly in the memory. Then the whole passage could be placed beside the diagram and pictures.

Endnotes

1. Scripture quotations in this chapter are from the New King James Version. copyright © 1979, 1980, 1982, Thomas Nelson, Inc., Publishers.
2. Kevin's illustrations in this chapter have been reduced to 75% and 85% for reproduction.
3. Edgar Dale, *Audio-Visual Methods in Teaching,* The Dryden Press, Inc., New York, 1952, p 22.
4. Robert M.W. Travers, "The Transmission of Information to Human Receivers," *Audio-Visual Communication Review,* vol. 12, pp. 373–385, Winter, 1964.
5. Primarily spiritual good behavior because the whole theme is on doing good instead of evil. The Hebrew word also means "good."

Psalm 1

1 Blessed is the man
  Who walks not in the counsel of the ungodly,
  Nor stands in the path of sinners,
  Nor sits in the seat of the scornful;
2 But his delight *is* in the law of the LORD,
  And in His law He meditates day and night.
3 He shall be like a tree
  Planted by the rivers of water,
  That brings forth its fruit in its season,
  Whose leaf also shall not wither;
And whatever he does shall prosper.

4 The ungodly *are* not so,
But *are* like the chaff which the wind drives away.
5 Therefore the ungodly shall not stand in the
  judgment,
Nor sinners in the congregation of the righteous.

6 For the LORD knows the way of the righteous,
But the way of the ungodly shall perish.

14

Memorizing Scripture, A Joyous Legacy

Jonathan Lindvall

I can honestly say that Scripture memorization is one of the most enjoyable parts of my children's home school experience. Many others have confided that, for their families, it is, instead, a dreaded duty. I readily identify with their dilemma because Scripture memorization hasn't always been such a delight for us either. Let me share our secret.

Jonathan Lindvall
Pastor Lindvall is administrator of Pilgrims School which offers an independent study program to home schooling families in the state of California. I have appreciated his clear thinking about Christian education, and I believe you will see why.

Is it really important?

I am the administrator of Pilgrims School offering an "Independent Study Program" to home school families. We provide such services as record-keeping, curriculum counsel, and accountability. Occasionally the accountability factor becomes a sticky point because we require several distinctive commitments. One of these is daily work on Scripture memorization.

From time to time some parent will object to this requirement to memorize Scripture. "We want our children to enjoy God's word," one sincere Christian parent said, "and forcing them to memorize Scripture will cause them to resent it instead."

Another suggested, "We want our children to focus on the content, not the form. We want to study and discuss the meaning of Scripture passages instead of working on rote memorization of the words. Remember, Paul said, 'The letter kills, but the Spirit gives life.'"

Although I have found such appeals well-intentioned, reasonable, and rather compelling, I have gently but consistently insisted that daily Scripture memorization is a distinctive of Pilgrims School that I believe the Lord has asked of this particular ministry. Rather than modifying our expectations on this point I have helped parents find other home school resources if they felt strongly that they should not submit to such requirements.

A biblical injunction

On one occasion I was challenged to show a mandate in the Bible itself directing us to memorize Scripture. I confidently quoted Psalm 119:11, "Your word have I hidden in my heart, that I might not sin against You." My friend responded, "That is a testimony – not a command." I returned with Joshua 1:8, "This book of the Law shall not depart out of your mouth; but you shall meditate in it day and night. . . ." He remained unconvinced, "That says to meditate in Scripture – not to memorize it."

Temporarily stymied I was certain it would be a simple matter to find a proof text to validate my position. I went to Strong's concordance and looked for the word "memorize." To my consternation the word was not to be found in Scripture. All my life I had been taught that Scripture memorization is important for growing Christians. Now, however, I was unable to verify this notion from the Bible itself. Perhaps I had been wrong all along. What was I to do?

It just happened that my family was, at that time, working through

Deuteronomy 6 as our memorization project. As I was doing a bit of word study on verses 6 and 7, I became quite excited and grateful for the Lord's timing in providing an answer to my dilemma. After giving the command which Jesus later quoted as the "greatest commandment" (Matt. 22:37, 38), Moses continued, "And these words, which I command you this day, shall be in your heart: And you shall teach them diligently to your children, and shall talk of them when you sit in your house, and when you walk by the way, and when you lie down, and when you rise up."

In studying the text I found first that the emphasis was on the words themselves and not just on the concepts. Then I found that this is the only case where the Hebrew word "shanan" is translated "teach." Its general meaning is "to pierce." It is usually translated "sharp" or "sharpen." Here translated "teach diligently," the idea is to "inculcate" or "insert" the very "words" of Scripture themselves into the child.

Then I came to the next phrase, in which Moses commanded fathers to "talk of them" (the words) in various lifestyle situations. I found in this passage a mandate to not only discuss the principles of Scripture with my children but to actually "talk of" the words themselves. When we individually contemplate the words of Scripture and consider their meaning in our lives we are fulfilling the Biblical exhortations to "meditate" on the word of God (Joshua 1:8; also Psalm 1:2). When we do this aloud together in our family it becomes effectively a form of corporate meditation.

While this passage is certainly a mandate to instruct children in the meaning of the Scripture, we also take it as the scriptural reason for regularly "rehearsing" the very words of Scripture "when you sit in your house, and when you walk by the way, when you lie down, and when you rise up." Such recitation would likely require previously memorizing the passages repeated or would, at the very least, lead to their effortless memorization, through verbal repetition.

The emphasis

It was at this point that an insight began to dawn on me. The emphasis in this passage is clearly on the frequent review of the words of Scripture more than on the act of memorizing them. Moses clearly taught that we should soak our children's minds in God's words by saturating their environment with Scripture. In verses 8 and 9 he continued, "You shall bind them [the "words" of verse 6] as a sign on your hand and they shall be as frontlets between your eyes. You shall write them on the doorposts of your house and on your gates." The emphasis throughout is specifically on the very "words" of the commandment and not just on the meaning behind them.

I was intrigued by this idea of repetition. Moses had told Joshua (Josh. 1:8), "This book of the law shall not depart out of your mouth. . . ." Perhaps an emphasis on oral recitation would be a key to success for my family as well. We had already begun a family tradition of quoting one or more Scripture passages as we sat down at our meals. Now I began a conscious plan of leading in rehearsing Scripture passages at times when the family was together riding in the car, at bedtime, and when we first got up in the morning.

The pleasure of recitation

Quickly I learned that children (and adults) rather enjoy quoting things they already know. When we emphasized memorizing new material the process took disciplined effort that admittedly was sometimes less than a delight. But, when the emphasis shifted to rehearsing together what we already knew, it actually became a delight. Young children, especially, love repeating words and phrases they are familiar with. We have all experienced having our early talkers drive us to distraction with the constant repetition of their most recent verbal acquisition– a radio or television commercial, a cute saying, a rhyme, and so forth. They seem like broken records repeating the same thing over and over. Children do this because God has given them an inclination to enjoy what they are familiar with and have thus mastered. As we tap into this inclination our children find great joy in rehearsing Scripture with us.

When I taught fifth grade in a public school I enticed students to memorize the Preamble to the U. S. Constitution. They would groan and complain about how hard it was until they actually had it committed to memory. Then they would, all of a sudden, change their mind about it. Students would compete for opportunities to recite the words. They would even come up to me at recess asking me to listen to them recite the Preamble. Why was this? Children simply love repeating what they have memorized.

Togetherness

Another key to the delight our family finds in Scripture memorization and recitation is that we nearly always do it together in unison. Thus, the burden is not on one individual's shoulders. What a joy to quote with others, helping them when they get stuck and being helped in turn. Your children will enjoy even the task of the initial memorizing if you do it together. They will not likely be as motivated, though, if you simply assign memorization tasks to them individually.

We completely avoid any sense of individual pressure to complete a memorization assignment. Each memory project is a family project in which we, the parents, are helped by our children to memorize the selected text. The older children enjoy memorizing right along with us, without ever having to recite by themselves. The younger children chime in as a matter of course just as they do with anything else the older ones do. We are very careful not to make this a source of stress to them.

More than isolated verses

Also, we memorize whole passages rather than isolated memory verses. This lends itself more readily to recitation. And children gain a real sense of accomplishment when they can point to a whole chapter they have memorized. You might start with some Psalms that are fairly short.

Initially it took only a minute or two for us to quote everything we knew. In time, though, our family had memorized more Scripture passages than we could generally quote in one sitting. Now we will spend about a half hour in the morning rehearsing Scripture together, taking turns selecting the next passage to quote. Although we do not take the time to quote them all each morning, we keep all of them fresh by making certain each is rehearsed at least once every few days.

A dream to pass on

Let me perhaps pass on a dream for your family. Isaiah 59:21 says, "'As for Me,' says the LORD, `this is My covenant with them: My Spirit who is upon you, and My words which I have put in your mouth, shall not depart from your mouth, nor from the mouth of your descendants, nor from the mouth of your descendants' descendants,' says the LORD, 'from this time and forevermore.'"

Imagine that! The Lord Himself is saying that our mouths and our children's mouths are to be continually occupied with His "Words." God wants us to pass on a heritage to our children, our children's children, and all future generations. This heritage is to result in continually speaking Scripture. I'm convinced God is calling us to develop lifestyle patterns – traditions if you will – that enable us to pass on godly routines to future generations.

Imagine the spiritual benefit your family might be reaping today if, for the last two years, you and your children had been memorizing a conservative average of two verses each week and could recite all of them today. Imagine the benefit after four years, or ten years of such a pattern. Think of the reward for a lifetime, and the for future gsenerations. This is my dream for my children.

A delight and a blessing

I began by saying Scripture memorization was the most enjoyable portion of our home school experience. As you can see I should really revise this to say "Scripture rehearsing" is delightful to us. Not only is it a joy but it allows us to fulfill the command referred to earlier (Joshua 1:8), "And this book of the Law shall not depart from you mouth." God promised in the same verse that if we obey this command, meditating in His word day and night to observe its mandates, we would "prosper" and our lives would "have good success." May this be fulfilled in each of our families as we, by God's grace, memorize, rehearse, and apply the Scriptures together.

Endnote

* This phrase from 2 Cor. 3:6 and all other Bible quotations in this chapter are from The New King James Version. Copyright © 1979, 1980, 1982, Thomas Nelson Inc., Publishers.

15

Enrichment Resources

Wherever you are, teaching resources surround you. This chapter will help you recognize them and give you a few ideas for using them.

Textbooks

It isn't that your textbooks will lack enough good material to keep your child busy, but learning achieved from other sources can enrich your teaching in several ways: it can brighten up your program; it can help your child see how school is related to real life; it can give the learning an up-to-date aspect; and it can help your child develop observation skills and be aware of his or her surroundings as sources of learning.

Textbooks are often considered as "predigested" material. Yes, but, to some degree, this is true of anything anyone writes beyond direct data like records of rainfall or messages from divine inspiration. Using other sources is fine. It's the topic of this chapter. We just need to keep our thinking straight.

Unit studies, casual learning, and making activities worthwhile

A few years ago I met an elementary school teacher who used Egypt as a framework for her whole curriculum. She read everything she could find about that country and prepared a big chart to show how it can all fit together. The necessary math, reading, and other goals are worked for as her kids learn about Egypt. Unit studies like this are popular with home schools, too. I discuss them in chapter, "Planning for Teaching."

The term, "unit studies," might also describe attention turned to whatever happens to seem of interest each day. As you can guess, such a curriculum brings vertical furrows to my forehead although I would encourage occasionally interrupting the routine to take advantage of a special resource.

To help keep activities which use resource material from becoming useless busywork, consider three cautions. First, Insist on active finding out. Tracing the borders of a map of your state or province may teach little more than tracing, a skill your child may already have mastered. To make the activity worthwhile, ask questions which help develop useful concepts. For example, if one boundary is a wavy line, help your child discover why. Have him or her know the neighboring states, where on the map your home is located, and so on. Collecting wild flowers is nice, but don't stop with collecting. Learn their names and something about where or how they grow. Use resources to look up information.

Of course you can easily run a project into the ground by expecting too much. Ten questions to answer about the map, if they all take looking up, could seem to a young scholar like a major research project. The younger the child, the simpler the project must be. The activity should end while it's still interesting. We discuss other aspects of teaching with projects in the chapters on reading and social studies.

The second point to remember is, Relate the new concepts to your basic curriculum. Choose, or guide your child in choosing, projects or materials with potential for complementing what you are studying in your textbooks.

The third caution is, Don't let the tail wag the dog. An experienced teacher might be able to build a major portion of the year's social studies program around Eskimos or the local newspaper and keep it balanced, but you may find it easier to arrive at your goals by following a good textbook for the major part of your time, keeping your projects as sidelines.

Projects or unit studies do take time – often more than you anticipate. Don't be afraid to skip minor topics in your prescribed program if you feel your students will gain more from the outside project and you need the time. You can still cover the major concepts of your curriculum, keeping a logical plan and sequence in your teaching.

> ***Quality Activities***
>
> ◆ *emphasize intellectual initiative,*
>
> ◆ *relate new learning to established concepts, and*
>
> ◆ *keep a steady focus on the long range objectives.*

Before discussing how specific items might be used to enrich your teaching, we need to remember that a child's developmental level changes rapidly and extensively in moving from kindergarten up through the elementary grades and into high school. Thus if a project isn't working well for your child, you may need to modify it or help with it. If you help, be sure to talk it over with your child and clearly define his and your responsibilities. If he has trouble, ask questions or make suggestions about where to look for information, but try to avoid doing his part.

A number of developmental factors determine readiness for any activity. For example, attention span, movement skills, reading ability, reasoning ability, and prior learning. These all, to some degree, affect interest, which we discussed in an earlier chapter as the best indicator of readiness. You don't need to know exactly what is best ahead of time, either. Just keep your child in mind, and if you see he is having difficulties, modify the task appropriately or talk about it for awhile and lay it aside.

It is well to let your older student plan the project as well as do it. This assures a good deal of motivation, too. You can discuss what is to be gained from the experience; then make only necessary suggestions as your young adventurer plans a course of action. Encourage being realistic – not biting off too much. If a simple goal is reached, further work could be considered.

Now let's consider several different categories of materials within easy access of most homemakers. These ideas can start you thinking about many more. As topics and concepts come up in your study materials, let your mind search around the home and into the community for resources to reinforce or expand the learning.

Print materials

Such a mass of degrading printed matter floods our world, that we sometimes forget about the great amount of good material also available. Your home school library may not count thousands of volumes, but with careful planning, you can surround your child with a rich environment, and borrow for more.

Magazines and newspapers contain readily usable material. Pictures, articles, and even advertisements can provide a great variety of good learning if managed right. You may want to subscribe to several periodicals. Check Appendices K and L in addition to those in subject matter areas. Another way to decide what you would like is to visit your public library. For magazines you want but can't afford, your librarian can help again. She (or he) can loan you magazines and may even give you copies of discarded older issues.

Periodicals and books can be used in many ways. The best ideas for your students depend on many factors. I can give you only some general suggestions, hoping you find them helpful in expanding your own ideas.

First of all, even though direction and keeping on target with the textbook objectives are important, a certain amount of free-time reading can be very worthwhile. You won't want to teach your children like you would control a nuclear reactor, deciding exactly what goes in and precisely measuring the output. Your job is more to provide the atmosphere of time, appreciation, physical comfort, and good reading matter.

Don't hesitate to allow time in your program to learn for the fun of it. Often ask your child about what was read. Discussion encourages more alert reading and reinforces the learning.

Taking another step in structuring the situation, you may talk over the objective with your young scholar and let him or her choose an article or book to help meet it. Material is easy to find on broad topics like controlling the relationship between people and wildlife, or seeing how authors use active verbs, or energy conservation.

At times you will want to assign specific articles or books to achieve particular purposes, and you may even wish to provide specific questions to answer.

Children can demonstrate their learning from special reading projects in many ways. You may ask them to underline a sentence that gives the author's key thought. You may have them choose ideas they feel are important or that they disagree with. They can write a summary in their own words. And for advanced learners, occasional formal reports are appropriate.

Scrapbooks are fun. Children too young to read may not have the fine motor control for cutting either, but they can tear and tape. A collage, or composite of several pictures glued to the same paper, gives opportunity to exercise creativity while learning from the pictures. Advertisements with prices and other numerical data can help connect math skills with the real world.

Weekly Reader provides articles and activities in particular subjects at various grade levels. For a Christian emphasis, God's World Publications offers excellent student periodicals. You can select a periodical for a specific grade range. Catalogs will give ordering information. Teacher's guides are sent along with the periodicals. This extra study material coming every week or month can add interest and be a helpful supplement to your regular textbooks. (Addresses in Appendix L).

The daily newspaper has more good instructional resource material than you might have imagined. In addition to following news events in a selected world area or on a specific topic, and learning math from the advertisements as already mentioned, you can clip news items and have your child make up headlines, then compare with what the paper used; you can follow the weather forecasts and make a notebook comparing expectations with what actually happened. You can graph the temperatures (not for lower grades), and on, and on.

Books are obviously important print resources even though you may not want them cut up and marked as much as your magazines and newspapers.

Your home school should also have reference books. A good dictionary is a must for every home with children growing up, even if they go to a classroom school. And, if at all possible, get an encyclopedia suitable for children, like *World Book* or *Book of Knowledge.* Bibles in various translations, a Bible dictionary, a concordance, and accurate Bible story books are also important reference material for Christian home schools.

Nonprint materials

Beyond books and other printed information sources, the home surroundings abound in valuable learning possibilities. Before discussing this potential, let's notice two more principles that apply to supplementary learning.

Learning sources should be appealing. Since interest probably influences success more than other factors do, students should choose their own projects as much as possible. But children's interests are scattered and changing. Starting a serious project every time an interest surfaces would spell failure and frustration. How does a parent know which ideas to encourage? Before you spend a thousand dollars on amateur radio equipment only to find that your child's interests have turned to horses or stamp collecting, it's wise to plan a "cooling off period" like the Federal Trade Commission requires for contract sales. Taking the time and effort necessary to learn the code, theory, and laws for passing the novice radio test would indicate more than passing curiosity in ham radio. Two weeks' delay in purchasing a skate board or a camera could help your youngster's judgment mature and might save money, too. I don't mean that you need to keep your foot on the brake all the time. Occasionally you will want to follow through right away. But whether slowly or quickly, encourage those interests that will help your young person build solid character and be prepared to live a full, productive life.

Sometimes children will follow your interests. But not always. Don't be surprised if their preferences are not exactly like yours. Be open minded, and judge from principle. Then when a project is chosen, you can double the fun *and* the learning by joining in. Of course, avoid the temptation to take over even when you know a better way. Be more like a consultant then a project manager. When appropriate, ask questions to stimulate thinking. Tolerating the bungles and botches of inexperience is a greater virtue than your interference to make a beautiful job.

Learning sources should nourish balanced development. Parents can easily let learning pursuits become unbalanced. For example, music is important, but we should not be so set on seeing our children show off our own high culture that we neglect their opportunities to learn to use tools. Or we should be careful that sailing or basketball or clothing construction doesn't crowd out the quiet time for aesthetic spiritual experience and the time to just relax. As your child grows and matures, stop now and then to check on what is happening. Do you see a good balance of mental, physical, social, and spiritual development – a balance between heart and head and hand?

Now let's explore the gold mine of teaching resources around your house. Your own kitchen is a first class science laboratory. You know it's good for teaching home economics, but with some simple equipment, most of which you can make or purchase inexpensively, it can also be a fantastic one-student lab. Follow the cues in your science textbooks to know what to do when, and how.

The sewing corner can become a learning center. Find a good sewing book, perhaps one for children. Spend time on clothing repair as well as on making new things. By the way, boys like to sew, too. And without the stigma of what classmates might think, they can pick up a very useful skill.

What fun the workshop can provide! Here safety rules are extremely important. Hair grows back and cuts heal, but sawed off fingers and eyes with metal chips in them don't have such good chances. If you are a mother and not used to working with tools, this safety caution may frighten you. Don't let it. Shops are safe when you make them that way. Safety is an important lesson in life.

I would say, no power tools for children in lower and middle elementary years. Small electric tools like a drill, a saber saw, or a sander could be used at the junior-high level or possibly sooner. In addition to ensuring greater safety, using muscle-powered hand tools helps develop good manual skills and coordination. A good rule for any sharp or heavy tool is, anticipate where the instrument will go if it slips. Then keep hands away from that place. During senior high years, major power tools are safe after training and *with supervision*. And as with sewing for boys, don't underestimate your daughters' potential for craftsmanship.

Next let's look outside. Digging in the dirt and stretching muscles can be great fun and, in the end, much more rewarding than sports. For your child to plant a garden, patiently cultivate it (with your encouragement and insistence), water it, and weed it, then to prepare the harvest for the table can bring real satisfaction. Making the yard look nice involves more than cutting grass and picking up leaves.

Consider giving your child complete control of a spot of ground. Provide counsel and help, but let his or her decisions stand. Learning comes from mistakes as well as from success.

Television

Television's impact on our society claims special attention. The typical American child spends more time watching television than attending school. If the TV is managing your whole household, I suggest you sell it, give it away, or let the trash man haul it off. Where home is school, control of the television set is imperative.

A generation ago my kids were kids and television was bad. But today's TV makes what I remember from then seem like children's stories. If you choose to have television in your home, handle it as you would a butcher knife around your baby.

Television is an effective teacher. Concerned parents who understand its potential don't want their children to watch violence. But if Mom and Dad watch the stuff, what can they tell the kids? Let's say you switch to "off" when the shooting programs start. But have you considered the effect of the other programs? What makes the comedy programs interesting? Deception. Selfishness. Sex. Think about it. And the commercials? Not much better. What motivates the quiz shows? We could go on.

While you want your children to develop impulse control, television is teaching them that they should have what they want *now*. While you plan for your children to become loving, caring people, television tells them that dishonesty is funny, that loyalty and purity are only a game, that hatred and the violence it inspires bring satisfaction, and that constant excitement is the reason for living. Although certain programs may be worth watching, parents who sometimes need to leave their children alone should consider the liability of access to a TV set. Even "good" children should not be expected to have the maturity and judgment of adulthood.

Now before you throw a brick through the TV screen, let's look at the other side of the coin. There *are* good programs, especially on noncommercial stations – programs that can enrich your teaching. In fact, with a video player, you can stop the tape at appropriate points to probe for understanding, invite discussion, or anticipate what might happen next.

To take advantage of television broadcasts, first plan. Look over program guides and make selections that seem to offer learning appropriate for your child's level and interests.

Some television programs pack a great amount of information into a short time. For your youngster, learning from them may be like trying to get a drink from a fire hydrant. You can do several things to help. Before watching the program, learn what you can from the program guide. Look up background information in the encyclopedia, or even in a dictionary.

Note taking is a great learning aid, but this skill which involves watching, sorting out what is important, condensing it to brief coded statements, and writing, all at once, is too much to expect from younger kids. They can *begin* to learn in the junior high years or maybe in the middle grades. You take notes. Then as soon as the program is over, discuss it. If you don't, not much will be retained, and some significant points may be entirely missed. If you have a VCR, record the program and watch portions of it again. Plan a quiz.

In keeping a television set under control, make specific rules instead of arguing with your children and running to turn off objectionable programs all the time. Decide what hours during the week the set may be on and what programs may be watched. Permit each child to suggest one special program each month (or oftener). And require all chores to be done well and schoolwork to be reasonably up to date before any TV watching occurs.

In the chapter on teaching reading, I express concerns about the children's TV program, Sesame Street.

The Internet

Your computer can open an expanding world of communication and information. If you have a modem, it can connect by phone line, through an Internet service provider (ISP). Look in your phone book and compare. Large companies like America Online and CompuServe (now under the same ownership) provide special services like news, discussion groups, magazines, etc. All will provide e-mail connection. Of course home education is only a small part of what interests people who use these services. You want your modem to run as fast as possible (or as fast as you can afford). The opportunities in cyberspace communication are changing rapidly.

Your children can learn a lot from the

Field Trip Ideas

Museums There are many types. Some are at colleges and universities.

Historical sites Get information from your travel or tourist center, or from a historical society.

A zoo Have your child write down animal names and match them with photos taken.

Birding Find someone who knows birds to take you out. Identifying birds is more fun than you might think.

Looking for minerals Find a rock hound to take you to collection sites and to help identify what you find.

Ecology sites Go to the seashore, a mountain stream, a desert, a swamp, or any specific wildlife habitat. Don't just run in and out again, but sit down, watch, compare, think. Take a notebook for drawings and observations. See what your child can discover about the plants and animals that live there. Read about them, and make a notebook.

An amateur radio station Your child can talk to someone by radio and maybe get a QSL card to prove it.

A TV or radio station Call ahead to arrange a time.

An airport Try to get permission to visit the control tower and to enter a plane to talk with the pilot. Airports for small planes are interesting, too. If you don't know a pilot, just go and start asking questions.

A construction site You might arrange two trips, first to see the action from a safe distance, then after working hours when the boss can take you through the site to explain what is being done.

A boat excursion

A courtroom

A legislative assembly or **other government in action**

An office

A garage

A printing press

An art shop Or where an artist is working.

right Internet sites. They can also find pornography, hate groups, and anything you can imagine. You may want to subscribe to a service that filters what is accessible.[1] Your ISP software may allow you to limit access. Even e-mail can be a risk from people who cultivate friendships for the purpose of exploitation. You will want to know what your kids are looking at just like you know where they are at night. Some home schooling sites have links to many other sites of interest. To get started, go to a major search engine where you can find sites relating to words you enter.[2]

Field trips

Field trips can provide outstanding learning experiences. If managed well, these educational visits to places outside your home classroom will not be time off from school, but one of the best kinds of school. Of course I'm not recommending that field trips or other educational "experiences" replace serious book learning.

In addition to brief field trips to places not far away, plan learning experiences in connection with your family vacation. Even weekend outings can be partly school time. But keep careful records if you are fulfilling state requirements. Incidental learning that occurs in routine travel would less likely be considered as school work by attendance authorities.

Teachers in regular schools would probably take their classes on field trips more often than they do if it were not for the extra work and supervision required. Handling 35 children on a field trip is not the same as teaching them in a classroom. Here again home schools have an advantage.

Planning and follow-up are even more important for field trips than for educational TV programs which are already designed for teaching. Relate learning trips to the rest of your study program. Read about where you are going or about what you expect can be learned there. Help your students make a list of questions to answer from the trip. For several children in different grades, the questions can be different depending on maturity. Information should be recorded on the spot in a notebook.

A camera makes the trip more fun. Notes should be written about the pictures as they are taken. Also, if your camera has an adjustable focus (and you can afford it) shoot pictures of plaques explaining what you are seeing. This is a quick way to get accurate information for a review at home. A portable tape recorder can preserve tour guides' explanations and answers to questions asked, or your child might use it in place of the camera for dictating posted information.

When you return from your trip, your child may profitably spend as much time as your visit took, making a booklet about the whole experience. Where you choose to go depends somewhat on the maturity of your student. Very young children typically visit places in the local community such as the fire station, the power plant, a bakery, the hospital, the police station, or a dairy. And don't leave out the place Dad works every day.

Risk of lawsuit for injuries and the nuisance of kids running everywhere handling things causes people in charge of some manufacturing plants and other interesting places to say, No, to field trips. If you are really in charge, and your kids toe the line, you could point out this better control factor. The small size of your group will likely be an advantage, as well. If you go, set strict rules ahead of time!

Resource guests

Sometimes instead of taking a trip to help your children learn, you can arrange for the outside information to come to them. Invite interesting people to share their special knowledge. They may be able to bring pictures and objects to demonstrate what they are talking about. Occasionally a resource guest may not understand the level of the audience, or may try to use the opportunity to advocate a special hobby horse or political position.

It is well to talk with the person ahead of time. You can prepare him or her for the thinking level of your children, and an opportunity to find out more about the topic to be presented allows you to do background study with them.

Children automatically absorb attitudes and information from their environment. Your biggest job as a parent-teacher is to manage it. Teaching is more than providing knowledge and skills. It's guiding the formation of character. And character is permanent.

Endnotes

1. BESS is a service for monitoring what comes into your computer. The staff continually checks sites and files that corrupt character. They act as an intermediary between your computer and the Internet. Send e-mail to bess@bess.net or call (800) 971-2622.

2. "A search engine" is an Internet site you reach by entering its address (called a URL) in a little window when you log on. You change where you first enter the Internet by highlighting the address of that location and entering another one. In CompuServe or America Online you may enter the URL directly into the "goto" or the "keyword" space. The software figures out that you want the Internet and sends you to that site. The first part of the address is http:// You can often leave that off. We have omitted it in the URLs we show in this book.

Several good search engines are at www.excite.com, www.yahoo.com, www.yahoo.com, and www.infosearch.com. The engines can send you to any of thousands of sites that have been registered with them.

16

Using Your Local Library

I expect you already consider the public library in your community as a resource. It can strengthen your program by opening learning sources not available in your home. In this chapter, we will look more at what to expect from the library than at library skills such as using reference books and the card catalog. You likely already know many of the skills and can figure out others as you work with your child in the library. And, with your library card, you can borrow books about library skills.

To benefit more from the library, don't be content with simply checking out interesting books. Help your child develop some of the skills not discussed here. What dictionary entries reveal, for example, is clear to you, but your child needs practice extracting information from them. The alphabetical order can be figured out from knowing the alphabet, but knowing quickly the position of a certain letter takes practice, and ordering words according to letters after the first letter, needs explanation. Many language arts books teach these skills.

If you want to teach your child high moral standards, spend some time talking about what makes a book worth reading. I share some thoughts on this in the chapter on teaching literature. Your explanation at home could be reinforced by discussing books you look at as you make selections in the library.

If your home schooling support group doesn't have a lending library, you might consider starting one. Various families could put their books into the library to be borrowed by others. Contributing families could be allowed to withdraw the books at any time or be paid a predetermined amount if they are lost. Obviously, good record keeping is important.

Except for added comments marked with brackets [ ] and some modifications in the subheadings, the remainder of this chapter has been abridged from the book, *Helping Your Child Use the Library* by Kathryn Perkinson.*

Getting children interested

Helping your child to enjoy reading is one of the most important things you can do as a parent and well worth the investment of your time and energy. . . .

By far the most effective way to encourage your children to love books and reading is to read aloud to them, and the earlier you start, the better. Even a baby of a few months can see pictures, listen to your voice, and turn cardboard pages. Make this time together a special time when you hold your kids and share the pleasure of a story without the distractions of TV or telephones. You may be surprised to find that a well-written children's book is often as big a delight to you as it is to the kids.

And don't stop taking time to read aloud once your children have learned to read for themselves. At this stage, encourage them to read to you some of the time. This shared enjoyment will continue to strengthen your children's interest and appreciation.

Simply having books, magazines, and newspapers around your home will help children to view them as part of daily life. And your example of reading frequently and enjoying it will reinforce that view.

While your children are still very small, it's a good idea to start a home library for them, even if it's just a shelf or two. Be sure to keep some books for little children to handle freely. Consider specially made, extra durable books for infants, and pick paperbacks and plastic covers for kids who are older but still not quite ready for expensive hardbacks. Allowing little children to touch, smell, and even taste books will help them to develop strong attachments.

How you handle books will eventually influence how your kids treat them. Children imitate, so if they see that you enjoy reading and treat books gently and with respect, it is likely that they will do the same.

When you read aloud together, choose books that you both like. If a book seems dull, put it down and find one that is appealing.

Your neighborhood library as a resource

If you are not familiar with the library, don't hesitate to ask for help. The children's librarian is trained to help you locate specific books, books that are good for reading aloud, and books on a particular subject recommended for a particular age group. The library also has many book lists, including ones like those mentioned above and probably some published by the library itself.

As soon as you can, it is a good idea to include children – even toddlers – in weekly trips to the library. Libraries are often open in the evening for working parents, and most will issue a library card to any children who can print their names and whose parent will countersign for them. See that your children get their own library cards as soon as possible so that they can check out their own books.

Although public libraries welcome children and may have special facilities for them, there are common sense guidelines for behavior that parents need to stress:

➢ Library books are everybody's property and should be treated carefully.

➢ Be sure that you and your children know the library's policies regarding loan periods and fines for overdue books.

➢ Explain to your kids that the library is there for the whole community and they need to be considerate of others' needs.

Keep in mind that it is your responsibility to see that your children behave acceptably and are not disruptive to others using the library.

When your child visits the library alone

Preschool children visiting a library should always be accompanied by an adult or teenager. Suggestions for parents of older children who will be visiting the library include:

➢ Remember that the library is a public building. Librarians are busy and are not able to supervise kids.

➢ Teach your children how to take care of themselves in public places, including how to deal with strangers, what situations are dangerous, and what to do if they feel threatened.

➢ Assess whether your children are comfortable being at the library for long periods. If going directly from school, do they need something to eat or some kind of physical or social outlet first?

➢ Instruct your children on how to be considerate of others using the library.

➢ Always pick up your children at least 30 minutes before closing time. In case you are delayed, give your children an alternative plan, such as calling a neighbor for a ride home.

All of these guidelines and policies are designed to protect children, not discourage them from visiting libraries. Kids are welcome.

Library services for preschoolers

Some libraries invite parents to bring in their children – no matter how young – for special programs, such as parent-child story hours in the evening. Here parents can learn finger plays, songs, rhymes, and other activities they can use at home to entertain and stimulate their infants.

The kinds of materials available for check-out for children ranging from infants up to age 5 vary among libraries. There will always be books, though – hard-backs, books with cardboard pages,

picture books, and often cloth books, paperbacks, and magazines. the variety of subjects is tremendous, with everything from baby colors to bicycle basics, and from bamboo to keeping bugs in a jar. When your kids ask you endless questions about where they came from and why the sky is blue, chances are good there's a book at your library with answers they can understand. Or, if your children have homed in on favorite subjects – whether dinosaurs or donkeys – you'll find lots of fascinating books for them at the library.

Almost all libraries also offer recordings of children's stories and songs. Many also offer cassette tapes, compact discs, video-tapes, book/cassette kits, and even puppets and educational toys. See what your local public library has to offer. You and your kids may be pleasantly surprised. And the only thing it will cost you is some time.

For school-aged children

Libraries take on another important dimension for children beginning school. In addition to recreation, the library is a place to find information, usually for help with schoolwork.

Most libraries offer a variety of programs for children. . . . For elementary school children, there are variations of the read-alouds and storytelling hours that often include discussions and presentations by the children themselves, as well as summer reading programs. For middle and junior high school kids, there may also be book talks, summer reading programs, creative writing seminars, drama groups, and poetry readings.

It is very important to find well-written books for your children at this stage [ages 7 – 9]. A story that will make them laugh or want to know what happens next will motivate them to read even though it's difficult. Your local public library is filled with such books, and the children's librarian is skilled at locating these treasures. A growing number of very informative nonfiction books are available as well.

Hopefully that sense of wonder and curiosity behind little children's endless questions will continue as your kids grow older. Encourage them to look up answers to their questions in dictionaries, encyclopedias, atlases, and almanacs. These are resources you may want to add to your home library. Even if you do, remember that your local library will have a larger selection and more materials on specific subjects, and the librarian will be glad to help your kids learn to use these resources.

[As a home teacher you may wish to ask your children to write brief papers which require finding information in a library. Here are ways to help them.]

📖 Ask your children questions. . . .

This helps children to clarify what they're trying to do. Help them to identify smaller components of the topic they're researching or to see the topic as part of a larger topic (brontosaurus is a subgroup of dinosaurs, which is a subgroup of extinct animals). These classifications will help them to identify useful references.

🕮 Suggest that they look up the topic in the library catalog, periodical guides, and reference books. the librarian will direct them and help them get started. Be sure they know how to use a table of contents and index. Suggest they start with something general about the subject and be prepared to consult more than one source.

🕮 Help them to break assignments into logical segments and avoid last-minute panics by setting deadlines for each phase of the work. Allow them plenty of time to gather the materials they need.

🕮 Help them to determine if the community library has the resources they need or if they need to check other information sources.

🕮 Encourage your kids to ask the librarian for help in locating materials and let them to their own talking.

🕮 Give them encouragement, advice, and a ride if they need it, but resist the temptation to take over an assignment. Let your children assume responsibility for researching and writing reports. It's the only way they'll learn the library skills that they can use all their lives.

One of the most important and frequently available library services for school-ages children is the summer reading program. Recent research has shown that kids who participate in library summer reading programs begin the school year with stronger reading skills than those who don't. So, encourage your kids to participate in such programs, particularly if they have any difficulty with reading.

The increasing number of computer software programs available at public libraries are of particular interest to school children. Since kids generally are more interested and at ease with computers than their parents, computers are often found in the children's section as well as the adult department. many public libraries offer training courses for children in using different software or educational programs. Be sure your kids – especially your teenagers – know what's available at your local public library.

For teenagers

Teenagers, of course, are more independent than younger kids, so parents will have a somewhat different role when it comes to helping them use the library and encouraging them to read for recreation. Just being certain that teenagers know what kinds of programs are available may be the best help you can give – that, along with setting the example of visiting the library and reading yourself.

Services for special children

If your children are gifted and talented, you may find that helping them to use the library offers special benefits and challenges. Gifted children usually have a love for reading and are able to learn on their own and advance to higher level materials at an earlier age. They tend to have a great deal of curiosity and desire for answers on a variety of subjects, so that they need access to a wide range of sophisticated sources of information. The public library can be a "learning laboratory" for these children, and very often they can make good use of its resources with relatively little assistance.

If your children are handicapped in any way, don't let this discourage you from introducing them to the world of books in your community library. The Americans With Disabilities Act, which took effect in early 1992, requires facilities and services regularly used by the public to be accessible to the . . . disabled. Even before this act, most public libraries eliminated barriers to physically disabled individuals and many offered programs specially designed to serve people, including little ones, who are developmentally disabled, hearing-impaired, blind, or physically disabled.

The kinds of library services vary greatly for children who have learning disabilities or who are mentally retarded. To find out what's available in your area, the best starting point is your local public library. If its programs do not address the special needs of your children, perhaps the librarian can rsefer you to other area libraries that do. [Library services are also available for hearing impaired, blind, and physically disabled persons.]

Endnote

* Kathryn Perkinson, *Helping Your Child Use the Library*, Published by U.S. Department of Education, Office of Educational Research and Improvement. In the public domain. 1989. 21 pp. From Consumer Information Center, P.O. Box 100, Pueblo, CO 81002. The material has been abridged. We have not used ellipsis points except when cutting parts of the author's sentences. Check their web site.

17

Support Groups

To write the article[1] which has been slightly abridged to become this chapter, ***Cindy Short*** *studied questionnaire responses from many support group leaders. From the wide variety of purposes, activities and people in these groups she found a wealth of ideas — ideas that give you reasons to join a group if you don't already belong to one, and ideas to make your group better if you do. Cindy helps her sister, Sue Welch, edit* The Teaching Home.

How do support groups get started?

There are several possibilities. Sometimes two home schooling families find each other and start meeting together for fellowship or to meet specific needs. Sometimes one person with a vision advertises an informational meeting or get-acquainted potluck or calls on other home schoolers to find those interested in starting a group. Some groups that have large memberships or that cover large areas will subdivide into smaller groups or refer newcomers to a newly forming group. Contacts made at a home school seminar or at church sometimes lead to the formation of a support group.

What purposes and objectives do support groups have?

Surprisingly quite a few.[2] A primary goal is usually *support and encouragement.* This can take two forms. The first is spiritual support and is accomplished by Christian fellowship, Bible teaching or study, memorization and meditation, and prayer.

In some groups, the fathers and/or mothers take turns preparing a devotional or Bible message for each group meeting. This is sometimes followed by a sharing time for prayer requests and a time of prayer for the needs of each family and of the home schooling movement. This kind of support is maximized in an all-Christian group, especially when all have similar doctrinal positions.

The second form of encouragement is moral support and is accomplished by just being with other home schoolers as well as by sharing common experiences. Needs and problems, as well as victories and solutions, are shared for the benefit of all. This occurs during group discussions or in one-to-one conversations. Friendships are formed between both parents and children, and children are encouraged by the attention of other adults.

A second goal of many support groups is the sharing of *information about home schooling* with each other and with those interested in getting started. This includes information about curriculum, methods of teaching, legal options, and seminars or books that are helpful.

A third goal, which is emphasized by some groups more than by others, is to provide *educational opportunities* that would be difficult for parents to provide by themselves. Some groups have been successful in arranging a skill exchange between families. One parent may be an excellent teacher of higher math or science and be available to tutor children whose parents have difficulty with those subjects. Another parent may provide coaching in creative or artistic skills. One group publishes a phone number in its newsletter for a "Grammar Hot-Line" to answer the questions of stumped parents.

Many groups arrange special one-time

presentations such as science experiments or craft demonstrations for the children at their meetings. Almost all support groups play some role in arranging field trips of an educational or enrichment nature. Some groups have well-attended regular classes on subjects ranging from art to science. Social and expressive skills for both parents and children are also taught or encouraged in many groups, directly or indirectly.

Another goal of support groups is to visibly *represent home schooling* to the community, to their relatives or friends, to local churches, to government and legislators, to a state home schooling organization, or to school officials.

A few groups have incorporated as a school or satellite program, and one includes families who want to supplement their children's public school education.

Who is involved in support groups?

Some support groups consist of members who are very similar to one another and others include families with great differences between them. One factor that can greatly affect the activities and atmosphere of a group is its policy about including or excluding unbelievers. Groups that have a written statement of faith may require that it be signed either by all members, by those who vote or participate in certain activities or only by the leaders. Other groups are all or mostly Christians by common consent. Some groups include activities such as Bible teaching and prayer that give the group a definite Christian emphasis. Others take a neutral position or even deliberately appeal to non-Christians and seek their cooperation and participation. Some groups consist all or mostly of families from one church or denomination and report very close fellowship and an absence of conflicting beliefs. Others find unity in their common faith in Christ and avoid doctrinal discussions.

Support groups may include both new and experienced home schoolers or all beginners. Experienced home schoolers can give valuable help and guidance to those just getting started. On the other hand, enthusiastic beginners often pitch in and help each other and organize innovative activities when they realize there are no "old-timers" to tell them what to do. They usually find by trial and error what works best for them.

Some groups tend to have only families with young children; others have some with older children or teenagers. The unique needs of these different age groups are sometimes difficult to meet in groups that do not have several in each age group.

There are various policies on the attendance of children at group meetings. Some groups hold meetings for parents only, some include children in all functions and some have planned activities or supervision for children separate from adults during meetings. The responsibility for supervision of children in the latter case is either delegated to one or two volunteer parents or taken by rotation of all parents. When children stay in the adult meetings, the parents are expected to keep them from distracting others or else take them out. Many groups have separate planning meetings for adults and include children in other meetings. A few have special meetings for mothers of toddlers or for families with teenagers to meet their unique needs.

Some groups encourage members to invite friends, relatives or school officials who are curious or skeptical about home schooling to visit their regular meetings. Others hold special meetings for the purpose of answering the questions of those interested in home schooling.

Support groups can include home schoolers from several counties or from just one community. One large group subdivides by zip code for some of its meetings to provide closer contact between members.

How are support groups organized?

There are two basic patterns for support group organization styles with some overlapping. The first is the small informal group. It is usually fairly new and is loosely organized. Leadership is provided by volunteers, by one or more members who see this as their ministry, or by rotation of responsibilities among all the members. Decisions are made either by the leader(s) or by consensus. There are usually no official memberships or dues. Funds are provided as needed by collection of donations, by one or more members' ministry of giving, or by equally dividing the cost between participating members.

The second type of organization is the larger, more formal group with a tighter structure. Leadership is provided by the group's founder(s) and/or by elected officers. Decisions are made by these leaders or by voting members. Sometimes a written constitution is adopted. Membership in the group may be associated with certain requirements such as signing a doctrinal statement, participating in a minimum number of activities, or paying dues. Privileges include voting, receiving a newsletter, and participating in certain activities. Some groups have different levels of membership, each with its own requirements and privileges. Membership lists are usually for members only and to be kept confidential. Funding for these groups' usually extensive activities and services comes from dues, newsletter subscriptions, and/or user fees.

As mentioned above, there is quite a bit of overlapping of these two styles. Some small groups are more organized and some large ones are less. Large groups often subdivide into smaller ones, at least for some activities. Some groups deliberately limit their size for more efficient operation, dividing in half when the group exceeds the limit. Some groups have experimented with formal organization and found that it caused a loss of fellowship and sharing. Large or formal groups find they need to counteract this tendency by providing ample opportunity within their total program for individual contribution and interaction.

How do support groups communicate with their members?

In small groups the leader will often contact each member personally by phone to announce meetings and activities. As the group grows beyond a few families, however, this becomes too time-consuming for one person to handle. At this point a phone chain or phone tree is usually started with each person calling the next person on the chain or with certain members each calling 3-5 others. Another use of the telephone is to have one or more members available to answer questions, channel newcomers to those who can help them get started, or refer requests concerning specific needs to volunteers who can help in those areas.

Sooner or later many if not most groups find mailing more efficient than phoning. This can take the form of occasional flyers announcing meetings and activities or of a regular newsletter. Newsletters are published with varying frequency, from weekly to quarterly. They can contain announcements of group activities or community events, articles on home schooling or scriptural topics, or creative contributions from members of the group – both adults and children. The newsletter is produced by an editor, by a team, or by each member taking a turn in rotation. Costs of printing and mailing are covered by dues, subscriptions, or donations from the whole group or individuals. Sometimes members provide self-addressed stamped envelopes for mailing.

Other printed material may include a welcoming letter or brochure for newcomers describing home schooling in general or the support group itself. Sometimes the support group prints its statement of faith in these materials to clarify its stand. Some groups print a questionnaire to identify the needs of members and evaluate the success of various programs. Membership applications sometimes provide the group with specific information about each family, such as names, ages, birthdays, curriculum used, experience level, hobbies, skills, interests, needs and availability to help others. Some groups distribute reprinted articles or brochures obtained from outside sources which they feel would be helpful to the group.

A few groups have advertised their existence in magazines or local papers and have gained new members in this way.

What do support groups do?

There is a rich variety of activities and services provided by the support groups we have heard from. The most basic activity common to most groups is the regular *group meeting*. These meetings are held from weekly to monthly, usually in someone's home unless the group is too large. Larger groups or those that include children often meet in churches, schools or rented halls.

Some groups open with prayer, Bible reading, and singing and include a devotional by one of the parents and a time of group prayer and requests. Others are conducted as business meetings using *Robert's Rules of Order*. There is often a speaker on some topic of interest to home schoolers and sometimes a workshop or discussion period centered on a specific topic or question. Some groups have a time for book reviews or the presentation of helpful articles, sometimes distributing reprints of these. Announcements are made regarding the group's activities as well as state and national events or news of interest to home schoolers. Sometimes a legislative crisis will call for discussion and action by the group.

Educational presentations are an important part of some group meetings. One group chooses a subject area such as American history, science, geography or literature as the theme for the year's meetings, and then subdivides the subject into smaller sections, covering one at each meeting. Families present material in various interesting and creative ways such as reports, plays (with costumes), poetry recitations, games, demonstrations, arts and crafts, songs, Scriptures, and even simulated radio or TV programs. Small children are involved in these presentations as much as possible with their parents and older brothers and sisters. Follow-up learning is included in the form of printed handouts and suggested activities.

Many group meetings include a time for free sharing between members, either as a group or in one-to-one conversations, and end with refreshments. Other meetings are held either before or after a picnic, sack lunch, or potluck dinner for fellowship. Sometimes the children make and bring the refreshments. A few groups have one person in charge of bringing food bought with group funds; others rotate the responsibility of contributing refreshments.

A common feature at many group meetings is a resource table including printed information, books and magazines on home schooling or curriculum displays for parents to take home, browse through, buy, borrow, order or trade. Some groups also have lending libraries.

During meetings that are not geared for children, some groups have planned and supervised activities for them in a separate room. These can include informal play, games, stories, crafts, entertaining or educational movies or even regular classes. Responsibility for these activities can be taken by one person or several either permanently or by rotation.

In addition to the regular group meetings, some support groups have special meetings for parents only or for parents of preschoolers or teenagers only. Another common kind of meeting is "Mom's Day (or night) Out," either for relaxation or business or both. Dads or baby sitters keep the children during that time.

Some kind of *planning* is usually required to make the group meetings go smoothly. Planning meetings may include leaders only, dads only, moms only, or the entire group. Or planning can be done by individual volunteers or by rotation, one or two families being responsible for each meeting.

Group *field trips* are a primary activity of many support groups. Responsibility for planning these can be one person's job for the year or taken in turns by one or two members at a time. Some groups have no official field trips, but individual families make their own arrangements, sometimes inviting the group or another family to join them. The lasting value of field trips is greatly enhanced by prior study of the topic as well as by follow-up activities.

Field trips can be of several different types. *Cultural* field trips can include symphony or other concerts and visits to art museums. In the area of *community services* there are public utilities, police and fire stations, courts, libraries, and hospitals, as well as private charities and nursing homes. Some support groups visit nursing homes regularly as a ministry to the residents. Various *occupations* can be explored by visits to businesses, factories, bakeries and newspapers or to the home or shop of a self-employed farmer, artist, or craftsman. The subjects of *science* and *history* can be enriched by trips to museums, exhibits, planetariums, and local events such as rock and mineral shows. *Nature* walks or hikes with or without a knowledgeable guide help children appreciate God's creation.

The ideal number and age range of children to be included in any given field trip depend on several factors and require careful consideration for best results. Many groups have learned by trial and error that smaller groups of children accompanied and well supervised by their parents learn the most from field trips. Some field trips are of more interest to one age group than another. Sometimes there are rules or requirements made by the place you are visiting that determine the size and age range of the group.

Support groups have field trips with varying frequencies, from two each week to one each quarter.

Several groups go beyond field trips or occasional educational presentations and provide *classes* in various subject areas for their members. Arts and crafts classes are sometimes taught by working artists and explore various media. Projects created may be displayed in an art show. Music, drama or puppetry classes may produce a musical or play or go Christmas caroling. Regular periods of sports or exercise are provided by some groups using public parks and gyms or church facilities. Sometimes home schoolers participate as a group in classes provided by the local park and recreation department. One group held science courses in entomology and chemistry, taught by a public school teacher. The entomology class collected insects and the chemistry class was centered in the kitchen observing chemical reactions commonly occurring there. One group had a parent teaching beginning readers in a phonics program. Sometimes groups will meet regularly but vary the subject from time to time to include enrichment in many areas.

Classes are usually held weekly and continue for a period such as six weeks or for the entire year. They are taught by volunteer parents with or without expertise or by outside professionals. Some require tuition; others ask for fees just to cover costs of materials.

Social activities are important to many groups. Potlucks and picnics are commonly enjoyed at regular intervals. Holiday celebrations may combine a special dinner with an appropriate program at Christmas, Thanksgiving, Harvest time (Oct. 31), or Valentine's Day. Another type of special dinner is the International Fair, which includes dishes and costumes from many countries.

Parties are given regularly by some groups, either for everyone or for a certain age group such as teenagers. A favorite is roller skating. Usually the support group or several groups together will reserve the rink strictly for themselves and provide their own music and supervision.

Many groups have park or sports days in the summer with games and contests or just general playtime.

Annual events that can be anticipated and prepared for all during the year are planned by some support groups. A program of various presentations by home-schooling families or individuals is one option. A variation of this is the talent night. Another is open house, which can include displays of the children's school work or special projects. Science fairs are another possibility. Some groups prepare a play or musical every year. Parts can be practiced mostly at home and then put together in a few rehearsals or worked on weekly in a class. Graduation or award assemblies give parents an opportunity to recognize their children's achievements. Each child can be recognized for something, whether it is academic progress or excellence in a certain subject or development of a character quality.

Support groups often hold or participate in *book and curriculum fairs* once or twice a year. These include displays by many different publishers and give home schoolers an opportunity to buy, sell, rent, trade, give away, or examine materials.

Seminars or workshops on various topics of interest to home schoolers are either hosted or planned by some support groups.

Several groups have *lending libraries* containing a variety of material helpful to home schoolers, and some even lend children's textbooks.

One group keeps a scrapbook of its activities throughout the year and produces an annual *yearbook.*

Such *services* as health screening and standardized testing are provided by some support groups. Others include consultations with certified teachers which meet legal requirements, or even a full-fledged umbrella school.

Support groups give home schoolers enhanced opportunities to help and encourage one another in accomplishing their common goal – to train their own children in every area of life.

Typical Support Group Activities

- *Meetings*
- *Field trips*
- *Classes*
- *Social occasions*
- *Annual programs*
- *Curriculum fairs*
- *Seminars*
- *Libraries*
- *Yearbooks*
- *Testing*

Endnotes

1. From *The Teaching Home,* "Support Groups," April/May, 1988, Confirmed, 1993, by the author.

2. Sample beliefs and goals statements appear at the end of Chapter 3.

3. For more information on the topic see *The Homeschool Support Group, a handbook for Christian leaders,* 1997?, Hearthside Productions, 15470 County Rd. 2, Leonard, ND 58052.

18

Developing Intelligence

The development and use of intelligence is clearly a primary purpose of education. We want our children to have it, but the actual nature of intelligence has not been so clear. Early in the 20th century, psychologists came up with the idea of a measurable "intelligence quotient" or IQ. Tests for it are first tried out on a typical group of kids, and the average score is established as the IQ level of 100. We may well question whether most individuals would be better off without the tests, but we are looking at a different question here. Isn't intelligence broader and more complex than what these tests test?

Howard Gardner thought so, and in his 1983 book, *Frames of Mind*[1], he identified seven areas of mental ability calling each one an "intelligence." Thus he has essentially redefined the term seeing it as the capacity for solving problems and for fashioning products in a context-rich and natural setting. The appropriate setting is determined by the particular intelligence. I would add a third capacity, that of being able to communicate in the "language" of the intelligence. All this will make more sense as we proceed.

Is this chapter really important to you? While understanding these concepts isn't among the bare essentials of home schooling expertise, keeping them in mind can help you provide a broader and richer learning experience for your children.

You may have kept your kids at home for their schooling feeling that you could offer them certain learning opportunities not afforded by classroom schools. Although you may not be more skilled than a good classroom teacher, you can certainly do a better job in some areas of instruction either because you have particular knowledge to share or because those areas require more personal attention than school teachers can provide. Will your efforts actually promote the abilities you are aiming for? To get an idea you will want to identify fundamental areas of intelligence. From the Christian viewpoint, we recognize that intelligence is a gift – a talent. We here discuss areas in which that gift may be developed and used for His glory.

We tend to want to know how intelligent our children are. The discussion in this chapter will direct us to rephrase the question asking instead, how are our children intelligent?

The seven intelligences

Linguistic intelligence This is the capacity to use words in speaking and listening, reading and writing, and for a variety of purposes. Words are vehicles for thought development.

Logical-mathematical intelligence In this area, abstract ideas are seen in patterns for predicting results. Skill in manipulating numbers and other symbols is used to develop logical relationships.

Spatial intelligence Here is the ability to perceive and imagine objects in space relationships. It includes a sensitivity to the effects of shapes and colors. The first two of the seven areas and, to some degree, this third one are what we usually think of as intelligence. Now we expand the definition:

Bodily-kinesthetic intelligence This is bodily movement abilities in dimensions including coordination, dexterity, and strength. It involves muscle control and touch sensitivity. Remembering that the brain controls body movements, we can see this as an intelligence.

Musical intelligence Defined as the

capacity to perceive, discriminate, transform (create), and express music. The person with musical intelligence is sensitive to the dimensions of music: including pitch, rhythm, melody, and tone.

Interpersonal Intelligence Understanding people, getting along with them, and being sensitive to them. Naturally one can also use this ability to deceive and hurt people.

Intrapersonal Intelligence Understanding of one's self (including the avoidance of self-deception), good self-esteem and, most important, in my opinion, self-discipline.

Why these seven?

In looking over the list we try to discern how these seven qualities could be intelligences. (I would describe them as fundamental human abilities controlled by the brain.) Then we are led to wonder whether there are really only these seven. Indeed others have been proposed, but the seven we have described seem truly fundamental. Gardner identified them after studying brain damaged individuals through the Boston Veterans Administration. He compared deficiencies in specific intellectual capacities with the location of the damage in the brain, thus relating them to functions of those locations. The sets of abilities associated with the right and left brain hemispheres are well known. The theory of multiple intelligence expands on that concept.

Another question is likely to come to the minds of serious Christians although people of other religious persuasions would ask it, too: Might the spiritual dimension be missing? Should spiritual perception be an eighth intelligence?

To help you relate to your own ideas, let me share how and why I see spirituality as a significant function. First, I believe that God is powerful enough to both communicate with humanity and to preserve His word. Thus I accept the Scriptural explanations of where we came from and where we may choose to go. I believe that, although the human anatomy and physiology may be described in generally the same terms as for animals, the two differ in a fundamental aspect: the ability to perceive and relate to God.

As a Christian, I believe that humans broke their love relationship with God and that the divine Christ came to reach out to us and bring us back into harmony with heaven. I also believe that, because love can only be voluntary, God never takes control of the expressions of that love. He never violates our opportunity to choose what we want to think and do (although our choices have natural consequences). While God does not program our behavior, He offers us hope of restoration from our natural evil tendencies, to a life of joy. The Holy Spirit appeals to us through our minds as we open them to His influence. We may accept God's grace, pledging our love, or we may refuse it. This involves communication with God, a privilege not given to any other creatures.

This relationship with divinity, however we choose it to be, involves the highest activity of the mind. Although it affects all brain functions, I see it as centering in what has been identified as the intrapersonal intelligence. In coming to this conclusion I, by no means, intend to imply that self is above God. By seeing God, we can know ourselves in the light of heaven. We can intelligently yield our wills to be transformed into the divine character, loving others as God has loved us.

Practical understanding

Over the years a number of models have been developed to describe the human thought processes. In a sense, the ideas of this chapter form one more model. Although I don't believe you should restructure your whole program for this one, understanding its concepts will make you a better teacher.

As you can see with a little reflection, none of the intelligences operate independently of the others. Musical development, for example, that moves toward performance, obviously requires a sense of the expressive quality of sound patterns. But other intelligences are tied in, too. Making music also requires well-developed muscular skills (the bodily-kinesthetic intelligence), spatial understanding in reading the musical staff, and even in acoustics (echoes, relationship between sound source and listener, placement of microphones). It requires mathematical skill to perceive timing and rhythm. It requires interpersonal skill (to play for the enjoyment of listeners, to play in ensembles, and to understand and communicate feelings). And it touches the intrapersonal area in being able to enjoy the sounds produced.

Because the intelligences work together, we all have them all. Furthermore, we all can develop in each of these dimensions. The wonderful lady I live with explains that she is waiting to get to heaven so she can sing. Actually, I hear her sing beside me in church and, although I haven't urged her to sing a solo, her singing is fine and could be developed (my opinion). Of course development means time and effort (and interest). No one can do everything in life, and she has superior abilities in other intelligences. While we have to make choices, we and our children can and should be capable, to some degree, in all seven areas, and we should excel in at least one.

Here I recognize exceptions. Some people have severe limitations, and although effort and some degree of development in each area is to be encouraged, they may not be capable of achieving the level of competence necessary for using intelligence effectively in the service of others. Recognizing our children's limitations, we must avoid making them feel that they are failures. Trying harder is not always the answer. There's a time to stop pushing and praise them for what has been achieved.

A number of factors determine the strength your child will achieve in the various areas. These include heredity, access to resources, the cultural and geographical environment, a healthful lifestyle, brain damage, and other situations in your family.

With the "multiple" definition of intelligence, we may view education broadly as intellectual development. From another viewpoint, human abilities are divided into the areas of intellectual, physical, social, and spiritual. The multiple intelligence theory doesn't ignore any of these. It simply sees them under an alternative definition of intelligence.

Critical moments in education

Gardner describes intelligence as capable of being "crystallized" for success. Experiences, often during childhood, inspire goals that fire the interest and lead to excellence. As a parent, your job is to plan for these opportunities. For example, positive experiences in art activities coupled with visiting a friendly artist at work who discusses his own creative process is likely to spark interest in the area. Sincere parents can help make Christ real to their children. Projects of helping others would strengthen spiritual, as well as interpersonal, abilities. In whatever intelligence, plan for opportunities for your child to get involved in activities that use that brain area. And don't be satisfied with just one or two areas. Your child won't likely become a genius in every

intelligence, but you should open the doors in each of them. Einstein was given a compass at age four. From that experience he developed a desire to explore the mysteries of the universe. Special musical experiences have launched the rise of many expert musicians.

In considering crystallizing experiences, Thomas Armstrong realized that unpleasant situations produce the opposite effect.[2] He calls them "paralyzing experiences." Suppose your little boy learns to love Jesus and His kind ways and begins talking about his own feelings. Then suppose someone responds in a sarcastic way with comments that such things are only for girls and grandmothers. Would it not impact the delicate structure of his inward thoughts as well as his future relationship to God? Your job here is obviously to steer your children away from negative encounters (without isolating them).

Of course some specific interests foster evil character traits. Others may simply be inappropriate. Just say, no when you need to or redirect the interest. For example suppose your girl who, prompted by her ability with numbers, wants you to buy a certain puzzle book when she already has three waiting for her attention at home. You aren't going to tell her how bad she is for wanting such a silly thing or how she is wasting your money for wanting more. Instead you will say, "Let's remember where this book is, and when you have finished more of the puzzles you already have, we can come back. If it's gone we can look for another one or get it on special order." In another approach, you might first ask her about the books at home. This might help her come to the conclusion that waiting (often very hard for children) would be a good idea.

Materials and methods

Below are a few broad activity areas to help the development of various intelligences. You can think of many more.

Linguistic Lectures, discussions, printed materials, brainstorming, word games, speech making, writing projects, reading silently and aloud, making an audio (or audio-video) recording of one's speaking, using word processors and "publishing."

Logical-mathematical Logical problem-solving exercises, math problems, scientific thinking and demonstrations, Socratic questioning, discovering relationships (classifications), puzzles and games, computer programming, logical sequence, Socratic questioning, and studying the reasoning process.

Spatial Diagrams and maps, observing and producing photography and visual art, videos, kit building, visual thinking exercises, and optical devices like telescopes or microscopes.

Bodily-kinesthetic Expressive movements, physical games, manipulative learning devices, field trips, plays, crafts, exercises for body maintenance and development, and physical activities of all kinds (cooking, cleaning, gardening, hiking, repairing, etc.)

Musical Singing (or humming or whistling), playing recorded music, playing an instrument, learning about music composition and pieces of music, seeing mood in music (and how music can influence people for good or evil).

Interpersonal Interacting in various ways with other people, group projects, conflict resolution, listening and caring practice, developing friendships, helping those in need, and experiencing relationships for teaching and learning.

Intrapersonal Learning to know God through prayer and Scripture study, developing personal life objectives, using personal time, practicing deferred gratification, keeping a diary or journal, understanding personal worth, and maintaining an atmosphere for good character development.

How to teach for development of all the intelligences

♦ Balanced development doesn't mean equal time for pushing each intellectual area. The intelligences naturally blossom at different times in childhood. For example, some of the abstractions associated with mathematics and logic occur later. During the early years, even within each area, some activities are more appropriate than others. How do you know? Try various things and watch your child's interest. Older children, say by age 9 or 10, should have little trouble with any of the areas. But the learning activities you choose for older children should still take into account their changing interests.

Also consider that good development for one intelligence does not require the same amount of time and attention as is needed for another. Your job here is simply to help your child to keep moving toward maturity and competence in all the areas.

♦ We should be sensitive to preferred learning styles while being careful to prepare our children to learn under varying circumstances. The ways people like to learn depend, to some degree, on the intelligences they have developed. People who enjoy physical activity, for example, would memorize well as they jog. As an aside, most of us could profit from learning, especially outdoors in the fresh air which makes the brain alert.

So how should you teach? As always, use common sense. To promoting certain intellectual strengths use methods that combine them in the teaching of your regular curriculum rather than just focusing on the development of the favored intelligence. For example, a child weak in interpersonal intelligence might be asked to do more interviews in social studies or to join a science club or to work with friends on projects. When learning drags, change tactics. Later, at appropriate times, bring in the less enjoyed ways of learning for a little practice.

♦ How you teach your children will depend, to some degree, on your own intellectual strengths, and on how your were taught. I suggest that you sometimes use outside help and resources, at least for your older children, in selected areas. Your spouse can be a big help here. Please don't take me too seriously on this point. Your kids are going to learn well even if you don't feel good at math or music. Will they have as good a chance at becoming a computer programmer or a concert pianist? Not quite, but then they may become good people people because of your strength in that area, and you can see to it that they have enough outside exposure to math and music for proficiency and so that they can take off in one of those directions if they should so choose.

♦ I also suggest that you stop now and then to think through how your child is progressing in each of the intelligences to see where you can improve. As your child matures, begin letting him or her carry more of the responsibility for learning. Talk over plans and objectives. Take your child's thoughts into account. Together press upward leading your child to bless others in many ways and find personal satisfaction in each area.

Endnotes

1. Howard Gardner, *Frames of Mind: The Theory of Multiple Intelligences.* Basic Books, 1983.
2. Thomas Armstrong, *Multiple Intelligences In the Classroom,* Association for Supervision and Curriculum Development, 1994, p. 22.

19

Thinking Responsibly

Our thoughts about our children's thinking usually focus on how to help the cranial wheels turn faster and with more precision. We want our kids to get the answers right and to produce impressive reports for their unit projects. We want them to get better marks on standardized tests. This is not bad. But is sharp thinking really our big goal? Brilliant minds can be selfish and deceptive. In thinking, moral responsibility must come before skill. As Solomon expresses it, "The fear of the Lord is the beginning of wisdom. . . ." (Proverbs 9:10) It's what comes first. ("Fear" here means awesome respect.)

Choices made day by day lead to habits, and habits harden in the kiln of life to become character. How your children think determines how they choose and hence, what kind of vessel they will become as they bake in the kiln. It's your privilege to help the great potter make your children masterpieces as you guide them to unselfish thinking.

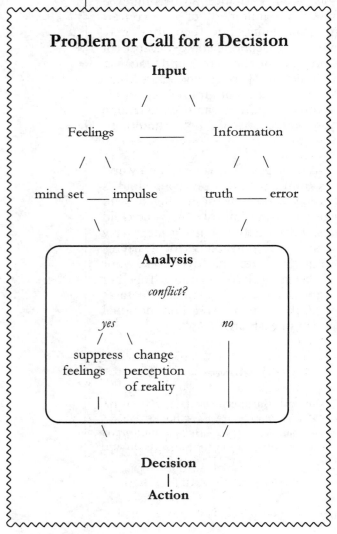

Problem or Call for a Decision

Input

/ \

Feelings ______ Information

/ \ / \

mind set ___ impulse truth _____ error

\ /

Analysis

conflict?

yes *no*

/ \

suspend feelings / change perception of reality

\ /

Decision

Action

Making choices

We constantly make decisions. We choose what to wear for the day, whether or not to get a drink of water and how much. In response to a friend, we choose words and body language. We even choose the thoughts we allow to run in our minds. Choices often involve right and wrong behavior. Victory over small temptations prepares us for the big ones. If we make the wrong decision about the extra cookie our tummy is asking for, how can we expect to stand for principle when it means losing our friends or our job? And, of course, our right choices give us the earnestness and credibility to guide our children.

The diagram in this chapter traces the general pathways in decision making.

Notice first the raw materials we use in making decisions. We decide by two basic influences, how we feel and what we know. Although feelings are often misapplied in making decisions, they do have a legitimate function. Love, after all, is a feeling. Our problem comes when we allow feelings to hold the reins to our moral decisions. True love, as with other emotions, must be guided by principle.

Our feelings are shaped by our general mind set which influences the impulse of the moment. Mind set is normal and proper. We have a responsibility to cultivate the right mind set and likewise to lead our children to naturally want to do right.

Information, the other factor in decision making, is basically knowledge of consequences in the light of principle. We must ask, How will a particular choice affect me? How will it affect others? Information may be right or wrong or incomplete. To minimize the chance of a wrong decision, we need to seek good information and to revise our paradigm as we learn more.

So we (and our children) must decide by what we know about consequences and by feelings that do not violate principle. To decide, we dump these two influences into our mind mill and turn the crank.

Conflict

Often our information calls for us to decide one way while our feelings are pulling us hard in another. How we resolve conflicts between what we know and how we feel is critical. To harmonize the two, we either suppress feelings or we change our perception of reality. Modern psychology tells us that suppressing feelings is bad, and it is if we keep them boiling inside. But when the feelings call for a wrong action, we must suppress them.

Suppression, however, doesn't mean we have to live with bad feelings. If you are a Christian, you have a solution. God is ready to change our feelings if we really want Him to. He can help us feel good about doing the right thing. David prayed, "Create in me a clean heart, O God; and renew a right spirit within me." (Psalm 51:10). This takes divine power as in the miracle of creation. Our part is to cooperate in placing our will on God's side. (Dan. 1:8; Job 13:15)

Secular psychology does offer a solution. It says, just learn to feel good about your bad feelings. If you hate your mother, that's okay. Just go and smash something to vent your feelings. Then you can relax. I don't buy that idea either logically or morally.

To resolve the conflict between feelings and facts without changing the feelings part requires working on the information. This means denying reality. This sounds very strange, but it happens. For example, people often imagine that health principles are for someone else, or they rationalize that stealing from an employer is okay because they work hard and deserve what they take. And what about "ethnic cleansing"? How could rational people support it? They are taught to trust their leaders who gradually persuade them that the target group is bad. As hate builds, killing is easier. This is what happened in the holocaust in Germany and has happened in the former Yugoslavia and in Rwanda. A similar self-deception was necessary to justify slavery, and it justifies people in walking out on their spouse in favor of another lover. Now what about you and me? If we want a new car or a new garment, don't we begin to imagine how bad the old one is? Sometimes we are right, but not always. (Read 2 Thess. 2:8–12; Phil. 4:11).

Before leaving this topic, I'd like to add that our minds should never be put in neutral allowing someone else to do our thinking for us.

Can a choice be made with a conflict unresolved? Following behavior we know is wrong means constant (and proper) guilt. We could try to ignore the conflict but in a sense we eventually change our view of one side or to some degree both.

A person may continue a wrong action, putting off a decision, but this is also a form of self deception. (See Acts 24:24, 25). Basically, we need resolution for a decision.

Teaching children to make wise choices

1. *Spend time with your children.*
2. *Model good behavior.*
3. *Create opportunities for young children to choose. Hesitate to interfere with decisions.*
4. *Teach principles as your talk about consequences.*
5. *Suggest alternatives when you need to say, no.*
6. *Always discipline in love; use consequences to influence changing wrong behavior.*
7. *Pray with and for them.*

So what about our children?

I have been describing this process so that, in helping our children face their battles, we can lead them to make the right choices. No one can guarantee that their children will make good choices, but we can do a lot to direct them in that path. The side bar shows some suggestions. You will find more elsewhere in this book.

Teaching your children at home gives you more opportunity to provide the guidance we have been talking about.

20

Thinking Precisely

Any teaching calls for thinking, but too often the thought process is essentially limited to storing and retrieving information. For information to be meaningful, it must be applied – its value must be tested. And that requires a higher level of thinking. If our children are to become masters of their minds rather than drifting along with the popular crowd, we need to fortify them against being programmed by the media, led by peers, and driven by their own sensual impulses. In preparing them to make right choices, we must direct their minds to high moral standards, as discussed in the preceding chapter. Then, with that point of reference, we can help them sharpen their analytical skills. Analytical thinking ability is the focus of this chapter.

Advertising today is a sophisticated technology for raking in profits on everything imaginable from cat food to pornography. Political candidates rarely make it into office without enormously expensive and deceptive assaults on our minds. Even religious ideas are "sold" by applying the best use of media and often by manipulation of the emotions.

Now I'm not against reasonable profits through honest advertising. Also candidates do need to pay for channels which can communicate their ideas. And to preach the gospel to the whole world as Jesus commanded, we need to use efficient methods. My concern is that our kids are bombarded by deceptive techniques as well as by good information. We dare not neglect to show them how to think for themselves. They need to look past the facades and hype to the real truth. They must be able to make decisions independent of tradition and popularity.

Although this chapter is about thinking, the cultivation of a clever mind is not enough. Good thinking must be guided by good motives. Let's help our children develop the courage to stand against the current – to do right because it is right.

Reasons to think

Have you ever tried to persuade someone to abandon a choice which they have based on totally weird logic? Let's take smoking for an example.

Tobacco shortens life, even for teens. It's a parasite sucking up time and energy; it's expensive; it restricts behavior; it offends far more people than it pleases; and it robs the national economy. In short it's just plain. . . . (Okay, I'm getting steamed up.)

Why then do people use tobacco? Why do they ever start when it's so hard to stop? Let's consider your children. What are the pressures on them? If your home is smoke free, they have a tremendous advantage. Guarding their freedom from the bondage of tobacco, alcohol and other damaging substances, by the way, is reason enough to home teach them. Children and teens read the billboards. The attitude of school peers communicates to them that smoking is "cool" – a powerful incentive for adolescents striving to establish identity. Is being cool for the moment sufficient reason to ignore the weight of evidence against smoking? If you ask a smoker, he isn't likely to tell you that the ads and his friends have been making a fool out of him.

The human mind, in such cases, does a

How to make a bad decision

1. *Guard your comfort zone*
2. *Make quick evaluations.*
3. *Depend on what you already know*
4. *Think scattered thoughts*
5. *Don't worry about consequences.*

little trick. It short circuits the logic process to justify wrong behavior. Motivation for picking up the smoking habit may include popularity, rebellion, or even the intrigue of the taste. The new smoker puts the eventual consequences out of mind – he puts a hold on clear thinking. When dealing with people, tact and courtesy are important. We don't change people by ridicule.

As already stated, ability to think logically isn't the whole answer. First your kids need a sense of moral responsibility. Then they will want to think clearly and, understanding some basic principles, they can more easily make good decisions.

How to approach the teaching of thinking

You can teach responsible thinking in conjunction with your regular subjects, so there's no need to stop to add a new subject. Although all good teaching promotes good thinking, direct instruction on the process of rational thought will make your children conscious of their mental processes and help them think wisely. Their approach to life as well as to academic learning will be greatly enhanced. Some recent textbooks do challenge the reasoning powers and promote decision making, but teaching materials often overlook this objective. Therefore you need to watch for opportunities to build thinking lessons on the concepts in your curriculum.

I suggest that as you teach you keep in mind the various thinking lessons offered in this chapter, watch for opportunities to present them, and keep track of what you have done. Later, as appropriate topics come up in your curriculum, you can return to thinking skills you have already worked through and rehearse them by assigning exercises that apply them. You may also want to read more about the teaching of thinking. My ideas for this chapter are largely drawn from the book *Infusing the Teaching of Critical and Creative Thinking into Content Instruction** which you will find reviewed in Appendix Q.

To infuse specific thinking skills into your curriculum, the following four steps are recommended. But don't wait until you are ready to apply all of them perfectly to begin helping your kids understand the principles of good thinking.

❈ *Introduction.* As you bring up the selected concept in your curriculum explain the importance of clear thinking in relation to it. Also you might outline the process you are about to help your child apply. As we look at specific thinking skills, this will make more sense.

❈ *Thinking activity.* Use verbal prompts to help guide the particular type of thought process you have chosen to develop. A simple chart which your child writes on is recommended. This clarifies and reinforces the structure of the process.

❈ *Thinking about thinking.* To help your child realize what is going on, you discuss the particular thought process. The fancy word for this analysis is *metacognition.* You need to back away from the activity you just guided for applying the skill to focus on the process of thinking. This is a higher level of abstraction and will likely be new to your child.

❈ *Thinking skill transferred.* Your discussion of the process in the previous step helps prepare your child to use it. This final step is simply reviewing the skill later by applying it to other appropriate situations. Your prompts will be needed less and you might simplify the process by not asking for everything to be written down on the chart.

The thinking domain

Schwartz and Parks describe what they call "the thinking domain."* They divide thinking skills into three types:

▲ clarification – understanding the situation,
▲ creative thinking, and
▲ critical thinking.

These three skills are applied to achieve the purposes of thinking:

▮ decision making, and
▮ problem solving.

We will begin with the purposes. When we better understand the overall process, we will return to sharpen the skills. To simplify, let's combine the two purposes. After all, if you are confronted with a decision, it's a problem to be solved.

To solve a problem

In looking for a solution, we consider various options and the consequences of choosing them. We may also identify the need for additional information. As we understand the situation better, we may modify our list of options. Finally we choose a solution even if it's to do nothing about the problem. All this is usually only a mental process. For example, when I go on errands in town I decide on a sequence for my stops. I settle on my route based on time constraints (when the people I need to see are in), on the total travel distance, on whether the success of a certain stop requires something I would get from another one, and so on. I'm sure you do the same thing.

Sometimes writing down all the options helps make a decision easier. For the many decisions we make every day, we don't generally think about the process we go through of sorting and adjusting. Poor thinking habits mean poor decisions. I don't know about you, but at times, I'm not very efficient or I make an unwise purchase or I find myself saying things I wish I hadn't said.

In helping your children learn good thinking habits, I suggest you assign problems to be resolved and have them sketch out the various thoughts as they go through the process. Later when the process is understood, little or no writing will be needed. Requiring decision exercises to be mapped out will help your children see the process more clearly and, hopefully, will make them better adult thinkers.

I have prepared a chart to make this convenient. You will find it with the other forms at the end of this book. To some degree an ideal pattern depends on the particular problem. The actual paths taken by our brains are generally too complex to be efficiently put on paper. Still a chart helps us see what is happening even though we may add some auxiliary steps that aren't on it. Also, for a particular problem, some of the suggested steps won't be as appropriate. Just omit or modify them. For younger children, you will want to simplify the process.

Problem solving example

The form shows six steps for solving a problem. Because you are likely to have some familiarity with stories in the Bible, I have chosen to illustrate the dilemma of the three friends of the prophet Daniel when they were asked to bow down to the golden image of Nebuchadnezzar, king of Babylon.

I'm assuming you are teaching Bible and have decided to explore the alternatives available to Daniel's friends. If you don't teach Bible, this is still a good dilemma to examine.

Situations that called for decision in literature or in history could follow a similar problem-solving pattern. Your children may already know how the story ends, but they should try to imagine the situation as if they didn't know the outcome.

You can find the story of Daniel's friends in the Bible book of Daniel, Chapter 3. I suggest you look at the blank chart (with the forms in the back of this book) and talk about the process briefly,

Solving a Problem

Or making a decision

Step A Define the problem

Choosing between the king's demand to bow and God's commandment not to. Not bowing meant death.

Step B Think of possible options or solutions

Suggested Options or Solutions

1. *Bow down as commanded*	6.
2. *Sit or duck so soldiers would not notice.*	
3. *Bow down and pray to the God of heaven.*	
4. *Leave the assembly*	
5. *Remain standing*	

Step C Circle the numbers of a few options that seem worth further consideration

Step D Consider consequences of selected options
Step E Judge options according to consequences

No.	Consequences Expected or evidence	Explanation	Value (Use +, -, circles, etc.)
	Escape being thrown into the fire.	*The king had made it very clear.*	+
	Disappointment for Daniel	*He had stood with them on the diet issue. Dan. 1.*	-
	Disappointment for God	*God had shown His love for them and they wanted to be loyal. Dan. 2:13-28.*	-
	Loss of entrance to eternal kingdom	*Daniel's vision explained the kingdom. Dan. 2*	-
	Escape being thrown into the fire.	*Reason shown above.*	+
	Deliberate dishonesty. Still lose the eternal kingdom.	*God's law prohibits dishonesty. Ex. 20:16*	-
	Bad example	*People would think they were worshipping the king.*	-
	Still bowing to image in God's eyes?	*God had forbidden image worship and other gods. Ex. 20:4, 3. (This applies to choice 1 as well)*	-
	Powerful example of loyalty to God.	*Thousands of leading people were watching. Dan. 3.*	+
	Death likely, although God could save.	*The king's word was law.*	-
	In either case, assurance of eternal life	*Like Abraham (Heb. 11;8-10) their objective was the eternal city.*	+

Step F Conclusion

To stand firm while speaking respectfully to the king.

then read the story up to the point of the problem.

The process

In teaching the process, you need to provide some guidance. Try to balance between saying too much and not saying enough. Let's look at the steps using the example. The bold italics represents what would be written down in going through the decision process. Before actually doing an exercise, you might want to just talk about the process using my example or one you have made up.

(***Step A***) The problem needs to be specifically defined. Trying to solve a problem without looking at it clearly, may lead to a poor choice.

(***B***) Brainstorm for solutions. Although you need to think of their potential in vague terms, try to postpone analysis. A variety of solution ideas at this point helps avoid overlooking unusual ones. When your child stops and you think there should be more options, wait a bit. Productive silence is okay.

Then you can ask questions to prompt more thought. For example, if you have my number 3 in mind, you could ask, "Might there be a way to please the king and God at the same time?" The answer in this case is, No, but that needs to be discovered later. After possibly more prompts, you could simply suggest the solution candidate. Your participation helps as long as you hold back from doing most of the thinking

It's nice to have several children working on the project. Interacting with a group is good experience. If other children are involved, you will want to put the brakes on the older or brighter ones so that all will have opportunity to participate. One way would be to ask the children to take turns.

For step **(C)** options that seem to have potential are selected for further consideration. How many is up to you. Following all of them may make the exercise drag out too long. Your student can note the choices by simply circling the numbers. He or she can always come back and choose a different one if appropriate.

In step **(D)** the selected options are examined using the first three of the four columns. Your child tries to think of all the significant consequences for the second column. After the process is started, you can ask your child a question, getting him to consider more consequences – perhaps how other people would be affected by the decision. Use an extra sheet of paper if needed.

In the third column reasons are given to back up each consequence. This practice helps develop careful thinking. Without a reason, the consequence is not likely valid. Younger children might skip this part. You may want to just talk about the consequences.

After processing all the selected options, your child moves to step **(E)**, "grading" the validity of each one. First mark consequences as for or against the option with + or –. Then go back and circle the + or – to indicate stronger reasons for and against.

Finally, **(F)**, looking at the weighted consequences, a conclusion is chosen. Usually it will be one of the selected ones, but a new solution combining some of the good factors is okay. Notice in the example I have chosen option 5 but have modified it somewhat.

As you come toward making a decision, you might discover that more information is needed. Then, if time permits, your decision is to wait. I suggest listing just what you still need to know. Of course if the information is available at the time, you just stop and find it before proceeding to the decision line. When you choose problems that grow out of your curriculum, this is all part of the learning. And please remember that the word, curriculum, for this author means what your set out to learn. Books and such are not "curriculum" but are curriculum materials or learning materials.

Sharpening the decision-making skills

We have looked at the whole process of problem solving and making decisions. This activity depends on skills in basically three areas which we listed earlier. They are (1) clarification – understanding the situation, (2) thinking creatively, and (3) thinking analytically (or critically). These more-specific skills may be sharpened by drawing applications from your curriculum as I have suggested for the general skill of problem solving.

Clarification

The first reason for clarification is to understand the problem to be solved. Is the immediate difficulty only a symptom of a larger problem that should be addressed? Have we otherwise misidentified the source or seriousness of the problem.? Clearly stating the problem helps avoid superficial or incomplete solutions. Also, as we begin to look at possible solutions, we need to make clear comparisons among the options. We can take two (or more) solution suggestions and write down how they compare feature by feature. For example, if the family has a hard time fitting into the car, we look first at general options. If we conclude that we don't want to leave some of the kids at home and we don't want to rent a bus every time we want to travel with the whole family, then we need to compare, point by point, various characteristics and circumstances associated with vehicles that could serve our need. At this point features are listed and consequences are compared.

Many of the important decisions we make are advocated or discouraged by people who surround us – salespeople, consumer groups, religious advocates, friends with opinions, and so on. It is important to evaluate what we read and hear. We need to ask several questions:

Is the information accurate? I recently saw a television report about arrests of people who got married before they were divorced from a previous spouse. They told their new lovers that they were divorced, while in fact, the divorce was only in process. Falsehood is usually supported by partial truth. Compare information with another source. Ask for documentation.

Is the information sufficiently complete? We expect salespeople to emphasize the good points of their products. Looking at competing products and reading consumer information helps us get a balanced picture. One company promotes its substitute for dietary fiber by showing that it is easier to swallow. The competition claims that their product has no "harsh chemicals." Neither of them admits that the best way to get dietary fiber is simply to eat food that is not highly refined. They can't make money when you buy whole grain bread and cook up fresh vegetables.

Is the argument sound? One type of deceptive argument leans on analogy. A certain writer has promoted the idea that God will not punish the wicked. Please note that this is an illustration. You may believe one way or another on the topic. My point isn't to convince you (although I wouldn't mind) but to insist that you have good reasons for your conclusions.

The writer explained that a mother whose child got burned on the stove would not punish the child for touching the stove because the bad experience would teach its own lesson. On hearing the analogy we correctly sympathize with the child and applaud the mother. However, before accepting the idea that sin brings no punishment beyond its direct consequences, we must ask whether the situation with sin is exactly like the analogy. To know the answer we may go a source of authority. I believe God has answered this question and others in His word.

Analogies are good for describing the

unknown in terms of the known. They stimulate us to seek an answer. However, they are not to be trusted in determining truth. Considering opposing viewpoints and putting aside our own emotional preferences are helpful in analyzing arguments.

Misjudging cause-and-effect relationships also leads to unsound arguments. Suppose you have a sore throat and drink some herb tea. If your throat feels better the next morning can you say that the tea cured it? No, because many other things were working in your life. Your natural body defenses may have been helped by the water in your cup or other factors, and not by the added flavor. To be confident that the tea caused the healing, you would have to do a comparison experiment with and without the tea while having a sore throat while keeping all the other variables the same. The better feeling is only a clue. You might want to try the tea again but you don't really know for sure. People with unnatural fears tend to draw strong conclusions on very slim evidence. Their imagination becomes their reality!

As you help your children understand these principles, have them analyze specific ideas they hear promoted. You may use current events in the news, ads, and so on. Unless you are familiar with the topic and all the pros and cons, it's a good idea to do some research on your own, too. History, literature, and the environment are good source areas for analyzing opinions.

Creative thinking

If we take the attitude that the old ways for facing certain kinds of problems are the only ways, we may be missing possible solutions. When the insurance agent noted that no fire plug is in the area of my new home, I tried a little creativity. I told him the river was not far away. But no luck. He reminded me that the river was frozen over during the winter. Of course wild ideas can turn out to be good ones, and sometimes they can be modified for workable solutions. Kids enjoy creative thinking.

Such creativity means striking off in new directions. It means challenging tradition. Brainstorming is looking for solutions, usually with other people, where no ideas are considered silly or are rejected out of hand. I'm not suggesting, however, that basic truth which you have already tested and proved for yourself be doubted in the name of creativity unless new evidence calls for re-examining them.

Critical thinking

Critical thinking needs to follow creative thinking in a rigorous analysis of ideas. It requires looking at thes reliability of information sources and analyzing arguments.

❈

Sound reasoning is important in the current atmosphere in our world. Many pressures clamor for the loyalty of our minds. Although more on this topic is beyond the scope of this book, I have shared the most important concepts. Even if you don't study beyond the relevant chapters in this book, your simple, cautious thinking (and from my perspective, dependence on the divine source of truth) will help you and your children avoid deception.

Endnote

* *Infusing Critical and Creative Thinking into Content Instruction, A lesson design handbook for the elementary grades.* Robert J. Swartz and Sandra Parks., 1994, Critical Thinking Press & Software, P.O. Box 448, Pacific Grove, CA 93950 (800) 458-4849. This is a large book nearly the size of *The Home School Manual.* See Appendix Q.

Areas of Learning

SECTION TWO

21

Planning for the Early Years

Human infants begin the journey of life with but little intellectual baggage. They are preprogrammed to know only a meager fraction of what normal preschoolers somehow classify and store behind bright little eyes. Consider the complexities of walking and talking – all mastered without the help of a certified teacher!

Why not give them an early start?

It seems only reasonable that instilling young fertile minds with skills for reading, math, and similar bridges to general learning would be a great advantage. In fact, an increasing number of parents are evidently interested in special early training for their kids. About 40% of three-and four-year-olds in the United States are in some kind of out-of-home school. 92% of five-year-olds are.[1] 53% of the younger group have mothers in the labor force, and 55% of the five-year-olds do (or did, according to an older report).[2] Parents are naturally interested in programs that provide for the kids during working hours. Programs with an academic emphasis will attract many of them.

But the push to get ahead by starting early raises certain questions. The principles of learning, for young children, are a little more complex than it would at first appear. For example, let me remind you that preschoolers who learn a second language apparently as easily as you and I learn half a dozen telephone numbers, also forget it unless they continue using it past the age of six or eight. Melvin, my own youngest, was conversing fluently in simple Creole and French when he was five, but knows almost nothing of either now as an adult.

Although the answers aren't always simple, we dare not take education in the first crucial years of life for granted. And it's not enough to accept the conclusions of skilled speakers or writers without examining the evidence on which they base their ideas.

In this chapter we first discuss research studies (and the debate about what they mean) so you can intelligently direct the education of your young child.

In the next chapter, we look at some specific teaching principles for helping preschoolers think and develop; and I'll suggest how a child for whom formal instruction has been delayed can be integrated into the stream of classroom education.

Delayed formal instruction

Formal instruction, as we usually think of it, requires sustained eye work, fine hand muscle control, confinement for seat work, coping with peer social interaction, logical thought processes, and so on. Just from this description and from what you know about your own children, you probably are beginning to see reasons for delayed school entrance.

Some of the most convincing reasons to wait come from studies comparing children who actually began earlier and later. For example, the following report from *USA Today* mentions two studies indicating that children who wait a year to start school get higher grades than those who attend first grade as soon as they are eligible.[3]

✦

A seven-year study of 70 children in the Cincinnati school system found:

➢ 81 percent of boys who waited had

above-average grades, while only 47 percent of the younger boys did.

➢ 100 percent of girls who waited had above-average grades, compared to 60 percent of those who started early.

The added maturity may allow development of coordination, vital to reading and writing skills.

➢ A study of 278 Nebraska pupils found those who began school as soon as they were eligible were more intelligent than their older counterparts, but got lower grades.

Young Children Are Not Ready

- *Young eyes can focus at close range, but certain evidence indicates that early close work is associated with nearsightedness. (More on this later.)*
- *Frequent confusion between similar letters and words means extra strain on an immature brain.*
- *Auditory perception — the brain's accurate interpretation of sounds — isn't mature.*
- *Ability to see a spatial arrangement and predict what certain changes would do to it, generally begins between the ages of eight and eleven.*
- *Young children are more susceptible to respiratory and other diseases, thus hardly braced for recycled classroom air.*
- *Because of the way young children reason, they have little defense against unwholesome peer influences.*
- *Without the ability to weigh issues for understanding right and wrong, little children in groups too large for good adult supervision hurt each other emotionally and sometimes physically. And*
- *Young learners thrive on action — running, jumping and climbing — not desk work with abstract ideas.*

✦

In a study of more than 190,000 South Carolina public school students in grades 1, 2, 3, and 6, significantly more younger students in each grade failed the state's standardized reading test.[4] Among the 16% who failed in grade 1, those born during the last three months of the eligibility period (the younger ones) had 58% greater odds of failure. By grade 6, the odds difference was still against the early starters, but was reduced to 13%. The advantage of waiting to enter school is even greater than these figures indicate, however, because children kept out by special request for a whole year (until age 6 by November 1) were not included in the study. Many of these excluded children were, no doubt, held out of school because parents or counselors realized that they were not ready. Thus the children reported on had a better-than-average chance for success. Also the odds of failure after the first grade would have been greater had repeaters been included and reported on by age.

These studies have looked at risks to *academic* success. Raymond Moore and his wife, Dorothy, see a number of additional reasons why children at the typical first and second grade ages are placed at risk by formal schooling.[5] The side bar shows characteristics they believe research studies reveal about these children.

Dr. Moore undertook a comprehensive search of the literature in areas that might show the dangers of early formal learning. Some of the hazards of "formal schooling" on this list apply only to the classroom, but most apply as well to formal home teaching.

Challenges to the idea of waiting

The public school political structure has not appreciated recommendations to keep young children away from formal schooling. Recently challenges have arisen from some in the home schooling community, too.

Two authors involved in home schooling early academic instruction have criticized the idea of waiting.[6] After a careful study of their arguments, I feel they have misunderstood the reality of the situation.

We need to ask, What happens when very young children are taught academically? In the school entrance comparison studies, we looked at the achievement of kids in certain grades – after they had been in school for a given number of years. We found early starting to be a disadvantage, but as a rule, they learned. In the same way, we would expect children to do better after the end of their first year of study if they wait longer before beginning. At the same time, a child with two years of preschool math will do better in first grade math than kids coming in without the extra study – that is, assuming the experience has not destroyed his will to learn. The point is: academic learning is not as successful for young children as it is for older ones.

Looking at how young children develop, my own conviction is that the Creator planned the early years as a special time to prepare good characters and strong bodies. That doesn't mean total abstinence from words and numbers or that early learning interests must be extinguished, but it does mean no strict academic thrust in those directions until much later when delicate young minds are better prepared for the complex processes.

Incidentally, I feel that many activities of typical kindergarten and early grade programs do not cause harmful academic stress.

Eye damage from reading

What about early reading and eye damage? Both of the early home schooling advocates address the issue. My critical reading of the research summary on myopia (nearsightedness), to which Moore refers, leads me to feel that, directly or indirectly, early reading tends to result in this eye handicap. The author, Francis A. Young, reports that ". . . a recent study of the Eskimo population at Barrow, Alaska . . suggests strongly that the early visual environment and early visual experience play an important role in developing and modifying the optical characteristics of the eye. . . ."[7]

In this study, 508 volunteer family members were tested for myopia. Those in the oldest groups (ages 51–88) had been children before reading was generally taught in their village and grew up illiterate. None were myopic. But their children and grandchildren had eye problems more like other populations. In one age group, 88% were afflicted! The changes reflect the introduction and increases in book learning.

So, should you prohibit early reading? We aren't quite ready to answer. There's another piece to the puzzle. Myopia usually develops between the ages of 10 and 14.[8] Eyes younger than that do not show any damage from early reading. It looks to me like reading habits of the early years continue during the vulnerable period when myopia actually develops. If that's true, you could solve this problem by not starting your kids in reading until age 15, but then they would be just a wee bit behind in their studies. Corrective glasses to reduce the close-vision strain have been suggested.

So early readers do tend to develop myopia, maybe from a secondary reason as I have suggested, or maybe by a process no one understands. Research does not tell us much about early reading and myopia because children's futures cannot be sacrificed on experimentation. Although we may not find, from eye research, much solid ground here for seriously delayed instruction, what we do know calls for restraint guided by common sense. Other points on our list provide greater reasons to minimize book learning in early years. Since myopia has been a concern, we have taken time to look at it here.

A very significant experiment in early learning – The Perry Preschool Project

While some educators are saying, hold off on teaching academics, others seem to be telling us to hurry up. Let's take a look at results from a major preschool experiment, The Perry Preschool Project. (now communicated as High/Scope). Each year between 1962 and 1965, three- and four-year-olds were selected from among disadvantaged children in Ypsilanti, Michigan, and admitted to a specially designed preschool program. Another group from the same community and with essentially the same backgrounds and characteristics, called the control group, was not admitted to the program, but was studied as a comparison. Eleven years later, tests and questionnaires showed the group who attended the special preschool program to have greater school achievement, more commitment to school, a more positive student role and decreased delinquent behavior.[9]

Several years later High/Scope Educational Research Foundation did a follow-up study.[10] They examined 95% of the original individuals, then at age 27. Those who had not been in the program had been arrested many more times (35% compared to 7% had had 5 or more arrests). Only a fourth as many were earning over $2000 per month. A third as many owned their own home. 35% more had been on social services. And only three-fourths as many had graduated from high school.

Figuring costs of the program adjusted for inflation and estimating for the lifetimes of the individuals, the researchers calculated that the public will gain $7.16 for every dollar invested.

One factor is of particular interest. Parents were trained to in how to foster their children's learning. This is a vital element.

We can conclude that preschool programs very likely do make a difference, especially for the disadvantaged. We cannot, however, say that school is a better early learning place than home, because the experimental programs involved strong home education components. We don't know what undesirable side effects the schooling might have had or for how many of the children. None were evident from the research reports.

Early academic emphasis in question

In a later study by the Perry Preschool Project,[11] 68 impoverished children were randomly assigned to three different preschool programs. One taught academic skills reinforcing frequent responses from the children. The second took the opposite approach of the "child-centered" nursery school allowing children to initiate their own play activities, with guidance from teachers only as requested. The third program used the project's High/Scope curriculum which combined child-initiated activities with teacher interaction in planning and discussing with children.

Interestingly enough, intelligence and

school aptitude for children from all three approaches turned out to be about the same. The three groups didn't appear different in other ways either until 1986, when the participants were evaluated at age 15. Then those in the group directly instructed for academic skills reported having engaged in delinquent acts at a rate of about twice what was reported for those in either of the other two groups! 44% of the direct-instruction group were classified as high-rate offenders compared to 11% of the nursery school group and 6% of the High/Scope group.

We could wish that the experiment had had larger sample sizes and a range of home situations. Still the astonishing difference in adolescent behavior certainly points to danger from the early, strong-academic emphasis. It's a risk I would not take.

The daycare option

The experimental programs we have described were certainly different from the typical preschool daycare services where you find less-qualified personnel, more children per adult, and little if any deliberate, planned learning or parent participation.

Working mothers of the approximately four million American children not cared for by other family members find a variety of solutions for their child-care problem. Some arrange for baby sitting, some leave their children with a neighbor who watches (or tries to watch) a flock of children for supplementary income, and some can afford services from a licensed daycare center. But even among licensed preschools, probably only a small fraction, for financial or other reasons, compare in quality with the experimental preschool programs I have described.

Research comparing children from daycare services to those who can stay at home raises serious questions about social development. The daycare children in one study were found to have worse peer relationships, more aggression toward other children (shown by hitting, taking possession without consent, and abusive language), more hostility toward teachers, and so on.[12] Some of this difference may have come from the typical home influences on the two groups.

Although a few preschools or daycare centers may, through well-planned effort, help their children avoid most of this negative social influence, we would expect most to be as bad as the negative reports declare or worse, since centers with obviously poor care would not be expected to submit to research studies. Reports of child abuse at a few daycare centers don't paint a fair picture of the vast majority, but if my children were still small, I would want a good reason before leaving them with someone I didn't know very well.

Montessori and Waldorf education

Montessori and Waldorf schools are increasing in popularity and are beginning to claim the attention of home school parents. We mention them here since they (especially Montessori schools) enroll many young children. While their methods apparently achieve certain good results, I have some concerns about their philosophical backgrounds which quietly influence the developing perceptions of children. From reading this book you will realize that these educational systems don't harmonize with my own understanding of truth. Let's look at a few of their basic ideas. Then you can judge for yourself.

Maria Montessori was an innovative Italian physician who turned her attention to children's education in 1907. Her "science of the human spirit" proposes to free the child from its ordinary limiting weaknesses such as laziness, disobedience, violence, etc., and to reveal its true nature of joy, and harmony with the environment.

The method taught to Montessori teachers "expresses an intangible inner commitment to certain absolute principles, the source of which lies completely within oneself. The realization of such an inner commitment with children creates a psychic condition within which the 'normalized' child is compelled to emerge."[13] The teacher's job is to observe, to respect individual liberty, and to stage the learning environment. The child is seen to be "the true creator of its own 'normalized' nature — a spontaneous expression of the mysterious creative power of the universe springing from life itself."[14]

You might contrast these beliefs with what the Bible says about the natural heart and the source of our strength and about looking to nature as God. (See Jer. 17:9, Rom. 8:7; Phil. 4:13; Deut. 4:19; Ex. 20:1–6.)

Rudolph Steiner, founder of the Waldorf School, was a German occultist who promoted his belief in "knowledge produced by the higher self in man" and in "spiritual perception independent of the senses." Beginnings of Waldorf Education date from 1913. The "essence of education," according to this philosophy, is a "releasing and freeing of forces and capacities that live in the child."[15] By properly relating to these changing forces, Steiner considered the child to be prepared as a citizen of both the earth and the spirit world. The young child is thought to be still charmed from its "pre-earthly origin," with objects and sounds around it echoing the "spiritual world." Children "awakened" too early from the dreamy experience are considered deprived of "spiritual strength" in later life.[16]

Steiner applied his ideas to more than education. Titles of some of the books transcribed and translated from his lectures are: *The Fifth Gospel, The Reappearance of Christ in the Etheric, Occult Reading and Occult Hearing, Metamorphoses of the Soul.*

For evaluating these ideas, here are some Bible texts that I, personally, find helpful: Ex. 19:31; Is. 8:19, 20; Jude 6; Matt. 25:41; Heb. 9:27; Eccl. 9:5, 6; Rev. 22:12; and Ezek. 18:20.

How does all this relate to home schools?

A good, early education program involving both classroom and parental guidance is evidently better than no program. But contrary to what some public school promoters would like to imply, evidence does not support the idea that little children from ordinary functional homes should be sent off to school as early as most of them usually are.

Responsible home education was not tested in these research projects, but evidence discussed in this book and the experience of numerous families support it as the ideal plan for young children. A good, out-of-home early education program is better for kids than having them unguided, but an organized nurturing home is best of all. And it doesn't need to cost all the money that is necessary for the successful preschool programs.

Endnotes

1. According to a census bureau report (the most recent one as of June, '94), there were 7,712,000 children in the United States of ages 3 and 4 in 1992. 34% were in nursery school and 6% in kindergarten. Of 3,832,000 five-year-olds, 7% were in nursery school, 80% in kindergarten, and 5% in elementary school. U.S. Department of Commerce, Bureau of the Census, (Education and Social Stratification Branch, Population Division), Washington, D.C. 20233.

2. Sally Lubeck, "Issues on Four-Year-Olds and Public Schooling," Condensed in *Education Digest*, October, 1989, from *Theory Into Practice*, Winter, 1989, p.3.

3. Copyright 1983, 1988, *USA TODAY*. Reprinted with permission.

4. Molly M. Jones and Garrett K.

Mandeville, "The Effect of Age at School Entry on Reading Achievement Scores Among South Carolina Students," *Remedial and Special Education,* March/April, 1990, pp. 56–62. According to the report conclusion, ". . . the wise school district may be one that sets a convenient official entry cutoff date, then welcomes and plans for all children within the full 12 month range of eligible birthdays. . . ." It is interesting to note that the primary author of the report was a "research and evaluation specialist at the South Carolina Department of Education."

Exclusion of repeaters in the study was necessary because test grades children would have gotten had they been in school or in the next grade are unknown. Still this limits our conclusions. The final figures make the picture look better than it really is.

5. For a well-documented report of the Moores' analysis of research, see their book, *School Can Wait.* For this and other good books by the Moores, write to Moore Foundation, Box 1, Camas, WA 98607. *Home Grown Kids* has lots of practical ideas for the early years.

6. J. Richard Fugate, *Will Early Education Ruin Your Child?* 1992 (2nd edition), Aletheia Division of Alpha Omega Publications, 404 W. 21st St., Tempe AZ 85282.

Doreen Claggett, *Never Too Early,* p. 159. This book has some excellent thoughts on Christian education. Published in 1989 by Dove, Melbourne, FL. It is also sold by Christ Centered Publications, 2101 N. Partin Dr., Niceville, FL 32578.

Fugate questioned the validity of some of Moore's research conclusions. His analysis, however, supported a good number of them, thus leaving validation for Moore's ideas. To many questions, all parties would give the same answers.

7. Francis A. Young, *Development of Optical Characteristics for Seeing. Early Experience and Visual Information Processing in Perceptual and Reading Disorders,* a publication edited by Young and D. B. Lindsley, National Academy of Sciences, 1970, pp. 35–61.

Young also reviewed the investigations of British scholar, James Ware and quoted from a comment about them which noted that "Children born with eyes capable of adjusting themselves to the most distant objects, gradually lose that power soon after they begin to read and write; those who are most addicted to study become near sighted more rapidly; and, if no means are used to counteract the habit, their eyes at length lose irrecoverably the faculty of being brought to the adjustment for parallel rays."

Young then observes: "The statements appear to be as valid as they were in 1813, and this concept, that the use of the eyes for near-work is responsible for the development of myopia, has a long history in ophthalmology and optometry, but there is inadequate evidence for supporting or rejecting it. Myopia usually develops between 10 and 14 years of age and usually tends to increase with time but to stabilize around 18 years of age." (p. 42).

8. Quoted above.

9. See L. J. Schweinhart and D. P. Weikart, *Young Children Grow Up: The Effects of the Perry Preschool Program on Youths Through Age 15.* High/Scope Educational Research Foundation, 600 N. River St., Ypsilanti, MI 48197. 1980.

10. See the monograph describing this 1992 study, *Significant Benefits: The High/Scope Perry Preschool Study Through Age 27. Address in the previous endnote.*

Factors considered in the cost savings were welfare, extra schooling, revenue from taxes, judicial system costs, and losses by crime victims. An estimated $88,433 in benefits are being realized from the $12,356 cost of the preschool program.

11. "What Makes a Good Preschool Program?" *High/Scope ReSource,* Fall, 1986.

12. Neal W. Finkelstein ("Aggression: Is It Stimulated by Day Care?" *Young Children,* September 1982) refers to studies finding undesirable social behavior in children who have had day care. Then he describes how one experimental center overcame aggression problems they found. See also three articles in a special section of the September 1982 issue of *Parents Magazine* entitled "Daycare Days."

13. A Few Clear Words About the Montessori 'Method,'" *Montessori News,* May 1984, p. 2. International Montessori Society, Silver Spring, MD 20910.

14. "Creativity," *Montessori News,* May 1984, p.4.

15. *Trade Announcement,* Anthroposophic Press, Winter/Spring, 1988, p. 8. Hudson, NY 12534.

16. *Trade Announcement,* p. 9.

22

Teaching in the Early Years

In the preceding chapter we discussed the importance and purpose of early learning and why we should not push academic instruction too soon. However, I am not suggesting that young children shouldn't be taught. In fact, a simple instructional program is a good idea for the typical preschool years and is even more important for a child of traditional school age. And such a program may appropriately be called "school." The cautions are in: (1) preempting the time needed for character formation through your companionship, (2) stifling the freedom for inquisitive exploration of the big world, (3) not providing adequate opportunity for critical physical development, and (4) bringing frustration for immature minds expected to wrestle with abstract number and word skills.

Preschool learning is also dealt with in several other chapters of this book. See especially, "Teaching Values," "Teaching Reading," and "The Lovely Game." Basically, be a loving parent. Spend time with your children. Talk with them (not just to them). Go places and do things with them. Read to them. Provide challenges to stimulate their intellectual and physical skills. Set a good example. And hold expectations for good behavior with gentle, steady firmness.

In the right environment children's natural curiosity will lead them to ask how things work. They will want to go and do and make and find out. The most important learning subject for early years, as explained in the next chapter, is values. The advantages you can give your own child are a good home environment and learning appropriate for young minds and bodies. Start slowly. Introduce activities as readiness becomes apparent.

Readiness skills

Following are comments in areas of development identified by editors of *The World Book Encyclopedia*[1] They surveyed over 3,000 kindergarten teachers in the United States and Canada asking them to list what they would like to see children coming into their classrooms be able to do. Rather than copy their long list, I'll comment about each of the areas.

Please don't think of this list as a sort of required curriculum that you need to hammer away at. These are only ideas to keep in mind as you interact with your child. In fact, some of the skills are better learned in kindergarten itself. Also keep in mind that, until readiness for any skill is apparent, waiting is better than pushing.

Size

Big and little and similar concepts come as you talk with your children. Use the terms and they will understand.

Colors and shapes

Playing with objects helps. You might use plastic building blocks kits. Just talk about colors and some shapes. Your child will pick up the ideas.

Numbers

Concepts develop as you show them to your child. I wouldn't push number concepts until kindergarten, then I would go easy. Just begin talking about how many there are of certain things. Then, as interest develops, encourage counting to ten. (At three one of my grandsons already knows numbers and letters and talks about hundreds and thousands, but that's unusual).

Reading readiness

Several basic readiness skills are shown in the reading chapter. Note they are not teaching reading but developing those skills that are important in learning to read.

Space relationships

This means understanding "above," "below," "inside," "up," and so on.

Time

Have a sense of how the clock changes and being able to interpret it. Some of what is typically taught here could well wait, but use your judgment as you watch your child.

Listening and sequencing

Listening to stories and taking about them is important. Children should begin to get the idea of show a story progresses in time. Relating this to their own experiences would help.

Motor skills

This means body movement coordination. Ordinary play and activities are the best teachers here. Certainly sitting and doing cutting and writing and memorizing activities are to take a low priority for small children.

Social-emotional development

This area, too, comes naturally in homes with caring parents. One thing to plan for is playing with other children and learning to share and be kind. Your child should know his or her name and be comfortable in the presence of strangers (while you are present, of course).

Examples of how to teach readiness skills

The same booklet[2] from which the preceding list was taken suggests ways to teach some of the skills.

For recognizing the primary colors: "Go for a color walk with your child. Look for as many things of one color as possible. Play a touching game with things around your house. As an example, ask your child to: 'Touch the blue book.' 'Touch the red chair.' 'Touch the yellow pot.'"

To teach counting through 10 and matching objects one-to-one: "In the bottom of each pocket of an empty egg carton, place different quantities, from 1 to 10, of small items such as buttons, beans, pegs, raisins, or peanuts. Ask your child to count the number in each pocket. . . . Make a game of setting the table. Ask your child to help you find a cup for each saucer, a fork for each plate, or a napkin for each place mat."

For awareness of letters: "Even before your child learns to recognize letters, make a point of printing your child's name on his . . . favorite belongings. . . ."

In developing the skill of storytelling: "Find a magazine picture that shows one or more children engaged in an interesting activity. Encourage your child to tell about what is happening in the picture. If you repeat this activity several times using different pictures, you can encourage your child to notice more details in the picture, to add imaginative touches, and to talk about how the people in the picture feel.

"As you read a favorite picture book, encourage your child to participate - first by joining in on favorite refrains, then by talking with you about what is happening in the pictures. When the story is very familiar, let your child "read" the story to you or to a younger brother or sister by looking at the pictures and telling the story."

Ideas you can use from High/Scope

In the previous chapter we discussed results of studies conducted by the High/Scope Educational Research Foundation.

Principles from the High/Scope plan for

preschool education may be adapted for home teaching without the usual dangers of early formal schooling. In the box on the previous page, I have sketched out the methods as I understand them.[3]

Although children in the program initiate their own activities, adults remain in charge. They provide activities from which the children choose. They help them plan, follow through, and evaluate. And they stimulate the thinking process. A balance is maintained between adult-suggested and child-initiated activities.

Probably the toughest part of following the plan is restraining your own impulse to make the decisions and solve the problems, thus countering the creativity and initiative you are trying to help your child develop.

Now let's put this in the context of a Christian home. Isn't our response to God's invitation based on the freedom of sanctified reason (Isaiah 1:18; Joshua 24:15)? As you encourage and join with your children in their projects of making and doing, you help them learn to think clearly. By word and action you hold up before them the beautiful plan of happiness God has given in His Book. And as you help them explore the wonders of creation, you ask for the Holy Spirit to influence their choices and plans ever leading them to reverence the One who made their minds.

Kindergarten

When children in the United States are five, most of them go to kindergarten. Although I feel that the "typical" program shown in Appendix G is not generally appropriate for five-year-olds, I recommend some of it in a low-stress, home atmosphere, and most of the rest may come along as a child matures.

My concerns aren't original. Since 1837 when the kindergarten concept was introduced, opinions of teachers and curriculum planners have been divided over the proper instructional approach. Some press for introducing numbers and reading skills. Others prefer to arrange for life experiences such as playing store and visiting museums where basic concepts are learned more naturally. For example, they would introduce the alphabet through songs and not stress specific phonics concepts. Both groups teach for muscle coordination and social development.

While you are emphasizing the building of good characters and strong bodies in the tender years, you can also watch for opportunities to direct your child's inquisitive mind, leading him or her to think and create.

In Appendix G you will find the topics typically covered during the elementary and secondary grades including kindergarten.

Preparing your children to begin traditional schooling

As children mature, they become ready to handle a more formal learning program, whether you continue to teach them at home or send them to the classroom. From my own observations, the age of six is too young for many children to begin formal school as we usually think of it. As we saw in the previous chapter, the home school has fewer of the problems that would jeopardize nervous systems and social adjustment, but caution is still in order. We need to look at the whole picture. The early years are a time for developing strong bodies and good characters. Intellectual development is important, too, but not much of it needs to come from books and none should crowd out opportunities to explore God's nature under the guidance of parents or guardians. Gradually more emphasis should be placed on academics. Children can advance in numbers and reading while they are younger and less mature, but the learning is often slow and tedious. Avoid both extremes – pushing too early and relaxing too long.

While you are waiting, go ahead and teach elements of subjects which you feel are appropriate. As time passes, gradually introduce more serious learning with sensitivity to the principles we have discussed.

When your child is mature enough and you have evidence to believe that the time has come for a more serious look at the 3 R's, you have the choice of school at home[4] or in the traditional classroom. In either case, I recommend that your child begin formal schooling with the grade children of his age are usually in. That means you would start an eight year old in third grade, not first grade. Why? (1) Learning materials for each grade are designed to appeal to the interests of children expected to be at that level. (2) Your child will probably not find adequate challenge in a lower grade. As an older child she or he will learn more quickly and will also understand from natural experience much of the previous grades' curriculum, so why waste time? (3) Peers will relate better if your child is not too different. And (4) classroom management depends on the general age level of the students.

If you plan to begin formal schooling with the third grade, I suggest you borrow sets of first and second grade books two or three months before formal school is to start. If your child really knows very little about reading and math, a gradual introduction beginning six or eight months earlier might be better.

I suggest a pick-and-choose approach to topics in the grades for children below your child's age level especially if you will be continuing to educate your child at home. A superficial understanding may tempt you to move too lightly over some areas. By checking carefully you will know. Some points are indeed less important and can be skipped. Concentrate on the foundation blocks. Small errors in choosing what to teach in your get-ready program can be amended later. Also, the review of essential ideas that appears in the beginning lessons of sequential subjects textbooks (notably in math), and an understanding teacher help fill in small missing areas.

If the idea of going through several grades in a few months seems unrealistic, remember that an older child beginning formal study will usually learn in an hour or so, concepts that might have taken days during younger years; and that he or she has already informally mastered many of the goals for the early grades.

A solid, early preparation, a good home atmosphere, and thorough study year by year will give your child a tremendous advantage.

Endnotes

1. From the booklet, *Getting Ready for School*, by the editors of *World Book*. © 1987 by World Book, Inc. For information on receiving a copy, write to: Educational Services Department, World Book Educational Products, 101 Northwest Point Blvd., Elk Grove Village, IL 60007.
2. *Ibid.*
3. "Child-Initiated Learning–What About the Teachers?" *High/Scope ReSource*, Fall, 1986. If you are serious about preschool education, see *Young Children in Action, A Manual for Preschool Educators*. $29 postpaid from High/Scope Press, 600 N. River St., Ypsilanti, MI 48198. Information phone number: (734) 485-2000; fax (734) 485-0704; info@highscope.org; Order by phone (800) 407-7377 or order by fax (800) 442-4329.
4. Some people reserve the word "school" for the type of austere disciplinary atmosphere they imagine all schools to be.

23

Teaching Values

Let's stand back and take a look at what we really expect from the education we plan for our children. Do we want people to be impressed by where they inherited all their intelligence? Or what good providers their parents are? Oh no, at least not at the conscious level. We want our children to be able to function well in the world they face. We want them capable of making a good living at something they enjoy.

And we really want even more from a Christian viewpoint. We want happiness now and in the hereafter. We want our children to relate unselfishly to people and to honor God. Most Christian parents expect their children to learn the three R's in school and religion in church, but in too many cases it just doesn't work that way. Peers and entertainment during the week teach a lot more values than the preacher can unteach in church.

Of what worth are skills in math, reading, writing, foreign language or playing a musical instrument compared with solid principles for living? If you had to choose for your child between wealth and beauty of character, which would it be? Often parents are so eager to gain an advantage for their young child that they concentrate most of their instruction time on training the intellect, taking for granted that values will somehow be absorbed. Or worse, parents might suppose that character development is a matter of chance – that since everyone has to decide personally, their only responsibility is to take the kids to church.

Values are learned just as certainly as knowledge is. All learning falls into three categories:[1] (1) cognitive–factual information and ways to handle it, (2) affective–values and appreciations, and (3) psychomotor– body movement skills.

Practically all schooling is directed toward cognitive development. Spiritual and moral values, our particular concern in this chapter, would come under the second area – the affective.

Often, well-meaning parents or teachers plan to teach values but end up changing only the cognitive. The ability to repeat a set of words isn't the same as believing the message they expound. For example, a child can say the Pledge of Allegiance to the flag without changing his patriotism, or repeat the twenty-third Psalm, without knowing the Shepherd it describes. However, learning sets of words can *play a role* in changing the feelings if we combine values (affective) teaching with the factual (cognitive).

Young children are open to accept their parents' values. Character, well developed in the first few years, lasts a lifetime. We discuss this more in the chapter "Early Education."

You may have heard of "values clarification." Be careful. Its focus is more on choosing values logically and applying them than it is on considering a specific set of values. From a Christian education viewpoint, I see this as the wrong emphasis. Clear, perceptive choice is important, but basic principles of right and wrong must be presented as absolutes. The topic is discussed more in the chapter, "Teaching Social Studies."

How to teach values

Teaching the heart isn't complicated. The first element is personal example. If you teach in your health class that sugar clogs up the body's defenses and then make a sweet roll the main part of your breakfast, what have your children learned? If you tell them that spiritual commitment is important without holding it in your own heart and actions, are you teaching any more than empty words?

Your own way of life is the most important method for teaching values, but it's not enough. Good values have good reasons. Talk it over. Young children like to do what Mommy and Daddy do, but adolescents want to think for themselves. Childhood habits are easy enough to carry into adulthood if they have been backed up with clear thinking.

Your third responsibility in teaching values, in addition to presenting your example and logic, is to control the environment. We learn through all our senses all the time, and we learn from all our associates. Talk to your children about the principles, then help them choose what they feed their minds–what they read and watch on TV, the places they go, and the friends they choose.

As a parent, you have potential for a greater influence in your children's choice of friends than you might think. Find other families with high ideals and invite them over for special occasions; plan outings together. Your children will quickly become friends with theirs. And the cross-family friendship will help them develop socially far better than classroom associations.

Finally, values are learned from beginning to end by spiritual strength – ours and your children's. Paul says that the natural man cannot accept or even understand the things of the Spirit of God "because they are spiritually discerned" (I Corinthians 2:14). Proverbs 3:6 admonishes, "In all thy ways acknowledge Him, and He shall direct thy paths," and Psalm 119:105 says, "Thy Word is a lamp unto my feet and a light unto my path." Spiritual values are learned from opening the heart to God through prayer and listening to His voice through the Scriptures.

Development of spiritual maturity–an ideal pattern

Psychologists have described in some detail the typical developmental characteristics of individuals as they grow from birth to full maturity. But development involves more than physical, mental, social and emotional growth. God's plan of education includes another dimension – the spiritual – growing "in grace, and in the knowledge of our Lord and Saviour, Jesus Christ." "Till we all come in the unity of the faith, and of the knowledge of the Son of God, unto a perfect man, unto the measure of the stature of the fullness of Christ" (2 Peter 3:18; Eph. 4:13). In Peter's second epistle, he lists areas of spiritual growth as faith, virtue, knowledge, temperance, patience, godliness, brotherly kindness, and charity (chap. 1:5–7).

The following list of stages in spiritual development explains my own understanding. You may expand or modify it according to your own viewpoint and use it as you plan strategies and choose materials for teaching values.

These stages are not automatic. Children need guidance for spiritual growth just as they do for physical, mental, social, and emotional development.

Ages 0-1. *Learning God's love through parental example and control*. Trust is developed and nurtured through loving care and guidance from parents. Self-control in later years has its basis in behavior patterns set from the earliest time in life. At this stage and for the next several years, parents stand in the place of God to their children. Habits of obedience to parents make obedience to God's will a natural trait in later life.

Ages 1-3. *Learning what God is like*. As the imagination develops, the child learns about God through stories of Jesus. Impressions are made through songs and a growing, trusting relationship with parents. Simple Bible stories plant seeds of knowledge which mature later in the behavior patterns. Character is basically set.

Ages 3-6. *Bible principles taken for granted.* The child learns the basis of what is right and wrong but expects parents to be in control. Good behavior is by habit and obedience rather than from principle. Verses of scripture may be learned to reinforce later growth. Object lessons from nature make lasting impressions.

Ages 6-9. *Guidelines for right living accepted as reasonable.* Specific do's and don'ts begin to make sense and are often observed scrupulously, while other behaviors are sometimes overlooked. It is easy for the child to see problems in other children and to expect them to be treated according to his or her own sense of justice. More of the Bible stories are learned. In addition to stories, principles for right behavior begin to make sense.

Ages 9-12. *Principles begin to be integrated into the lifestyle,* rather than being just acceptable isolated rights and wrongs. The controversy between good and evil begins to make sense. Even though a somewhat fuller picture is formed, the focus still seems to be more on behavior than on a relationship with God. Skill is increased in comparing scripture with scripture.

Ages 12-16. *Biblical principles applied to a growing personal dependence on God.* The prayer life grows to be more of a connection with God. God's word takes on deeper importance and significance. Opportunities to share God's love in simple ways are taken advantage of. With increased adolescent independence in thinking, parental values are no longer taken for granted. Disparity between church members' lives and church or Bible standards provides a new kind of temptation–to excuse personal misbehavior. This crucial time in life when the emotions call for independence is often a turning point. A previous trust relationship allows the youth to accept parental counsel, and principles learned can help form the new value structure. The new-birth experience marks an abrupt change for the person who turns to Christ from a life deep in sin. In the more ideal spiritual growth pattern, as I see it, the child, ready to accept responsibility for personal decisions, renounces sin and makes the new-birth commitment at around the age of 10 to 14. (On this topic, terminology and theological understandings differ.)

Ages 16-20. *Total dependence on God, living by faith.* New spiritual concepts enrich the relationship. A reasonably good command of the Scriptures prepares the individual for serious witnessing and leading others to a decision for Christ.

Ages 20 and onward. *Settling of convictions.* Searching and testing of God's way subsides. Major questions about Christ's being both Lord and Master have already been decided in the thinking. Gradually, as the years progress, the faith becomes unshakable. Growth continues in understanding God's will and in relationships with others. People are seen as those for whom Christ died. Each is valuable. The burden of being a representative responsible for the souls of those who need to be warned becomes serious. Divine providence is accepted, and faith holds onto the continued, ever-growing relationship with God and confidence in His Word.

Bible Study

The Word of God should be the major source of study for developing values because through it we understand our Creator and Redeemer, and we see how God relates to people. From Bible study we can expect (1) to think more deeply, claiming the promised guidance of the Holy Spirit, (2) to be safe from deception, (3) to build a personal value system, (4) to develop a sensitivity to people's needs, and (5) to grow in our personal relationship with God.

Scripture study deserves more than incidental consideration in the curriculum. For young children, read and discuss Bible stories written for their level of understanding, or review the stories yourself from the Bible and tell them in your own words. Add stories showing how God leads people in our day, too. Get children busy acting out the Bible stories, making felt or sandbox representations, writing about stories or principles, and so on, according to age.

Older children need to learn to dig out life principles from their own Bible reading. Have them choose a verse or several verses and think about them. Then discuss the passage with them. Don't just say what you think, but give them a little time to develop their thoughts into words. You can ask questions to lead to better understanding, and of course, do some explaining when it's appropriate. This is an opportunity for you to learn, too.

Youth can learn to find Bible answers to their problems and to share God's love with others. They can look at longer passages of Scripture to see the context of particular verses.

At all levels, have your children memorize scripture. For small children just a few simple words from a chosen verse will suffice. Older children can memorize more. (Jonathan Lindvall has provided a whole chapter on this topic.) Also it is helpful to remember what chapter and book certain passages are in. For example, you might remember that Luke is the writer that told the story of the walk to Emmaus. You might also remember that it is near the end of his gospel account. Then it won't take but a few seconds of scanning to find it.

You can study Bible topics systematically letting the idea of one Bible writer lead you on to explore other passages that might clarify them. Use reference books, like a concordance and Bible dictionary. (Strong's Concordance is good and inexpensive for its size. Even though it is for the King James Version, you can find almost anything with it.) Commentaries are good, too, but do your own thinking first. In other words, do your basic study in the Bible using the commentary for extra ideas. Never make the commentary your main focus of study. Compare different Bible versions.

Help your older children make notes. I like to use a wide margin Bible, and I make lots of notes in it. I use a good quality mechanical pencil so I can erase when I find my ideas need changing.

Always pray before reading the Bible. Not to open our minds to divine help is to be led into misunderstanding and doubt. The same Spirit that inspired the Bible writers is needed to help us understand them correctly.

Commenting is just as easy as sharing your thoughts out loud. You can comment on the passage as you read it, making your own applications and explaining the difficult parts, or connect it to other portions of Scripture. The children will see the difference between your reading the Word and talking about it, while benefiting from both. This is more than can be said for many Bible programs that substitute Bible stories for the Bible and give comments on the Bible equal weight with the Word itself.

Are you weak in some areas of Scripture, like just about everyone else? Good for you for being honest! Then you can use a good commentary, and let the children help you find answers to some of your questions. Also teach them how to use a Bible dictionary and a Bible encyclopedia.

To teach values:

1. *Appeal to your child's reason.*
2. *Follow through with your own example of consistent enthusiasm and earnestness.*
3. *Shape the environment.*
4. *Direct mind and heart to the Source of all Wisdom.*

Bible storytelling (by Gregg Harris)[2]

A child whose heart is filled with

accurate accounts from the lives of people in the Bible is able to make right moral decisions much more consistently than a child who has only been given a list of rules and a lot of spankings. Current events in the church today warrant a return to this kind of Bible storytelling.

Rules are important. The Ten Commandments are still the basis of all God-given law. But only 15% of God's Word comes to us as commandments. The other 85% is recorded as history.

Storytellers tend to distort the Bible stories freely for the sake of younger children. Distortions come in various ways. We can add ideas for which there is no basis in the biblical account. Some publishers have Noah giving altar calls like a modern day preacher. Other publishers distort some stories by editing the plot to achieve a "G Rating." The story of Samson comes to mind. In other words, accuracy is being sacrificed to modern tastes of what is appropriate for children to hear.

Gregg Harris is president and speaker for Christian Life Workshops. He writes and publishes books and other materials under the company name, Noble Publishing. We have reviewed several of his major products.

Beware of this tendency in your own storytelling. Don't say that something happened if it didn't happen. And don't skip over something that the Bible includes as part of the story. If you feel a particular story is inappropriate for a very young child, just don't tell it yet. But for the child's sake don't distort the story when you do tell it.

Handled accurately each Bible story will accomplish God's purpose. Study each character's life story as God recorded it, then, at the right time, tell it like it is, warts and all, to your children.

I'm convinced that a child raised on accurate Bible stories would know that people, even God's people, (himself included) are still people.

The Bible told him so!

Reality

Gregg Harris has suggested making the Bible real to children. I would just like to build on his advice by sharing a serious concern. The cartoon approach, popular in Bible materials for children, is a "quick fix" to get kids interested, but the end result may be disaster.

Imagine you are a little child, growing up in today's world. In the pictures and stories you hear, Jesus and Noah and especially Jonah are presented at the same level of reality as Garfield or Cinderella. The songs often match the pictures. You try to believe in Santa Claus. But in a year or so that becomes "little-kid stuff," and pretending doesn't get you more presents anyway. As an adolescent, social life appeals to you, and this becomes the big thing in connecting you with religion. Later you are interested in making money and getting ahead in the world. Why then God?–except as a sort of eternal-life insurance just in case there was something to it.

Then what about Abraham, Jesus and Santa Claus? You will teach them to your children, of course. Have they not become part of your cultural tradition?

Coming back to the present, I think you can see my point. Certainly we need to use bright pictures and cheerful songs. Friends are important, too. But let's focus our search for happiness on the reality of eternity.

Endnotes

1. See Benjamin Bloom, et al, eds., *Taxonomy of Educational Objectives, Handbook I: Cognitive Domain.* 1956. McKay. Objectives for the affective domain were worked out by David R. Krathwohl and others. See *Taxonomy of Educational Objectives, Handbook II: Affective Domain.* 1964. McKay.
2. From *The Teaching Home.*

24

Developing Strength of Character

Kay Kuzma

What would you do if:

. . . bags of money fell out of an armored truck, and the truck kept on going down the freeway?

. . . you found a wallet loaded with ten- and twenty-dollar bills and no one was around?

. . . you opened a briefcase that was filled with cash and no ID?

. . . a waitress had not picked up the tip from the previous customer?

The answer is simple, isn't it? You would return the money. You would do everything possible to find the rightful owner. Would you? Well that's not what most people would do. "Finders-keepers" seems to be the moral code that many adults are living by today.

God's moral code is clear: "Thou shalt not steal." And yet many rationalize dishonest behavior. "Society owes it to me because of the way I've been treated." A Christian variation is, "I was praying that God would help me get some money – and suddenly there it was." Others make their moral decisions based on who the victim was. For example, they reason that it's worse to keep the money if the person is poor than if he is rich. It's even less objectionable if it's an institution or the government that is cheated.

Influences that affect choices as children mature

What makes a child, who knows what is right and what is wrong, choose against his conscience? It has to do with the development of moral decision making.

A vast amount of research has been done on this subject in the last few years, and most findings agree that a developmental pattern influences the way a child makes decisions.

Before two years of age the child has little, if any, understanding of right and wrong. We hope he has been conditioned or taught to respond to the word "no," but other than that, he basically follows his impulses.

***Kay Kuzma** is a child development specialist with a doctorate in early childhood education and the president of Family Matters. For more than twenty years she has served as an educator, consultant, author, and speaker providing leadership in the field of child raising and family life. Dr. Kuzma hosts the Family Matters radio and television programs and provides guidance for its educational activities. See Appendix C about receiving their free newsletter.*

At home, in Tennessee, Kay is the wife of Jan W. Kuzma, a research specialist. Their three children are now grown.

I was delighted that Dr. Kuzma was willing to contribute these valuable insights. For this chapter, she adapted the heart of her book, Building Your Child's Character From The Inside Out. *Her newer book is* Easy Obedience, *reviewed in Appendix N.*

Between two and four years of age a child begins making decisions based on whether he will be rewarded or punished for a behavior. The child is self-centered, and his primary thrust is to do what he wants to do. His decisions are based on whether or not he will get caught and punished.

The next stage is to conform, because it is the acceptable, or the nice thing to do. Good children don't lie, cheat, steal, or disobey. Kids between five and ten many times decide what they will do because they don't want to be embarrassed or made fun of. When they choose to abide by the rules it is often because they would be ashamed if others saw them disobeying. You can see the importance of good role models and peer influence during these years. I remember when I was growing up I wouldn't think of going to a movie because none of my friends went to movies and I didn't want them to think I was a "bad" person!

During the later school years children become almost legalistic in following their own internal moral code, which to adults is not always very rational. They will fanatically defend the rules for a game, but think nothing of cheating on a test. It is during this time that they become very vulnerable to doing what authority figures tell them to do. A common plea is, "But Mrs. Jones told us we could. . . ."

This can be a very dangerous stage for determining whether something is right or wrong, because kids tend to follow a Pied Piper rather than thinking things out on their own and coming to a rational decision about what they should do. Much of the research on children who have a strong religious background and find themselves in a restrictive environment indicates that these kids tend to plateau at this level for the majority of their moral decisions, rather than moving on to a more sophisticated stage.

The final level, and the stage at which most adults should be making moral decisions, is to have an internalized set of moral principles to judge whether something is right or wrong. Individuals who make principled decisions consider questions such as: How will it affect others? What if everyone were to do this? What does God say about this behavior?

Without an internalized moral code, the child will be swept away by the various pressures: the pressure to win, the pressure to be accepted; the pressure for attention; the pressure for self-gratification, etc.

Developing strength of character

How can you protect your child against the Pied Pipers of the world and help him develop a strong internal moral code based on principles?

1. Help your child feel good about himself. Kids who know they are special don't have to "buy" acceptance by saying yes to questionable activities.

2. Establish a biblically based moral code for your family. The earlier you take a strong stand as to what is right for your family, the more likely it is that your child will accept these standards and internalize them. The kids may not always like them, but they will respect the rules if they are reasonable and easily understood.

3. Encourage your child to think through why an act is right or wrong. A child doesn't start making decisions at a basic level and immediately jump to decisions based on principles. There is a pattern to the development of a child's thinking and decision making. A child making a decision because it's the acceptable thing to do is a step above the child deciding on the basis of reward or punishment. It has been found that a child moves from one stage to the next more quickly if he has many opportunities to interact with others who are making moral decisions just a little ahead of his level of thinking. Kids learn from other kids, particularly from older ones.

Take advantage of this. Pose various moral dilemmas and ask your children what they would do and why? The rationale is a significant factor because it indicates on which level the child is making the decision. For example, you might ask, "What would you do if your family didn't have enough food and the neighbors had plenty, but wouldn't give you any?"

If the child says, "I wouldn't steal because I might get caught." He is making the right decision but for a very low-level reason – based on punishment.

If the child says, "I wouldn't steal because Christians don't steal," he is at the level of conformity, based on whether it is an acceptable thing to do.

If the child says, "I wouldn't steal because my mommy says stealing is wrong," that would be the next level – choosing not to do something based on some authority.

Finally, if the child says, "I wouldn't steal because God says, `Thou shalt not steal,' and if everyone stole, then no one could trust anybody," this would be a principled decision.

4. Encourage your child to make his own decisions, to defend them and to take responsibility for them. Many children make decisions merely by choosing the path of least resistance. Help your child to realize that by just going along with what somebody else says, he is actually making a decision. Don't allow him to blame his buddy if things don't work out. He must take the responsibility for making his own decisions. Reinforce this fact by role-playing a courtroom scene, where the child is being accused of something because he happened to be with the kids who did it. Have him answer this accusation without blaming anyone. It's hard to do! Our natural tendency is to blame others rather than accept the responsibility for our own decisions.

5. Don't shield your child from the consequences of a decision. If a poor decision is made and the child doesn't like what happens to him because of it, he will probably make a better decision next time.

6. Allow your child to do things on his own. If you are constantly in control of your child's life, deciding every move he should make, the child doesn't learn much about self-control. Why should a child internalize a moral code, when the folks or the school authorities make all the decisions for him? He doesn't have to consider what is right or wrong.

7. Don't always shelter your child from the windy weather. Hardship develops character.

When things come too easily to a child, there is no reason to develop character traits such as perseverance, courage, determination, or thrift. If a child never feels rejected, she doesn't realize the value of loyalty, cooperation, and acceptance. If there has been no pain, there is no need for sympathy, compassion and care.

How to Help Your Child Build Character

- *Help your child develop a healthy self-image.*
- *Provide family standards.*
- *Encourage thinking about right and wrong when making decisions.*
- *Encourage him to make his own decisions and to take responsibility for them.*
- *Allow him or her to shoulder the consequences of a decision.*
- *Avoid controlling your child's every move.*
- *Don't shelter him from hardships.*

Children should not be overprotected from the little stresses and strifes that come their way. Experiencing natural or logical consequences for their behavior, learning to cope, finding out about one's resources and abilities in life's little winds, help to prepare a child to withstand the big storms that we all must face sooner or later.

Research on moral development

I have gleaned the following general principles from the research in character development that has been done in the last sixty years. Don't be discouraged with these findings. Just because the majority of kids tend to behave a certain way doesn't mean that your child will do the same. Your child can be the Daniel who has the internal moral code to stand for right. But daring to be a Daniel doesn't happen by chance!

1. Character is specific, not general. In other words, if a child cheats in one situation, it does not necessarily mean he will cheat in all situations. Cheating strongly depends on the nature of the situation, i.e., the risk of detection, the punishment, what the child learned in similar situations, and an awareness of the implications of his behavior.

2. Knowledge and intentions do not necessarily correspond with behavior. In other words, the fact that children know what is right and plan to do what is right, does not mean they will follow through. This points out the importance of internal control. When children are warned that other kids may yield to temptation, even though they know better, they can learn to avoid strong temptations and to pray for the Holy Spirit's power to resist.

3. Children tend to conform to group standards and customs, even though these may differ from what they have earlier declared their standards to be. Note the power of peer pressure! Encourage your child to choose friends who have a positive influence on their lives rather than a negative one.

4. Children tend to be more like their friends than their classmates. The strongest influence noted in the research, came from friends who were also classmates. The closer the friendship and the more time spent together, the more influential they were.

5. Children change with age. As they grow older they appreciate ideal standards and social norms, but they also become more deceptive when they deviate from these standards. So, merely knowing the standards does not guarantee better characters.

6. Resistance to temptation is somewhat related to intelligence. If a child can be encouraged to think about the moral implications of her conduct, there is a possibility that her behavior can be changed.

7. Parental and teacher influence is very important. For example, the homes which exhibit a negative parental example (parental discord, poor discipline, unsociable attitudes toward children) seem to produce children who are most dishonest. But where parental examples are favorable and the school supports the parental values, the chances of children being honest are greatly improved.

8. Actively religious families tend to produce children with well-developed characters, but church attendance or affiliation alone does not guarantee this.

9. Parental discipline has an effect on the level at which a child will tend to make moral decisions. The overly permissive parent has children who function on the lowest levels. Authoritarian practices are more likely to produce conforming or legalistic traits. Democratic discipline, however, produces kids who make reasonable decisions based on principles.

10. Friends and associates act as reinforcers and models of character, rather than originators of moral values and behavior patterns. It's your job to build the foundation.

11. Schools tend to encourage a more conformist type of behavior rather than a principled type.

This disturbs me, especially when I look at some of the findings on why children reject religion. One of the main reasons seems to be that kids feel the authoritarian figures in their lives are too restrictive and they end up rebelling against them and God, too. If we encouraged principled decision making, rather than conformity, would we have less teenage rebellion?

12. Children need to be taught how to be good as well as how not to be bad. Parental reasoning, plus concrete suggestions for making things right once mistakes have been made, appears to be most effective in helping children develop consideration for others. Parental guidance, instruction, and involvement are all vitally important.

IN-factors

In summary, the research in character and moral decision making supports three important points:* The *influence* of close friends and the pressure to conform to group standards has been documented. Parental *information* is important, especially when teaching children what they should do to right a wrong they have committed. And finally, the most important of all, is *internal control*. It's only with a strong sense of internal control that a child can choose to be different – can dare to be a Daniel and choose right from wrong.

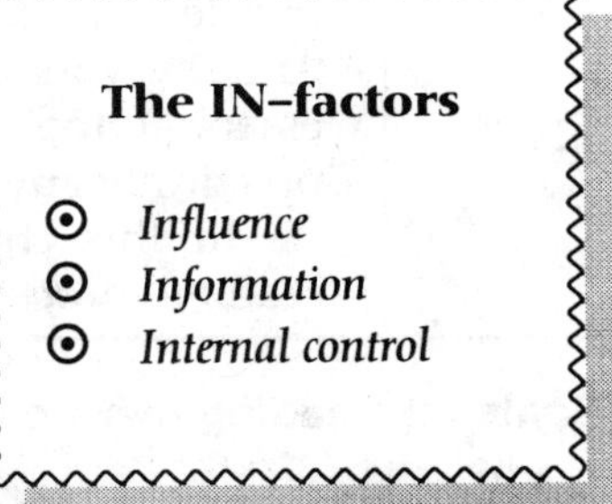

* The IN-factors are discussed in Dr. Kuzma's book from which this chapter was adapted.

25

Teaching Reading

When children begin to realize that information and ideas and stories are locked up in visual symbols, and when they feel like they could figure them out, they want to be able to decode words. Learning to read is like working on a puzzle. It's a key to the grown-up's world. And as you and I know, reading is an essential tool for all serious learning in practically any area.

In this chapter we will examine the reading process, and I will suggest how you might help your child develop this essential skill.

Goals for Reading Instruction

📖 *Recognize the visual symbols for words in an ever-expanding auditory vocabulary while developing an intuitive understanding of how letter combinations represent word sounds, and component meanings.*

📖 *make sense from blocks of reading material. Be able to analyze and evaluate.*

📖 *Read fast and accurately with proficiency in both silent and oral reading.*

📖 *Choose reading matter in harmony with life goals.*

📖 *Remember what was read and be able to apply the new learning.*

📖 *Enjoy reading.*

Among the secular subjects in the lower grades, reading is number one, and math comes closely behind. Reading is part of the broader area of language arts which includes spelling, grammar, writing, speaking and listening. At first, most of the teaching–learning effort goes toward reading. In the middle grades, the other language arts areas begin to get increased attention. And at the junior high level and beyond, the class is called English. In senior high, literature becomes more important while study is continued in grammar, composition, and sometimes speech. Then when the "cream of the crop" enters college, a good portion of them still can't read and write well enough for serious scholarship, so they take composition courses which re-teach some of what should have been learned in elementary and high school.

We wouldn't expect everyone to follow the college trail, but all should make the most of their mental ability. Too few do. Poor reading ability is no doubt the roadblock to learning for many.

Are poor readers just too "dumb" to have learned to read well? I firmly believe not. Practically everyone has ample intelligence. Your child's future depends to a large extent on reading skill.

What do we mean by being able to read? Can a person who is able to pronounce a variety of words read? Is knowing word meanings reading? Having in mind what we expect gives direction to our learning. I suggest you consider the long-range goals shown in the side bar.

Laying the groundwork for reading success

Scholars have identified an impressive array of prerequisite skills a child needs to be ready to learn to read. The suggestions we offer here for guiding your child's development are simple and important. Most of these experiences you would provide for your child as a caring parent anyway. Still, understanding what promotes good development will make your caring more purposeful and probably more successful.

The first question to address under reading readiness is how to know when the informal preparation stage is sufficiently completed so you can begin teaching your child to read printed words and sentences. Elsewhere in this book we discuss the concept of waiting until a child has achieved a degree of physical, mental, and social development before beginning formal instruction. Let me just remind you here that most of us are tempted to jump too fast in our eagerness to convey what seems so simple and natural for us. Of course, the shift to more direct teaching should be gradual.

Serious educators have been concerned about the damage structured reading instruction can have on children who are too young for it. Seven national professional organizations directly or indirectly involved in fostering good reading instruction published the following statement:

"A growing number of children are enrolled in prekindergarten and kindergarten classes in which highly structured pre-reading and reading programs are being used.

"In attempting to respond to pressures for high scores on widely used measures of achievement, teachers of young children sometimes feel compelled to use materials, methods, and activities designed for older children. In so doing, they may impede the development of intellectual functions such as curiosity, critical thinking, and creative expression, and, at the same time, promote negative attitudes toward reading."[1]

Some would disagree with this concern. Of course the appropriate time and type of structured teaching depends on the development of the child; but caution is appropriate. In the chapter, "Planning for the Early Years," I describe a significant study of reading failures in South Carolina.

How people learn to read

No one really knows for sure how anyone learns anything, but we do understand enough to choose reasonable teaching strategies. The steps which follow are not teaching levels, although teaching may be implied from them. They are stages of an individual's development in learning to read. The process starts long before the child begins to decipher the printed symbols we call words and sentences, and it continues on through the achievement of mature reading ability.

1. Develop spatial-visual perception. That is, make sense from what is seen. Distinguish sounds and associate them with people or events.
2. Associate spoken words with physical objects and with simple ideas. Figure out the muscular process of producing words. These, by the way, are utterly complex skills based on practically no prior experience and little, if any, conscious teaching. Yet they are learned!
3. Understand the time relationship of sequences of events, and be able to conceptualize a sequence from its narrative description. This means stories make sense because stories depend on a time sequence. Then later, complex trains of abstract logic may be understood.
4. Begin to recognize visual (printed) words — which are symbols of spoken words which, in turn, are symbols of objects and ideas. This complex process is different for each individual.
5. Recognize more words by: linguistic cues (comparison with similar words or root meanings), contextual cues (seeing what word would make sense in the sentence), and cues from letter patterns in the word.
6. Perceive meaning for whole stories or blocks of text as reading speed picks up.
7. Understand meaning from a flow of printed words often completely bypassing the sounding-out process, even mentally.

Sesame Street

As you would expect, I believe that little children are often instructed in reading skills too early and too intensely. Psychologist Jane Healy has studied this particular problem and would agree. One object of her concern involves the popular children's television program, "Sesame Street." In her book, *Endangered Minds: Why Our Children Don't Think*, she explains why the program is bad news for reading.[2] My own reasons are similar and echo many of her ideas. Looking at the dangers of this program helps us recognize inappropriate teaching practices in other settings.

- "Sesame Street" leads people to assume that preschoolers should be taught to read. Of course parents need to be laying the foundation, but they should not push their child into even simple reading. Chickens don't lay eggs until they arrive at a certain level of maturity.

Not until after children have mastered the process for learning and using spoken words and they have achieved other physical and mental developmental characteristics are they are ready to take on the next level of abstraction – dealing with visual words. Before they have good tools, they are not ready for the task. Trying to force this readiness brings frustration and takes up the time needed for necessary developmental tasks.

Children achieve cognitive development through physical interaction with their world, social play, and listening to good reading material.

Many or most young brains are not ready for learning the alphabet – the abstract association between graphical symbols and specific voice sounds. In fact, as Jane Healy reports, many experts blame early pressure to learn letters and their sounds for learning problems like dyslexia.

- Most adults today have poor handwriting. The skill requires fine muscle control. Healy believes television is to blame because it absorbs time that used to be spent in manipulative play experiences during which the nervous system learns to control young hands. For the appearance of my own handwriting, I have always blamed impatience and too much note taking during lectures. Now I have a better explanation (excuse).
- Letters and numerals have been overemphasized by "Sesame Street" with little building of verbal and reasoning skills. Kids taught this way tend to think of reading as knowing the alphabet instead of as getting meaning from print. Oral language development leads to later success.
- Children need to learn how to link concepts for understanding. Learning unrelated bits of information does not help build that skill.
- Phonics requires listening skill. The television program's visual approach leaves children with little opportunity to practice careful audio discrimination.
- For understanding, the nervous system needs to mentally organize the array of visual input. Overstimulation tends to block this process.
- The program does not encourage aggressive figuring out. Thinking is not encouraged, and concepts are not established. Letters that jump around and tell their names while kids passively watch, leads to lazy thinking. Poor students are passive learners. They give up when something isn't obvious.
- Active memory strategies are not developed. Children need the ability to keep sensory input in their working memory long enough to develop an understanding which can be remembered.
- Children's attention is held by rapid movement, bright colors, and abrupt noises. This dulls their ability to calmly ponder what they read.
- The lack of ability to visually conceptualize ideas and scenes from printed words keeps too many American children from success in solving math and science problems as well as hurting reading comprehension. Too much television viewing of any kind is damaging in this respect.
- Rocky music and other harsh stimulation must certainly have its effect on character, especially in the tender, formative years.
- As I say elsewhere in this book, I believe that the Creator has a better plan for the early years. Children need the time and environment to develop strong bodies, good characters, and the calm base for intellectual development. We should never sacrifice this for television or even books, although some books and even some TV (if you can find a good program or tape) may be appropriate.

Reading to children

Aside from providing love and protecting life and limb, probably the most valuable help parents can give their children toward becoming good readers is to read to them. This is the message of Jim Trelease's book, *The Read-Aloud Handbook*.[3]

Children need to hear the comforting and controlling sound of their parents' voices even before they can understand words. Read or simply talk to your infant. Your words may not make sense, but your tone of voice does. And you are establishing a communication channel. As your child becomes old enough to understand words, you will want to speak clearly and simply, but avoid trying to restrict your vocabulary too much. Such limited communication not only stifles vocabulary building but tends to reduce what you say to a few simple command words – hardly a basis for a growing relationship.

Talk things over with your child explaining your actions and sharing your feelings (as long as your own behavior is mature).

Also, sing. Your child's sense of melody and rhythm can develop naturally; and music conveys feelings of love, security, and inspiration while it teaches words and concepts. Some parents like to sing religious children's songs to begin preparing their child for a trust relationship. Resist the temptation to consider yourself a nonsinger. This is your chance to practice. Get a simple recording of children's songs as a guide.

As parents, your own skill with words will greatly influence your child's learning. An extensive vocabulary heard at home will make reading growth easier especially for your middle-grade child. When familiar words pop up in print, they are recognized and reinforced. You don't just switch on rich vocabulary, but you can build slowly. Of course, reading itself can expand vocabulary for both you and your child.

Another skill you need – one not as directly fostered by reading – is clear, correct enunciation. The reason is obvious. Words incorrectly pronounced get incorrectly spelled and aren't easily recognized in print. Have you ever heard anyone say something like, "Gimme sump-em te-eet"? Words mumbled and slurred are bad teachers.

A look at the backgrounds of good readers provides clues about what might be important. Children who read early and who begin learning well in school generally (1) have been read to regularly, (2) come from homes with a variety of printed material, (3) have had paper and pencil readily available, and (4) have experienced interest in their reading and writing from people at home.[4]

Reading to your children can help build their vocabulary, expand the horizons of their big, new world, build memory patterns as stories are repeated, and increase capacity for time sequences and cause-and-effect relationships. Reading time, unlike TV watching, is a time for physical closeness and sharing between child and parent – a time to reflect and discuss. And while children are being read to, they pick up information such as how words are arranged on the page, how the pages turn, and they even begin recognizing some words by sight.

Let me suggest some guidelines for reading to your children. Most of them you can find in a different form and explained more fully in Jim Trelease's book which I already mentioned.

🕮 Set aside a regular time for reading each day. In fact, you might want a devotional reading time as part of your daily program. Then you could read more at other times, too.

🕮 Allow time for questions and discussion. Expect interruptions. Ask some thought questions from time to time.

🕮 Keep the length of your reading time and the choice of material within the maturity level of your child. But don't be afraid to try something now and then on the difficult side. You can interpret and simplify as appropriate.

🕮 When you read to several children at once, remember that older ones still enjoy picture books, but younger ones might not appreciate the longer, more involved stories.

📖 Most people need practice reading aloud. Maybe you do, too. Don't read too fast. Use expression and emphasis, letting your tone follow the story mood. To make your reading better, read the story first to yourself.

📖 Fathers should read to their children (and to themselves in the children's presence) as often as possible to help avoid the idea that reading is for girls. And, of course, Dad shouldn't miss out on this opportunity for bonding.

📖 Control the TV; don't compete with it. Offer to read during times already designated for the set to be off.

Preparation in four areas

Language development: Plan opportunities that encourage talking and listening. Your child can develop by playing with a toy telephone or a tape recorder, acting out stories, describing an object for another person to guess, or giving directions to a blindfolded person. Ask your child to follow directions to find special gifts you have bought. Stop in the middle of a story and ask what might happen next. Also, being a good listener yourself helps your child to develop meaningful talk.

Visual perception: In order to read, your child must see clearly and have the mental capability to interpret what is seen. Both come naturally as time passes, and they can't really be rushed much. However, watch for eye strain, focusing problems or one eye not getting used. Being able to interpret partly symbolic pictures indicates readiness to understand the printed symbols we use for words.

Auditory perception: As with seeing, both the ability to hear and to interpret and differentiate between sounds are necessary for reading. This is because reading is understanding printed symbols by comparison with previously understood sounded symbols. Hearing problems are usually easy to detect. For a simple ear test, rub your finger against your thumb and see how far away from each ear your child can hear it. Compare the results with your own hearing.

Motor development: Here "motor" means muscle control. Writing is appropriately taught along with reading, and writing takes fine motor control – being able to accurately use a complex array of hand and arm muscles. Before that, the visual impulses and the muscle control must be coordinated in the brain; and before that, or with it, use of the large muscles needs to be developed. All this takes time, and activities like running, jumping, climbing.

Some of the most important preparations for learning to read are the simplest. Find interesting activities to share; read and talk together. You will find workbooks offering reading readiness preparation, but they don't substitute for the preparation we have talked about here. And they wouldn't be very helpful until your child is practically ready to learn to read anyway.

When your child wants to know what certain words say, tell her (or him). Show her how to write words when she asks. Let her watch as you read. As this interest ripens, you can begin very brief phonics lessons. One day your child will be reading without any great amount of conscious direct teaching.

My only cautions would be: don't push for skills when immaturity says, wait; and don't let academic preparation steal time from the crucial balanced development. Young children need physical activity and a close caregiver bond for physical and moral development.

Organizing your reading program

Now suppose your child is mature enough to begin a serious attack on reading skills. You have read to him or her and have provided an atmosphere for vocabulary building and for correct pronunciation and grammar. Probably he or she is already familiar with most of the alphabet and recognizes a number of words by sight. What's the next step?

Your reading tools are phonics programs, reading skill building materials, and items to read, principally books. Your choices are how much you will use of which. Once you have begun, the decisions aren't so hard because you will judge, to some degree, by how your child is learning. We will talk about phonics as word-attack skills in another chapter.

Some programs guide you in teaching phonics and leave you on your own for skill building. Some carry on with more reading and spelling and all the rest. Standard textbooks would continue with reading practice through the lower grades, often with other books for spelling and the rest of what is known as language arts. After reading the other chapters in this book on teaching reading, you will have some ideas to try out. As long as you are sensitive to your child's learning and follow through with consistent care, you will be a success.

I have only one minor observation. I would feel more comfortable, after the introductory instruction, in using materials created by more than a single individual. On the other hand, it might not matter.

Next, let's consider some components or characteristics to plan for in your reading program.

Reading for fun

Even with well designed readers and appealing selections, some students seem to see all the reading they are expected to do for learning specific skills as hard work. What can be done to get these children to enjoy reading so they will read more and become really good readers?

🕮 First, consider that your child might not be ready. If readiness seems to be the problem, put everything on the shelf for a while. If you believe the child is mature enough, you wouldn't want to wait long before trying again, perhaps with a fresh book or something special. Work on stimulating interest.

🕮 Next, let your child see you reading. If you don't read much, make a change. Do you think you could help your child build sustained interest in camping or sewing without getting involved yourself? The same goes for reading.

🕮 Then, plan a short time each day for silent reading without being accountable for reports or answering questions.

🕮 Keep good books within reach. Occasionally read the first chapter of a book to your child as an enticement. (I will never forget the day my mother polished just one of my shoes.) Make fun trips to the library, and buy books to keep.

🕮 Television has been seen as the number one enemy of learning to read. But this doesn't need to be so, as we discussed in the chapter, "Enrichment Resources." Of course undisciplined TV viewing threatens mental health, character development, and indeed, every noble pursuit requiring the time it absorbs.

Teaching for comprehension

Decoding and word recognition are certainly important, but your child also needs to be able to make sense from reading material. Good readers constantly analyze what they read by asking themselves questions. They compare the new information with their own knowledge; identify the main points, relating them to the overall theme; and anticipate what the author might say next.

Success in reading comprehension depends fundamentally on the reader's approach to the material. Too many students consider school as something to finish – a process to be endured while waiting for more important things in life. When they read, they hope the material will be interesting and that some of it might stick long enough to be useful on the test. The more successful approach is to be aggressive instead of passive.

Aggressive scholars view a reading assignment as they would an old prospector who knows about a lost gold mine. Rather than enduring the old man until he says what he has to say, they sit on the edges of their seats asking him questions and checking to be sure they understand what he said. They sketch maps and take notes. They reinforce their memories by restructuring ideas from their notes and discussing them with friends. So intelligent reading requires more than sending words through the mind. In the box are some suggestions for learning from reading. I have taken a slightly different approach to these same principles in the chapter, "Techniques for Teaching."

You can see that these skills would be a bit much to expect in the early grades. Instead, you can keep the aggressive learning principles in mind as you teach. Invite consideration as you teach what is important about a topic. Ask questions to relate it to the child's experience. Check to be sure all points are understood. And help your child sum up the topic. The inquiring approach you show can surface later in your child's own reading ability.

For her (or his) reading assignments, talk over the title (and the topic) before reading begins. If she is reading aloud, stop her now and then and ask questions. At the end discuss the reading, not by doing most of the talking but by asking questions, prompting comparison with other ideas, and by probing for personal meaning. Also be sensitive to not make the process tedious. If she dosen't remember something that she read, don't treat it like a big mistake, just talk it over and move on. Keep reading fun.

The key-word method

Two early-grade teachers, Pam Palewicz and Linda Madaras, have developed their own way to teach reading. I would not depend on it for the backbone of a reading program, but it could certainly work for a period of time or for an added help.

The idea in brief involves getting children to learn from words they choose and copy, and stories they tell or write. The plan requires more individualized work with children, but that's the way you teach in home schools anyway. The points or steps which follow have been condensed from the book, *The Alphabet Connection,*[5] (and filtered through my thinking):

1. Teaching with the key word plan begins after the alphabet is mostly learned. You ask your child to choose a word for you to write on a card. Work with several words at a time, but don't start them all at once. It would be all right to add more words before all are learned, but not too many. If your child doesn't think of a word, prompt with questions.

2. You will write the words at first. Your skill in printing isn't important, but size is. Make them big.

3. While you are writing the word, sound out the letters.

4. Repeat the word and ask the child to say it. Then go over the letter sounds again.

5. Depending on your child's writing ability, either hold the hand with a finger extended to trace over the letters, or ask him to trace over the letters with pencil or crayon. Touch and movement are important in teaching young children. If you have delayed the beginning of formal schooling, as we discuss elsewhere in this book, muscle coordination won't be a problem.

6. As abilities permit, ask your child to copy the word in space you have left at the bottom of the card.

7. You can ask the child to draw a picture of the word, but not on the word card itself to avoid remembering the word by the picture.

8. Ask your child to tell you a story about the picture. Three to five sentences are enough. You write the story from dictation on the card with the picture.

Children won't think of simple words like articles and prepositions when asking for new key words, but they can learn them from seeing the stories on their picture cards.

9. After the story is copied down, read it back. Your boy or girl will probably hear grammar mistakes as you read and correct them. If mistakes aren't noticed, you can casually correct serious ones.

10. Then you can ask your child to look at the story and find all the words that are the same as the key word the story is about. Other words might not be recognized yet.

11. When your boy (or girl) is mature enough, ask him to copy the story word-for-word below the words you wrote on the card.

12. Have your child think of new words. Start new cards and new stories.

13. The stories can be shared with other children or family members as the child begins to read them.

14. Begin reviewing after a few words are on cards. Also review sounds made by letters and letter combinations. Review and add new words about three times a week. If the list gets too long to learn effectively, discuss which words to eliminate.

In thinking over this technique, we need to ask whether it might not take on a more casual approach with children for whom formal reading instruction waits for a little more maturity and natural interest. Then when the child is older, key-word cards won't be apt to play a very big role. The method does sound like fun and might be worth trying a time or two even when using another basic plan.

Reading as part of a broader educational view

After initiation to reading, the subject is best taught in connection with other language arts subjects. Speaking and listening skills might be added first, then writing and spelling. With adequate maturity, teach literature and more writing with grammar. Integration isn't as hard as it might seem. Your structured textbook program might already do this to a degree. To help connect the language areas, just comment on what you see important about one subject while teaching another – spelling in reading, grammar in literature, writing down spoken words, phonics in spelling, and so on. Then, also, make reading important in studying subjects outside of language arts, while you encourage general learning from the reading class.

Choosing what to read

For parents who view education as character development, reading instruction must deal with the question of *what* to read as well as with how. We often lament the evils of television, forgetting that the printed page can produce many of the

How to Tackle a Reading Assignment

(1) Think of what the title might imply and wonder what the article will tell about it. Maybe formulate questions you want the author to answer for you.

(2) Read the introduction asking why the author believes the topic is important and thinking how it might relate to your own interests and previous knowledge.

(3) Glance at the subtitles and consider them in the same way.

(4) Read attentively trying to identify the author's main points. Underline and make notes in the margins (or write on your own paper).

(5) Clarify any new words.

(6) See if your questions were answered and add significant points you didn't think to ask about.

(7) Return later to review.

same effects.

Many parents and educators today seem to feel that a balanced education requires access to everything in print. They oppose parents who want certain books removed from school libraries. Christian parents and all concerned parents need to remember that children are a responsibility, that they are by nature dependent, giving us the privilege of guiding their moral as well as their physical development.

Principles for Teaching Reading

- *Good reading ability is important. Doing a good teaching job will pay off in later life.*
- *No teaching technique is a unique solution.*
- *Preparation for reading begins long before the child concentrates on words in print.*
- *When it's time to learn, follow an organized plan. Occasional visits to the library won't likely be enough to develop good readers with a breadth of language skills.*
- *Make reading both a science by teaching specific skills, and an art by encouraging reading for fun.*
- *Control the television set or get rid of it.*
- *Teach for comprehension by getting your children to be aggressive readers — to ask questions about what they read.*
- *Integrate reading with other subjects, especially writing and spelling.*
- *Education, in its deepest sense, is character development. What children read is even more important than how.*

Everyone would agree that young readers need material that is interesting, intellectually stimulating, a little challenging, and a model of good writing. But if we recognize that values and attitudes are more important than skills in math and reading, and if we consider relationships to be more important than knowledge, we will want to take a close look at the material we provide for reading practice, to see whether, in some cases, the risk from side effects might outweigh the therapeutic value.

In the another chapter, we look at purposes and dangers of teaching literature, and I will suggest a list of criteria for judging reading material or literature. Instead of creating a dull existence, high standards in reading and viewing lead to deep satisfaction, unshakable mental stability, and lasting happiness.

As you consider what your children should read (and watch, and hear) you may sense the importance of your own reading and television habits. Children learn values from their parents. You can't fake it. If you need to make a change, now is not too soon.

Your children's future probably depends more on learning to read than on any other traditional school subject. Do your best, ask for help when you need it, and check your progress every year or so with outside exams.

◆

We will look closely at the phonics question in another chapter.

Endnotes

1. "Reading and Pre-first-grade: A Joint Statement of Concerns about Present Practices in Pre-first-grade Reading Instruction and Recommendations for Improvement." *Young Children*, September 1977, pp. 25, 26.

2. Jane M. Healy, *Endangered Minds: Why Our Children Don't Think*, pp. 222–234. Simon & Schuster, 1990.

3. Jim Trelease, *The Read-Aloud Handbook*. Penguin Books, Middlesex, England and New York, 1982.

4. Summarized by Jim Trelease (reference above). See Dolores Durkin, *Children Who Read Early*, Teachers College, 1966.

5. Pam Palewicz and Linda Madaras, *The Alphabet Connection*. Socken Books, NY, 1979.

26

Phonics, a Realistic View

Ruth Beechick

Home schooling parents practically all favor phonics for their children. They are beyond debating "yes" versus "no" and can move on to the next questions of how and when.

Common questions

Many ask, how early should I start? Though whole books are devoted to this question and its concept of "readiness," it has a quite simple answer when you are concerned with just one child. All you need to do is to start teaching the reading or phonics system you have chosen to use. If your child can learn it without undue effort, he or she is ready. If not, it is better to wait.

Another common question is: Should I teach all (or most) sounds first, before reading? Some phonics systems advocate that you do. But I believe it is better to have children practice reading as much as possible while they are learning phonics. It strengthens and speeds their learning if they *use* phonics instead of just learning *about* phonics, even at the beginning stage of reading.

Some reading programs are designed to help children sound out words right from the start. "Linguistic" systems, for instance, may begin by teaching the short sound of **a** and a few consonants, then follow immediately with sentences such as "Dan can fan." More sounds are added gradually, and reading practice is provided all along the way. In this type of system, rules are not given to be memorized. Instead, children figure out rules for themselves. The orderly presentation of sounds leads to seeing patterns and generalizing these into what we call rules.

Some phonics systems have adopted features that the linguists introduced. They may begin with short vowel sounds and adapt the practice reading material accordingly. And they present only a few rules to memorize.

Why is the short sound taught first? Because it is used more often. For instance, the short sound for **a** is used 70% of the time while the long sound is used only 25% and all its other sounds comprise the remaining 5%.

Other phonics systems teach many rules and a lot of information about sounds and their spellings. Much of this is supposed to be mastered *before* children start to read, and all the rest is to be mastered soon after. The promotion of these phonics systems among home schoolers has led to the appearance of another question.

Phonics for children who already read

"My child already reads; do I need to continue with all this phonics?" Usually the question is accompanied by a naming of books, perhaps classics, that the child reads and which show that he (or she) is definitely past the "decoding" stage of reading, and maybe past the fluency-building stage too, and is into the stage of reading for information and enjoyment.

Obviously such a child already knows quite a lot of phonics. If he has not been taught it, then he has figured it out for himself. He may not be able to recite rules as they are given in any particular phonics program, but he is beyond that. He can *use*

Dr. Ruth Beechick *is a professional educator and author whose writings have included numerous articles and books on home education. She is Director of Education Services in Arvada, Colorado.*

the rules. He can apply his phonics knowledge to the task of reading, which, after all, is the ultimate goal of teaching phonics. To continue plowing through a basic phonics book with such a child amounts to overkill.

In former generations parents made a rather simple job of teaching their children to read. Susanna Wesley wrote that she took one day to teach the letter sounds to each of her children. It is only in this century that we have the work of modern linguists and the great amounts of information that they have compiled about the sounds and patterns in our language. Do we need to teach it all to young children?

Three levels of understanding

To help us decide how far to go with phonics teaching, I have proposed thinking of phonics information in these three levels: 1) pupil level, 2) teacher level, and 3) publisher level.

Pupil Level. On the pupil level I would use at the beginning only the amount of phonics needed for learning to read. Later on, more phonics which is helpful in spelling could be added. This principle is especially important for children who have difficulty learning to read.

Children don't need to know terms like "digraph" and diphthong" in order to read. They don't need to know that they will meet the blend **br** more often than **bl**. Beginning readers don't need definitions for "consonant" and "vowel." (Can *you* define consonant and vowel?) When stripped to the bare essentials, reading requires only knowing what sound to make for each letter or combination of letters. Many children have learned to read not even knowing the names of the letters. Of course, letter names are needed later for using a dictionary and other purposes, but for beginning reading they are not essential.

Once children catch on to the phonics principle, some of them forge ahead and, with only a little help, are soon reading at whatever level their vocabulary and understanding will allow. Others continue to need systematic teaching of phonics for a time, to become better readers.

Teacher Level. Any adult who reads has quite a lot of phonics knowledge, surely enough for teaching a child to read. Many people think they don't because they cannot call the rules to mind out of context. And they are intimidated by words like "digraph" in a teacher's manual. But these same people have no trouble explaining how they sound out words. For instance, they could explain why *found* and *ground* are pronounced as they are. They also could explain about *fight* and *might*.

If you are one of these intimidated people, it may help to know that the phonics experts have many differences among themselves. They quibble about little matters like whether **u** following **q** is a silent vowel or if the two letters should be considered together and called a consonant and whether we should teach that **ough** has six sounds or if we should teach that it is a "wild sound." Some say that **igh** is a spelling for long **i** sound, and others say that **gh** is silent before **t**. In other words, phonics is not neat, and if you feel that you don't have it neatly stored away in your brain, that is just normal.

For the teacher level it is probably enough to know the major vowel and consonant sounds and to be able to understand explanations of the rarer sounds and the various letter "teams" when they are explained in the teacher's manual of the phonics program you are using.

Publisher Level. The pupil or teacher will lose nothing if they don't know that **br** is used more often than **bl**. But developers of phonics systems do need this kind of information so they can teach items in the best order. The **ough** sounds present another example of decision-making at this level. The curriculum writer must decide whether or not to teach the six sounds (tough, trough, though, through, thought, bough). The writer should know that students are going to run into only 15 to 30 such words in their reading, depending on the difficulty of the books. Is it worth the effort to memorize the six sounds? Many such decisions must be made at the publisher level, and there is now a great amount of computer generated information available to help them in this task.

Curriculum developers should also be aware of common problems that children have. For instance, many have difficulty with the short **e** sound. *Pan* and *pen* sound alike to them. So do *pin* and *pen*. With this knowledge, writers can arrange to teach the short vowel sounds in a better order. Some good systems teach short **a** first, then **i** or **o**. Although **e** is the second vowel in the alphabet, it need not necessarily be taught second.

Your level

As teacher, your level of knowledge can overlap the publisher level as much as your interest and time allow. You may arrange your own phonics program and make many decisions about what to teach, and in what order. Or you may use published programs and leave most of the decisions to them. But even with published programs you can find yourself modifying as you go along.

For instance, many programs do teach the vowels in alphabetical order in spite of the problem mentioned above. If your child happens to have great difficulty with the **e**, you can try skipping to the **i** section and see if he catches on any easier. Another flaw in many programs is that the sound /**s**/ is taught on a page with words like *sat*. (The slash marks indicate the sound, not the letter.) And then the next page includes practice words like *has*. "Oh yes," you may say, "**S** sometimes sounds like /**z**/." If you don't happen to mention it, your child may simply enlarge his rule about what the /**s**/ sound includes. Children adjust and learn in spite of our adult bungling. Minds are powerful.

Many teaching parents must also make a decision about the new question: Should I continue with all this detailed study of phonics now that my child has "caught on" to reading? A little common sense will help.

The Place of Decoding in Learning to Read

Prereading Stage The child gets ready for reading by being read to, seeing people read, and learning what books and reading and writing are for. Talking and thinking and learning about the real world are essential, too. They prepare the child for the book world.

Decoding Stage The child catches on to the system — the code by which we put sounds on paper. And he is able to use at least major parts of the code.

Fluency Stage The child reads easy materials for a year or two. This gives him lots of practice and makes decoding automatic so he can concentrate more on the content instead of the process of reading. An important stage that should not be skipped or hurried.

Information Stage The child reads a variety of materials for pleasure and information. Reading moves beyond being a goal itself and becomes a tool for reading other learning goals.

High School Stage The student uses higher thinking skills as he reads. For instance, he can understand other people's views better than before, and can analyze issues from more than one viewpoint. He uses more advanced study strategies.

College Stage The student can handle difficult abstract and specialized materials. He can analyze knowledge from many sources and compare and synthesize for his own thinking and writing.

Susanna Wesley probably only had what amounted to the teacher-level knowledge of her time. But in our century we have the expert level, or the developer level. Because we have it, we tend to teach more and more of it. At some point we must ask whether we are teaching phonics for phonics' sake or teaching it for reading's sake.

27

Decoding Words

The place of phonics in teaching reading has always been a hot issue. And, as with most volatile topics, intelligent answers aren't quite as simple as the questions. I hope to help you make sense out of what you hear, and give you a basis for sound planning in teaching your own child.

Phonics is the relationship between the individual sounds in a word and the letters that represent them. Everyone agrees that readers need to understand how sounds relate to words. The issue involves how this should be taught. To explore this area, let's first trace the history of education as it involves reading. (You could skip it if you are in a hurry). Then we will look at the options for teaching the basics of how to read.

How the curriculum has changed

Looking back helps us view modern pressures on the curriculum in perspective. An expert in the history of education might see events a little differently from the way I sketch them below, but this can give you a fair idea.

📖 Education for the European elite class during the Middle Ages is described in my chapter, "Structure for Learning."

📖 Not until after the US civil war in the 1860s did education slowly begin to become widely available to common people. I explain a little of this history in the chapter, "Keeping Peace With School Authorities."

📖 At the entrance of the 20th century, elocution – or public speaking employing gestures and vocal delivery – was considered an important art. Thus the reading program in schools employed oral reading with inflection, distinct pronunciation and, of course, phonics. This was McGuffey's time.

📖 A change occurred when good methods of standardized testing were developed, and educational measurement promised to find scientifically accurate answers to every problem. Researchers discovered that students well-trained in oral reading tended to read slowly. Silent reading then became a primary concern, and teaching techniques began emphasizing quick word recognition. The new challenge was "see and say," rather than "sound it out."

📖 Then the project method came into vogue. Instead of the various school subjects taught one at a time in isolation, projects were chosen that required application of math, reading, social studies, science, and so on. Learning was shown to have a purpose beyond pleasing the teacher and getting good marks on a report card. Tests showed better achievement from schools trying the new method, likely influenced by the higher expectation of the students involved.

Teaching through projects (reincarnated recently as the unit study method) is still a good idea and works well for home schools. That is, it's good if you are alert and avoid its pitfalls. For one thing, projects don't tend to foster the reinforcement of basic skills so essential to thorough learning and remembering. Other points are covered elsewhere in this book.

📖 As the project method was adopted far and wide, basic skills, including reading, began to suffer. Neither word recognition nor phonics drill was getting much attention.

📖 In the 1930s and again after World

War II, schools were loudly criticized (although students were learning well) and they turned back to more basic skill-building.

- In 1955 Rudolph Flesch published his book, *Why Johnny Can't Read.* The answer? Neglect of phonics instruction. A sequel appeared in 1979.[1]
- Then in the 60s the cry became, "We want it relevant," and drill (and, to some degree, phonics) wasn't.
- In the 70s national test scores began to slip and the watchword was "back to the basics."
- The 80s could be characterized by a call for life application and realistic preparation for a changing job market. Skills for processing numbers and words were emphasized a little less.
- In the 90s, the emphasis has been on usefulness of learning as indicated by abilities achieved. The call for the various states to specify outcomes in their lists of achievement objectives has been viewed with suspicion by many who are concerned about public education. I discuss reasons for caution in the chapter, "Developing an Educational Framework."
- In reading, "whole language" has been popular in many schools but has gotten a bad reputation and phonics is again in vogue.

I have oversimplified some of this so you can see the bigger picture. The educational pendulum swings back and forth. Good school teachers have always worked for what they feel is best for kids and home teachers should, too.

Incidentally, I don't believe that a lack of relevance or a lack of basics or a lack of phonics or too much phonics or prescribed outcomes has been the real problem in schools. Drugs, sex, alcohol, tobacco, violence, TV, broken homes, teacher unrest, and similar influences are certainly more prevalent now than in the past and can't help but interfere with the operation of schools.

In spite of this, national test scores have been steadily improving, perhaps due to better methodology. I discuss this in chapter 2.

Clear thinking about phonics arguments

What is the great point of controversy about how children should be introduced to reading? Some feel that decoding skills, specifically phonics, should be taught thoroughly as a foundation before any reading occurs beyond words or sentences for which the rules have been learned. By blending the succession of sounds made by letters or letter groups children are to be able to decode words and become good readers. Without this, it is felt that they will be poor readers and spellers.

At the other end of the argument are those who feel children should, with a few words recognized from sight, begin reading words as they naturally appear in stories. This is believed to help them learn better and faster without sacrificing the knowledge of the combinations of letters that make up the words. New words are recognized by comparing them with known words.

I began a serious investigation of this topic in the early 80s soon after I began writing about home education. Although I make a conscious effort to be objective, I didn't begin my study of the reading-methods debate without some ideas. I felt children should be taught a modest amount of phonics as the key to decoding words. My wife is a better reader than I am, and she studied phonics as a child. I vaguely remember a little phonics instruction and more clearly remember learning whole words. For both of us, this was in the early 40s. This is good personal-experience evidence, although with a rather small sample size for research reliability. Incidentally, my reading skill has gradually improved. It took a jump during the time of my doctoral studies in the late 60s and again in the 80s.

As mentioned earlier, kids are amazingly adaptable. If we can motivate them, they will learn even with faulty methods. Still, there *are* principles for good learning and we all want the best for our kids. This a call to listen with both ears, separating fact from inference and trends from anecdotes.

As we consider a topic of this nature, we need to cut through the emotional level of favorite ideas and sensationalism. Reading methods are sometimes denigrated or elevated on the basis of claims about sinister motives of teacher educators and about particular methods of instruction. Thus people are often frightened into choosing or avoiding particular materials or methods.

Let's look at the options beginning with specific phonics approaches and ending with a plan developed in recent years.

What Phonics Instruction Does

⌘ *A systematic and logical instructional pattern in any subject tends toward more successful learning.*

⌘ *Children often enjoy decoding, and the experience strengthens confidence.*

⌘ *Phonics instruction builds the habit of looking closely at words. Seeing them more clearly, the mature reader processes them more efficiently.*

⌘ *Knowing phonics principles make decoding easier.*

⌘ *Reading decoded words develops them into sight words and builds the reader's inventory.*

⌘ *Knowing more words makes it easier to recognize new ones.*

🕮 Some home schoolers, concerned about giving their children a solid reading foundation, like to use reprinted editions of the old McGuffey readers, evidently feeling that in the "good old days" educators really knew how to teach. McGuffey used a phonics approach although he considered whole word memorization to be an option.[2]

🕮 For several editions of *The Home School Manual* prior to this one, I have included a specific phonics methods chapter by Frank Rogers – with no regrets. Let's consider the case he makes for what he calls "vertical phonics." Rogers' system follows some of the principles in the *Writing Road to Reading* method. He believes, differently, however, in many ways including, ❃ that reading is the road to writing, ❃ that children should learn the names of the letters before phonics instruction; and ❃ that word decoding can start with knowing the sounds of just four letters.

He is very methodical. For him, the child is to be taught all the significant sounds of each vowel, each consonant, and certain letter combinations in the order of how frequently they occur in general reading material. For example, to discover the correct sound of the letter *a* in a particular word, the first sound tried is the one *a* makes in the word, "at." If that sound combined with the other letters doesn't make a word he or she recognizes, the sound of *a* in "ate" is tried; then its sound as in "all." The *a* sounds in "again" and "any" must be treated as exceptions.

In the more popular phonics method, the short vowel sounds (which occur in more words than others) are taught first. To Rogers, this is like learning the names of the presidents by memorizing all their first names, then going back to learn the last names. We have had some good discussions about how learning presidents is different from learning words, so he may hesitate to use that analogy. But learning presidents' names together does describe his system. As he sees it, vertical phonics is first logical, then it works so it must be the best.

🕮 If we change uniforms and join the ranks of believers in the more popular phonics methodology, we find a defensible logic fortress there, too. By first teaching the short vowel sounds – the ones occurring most often – kids can decode more words earlier. The logic of this plan isn't as nice, but the plan seems more natural, with simpler attack rules. Without solid research, we cannot say which is better or if it matters. As far as I know, kids learn well either way.

🕮 Practicing with word families is another approach. Certain letter combinations are learned by lists like "Sam, ham, jam, dam slam." This method, too, is backed by good learning rationale, especially if taught with rhyming stories. In one of *Bob's Books* booklets, which I have reviewed, I remember two lines in a story: "Into the tent the ten men went. Then to bed the ten were sent." Even without cute stories, the supposedly dull lists of words hold a pleasant challenge for the young student. In reading "mop, drop, stop, crop, pop" I can see how the easy decoding allows the child to focus on word differences while the "op" word-pair sound settles into the subconscious.

📖 Advocates following these three approaches feel, to varying degrees, that words should not be taught before the rules that govern them. This has a certain logic, but so does the argument that Mark Thogmartin uses. As you can see from his chapter, He uses children's story books. The teacher sits with the child and, when a word appears that doesn't make sense, assistance is provided to help analyze it, thus teaching a sort of phonics. Interest in the story provides incentive and a context for remembering the new word as well as the letter patterns in it.

Neither analogies nor success stories are reliable evidence for a "best" way to learn to read. They may appear convincing but we need to be careful in accepting them as arguments.

Phonics and new information

From reading Rudolph Flesch's 1979 book, *Why Johnny Still Can't Read,* I learned that the phonics issue was emotional and political. The educators (and politicians) hadn't listened much when his earlier book came out in 1955 and again he was taking his case to the people. Unfortunately, politics still drives reading methodology in US schools. More on this later.

I have questioned the relative importance of one reading approach over another as discussed earlier in this chapter. Now, just as I'm already late in getting this seventh edition to press, I discovered some information you may not have known about. I'd like to share some of it.

Phonics offers a nice way to analyze words and, as we have seen. It follows logic. But some have questioned whether it provides a suitable model for effective teaching.

In the 60s the reasonableness of phonics instruction was questioned by Theodore Clymer.[3] He took four popular reading programs and identified 45 clearly stated phonics generalizations in them. Then he looked at the words used in those programs. Among the rules he listed as being taught in the four programs is "When there are two vowels, one of which is a final *e,* the first vowel is long and the *e* is silent." It was seen to work with *bone, came, date,* and *time.* but not with *done, come, have,* and *were.* This is not too surprising because there are exceptions to phonics rules (all but one of his 45 have exceptions). The problem Clymer saw was that more than a third of the words in the texts classified as exceptions to this rather fundamental phonics rule just described! In fact, of the 30 rules involving vowels, only half worked 60% or more of the time in the reading texts. The more reliable phonics rules tend to apply to the less frequently appearing patterns. Several other researchers did studies to test his results and got similar results.[4]

At about the same time, other researchers were asking if children were even able to identify the phonemes. D.J. Bruce[5] found that none of the five- and six-year-old children in his study were able to remove a phoneme from a given word to make a new word. For example, they could not take the word *fork,* remove the /k/ sound, and say the new word *for.* Seven-year-olds succeeded on an average of 2 out of the 30 words. At eight and nine years (by the time they would have been reading well) the kids could score 50%.

How can children figure out new words in a story without sounding them out? In 1965, Kenneth Goodman[6] took a group of children to see if they could recognize words in context. For each child, he found a list of words on which only a few words were not recognized. Each child was then given a story which used all the words on his or her list. Instead of the unrecognized words, only blank lines appeared. When reading the stories they were able to recognize, from the context, most of the words they had not known in isolation. If they had used letter-sound correspondences to read the words, they should have done at least as well reading the words on the list. One might think children would learn errors this way or that they would not easily remember the new words, but this does not appear to be the case. Children are guided in analyzing letter sounds for these words as they are in phonics methods.

In colonial times, charts like this were attached to small paddles and protected with a transparent layer of an animal horn. Thus the term, "horn book."

An interesting comparison between whole language (learning from context as well as other cues) and phonics instruction appeared in the statistics from The National Assessment of Educational Progress (NAEP) test of fourth-grade readers.[7] Teachers were asked to identify their teaching method as "whole language" or "phonics" and the degree of emphasis they gave it. There was no apparent difference between student scores of "moderate" emphasis teachers. However, scores of students with "heavy" emphasis teachers of whole language were 9% higher than those of heavy emphasis phonics teachers. Other studies have shown similar results but are not as impressive statistically because they were conducted with specific classes rather than with the masses of kids across the nation in the NAEP. We must also not miss the point here that, although not scoring quite as well, children with phonics instruction were learning reasonably well.

See the notes at the end of this chapter for more about phonics and whole language.[8] It is not a matter of one all good and the other all bad.

How are children guided in learning from continuous (whole language) text? ✓ We described the key word method in the reading chapter. ✓ "Shared reading" is another technique. A story where illustrations that show the story are discussed, then the teacher reads it pointing to the words. After several readings, over a period of days, children memorize the language and "read" to the teacher and to each other as they figure out the printed words. I have seen a variation of this using Bible passages with words to be learned shown in bold face. After reading a passage several times, the teacher can stop at the special words, point to them, and have the child say them. This would logically (but maybe not strictly the whole-language way) be done after, or in connection with, helping the child know the sounds of the letters and letter-groups or phonemes. ✓ Mark Thogmartin's chapter explains his ideas for teaching.

In this initial stage of building a sight vocabulary, I would also help my child analyze the word by blending the letters left to right phonetically, discussing any variations from the expected such as in the diagraphs "ch" or "th" or other phonemes.

How children recognize words

Research we have discussed reveals that children learn new words better from story contexts than from traditional phonics, although we see a little of each method in the other. How do minds do so well at recognizing new words in print without learning a large set of letter-phoneme relationships? Phonics advocates tend to claim that these children are just memorizing the whole words, a seemingly impossible task given the number of words in a good vocabulary.

Let's stop a minute here. Learning whole words without relating to the sounds of their letters, as was in vogue when I learned to read, is now condemned by both whole language advocates and phonics people. This is my excuse for being a not-so-good reader. But I lose at least part of it because my younger brother, whom I taught to read in sessions after I came home from school, is an excellent reader. Nice try. Well, maybe I'm a good teacher. Sorry, that's only a distraction. Let's get back to the topic.

Until 1972, whole language people didn't have any good explanation for how good reading happened without traditional phonics. Then Donald MacKay[9] studied speech errors resulting in words with parts replaced from other words in the sentence. For example, "Fix the big mixture" could become "Mix the big fixture." The brain hears "fix" as /f/+/ix/ and "mix" as /m/+/ix/. In this type of error, word parts tend to get hooked up in the wrong way. The slash marks (/ /) here indicate sounds instead of printed words.

MacKay's study led him to describe syllables in spoken words as heard into two parts: (1) any consonant sound that comes before the vowel sound, and (2) the vowel sound with any consonant sound that may come after it. The two parts are now known as *onset* and *rime*. These two sound parts for "fix" are /f/+/ix/. If no consonant precedes the vowel, then the word has only a rime. Let's take a few more examples: "home school" = /h/+/ome/ /sch/+/ool/. (The *h* by itself in "home" doesn't seem like a significant word part until we compare with "Rome" which is /r/+/ome/.) "ice" is only /ice/ – no onset.

The phonics breakdown for "school" would be /s/+/k/+/oo/+/l/. Studies verify that the brain tends to lump the phonemes into larger chunks, seeing words as onset and rime, and to make letter-sound correspondences using them.[10]

Several studies have shown that children recognize new words better from analogous words than from their

Raw material for learning from whole language

- ⌘ *A predictable story line so attention can be on new words.*
- ⌘ *A few, but not too many, new words (like 1 in 20).*
- ⌘ *A background knowledge of the topic being discussed*
- ⌘ *Familiarity of the word flow of print (from being read to)*
- ⌘ *A relatively large sight-word vocabulary*
- ⌘ *The availability of many suitable children's stories.*
- ⌘ *Patient instruction which protects from the pitfalls.*

knowledge of phonics.[11]

In summary, rather than seeing the letters in words as phonemes, children tend to group the letters into onsets and rimes. The rimes are actually conceptual groups of phonemes. When encountering new words in print, the mind remembers two parts of syllables (and, of course, whole syllables) in known words and judges the new word by parts from the old ones. According to the whole-language advocates, this means that children don't need to separate all the sounds and blend them into words before learning to read but they separate the sounds naturally as a *result* of reading.[12]

What happened in California?

Unless you are familiar with the reading controversy, California might not seem relevant to reading. The state chooses educators who are experts in their curricular areas to set up standards for instruction. This is done every seventh year. When the standards are out, textbook publishers get busy preparing or revising their books because California decides what books its schools may choose from. Being the country's largest buyer, they have the greatest influence. The following year the textbook lists are composed.

In 1986 the group working on reading had been excited by the research showing the effectiveness of whole language reading methods and had established standards accordingly. Many citizens are advocates of traditional phonics, and Congress consequently asked Marilyn Adams, who works with a private research firm, to find out how to teach phonics better. Whether the method was effective was not the question and was not part of the support gathered to back the objective of her book, *Beginning to Read.*[13] The research we have discussed about the difficulty in identifying phonemes was cited, and the goal became "phonemeic awareness."

In California, the 1994-'95 Framework Commission reaffirmed the 1986 decision noting that teachers needed more preparation with the methods, which I assume may not have been followed carefully especially with the appearance of the "phonemic awareness" book.

In 1995, the results of the recent national examinations (NAEP) was published. California was *not* at the top or even near the top, although children were reading. They were next to the bottom of the 39 participating states. No state should be near the bottom of such a list! Or so it seems. What could be the matter? Whole language, of course! The title of a *Los Angeles Times* report expressed the prevailing sentiment. "Dole Sees Problems in Schools and Blames Liberals."[14]

Conclusions were not based on an examination of the situation.[15] The following facts were ignored in defending the move to change reading instruction: ✓ The size of classes in California was the largest or next to largest in the nation (depending on when they were measured). ✓ The state's school libraries were among the poorest. ✓ California's Hispanic students scored the lowest of any ethnic group in any state. Their scores influenced the average. (Scores of California's non-Hispanic groups matched those in other western states). ✓ Twenty-five percent of the state's population were new immigrants. ✓ Only 2 percent of the teachers had been exposed to whole-language methods and sample lesson plans were only in preparation. (We may infer that some would have been teaching phonics and some would have let the children "read" without proper instruction.)

California's new superintendent of public instruction authorized a Reading Task Force under the direction of a citizen who was prominent for promoting the phonics system. No reading professionals and not even any teachers below the fourth grade were on the committee. They recommended "an organized, explicit skills program that includes phonemic awareness, phonics, and decoding skills to address the needs of the emergent reader."

In the meantime, in the cycle of their appointment, 110 professional educators established the list of recommended books, and the state board, in a rather unusual decision, promptly removed from the list books from two publishers of "predictable" books. Then in the middle of the cycle a new group of teachers was asked to write another framework. Next the legislature established a bill requiring books to include phonics, and teachers to be proficient in teaching it. Then the legislature acting through the fall of 1996, changed from their call for "balanced" reading instruction to a position of actively discouraging materials that enable children to figure out words in print in the natural way.

This is the story of California. It is why the nation's schools (and those in other English-speaking countries) have returned to a heavy emphasis on phonics.

The new phonics rationale

Before learning most of what I have just shared, I found an article entitled, "Research-Based Reading Instruction: The Right Way."[16] It sounded good but was not what I expected. Because the author, Bill Honig, has clearly articulated the strong phonics position in language that appeals to educators, I'll share some of his thoughts with a few comments.

After describing the nation's reading failures, Honig explains that the solution is to be found by looking at poor readers in the upper grades. He writes of "a powerful and persuasive consensus " of educational, cognitive, and medical researchers, as well as our best teachers, "about the causes and cures of reading failure." The more than 10,000 teachers he asked to describe them, report that they have "poor decoding skills." And he adds that they struggle with too many individual words not knowing how to tackle new ones. They are also weak in vocabulary, spelling, strategic reading, etc. all because of reading failure.

Honig points out that first grade decoding ability predicts 80 to 90% of reading comprehension in second and third grade and 40% in the ninth grade. "Predicts" is the correct word. We cannot say that good decoding *causes* good comprehension. Both poor decoding and poor comprehension must, to some degree, be caused by the same inadequate language ability. Reasons could be homes where English is not spoken or where children are not read to, or where children are not mature enough to begin school, etc. Also, we may assume that most of these children would not have learned the word-attack skills promoted in whole language programs. Likely lack of success with either type of program would lead to poor comprehension.

According to Honig, "No method but full alphabetic screening of a word produces fast enough retrieval for the huge numbers of words in English. . . . Context-driven decoding, even aided by partial alphabetic clues, is too slow and unreliable to serve as a fluent decoding tool." Although this sounds logical, those who teach whole language carefully would disagree. The research we looked at and more that we haven't, clarifies that kids can learn well with good whole language instruction. According to the NAEP test results, they learn better.

My opinion

I would read to my kids letting them watch. We would talk about the stories. I would teach the alphabet and the sounds the letters usually represent and let them play with plastic letters or make letters with strings of clay. When they were ready I would let them see what words in the story were saying. I would explain common letter-combination phonemes and let them enjoy some phonics exercises. Then I would apply the principles we have discussed and which Mark Thogmartin explains in his chapter including stopping to help them sound out words. In brief, I would combine good principles from both methods.[17] And as reading began, I would apply whatever method helped. You might do something different. Your kids will learn, too.

Teaching your beginner

If your reader learns to stop often (maybe not always) to figure out new words using word-attack principles and confirmed by the context, reading skills will develop.

Lack of success may not be from using the wrong methods. It could be a signal to wait for more maturity. Pushing is a temptation because you want the excitement of seeing your child learn to read. Use restraint. Pushing too soon or too hard could bring frustration to a child who is not ready. Unless your child is way past the typical reading age, don't hold out the carrot saying, as soon as you can read, you can enjoy such-and-such.

Whether with traditional phonics or a more casual approach, be diligent. You need to spend time with your child to help him or her avoid rushing over words which are not understood. Even with a word or two blocked out, most sentences can be understood correctly. (The principle is called "close.") If your reader is depending on this, however, for meaning and not stopping to learn the words, carelessness develops and reading skill is in danger.

In our teaching, we must avoid letting kids bypass the thought process by telling them a word before they have tried to figure it out or by letting them by with too many wild guesses losing their opportunity to understand the sentence. Neither should we hold them to instant perfection. We don't in any other type of learning. In our own learning, we begin imperfectly and move to excellence.

We must also avoid the idea that pronouncing strings of words is reading or that pronouncing individual words indicates knowing what they mean.

Good readers have good habits of concentration and looking at the words. They also figure out, perhaps unconsciously, how letter combinations affect word sounds.

Endnotes

1. In 1955, Rudolph Flesch created a great stir by his book, *Why Johnny Can't Read.* He correctly condemned the look-say instructional method of whole word memorization only, but his solution wasn't, in my opinion, as good as it might have been.

2. *McGuffey's Eclectic Primer,* Rev. ed., 1909, p. iii.

3. T. Clymer, 1963. "The Utility of Phonic Generalizations in the Primary grades." *The Reading Teacher* 16: 252-258.

4. M. H. Bailey, 1967. "The Utility of Phonic Generalizations in Grades One Through Six." *The Reading Teacher* 20: 413-418.

5. D. J. Bruce, 1964, "The Analysis of Word Sounds." *British Journal of Educational Psychology* 34: 158-170.

6. Kenneth Goodman, A Linguistic Study of Cues and Miscues in Reading." *Elementary English* 42: 639-643, 1965. First graders correctly read, in the story, nearly two-thirds of the words missed on the list, second graders, 75%, and third graders 82%.

7. I. Mullins, J. Campbell, and A. Farstrup, 1993. *NAEP 1992 Reading Report Card for the Nation and the States.* National Center for Education Statistics. The score ratio for whole language / phonics rated as "little or no emphasis" was 218/222.

8. Jeanne Chall wrote: "a code-emphasis method – i.e. one that views beginning reading as essentially different from mature reading and emphasizes learning of the printed code for the spoken language – produces better results, at least up to the third grade." Jeanne S. Chall, *Learning to Read: the Great Debate.* McGraw-Hill, New York, 1967, p. 307. The book was revised in 1983.

In a 1988 article, Marie Carbo challenged Jeanne Chall's conclusions that a code emphasis (bottom-up) is more effective than a meaning emphasis (top-down), and Chall responded in the same journal citing more studies that Carbo hadn't mentioned. Then, in an article, "The 'Great' Debate – Can Both Carbo and Chall be right?"[4] (*Phi Delta Kappan*, 1989, pp. 276–283.) Richard L. Turner reviewed the studies Chall had used in support of her ideas and found all but nine of them to have flawed methodology. From the few studies with a good research base, he concludes that systematic phonics is a little better than the whole-language approach until the beginning of the second grade, but after that, the difference disappears. I don't know why these results differ from those drawn from the NAEP scores. They would have been older studies.

Also see my comments in Chapter 2 under "Public Schools" for research reports of general success of schools including a report on reading success in the US and New Zealand.

Nancy Larrick, "De-trivializing our methods of reading instruction," *Phi Delta Kappan*, November 1987, pp. 184–189. Children in one of the most difficult New York City school districts, many of whom didn't hear English at home, showed remarkable success in reading. They were part of the Open Sesame project which uses large numbers of ordinary children's books instead of the typical basal readers. In this method (1) the teacher reads systematically to the children; (2) they are encouraged to read from many library books displayed in the room; (3) activities such as dramatization, discussion and illustrations make the books that are read to them more memorable; (4) key words (at the kindergarten level) are chosen by the children and displayed on cards around the room; and (5) the most interesting characteristic – phonics is not stressed. It is taught as children ask for help with their writing, and in quick crash courses before taking standardized tests.

By late spring, 1987, all 350 first graders in the Open Sesame project were reading in English, and all but three (who had been in this country less than six months) passed a comprehension test given by a school district evaluator. The project is based on an earlier research study comparing ten second-grade classes learning from this approach with ten more using conventional readers.

9. Donald D. MacKay, 1972. "The Structure of Words and Syllables: Evidence from Errors in Speech." *Cognitive Psychology* 3: 210–227.

10. R.E. Wylie and D.D. Durnell, 1970. "Teaching Vowels Through Phonograms." (The terms "onset" and "rime" had not yet been coined.) Also R. Treiman, 1983. "The Structure of Spoken Syllables: Evidence from Novel Word Games." *Cognition* 15: 49–84.

11. U. Goswami, 1986. "Children's Use of Analogy in Learning to Read. . . ." *Journal of Experimental child Psychology* 42: 73–83. U. Goswami, 1992 and F. Mead. 1992. "Onset and Rime Awareness and Analogies in Reading." *Reading Research Quarterly* 27: 150–162. M. Moustafa, 1990. *An Interactive/Cognitive Model of the Acquisition of Graphophonemic Systems by Young Children*. Ph.D. Dissertation, University of Southern California.

12. Margaret Moustafa, *Beyond Traditional Phonics, Research Discoveries and Reading Instruction.* Heineman, 361 Hanover St., Portsmouth, NH 03801-3912. 1997. p. 51. This book has been the souce for much of the material in this chapter. I've left you plenty to read.

13. Marilyn J. Adams. 1990. *Beginning to Read: Thinking and Learning About Print.* Cambridge, MA; MIT Press.

14. E. Chen and R.L. Colvin, *The Los Angeles Times*, July 18, 1996.

15. Mustafa, *op cit.* pp. 35, 36 She explains more problems with the condemnation of whole language.

16. Bill Honig, "Research-Based Reading Instruction: The Right Way," *Education Digest*, Dec. 1997, pp. 15–22. Condensed from *The School Administrator* Sept. 1997. Honig, who is President of Consortium of Reading Excelence, in Emeryville, Calif., has also written *Teaching our Children to Read: The Role of Skills in a Comprehensive Reading Program*. Corwin Press.

17. An Illinois school was concerned that their whole language program needed more phonics. They found the combination successful. Kathy Batjes and Theresa Brown. ERIC Report ED409539. Improving Reading Achievement of First Grade Students by Integrating Phonics Skills into a Whole Language Curriculum. May 1997.

Also, Barbara Matson. "Whole Language or Phonics? Teachers and Researchers Find the Middle Ground Most Fertile. The Great Reading Debate. *Harvard Education Letter* (v12 n2 p1-5 Mar.-Apr. 1996).

28

More Than Phonics

Mark B. Thogmartin

Often children who come to me for special reading instruction appear not to need the help. They have already learned how to say the words they see but are unable, after completing a selection, to explain very much of what they have read. In whatever approach we take to reading instruction, making sense of print should be our fundamental goal.

Mark Thogmartin *is a reading specialist teaching near his home in Ohio. He is author of the book,* Teach a Child to Read Using Children's books, *reviewed in Appendix O*

Previous chapters discuss how to prepare your child for reading. I would like here to emphasize the importance of a literate lifestyle. Children need to see you reading and writing, and they need you to read to them. Some children learn to read simply by experiencing the written word many times a day with their parents or other adults. But most need some type of focused instruction to help develop the self-improving strategies needed as the text becomes increasingly difficult.

Home schooling parents usually choose a strong phonics approach to teaching reading because they believe phonics works. They generally use one of the many programs on the market, and their children become good readers.

To deny the importance of phonics instruction is a little like saying breathing is optional, but literacy requires learning more than how to decode printed words. A number of skills are essential to receiving the visual communication of an author's message. Pick up a medical journal at the library sometime. You may be able to pronounce all the words on a page while understanding almost nothing. Only a person having had a special range of experiences would be able to fully comprehend the message in such a journal.

Children learn to talk by being immersed in real conversation all day long. We do not give them formal talking lessons nor do we have them memorize rules governing our use of the spoken words. We just talk to them and with them, and we gently adjust their misuse of language in natural conversation. If our child says, "Grandma flied in the plan," we would probably respond by saying something like, "Yes, Grandma flew here from Florida," using the correct form of the verb, fly. By repeatedly hearing the proper use of words, children incorporate these conventions into their own conversation. The human brain has an amazing capacity to accept, reject, or refine thousands of "rules" based on experience alone.

Because children are not as surrounded day in and day out by print as they are by speech, reading instruction needs to be more purposeful and explicit. This can be accomplished through "real" children's literature as a primary tool with phonics as a major part of the process.

Balance in reading instruction

We read for the purpose of getting meaning from print. Although children understand this, they often comprehend poorly. A variety of cues help us understand. Letters and words are our primary source of information but there are others. As mentioned at the beginning of this chapter, I have worked with many children who, while skillful in applying the rules of phonics, understand little of what they read.

As your child looks at letters and

words, encourage listening with a comprehending ear to the entire story. If she does not stop occasionally when a word or phrase does not make sense, she is word calling and not listening to the story. Or if she is happily "reading" a wonderful story that does not match the text, encourage her to watch more closely.

The following incomplete sentence demonstrates my observation. *The boy kicked the b_____.* Most children can easily supply an unrecognized word, or at least think of one that makes sense, even with only one letter as a cue. Suppose this sentence in its complete form appeared in a story, and the child read the word *blue* instead of *ball*, continuing without hesitation. We could assume she is mostly concerned about saying words and is not thinking about meaning. If she makes a mistake like reading, "The boy kicked the *tree*." she would need encouragement to watch the print more closely. This simple example shows the value of instructional elements beyond sounding out words.

After your girl has made an error like reading *blue* for *ball*, you might ask her if what she read made sense or if it sounded right. Teach her to anticipate what word is coming next and to quickly verify it with her eyes while following the flow of ideas to see if it all makes sense. This powerful strategy takes into account the entire act of reading – relying on both print and meaning. It also helps a child become a fluent reader early on, reading with expression instead of calling . . . one . . . word . . . after . . . another. So how can this kind of instruction take place while the child recognizes relatively few words?

Predictable books as teaching tools

Certain elements in "predictable books" make them easy for young children to read. (1) They usually have a repetitive pattern that children can follow after the first few pages. (2) They present concepts familiar to children. (3) Illustrations usually match the text. And (4) predictability is increased by rhyme and rhythm, cumulative patterns, or familiar sequences. The popular children's book, *Brown Bear, Brown Bear, What Do You See?*[1] is a delightfully illustrated predictable book that beginners can read with little or no help after hearing it once or twice.

The book's title is also its first line. The bear sees a red bird, then the red bird is asked who it sees and responds that it sees a yellow duck, and so on.

Among children's books commonly found in US public libraries, I have identified some 600 that are predictable and easy to read.[2] Your librarian can point you to these and many other suitable ones.

As you use such books, instructional opportunities in all aspects of reading will come up. I've been doing this for several years in a program for only the lowest twenty percent of first-grade readers. Using predictable books, we work with the children one-on-one for thirty minutes each day. Our goal is to help them learn to read as well as or better than average students within twelve to eighteen weeks. We reach our objective for approximately three-fourths of our students. Even children who do not "graduate" from the program within this time period achieve much more than they otherwise would. Remember we work with only the poorest readers. Children who are not disadvantaged and who have their moms or dads as tutors will certainly excel with this kind of book-based reading program.

Teaching strategies

So how is it done? You may wish to apply the ideas I'm about to explain, taking one of two basic approaches. You could follow methods from a phonics package in conjunction with the reading of children's books, or you might teach phonics and other skills using only children's books and a few simple tools I'll describe later. Either is fine as long as you make meaningful reading your ultimate goal.

Prior to beginning this program, your child should know most of the letters and their common sounds. In families who value the written word, children usually gain this knowledge through purposeful activities like writing notes, playing letter games, typing on the computer and, of course, reading aloud. Teaching the letters and their sounds does not require a packaged program as long as you regularly talk about them in your normal literate life with the child. Letters or sounds still unfamiliar will be learned as you continue the activities I recommend.

Before reading a book, make sure it is within your child's ability. The topic of the book should be familiar to your child. He should already understand most of the words used. He should also be able to catch on to the nature of the repetition and see how the illustrations relate to the text.

Introduce the book by talking together about it while looking at the pictures. Use the words in the story as you discuss the pictures. Possibly have your child locate and read already familiar words. Have him find one or two more difficult words by telling him the word and asking what letter he would expect to see at the beginning and/or the end.

After introducing the book, turn back to the cover and read the title again. Have him read the title page. Then let him start out on the first page with whatever help you need to offer. After a page or two, if you've chosen an appropriate book, your child should be able to continue on his own. If you think he is only "reading" the pictures, have him point at each word as he reads. This will make him watch the text. He will soon learn the most common words by seeing them frequently. Encourage him, as much as is practical, to use expression when he reads. Don't let him sound like a robot.

When the child makes an error, or when he hesitates on a word, wait awhile before jumping in. See if he can use what he knows about print to figure out the word or else his mistake. If he says a word that does not match with the print, have him go back to the beginning of the sentence and try again. Ask him to watch more closely as he reads. If he still doesn't catch his mistake, point directly at the problem word, tell him what word he read, and ask if this word starts like it. Then help him sound it out noting the letters and letter combinations. Ask him to go back and try again. If he reads the word correctly, help him check to make sure by seeing if it makes sense and if the rest of the letters in it sound out to make the word. I will discuss more detailed phonics instruction techniques in the next section.

If, although watching closely, the child misreads so that the text doesn't make sense, stop him at the end of the sentence and ask if the word sounded right. You may have to go back and read the sentence like he read it for him to be able to hear what he read. He will probably realize his error. Then you can point him to the problem area. Focus on the word together, letting him do most of the work. Give as few hints as possible.

Point out only what he could have picked up from the text or from the meaning of the story. For example, if he hesitates on the word *tree* his reading skill would not be helped by saying "You know, it's one of those things that you climb and that you find in a forest." This kind of prompt is useless in helping a child figure out unfamiliar words because he would not have been able to generate the comparison on his own. It would be better to tell him to think about what was happening in the story and to look at the *tr-* at the beginning of the word. Then tell him to go back to the beginning of the sentence and try again.

As he becomes more proficient, he will begin to do this kind of monitoring on his own. He will often stop, go back, and correct himself. You should encourage this.

He is putting together all the skills involved in fluent reading. Good readers always read to make sense and they watch the print closely to be sure it matches what they are reading. Gradually increase the difficulty of the reading material as your child grows in ability.

Phonics instruction while reading

In her chapter, "Phonics, a Realistic View," Ruth Beechick identifies three levels of phonics understanding: the pupil level, the teacher level, and the publisher level. In discussing the pupil level, she suggests using only the amount of phonics instruction necessary to enable the child to read. I concur. This means that the child needs to know only the sounds for the letters, and the sounds they have in the more common blends. How can this be accomplished in the program I am describing?

Linguists – people who study language – have discovered through research that children have a natural tendency to look for the biggest recognizable "chunks" of letters when attempting to read unfamiliar words. In single syllable words, these chunks usually consist of a beginning letter or letter blend called the onset, and then the rest of the word called the rime. For effective phonics instruction, help your child follow her natural inclinations to look for these recognizable chunks.

In our example with the word *tree,* looking at its chunks turns up several leads. If the child knows the word *see,* you could make a connection with the *-ee* chunk. Using the chalkboard or other writing surface, show her that *-ee* sounds the same whenever it appears. Start by making the word *see.* Then make other words like *bee* and *fee* asking her to read each word as your write it. Then add the *tr-* chunk to the *-ee* chunk and talk about how you would pronounce it. Whenever possible ask her to make the word herself and to follow under it slowly with her finger as she combines the phonetic sounds. This letter-and-word work is done in quick episodes as you read the story. After you have successfully examined a word, go back to the story and read again the part containing it. The whole process is very profitable but can be overdone. Stopping to analyze a word more than two or three times in a brief children's story could quell interest in the process.

While reading, you can isolate a chunk of familiar letters by simply covering part of the word with your fingers. For example children soon learn the often used *-ing* chunk. If your child has difficulty with a word such as *playing,* you can help her isolate the word *play* by covering up the familiar *-ing* chunk with your finger. The

exposed word *play* is now much easier to recognize or sound through.

Of course, early in your reading instruction, you will want to teach your child how to effectively sound through simple phonetically-regular words. Use simple two-, three- or four-letter words to demonstrate the process. Words like *at, in, man, bed, frog,* and *trap.* Show your child how to run her finger under the letters sounding each one while blending them to pronounce the word. Sounding individual letters or chunks without blending them makes it hard to hear the word. As your child comes to an unfamiliar word while reading a story, ask her to first think about the story, sound the initial letter, then quickly scan the word for familiar chunks. If these strategies are unsuccessful, encourage her to sound through the word.

Skill in sounding out words phonetically is important. I suggest trying other strategies first only to keep a balance between learning the phonics and striving for comprehension. Too many long pauses break the chain of thought.

In my lessons, I include a special segment for purposely working on letter sounds and word identification. For this I spend a few minutes with magnetic letters or the dry erase board on a chunk or phoneme that I realize needs practice. The rest of the lesson is spent in reading several books at the child's level, most of which she has read before. I introduce no more than one new book a day.

Writing to learn phonics

Writing a story with the child is another valuable phonics activity. This story usually does not need to be longer than a sentence or two. Suggest writing on a topic from a book you just read or about something that interests him.

Talk about letters, sounds, and chunks as you write. Practice writing irregular words – ones that do not follow the basic rules of phonics like *the, saw, was, of, love,* or *come.* When such a word comes up in the story, point it out and have your child write it three or four times for practice. Then ask him to use it in the story. More regular words should be pronounced slowly, listening for the sounds. Guide him through those tricky silent letters. Talk about frequently occurring letter combinations including blends such as *bl-, br-, dr-,* and *fl-*, and chunks like *-at, -in, -ike, -ing,* and *-ed.* The more you and your child work with letters, chunks, and words, the more familiar they will become. The story writing part of your lesson also provides opportunity to talk about capital letters and punctuation. Just remember to introduce new concepts gradually, not expecting immediate adherence to every rule. When your child finishes writing the story, have him read it back to you. Return often to earlier stories he has written. Your going back to them will help him value what he has written.

Real books and real writing provide a balanced reading program for your child. The enjoyable nature of this approach stimulates interest and leads to success. It helps children sense the importance of word skills.

Examples of Predictable Books

These books, graded into levels of increasing difficulty, can be used to judge the levels of other books you see. Most of them can be found at your local library. Your librarian can suggest others of similar difficulty for each level.

Emergent (Beginning) Level

1 Hunter by Pat Hutchins (Greenwillow, 1982)

Have You Seen My Cat? by Eric Carle (Picture Book Studio, 1987)

Preprimer 1 Level

Brown Bear, Brown Bear, What Do You See? by Bill Martin (Holt, Rinehart, & Winston, 1984)

Who's Counting by Nancy Tafuri (Greenwillow, 1986)

Preprimer 2 Level

The Chick and the Duckling by Mirra Ginsburg (Simon & Shuster, 1972)

Five Little Ducks by Raffi (Crown, 1989)

Preprimer 3 Level

All by Myself by Mercer Mayer (Western Publishing, 1985)

Five Little Monkeys Jumping on the Bed by Eileen Christelow (Houghton Mifflin, 1993)

Primer Level

Dear Zoo by Rod Campbell (Simon & Schuster, 1986)

The Carrot Seed by Ruth Kraus (Harper, 1989)

First Grade Level

The Very Busy Spider by Eric Carle (Philomel, 1985)

Goodnight Moon by Margaret Brown (Harper, 1947)

Second Grade (First Half) Level

The Last Puppy by Frank Asch (Prentice-Hall, 1980)

Little Bear by Else H. Minarik (Harper, 1957)

Second Grade (Second Half) Level

Frog and Toad Are Friends by Arnold Lobel (Harper, 1970)

Stone Soup by Ann McGovern (Scholastic, 1968)

Editor's note:

Some home schooling authors (and hence some parents) are strongly opposed to any reading method that does not begin with intensive phonics which requires memorizing the sounds of a long list of phonemes before reading more than a few words. You might wonder why this author has taken a somewhat different approach.

The instructional method outlined by Mark Thogmartin has been adapted from a program known as Reading Recovery. In the 60s New Zealand teacher and psychologist Marie Clay began observing successful reading teachers. From what she learned she developed Reading Recovery which has been successful in her country and is now widely used in the US and elsewhere for children who risk becoming poor readers.

Is it better for your children than an intensive phonics program would be? The answer is not simple. Children adapt to many different methods, and the traditional phonics idea is not necessarily a bad one.

The only study I am aware of which compares the two methods concludes that Reading Recovery is more effective.[2] Nearly 400 children in several school districts in England participated in the study. Reading Recovery methodology requires more individual-child or small group instruction. This could answer for some of the advantage.

Testing during the second year showed that Reading Recovery had lost much of its advantage over the ordinary instruction (neither of the methods in question) which half of the kids received in each of the schools and the Phonological Training had lost all of it. Since this basically a whole-language approach, you may consider the research I describe in my chapter , "Decoding Words."

This program seems to lend itself well to home schooling where you can spend more individual time with your child than would be possible in a classroom. The fact that you want to teach them means you will also likely inspire them to succeed whether you use one method or another.

What would I do if I still had young children to teach? I explain in the chapter mentioned above.

Endnotes

1. Martin, B., *Brown Bear, Brown Bear, What Do You See?* by Eric Carle, 1984, Holt Rinehart, and Winston.

2. Kathy Sylva and Jane Hurry, Thomas Coram Research Unit, "Early Intervention in Children with Reading Difficulties: An Evaluation of Reading Recovery and a Phonological Training." *Literacy, Teaching and Learning.* vol. 2, No. 2, 1996.

29

Teaching Literature

To know how to relate to the teaching of literature, we first need to ask what good literature is and why it comes into the curriculum in modern schools.

We might argue that literature is anything that can be read. But what is "good" literature to those who are supposed to know? And why do certain selections find their way into textbooks?

From my observations, three characteristics qualify reading matter as literature worthy of study.

1. *Meaning*. A selection must provoke thought, often expressing the writer's wisdom. Even if the thought is not serious, the words must do their work well to get classified as literature.

2. *Good writing*. Good literature shows excellence in writing skill.

3. *Wide recognition*. For writing to be classified as "great" literature its quality must be recognized by many people.

Objectives for studying literature

From these three characteristics of important literature we find three reasons for studying it:

1. To learn and/or be entertained by, thought leaders of the present and past.

2. To improve self-expression by being exposed to, and by analyzing, good writing.

3. To be able to refer to ideas from commonly known literary works as an aid in communication.

The hook

My words here are addressed to Christian parents, but anyone who senses the importance of character development will find them significant. We are all influenced by what the rest of our society considers important for education. We have always heard that Shakespeare and Poe and Emerson and a long list of others were the "greats" of literature. And we believe our kids must learn from these supposedly great men and women. To do otherwise would seem as uncultured as going barefoot to a formal dinner. But if our values are set in the framework of eternity, we recognize that some people whom the world considers great have, in reality, worked against the glory of God and would teach us, directly or by inference, to do the same.

Then what about the purposes for teaching literature? All the authors found in popular school literature for children and youth show at least the first two of the three characteristics I have listed. And it's right that they should. Certainly we want meaningful reading matter and a demonstration of good writing skill. And there may even be value in the third objective–an introduction to the authors. But in addition to these criteria, those of us who look for wisdom from above for ourselves and our children expect more. We want literature that lifts, that builds character.

Suppose we do recognize some wrong ideas in certain recognized works. Shouldn't we be able to read for "literary value" even though we disagree with some of the ideas? Can't we read all the famous authors and get the spiritual "vitamin supplement" from our Bibles? Here's the problem: "Good" literature is philosophy skillfully expressed. Writing without significant art and purpose is just not good writing. Whether in a story or an essay or a poem, if it's good literature by the standard of the world, the author writes with power. He drives the message home.

He teaches his philosophy. And, although we use different terms for it, philosophy amounts to the spiritual essence at the heart of religion. Philosophy defines values. It decides purpose for life. Instead of seeking this meaning from secular literature, I look to God as revealed in His Word, and I think you do, too.

Influence

For the Christian, the whole basis of child training rests on the idea of learning through influence (Prov. 22:6; 2 Cor. 3:18; Heb. 12:2). Alexander Pope, sixteenth-century English poet, expressed the problem of evil influence very well:

Vice is a monster of so frightful mein
As to be hated needs but to be seen;
Yet seen too oft, familiar with her face,
We first endure, then pity,
*then embrace.**

The Apostle Paul put it in the positive:

. . .
whatsoever things are true,
whatsoever things are honest,
whatsoever things are just,
whatsoever things are pure,
whatsoever things are lovely,
whatsoever things are of good report;
if there be any virtue,
and if there be any praise,
think on these things (Phil. 4:8).

As adults, we are influenced by what we see, otherwise there would be no advertising. How much greater then is the power of influence on children who have not developed the ability of discrimination and on youth who are novices at it? Most literature which the world considers great, generally has certain enduring qualities. But when laced with distorted values, we teach or study it at great risk.

For the unavoidable evil that surrounds us, we can claim strength from the admonition of Isaiah 33:15, 16:

He that walketh righteously,
. . .
that stoppeth his ears
from hearing of blood,
and shutteth his eyes from seeing evil;
He shall dwell on high.

Also remember, as parents, that what you feed your own minds opens the door wide for temptation for your children even years later, after they have flown from the family nest.

We have addressed the question of reading matter, but the total mass of sensory input, including television and even private conversation, must stand up to the quality of heaven.

Then what can be studied?

When you look closely, many famous literary works don't pass the test. (For me, most don't.) Of course, some do. Certain selections from an author may be good while others are objectionable. And many works that aren't famous still teach good value and writing quality.

Of course nothing equals the Scriptures for literary quality in depth of truth. To see them as literature in the secular sense, is good. But when you examine the deeper meaning of God's love letter to us, the words of inspiration become a treasure beyond value.

In the final analysis, "Where is the wise? where is the scribe? where is the disputer of this world? hath not God made foolish the wisdom of this world? . . . He that glorieth, let him glory in the Lord" (1 Cor. 1:20, 31).

On the next page are criteria for choosing literature and whatever we feed our minds.

Criteria for Choosing What to Read (and Watch)

God's character may not be distorted. It has been Satan's purpose since the beginning of sin to obscure the true character of God. Several common misunderstandings are: (1) that God is unjust and selfish, (2) that He is unmerciful and capricious, (3) that He doesn't care how people behave, and (4) that He doesn't exist at all leaving them to be their own gods.

Any people the reader is led to identify with, whether story characters or authors, must be worthy of emulation. Flaws in character justified by the author are probably the most dangerous. Consider, for example, deception which achieves apparent good, or that is designed to create a laugh, and impurity presented as clever and desirable.

Words or phrases that dishonor God's name or His attributes should be avoided. The major problem in exposing ourselves to profanity is that, by repetition, these emotional expressions become engraved in the thought patterns. Then when the emotion others have used them to express occurs, the words tend to surface. Many common expletives are only camouflaged profanity — "Gee" and "Gosh," for example.

The mind must be kept receptive to the impressions of the Holy Spirit. Prayer and the study of God's Word are the Christian's lifeline. Reading that feeds the appetite for excitement or that leads to a dream world (even if from Christian publishers) dull the spiritual perceptions and tend to leave the mind indifferent to communion with heaven.

The emotions and attitudes developed toward other people must lead to respect, sensitivity, valuing human life, and in brief, to love. Too much of what we read and see tends toward hatred, suspicion, prejudice, and the poisoning of vibrant, fulfilling relationships.

The reader must be left a better person. Asking what is wrong with a selection is not enough. There must be something right about it before we can expect time and interest to be spent on it.

Endnote

* Pope, *Essay on Man*. Epis. ii, l.217.

30

Teaching Writing

You already know why writing skill is important. It's a vital tool for exchanging the ideas necessary to develop human relationships. But there are more reasons to write. Beyond communication, the writing process reflects, reinforces and develops thinking. This is true of speaking, too, but writing allows the time for considering and adjusting.

The ability to write well requires instruction and practice. You can help your children learn this essential skill even as your own ability grows.

Encouragement for writing

To lay the foundation for writing and other communication skills, make your home a place of words. Talk with your children about places you go and things you see. Ask questions to stimulate their thinking. Intelligent discussion of shared experiences helps younger children develop ability in using language.

Let your children observe you talking, writing on paper and with a computer. They should know that you read and that you listen to or watch informative programs. Places of worship are generally rich in communication experiences.

In guiding your children's writing, you help most effectively by getting them to think for themselves. Instead of being a literary critic, help them discover what they want to say. Instead of trying to correct every mistake, be available as a resource for spelling, punctuation and usage. Show your pleasure with their work.

As you help them improve their writing, let them know that you revise and correct your work, too.

Gifts like pens, pencils, a desk lamp, paper, and stamps help make writing fun. A booklet for a diary or journal may begin a rewarding experience, especially if it can be kept private. A dictionary provides spelling help as well as other interesting information about word origins, synonyms, and pronunciation. A typewriter or computer with a word processor can be an important learning tool once keyboard skills are adequate.

Writing Activities Suitable for Younger Students

By Cynthia J. Stark

❋ *Write a poem (Look at simple poems for style ideas).*

❋ *Interview someone (Plan questions and write about the answers).*

❋ *Finish a story from a few sentences which will be its beginning.*

❋ *Write a new ending to a story you have read.*

❋ *Keep a journal of books read, and write a response about each one.*

❋ *Make a sentence-building game which uses words from cut-up sentences.*

(a) Make up simple sentences on index cards.

(b) Cut them up according to parts of speech.

(c) Create different sentences identifying the parts of speech.

The first four of these activities would be good practice also for older students. (tw)

Because, with a computer, text can be easily moved around and changed, more of the energy goes into thinking and creating and less into the mechanical effort of getting words to look good on paper.

Look for reasons to write

Real purposes make writing (or any other kind of learning) much more interesting. For this kind of opportunity, classroom schools can't match homes. If you are following a textbook or packaged program, look for chances to substitute activities touching the real world.

One such real-life activity is letter writing. Share appropriate letters you get – especially parts your child might be able to relate to. Ask your friends and relatives to write special letters to your child, or to include notes in letters they write you. Writing is more fun when people respond. Pen pals provide more letter-writing opportunities.

Your child can also write to request free and low-cost items. Check your library for *Freebies* magazine or *Free Stuff for Kids*.[1] Other writing "jobs" include making grocery lists, taking telephone messages and preparing invitation notes.

The greatest writing joy may be in seeing one's work in print. But selling or even giving writing to a publisher is not easy for the vast majority of would-be adult writers. For children, it's usually only a dream. Look for periodicals that accept children's work. You might suggest that student compositions be included in your support group newsletter. Or your group could publish one or two special issues a year with deadlines announced well in advance.

Consider helping your children publish their own booklet of poems and stories. My first publishing venture was on a toy cylinder press using rubber type. I "printed" a sort of family news report and sent it to all the relatives. It even featured the first part of a still-unfinished nature story – all of three or four sentences. Now in the days of computers and photocopy machines, homemade publishing is easy.

The writing process

How you or your child goes about getting words on paper in an acceptable form depends on what you write. Copying a phone number or attaching a sticky note to a check doesn't take revision and a spell checker, but for most writing, quality requires following certain principles.

Planning Collecting ideas in your mind, finding or verifying factual information, and then developing an order of presentation; these are first steps in all but trivial writing.

Making detailed outlines, 1,2,3, and a,b,c, is a good exercise for analysis or organization of existing material, but for writing usually by the time the outline is perfected you could have written your paper. I start by thinking a bit then writing a few cryptic notes in pencil. To get order I write between lines or use arrows.

The draft By the time serious words start following one another on the computer screen, the order is already changing and new thoughts are inserted. For a draft, getting words into a form someone else could read is more important than spelling, grammar or even accuracy. Thus mind energy is devoted to a logical progression of ideas as words are arranged to make sense.

Whenever I write more than a sentence or so and send it off without reading it over, I'm sorry. Care is needed to be sure words make sense and stupid mistakes are avoided. Basically more formal writing needs more revision.

In the days before word processors, people did manage to write decent letters, even by hand. I enjoy seeing nice handwriting. It's becomind a rare art form.

You don't need to expect a draft of every writing exercise. Use your judgment.

Revision This often long part of the process takes the least explanation. Rewriting offers an opportunity to expand and, more important, to cut superfluous material as the work is refined. Leaving work to be rewritten later allows approaching it with a fresh mind. Several drafts are often needed. Be careful not to expect too much from your young student. Writing is hard work but it needs to be an enjoyable challenge. Use your judgment to know when the work is good enough. The future will bring more opportunities to learn.

Editing This means checking for clarity in the flow of thoughts as well as for correctness in facts, spelling, form, usage, and grammar. In practice editing occurs during the revision process. At the end it may be well to concentrate on it a little more.

Presentation Sometimes you will be the only recipient of your child's writing piece, but sharing in a wider circle is important especially in home schooling. Sometimes your student can read the work aloud, sometimes a poem or other brief writing project can be posted, maybe with art work. You can think of other ways including publication.

Safety in handling tools – the computer

You have probably grown up around computers or know about them even if you don't own one. To ignore them in this age is like ignoring the automobile when it became useful and affordable.

One side effect of using a computer or typewriter, however, is getting less practice with handwriting. Help your child work for a balance.

I expect you have also been awed by the mass of information available through the Internet. It's both good and bad, true and false, useful and trivial advertisement. CD-ROMs store up to 65 megabytes of information, accessible in a second. Now technology is beginning to pack seven times that much onto the same little disks. As a point of comparison, the files for this whole printed book take about 2.2 megabytes without the graphics (which take lots of memory). Removing the word processor formatting codes (which don't show) leaves just the text. That would take only 0.8 megabyte!

Both the Internet and the CD-ROM offer resource information for student writing. Educators are beginning to notice, however, that fancy-looking papers with illustrations and graphs (which sometimes don't apply) are letting students bypass the thought and analysis process. You see, we teach writing not only as a communication tool, but as a way to develop thinking skill – as a way to gather information and process it, judging what is important for a particular objective and what is true.

In an age of instant access, cut and paste is easy. With a little touchup a coherent message can be formed. All without being processed by the mind. This is okay for collecting quotations or editing someone's work, but good writing skill comes from struggling with text.

Should you ask your child or youth to write without gathering information through the computer? Maybe, as some kind of special exercise, but not for all their writing. If you and they are aware of the hazards, it can be a great tool. Certainly they will want to clip a paragraph to quote now and then, too, but expect them to do the writing from what they learn. Expect them to dig for information rather than grabbing what catches their eye and presenting it as a collage of disconnected ideas they have barely read through without processing and considering – without making them their own or climbing on them as a ladder to their own better conclusions.

The people we write for these days are already overloaded with information. This is the challenge to help our children strive for excellence and significance in writing.

Grammar and marking papers

Serious communication in business and in other contacts with important people demands good grammar and spelling. So should children begin as perfect writers by these standards as soon as they are old enough to understand the rules? I could get in trouble with some of you here when I say, no. Let me explain.

None of us can concentrate seriously on a lot of things at once. Suppose your area government decided that the citizens should use good grammar, so they added that requirement to the driving tests. As soon as you are sixteen or whatever the magic age is, you go for your test. The multiple choice items could be wrong for errors in the law or in grammar. When you nervously go out for your driving test every word is scrutinized by the officer, and you can't just be silent because you have questions to answer – in complete sentences!

Putting words together for reader impact requires concentration. As your child's words gel, encourage the brain energy to be focused on the creative process. The editing step of the writing process can come later.

How perfect you expect your student to be depends on many factors. Just remember that your goal isn't marking all the errors in red. It's helping your child grow. Sometimes the growth is helped by a red mark (or better, by courteous blue or black one). Make your more emphatic marks and comments about the good things you see.

Some writing can be informal – done for the sense of accomplishment with no grading at all. You don't need to mark a paper. Discussion may be sufficient although the marks can help your child remember what should be improved.

Can writing be taught successfully without directly teaching grammar? Perhaps for kids from homes with very accurate language.[2] Then the rules can be looked up as needed. In most cases, however, I favor the idea of teaching some grammar. One can write well without knowing definitions for terms like *clause* and *phrase, antecedent* and *transitive,* but we need the more important of these for communication about what we write.

Ideas for teaching

Here are some suggestions to help your child learn from his writing. Rather than a list to be processed, these are ideas to plug in where they fit in guiding the rewriting and editing process: (1) You could ask for thesis sentences to be identified. (2) Ask your student to read the paper aloud. Needs for improvement not *seen* can sometimes be *heard.* (4) Your written (or spoken) questions can call for consideration of problem spots. For example, you can challenge superfluous material by asking how it contributes to the theme. Or you could question wrong information. And (5) papers may be exchanged with a home schooling peer for suggestions.

To teach writing beyond the elementary years, I recommend using an English textbook for general direction.

As I have implied in the chapter on teaching reading, language arts skills aren't learned in isolation. Learning to listen and talk prepares children for both reading and writing as well as for speaking. And these communication skills need to be practiced while studying science, history, math, and the other school subjects.

Writing skill develops slowly. The program you use should introduce concepts and activities in progressing complexity. Being sensitive to your child's level of ability, you can adapt your instructional material to his or her needs.

Expect your curriculum to include a wide variety of writing experiences. People learning to write, need to practice with different forms (letters, essays, stories, etc.), different purposes (to inform, persuade, describe, etc.), and for a variety of audiences.

Reading skilled authors helps build writing ability. Assign or help your student choose good literature. Discuss it and encourage analysis of the writing in selected passages.

Keeping your child's writing (or samples of it) in a file folder allows you to assess progress. Also, in case you are questioned by authorities (or relatives) a collection like this shows that your child is really learning. And it's a source of keepsakes for remembering childhood experiences. Date each article.

As your young writer develops, she (or he) may begin pressing the limits of your own competence.[3] Then consider asking someone with advanced ability to mark occasional writing assignments and to discuss them with her.

My comments under the subheading, "Feedback," at the end of the chapter, "Techniques for Teaching," are particularly appropriate for teaching writing.

In your own response to your child's writing, concentrate more on content and creativity than on technique. All three are important, of course. But if your interest emphasizes the flame, then finding and chopping the wood will have its own purpose.

How to Learn to Write Well[4]

✍ **Clear thinking.** *Sometimes the child needs to have her memory refreshed about a past event in order to write about it.*

✍ **Sufficient time.** *Children may have stories "in their heads" but need time to think them through and write them down.*

✍ **Reading.** *Reading can stimulate a child to write about his/her own family or school life. If your child reads good books, (s)he will be a better writer.*

✍ **A meaningful task.** *A child needs meaningful, not artificial writing tasks.*

✍ **Interest.** *All the time in the world won't help if there is nothing to write, nothing to say. Some of the reasons for writing include: sending messages, keeping records, expressing feelings, or relaying information.*

✍ **Practice.** *And more practice.*

✍ **Revising.** *Students need experience in revising their work — that is, seeing what they can do to make it clearer, more descriptive, more concise, etc.*

Growing in writing ability

Preschool or early grade children can tell a story as you write it down. When you read it back, corrections can be made.

Don't expect writing for younger children to be as polished as for older ones. After all, writing won't be more mature than the child's basic ability to process language. Common sense will help you know what to expect for the steps in the writing process which we have just discussed.

Endnotes

1. See *Freebies* magazine in Appendix L. They also publish a book, *Freebies for Kids*, which is relatively inexpensive.
2. See my review of *Writing Strands* in Appendix P.
3. Many books will describe the basic rules of English grammar. One is *Test Your Grammar* from Usborne. 32 pp., 1994 $5.95. Another is *Errors in English and Ways to Correct Them* by Harry Shaw. Harper & Row, Publishers, 10E 53rd St., New York, NY 10022, 1986. A collegiate dictionary will have a punctuation and grammar chapter.
4. The list in the side bar was adapted from *Help Your Child Learn to Write Well*, Office of Educational Research and Improvement, U.S. Department of Education, Washington D.C. 20208, 1985. Read the whole booklet on the web at http://www.ed.gov/pubs/parents/Writing/index.html.

31

Teaching Handwriting

Barbara Getty and Inga Dubay

In the cities of the world, millions of typewriters, copy machines, fax machines, and word processors are cranking out endless streams of reams of paper in our effort to communicate the written word—to get information from one place to another.

Most of the words we read today are made by machine. But even in this computer age, the simple handwritten note is an essential part of everyday life. Children are required to use handwriting daily at school, and most adults use it daily in their work and in their personal lives—there will always be a need for handwriting.

Professional writing, from novels to newspaper articles, usually is done on word processors, but from a practical point of view, handwriting will persist in everyday use for two simple reasons—it is convenient and it is personal. A young woman working alone in a northwest forest fire lookout station complained that the letters sent by her family were printed by computer and were too impersonal. What's more, her brother didn't even bother to tear off the perforated edges or sign his name. She pleaded for handwritten messages. Handwriting counts!

Until the turn of the 20th century, handwriting was a major discipline in the classroom. In American schools, the general practice has been to introduce young students to a drawn manuscript alphabet known as "ball and stick." Many of these letters require a cumbersome series of strokes.

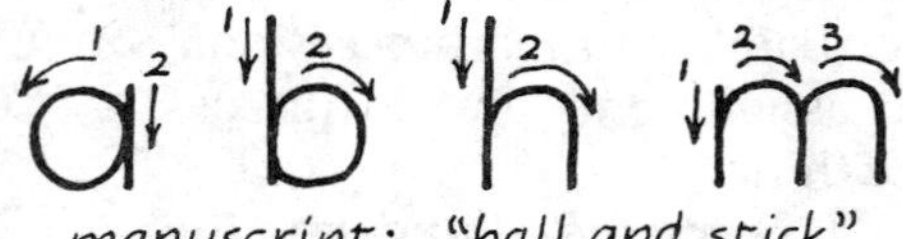

manuscript: "ball and stick"

As students are just gaining some mastery of these forms, usually at the beginning of third grade they are asked to abandon their new skills and learn to write a different set of 52 letters known as "looped cursive." This frustrates and confuses many learners.

bridge *bridge*

manuscript looped cursive

Paradoxically, the looped cursive that is generally taught in upper grades stems from letterforms inscribed by copperplate engravers and not from letters designed for handwriting. When these forms were taught as a major subject with hours of practice, an elegant hand could be the reward. But in this modern age, school systems are increasingly reluctant to devote much time to handwriting as a classroom course, and most teacher-training programs neglect instruction in handwriting. Consequently, handwriting is on the bottom rung of the educational ladder and in many instances deteriorates to the point of illegibility.

Many schools throughout the nation are now adopting italic, an old yet innovative, simple yet elegant approach to handwriting.

This contemporary italic handwriting system presents one simple lower-case alphabet: basic italic. Note that these letters are cursive in nature from day one, since most of the letters are written in one stroke with no lift of the writing tool.

a b c d e f g h i
j k l m n o p q
r s t u v w x y z

BASIC ITALIC LOWER-CASE

Cursive italic retains the same letter forms and the writer merely joins them together—a sort of "joined printing." This eliminates the transition phase that traditionally occurs when changing from ball and stick to looped cursive.

a quick brown fox

BASIC ITALIC

a quick brown fox

CURSIVE ITALIC

Cursive italic capital letters retain their basic forms except for optional flourishes.

A B C D E F

BASIC CAPITALS

A B C D E F

CURSIVE CAPITALS

The lifetime ability to handwrite legibly is as important as the other basic aspects of communication — reading, speaking and listening. But unfortunately, handwriting is understressed and undervalued. An article in TIME magazine a few years ago stated that this country's estimated business losses due to illegible handwriting (handwritten instructions, bookkeeping figures, addresses, etc.) amount to $200 million a year.

Where interoffice memos & notes are written by hand, there is an awakening to the need for a personal touch. Business executives are encouraged "to take a few minutes to write a handwritten note using the finest of fountain pens and stationery. The letter — not the fax, the phone, or the computer — is the heart and soul of networking."[1]

"It is interesting to note," says another writer, "that even with the invention of the typewriter, letters continue to be handsigned, and even memos are initialed. This aspect of writing will continue to play a role in our culture. It is difficult to imagine a time when love letters between young men and women will end up on floppy disks stored in an attic."[2]

For the last 5,000 years, cultures have been recording their history in written form; and although our system of communication known as handwriting may continue to undergo changes, it is here to stay — and those who want to leave a legible mark may find italic the way to write!

Explanation By Ted Wade

You have just read the preface from the book *Write Now*[3] which teaches the system developed by its two authors. Of course, there are other publishers who believe in what they teach.

Standing somewhat in the middle between the original "Palmer method" and this new "italic handwriting" is the D'Nealian system. As Barbara Getty and Inga Dubay explained to me, D'Nealian takes the right direction by getting rid of the awkward "ball and stick" letterforms for the primary grades, but the cursive retains loops and is difficult to write legibly. Also serifs (or what D'Nealian calls monkey tails) are added. Young children tend to distort them. For all of the other systems, including D'Nealian, the loops often get tangled by adults who want to write small enough for college ruled notebook paper.

In contemplating the idea of this chapter, I was wondering about the efficiency of a system that might be slower and more awkward than the common cursive. So when I examined John Holt's book, *Learning all the Time,* for review, his experience with a fifth-grade class caught my attention.[4] He was having the children compete with themselves in writing faster. After half a minute he would stop them and they would count how many words they had written copying the alphabet sentence, "The quick brown fox jumps over the lazy dog." Three of the students using manuscript printing were apparently writing faster than he could. "I must have counted wrong," he reports, "these ten-year-olds can't possibly write fat manuscript letters faster than my itty-bitty superspeedy cursive." He had them all take another timing while he made his own pen "fly." The results were the same, and two of the three were writing neatly!

Even more important than choosing an efficient system is realizing that developing good handwriting is still of great value.

Endnotes

1. Don Wallace, "Sending the Right Message," *Success Magazine*, April, 1989, p. 62.
2. Keith Schoville, *Sign, Symbol, Script,* University of Wisconsin, Madison, 1984, p. 82.
3. Barbara Getty and Inga Dubay, *Write Now* © 1991, by its authors. Used by permission. Further information on this book and on the *Italic Handwriting Series* is found in Appendix P under "Handwriting."
4. John Holt, *Learning All the Time* © 1989 by Holt Associates, p. 39. Reviewed in Appendix J.

32

Teaching Math

I have always admired Monroe Morford's ability to teach math, so I asked him to share some of his wisdom with you. The dialogue which follows was transcribed and edited from a cassette tape we made just for this book. Many people aren't successful in math. Monroe doesn't believe failure is necessary for normally alert people, and I agree. The textbooks you use will give you good ideas about what to teach, but as you "listen" to our discussion, try to learn how to help your child avoid the dead-end math street that has been the final destination for so many people.

Helping children understand math

(An interview)

Morford> The major thrust of what parents need to realize is that they cannot *teach* their children mathematics in the way that word is usually used. The best they can do is to provide the experiences from which the child will learn. In other words, they can't teach successfully by telling the child, "Now, this is what you are supposed to know." It isn't going to happen. At least not in a beneficial way. Children may remember what they've been told for a day or two, but that is not going to develop mathematics. What parents or teachers must do is provide the materials, the kinds of experiences with which the child may interact, and as a result, add new concepts to his previous understandings.

Wade> What pattern do parents or teachers sometimes use that doesn't result in genuine realistic learning?

M> Most textbooks start out very nicely by developing concepts with groups of items to be counted. Children get the idea that when they see four items that this means four, and that the word four is an abstraction, not of four apples or four oranges or four balls, but an abstraction that relates to all of those things. Then they start building on this. Kindergarten or first grade exercises ask children to draw circles around items or mark every group that has four items in it, for example. And this goes fine on over to a certain point. Then the children are shown, through these exercises, that with a group of three and a group of four, they end up with a group of seven. And this is written down for them: 4 + 3 = 7. Then most teachers just leave all of this concrete experience behind and feel, "Well, the child has seen it once. Now he's supposed to know it."

I think the parent must take the position that whenever the child does not come out with the seven having been given the four and the three to add together, that he not be told, "It's seven. Now remember it." This wrong answer is merely a signal to the teacher or the parent that the child has not grasped that reality yet. You must go back and go through the reality again, until the child gets the abstraction established. When he sees four objects and three objects, he must get through to the seven, by whatever mental processes it takes for him to tie them together. In other words, if he can't look at four and three and come through with a short-term seven, there's no point in just telling him the answer. You will then only

> *I've known* **Monroe Morford** *and his wife for a long time. In fact, they were teaching in Uganda when my young family lived in the neighboring country of Rwanda. Since our dialogue for this chapter occurred, he has spent a number of years in Egypt teaching in a Christian school and a year and a half in south Sudan starting a secondary school. He now lives in Northern California.*

transfer him over to trying to remember, which is not going to build his understanding.

W> Would you say then that teaching needs to be for the purpose of understanding meaning?

M> All teaching must make sense, and providing practice must go along with explaining. Whenever you recognize that the student is not able to do the exercise–to put into practice what you thought he had learned, go back and provide the realities to go through the learning again.

W> This sounds like what we called new math a few years ago, where the designers of the mathematics curriculum were very theoretically oriented and wanted the children to know the fundamental meanings of mathematics, feeling that that was much more important than all the drill and exercise. They caused a great revolt which is still going on in the back-to-basics movement.

M> Knowing the fundamental meanings was the intent of the modern mathematics concept but it isn't what the movement produced. It produced some very precise mathematical language stuck back into first, second, third, fourth grade which the teachers didn't understand and only gave as more stuff that the kids had to remember rather than as a set of activities through which they were to learn the concrete ideas. That's what went wrong with new math. Many teachers like me were teaching modern mathematics or new math ten years before it got out in books, and are still teaching it today using now the more fundamental – as the word is used – back-to-basics textbooks. We just continue to do what we have always done – to teach kids to look at reality and think and know why.

W> Do you see any danger in the extreme position of the back-to-basics movement?

M> Oh, yes. Because it will merely give the people who have always said drill-drill-drill more chance to beat kids over the head. This will produce in children who have enough determination on their own to find out why, a little faster action. They will come through with a little more precise reactions in their work. This will be true for maybe the top twenty percent of kids who will think in spite of the teachers rather than because of them and will come up with their own reasons why they are able to see it through. And it will also produce at the other end a lot more frustrated kids who are just anti-mathematics because they get totally frustrated with trying to remember what they are supposed to remember but can't. The drill is supposed to be producing more results, and it's producing less for all but this top group. For the majority, it's only more confusion and more frustration.

W> Would you say that too much drill is probably not a good thing – learning number facts and so forth?

M> First, I want to pick apart your words. Too much drill without understanding merely causes frustration. Not enough practice after understanding will leave it not well enough developed. There's nothing wrong with practice. Practice is good. But drill without understanding is debilitating to the mind just like bad food is to the stomach.

W> That makes sense to me.

M> Let's say that an individual has a set of cards – multiplication facts, addition facts, or whatever – and he's holding them up giving the child one or two seconds to respond. Maybe he has a ticker set up and every time it ticks he lays one down and picks the next one up. The person giving the drill may be keeping track by laying them into separate piles–the ones the child knows and the ones he doesn't. Nothing wrong with this. I do it with my grandchildren. I do it regularly with children I'm working with. Whether you are helping develop concepts or giving meaningless drill is determined by what happens when you've gone through and you've given them their second or two seconds or whatever it is that you're allowing them per card. And you have your stacks of the ones that they knew and the ones that they didn't know. Now what do you do afterwards? That's the critical issue.

Suppose you pick up the pile the child didn't know and start going through them again, and the child isn't able to respond within the period of time. You can see him start counting on his fingers, or whatever else you don't want to happen. Now what's your action? If for example, one of these cards you hold up is eight and seven, and the child doesn't know eight and seven are fifteen. So you say, "Fifteen." Nonsense! You haven't helped him. You've only frustrated him. He may remember now that you told him it was fifteen, but that doesn't help. It only creates more fear and frustration. He's going to forget it again next time.

W> All right, what would you do instead?

M> Instead, I would go back to whatever basic concept I had been using with the child to help him gain a reality. Up to ten probably you deal with looking at objects and counting them up. The child who can conceptualize combinations up to ten, will do so through some reality handling of the situation. When you get above ten, he's got to move to some kind of an abstraction or else count fingers. And thereby, he must move into a two-step process of some sort. If you're back at the three-and-four stage, you lay down again the three and the four and let him look at them and count them up and establish whatever reality he makes of it. This is something you can't establish for him, although you may help him a little bit.

If, for example, you know he knows what five is – he can see five all right without having to count it up – then maybe you take one of the three and stick it over with the four, completing a five and leaving the two from the three. Then with the two and five he comes to the seven. This is one way of helping him establish his reality of whatever the problem is. In the end, he will probably do it on his own, because most children do. The reality situations up through ten they figure out some way in their own little minds – putting things together that they understand, and it comes through because they can see it.

But now, let's go back up to the eight-and-seven situation. Instead of saying "The answer is fifteen," you ask the child, "How many more do you need with the eight to finish up a ten?" He will say "two more." All right, where are you going to get that two more? From the seven. Okay, take the two from the seven and what's left? Five. What does that make? He'll come up with the fifteen.

As an alternative, dominoes with up to five dots per side or score-keeping tally marks can help build reality relationships. For example, by placing a 5|3 and a 5|2 side by side the child can visualize 8 + 7. This is then the same as 5| + 5| and |3 + |2, the two fives making ten with the three and two added for fifteen.

In preparing for this, the child must be encouraged to line up dominoes to match corresponding pairs. For example, 5|1 for 6 and 5|2 for 7 are compared to 5|4 for 9 and 5|5 for 10. This way he gets a feel for what happens as more dots are in the combinations.

Returning to the problem of recognizing the sum of 7+8. If you feel he didn't follow that through too well, maybe you want to go back and ask him the series of questions over again. As he lets this turn around in his mind three or four times, it becomes hisvreality, so the next time he sees seven and eight his mind takes that cycle, in maybe a second and a half. The next time he does it, it may take three-quarters of a second. The next time it happens in a tenth of a second. In other words, after several cycles of that set of thinking he comes out with it as though he had memorized it. But he actually has built up a mental pattern that works for him to develop it.

W> Would you say that some of the

number combinations, for example, the ten and the five, are more easily conceived and therefore remembered than other number combinations such as the seven and the eight.

M> Oh, yes. It always is, because the child has ten fingers, five on each hand. He has gotten used to that; that's a reality with him. He doesn't have any trouble with ten and five making fifteen because he's done that with his own fingers.

W> Of course, he's counted by tens. That's the same as counting by one's except with the zeros.

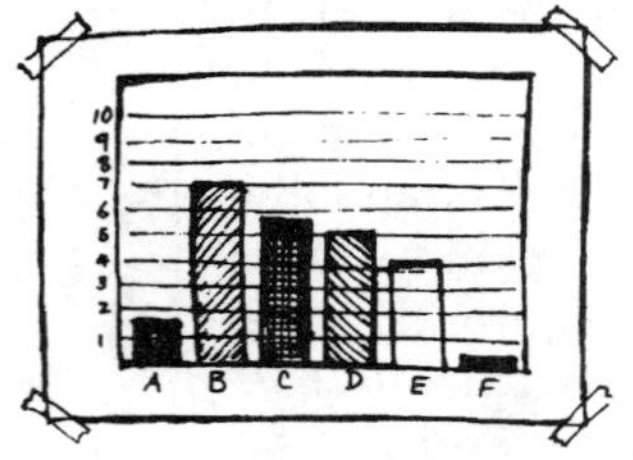

M> Exactly. And this is, of course, what he deals with. These are the realities. And you don't have him memorize ten, twenty, thirty, forty. You have him look at it and get a connection between the words of two and twenty, three and thirty, four and forty, and let him build up his own meaning of counting by tens.

W> Then are you saying that, because some number combinations are more easily understood and remembered than others, we might best teach those more complicated number combinations by relating them to the simpler ones?

M> Always. This is the whole issue, I think, in mathematics instruction – if you want to call it that – carrying out some kind of experience that a child grows from. And to me, you see, this is where teaching methods are quite different. Some people – in fact, most people – would say when you're teaching them you tell them what the answers are and they're supposed to remember. Or you tell them how they're supposed to think. Mathematics instruction is not telling them how they're supposed to think, but finding out what they do think and helping them tie in new ideas. You may choose what you supply to them as the next thought of development so that it will lead them into patterns of thought that you want, but you don't tell them, "Now this is the way you think." Because then you have started taking them out of reality again and told them, "Now you do it my way." You've got to lead them if you want them to do it your way; you've got to lead them to right understanding from where they are through some logical thought of their own.

If the teacher does not understand the child's physical and emotional maturity level, he may try to toss ideas to the child that are like his own, but the child may not yet be ready to work with them. So knowing the child's viewpoint is very important in tying new learning to already established reality.

This is where the whole idea of the psychological development, that Piaget's research has shown us, fits in. You must recognize developmental levels as important steps and not try to jump ahead of them with your instruction.

Up to this point, early learning – learning number combinations – basically is all we've talked about. But the same idea carries on throughout. Any kind of experience the parent or teacher provides for the child to do should be connected with some kind of reality. For example, as we move on, instead of just saying to the child, three times four is four three's added together or three fours added together, you give him pennies or dimes or something else in a pile on the table. Then you move out four, then four more, and four more beside them, thereby having a group of twelve in the combination of three groups of four. Then moving on through other multiplication facts he continually repeats this idea until, whenever he sees any two numbers multiplied together, he immediately thinks of them in terms of groups. He won't be working through this concept of adding groups his whole life, but he will make the move over to simply seeing the numbers.

W> It seems like much of mathematics is learning to do things easier. Perhaps if we try to help our children see math as fun ways to achieve easier results, that might help them see why it's important. For example, in multiplying four times three, it's a lot quicker to add by groups of three's than it is to count to twelve.

M> Before the child goes, for example, to multiplying seven times three, he has probably gone through the experiences of learning to add groups. Let's say he cannot remember three times seven but knows that three times four is twelve. And he knows that three and four are seven. And so his seven can be broken up into a three and a four. Then he can see how three times three is nine and three times four is twelve. Adding the nine to the twelve gets the twenty-one.

Now to the person who is saying, But that's a lot of work, why not just know that three times seven is twenty-one, I agree at the end result. But in the growing experience that going through those steps of thought is building up what I call electrical circuits in the brain. This is programming the computer so that it will do it instantaneously for him at a later point. And sure, that takes longer to go through than it does to tell him that three times seven is twenty-one. But, having that experience several times establishes a circuit in his brain which works for him. Many children, just counting by threes adding three to each number in their minds as they go along, will automatically build these electric circuits.

So the next day when you say to a child with this background, "What's three times seven?" his eyes roll a second and his mind retraces that counting. He doesn't go through now and count up, three, six, nine, twelve and so forth and add each time to do it. His mind established a pattern of thinking the previous day, and he says, "Twenty-one." He doesn't remember in the sense that we usually use that word, pulling it out of memory from having been told. His mind retraced the pattern of thinking and came out with the result. The child who has not established that kind of thinking doesn't have a memory pattern to turn to.

W> I think in my own experience, I understood the concept of what multiplying meant having seen it in some rudimentary examples such as three times four. Then I extended that and took the more complex combinations for granted and memorized them.

M> Well, I don't think you actually memorized them. I think, in your play time or whatever else as a child, your mind went back through those things and you just established those realities for yourself. The teacher didn't have to do it. In other words, people who have developed their mental capability just do these kinds of things. We plan our teaching assuming that everybody functions like these individuals who have had basic understanding built up for them.

My main point here is, everybody doesn't function like that. Some get to a certain level, and the pattern breaks. We keep teaching, assuming growth is going on, but it isn't. When we discover a problem we have to look for the point where learning stopped. As long as the child is moving on his own, fine, just let him grow. Keep tossing out new ideas for him to think about. But as soon as you see he isn't grasping an idea, that he's striving to pull it from somewhere because he's supposed to, this should be your signal to stop. Move back for him, trying to find out where his reality or clear understanding actually is and where you can tie in to begin building up the structure of understanding you assumed he had.

Of course, encourage him to make these realities all along. Suggest to him, for example, that maybe while he's going somewhere today he can look around at windows of a building and count them trying to see groups of two or groups of three, so he can begin to see certain reality patterns that you are trying to help him build.

W> Maybe we should bring in a point of how people learn. It's very possible for a person to understand something superficially – just understand it without having it internalized so that he thinks, yes, it looks reasonable. If the teacher doesn't recognize this difference between superficial assent to the reasonableness of a concept and understanding the concept well enough to be able to explain it, he could misjudge what learning is taking place. When the child says, "Yes, I understand," we are tempted to move quickly on to something else without going over the idea or coming back to it enough to establish it well.

Developing a multiplication table

X	1	2	3	4	5	
1	1	2	3	4	5	6
2	2	4	6	8	10	
3	3	6	9	12		
4	4	8	12	16		
5	5	10	16	20		
6	6	12	18			
7	7	14	21	28	35	

M> An important thought in this is that instead of asking the child, for example, to go back to the multiplication tables when he doesn't remember that six times seven is forty-two you can say, "Well, how do you think?" Don't ask him what's six times seven again. You just found out he doesn't know. Or maybe even after you told him it's forty-two, you turn around and ask him to see now if he remembers two minutes later. That is not helping the mental patterns. Ask him how he could get at six times seven. Let him verbalize to you what he understands. And if he can't come up with any logical thought process, then you know you're certainly in the dark to tell him what the answer is. He needs to come up with a way to work toward it. You've got to go back and help him build the pattern over again. Don't tell him what the pattern is, but have him build it. Because as soon as he's built it himself, even though he doesn't realize it, he will have a much better learning experience.

At this point multiplicaiton tables may be developed based on the idea of area. Let the child make his own. In the process thought patterns will be formed that bring about understanding and ability to remember.

It's the teacher's job to seek real things in the student's daily experience that can be handled, drawn and seen to which new ideas may be attached. For example, scores in a game are ideal for developing the concept of positive and negative numbers. Pick a game that your children know how to play and that has situations where they lose points for doing something wrong and can even "go in the hole" if they do wrong things often enough in comparison to doing right things. Then start watching the score. You gain four points this time; next time you gain three points; next time you lose five. Where are you? They know how to add up those scores. They have experienced it in their reality development; and when the idea of negative and positive numbers is tied to that game reality, they have no trouble remembering what to do with figures on paper.

W> Would you like to talk about asking questions?

M> Well, only to re-emphasize that, as far as possible, to help a child with a problem he can't attack you should use leading questions. You can ask, "What is it talking about? What have we done with that before? Can you make any sense out of the problem situation you're seeing?" So that rather than telling him what's going on or asking him to give specific answers to a problem, try helping him relate to his own thinking process so that he can conclude what he's supposed to do. Of course, I think this is important for any subject, not just for mathematics.

Going on then to another idea, it's very important that the teacher realize the sequence of topics which builds the structure of mathematics. When, for example, a child doesn't know the multiplication facts, you should question whether or not he knows the background items required to get them. You realize that before you can multiply, you have to know how to add. Before you can divide, you must understand the concepts of multiplication, and you must be able to reverse that concept. The best test to find out whether a child knows his multiplication facts is to ask him to tell you what possible numbers he could multiply together to get a certain number. For example, "What numbers would you multiply to get thirty-six?" Of course, the child should be able to come up with six times six, four times nine, two times eighteen–not immediately, but with some dwelling on the idea. He arrived at the fact that thirty-six was the result of multiplying four times nine. If he can do this throughout the multiplication tables, then you can be very confident that he knows his multiplication facts, and furthermore, that he now is ready to do division.

W> Then you can say, given thirty-six, if two is one of the numbers, what's the other one?

M> Then he is ready. Then division makes sense to him. He has no problem knowing what he is doing or why he is doing it. And when you go to fractions, if division has not been established as meaningful, then to talk about dividing by four or about finding a quarter of something won't make sense either. Or it will make sense only as far as he can mechanically cut up a whole into equal parts. A child can usually look at a thing and divide it up into six parts and so he can handle one-sixth. But when it comes to combining that one-sixth with two-thirds, unless he has this concept of division as being a dividing up into parts and then taking a certain number of those parts to formulate a fraction, there's no hope that the fractions are going to work correctly for him. The concept that division comes out of multiplication must be understood.

W> What part to you think that frustration has in math learning disabilities?

M> Frustration is probably ninety-nine percent of everybody's problems in mathematics. It's the frustration of not being able to remember and not having any way to go back and build.

W> Do you think perhaps frustration leads to a desire to avoid the topic in order to avoid some of the problems expected?

M> All human beings are animals biologically, and we respond as animals except as we consciously decide to do otherwise. We know from research on animal learning or animal deterrence, that desire to achieve a goal is completely canceled by frustration. The quickest way to stop a rat from wanting to run a maze is to formulate some kind of frustration in the maze. If he's frustrated, he will stop trying, even though he's half starving to death. Learning is the same. A person may want very much to learn, but he won't have the courage to get at it unless the frustrations can be eliminated.

Of course, my point of view is that anything not meaningful that you try to remember only frustrates because it immediately builds fears that you will forget. Fear causes frustration and frustration creates more fear and more desire to not come in contact with the subject.

Building foundations

I would like to add just a few thoughts to the discussion with Monroe Morford. First, on building foundations. In the chapter, "Planning for the Early Years," we discussed not pushing formal learning too early. This advice is certainly true in teaching mathematics. You probably won't have time to study developmental psychology, but you can recognize that small children think differently. You can be sensitive and perceptive. If your child isn't understanding, and he or she is under seven or eight years old, slow down. Young brains don't find it easy, for example, to see how something can change shape and still have the same total volume, and they can't easily imagine abstract things. In fact, the kind of abstract study required for algebra is difficult before the adolescent years.

Physical objects are important. Little kids need to touch, see, count and move around. One of the best ways to teach place value (the concept that digits are worth more the farther they are to the left in a number) is by using small sticks (Cuisenaire rods). You can buy them or make them. Help your child bundle some by tens. Ten bundles of ten are a hundred. Show how they are easier to count in bundles and how they are like the way we write numbers. Another way to discuss place value is with money. The pennies, dimes and dollars will show that one is worth ten of another.

You can make up the exercises. For example, looking through a catalog and laying out the money necessary to purchase some treasured item is both fun and educational. You can also buy or make sticks for teaching place value and understanding quantities. Get lots of them. They can be bundled in tens and in hundreds, or used to explain other ideas.

Visit a school supply store or look through educational materials catalogs to get other ideas. Appendix Q deals with mathematics.

Keeping skill from fading out

An advantage parents often think of for home teaching is that their children (always the brightest, of course) don't have to sit and be bored while the teacher drills and repeats to get the rest of the dumb class to catch on. As Monroe has told us, drill without understanding is debilitating, but practice (with understanding) *is* needed to get the idea nailed down. In my teaching and learning experience, knowing how to work a problem doesn't mean it's safe to go on. The know-how must be practiced a little more than would seem necessary, to keep it from blowing away in a storm.

Problem solving

Even kids who can accurately manipulate figures in long division and fraction exercises, often don't get to first base with simple word problems (story problems). Let's face it. Our society (partly through TV) teaches kids to be absorbers more than thinkers. For your child, you can be sure concepts are understood all along.

To line up figures in certain ways and to put digits in various places may get the "answer," but the "why" is important, too, as Monroe Morford told us. When word problems come in your textbook, go through them slowly enough for your child to make sense out of what you do. Children are tempted to feel (sometimes by the way we teach them) that when they get the result of their calculation, they have somehow achieved success in math. Just remember to press the idea that understanding is more important than coming up with the "right" number.

I read an article not long ago by someone who felt that word problems were irrelevant. You may wish your teacher had thought so, too. "If the stage-coach leaves Mosquito Junction at 4 p.m. going 28 km/hr, and. . . ." But who cares how long it took to catch up with the wagon train? And stage coach drivers didn't know about kilometers, anyway! Actually, the difficulty isn't so much with the stage coaches and times for getting a fraction of a job done. It's the temptation to try to remember whether to divide or multiply, when working a set of problems having similar situations. In other words, trying to learn a procedure without understanding what is going on.

Helping your child figure costs and quantities for a lemonade business is an excellent learning experience. Home life, however, just doesn't happen to provide for exercising some of the abstract thinking or the repeated application that apparently builds continuing competence in math.

I should qualify my concerns. Any time you can find a good live situation for practicing math, by all means put it to work for you. It will be more appealing and better remembered than the book problems. Just don't imagine that you can toss the book out the window unless you are sure you have taught and reinforced all the skills needed for a good mathematical foundation.

Perhaps even more important than learning mathematical processes taught by certain word problems, is developing skills for tackling complex situations – for analyzing them and using what is known to find out what isn't.

In a side bar, I'll suggest a list of steps in the logical process of solving word (or story) problems. As you can see, they are more appropriate for upper grades or high school. If your concern is lower grades, however, study it anyway. Understanding the principles yourself will help you get the right approach to guiding your child. Not everyone will use this same attack. Sometimes steps can be skipped. But seeing a sensible plan will help you help your child conquer word problems.

How to Solve a Word Problem

1. Understand the situation without much concern at first for the numbers.
2. Identify the question. Know what you are looking for.
3. Think backwards if the problem is very complex. Remembering what you are looking for, ask yourself what you would need to know to find that answer. Then look at your problem again to see what information you actually have.
4. If some of the needed information is missing, see if you have other facts that would, in an added step, lead to the missing information for the basic solution.
5. If you are in a blind alley, back up and look at your question again. Does the given information prompt you to think of a different way to get to your answer?
6. Draw a sketch of the situation. This can help you visualize relationships in the problem.
7. If you think you have found a plan for solving your problem but aren't too sure, try it using very simple numbers — numbers you can think through to a solution without getting bogged down in the calculations. If your process works, you likely have a good plan.
8. Carry out your plan, with careful attention to calculation accuracy.
9. Compare your solution with the "question." Is what you came up with actually what was requested in the problem? Have you used the correct units of measure to express your answer?
10. Examine the numerical value of your solution. Does it make sense in terms of the reality of the problem situation?
11. If you can, use a check method to verify your solution.

Computers

First let's talk about calculators. They are really special-purpose computers. And they are now a permanent part of our world. Kids should know how to use them, but that doesn't take long. Although your children may have less need than your generation has for pencil-and-paper calculation, that skill is still important. Your children won't learn it if they use calculators all the time. You need a firm policy. I suggest you permit calculators to check exercises already worked (with mistakes corrected by hand) and whenever you or the textbook specifically calls for them.

Computers are becoming more prevalent and less expensive. They aren't taking the place of books and they won't. Your child will need to know something about them to face the world he or she is preparing for. "Computer literacy" is a topic which may fall into the school subject category of math. Newer textbooks will deal with it. If yours doesn't, get some information from your library or a local bookstore or from a computer store.

I won't try to tell you about them here except to say that most information you will run across will come under categories of (1) knowing what they can and can't do, (2) knowing how to operate them, and (3) knowing how to program them. The first two aren't difficult to know something about. The third – programming or telling them how to "think" – although not as important as the first two, is worth adding to your curriculum. Only a few people in our society need to be experts in this area, but more of us need to know enough to work intelligently with a programmer and to write simple programs or to make minor modifications. And the building of a logical procedure for telling the computer what to do (which is what a computer program is) builds reasoning skills.

As teaching instruments, I don't believe computers will take over the job of textbooks, although we are beginning to see some real changes. More and better software is appearing. For most home schools, however, learning by computer is still somewhat limited by its expense.

One lady told me how excited she was about home schooling. She felt that she would just get a computer to do the teaching while she went off to work! Sorry, it doesn't work that way. Even if finances aren't a consideration, computers can teach efficiently only a fraction of what kids need. If you have access to a computer and the appropriate software (programs) by all means use them, but view them as a supplement to your main program.

A computer could be an asset to your home school in several ways:

- Teaching programs in many areas (not just math) provide interaction and feedback.
- First hand experience would better prepare your child to face the world which uses computers extensively.
- Word processing software (prepared instructions you can feed into your computer to tell it how to receive and handle words) is a convenient writing tool as long as your child still has ample practice in handwriting neatness. A spelling checker (now a part of the word processing package) may also teach if used conscientiously.
- Computer programming (the writing of coded instructions to tell your computer how to manipulate information you will give it) is an interesting challenge and provides practice for organized, logical thinking.
- The novelty of thought interaction with a machine brings added interest to your home school.

Computer games may subtract more than they can add to your child's education. Consider the hours they absorb and what most of them teach about kindness to others. I'm not making a blanket condemnation but would like to encourage you to think it through.

Curriculum standards

The National Council of Teachers of Mathematics has published curriculum standards for changes their study groups feel should occur in mathematics instruction. They believe the changes are needed to prepare people for a more technological society and to enable them to extend their learning. Five general goals for children in grades K–12 are:

(1) that they learn to value mathematics,
(2) that they become confident in their ability to do mathematics,
(3) that they become mathematical problem solvers,
(4) that they learn to communicate mathematically, and
(5) that they learn to reason mathematically."[2]

This calls for a variety of experiences including opportunities to explore, guess, and correct mistakes; also to conjecture and to defend value judgments.

The study groups have outlined what ought to be added or given more emphasis and, realizing that only so much can be taught in the school year, they have also suggested what is less important. Basically they want to move toward more realistic learning – realistic in helping children be able both to make sense out of mathematics itself and to apply it more directly to real situations.

I'll extract here only a few high points from the rather detailed report. These aren't intended as a full curriculum scope chart, but you may find them helpful in selecting materials. And I hope you will look for ways to implement some of them whether the program you are following covers them or not.

For grades K - 4 Increased attention should be given to: number sense, estimation, understanding the meaning of operations (addition, subtraction, multiplication, division), meaning of fractions and decimals, mental computation, reasonableness of answers, selection of appropriate computational methods, geometric relationships, spatial sense, process of measuring, use of variables to express relationships, word problems with a variety of structures, looking for patterns and exploring chance (how often a random event would occur).

Less emphasis would be given to: early reading, writing, and ordering numbers symbolically, practicing special-case operations (subtraction without renaming, long division without remainders), complex paper-and-pencil operations, and use of clue words to determine which operation to use.

In teaching you would emphasize: manipulative materials, discussions, explaining why mathematical processes work, writing about mathematics, solving problems to teach principles, and use of calculators and computers. You would place less emphasis on worksheets, rote practice, and memorization of rules (number facts still need to be memorized).

Grades 5 - 8 You should expect more emphasis on: pursuing open-ended problems and problem-solving projects; formulating meaningful questions to attack problem situations; reasoning skills (in spatial contexts, with proportions and from graphs); practice inductive and deductive reasoning; relating mathematics to the outside world and to other school subjects; sensing the meanings of numbers and operations; using estimation; understanding proportion, percent, and fractions; seeing and using functional relationships (how one mathematical event affects another); understand algebraic variables, expressions and equations; the use of a variety of methods to solve linear equations; informal investigation of inequalities and nonlinear equations (ones with exponents); analysis by statistical methods; use of models to understand probabilities; using geometry to solve problems.

Less emphasis would be given to: routine one-step problems and those categorized by type (coins, age problems, etc.); worksheets; relying on answer authorities; memorizing rules; tedious pencil-and-paper computations; learning procedures, such as cross-multiplication, without understanding; and memorizing formulas and vocabulary.

As a teacher you would involve your students in active exploring, conjecturing, analyzing and applying mathematics; using the computer and other technology. You would be more a facilitator of learning than a fountain of information. You would place less importance on memorization.

Grades 9 - 12 The major new proposal for high school mathematics is a core curriculum where all students are exposed to certain key topics. Students with stronger backgrounds and who expect to attend college cover the areas in greater depth and for all four years. This will take a few years to transform the schools and when it does, I expect that we will still have courses with much the same labels. The big difference will be more integration and crossing the lines between the areas of study. In the meantime, look in the directions outlined below for differences that will improve the mathematics your youth studies.

For algebra: You would change the emphasis by expecting students to: use real-world problems in learning theory; use the computer to aid understanding and to solve problems; explore number systems; and learn matrices and their applications. Less emphasis would be given to: word problems by type (coins, digits, completion of work, etc.); factoring; logarithm calculations; determinants in systems of equations; and conic sections.

For geometry: Increased attention would be given to integration with other study areas and real world modeling; coordinate and transformation approaches; deductive arguments expressed in words; and three-dimensional figures. Less attention would be given to Euclidean geometry as a complete axiomatic system; proofs of various kinds; inscribed and circumscribed polygons; and analytic geometry as a separate course.

For trigonometry: Students would use scientific calculators and computer graphing utilities. They would emphasize connections among the right triangle ratios, trigonometric functions and circular functions. They would spend less time verifying complex identities, use of tables and interpolation and with paper and pencil solutions of trigonometric equations.

For functions: Expect integration across all topics and grade levels; connections among a problem situation, its model as a function in symbolic form, and the corresponding graph; functions checking the reasonableness of graphs; and functions modeling real-world problems.

Outcomes

Your math instruction guide should list appropriate expectations for your teaching. Take time to examine them and to discuss them with your students. Mathematics is important for several of the general goals I list elsewhere in this book. I just want to point out that, although math appears to be the least likely subject for expecting moral values goals, there are several. Don't forget to tie them into your teaching. I would list: honesty, accuracy, respect for property (your own, other people's, and God's), a sense of the value of time, and responsibility for providing and using resources wisely.

Prepare your children to experience the pure pleasure of mastering the abstract. As a bonus, they will achieve the practical competence for handling numbers which is so important for the complete individual.

Endnotes

2. *Curriculum and Evaluation Standards for School Mathematics*, © 1989, p. 5 and elsewhere, The National Council of Teachers of Mathematics, Inc., (1906 Association Dr., Reston, VA 22091), See my review of Open Court *Real Math*• in Appendix Q.

33

Teaching Science

Children in our modern society face a mostly artificial environment – from Big Bird and cartoons, to junk food, to competitive sports. Science can open the door to the real world, and kids usually enjoy the experience.

What is science?

Science is observing and explaining nature. It's looking for interesting situations and events, then trying to explain cause-and-effect relationships or checking out someone else's explanations.

We study science as *process* and *content.* Process describes the ways of exploring science. Content tends more to be the facts and explanations – the end results of the process. From process, we learn how to think. Content is what we think about.

The process skills are: observing (measuring, testing); interpreting (reading between lines, explaining); classifying (organizing, comparing); communicating (getting and giving information, using numbers to express and analyze values); and predicting (explaining, making theories, testing hypotheses, judging importance).

The content part of science is obviously descriptions of objects–maybe the different kinds of blood cells or the metals that can be easily magnetized. It also includes purpose and relationships: What do the white blood cells do in the body? Where do they come from?

Then considering the process aspect, we see that the science class has more to offer than information. The process skills are important for perceptive thinking. They are ways to learn and understand the facts of science, they are skills used by the scientist, and they provide skills for relating to knowledge outside the area of science.

Why science belongs in your home school

A study of science can help develop attitudes of enjoying and conserving earth's natural resources and a respect for the One who provides them for our happiness. In studying nature we see the hand that made and guides all things. We already mentioned the importance of developing rational thought processes. Knowledge is important, too. Knowledge includes specifics, processes, concepts, generalizations and unifying principles.

Deciding what to teach

You can teach smorgasbord style, just bringing in interesting things whenever you find them, but after the preschool or early grades I recommend using textbooks. Get ones you like. If evolutionary concepts are objectionable to you, look for them before making your choice. Then use your books as a general guide, but don't feel you need to cover everything. Add learning from field trips and explore questions that come up. Invite people with knowledge in science areas to come in.

My older son, Tim, was five or six when I took him down into the mechanic's pit where I had been changing the oil in our car in Africa. We talked about how the engine turned the drive shaft which turned the axle to make the wheels go around. We traced the path of the exhaust and talked about what the muffler did. He was totally interested, and absorbed more than I thought he would. He learned about cars and wheels while I learned about children.

The study of science content (natural

science, not social science) may be divided into the general areas of: (a) life science or biology (botany, zoology and health), (b) physical science (chemistry and physics), (c) earth science (geology and weather), and (d) astronomy.

The process part of science is more prominent in the elementary grades. Beginning at the junior high level, the laboratory and special exercises cover process skills without identifying them particularly.

Through the sixth grade, textbooks are generally divided into units featuring topics from the various general areas. Often the three junior high years will cover the areas of life science, physical science, and earth science; although biology sometimes comes into grade 9. Students not headed for college often take only "general science." Physics and chemistry are usually electives in the senior high years. Also see Appendix G, "Typical Course of Study."

How to teach science

We have already suggested using textbooks as resources and for part of what you cover. As a busy teacher, you won't have as much time as you would like for adventures such as finding bird's nests. But do make science more than reading the chapter and answering the questions at the end.

Kids enjoy laboratory time. For elementary school, this is much simpler than what you might remember from your high school or college chemistry class. Your textbooks will give you ideas. Don't try to perform every experiment suggested. Just have your young scholar help you pick a few that seem especially interesting. You may have to buy a candle or a magnet, but most experiments won't use exotic equipment. And remember that labs are for exploring. Refrain from explaining too much. Ask leading questions. Guide your children in finding answers.

Projects are worthwhile if they don't run away with too much time. Help guide their design to avoid unproductive busywork. Plan to have your child participate in a science fair if a nearby school is having one.

News magazines include a science section. Add appropriate reports to your study sources. Consider subscribing to a science periodical published especially for schools.

Field trips are great learning experiences. We discuss them in the chapter entitled "Enrichment Resources."

The next chapter tells you much more about teaching science.

Science for preschoolers

Small children are naturally curious. Teaching them science means providing things to investigate and asking questions to keep them from wandering off too quickly. For instance, where do ants go? what happens to ice when it melts? Go for nature walks and watch for interesting things. Find nature books in the library. Your older children will like the nature adventures, too. They can help plan them.

Concepts for character

Jesus, the master teacher, used parables effectively for adult audiences. Spiritual truths were associated with the common things in nature – sheep, weeds, grapevines, flowers, even the weather. Later as the people saw the objects again, the lessons would come back to their minds. As you work with your children, be alert to opportunities to draw parallels between nature and life principles. For example, think what might be taught from an experience with poison oak or poison ivy, considering the delay between contact and reaction. Such lessons don't require long discourses, just a sincere comment at the right time. Your child, if old enough, will enjoy discovering object lessons. You can discuss them together.

The changing science curriculum

Brian Ray also deals with this topic briefly at the end of the next chapter. If your time is limited you could skip over the discussion here for now. (But come back when you can, or have your student read it.)

In becoming a better home teacher, you should know about the thinking of science curriculum makers because: (1) Although you are probably using a textbook or an instructional package, it's well to consider the recommendations discussed here as you think of directions for enrichment – for ideas that can make science more practical for your child's future. (2) Knowledge in this area can give you ideas for evaluating the curriculum materials you select. Of course, reading a few paragraphs here won't make you a curriculum expert, but it can help you ask some of the right questions.

The American Association for the Advancement of Science has set up a national council for what they call "Project 2061." (The year 2061 is when Comet Halley is to return. Your children will likely see it if this old world lasts that long). The council has completed the first phase of its work. They have outlined goals for what they feel is scientific literacy. The recommendations look good to me. Here they are, stated in very general terms:

❄ Being familiar with the natural world and recognizing both its diversity and its unity.

❄ Understanding key concepts and principles of science.

❄ Being aware of some of the important ways in which science, mathematics, and technology depend on one another.

❄ Knowing that science, mathematics, and technology are human enterprises and knowing what that implies about their strengths and limitations.

❄ Having a capacity for scientific ways of thinking.

❄ Using scientific knowledge and ways of thinking for individual and social purposes.

These recommendations are expanded in a book available from the AAAS.[1] They are more briefly stated in several pages of a summary booklet from which I am quoting (and which I recommend).[2] They are to give direction for grades K – 12. And they are described under the following areas of understanding:)

The scientific endeavor. It is felt that everyone should know how the use of science relates to life. This understanding necessarily involves mathematics and technology.

Scientific views of the world. Science knowledge makes the world more comprehensible and interesting, although everyone does not need the same level of understanding of concepts and principles.

Perspectives on science. Scientific literacy includes understanding science in the light of cultural and intellectual history and knowing about some special ideas that involve science, mathematics, and technology.

Science habits of mind. These include positive attitudes, reasoning skills, computational ability, observation and communication skills, and critical-response skills.

Many of the topics already being taught in science classes are included in the new recommendations, and new areas have been added. The emphasis is not on learning more, but on learning better.

"One difference is that boundaries between traditional subject-matter categories are softened and connections are emphasized. Transformations of energy, for example, occur in physical, biological, and technological systems. . . .

"A second difference is that the amount

of detail that students are expected to retain is considerably less than in traditional . . . courses. Ideas and thinking skills are emphasized at the expense of specialized vocabulary and memorized procedures. . . . The council believes, for example, that basic scientific literacy implies knowing that the chief function of living cells is assembling protein molecules according to instructions coded in DNA molecules, but that it does not imply knowing such terms as "ribosome" or "Deoxyribonucleic acid."

These recommendations would not limit deeper study by capable and intersested students, but they set a broad base for that continued education, and they outline the learning for life preparation which everyone needs.

For the committed Christian, a fourth connecting area of understanding enters the scene: *a knowledge of the Creator through His Word and His nature.* In fact, only in the light of divine science do natural science, mathematics, and technology have real meaning.

Success

You don't need to know all about science to be a good science teacher, although preparation is certainly recommended. The most important way to get kids to learn is to get them interested. For them to be interested in a topic, you must be, and you must show interest in their discoveries and projects. This is particularly true for science.

Endnotes

1. *Science for All Americans,* Summary, pp. 4, 5. American Association for the Advancement of Science, 1989. AAAS Books (Dept. 2061), P.O. Box 753, Waldorf, MD 20604.

2. *Science for All Americans,* Integrated Report, AAAS, $14.50 (Plus tax if MD).

34

More on Teaching Science

Brian D. Ray

The curiosity that is characteristic of young children should continue long into life. You can strengthen this natural gift and enhance thinking skills by helping your students understand the nature of science and by engaging them in the "scientific enterprise." Science involves (1) a body of knowledge, (2) a way of thinking, and (3) a way of investigating. Believers in God find it exciting to realize that He invites their investigation of the natural world He created. The unfolding of His handiwork calls forth their praise and honor.[1]

Courage from research

Science appears to be one of the strongest subjects for home educated children when it comes to standardized achievement tests. Also there is research evidence that they develop formal thinking abilities earlier than average and have higher intentions to do science. I'm not sure exactly what caused these positive findings, but it just may be that the home school environment is "a natural" for capitalizing on children's inalienable interest in the creation.

Science and thinking ability

As your children's interests mature, you will want to discuss their questions with them and help them find answers. Science educators point out that science may be the most ideal school subject for improving thinking ability because it emphasizes inquiry. You can, no doubt, appreciate this position from your experience answering questions like, "Where does the water in the faucet come from?" (From the reservoir; from the river or stream; from the fallen snow; from the sky; from the clouds; from the evaporation process from the ocean.) "Wow Dad! What is evaporation?"

Or, a public television program that refers to evolutionary theory which you don't accept may prompt questions about where whales and shrews and humans came from. This is your opportunity to study up and compare for your child the evolution model and the creation model as ways to explain the origin of life. (I personally believe that it serves our children and society well to make sure our students are knowledgeable about the major teachings of modern science, whether we agree with them or not. In fact, a critical examination of theories, and the information and assumptions upon which they are based, will give students a better grasp of science and honest thinking.)

Brian D. Ray *is president of the National Home Education Research Institute (See Appendix C). Since 1985 he has managed a clearing house for research information on home education. He holds a Ph.D. degree in science education and an M.S. in zoology. Brian and his wife teach their six children.*

Science as a body of knowledge

Modern science textbooks help expose your students to the generally accepted body of knowledge in the sciences. This is the first of the three aspects of science I identified earlier. You would not expect to select these knowledge concepts yourself unless you had recently studied a broad range of science topics. Texts let you know what the "experts" think science students should learn as they progress from age 6 to 18 and beyond.

Other ways to learn science as a body of information include lectures and television programs. Even fairly young students can learn from lectures, particularly if they are interested in the topic. Second, successful learning is more likely if they already have an organization of related information in their minds. Lectures are available at local colleges, libraries, zoos, planetariums, and museums. Make use of them.

Science as a way of thinking

In approaching science as a way of thinking, students should understand the *nature* of science. Scientists generally agree that the work they do is based on empirical data. However, the degree of objectivity practiced in the collection and interpretation of that data is subject to debate. Further, "science is based as much on assumptions as on facts, and a change in an underlying assumption may force a restructure of science just as a change in an axiom can force a restructure of geometry."[2] Science thinking also includes concepts such as inductive and deductive reasoning, cause-and-effect relationships, and evidence versus proof. As the teacher, you will be intrigued by reading about the philosophy and nature of science. If you have time for this advanced study you will be able to give your students a broader and richer understanding. Science as a way of thinking has both merits and limitations.

Science as a way of investigation

You and your students get to explore! Science investigation may involve demonstrations, laboratory studies, field trips, or science projects.

A demonstration serves to gain attention, illustrate a principle, or initiate further exploration by students. For example, you could place a few drops of blue food color dye in a clear glass of water and watch what happens over the next few minutes. You can ask your children to describe what they see. They can ask you questions or you can ask them. Then you discuss the process of diffusion. This could lead to a laboratory investigation of diffusion rates through different liquids (for example, hot water, salt water, and sugar water). To be prepared to answer some of their questions, you can study diffusion before the demonstration. Or you can ask and learn with them. A number of books are available on science demonstrations and "experiments."

Laboratory work immerses students in firsthand experiences which help them learn how to be scientific. Such activities must be a part of science in your home school. Experimenting is essential to the scientific enterprise. Laboratory work motivates learners by letting them experience science. It gives them opportunity to improve their science process skills. Process skills are those mentioned in the preceding chapter and others such as space/time relations, defining operationally, formulating models, controlling variables, and experimenting. Current science education books discuss these skills in detail.

I'd like to emphasize one very important aspect of the experimenting skill: the controlled experiment. Perhaps your children have noticed a relationship between the temperature of liquids on the stove and how fast bouillon cubes, sugar, gelatin, or other substances dissolve in the liquids. They could do some planned manipulation of an independent variable (temperature of 2 cups of water) and observe how it affects a dependent variable (time for a sugar cube to dissolve). They would hold the water at a certain temperature and see how many seconds were required. Then they would take another cube and repeat the process using fresh water at a different temperature, and so on. Careful record keeping is important. After examining the data they could end with a conclusion or final hypothesis about the relationship between water temperature and dissolving time. (The procedure could be repeated for a number of liquids and substances to be dissolved.)

In a simple controlled experiment, one variable (independent) is allowed to vary while all other factors are kept constant to determine how the manipulated variable affects the dependent variable. Controlled experiments are a powerful way to establish cause-and-effect relationships.

You may want to help your young scientist with controlled experiments in the biological realm. Maybe he has noticed that sometimes ants move slowly and sometimes they move fast. You could set up containers (some at room temperature, some a bit warmer, and some on cooling ice) to investigate the effect of ambient temperature on the activity level of ants. Then you could relate this to the regulation of body heat of various types of animals.

Long term science projects around home or participation in science fairs may also interest your students. These give them an opportunity to make plans in some detail. They will have to use foresight and begin to think beyond the 15 minutes of reading, the 5 minutes of demonstration and discussion, or the 60 minutes of a laboratory experiment. It also engages them in science activities that are more like what scientists actually do. Resources on projects and science fairs cover a range of topics such as insect and rock collections, to more complex experiments like the effects of ultraviolet radiation on the growth rates of algae, and designing an efficient solar water heater.

Inquiry

One approach to investigation is a process known as inquiry. Inquiry is the process of asking questions and seeking out answers. It involves observing nature, making predictions, manipulating variables, and verifying assertions. Inquiry means figuring things out, rather than being told. Inquiry often leads a student to "discover" principles. Although learning from textbooks is important and efficient, the skill of investigation is developed by also figuring out what questions to ask and where to seek the answers.

Field trips

There are many ways to go on field trips. For example, just pay to go to the local science museum and let the docents teach you and your children, or you might plan to visit a local river delta and spend hours ahead of time studying about plants and birds you might see. You might allow your students at the river delta to stop, look, and listen at will with no follow-up, or you could require taking a field book for observations of preplanned aspects of the ecosystem. Later they could discuss their experience and write about it, or they could do in-depth study of particular aspects. Field trips offer a wide variety of ways to get excited about science.

A science project for home schools

Gardening is convenient, economical, practical (for city and country dwellers alike), wholesome, appropriate to whole-family involvement at many levels, and it's loaded with opportunities to engage in science. But how do you relate gardening to science? Book stores and garden centers are replete with volumes on how to garden. Open to the table of contents of a "how to" book and you will find topics like soil chemistry, rotating crops, soil composition, cover crops, suitability of certain varieties to your climate, biological control of pests, and composting. You can probably guess from a list like this that there is much to discuss and learn in a simple vegetable garden.

Related to chemistry, you will learn about pH (that is, acidity and alkalinity) and getting it balanced in your soil. The topic of cover crops could develop your understanding of nitrogen fixation. Biological control will open a whole new world to you and your child concerning the beautiful balance in nature between pests and predators (or diseases). Practicing biological control in your garden might also make your vegetables safer to eat.

Finally, a garden just isn't complete if you aren't doing some semi-serious composting. Composting is a great way to improve your soil composition and learn about the roles of fungi and bacteria in the ecosystem. And if that isn't enough to thrill you, the giant earthworms and little red worms roaming in your compost will delight your preschoolers and perhaps motivate your older scientists to start a fishing bait business.

If you've never tended a garden before, consider starting small. Learn a little about growing food and related science principles. Later you can expand the project.

Science equipment

Some parents worry about the expense of equipment for teaching science. They imagine needing a fancy microscope, a computer hooked up to test instruments and loaded with experiment simulation software, a fancy chemistry set and much more. Of course it's nice to have a laboratory in your own home (and to share it with other families). But expensive equipment is not necessary to help your child be scientifically literate. He (or she) can certainly master knowledge without it. He doesn't need it for inductive and deductive reasoning, considering data, and discussing assumptions. Finally, experiments in the kitchen with household items, learning about and producing rich compost, and informative and enjoyable trips to a local park can all be done without expensive material aid.

STS

A current emphasis in science education is called science, technology, and society (STS). I already discussed the meaning of science. Technology is applied science. It's the translation of scientific knowledge into processes or products that may benefit people (for example, computer chips, nuclear reactors, chemical pesticides, and abortifacient chemicals). Science and technology both exert great influence on society. They have an impact on our lives. Many science educators believe that people should be scientifically and technologically literate. This includes the idea thsat they should be able to understand technology and thus be able to judge the appropriateness of its use. Such understanding involves the discussion of values and ethics in this modern society. Science educators don't all agree on whether STS should be a central theme of science education. You may think about it and decide for yourself. Regardless of your decision about the centrality of the STS theme, be aware that the study of science (and technology) will certainly raise questions in the minds of your students about the ethics and values involved.

You have exciting times ahead as you help your students experience the scientific enterprise. Stop with them to touch, smell, classify, hypothesize, experiment, and look in wonder at the creation about you. Use science to instill in them an awe for the Creator. They may one day use their knowledge of science to bring a stranger to the Lord, or to develop a new cure for a crippling disease. Get on with science!

Endnotes

1. Ruth C. Haycock, *Bible Truth for School Subjects Volume III: Science/ mathematics.* Whittier, CA: Association of Christian Schools International, Whittier, CA. 1981.

2. Alfred T. Collette and Eugene L. Chiappetta, *Science Instruction in the Middle and Secondary Schools*, Second Ed., Merrill Publishing Company, Columbus, OH. 1989. p. 31.

35

Teaching Social Studies

If we define education as preparation for life, then social science education is that part of the preparation involving an understanding of human relationships. For example, consider what is studied in several of the major social science branches: history – the development of civilization; government – the process of control and cooperation of social groups; economics – exchange of goods and services; and geography – how people relate to the land.

Social science education at elementary and secondary levels is called "social studies." The object is to expand children's understanding of how people live and relate to each other. It also lays the groundwork for continued study in the general knowledge area of the social sciences.

To the extent that teaching social studies helps prepare our children to resolve tension and misunderstanding in our troubled world, its value is obvious. And for those who feel a responsibility to share the Christian's good news with all the world, this area of study is even more important.

Standardized tests cannot reliably measure grade-level learning progress in social studies for lower and middle grades and, therefore, are not used much in this subject as an indication of overall scholastic achievement. This is because values (important learning for social studies) aren't measured with pencil and paper, and because understanding the concepts of the subject depends very little on sequence and thus not on grade level. Therefore, the fact that key testing for achievement focuses on math and language arts, does not imply that social studies is unimportant.

In this chapter we will (1) look at the development and rationale for the modern social studies curriculum, (2) discuss how you might plan for this area of learning in your home school, (3) consider the use of resources, (4) express concern about some recent approaches to teaching social studies, and (5) close with a note about teaching Bible.

We discuss more directly preparing children for good social behavior in the chapter, "Social Success."

The social studies curriculum

Traditionally, schools have taught geography as lists of cities, countries, mountain ranges, rivers, climates, exports and stereotypes of how people of other cultures lived and dressed. History has been mostly key people, wars and dates to relate them. By request of legislatures, classes in government were added to geography and history.

In the 1950s and early 1960s, the "new social studies" took over–or tried to take over–with the purpose of teaching concepts instead of disconnected facts. Of course, concepts had always been important, but few teachers or textbook authors had seen beyond the easily measured memorization of names and places.

The new course material was prompted by ivory-tower experts in the various social science disciplines and turned out to be a little tough and also seemed irrelevant for many elementary school kids.

Now, since the late '60s, educators have improved the curriculum by teaching how to use the basic concepts. Thus, the end purpose of social studies has become decision making. Discrimination, drug abuse, crime and war are irrational.

The new emphasis promised to help oncoming generations use better judgment. Although "perfect" social studies teaching won't bring world peace, the goal of learning to make rational decisions based on understanding is certainly better, in my opinion, than the traditional emphasis.

Decision making has meaning only in the context of concepts; and concepts are derived from facts. To take it a step further, understanding factual information requires certain skills. In social studies, these skills are: finding information in books, distinguishing between reality and opinion, interpreting maps, and so on. Putting all this together, you can see that to reach the goal of rational, informed decision making involving societal issues, our curriculum needs (a) instruction for developing information skills, (b) key facts of what is and what was, (c) concepts that make sense from the facts, and finally, (d) guidance in forming rational decisions by applying a set of values to the facts and concepts.

Of course, all this is a big order – too much to master in the first six or eight or twelve years of school. But by tipping the balance early toward concepts and skills, the foundation is hopefully set for the learners to apply information wisely in their life roles as members of family, business and social groups and as responsible citizens.

Social studies in your home school

I've sketched the usual curriculum approach and sequence of topics for teaching social studies, not because you have to do the same things in your own program, but rather to let you see what seems important to professional educators, and to broaden your consideration of goals you will want to keep in mind as you teach from day to day.

If your program is religiously oriented, you may want to bring specific values to your teaching in the areas of attitudes toward people, and principles for decision making. Later in this chapter when we discuss values and moral development, you may form more opinions along this line.

As I think about the whole curriculum for the elementary school, I feel that social studies would need less emphasis than some other subjects. It might best be "taught" informally for the first several grades. In fact, even the typical classroom

Study Sequence in U.S. Schools

The general areas covered in grades one, two, five and eight are usually the same across the country. We will list them and fill in with a typical pattern for the others.

K Self-discovery, people who help us, health habits. (Similar to first grade.)

1 Family, school, other cultures, safety, courtesy.

2 The neighborhood, the local environment.

3 The community, cities, business and industry, pioneers.

4 State government and history, regional geography, world cultures.

5 The United States: history (including recent history), geography, culture (including cultural problems), relating to neighboring countries.

6 The Western or Eastern Hemisphere. Usually selected examples and then generalizations.

7 The hemisphere not taught in the sixth grade or, more likely, world culture, world geography and nation groups.

8 U. S. history.

9 or **10** World history.

11 U. S. history.

12 U. S. government.

program is very low key for the early years. I suggest you center your teaching through grade two or three on experiences like field trips, learning to relate to relatives and friends, and on discussion. I do feel you need to plan, actually spend purposeful time, and keep a careful record. Your child will enjoy thinking of it as "school" but formal evaluation beyond progress notes in your log book would seem unnecessary.

By planning, I mean schedule a field trip or cultural television program every week or so on a somewhat regular basis. Then after each event, sit down and discuss it. A scrap book, souvenirs, or drawings could help make the experiences more meaningful. Read about field trips in the chapter on educational resources, and leaf through some lower grade textbooks to get more ideas of what to do.

After these early informal years, I suggest you follow a textbook or planned program but actively look for reasons to deviate from it. The reasons might relate to: (1) Unique characteristics of your community (a military base, a tourist town, a foreign country), especially if you are apt to move away. (2) Special needs of your child. (A death in the family could prompt a study of dying.) (3) Opportunities that arise. (Dad may need to attend meetings where your child could learn new things.) (4) Interests that develop. (An uncle may be elected judge, or friends may leave for mission service.) If you expect to omit part of a preplanned program, you will want to remember to arrange for the substitution.

Planning a unit on a special topic

Exploring a topic away from the path marked out by your textbook or guided learning program could turn out to be of little value unless you plan and follow through carefully. Work with your student to develop a project or unit plan. Consider including the following elements:

✓ *A title* to express the general topic or the initial point of interest. Your title might be the last part of the plan to be finalized.

✓ *Questions* to be answered. Some preliminary investigation may help you know what you might want as outcomes. Questions could be added or dropped as work progresses.

✓ *Skills* to be developed.

✓ *Attitudes* expected to emerge or be reinforced.

✓ *Resources* you expect to be used.

A brief description of the planned *culminating activity*. This will probably be a simple written report, but could instead be a slide show, a play, a map, a lecture or whatever seems appropriate. Some written record is especially important if there is a chance it may be needed to substantiate the validity of your home school.

✓ An expected *completion time.* Be realistic.

✓ *An evaluation,* particularly if attendance officials are breathing down your neck. Even if they aren't, your child will appreciate your appraisal, and expecting it will help him or her see the project as serious learning. Your evaluation may be very brief. It could be a note on the student report mentioning how well objectives (expressed as questions, skills and attitudes) were met and recognizing good work in particular areas. Consider evaluation (or participation in it) by someone outside the family.

Current events

A study of current events could add a little life to your social studies program. But as you can probably imagine, world watching without purposes in mind could easily become an exercise in gathering information pack rat style.

To make current events provide valuable learning, here are several possible outcomes to keep in mind:

🕑 Issues and actions in history

become more meaningful when related to similar situations today.

◷ Knowing what kinds of information the media offers and how to find them, opens channels for future learning.

◷ Careful guidance can bring a young learner a better perception of bias and objectivity in reporting. Ego-supported opinions, financial reward, political pressure and cultural background can be seen to affect all kinds of information provided for the public.

◷ The process of government operation can be illustrated by noting media reports of current activities.

◷ Variables that influence the ever-changing atmosphere of our society could be identified. These might include supply and demand, group or individual self-interest, protection of freedom, oppression from the strength of numbers of other sources of power, withholding or distorting information, possession and allocation of natural and financial resources, and so on.

◷ Value judgment may be practiced.

◷ Following a particular story over a period of time helps clarify the complex factors that influence human action.

Of course, the media also provides interesting information in areas other than social studies. You can think of ways all the subjects of the curriculum could be reinforced with attention to selected media excerpts. Especially consider how news events and reports can give meaning to your spiritual instruction by illustrating Bible prophecy, interaction between good and evil, and principles of justice and mercy.

I really haven't listed these possible outcomes to impress you with the complexity of teaching. The idea is that you should plan for meaning and purpose in your use of media reports. You probably won't use this list as a starting point. I see current events more as resources to reinforce important ideas from your teaching plan than as a separate subject to be studied. As concepts come up in your school program, look for reports of recent events to reinforce them. Occasionally you may also want to discuss principles not related to what you are currently studying when news items illustrate important lessons especially well.

In addition to radio, TV, newspapers and news magazines, several current events sources prepare material specifically for school use. World News of the Week is a poster-type publication dealing with a range of topics including: people, issues, careers, arts, science and recreation. Both the *Scholastic* and *Weekly Reader* families of classroom magazines provide resources for social studies (and for other subjects). Christian families will want to consider *God's World*. New York Times and Newsweek also publish materials for school use (although the Newsweek materials may be unsuitable for lower grades). See Appendix R for social studies resources.

Remember

☑ Being true doesn't make an event worthy of contemplation. Be selective. Give priority to character development. Material published for schools would be less objectionable than the public media in this respect.

☑ Current events may sometimes offer lessons of more importance than some of your regular program. Just keep your objectives in mind, and don't let the broader view get crowded out.

☑ Media sources alone cannot provide the structure of fundamental concepts you would expect to find in social studies curriculum materials published for school use. In other words, a subscription to a news magazine would hardly constitute a social studies program.

Other resources

In both my chapter on enrichment resources and Margaret Savage's "headpecker" chapter, you will find lists of resource suggestions. More could be added. As you consider a particular concept you want to teach, think also about where you might go to learn more about it.

If decision making is important in your curriculum as I have suggested, then seeing the process in action on real issues would be valuable. You could visit a legislative assembly or a city council meeting. Attendance at a public hearing may be worthwhile since it is a vehicle for citizens' voice in government decisions. Business and church board meetings probably wouldn't welcome visitors, but some church or civic *committees* might.

Also, it would be well to create the opportunity for your child to experience the role of committee member. Family council time teaches early lessons along this line, but for older children, it would be well to arrange for peers to help make group decisions. For example, the group could plan a joint family picnic. Supervise as appropriate, keeping quiet except to head off really serious problems and to help get everyone involved.

Values and moral development

Intelligent decisions are based on facts but also depend on value judgments. Thus in teaching young people to make wise decisions, educators have felt a need to help them choose moral principles and apply them to the factual information. The training emphasis stresses the importance of choosing and not what the choice should be (apparently because morality is the realm of church and not state).

According to the popular concept known as "values clarification," values are carefully selected after considering alternatives, then they are prized, and finally established by consistent application.

Sensing the importance of learning to make wise decisions, you will want to remember the idea of identifying values as you discuss societal issues with your children. For example, it is easy to decide what is right or wrong about the "equal rights" movement, but upon what value principles is the judgment based? Learning the historical facts about dropping the atomic bomb on Japan is of relatively minor importance without personally relating to the moral decision involved.

For those who recognize a source of authority – a standard of right and wrong – outside of humanity, I see several dangers in the values clarification process as it has been commonly understood: (1) choosing values in an atmosphere of neutrality teaches implicitly that the choice of particular values is unimportant as long as it is clear. (2) Even when teachers don't conceal their own values, students are urged to choose freely, and the teacher's bias could be an objectionable influence. And (3), although a child or youth may bring to school a good set of values from home training, peer pressure in a secular environment is often too great for the expression of values much different from the group norm.

Another recently popular concept related to decision making is Kohlberg's theory of moral development.* According to this idea, an individual moves through six stages to arrive at full moral maturity. Briefly summarized, they are: (1) Decisions depend on obedience, prompted by fear of punishment. (2) Personal benefit influences decisions. (3) Approval from authority becomes a motivating force. (4) Respect for authority and rules govern behavior. (5) Action is governed by a system of rules seen as reasonable. By cooperative agreement, the rules may be modified. And finally, (6) decisions are based on what the individual considers to be high ethical and consistent principles. Personal judgment, rather than exterior standards, guide behavior.

Kohlberg saw higher levels as better and believes children should be helped to advance from one stage to the next.

For the person who feels no particular responsibility to God, or for someone who believes that a relationship to God is independent from relationships to other people, this theory of moral development is a reasonable explanation. However, I see a subtle element of humanism. To me, the theory says that we gradually mature until, in stage 5, we intelligently conform to a standard we see as just. Then, as I understand the intent of stage 6, we "advance" to become our own standard of behavior.

By modifying this last stage as Kay Kuzma has done, we may outline the process in a form acceptable to people who recognize the authority of God. See her chapter, "Character Development."

The development of ideas I shared with you in the chapter, "Inspiring motivation," is a response to Kohlberg. I have related moral development to motivation or purpose. The first stage I call the *personal comfort stage.* Next is the *caregiver approval stage,* then the *selected friends stage,* and finally the *unrestricted stage,* which the majority of individuals never fully reach. Instead of developing to the point of independence from imposed standards, I see individuals as developing ideally toward unselfishness.

Bible in the context of social studies

If your school has a religious orientation, notice that many of the principles discussed in this chapter apply to teaching Bible. The topic is also discussed in the chapter on teaching values.

For example, Bible facts have meaning as they illustrate concepts, and concepts must lead to rational decisions. You might want to consider concepts in the areas of: (1) God's character – how He relates to us, (2) where we came from and how we arrived at our present condition, (3) His present and future purpose for us, (4) how we may choose to relate to Him, and (5) how we relate to others.

Then, returning to social studies and other subjects after studying the Bible, the values required for good judgment are clear and need not be pumped from a dry well.

Endnote

* Lawrence Kohlberg, "The Cognitive-Developmental Approach to Moral Education," *Phi Delta Kappan,* 56 (June 1975),

36

Introducing Geography

Carol Fromboluti

*This chapter was written for teaching young children. You will want to go beyond it for middle and upper grades geography. It has been taken from a small book prepared by the Office of Educational Research and Improvement, U. S. Department of Education.**

As you guide your children in the suggested activities, talk about them or ask questions appropriate to their level of understanding.

FOREWORD

Remember thumbing through an atlas or encyclopedia as a child, imagining yourself as a world traveler on a safari in Africa, or boating up the Mississippi River, climbing the peaks of the Himalayas, visiting ancient cathedrals and castles of Europe, the Great Wall of China? We do. The world seemed full of faraway, exotic, and wonderful places that we wanted to know more about.

Today, we would like to believe that youngsters are growing up similarly inquisitive about the world. Perhaps they are, but recent studies and reports indicate that, if such imaginings are stirring in our youngsters, they're not being translated into *knowledge*. . . .

Youngsters who grow up around maps and atlases are more likely to get the "map habit" than youngsters who do not. Where there are maps, atlases, and globes, discussions of world events (at whatever intellectual level) are more likely to include at least a passing glance at their physical *location*. Turning to maps and atlases frequently leads youngsters to fashion, over time, their own "mental maps" of the world – maps that serve not only to organize in their minds the peoples, places, and things they see and hear about in the news, but also to suggest *why* certain events unfold in particular places.

Helping every child develop his or her ability to use maps and to develop mental maps of the world ought to become a priority in our homes and schools. For, as we all know, our lives are becoming an ever tighter weave in interactions with people around the world. . . .

[The booklet from which this chapter is taken] is designed to help parents stir children's curiosity and steer that curiosity toward geographic questions and knowledge. It is organized around the five themes recently set forth by geographers and geography educators across the Nation – the physical *location* of a place, the *character* of a place, *relationships* between places, *movement* of people and things, and phenomena that cause us to group places into particular *regions*.

We encourage parents to get to the fun part –that is, the activities. The games, maps, and suggested activities that follow, while informal and easy to do, can help lay a solid foundation in experience for children's later, more academic forays into geography.

INTRODUCTION

Most of the suggestions in [the book from which this chapter was taken] are geared to children under 10 years of age. . . .

To help focus your awareness of the issues, we will begin each chapter with a brief description of the theme. This description includes examples of questions geographers use as they strive to understand and define the Earth, for geography provides us with a system for asking questions about the Earth.

LOCATION: Position on the Earth's Surface

Look at a map. *Where are places located?* To determine location, geographers use a set of imaginary lines that crisscross the surface of the globe. Lines designating "latitude" tell us how far north or south of the equator a place is. Lines designating "longitude" measure distance east and west of the prime meridian – an imaginary line running between the North Pole and the South Pole through Greenwich, England. You can use latitude and longitude as you would a simple grid system on a state highway map. The point where the lines intersect is the "location" – or global address. For example, St. Louis, Missouri, is roughly at 39° (degrees) north latitude and 90° west longitude.

Why are things located in particular places and how do those places influence our lives? Location further describes how one place relates to another. St. Louis is where the Mississippi and the Missouri rivers meet about midway between Minneapolis–St. Paul and New Orleans. It developed as a trading center between east and west, north and south.

Directions

To help young children learn location, make sure they know the color and style of the building in which they live, the name of their town, and their street address. Then, when you talk about other places, they have something of their own with which to compare.

✽ Children need to understand positional words. Teach children words like "above" and "below" in a natural way when you talk with them or give them directions. When picking up toys to put away, say, "Please put your toy into the basket on the *right*" or, "Put the green washcloth *into* the drawer." Right and left are as much directional terms as north, south, east, and west. Other words that describe such features as color, size, and shape are also important.

✽ Show your children north, south, east, and west by using your home as a reference point. Perhaps you can see the sun rising in the morning through a bedroom window that faces east and setting at night through the westerly kitchen window.

✽ Reinforce their knowledge by playing games. Once children have their directional bearings, you can hide an object, for example, then give them directions to its location: "two steps to the north, three steps west. . . ."

✽ Use pictures from books and magazines to help your children associate words with visual images. A picture of a desert can stimulate conversation about the features of a desert – arid and barren. Work with your children to develop more complex descriptions of different natural and cultural features.

Maps

Put your child's natural curiosity to work. Even small children can learn to read simple maps of their school, neighborhood, and community. Here are some simple map activities you can do with your children.

✽ Go on a walk and collect natural materials such as acorns and leaves to use for an art project. Map the location where you found those items.

✽ Create a treasure map for children

to find hidden treats in the back yard or inside your home. Treasure maps work especially well for birthday parties.

✽ Look for your city or town on a map. If you live in a large city or town, you may even be able to find your street. Point out where your relatives or your children's best friends live.

✽ Find the nearest park, lake, mountain, or other cultural or physical feature on a map. Then, talk about how these features affect your child's life. Living near the ocean may make your climate moderate, prairies may provide an open path for high winds, and mountains may block some weather fronts.

✽ By looking at a map, your children may learn why they go to a particular school. Perhaps the next nearest school is on the other side of a park, a busy street, or a large hill. Maps teach us about our surroundings by portraying them in relation to other places.

✽ Before taking a trip, show your children a map of where you are going and how you plan to get there. Look for other ways you could go, and talk about why you decided to use a particular route. Maybe they can suggest other routes.

✽ Encourage your children to make their own maps using legends with symbols. Older children can draw a layout of their street, or they can illustrate places or journeys they have read about. . . .

✽ Keep a globe and a map of the United States near the television and use them to locate places talked about on television programs, or to follow the travels of your favorite sports team.

Additional Activities

Children use all of their senses to learn about the world. Objects that they can touch, see, smell, taste, and hear help them understand the link between a model and the real thing.

✽ Put together puzzles of the United States or the world. Through the placement of the puzzle pieces, children gain a tactile and visual sense of where one place is located in relation to others.

✽ Make papier-mâché using strips of old newspaper and a paste made from flour and water. If children form balls by wrapping the strips of papier-mâché around a balloon, they will develop a realistic understanding of the difficulties in making accurate globes. They can also use papier-mâché to make models of hills and valleys.

PLACE: Physical and Human Characteristics

Every place has a personality. *What makes a place special?* What are the physical and cultural characteristics of your hometown? Is the soil sandy or rocky? Is the temperature warm or is it cold? If it has many characteristics, which are the most distinct?

How do these characteristics affect the people living there? People change the character of a place. They speak a particular language, have styles of government and architecture, and form patterns of business. How have people shaped the landscapes?

Investigate Your Neighborhood

✽ Walk around your neighborhood and look at what makes it unique. Point out differences from and similarities to other places.

✽ Show your children the historical, recreational, or natural points of interest in your town. What animals and plants live in your neighborhood? If you live near a harbor, pay it a visit, and tour a docked boat. You can even look up the shipping schedule in your local newspaper. If you live near a national park, a lake, a river, or a stream, take your children there and spend time talking about its uses.

✽ Use songs to teach geography. "Home on the Range," "Red River Valley," and "This Land Is Your Land" conjure up images of place. Children enjoy folk songs of different countries like "Sur Le Pont D'Avignon," "Guantanamara," and "London Bridge." When your children sing these songs, talk with them about the places they celebrate, locate them on the map, and discuss how the places are described.

Study the Weather

Weather has important geographic implications that affect the character of a place. The amount of sun or rain, heat or cold, the direction and strength of the wind, all determine such things as how people dress, how well crops grow, and the extent to which people will want to live in a particular spot.

❋ Watch the weather forecast on television or read the weather map in the newspaper. Save the maps for a month or more. You can see changes over time, and compare conditions over several weeks and seasons. Reading the weather map helps children observe changes in the local climate.

❋ Use a weather map to look up the temperatures of cities around the world and discover how hot each gets in the summer and how cold each gets in the winter. Ask your children if they can think of reasons why different locations have different temperatures. . . .

❋ Make simple weather-related devices such as barometers, pinwheels, weather vanes, and wind chimes. Watch cloud formations and make weather forecasts. Talk about how these describe the weather in your town.

Learn About Other Cultures

People shape the personality of their areas. The beliefs, languages, and customs distinguish one place from another.

❋ Make different ethnic foods. . . .

❋ Read stories from or about other countries, and books that describe journeys. Many children's books provide colorful images of different places and a sense of what it would be like to live in them. Drawings or photographs of distant places or situations can arouse interest in other lands. *The Little House in the Big Woods, Holiday Tales of Sholem Aleichem,* and *The Polar Express* are examples of books with descriptions of place that have transported the imaginations of many young readers. . . .

RELATIONSHIPS WITHIN PLACES: Humans and Environments

How do people adjust to their environment? *What are the relationships among people and places?* How do they change it to better suit their needs? Geographers examine where people live, why they settled there, and how they use natural resources. For example, Hudson Bay, the site of the first European settlement in Canada, is an area rich in wildlife and has sustained a trading and fur trapping industry for hundreds of years. Yet the climate there was described by early settlers as "nine months of ice followed by three months of mosquitoes." People can and do adapt to their natural surroundings.

Notice How You Control Your Surroundings

Everyone controls his or her surroundings. Look at the way you arrange furniture in your home. You place the tables and chairs in places that suit the shape of the room and the position of the windows and doors. You also arrange the room according to how people will use it.

❋ Try different furniture arrangements with your children. If moving real furniture is too strenuous, try working with doll house furniture or paper cutouts. . . .

❋ Ask your children to consider what the yard might look like if you did not try to change it by mowing grass, raking leaves or planting shrubs or trees. You might add a window box if you don't have a yard. What would happen if you didn't water the plants?

❋ Walk your children around your neighborhood or a park area and have them clean up litter. How to dispose of waste is a problem with a geographic dimension.

❋ Take your children to see some examples of how people have shaped their environment: bonsai gardens, reservoirs, terracing, or houses built into hills. Be sure to talk with them about how and why these phenomena came to be.

❋ If you don't live on a farm, try to visit one. Many cities and states maintain farm parks for just this purpose. Call the division of parks in your area to find out where there is one near you. Farmers use soil, water, and sun to grow crops. They use ponds or streams for water, and build fences to keep animals from running away.

Notice How You Adapt to Your Surroundings

People don't always change their environment. Sometimes they are shaped by it. Often people must build roads *around* mountains. They must build bridges *over* rivers. They construct storm walls to keep the oceans from sweeping over beaches. In some countries, people near coasts build their houses on stilts to protect them from storm tides or periodic floods.

❋ Go camping. It is easy to understand why we wear long pants and shoes when there are rocks and brambles on the ground, and to realize the importance to early settlers of being near water when you no longer have the convenience of a faucet.

❋ If you go to a park, try to attend the nature shows that many parks provide. You and your children may learn about the local plants and wildlife and how the natural features have changed over time.

MOVEMENT: People Interacting on the Earth

People are scattered unevenly over the Earth. How do they get from one place to another? *What are the patterns of movement of people, products, and information?* Regardless of where we live, we rely upon each other for goods, services, and information. In fact, most people interact with other places almost every day. We depend on other places for the food, clothes, and even items like the pencil and paper our children use in school. We also share information with each other using telephones, newspapers, radio, and television to bridge the distances.

Travel in Different Ways

❋ Give your children opportunities to travel by car, bus, bicycle, or on foot. Where you can, take other forms of transportation such as airplanes, trains, subways, ferries, barges, and horses and carriages.

❋ Use a map to look at various routes you can take when you try different methods of transportation.

❋ Watch travel programs on television.

Follow the Movement of People and Things

❋ Play the license plate game. How many different states' plates can you identify, and what, if anything, does the license plate tell you about each state?

You don't have to be in a car to play. You can look at the license plates of parked cars, or those traveling by when you are walking. Children can keep a record of the states whose plates they have seen. They can color in those states on a map. . . .

✽ Go around your house and look at where everything comes from. Examine the labels of the clothes you wear and think of where your food comes from. Why do bananas come from Central America? Why does the milk come from the local dairy? . . .

✽ Tell your children where your ancestors came from. Find your family's countries of origin, and chart the birthplaces of relatives on a map. You can plot the routes they followed before they arrived at their present location. Why did they leave their previous home? Where do all your relatives live now?

✽ Have your children ask older relatives what their world was like when they were young. They can ask questions about transportation, heating and refrigeration, the foods they ate, the clothes they wore, and the schools they attended. Look at old pictures. How have things changed since Grandma was a child? Grandparents and great aunts and uncles are usually delighted to share their memories with the younger generation, and they can pass on a wealth of information.

Follow the Movement of Ideas and Information

Ideas come from beyond our immediate surroundings. How do they get to us? Consider communication by telephone and mail, television, radio, telegrams, telefax, and even graffiti, posters, bumper stickers, and promotional buttons. They all convey information from one person or place to another.

✽ By watching television and listening to the radio, your children will receive ideas from the outside world. . . .

✽ Ask your children how they would communicate with other people. Would they use the phone or write a letter? Encourage them to write letters to relatives and friends. They may be able to get pen pals through school or a pen pal association. . . .

REGIONS: How They Form and Change

How can places be described or compared? *How can the Earth be divided into regions for study?* Geographers categorize regions in two basic ways – physical and cultural. Physical regions are defined by landform (continents and mountain ranges), climate, soil, and natural vegetation. Cultural regions are distinguished by political, economic, religious, linguistic, agricultural, and industrial characteristics.

Examine Physical Regions

✽ Help your children understand physical regions by examining areas in your home. Is there an upstairs and a downstairs? Is there an eating area and a sleeping area? Are there other "regions" in your home that can be described?

✽ Look at the physical regions in your community. Some neighborhoods grew up around hills, others developed on waterfronts or around parks. What physical regions exist in your hometown?

Examine Cultural Regions

✽ Take your children to visit the different political, residential, recreational, ethnic, and commercial regions of your city.

✽ Give children geography lessons by tying in with ethnic holiday themes. . . .

✽ Compare coins and stamps from other lands. They often contain information about the country. You may be able to find stamps from other countries where you work, or your children may get them from pen pals. Stamps tell many different kinds of things about a country, from its political leadership to native bird life.

✽ Learn simple words in different

languages. Teach your children to count to 10 in other languages. They can also learn simple words like "hello," "goodbye," and "thank you." Look at the different alphabets or script from various regions. All these activities expose children to the abundance of the Earth's cultural treasures. Many libraries have language tapes and books, some especially for children.

✵ If you have friends who are from different countries or have either traveled or lived abroad, invite them over to talk with your children. If they have pictures, so much the better. What languages do they speak? How are their customs or dress similar to or different from yours?

List of Basic Geography Terms

[As you do activities with your children, use words like these. Be sure they are accurately understood. Use a dictionary.]

Altitude	*Equator*	*Mountain*	*Reef*
Atlas	*Glacier*	*Oasis*	*Reservoir*
Archipelago	*Gulf*	*Ocean*	*River*
Bay	*Hemisphere*	*Peak*	*Scale*
Boundaries	*Ice shelf*	*Peninsula*	*Sea level*
Canal	*International date line*	*Plain*	*Strait*
Canyon	*Island*	*Plateau (or tableland)*	*Swamp*
Cape (or point)	*Isthmus*	*Physical feature*	*Topography*
Cartographer	*Lagoon*	*Population*	*Valley*
Continent	*Lake*	*Prime meridian*	*Volcano*
Degree	*Latitude*	*Range (or mountain range)*	*Waterfall*
Delta	*Legend*		
Desert	*Longitude*		
Elevation			

CONCLUSION

Geography is a way of thinking, of asking questions, of observing and appreciating the world around us. You can help your children learn by providing interesting activities for them, and by prompting them to ask questions about their surroundings.

Set a good example, and help your children build precise mental images, by always using correct terms. Say, "We are going north to New York to visit Grandma, or west to Dallas to see Uncle John," rather than "up to New York" or "down to Dallas." Use words such as highway, desert, river, climate, and glacier; and explain concepts like city, state, and continent. . . . Like any other field of learning, geography has a language of its own. . . .

Expose children to lots of maps and let them see you using them. Get a good atlas as well as a dictionary. Atlases help us ask, and answer, questions about places and their relationships with other areas. Many states have atlases that are generally available through an agency of the state government.

The activities suggested in this booklet are only a few examples of the many ways that children learn geography. These activities are designed to help parents find ways to include geographic thinking in their children's early experiences. We hope they will stimulate your thinking and that you will develop many more activities on your own.

Endnotes

* *Helping Your Child Learn Geography*, by Carol Sue Fromboluti with foreword by Bruno V. Manno, Deputy Assistant Secretary for Policy and Planning, and Kirk Winters, Research Associate. U. S. Department of Education, Office of Educational Research and Improvement. 1990. It has since been slightly revised. Not all of the material from the booklet is included in this chapter. It is attractively illustrated and comes with an outline map of the United States. Current price is less than a dollar, from Geography, Consumer Information Center, Pueblo, CO 81009. For foreign addresses, inquire at a U. S. Information Center. This material in this chapter is in the public domain and permission has been granted to reproduce it.

37

Teaching a Different Language

By Donna Faturos

Hoping to inspire my sons with my fascination with foreign languages, I decided three years ago to teach them German. I soon discovered that finding interesting foreign language materials for a home school was not easy. Most readily available textbooks were geared for classroom use and assumed the presence of someone who spoke the language. While that was not a problem for me, I realized that it would be for many families. Further, the heavily grammar-oriented methods favored by high school and college courses were inappropriate for my elementary school children. Since I found no existing curriculum that was entirely satisfactory to me, I came up with my own, incorporating materials from many sources. Has it worked? My sons, 9, 11, and 14 [fall 1993], enjoy their study of German and are eager to learn other languages.

In this chapter, I will touch on choosing a language, selecting materials, introducing the language to younger children and finding resources.

*For as long as **Donna Faturos** can remember, she has been fascinated by language. During her high school and college years, she studied six foreign languages. She revels in grammar and syntax, and she enjoys expanding her vocabulary. To understand and use another language brings her great satisfaction.*

This chapter records some of the key points she makes in her lectures at home schooling conferences. She likes to help other families design workable study programs for their children.

Calliope Books, her enterprise for selling foreign language materials, is listed in Appendix U.

Donna is also the home schooling mother of three boys.

An unappreciated asset

The state of foreign language instruction in the United States is dismal. Last November, columnist James Kilpatrick noted that, "In 1990, the most recent year for which data are available, barely one-third of all high school students were studying any foreign language. Even that pathetic figure is misleading, for those students, on the average, completed only one year. This is just about enough to teach them how to mispronounce 'bonjour.'" In spite of this obvious inadequacy, many Americans are unmoved by such statistics. A lot of people seem to feel that foreign language study is an interesting, though not essential, part of one's education.

There are many compelling reasons to be able to communicate in another language. Like it or not, our world is shrinking. National borders are not the cultural barriers they were in our grandparents' day. Multinational companies are commonplace, and news from around the world reaches us with unprecedented speed. The world has indeed become our neighborhood, and the easy flow of communication between peoples is crucial. Understanding only one language, even if it be an international tongue like English, is increasingly a handicap.

To me, the satisfaction that comes from

being able to read a newspaper or book, or to watch a foreign film, without relying on a translator's interpretation, is equally important. What a difference between the rich dialogue and subtleties of the foreign language and the adequate but uninspiring subtitles in English. Consider also the wealth of fine writing that remains untranslated, out of reach to those who know only one language.

Choosing a language to study

The first step in tailoring a language program for yourself or your child is to decide which language to learn. Choosing a language to study is a personal matter. Living near an ethnic neighborhood, having foreign-born relatives, or just being intrigued by the sound of a particular language may all influence the choice. It is true that some languages, especially highly inflected ones (German, Russian, Latin, and Polish, for example) demand a greater understanding of grammar than do simpler languages (such as Swedish, Italian, French, and Spanish), but these difficulties should not deter you.

Children often have their own ideas about what language they would like to learn. At a recent home school conference, a woman told me that her daughter was determined to learn Japanese. Mother, on the other hand, believed Spanish to be the logical choice because the family would soon move to a state with a large Hispanic population. I suggested encouraging her daughter's interest and giving her easy Japanese language materials. Once they move, I pointed out, her daughter will probably realize, on her own, how important it is to know at least some Spanish.

My own children, on the other hand, were interested in the idea of learning a foreign language, but had nothing particular in mind. I decided to teach them German for many reasons. Either way, listen to your children's thoughts before making a decision. They may surprise you.

Consider how your child might use the language

After you have settled on a particular language, French, for example, think about what you hope to achieve and set a reasonable goal. What you expect your child to receive from language study will guide your choice of materials. If he or she is interested in learning just enough French to chat with a neighbor, a conversational course covering basic grammar is sufficient. On the other hand, if he or she yearns to read Molière, a different, more extensive vocabulary and a greater command of French grammar is needed. If you are not sure how involved your child may become, you may start with one of the easier language programs and progress from there.

Selecting learning materials

Use common sense in choosing among the bewildering array of available language courses. Someone who is familiar with the product you are considering or a review in a home schooling publication can provide valuable opinions. Even if you do not have access to this kind of information, the following guidelines can help you make a more informed decision.

If your child is a beginner, limit your choices to courses with cassettes, records, or CDs. He or she needs to hear the language spoken clearly and accurately. Look through the textbook and, if possible, listen to a bit of the tapes that accompany it. Is the print in the book adequate? It sounds trivial, but print that is too tiny or too faint could become annoying and eventually derail your language program. Along the same lines, if the book contains writing exercises, will it lay open so you can work with ease – without needing to wrestle it.

Next read through some of the grammar explanations, beginning with something familiar, like verb conjugation or definite articles. Are the book's instructions understandable or is the terminology too technical for you? Do the little grammar charts make any sense? Does the book give enough examples for you to understand what you are learning and how it is used in a sentence? Words sometimes work differently depending on their context. Examples in the book should make the grammar clear to you. What about the dialogues and stories; are they interesting? You cannot expect fine literature in an elementary text, but neither should the material be boring.

If you are able, listen to a little of the audio portion of the course. Are the voices on the beginner's tape speaking clearly and at a slow to moderate speed? Is sufficient time provided for you to repeat or will you have to keep stopping your tape player? Also, tapes that leave too much blank time between phrases could be boring. I bought some German tapes for my children to "field test" for possible inclusion in my catalogue. The German was clear and understandable, but the pauses were so long the boys pretended to fall asleep between sentences. Those tapes are gathering dust somewhere in the house.

Beginning to learn a new language

Choosing the right materials for your child will depend on his or her age and ability. Small children can learn some basic vocabulary and become accustomed to the sounds of another language using any of the simple song and activity tapes that are available; learning through music is effective and fun. I also suggest a very simple picture book in the language to use in the same way you might use a picture book in English: naming the things in the house, the yard, and so on.

For elementary school age children, good introductory programs are available to teach basic language functions (greetings, counting, talking about themselves and their families, etc.) while still being enjoyable to use. This was an important point with my own children. They were more inclined to use materials that did not look like "official" school work. If you are using a book-tape combination, it is preferable for each child to have a copy of the book. If no book at all comes with the tape, consider creating your own, cutting pictures from magazines and labeling them with words from your tape. Your children would enjoy helping.

One of the smartest things I did for my sons was giving each of them an inexpensive personal cassette player with headphones. I no longer had to listen to the same cassettes over and over, and the boys were able to do part of their German lessons on their own. Choosing the time and place to work gave them a sense of independence and control. And they could listen to a favorite song or story as many times as they wished without sibling criticism.

Introducing grammar

Once your child has a rudimentary vocabulary in the new language, you can start introducing basic grammar. Using technical grammar terminology is unnecessary. Nouns are "naming words," verbs become "doing" or "being" words. Adjectives and adverbs are "describing" words. Here again you can use a picture book, either purchased or home made. Begin with nouns because they are the easiest to identify and understand: "the dog," "the baby," and so on. Next, you can add two or three verbs: "to be," "to eat," and "to play" are often the most useful. Now, "the baby eats," and "the dog plays." When your child understands the function of verbs, then adjectives and adverbs can be included to make the sentences more interesting: "the brown dog is playing" and "the little baby is eating." Not only will this prepare your child for a grammar-based language program, but it should help him or her understand English grammar as well.

For many people, the thought of learning grammar is enough to deter them from studying a foreign language. Perhaps we share collective elementary school memories of underlining and circling parts of speech, exercises that had no relevance to our lives at the time. In defense of such activities, I would point out that a firm understanding of grammar is indispensable to learning another language (or to communicate effectively in English, for that matter). This understanding enables us to build sentences and to recognize and correct many of our mistakes.

If your background in English grammar is weak, consider purchasing a basic grammar book to use alongside your foreign language text. Read through a few sections of any book before buying it. Beware of ones that make simple grammar concepts incomprehensible.

Teaching suggestions

Repetition is an important key to learning a language. You learned by repetition to understand your native language when you were small. Set aside a small period of time, every day if you can, for your child to work on language study.

College language labs provide for hearing yourself repeat phrases in response to a master tape or to your instructor. It is a humbling experience. At home, you can simulate this by using a second recorder to tape sentences your children repeat while listening to the publisher's cassette. You will find that mistakes are easy to pick out. When your children become more comfortable using the new language, seek out people who speak it well so they can practice talking to them. Foreign-born people have been eager to help me learn their language. No matter how badly I botched their mother tongue, they were patient and encouraging. The experience improved my use of the language and went a long way toward building up my self-confidence.

Learning another language is an exciting and rewarding experience, well worth the time invested.

38

Making Music

Velma Woodruff

Few areas of teaching give such a variety of choices and offer so much in permanent returns as does teaching of good music.

The joy of music may be expressed by singing, by whistling, by playing an instrument, or by listening to music that matches your mood, whether that be meditative, happy, or serious. Who doesn't love to be in a home where the little ones sing while they play, the father whistles as he works, and the mother snatches a moment to play a lively tune on the piano?

Listening to great music is a pleasure to those who know and understand it. Cheap and trivial music needs no disciplined training so, without direction, our children naturally lean toward the popular music of the day, which is dominated by lusts of the broad road – rebellion, sex, and drugs.

Students who sing or play an instrument find it easy to be members of groups such as choirs, bands, or orchestras, giving them a sense of identity and opening the way for friendships with other young people.

Children in today's world rarely have opportunity to participate much in their parents' vocation, which may leave them with a large amount of free time. Learning music can be an excellent choice to fill some of this void.

Quite apart from the subject itself comes an added dividend in character development. A well-organized music schedule in the home involves a plan for regular practice, diligent attention to details and accepting responsibility for practice. Thus it is one of the best methods to teach regularity, carefulness, responsibility, dependability, and self-discipline.

__Velma Johnson Woodruff__ has taught music for thirty years. She has studied in Vienna and has played in symphony orchestras. And she taught her children at home before it became a popular choice for concerned parents. You will appreciate the practical approach of her chapter. Her husband has taught mathematics for twenty-five years at Chattanooga State Technical Community College. The Woodruffs live in a rural area near Rock Springs, Georgia. To get to know Velma and her family a little better, read her story in the chapter, "Planning Social

Pitfalls and progress

Does music have any pitfalls? Yes, indeed! You may be tempted to lose your temper with the child who dawdles, is careless, or who argues, but practice sessions should never become times for shouting matches or negative comments about the student. Communicate clearly what is expected during the practice time and then calmly and consistently enforce it.

Inordinate pride by parent or child may be another pitfall, as is the opposite problem of making unflattering comparisons with others. Both pride and self-condemnation are unhealthy emotions. Satisfaction and the recognition of a job well done are commendable attitudes.

When should music education be started? As early as possible! More and more young mothers who have kept abreast of the studies showing the influences on developing fetuses, play records and sing to their babies before they are born.[1] And mothers, for generations, have sung lullabies to their little ones to calm them and put them to sleep.

Preschoolers usually love to learn songs from Mommy, Daddy, or from recordings. Many can sing on pitch and with delight by the age of two or three.

Recorded band music by John Phillip Sousa makes marching with Mommy and Daddy a special time of day. Clapping in rhythm, beating a toy drum with the music, bouncing balls in rhythm, or playing games such as Farmer in the Dell (where singing is an integral part of the game) are other ways to teach valuable musical skills.

In some homes music is part of the bedtime ritual. After stories, prayers, and good-night hugs, good music is played softly while the child falls asleep. What a wonderful teaching opportunity to enhance appreciation for the best in sound!

Eight years old is considered by many professional teachers as the ideal age to start lessons and formal training, although it is possible to do so earlier if your child is ready and interested. (Notice that it is the child who needs to be ready. Beware of pushing.)

Very young children may learn poor habits in their practice unless closely supervised. Practice time needs to be differentiated from play time.

How to Choose a Teacher

If you as a parent know music, you may be the one to teach your child yourself; otherwise, find a competent teacher by inquiring of other parents with young children who have found a satisfactory instructor.

Practice Time

For the first two or three years of study, it would be ideal if you as the parent would sit with your child as he (or she) practices, or, better yet, play your instrument with him, especially if he is learning a stringed or wind instrument. If he is practicing the piano, name the notes with him, count with him, sing with him, admire his progress, and encourage him. (This is recommended even if another person is the teacher.) In this way music becomes a joy and a tie between the parent and child instead of lonely, boring sessions.

Another important consideration is the length of the practice time. No young child should practice more than twenty minutes at one sitting. Older ones and adults should take a break after thirty minutes. If an hour of practice is the goal, then practice at two or three different times in the day.

It cannot be emphasized too much that practice times should not focus merely on listening for mistakes. The purpose of practice should be to sharpen skills and learn pieces well, aiming toward perfection of technique and expression. To take the negative view and emphasize mistakes is to shift the reason for learning music from beauty to stress. Students who learn music with the attitude of merely finding mistakes usually listen to music in the same way and are often very critical, missing entirely the fact that music is to be enjoyed.

The use of a chart where each practice period is rewarded with a star or sticker of some type is excellent incentive for young learners. A pretty sticker for each piece well learned is another possibility. The main reward, though, is that you as the parent notice the progress and give suitable commendation.

Teach self-discipline. Later success in music depends on learning to set attainable goals for each practice period and then working diligently until those goals are reached.

Who Should Learn Music?

Not every child needs to enter a formal study of music to be happy in life. However, an elementary knowledge of music gives a nice balance to a person and is certainly to be encouraged.

Probably no child has ever chosen to

practice regularly for the eight to ten years required to become truly proficient in playing an instrument such as the piano, the organ, or one of the symphonic instruments. When a child has tired of the newness of study, you need to decide whether or not to press for continuation.

No decision is right for every situation. Unnumbered adults who were allowed to quit their study after a year or two look back and wish their parents had insisted they continue. There are also many adults who are grateful that their parents had the foresight to require that they study music for a certain length of time – usually through the eighth grade or sometimes until the end of high school. A very few were made to keep on with their music and they hate even the mention of the word. Almost all of this group had parents who either belittled them, shouted at them, or sent them off to a lonely room by themselves.

A very small percentage of children are either tone-deaf or have no rhythm. For these, trying to please a parent with their music is a frustrating job and they should be encouraged to try other equally interesting and satisfying endeavors such as art, sewing, auto mechanics, or any of a host of other activities. However, be slow in making a final judgment; many children *seem* to be deficient and later overcome their limitations, especially if they have careful, understanding help.

Learning To Listen

I suggest getting a set of recordings specifically produced to teach music appreciation for children. One such set called *Music Masters* is an outstanding introduction to classical music. (See Appendix T.)

Other children's music includes "Peter and the Wolf" by Sergei Prokofiev, "Child's Symphony" by Franz Joseph Haydn, and "The Carnival of the Animals" by Camille Saint-Saens. Please explain these compositions to your child if the record you buy does not.

For going-to-sleep, consider the music of Johann Strauss, Antonio Vivaldi, or Wolfgang Amadeus Mozart. Try compositions such as the The Nutcracker Suite by Peter Tchaikovsky, the Moldau by Bedrich Smetena, The New World Symphony by Antonin Dvorak, or the Nocturnes of Frederic Chopin. In fact, almost any of the great music will fit into this category.

Good music is loved more after many repetitions, so play the same compositions again and again and again.

Singing

Formal lessons in voice are usually not recommended on the elementary school level, but that doesn't mean that children shouldn't sing. Teach several songs a week, explaining how to read the music and the words. Sing *with* your children and, if possible, let them sing by themselves.

If a child is unable to stay on pitch, patiently have him listen and try to match the tones of your own voice or those of an instrument. If this takes many days, many months, or several years, don't give up. Such children almost always succeed at last.

Instrumental Music

Instrumental music may be introduced through a flutophone, a recorder, or a keyboard of some type. Many children, at an early age, will want to learn an instrument with greater potential such as the piano or the violin (which comes in sizes from one- sixteenth to full). As the young musician grows in stature and lung capacity, the whole range of wind instruments (which come only in full size) become available. Which instrument to choose depends on finances, the availability of a good instructor, and the interest of the child.

Stringed Instruments

If stringed instruments interest you, consider putting the family together as a group. If you have one child, you and the child make a duet, or with your spouse, a trio; more children make the group larger. If you all get instruments at the same time (such as violins, a viola, and a cello), you could take lessons together, practice together, and learn together.

A class instruction method such as *String Builder* by Samuel Applebaum, Books I, II, and III, published by Belwin, Inc., allows the whole family to progress together. *Miniatures for Strings* and *Pieces for Pleasure,* both by Noah Klauss and published by Pro Art Publications, Inc., offer delightful and easy pieces to supplement the method book. Another such book is *Brentwood String Orchestra Folio* by Leon Metcalf, published by Pro Art.

The *Suzuki Violin Method* has gained much attention. If taught by a professional who understands the whole concept, it can be very effective.

Set a scheduled time for group practice and stick to it. From the time our three oldest children were six, seven, and nine, we arose each morning at 5:30 a.m. for devotions, a glass of juice, and ten minutes of physical exercise before practicing for thirty minutes from 6:00 to 6:30. Why so early? Because at that time Daddy could be with the group and learn cello and that made it extra special!

Nothing is as easy as it sounds, though, so don't expect everyone to be on hand with a smile every day. Know ahead of time that it will take hard work, lots and lots of patience, and enough leadership from one or the other of the parents (decide which ahead of time!) to keep things going. No matter what happens, keep things on the happy side. Make this a time your children will remember with joy.

Each instrument needs to fit the player. For violins and violas, have the child stretch his left arm out parallel to the floor under the instrument (which is held under his chin). His fingers should be able to curve up enough to bend around the end of the scroll.

****

Suggestions For Teaching Piano:

(Most of these ideas apply to other instruments also.)

Goals for a beginning student include:

- learning proper position at the instrument
- using the proper hand position
- reading and following the fingering as given
- learning to read the notes and rhythm
- becoming proficient at sight-reading
- developing a love of music properly played

To achieve these goals:

- Be firm, but kind, in expecting regular and proper practice. Keep a permanent book with the lesson assignment and a record of practice. Give stars or other awards for goals met.
- Give the student lots of material so he will have to read a variety of compositions. As soon as they are learned well, go on to new pieces.
- Never demonstrate the piece before the student has learned the notes. To be able to play by ear is a talent, but to be unable to read music is a tragedy for a person who wants to be a musician.

Practice Suggestions for the Piano Student:

- Sit straight and tall. You'll look better and play better.
- Keep fingers curved and wrist in natural position – neither high nor low. (In order to do so, your fingernails must be short.)

- Practice regularly every day.
- Do not neglect *s l o w*, meticulous practice.
- Follow the fingerings as given.
- Count evenly. If you have a metronome, use it often, setting it at a slower-than-normal pace.
- Practice small sections of a composition. If you encounter a difficult passage, work that portion slowly (with separate hands if needed) until that part becomes easy.
- Before you begin a piece check: clef signs, key signature, time signature, tempo
- Pay careful attention to phrasing, staccatos, and other markings.
- When you have learned to play a piece without fumbling, try to play it with the feeling you believe it should express. Avoid sacrificing accuracy.

Sight Reading

Many music teachers pay little attention to sight reading, spending a great deal of time on each piece, and, in extreme cases, spending the whole year on a half dozen pieces that are memorized and perfected to the last staccato. They also find that the easiest way to teach is to demonstrate every composition that the student is to learn. For the student with a good ear, this becomes a real trap, because he is able to mimic the teacher without learning from the printed page.

This produces boredom. It is an unusual child, indeed, who can practice the same pieces week after week and still retain interest. And, worse yet, a student taught in this way may never become an excellent sight-reader.

Compare this with teaching a child to read a book. If the child reads the same pages over and over, memorizing each one before proceeding, he will not be able to read new material with ease. The same thing happens with the reading of music. The only way to produce real skill in sight reading is to encounter new music every day. For this reason, I suggest that students do many books on each level, going on to the next level only when they can read their present assignments with ease.

Just as a student learning to read learns memory verses from the Bible, the Pledge of Allegiance, or some poetry, the music student should memorize one or two compositions a year and perfect them as much as possible, while continuing to learn from six to twelve other compositions a week, depending on ability and amount of practice. If the student is unable to read well enough to finish at least four or five pieces a week, consider giving him some easier material.

In addition to covering a large amount of material, the student should always learn his assignment from the printed page, not from a demonstration by a teacher or parent. Playing by ear has an important place in music, but on the material chosen to teach the reading of music, it should not be allowed.

The above paragraphs are aimed particularly at the beginning student. When a student reaches difficult music, he will, of course, learn fewer pieces and take much longer on each one. In advanced piano he may spend a semester or even a year on a composition.

***Piano Teaching Methods:* Preparatory Level**

It is suggested that the student plan to practice five hours per week, preferably in twenty minute segments and certainly never longer than thirty minutes at one time.

All pieces should be practiced six times each day in the following manner:

Play while naming notes aloud. (Twice)
Play while counting aloud. (Twice)
Play and sing. (Twice)

Be sure that a proper hand position and correct fingering are used, along with correct position at the piano. (The student should sit so that elbows touch the body when they are swung in front of it while hands are in playing position.)

Choose any ten or twelve of the following books or other good primer-level piano music: (Starred books are especially good.)

**Steiner Piano Course, Junior Approach*
**Piano Student* by David Carr Glover, Primer
**Church Musician* from the Glover Sacred Piano Library, Primer
**Teaching Little Fingers To Play* by John Thompson
Piano Repertoire from Glover Piano Library, Primer
LESSONS, David Carr Clover Method for Piano, Primer
Michael Aaron Piano Course, Primer
Belwin Piano Method by Weybright, Book I
Schaum Piano Course, Pre-A (Green Book)
Sight Reading by Schaum, Book I
Easiest Piano Course by John Thompson, Book II
Childhood Scenes by Ward
Hymn Primer by Schaum
Piano Course by Mark Nevin, Preparatory
Melody All The Way by John Thompson, Preparatory Book
**All students should do the *Piano Theory Primer* by Glover.

Piano Teaching Methods: Level I or Grade I-A

Students should continue to practice five hours a week, with the longest time period at one setting remaining at thirty minutes. Finger and hand position, body position, and proper fingering remain important considerations.

Pieces should be practiced five times each day in the following manner:
Play while counting aloud. (Twice)
Practice three more times.
Slow, careful practice is essential until all the details of the composition are properly learned.

Choose ten to twelve books from the following list or from other good Level I or Grade I-A piano books:

Piano Student from the David Carr Glover Piano Course, Level I
**Modern Piano Course* by John Thompson, Grade I (first half of book)
**Schaum Piano Course A* (Red Book)
LESSONS by David Carr Glover and Jay Stewart, Level One
Piano Repertoire from Glover Piano Library, Lev. I
Michael Aaron Piano Course, Book I
Belwin Piano Method by June Weybright, Book II
Mark Nevin Piano Course, Book I
Making Music At The Piano, Book II, by Schaum
Sight Reading, Book I by Schaum
Melody All The Way, by John Thompson, Book I
First Grade Studies by John Thompson
Hymn Tunes You Like Arranged for Piano by Mark Nevin (Published by Schroder & Gunther, Inc.)
Child's Book of Hymns for Piano, Compiled & Arranged by Rob Roy Peery (Published by Lorenz Publishing Company)
**All students should do *Piano Theory*, Level I, by David Carr Glover

Piano Teaching Methods: Level II or Grade I-B

Continue the practice periods as outlined in Level I-A.

Choose ten to twelve books from the following list or from other Level II Books.

Piano Student, Level II by David Carr Glover
Piano Repertoire, Level II by David Carr Glover
Modern Piano Course, Grade I (last half) by John Thompson
Steiner Piano Course, Book 2
Schaum Piano Course B, Blue book
Making Music At The Piano, Book 3, Schaum
Church Musician, Level II, from David Carr Glover Sacred Library
Belwin Piano Method, Book 3, by June Weybright
LESSONS, Level II, from David Carr Glover Method for Piano
PERFORMANCE, Level II, from David Carr Glover Method for Piano
Melody All The Way, Book I-b by John Thompson
Program Solos, Level 2, by David Carr Glover
***Piano Theory*, Level II, from David Carr Glover Piano Library.

An Added Dividend: All Three Levels

If you want to make the best use of the books, go back and review each one after all pieces are well learned and the book is "finished." This time though, have the student (1) name notes, (2) count aloud, and (3) play. If he has done it "perfectly", go on to the next piece. Continue through the book, playing each piece only three times or until it is perfect. (After the preparatory level, the notes are not named, so the piece is played only twice or until it is perfect.) This applies only through Grade One. However, it is always good for students to browse through their finished books, enjoying their favorite compositions.

Endnote

1. Thomas Berny & John Kelly, *Secret Life of the Unborn Child* (New York: Dell Publication, Division of Bantam, Doubleday & Dell, 1982).
2. Henci Goer, "The Fascinating World of the Unborn," *The Reader's Digest*, November 1989, pp. 152, 153.

39

Music and Values

Learning the beauty of sound patterns deserves a place in a well-rounded education.

Any good musician would applaud this bit of profound wisdom (or would, at least, smile politely). Notice that I did not say "music." In our modern world, the term has taken on a broader definition than I associate with "beauty." In music, as in other art forms, "expression" is now the dominant characteristic. Beauty can be expressed, but so can feelings associated with violence, chaos, abandonment of responsibility, sexual passion, intoxication, spirit possession and many other evils.

Music as a language

Music, after all, is a language of the emotions. Music not only *expresses* emotions, but it also creates and reinforces them. The choice of music is therefore *not* arbitrary, as some would argue. It does affect behavior. Although the sounds you hear don't *force* your behavior, they make you susceptible. Add other influences such as the mood of people around you, the lyrics, darkness or light, your past experiences, hormonal drive, or other pressures, and you are drawn like a little iron scrap to a magnet.

Of course emotions are not all bad. Good feelings, under the control of unselfish reason, are what joy and happiness are made of. And music is a gift that makes them *glow*.

Choice

As in literature, which we discussed in another chapter, it isn't safe to follow the tastes even of people we admire. What you listen to influences your children, through their respect for you, and because they develop a taste for what they hear.

Elements of good and bad in music aren't always obvious. Here are some principles to consider:

Feelings of joy, peace, strength, praise, pity, sorrow, etc. are appropriate to express because we want to strengthen them.

Lyrics or scenes associated with music can make it objectionable. That's obvious. But also, good lyrics don't transform bad sounds into good ones. Both sounds and words must be good. In fact, bad sounds communicate to the subconscious that the good words are a lie.

Personal taste cannot always be trusted for quality in music any more than it can for food. *Sounding* like good music doesn't make it good.

Because music is a language of emotions, it has tremendous power for good or evil.

Rhythm and repeated phrases are important for music. They contribute beauty through expectation and order. However, a heavy beat that distorts natural, regular patterns and that tends to control the listener is dangerous. Such rhythm is used in the voodoo spirit-possession ceremonies. To varying extents, a strong beat has the hypnotic effect of causing people to relinquish the self-control for which they are responsible to God. Natural rhythm moves in a sequence of strong and weak beats like a well controlled mechanism. When the beat

pattern is given a distorted sequence (with beats where they don't seem to belong), it builds unnatural feelings in the listener. Music with perverted rhythm experienced by a group tends to draw them into the group norm. Mob attitude begins to emerge (even when violence isn't the objective).

Music, by its nature, is an experience that unfolds along the dimension of time. Rhythm tends to keep the flow going. The music experience, like a story, also develops by presenting uneasiness or expectation and following it by resolution. These are sequences of harmony (several pitches sounded together). Slightly discordant sounds are resolved as they are followed by ones that more naturally harmonize. Withholding this resolution brings distress

and is another element that fires rebellion.

Friends are known by the company they keep. So is music. Participation in modern rock music is generally associated with drugs, alcohol, sex, and rebellion.

Changes in the tastes of our society are not necessarily bad, but most changes in musical taste over the past 40 or 50 years have introduced a subtle danger. The beat and harshness of "music" we hear have gotten stronger without most people even noticing. Of course music isn't good because it's old or because you or I of the older generation like it. This is a point we and our children need to understand. Objection to anything must not be based on what group likes or dislikes it – or on how new or old it is.

Unfortunately most contemporary religious music has been corrupted with the kind of beat and poisonous sounds we have been discussing. Even children's songs are affected.

The distinction between right from wrong in these areas may not, at first, be obvious. If the supposed religious song tends to carry you along with a catchy tune or to whip up your emotions, rather than drawing the heart out toward God, beware. Excitement is appropriate, but any music, religious or not, is wrong if it produces an excitement tending to dull the reasoning powers. It's wrong if it gets in the way of calm self-control or of personal communion with God.

And in choosing songs, don't forget to take a careful look at the lyrics or actions. It takes more than a few nice-sounding words to make an acceptable message.

Music and children

Velma Woodruff's chapter deals with teaching and learning music. I'll just add a few thoughts: While still very young, most children begin to understand and communicate melody. I believe their musical ability for life is enhanced by parents who sing to them and encourage their singing from the earliest years.

Of course abilities of different individuals aren't the same, but even those who show very little talent can learn to make and enjoy music. My oldest son, Tim, seemed bright enough but he just couldn't sing. My wife taught him a little about the piano, but he showed no sense of rhythm.

We figured everyone doesn't have to be a musician and didn't try to push him. Then one day, when in the eleventh grade, he greatly surprised us. He came home on leave from boarding school, playing a borrowed French horn! He had found a friend who showed him how. He now enjoys good music and reads music very well considering the few years he spent learning. He has sung in choirs and has a good sense of rhythm.

As in other subjects, parents can teach music if they know a little themselves. Of course this is a convenient area to turn over to an out-of-home teacher for weekly lessons. A music teacher will probably arrange recitals, inviting parents to hear all her or his students. (Home teachers can arrange them, too, and they can suggest that their children play for appropriate programs.) Recitals challenge individuals for excellence, and playing when others do makes it more interesting. Few are prepared to teach music to their own children for very many years.

In my own experience, the weekly music lesson didn't provide as much technical information as it did stimulus to keep practicing. Of course both are necessary.

Reaching for excellence

I believe everyone needs to know some music just as we all need to learn to draw simple pictures. But when it comes to learning advanced skills, we need to consider the substantial investment and the many hours spent in practicing.

Life is short. Objectives other children are committing major portions of time to may not be the best choice for your children. Give them a chance to try different areas of personal development and to talk with people who have achieved ability in them. Then according to interests and talents, encourage more serious learning in the chosen areas.

Principles for Choosing Music

Music is a powerful force on the emotions. Feelings it develops must be uplifting.

Personal taste cannot always be trusted.

Lyrics must be significant and appropriate, but good words do not salvage bad sounds.

Rhythm may be misused to cause distorted attitudes.

Harmony may be misused to develop unrest.

Social aspects of certain music may lead to evil.

40

Teaching Art

Like pieces of a puzzle, each area of learning has its special place. And art is an essential piece in the balanced education picture. The arts and crafts you teach your children will provide excellent opportunities to polish their personalities and help them find life more meaningful. Each child has unique talents. Experiencing fine arts offers discovery, use of creativity, and enjoyment of beauty. It helps develop the special abilities God has given.

*I found **Sandy Ballard** in Colorado teaching her boys, and full of ideas about planning and organizing materials for home school. **Kim Solga's** contribution has greatly enriched it. Kim lives in Northern California and publishes* KidsArt News. *(See Appendix T.)*

The sections by Kim Solga and by me are identified. All the others are from Sandy.

Teaching art in the home classroom also allows you as the teacher to participate in the creative learning experiences. It can be a beautiful growing experience for both you and your child. With your involvement, remember that your child will be doing the work. If you tend to be a perfectionist and do it for him, you lose the most important things you are trying to teach. You should, of course, teach for neatness and carefulness, but remember that children work according to their age and experience.

For success in teaching, be genuinely interested in art yourself. Then spark that interest in your child. Visit galleries, craft stores, and museums. Talk over the types of things he or she would enjoy learning and doing. Then together plan the art projects you have chosen.

Helping your child enjoy beauty by Ted Wade

Technically speaking, what we teach young children is more crafts than art, but art grows from the crafts and, as long as we watch our words when talking to "real" art lovers, we can use the word *art* to mean this curriculum area. The art we ultimately aim for is more than making pictures. Seek experiences that help develop a love for beauty. When you see something nice, whether in an art gallery, in nature, in architecture, or anywhere, take time to talk with your child about what makes it beautiful. Visit a craft store and ask your child what might be fun to do or make.

Also a note on developmental psychology: Spacial perception is not well developed in young children, so don't worry if your preschooler doesn't get proportions right. Fine muscle control comes later, too. That is why finger paints work better than detailed drawings during the early years. (tw)

Planning

To begin, you might plan your art area layout and decide how to decorate it. You will want a place for pictures, a bulletin board, and some shelves for storage and display. Even if you need to teach art in the same place the other school subjects are studied, you will want to make it as suitable as possible. Kim Solga will share some ideas about setting up an "art center," after we finish looking at the basic ideas of planning.

Prepare for your art classes in advance. First, choose a general area of interest. Then:

(1) Decide when and how long you want your art classes.

(2) Make a list of possible projects.

(3) Plan according to seasons and events, student abilities, resources and materials available, and practicality for your situation.

(4) Organize your materials in advance so that you are sure to have everything you need.

As you plan and teach, keep the following suggestions in mind:

(1) Teach your child to enjoy looking at, touching, and making pretty things. Wherever you are, you can teach him or her to observe and appreciate the surroundings. In the home, at church, outdoors in nature, and even in the grocery store, you can help your child notice simplicity, beauty, organization, and neatness.

(2) Choose projects within your child's capabilities and interests. For each project in this chapter I have suggested appropriate grade levels. The projects appear in order of increasing difficulty. As you become better acquainted with your child's potential, you may wish to expand into more difficult projects. Flexible instructions allow opportunity to use imagination. Plan projects to be more than just busy work. Use them to help your child build a positive self-image. If you begin a project for which your child shows positively no talent, change projects rather than apply pressure. Always offer appropriate encouragement and appreciation, while at the same time promoting thoroughness, carefulness, and the importance of doing one's best.

(3) As already mentioned, do not do your children's work for them. Sometimes in a joint project, you can do one part, such as a frame, while your child makes the picture. But don't redo his or her handiwork.

(4) Choose activities that are practical for the home classroom. Many nice art activities use materials you already have on hand or that are easy to buy. You don't need to choose elaborate and expensive projects that require a lot of materials you will use only once.

(5) In developing your art program, use all the resources around you that you can think of. For instance, take advantage of your local library for art and craft ideas that will expand beyond the suggestions given here. Look in bookstores and school supply stores for good books. Find an older person in your church or community who will be willing to teach you and your child an artistic skill that is new to both of you such as knitting, quilting, crocheting, ceramics, tatting, etc. Or enroll your child in special art classes.

The art activity area by Kim Solga

I suggest you designate an area in your home as an art center. It should be near running water, have a washable floor or protective rug covering, and be stocked with all kinds of art materials as suggested in the paragraphs that follow. Above all, it should be easily accessible to your children so they can come when they have free time, and work on projects without adult direction.

Teach the necessary skills of cleaning up after projects. Even preschoolers can learn how to clean brushes and set them on their handles to dry, put the covers back on the felt pens, set the crayons in the box and throw away paper scraps. Children should wipe up their own paint spills and put the clay back in the bags. Only by being patiently taught to take care of their art tools and materials will children develop responsibility in working alone on their art projects.

Art is learned from more than the projects you assign and the techniques you introduce. Really creative work takes place when children decide for themselves what to make – what to do with the art skills they've learned. Encourage your students to work on their own, give them the time freedom for it, and praise their creations!

Suggested general materials

Arts and crafts materials may be purchased at most discount stores, office supply stores, and some supermarkets. Stores that sell only art supplies are nice, but often charge more. I would use them only for specialty items that cannot be purchased elsewhere.

Basic tools and space needs: pencils, scissors (blunt ends for the very young), tempera paint, string, glue, paper of various types, ruler, ink, crayons, tape, water color felt pens, and a special table.

Materials to save: oatmeal boxes, magazines and catalogs, small glass jars (with lids), empty spools, foil, cloth scraps, ribbon scraps, seeds, old pictures and cards, talcum powder, old crayons, old toothbrushes (sterilized), old candles, newspapers, old aprons or shirts, hair spray.

On selecting materials by Kim Solga

Children, especially young ones, should be given nontoxic art materials. Many items sold in art stores, even some made for children's art, are not safe! To be sure, look for the official "CP" or "AP" nontoxic label on paints, glues, inks, clay or anything that might end up on children's fingers and mouths.

Children's scissors should cut as easily as your best sewing scissors. Nothing is more frustrating than trying to cut paper with cheap tin scissors. Several companies manufacture very well-crafted embroidery scissors with blunt ends – perfect for youngsters.

Art materials for very young children are often over sized – fat crayons, wide handled brushes, giant felt pens. These jumbo tools may be harder for tiny hands to grasp and use than the normal sized items. Be sure to provide both large and regular sized pencils, crayons, brushes and chalk for preschoolers so they can experience both and choose tools they are comfortable with.

Materials to gather from your community by Kim Solga

Paper trim scraps: Print shops often have boxes full of "trim scraps"–the edges of paper trimmed off in commercial printing jobs. These papers are in many weights, textures and colors–luxurious papers you could never afford to buy for kids, and in the tiny sizes they love. Ask if you might have a few of these throw-aways now and then.

Hardwood scraps: Ask a cabinet maker. Use these with glue to create wood sculptures and mosaics. Nailing hardwoods doesn't work well, especially for kids. Paint and draw on them.

Softwood scraps: Find these by asking at a construction site. Use them with glue, nails, and paint. Carve them to make woodblock prints. Wrap needlework and pictures around blocks to make plaques. There's no end to what you can do with wood scraps. Even sawdust can be glued to paper or sculptures for great textures.

Posters: Hardware stores, supermarkets, card shops and other retail stores often discard advertising posters. These can be folded and stapled to create big sculptures. They can be cut into interesting areas of color, letters and shapes; or they can be painted and glued. You may even be able to find full-sized billboard papers from an advertising company. These are heavier than wallpaper and have truly giant figures and shapes.

Leftovers from manufacturing: Visit small manufacturers and craftspeople in your community. Find out what child-safe materials they might be tossing away. Dressmakers or tailors would have scraps of fabric, lace, and cords. A tile store might discard discontinued or broken tiles and linoleum scraps. A shoe repair shop might give you bits of leather. A newspaper publisher would have thin aluminum printing plates (not best for small children).

Big cardboard cartons and Styrofoam blocks: Check with an appliance store or just drive around behind now and then to see what they have set out for trash pickup. These materials can be cut with a hacksaw which is less dangerous for children The big cartons might make nice playhouses if used with adequate supervision.

By asking you may receive art materials in abundance while making friends and educating your students on commerce in your community.

Projects

In the rest of this chapter you will find suggestions for projects to get you started. Change and experiment with them as you wish. and by all means, don't limit yourself to just the ones listed here. These are just to spark your interest and imagination. Don't view them as a series to be dutifully completed.

For each project I have shown: a title, a suggested grade level, the general type of project, materials needed, and directions and ideas.

CARD MAKING

Suggested level: All levels.

Project: Designing and making all types of greeting cards.

Explanation: Card making is fun for everyone and simple to do. Handmade cards with that "personal touch" mean so much more. You can make cards for: birthdays, Christmas, Valentine's, weddings, Mother's Day, Father's Day, graduations, get well, friendship, and special family occasions.

A variety of techniques may be used. Some of the other art project ideas work well for making cards. For example, see: leaf prints, pressed flowers, potato prints, rubbed prints, scratchboard, and spatter painting. and you can also use ink drawing, pencil drawing, water color painting, pastels, silhouettes, and even crayons.

Materials: Choose any heavy paper such as index stock, tagboard, construction paper, bristol board, or lightweight cardboard.

To fold the cards consider: (1) a regular book fold, (2) a top- down fold, (3) a top-down fold with the top shorter, (4) a three- panel fold with sides folded in, (5) a regular fold with a window cut in the front. Before folding, you will want to plan the card to fit an available envelope or one you make.

Special materials you might want to use: paper lace; bits of ribbon; dried flowers, leaves or ferns; border designs; glitter; foil; metallic paper; soft fabric; wall paper; stickers; gummed stars; or doilies. To deckle the paper edges for your cards, use a heavy paper (construction or water color). Draw a line along the edge to be deckled and paint a water strip down that line on one side of the paper. Turn it over and do the same thing on the back of your first water line. When the paper is saturated, place a ruler along the line and tear the paper *upward.* Smooth down the edge and let it dry.

To make parchment-like paper, dip a soft cloth into salad oil and rub both sides of any kind of paper. Let the paper dry for two days, and it will look like parchment. Typing paper works well for this.

STRING PAINTING

Suggested level: Preschool and lower grades.

Project: Painting with string on construction paper.

Materials: For this project you will need sheets

of light- colored construction paper (12 by 18 inches is suggested), two or three pieces of string (18 inches or longer), two or three colors of liquid tempera paint, a large magazine, bowls for the paint, and some newspapers.

Directions: (1) Fold the construction paper in half in either direction. (2) Unfold the paper and lay it open on the newspapers. (3) Pour the paint into a bowl. (4) Carefully dip a piece of string into the paint. (5) Take the string from the paint and lay it on one side of the paper in an interesting pattern, leaving a bit of the string showing at the bottom. (6) Fold the paper over land lay the magazine on the top. (7) Press down lightly on the magazine with one hand and quickly pull the string out of the paper. (8) Remove the magazine and unfold the paper. (9) Let the picture dry and then repeat the process, using another piece of string and another color of paint.

This will produce an interesting and unique painting. Using more than three colors will usually make the picture unattractive.

MILK PAINTING

Suggested level: Preschool and lower grades.

Project: Painting.

Materials: One-half cup of milk powder, one-half cup of water, dry tempera paint.

Directions: (1) Mix the water and milk together and stir until dissolved. (2) Add the desired coloring. (3) Use as you would any paint.

This is an excellent paint medium for the little ones to use. Give them a specific assignment to paint. For example: a day at the beach; when the family goes camping; winter fun; a day at Grand-mother's house; springtime in my front yard; my favorite pet; a birthday party; Christmas fun.

Mix only the amount of paint to be used at one time. This paint dries to a glossy finish and is not dusty.

SCRATCHBOARD PICTURES

Suggested level: Preschool and lower grades.

Project: Scratching through ink-covered poster board to make pictures.

Materials: In doing this project, you will need heavy paper such as tagboard, poster board, or light cardboard. You will then need crayons, dusting powder, and black India ink (which may stain clothes), or black tempera paint. You will also need something sharp to scratch through the ink. For the younger children, the best thing to use is a mechanical pencil with no lead. A straight pin or sewing needle can salso be used with caution. You will need newspapers to put under the painting.

Directions: (1) Choose the size of picture you wish to make. A good size for little ones is 8 by 10 inches. (2) Using the crayons, color the entire page heavily with wax. Be sure to use the lighter colors, as the dark ones will not show up when they are scratched. (3) Check the picture to make sure the child has filled in the entire sheet. (4) Dust the picture with talcum powder. This will help the ink or paint adhere to the wax. (5) Cover the entire board with India ink or black tempera paint. (6) Allow the picture to dry. (7) When the paint is thoroughly dry, let the children begin to scratch through the ink and watch the colors show through. (8) Have the children scratch a particular subject such as a family picnic, a fall scene, winter fun, etc. (9) If the child makes a mistake, it can be blocked out by touching up the picture with a bit more ink. Be sure to let it dry before they start scratching again.

FINGER PAINTING

Suggested level: Preschool and lower grades.

Project: Painting.

Materials: To do this activity, you will need newspapers, old shirts or aprons to protect clothing, paper (typing paper or butcher paper, or regular water color paper), and finger paints.

Directions: (1) Cover work surface with newspapers. (2) Wet the paper and choose one or two colors of paint. (3) Spoon about one tablespoon of one color of paint onto the paper. (4) Smear around with the fingers. (5) Using one finger like a pencil, draw a pattern or picture. (6) The surface can be worked with for several minutes, but soon the paper will begin to tear, so encourage your child to work in a short time. (7) Set aside the picture to dry.

Finger painting is best with only one or two colors because the paints mix together and more colors will result in a brown. Two recipes for finger paint are given later in this chapter.

PUFF BALL ART

Suggested level: Preschool and lower grades.

Project: Sculpting with cotton balls.

Materials: To do this unique and fun project you will need a bag of cotton balls, a cookie sheet, some small bowls, food coloring, a cup of flour, and a cup of water.

Directions: (1) Mix the water and the flour together until you get a smooth solution. (2) Divide it into the bowls and add a few drops of the desired food coloring to each bowl until you get the color you want. (3) Drop in the cotton balls (one at a time) and twirl them around with your fingers until they are completely coated with the solution. (4) Carefully lift out the balls and place them on a lightly oiled cookie sheet. The cotton balls will retain their shape with a little puff. Don't squeeze them or you will lose the air that is inside. (5) Create any shape or design that you wish, making sure that the cotton balls touch one another. This will make them stick together as they dry. (6) Bake in the oven at 300 degrees for one hour. (7) Let the shapes cool before removing them from the cookie sheet.

If you wish to have brighter colors, do not add food coloring to the mixture, but rather paint them with tempera paints or water colors after they have cooled. You can use the shapes to write mottos, your name, or a favorite saying. You can make animals and bugs (caterpillars are favorites). and you can make many attractive flowers, too. If you wish to make smaller parts for heads, tails, ears, etc., just pull the puffs apart before you dip them in the mixture to make smaller puffs. They will become hard like beads when they bake.

SPATTER PAINTING

Suggested level: Preschool and lower grades.

Project: Spattering tempera paint on paper.

Materials: For this art project, you will need tempera paint, art paper, a stiff toothbrush, scissors, a blunt knife (a table knife will do), straight pins, and newspapers.

Directions: (1) Draw some designs or interesting shapes. Silhouettes would be pretty. (2) Cut out the patterns. (3) Lay your drawing paper on some newspaper and pin the shapes on top of it. Be sure to leave margins around the edges of the paper. (4) Mix your paint. (5) Dip the toothbrush in one color of paint and hold the toothbrush slightly above the picture bristles down. (6) Draw the edge of the knife *toward* you across the bristles making the paint spatter. (7) Repeat the process with one or two more colors, removing some of the shapes if desired. (8) Put aside the picture to dry.

WAX PAINTING

Suggested level: Preschool and lower grades.

Project: Washing paint over a waxed surface.

Materials: This art activity requires drawing paper, tapered candles, crayons, tempera paint, a paint brush, and a pencil.

Directions: (1) Decide on a pattern or picture you wish to paint. Lightly sketch or trace it on your drawing paper with a pencil. (2) Using a sharpened candle, or a white crayon, draw over the sketch, leaving a heavy coat of wax. (3) Thin the paint with water. This is called a wash. (4) Brush the paint over the design, and your picture will appear. (5) Let the picture dry.

For a different effect, use a light-colored crayon to make contrasting colors in your picture. (Darker colors don't show up well.) For example, you could use a bright yellow crayon and deep blue paint.

MURALS

Suggested level: Lower and middle grades.

Project: Painting, cutting, pasting to make very large pictures.

Materials: A large sheet of butcher paper or newsprint, lightweight colored construction paper, scissors, glue, pencils, and water paints.

Directions: (1) You might want to begin this project with a discussion of plant life and ask the children what changes they notice in the fall. (2) Let them bring, show, and talk about the leaves, flowers, seed pods, and insects which they have gathered. (3) Decide what kind of mural you wish to make, and have the children draw a small sketch of the picture they wish to create. (4) The parent-teacher might prepare the background for the mural (hills, trees, roads, sky, and such background objects), and let the children arrange the ideas. (5) Show the children how to arrange the shapes attractively. (6) When they have decided on a particular arrangement, begin gluing the objects or construction paper cut-outs of them to the background. Continue with this until you have the desired picture.

A mural is a very large picture. Parents should plan its size to fit the space where it will be displayed. I suggest at least 2 by 3 feet.

For an autumn mural, you might want to use leaves, flowers, ears of corn, pumpkins, birds, frogs, cats, a big moon, etc. For a winter scene, you could use cotton, artificial snow, cut-out snow men, snowflakes, houses with snowy roofs, children playing in the snow, and so on. For a spring picture, flowers and springtime activities would be appropriate.

POTATO PRINTS

Suggested level: Lower, middle and upper grades.

Project: Stamping pictures with a carved potato.

Materials: Several large potatoes, tempera paint, paint brushes, a sharp knife, drawing paper, and newspapers.

Directions: First plan your picture or design and make a sketch. Make it very simple. Cut one of the potatoes in half with a straight cut. (If your potatoes are too soft, you can soak them in water.) Cut your design into the surface of the potato digging down to remove materials from all but the areas you want to print. Mix your paint. Brush it onto the cut surface and press the potato on the paper. Repeat the process using different colors or designs to get the effect you want. A stamp pad will work to apply the color if you don't mind getting potato juice on it.

This is an excellent project for making your own gift wrapping paper.

RUBBING PRINTS

Suggested level: Elementary and secondary grades.

Project: Learning to understand textures.

Materials: Medium to thin paper (typing paper is good); crayons, pastels or charcoal; hair spray or spray varnish.

Directions: Lay your piece of paper over a rough surface and rub it with the desired medium. Crayons work best for your first try. When using charcoal or pastels, spray lightly to seal the finish to avoid smearing. Cheaper hair spray seems to work better than the more expensive brands.

Surface ideas: Bricks, rough wood, screens, sidewalks, wire fencing, manhole covers, etc.

Cut the prints into interesting designs and put them together on a larger piece of paper to form a picture or pattern. You can use the idea to make a game. Cut several different patterns and place them on one side of a piece of construction paper. The person playing the game then tries to guess what the prints are made from.

A similar art project would be making pictures of objects like coins by placing a piece of paper over the surfaces and rubbing over them with the side of the pencil lead. A child can make his or her own math problems by tracing various combinations of coins and figuring the totals.

TIE DYE

Suggested level: Upper grades and high school.

Project: Design from uneven dying.

Materials: Fabric (clothes, scarves, ties, etc.), fabric dye (one or several colors).

Directions: (1) Prepare the dye as directed on the package. (2) Tie several knots very tightly in the fabric to be used. (3) Dip the fabric according to the dying instructions. (4) Remove the fabric, let it dry partially, then untie the knots and continue the dying process. (5) If you wish to dye it again, retie the knots in different places, and use a different color of die. (6) When using more than one color, begin with the lightest first. Use colors that go well together. If you mix red and green, yellow and purple, or blue and orange, you will get a brown color.

BATIK

Suggested level: Upper grades and high school.

Project: Fabric design with dye.

Materials: Fabric (scarves, ties, table cloths, clothes, etc.), fabric dye (one or more colors), paraffin wax, half-inch flat bristle paint brush, newspapers, iron.

Directions: (1) On scratch paper, draw sketches of designs for your fabric. You could make swirls, large flowers, different sized dots, squares, fruit and vegetable shapes, etc. Plan for the color to soak into the areas you won't be coating with wax. (2) Melt the wax in a double boiler–a pan of boiling water with another pan inside it with the wax. (3) Spread fabric out over the newspaper. (4) Using the paintbrush, apply the wax following the chosen design. Don't spread the wax too thick. (5) Let the wax set. (6) Mix the dye according to the directions on the container. It should be warm, but not hot, because hot dye would melt the wax. (7) Wad up the fabric and dip it into the dye. Soak it for the directed time. (8) Remove the fabric from the dye and hang it up to dry. (9) When the fabric is dry, place it between layers of clean paper and iron with a medium heat to remove the wax. As soon as the paper becomes saturated with the wax, change it for fresh paper.

You may repeat the process, using a different color of dye for a variety of effects. The wax will crack when you put it into the dye. This gives a pretty marbled effect. Experiment for fun.

STRING ART

Suggested level: Upper grades and high school.

Project: Making designs with string run from point to point on a board.

Materials: Pencil, poster board (8 by 10 inches suggested for beginners), large needles, several colors of embroidery floss.

Directions: (1) When you have an idea of how designs can be formed with string, make a scratch paper sketch of what you want. (2) Draw your design very lightly on your poster board. (3) Choose a beginning point and make a dot. Follow all around your sketch lines placing dots evenly. (4) Using a needle (darning needles work best), go back and poke a hole through each dot. (5) Now choose a color of floss, and thread an embroidery needle using two or three strands of floss. (6) Tie a knot in the thread and pull the needle through from the back side of the board to the front. (7) Cross back and forth to opposite points on the board, making a pattern. The longer strokes should appear on the front of the card to form the pattern, with the shorter segments on the back. (8) You can use one hole several times to get an interesting effect.

Alternate idea: Instead of making holes in cards, you can cut a small piece of three-eighths or half inch plywood. Sand the edges. Cover the board with a piece of thick, solid color cloth wrapping it around the edges to attach to the back. Draw your sketch on paper. Lay the paper on the board. Then following the points on your sketch, drive small finish nails through paper and cloth into the board. Your pattern is formed by running the thread from nail to nail. Patterns with lots of long straight lines work best. If you wish, you can get painted nails used for paneling.

NATURE'S ART

Suggested level: Middle grades, upper grades and high school.

Project: Using leaves and flowers to make prints.

Materials: Drawing paper, writing paper, card-type paper or any desired work surface. You will also need water paints, drawing chalk or pastels, pencils, and glue. You will then find leaves, flowers, and other objects in nature that can be flattened or pressed.

Directions for making leaf prints: (1) Gather different leaves from your yard, or a public park. (2) Choose a color and paint one side of the leaf, covering it well. (3) Lay the painted side of the leaf down on the paper which will become the finished picture. (4) Place another piece of paper on top of the leaf and press firmly over the entire leaf. (5) Put special emphasis on the center vein and the edges of the leaf. (6) Remove the top paper and the leaf, and allow the print to dry.

You can use this idea for making stationery, pictures, or even greeting cards. If you wish to have more than one leaf on the picture, wait until the first print is dry, then make another impression using another color. If your leaf is green and you treat it gently, you can wash off one color of paint and use the leaf for another.

Directions for making pressed flower pictures: (1) Collect leaves, flowers, ferns, and other small plant items all year. (2) Press them between pages of a book for several days until they are thoroughly dry and flat. (3) Choose your paper or board material. (4) Arrange chosen pieces into an attractive design. (5) Lightly sketch a guideline if necessary. (6) Remove the pieces and begin gluing them back on, going from the background to the foreground.

Dried flowers can be painted with water colors for brighter colors.

BASIC DRAWING

Suggested level: Middle or upper grades and high school.

Project: Introducing the basics of drawing techniques.

Materials: Sketch pad or drawing paper (typing paper is good for beginners), several drawing pencils, kneaded eraser, hair spray or spray varnish.

Concept: Many people believe that they just don't have the magic touch to be able to draw, but in reality most people can learn to draw well. The ability to draw is a basic for learning to paint pictures. It does take time, but the skill is well worth achieving.

Directions: (1) Begin by helping your child see basic shapes in real objects. Look for squares, rectangles, circles, and triangles. Then study what happens to these shapes when they are tipped–when the viewing angle is changed. Talk about parallelograms, ellipses, and so on. (2) Have your student practice drawing the basic shapes and the tipped shapes. (3) Look around your home for shapes to draw. For example, the clock face, the refrigerator, a tent, and so on. (4) With an understanding of shapes, detail can be filled in. (5) A full description of drawing techniques involves more than we can deal with in this chapter. Purchase some good drawing books. By copying the pictures in them and trying out the ideas they present, drawing can improve.

WATER COLOR PAINTING

Suggested level: Middle and upper grades and high school.

Project: Painting.

Materials: A pad of paper suitable for water colors; three round brushes – small, medium, and large; a set of water color paints – black, white, red, yellow, blue, orange, purple and green; a container for water; and a pencil.

Directions: (1) Choose what you would like to paint. (2) Very lightly sketch areas to be painted. For example, draw a line to separate land from sky, block out grass, mountains, and so on. (4) Paint from the background to the front of the picture. (5) Let each color dry thoroughly and add any fine details last.

You may also want to experiment with washes (thin paint). Get your paper wet and using a large brush, paint in several areas. If you want a special effect, you can let the paint run where it will. Be careful not to use too many colors or everything will turn an ugly brown. As the paper begins to dry, paint in the details to make the areas look like flowers, animals, birds, and so on.

Paint recipes

FINGER PAINT RECIPE

1 (Yield: 2 cups)

½ cup white flour
2 cups of water
1 tablespoon of glycerin
1 teaspoon of borax
several small jars with lids for storing paints.
food coloring or poster paints

(1) Mix the flour with ½ cup of water to form a paste. (2) Add the rest of the water and cook over low heat until the mixture is thick and clear, stirring constantly. (3) Cool the mixture and then add the glycerin and the borax. If the mixture is too thick, you may add a little more water. (4) Divide the

mixture into the jars and add the desired color. This recipe dries to a matte (dull) finish.

FINGER PAINT RECIPE
2 (Yield: 2½ cups)

½ cup of cornstarch
¾ cup of cold water
2 cups of hot water
2 teaspoons of boric acid
1 tablespoon of glycerin
several small jars with lids
food coloring or poster paints

(1) Mix the cornstarch with ¼ cup of cold water and make a paste. (2) Add the hot water, stirring quickly and vigorously to prevent lumps. (3) Cook the mixture over low heat and stir it constantly. (4) Remove the mixture from the heat and add the rest of the cold water and also the boric acid. Stir until it is well mixed, then add the glycerin. (5) Divide the mixture into the jars and add the desired coloring. This paint dries slowly and has a glossy finish.

Modeling mediums

Following are recipes for doughs or clays that can be made right in your own kitchen with common ingredients. They work very well for modeling and sculpture projects in the home school. Just follow the directions carefully and let your child's imagination go as he (or she) creates objects with his own hands. Remember that gentle guidance and help may be needed, and it is even more fun if "teacher" participates too! The most important thing to remember, especially for the preschoolers is DO NOT EAT THE DOUGH!

Here are a few suggestions for using the modeling mediums (or "media" if you prefer to call them that): (1) Roll into long "ropes" and write names, mottos, greetings, and so on. (2) Make braided baskets. (3) Make your own flower pots. You will probably want to bake your pots. (4) Roll into "ropes" to make picture frames, round as well as square. (5) Make wreaths. (6) Roll out to about 3/8 inch thick and cut out decorations for Christmas. (7) Make flowers, statues, 3-D pictures, animals, and so on.

Where directions call for shellac, you might try a spray varnish. Look for it with the spray paints. Just get a clear color.

MODELING DOUGH
(Yield: 1 cup)

¾ cup of flour
½ cup of salt
1½ teaspoon of powdered alum
1½ teaspoon of vegetable oil
½ cup boiling water
food coloring

(1) Mix the dry ingredients in a bowl. (2) Mix the oil and water together, stirring quickly. (3) Add the oil and water to the dry ingredients and stir until blended. (4) Add the desired color of food coloring.

Use the dough as you would any commercially available dough. It will dry overnight if left out in the open air.

PLAY CLAY
(Yield: 1½ cups)

½ cup salt
½ cup hot water
¼ cup cold water
½ cup cornstarch

(1) Mix the salt into the water and bring it to a boil. (2) Stir the cornstarch into the cold water. (3) Add the above two mixtures and stir vigorously to avoid lumping. (4) Cook the mixture over low heat, stirring constantly until it thickens. It should become like pie dough. (5) Remove the mixture from the heat and let it cool. (6) Knead the mixture until soft and pliable.

This is an excellent dough to roll out and use for flat items and Christmas decorations. It can be dried in the air overnight, or in the oven at 200 degrees for one hour.

SOAPSUDS CLAY
(Yield: 1 cup)

¾ cup of powdered soap (Different from detergent; Ivory Snow)
1 tablespoon of warm water

(1) Mix the soap powder and the water in a bowl. (2) Beat with an electric mixer until it forms a clay-like consistency. (3) Mold into figures and objects. The mixture dries to a hard finish.

HARDENING CLAY
(Yield: 1½ cups)

1 cup baking soda
1/2 cup cornstarch
2/3 cup of warm water

food coloring
shellac

(1) Mix the soda and the starch in a pan. (2) Add the water and stir until the mixture is smooth. (3) Cook at medium heat and bring to a boil. It should look like mashed potatoes. (4) Remove it from the heat and let it cool. (5) Knead the clay well when it is cool. (6) Add food coloring to the clay, or use it as it is, to be painted later. (7) Let the objects dry. (8) Cover them with shellac.

This mixture hardens rather quickly, so it is not good to use if you just wish to play with it for a while. You should have project in mind before you make it.

BREAD DOUGH CLAY
(Small yield)

1 slice of white bread
1 teaspoon of white glue
1 teaspoon of water
food coloring
shellac

(1) Cut off the crust of the bread. (2) Pour the glue, then the water, into the center of the slice of bread. (3) Knead the bread until it is no longer sticky. (4) Add the food coloring as desired. (5) Shape the clay into flowers or objects as you wish, and then let them dry overnight. (6) Finish the pieces by shellacing them. If you want to make more than one small object, you will want to prepare larger quantities.

BASIC BREADCRAFT

4 cups of flour
1½ cups of warm water
1 cup of salt

(1) Mix the above ingredients. (2) Cover and refrigerate for half an hour. (3) Roll out and use as "ropes," baskets, writing, or decorations. (4) Use cookie cutters to make ornaments, if desired.

GINGER DOUGH

2 cups of flour
1 cup of salt
5 teaspoons of cinnamon
or instant coffee
¾ to 1 cup of warm water.

Follow the directions as shown for "basic breadcraft."

BRICK BREAD

1 package of yeast
2 tablespoons of sugar
¼ cup of warm water
2 tablespoons of salt
1¼ cup of scalded milk
5 cups of flower
1 tablespoon of shortening
2 eggs
1/4 to 1/3 cup plaster of Paris

(1) Mix the yeast in the water. (2) Add the shortening to the scalded milk and let it cool. (3) Add the sugar to the yeast, then add the milk mixture with the salt and one egg. (4) Mix. (5) Start adding the flour, one cup at a time. (6) Mix with a spoon, then knead with your hands, adding the remaining flour until the dough is no longer sticky. (7) Set your oven on warm. (8) Grease a bowl and set it inside the oven to warm. (9) Then set the mixture in the warm bowl, cover it, and let it set for ten minutes inside the oven. (10) Let the dough rise for one hour, punch it down, and let it set for another ten minutes. (11) Punch the dough down again, and knead in the plaster. (12) "Flour" a board with plaster of Paris, and shape your dough into desired forms or objects. (13) Let the shapes rise for one-half to one hour. (14) Bake on a foil sheet at 350° F for fifteen minutes. (15) Brush with a beaten egg and bake another fifteen minutes. (16) Reduce the oven temperature to 150° F and bake the projects for eight hours. (17) Turn the pieces over after about six hours. They should sound hollow. (18) Varnish the objects several times, letting the varnish dry thoroughly between coats.

41

Skills Development

Edwin Myers

I still remember the day when I found out that my oldest son, who was just finishing up a second grade math workbook, couldn't add:

"Say, Matthew, what's 7 + 4?"

"Uh, 7 + 4?" Matthew replied. "Let's see . . . 7, (and his fingers went under the table as he whispered slowly) 8, 9, 10, 11 . . . 11!"

Edwin C. Myers, Ph.D. *directs The Providence Project. The teaching concepts apparent in some of the materials he has developed interested me, so I asked him to share them with you. The computer graphics art in this chapter is also his contribution. He lives north of Wichita.*

Almost every problem I asked him went that way. Actually, I shouldn't say he couldn't add, because, in a way, he could. He understood the concept of addition and he could use a concrete procedure (counting fingers) to get the right answer – the majority of the time – after 7 or 8 seconds!

I was disconcerted by the fact that Matthew could complete his first and second grade math workbooks in an entirely acceptable manner and still have addition skills that were far from the point of real, practical usefulness. His experience was a classic example of the limitations of *knowledge without know- how.*

Toward self-reinforcement

One important way to judge the adequacy of a basic skill is to ask, "Has this skill become self-reinforcing?" We want our students to get to that delightful point where they "take off and run" with the skills they have been introduced to. This happens when they get "over the hump" of their initial awkwardness, and realize that their new skills make them more capable. Seeing the benefits of their enhanced skills, they start using them on their own.

Many students never get over the hump in one or more key skills. Because the skills in question aren't used, they wither away instead of being self-reinforced. A good example of this tendency is the might-have-been-typist. Many of us have perhaps taken a typing course in the past. We probably recall the unpleasantness of having to practice a skill that simply seemed to rob us of time for doing other activities that we were more comfortable and adept at. And, besides, we could write as fast or faster than we could type anyway! If we never got over the hump to where correct typing paid off in speed and accuracy, chances are we would have lost much of whatever typing skills we once attained.

How do we get over the hump? That's the question. But before we can understand getting over humps, we must know where they are – what each of our students faces at his own particular level of skill development. So let's first take a look at the humpy skills landscape.

The skills chain

Most tasks in which we would like our students to become proficient require a whole suite of skills – something I like to call a "skills chain." For example, we may casually think of the task of solving the math problem $5 + 2 = \_\_\_$ as calling for the use of the addition skill. With a little reflection, however, we realize that even this rather basic problem requires competence in several skills. These include:

visual recognition of the numerals written on the page, a mental concept of the values to which the numerals correlate, perception (at least at some level) of the meaning of the "+" and "=" signs, familiarity with other numbers (like the answer "7") which do not appear in the problem at all, and sufficient verbal or manual skill to say or write down the answer.

Take the long division problem, *628 ÷ 13*, for example. To solve it, one must: recognize the numerals and the division symbol and know their mathematical significance, estimate the various digits of the quotient (a multiplication skill), place them over the correct digits in the dividend (a place-value skill), multiply by the divisor (this may include the "carrying" skills of addition), subtract to find remainders, and so on. All the skills used in the *5 + 2* problem are still very much needed in the *628 ÷ 13* problem. Now here's the rub: a weak link in the skills chain, even a weak addition link, jeopardizes success.

The general principle is that *the quality of performance in any given task is limited by the weakest link in the required skills chain.* A corollary principle is that *a weak link in the skills chain at any given proficiency level will adversely affect performance at all higher proficiency levels.*

What does all this have to do with the skills humps we were talking about earlier? Just this: a weak link in the skills chain is simply a skill which has never gotten over the hump! To complicate matters we sometimes fail to detect the humps along the road to proficiency as soon as we should.

A weak link in the skills chain may not be apparent until we hang a heavy performance weight on the chain. For example, a student may habitually resort to mental finger-counting to solve simple addition problems like *5 + 2*. We may not notice this, and our student may not think it's any big deal either. Later though, when he encounters problems where he has to find *5 + 2 + 8 + 3 + 6* on his way to getting the answer, or when he's doing a problem like *628 ÷ 13*, in which additional skills need to be "second nature," the substituted addition link that once seemed strong, snaps. Then our student bogs down and becomes discouraged.

Over the hump! – *Points to remember*

▲ Don't presume that *knowing about* is the same as *doing well.* In the midst of such questions as, "Can my child describe it?", "Can my child give an example of it?", "Can my child classify it?", and so on, don't forget the importance of the question, "Can my child *do* it?"

▲ Try to raise the proficiency level of each new skill a *bit higher than it needs to be* at that particular time. Why? Because as soon as the very next skill is introduced, the previously learned skill will need to function at this higher (i.e., confident, natural, over the hump) level, or it may become a weak link in the skills chain.

▲ Try to cultivate a *diagnostic* frame of mind as you evaluate your children's performance. When your kids are having difficulties, ask yourself, "What's the real problem here?" Try to be specific with your answer.

▲ Give your kids a daily workout with

"academic calisthenics" in several key skills areas, if possible. These can take the format of brief, daily performance drills which focus on factual and procedural, nuts-and-bolts *doing*. Drills with goals for both speed and accuracy make weak areas stand out like sore thumbs, and provide a great way for student and teacher to measure proficiency and recognize improvement. One series of such drills is the Providence Project's *Learning Vitamins*. (See Appendix Q.)

▲ Finally, in connection with regular drills, it's well to set *performance standards*. By this I mean that advancement to higher-level drills should depend on successful mastery of earlier drills. In this way we can help give our students the humility and honesty to acknowledge where they are, and the pleasure and gratitude that comes from getting over the humps with God's enablement and provision.

Helping Learners Build Skills

- Knowing doesn't mean being able to perform well.
- Barely enough isn't enough.
- Be alert to specific learning needs.
- Speed drills reveal skills that need improvement.
- Set standards according to past achievements.

42

Learning From Work

We teach our children an impressive array of academic subjects. We also provide other experiences to help them mature. But preparation for practical, responsible living which common labor teaches best we somehow take for granted. The home school family environment is excellent for work education, but it takes more than being home.

Work education doesn't fit a neat little box like we use for math or spelling. And neither is it mastered simply by having a job and making money. Let's consider what we expect work education to contribute to the total development of our children. Then we will look at how work might teach at various stages of maturity.

I see objectives for work education in the three major groups: job skills, applied knowledge, and attitudes for success.

Job skills, specific and general

The first thing we think of that might be learned from a work experience is skill development. Yard work, for instance, teaches plant and lawn care. It teaches operation and maintenance of yard equipment. But how much help are these specific skills for later work as a cab driver, then as an accountant? More than it might seem. The unrelated skills provide the ability to work at a different job when employment in the preferred field is not available. And there are less-apparent values which we discuss later.

Work experiences can also teach general skills important for future employment and for efficient, intelligent living. Most of these general skills can be grouped into categories of: (1) caring for personal needs, (2) dealing with people, (3) working with ideas, and (4) handling materials.

Here are a few examples to show what we mean by general skills: keeping skin clean and fresh, using common hand tools, making people feel at ease, using a stove to prepare food, applying paint evenly and quickly with a brush, delegating responsibility in organizing people for a large task, using a typewriter or computer keyboard, arranging objects for visual appeal, and remembering instructions.

The difference between general and specific skills is somewhat arbitrary. The reason for making a distinction in our discussion here is to bring out the idea that even uncommon tasks are accomplished by a combination of more general skills, and that these abilities transfer to other jobs. Thus using a Philips screwdriver in the job of hanging kitchen cabinet doors improves the ability to work with the same tool on the instrument panel of an automobile, and the sensitivity to damaging the screw by too much force even transfers to picking cherries. When we analyze just about any task, we find skills or skill components that are general and thus may be applied in many other tasks.

Applied knowledge

In job knowledge, the second category of objectives, factual information is acquired, although not always as efficiently as with books. A person isn't apt to take a job on a cargo ship to learn the names of a few major seaports.

Knowledge seen in application, especially for young children, is easier to learn and remember. Keeping track of money earned for little jobs teaches more accounting to a third grader than careful explanations, even in simple words.

Attitudes for success

What we have said so far is more or less obvious and similar to what you would have expected as benefits of practical work. Now we come to the most important value of work education – the formation of attitudes. Consider this list of character traits that work experience might be expected to develop. Many more could be added.

- Perseverance
- Responsibility
- Sensitivity to people's needs
- Respect for authority
- Cooperation
- Adaptability
- Balance: physical, mental, social, and spiritual
- Setting priorities
- Sense of purpose
- Contentment: protection from covetousness and envy
- Integrity
- Sense of value of resources: time, effort, money
- Patience, deferred gratification
- Self-worth

Of course, factors other than work also contribute to the development of these attitudes. The example of parents or friends, and good reading are fundamental and inescapable influences. But observation is still theory. Only through the experience of personal application can anyone actually claim possession of an attitude.

As they mature

For the young child, work and play are the same. It's all fun. To keep work enjoyable, begin guiding toward responsibility while your child is still a toddler. As understanding develops, teach responsibility. Regular eating habits, potty training, keeping quiet in church and putting toys away are important early training objectives.

A little later, expect your child to "help" make the bed, bring clothes for the washing machine, fix lunch and do similar tasks you could perform much easier by yourself. Plan activities for developing attitudes of fulfillment through helping meet the family needs, and of acting by principle rather than feeling. At the same time you will be teaching skills in muscle coordination and in following instructions.

As time goes on, expect your child to assume more regular responsibilities around home. At this third stage, the child may also fulfill personal needs such as room orderliness, grooming and clothing care. Following through on responsibilities, however, doesn't come naturally for most children. You will need to supervise and encourage. And when progress dwindles, your talk will be heard best while you help (not take over).

Also don't expect so much that no time is left for relaxation, personal creative pursuits, and spiritual growth.

By the way, try to imagine how your children could learn all this if you pack them off to a child care service so you can work during their tender years. I wouldn't argue that it's impossible, but it's certainly not likely to succeed as well.

At the fourth stage, after your child has shown a reasonable degree of responsibility at home, it may be time for an outside job. Children are generally optimistic and try to swim the English Channel as soon as they can paddle across the pool. They need your counsel. Also, children are easily influenced. You will want to know that your child's working environment is a good one for character development and for physical safety.

Appropriate jobs for children include delivering papers, doing yard work and baby-sitting. During less mature years, such jobs need close supervision. Baby-sitting, for example, could be done in the child's own home with parents present. A parent could go with the child on some jobs.

Also investigate volunteer service work. In addition to such activities as helping in hospitals or nursing homes or in community cleanup projects, your child might enjoy the learning experience of working without pay for a business person.

Being responsible to someone outside the family gives working a sense of seriousness. Someone other than Mom or Dad expects a good use of time and energy. To make the experience more meaningful, take time to talk things over now and then. Talk with the employer, too. You will probably hear more positive than negative comments because, from my experience, home schooled kids tend to be excellent workers.

Young people of high school age are ready for more serious employment commitments – perhaps even a full-time summer job. When a new job begins, you and your offspring should make a list of learning objectives for both character development and job skills. Then every month or two you can discuss progress, thereby keeping those goals fresh in mind.

Parent teachers who work side-by-side with their children and youth can build trust relationships that open channels for communicating life values. Making bread or chopping onions together builds a different understanding than other types

You really weren't supposed to see this. We have a new chapter on the topic of chores and I told Deb we wouldn't be using her work which has appeared in several editions of *The Home School Manual.* Besides, I needed to save the space. But I thought you might appreciate both this and the new chapter so I squeezed it in.

Chores (by Deb Deffinbaugh. See Timberdoodle in Appendix Z.)

Children would usually rather play than work, and moms sometimes find it easier to do a job themselves, than to plead with a child to undertake the responsibility. Here are some ideas that have worked in our family.

1. Inherent in the assigning of each job, is the need to be explicit in your desires. In our family, when a child assumes a new chore, she is told how to do it. This often means that Dan or I take enough time to walk her through the assignment, detailing not only our expectations, but also why we do what we do, dangerous aspects to the job, and even tips on how to make it more efficient or pleasant.

2. Next we give our children a checklist to refer to, that reiterates our expectations for that chore. Then, when they feel they have completed it, they can check their list before they ask us for our approval. This saves a lot of "I forgot I had to. . . ."

3. For following through to completion, two big criteria are, inspection and checkpoints. We have found true the adage that when it come to chores, children will do what you inspect, not what you expect! Checkpoints are simply regular times during the day for reaching goals. Our checkpoints are mealtimes. Before our children eat, they must have performed certain tasks. By breaking jobs into manageable chunks, we eliminate overwhelming amounts of chores just before free time.

4. One final thought to moms: Examine what you are doing in a given day, and ask yourself, "Can this be delegated?" As a keeper of the home, delegation is vital.

For those who plead that their children need time to play, we encourage teaching children how to work smarter (faster), not harder. Most children who spend enormous amounts of time doing chores either lack that instruction, or are dawdling.

Moms who prefer to do a job themselves rather than teach their child to do it, make us uneasy. Just about everything is that way, from feeding to reading. Working in the home is an integral part of growing up, and the wise parent is one who recognizes that this short term bother will result in the long term benefits of a mature child of encounters. Christian living is seen as real and practical, and academic responsibility becomes a natural extension of the relationship. The adult supervises, but with sleeves rolled up.

After high school, work education continues as youth in the spirit of adventure explore their world with new freedom.

Throughout life, useful labor molds and preserves the person who has made God first. At the age of forty, Moses fled to the desert of Midian to learn humility herding sheep and in communion with His Creator. The broader an individual's early base of experience has been, the easier it will be to face the changes that come through the years.

Character is values built into life as governing principles. Reading about values and being able to explain them are important; but values touch the heart when they are seen in Christ and in the lives of parents and others. Then they are firmed up as internal principles as they are put into practice.

Choosing work experiences

In looking for jobs that educate, useful experience and environment count more than high pay. The biggest job "bargain" for an individual at any level of maturity is a task that involves physical exercise, health-stimulating fresh air, a relaxing emotional atmosphere, and a closeness to God's creation.

Gardening may best answer to that description. Digging, cutting, and hauling provide varied exercise; gardens are generally outside; plants don't talk back; effort of mind and body produce predictable, noninstant results; and the work is a partnership, because, as in the spiritual garden, Paul may plant, Apollos may water, but God gives the increase (1 Cor. 3:6).

In the following section are practical ideas for teaching job responsibility.

Character quality, the end purpose

Our complex society offers a vast array of good learning opportunities that compete for our children's time. Christian parents would agree that the formation of a Christlike character is of more value than any other learning. But why is practical labor so important in shaping lives?

Cutting grass, helping sick people, and carrying cement don't by themselves insure good character. But practical work experiences like these provide opportunity for our children to take actual possession of the principles they have seen and read about. Jesus learned the Scriptures from godly parents. He also was "subject unto them" (Luke 2:51). He spent many hours at Joseph's carpenter bench and in helping with the daily family chores. And He "increased in wisdom and stature, and in favour with God and man" (verse 52).

43

Teaching High School

As you probably remember from your own schooling, the teaching approach changes abruptly when high school begins (and again for college). In elementary school you went each day for whatever learning experiences your teacher had planned. If you put your heart into it, you learned. As you got to higher grades you probably had some homework. You were responsible to one teacher in early grades and later your home room teacher tried to see to it that you kept on course.

When you climbed, with some uncertainty, into the high school canoe, they gave you a paddle and a map to the various class islands and gently pushed you off from shore. Adolescence had already begun and you had been indeed eager to paddle your own canoe. Now, in a way, you were doing it. There were plenty of navigational aids and caring people, but you had more of the responsibility. If you were like many youth, your judgment was a little immature and you stopped for fishing at the wrong time now and then, but you made it.

I have reminded you of this change in approach to help you see that it matches a change in the development of children. In my opinion, the schooling change could be a little less abrupt (and it is with the junior high school and big elementary schools). In your home teaching, if you have been too much of a mother hen helping your child scratch for every bug, this is the time to ease more of the burden onto your young chickens. Actually good high school teaching makes the kids feel responsible, and it also has many ways to monitor and advise those who start on unprofitable fishing trips.

Grades 9 to 12 are traditionally considered high school here in the United States. A common refinement has been for grades 7 to 9 to be junior high and 10 to 12, senior high. Middle school begins somewhere before junior high.

Can you teach them at this level?

The answer isn't as simple as it was earlier. It depends on your own competence in the subject areas and on your students. Dr. & Mrs. Lanier offer practical advice on this in the next chapter. A few young people have the ability and self-control to dig out information from books and source people, but most would have a hard time understanding much chemistry without someone to explain at least those areas that begin to get confusing and to guide in the experiments.

In connection with these thoughts, read the chapter, "Educating for Superior Achievement." The Colfax boys had an excellent secondary education. To a large degree they set their own direction. I suspect that they missed some learning that typical high school kids get, but then the curriculum is somewhat arbitrary. No one can learn everything important especially in the first 18 years of life.

If I had it to do over from what I know now, I would want my high school age children to do some exploring into their own intellectual interests, I would have them involved in some group learning experiences – perhaps in a good classroom school. I would include correspondence courses to make sure the fundamentals were learned. And I would want them to dig more into the rich treasures of the Scriptures.

Choosing a high school level correspondence program

One good way to arrange for high school instruction at home is by "correspondence." As you can see from Appendix B, many state universities and private institutions offer high school correspondence study.

In choosing a secondary correspondence school or an individual course, you will want to consider the quality of the instruction offered, the services provided by the school, and the costs.

Courses vary somewhat in quality and philosophical approach even within the same school just as they do with different teachers in a traditional school. Although there is no way to be completely certain of satisfaction, most of the schools I am familiar with take a serious professional attitude toward the programs they offer, and produce good courses. The course description in the school catalog will give you clues about whether or not you are getting what you want. For a better idea of what the course is like, you could try to find a copy of the textbooks to examine.

For a half unit – a course in one subject for half of a school year – you should expect ten to fifteen lesson submissions and one or two supervised examinations. Part of each lesson is a printed commentary from the course author representing what a teacher might say in class. This presentation usually ranges from less than a page to half a dozen pages. The amount and type depend on the information available in the other study materials.

In addition to the commentary, most lessons have an assignment to send in to the school for grading. Sometimes lessons include self-check exercises. Often workbooks, audio or video tapes, lab equipment, or other special learning materials are used along with textbooks.

The school receives lessons, logs them in, has them graded, records the results, and mails them back.

Transcripts are issued for satisfactory course completion, but not all schools offer diplomas. Most students supplementing their classroom education take only one or two correspondence courses. Those who do want to complete their studies by correspondence can sometimes get a diploma through a local high school if their correspondence school doesn't offer one.

Examinations are administered outside the home. The student sends in exam request forms at appropriate points. State universities often have designated examination centers scattered throughout the state. Those who study from an out-of-state university or from a correspondence school which is not state sponsored arrange for an acceptable supervisor, usually at a nearby school.

Correspondence schools do not serve hot lunches or pick up their students in buses, but they do provide services beyond receiving tuition and mailing study materials. Some of the help and guidance a teacher in the traditional school would give a typical student is anticipated by the correspondence school and included in the study guide. The correspondence teacher grades the lessons and tests, and writes notes to encourage students and to help them understand their errors.

At least one university correspondence school expects supervisors of its high school students to do more than proctor the examinations. They are to be "links" between students and school to offer encouragement and guidance.

Although talking with the teacher on the telephone will not often be a great advantage with well-designed courses, occasions may arise when a short conversation could clear up a misunderstanding blocking progress on the course. Some schools encourage direct contact with teachers and will give you their phone numbers. Some will not. To find out about the policy you may need to ask. A few schools have toll-free phone lines to the school offices.

The prompt return of graded lessons is certainly desirable since students not only are rewarded by the results of their work but also learn from their errors. Unfortunately the lesson handling process is generally slow. Delays in returning lessons usually come from the teachers who are, in most cases, employed full time in a typical classroom, and who grade lessons as a sideline for supplementary income. Sometimes graduate students do the grading. Lessons are checked in, sent to the teachers, received back for grades to be recorded, and returned to the student.

Several schools use a computer to help grade some courses. This allows them to have lessons back in the mail quickly. Objective type responses such as multiple choice can be handled efficiently by the computer which not only indicates the mistakes but can give information to help the student find the right answers. Computers would not be used for subjective work such as art and English compositions which are better graded by "live" teachers.

Being able to retake a test is usually better than repeating the entire course. I would check school policies on this.

Mandatory school attendance ages generally cover most of the high school years as well as all the elementary years. Accreditation is important, but the primary issue is your receiving authorization to not send the young person to a traditional school. Credit acceptance may depend more on whether or not the high school you ask to honor the credits feels the student should be studying outside the traditional system, than it does on the qualifications of the correspondence school.

Be sure the courses you choose lead to the goal you want – presumably graduation. If you plan for your young person to graduate from the correspondence school, say so when you enroll and be sure you are getting necessary courses into the program. Verify that the school actually offers a diploma and that your son or daughter can qualify for it. High schools generally have a limit on the number of correspondence credits they accept toward graduation. In practice, however, if a student has a good reason for being out of the traditional school, arrangements can be made to accept the credits. A visit with a local school guidance counselor might be worthwhile.

Charges for courses vary considerably. When comparing tuition, note that some schools charge an additional fee for the study guide. Some schools have a "registration" fee which you will need to pay with each course or each time you send for a group of courses.

Know what reimbursement is made if it becomes necessary to drop a course. If the policy is not printed on the enrollment form, you may wish to write it in yourself before you sign. Keep a copy. If a particular course turns out to be unsatisfactory, most schools allow another course to be substituted for it. Check the costs and time limitations.

Also find out how much time is given for completing a course. Most schools give you a year, but for an additional fee they will grant an extension.

Appendix B lists most major high school correspondence schools in the U.S. Not all university schools offer courses at the high school level. And some who do, use materials from a major school like the University of Nebraska.

Admission for higher education

Even without a high school diploma most universities will accept students who show a reasonable possibility of succeeding. Scores from the SAT (Scholastic Aptitude Test) or the ACT (American College Test) help them decide. If you are interested in this plan, consult with someone in the university admissions office and, if possible, get written verification of their policies. Bookstores and newsstands sell books to coach preparation for the tests. The universities can tell you when and where they are given.

Shortening the high school m isn't necessarily wise, however, even if the college will accept the enrollment. I would look for readiness in study habits, social maturity, and proficiency in important subject areas which are more efficiently learned at the high school level.

Designing a high school curriculum

First let me remind you that a "curriculum" is a long-range study plan or an available area of study involving a series of individual courses. It is a set of learning activities planned for a specific purpose. Unfortunately most uses of the term in home schooling circles assume it to mean a particular set of *materials*.

Maybe I've been brainwashed by the educational establishment, but I feel (with a few exceptions) that the typical high school curriculum outline is a good background of the secular knowledge important to function efficiently in the adult world. When it comes to what is actually taught in some of the courses – theories that clearly conflict with what God has revealed – that's another matter. What I'm suggesting is that the lineup of courses such as are listed in Appendix G, "Typical Course of Study," (assuming that they are taught in an acceptable way) is a good point for beginning to decide what is important. In my introduction to that appendix, I mention what I feel might be added. Also, the list contains a few advanced courses of various kinds. Some of these could wait for college. Or if they are taken earlier they might be waived at the college level.

From a list like this you and your son or daughter can build what you see as important. The choice of some of the more intellectual courses like advanced math and science should depend on the ability of your young person and on plans for continued study. High schools generally have two streams. It would be worth talking with a counselor at a local high school to get ideas about consequences of studying certain areas. Taking a battery of tests is sometimes helpful.

I have described the typical correspondence schools as usually operated by universities. A number of religious organizations also offer home study courses. Some of them operate just as these correspondence schools do and some quite differently. Also several proprietary schools offer good high school programs. I am not recommending one approach above another. You might appreciate a nontraditional program. Compare it with the "Typical Course of Studies" already mentioned.

Making your own curriculum carries some risks. A visit to the fire station meets elementary school learning needs quite well, but being a volunteer fire fighter hardly substitutes as social science for a youth. Of course the traditional curriculum is not the only way. If you plan college education for your youth, just be sure he or she is challenged in the study areas needed for a good base.

Other learning for adolescents

In these years, social and moral development can come to maturity under the guidance of wise parents. Consider the chapters on work education and social development. For the Christian youth, it's a time to learn to walk with the Lord and to learn how to share the joy of Christ with others. See my description of the development of spiritual maturity in the "teaching values" chapter.

Adolescence is a time for making giant leaps toward adulthood. It's the ripening of the fruit of character development – the last significant opportunity for parents to make an impact on young lives.

44

Teenagers Taught at Home

David and Laurie Lanier

Things change when children become teenagers. Newspaper articles, talk shows, and numerous books and articles attest to the interest parents have in minimizing the turbulence expected in the family while children are teenagers. These concerns also find their way into the minds of parents who home teach.

In this chapter we discuss factors parents should consider when home schooling children in high school.

A prologue to adulthood

We reject, on principle and by experience, the idea that adolescence must be turbulent. We know of many cases where families have led children to, through, and beyond their teenage years in a spirit of love and unity. Granted, expectations may need to change from time to time, and the crucial role of communications can never be underestimated. Parents must constantly remind themselves that this six-foot, freshly shaven, deep-voiced individual requesting to use the car tonight is no longer the little boy whose ability to cross the street brought them anxiety only a few years ago. And while struggles and disagreements may arise, they need not strike fear into the parents' hearts.

On the contrary, the teenage years can be vibrant and exciting with shared expectations and mutual respect. Communicating to our children that we expect their teenage years to be problematical is unfair. Expressing dread of their adolescence contributes to the fulfillment of our "prophecy."

We should communicate early to our children that they "get to run the farm" when they become young adults. They should be groomed from a young age to believe that by the end of their adolescence, they will be prepared with the abilities and maturity they need for their role in adult life. We should clearly state our intention to not withhold any prerogatives of adulthood. The teenage experience may be seen as a joint project for the development of a young man or woman whose character all can admire. Such an understanding goes far toward making the teen years a pleasure.

The Laniers teach or have taught their own four children at home. Chris, Julie, and Sarah are in college or beyond. Abigail is in ungraded special education at home.

David Lanier holds a Ph.D. degree and is a licensed psychologist. His wife, Laurie's background profession is nursing.

Directions for learning

Total responsibility for study needs to be developed by the end of high school. The move toward independence should be already clear by the ninth grade.

We believe that the parents still have the primary responsibility for supervising the curriculum for the high school student. Many teenagers will not see the relevance of a course in United States history or English literature. Nevertheless, parents should require learning in appropriate areas. Beyond the minimum standards, however, the youth should be given an ever-increasing role in his own education. Courses of particular interest such as clothing merchandising, Russian history, automobile mechanics, or American Sign Language, should be planned into the school day.

To accommodate a wide variety of classes it may be advisable to adopt a college format where classes meet two or three times per week rather than daily. Long-term assignments can be established early in the semester. Or the elective topics may be studied intensively in blocks of several weeks while the standard curriculum continues through the semester.

Learning from an older sister

Many home schooled teenagers will have moderately clear ideas of what they intend to do following high school. It is altogether appropriate to encourage becoming acquainted with the fundamentals of those disciplines while still in high school. Other youth may not have any inkling of what they want to do "when they grow up." They should be exposed to a wide variety of vocational or academic options. In fact, options are also important for confirming or changing plans of students with established ideas.

By high school many home students will have begun a business which requires some of their time. Such activities should be encouraged as long as reasonable performance is maintained in the academic studies. Some will wish to participate in projects such as community cleanup campaigns, political activities, helping someone build a house, or travel to another country. Reasonable accommodation to such opportunities, whenever feasible, provides experiences for maturing. More broadening of horizons may be appropriate after high school or during college years.

Attitude is crucial

Hopefully your youth will be eager to satisfy basic requirements for continued studies. We believe that the principle of finishing the broccoli before eating ice cream applies to school, too, especially for high school. For a variety of reasons, not the least of which are the college entrance requirements to be discussed below, the adolescent needs to learn that doing what is desired may not replace doing what is required. It is only reasonable that the requirements you place on him should take into account his unique academic, social, and personality characteristics. By the time a child graduates from high school he should be able to bring the same amount of energy to an unpleasant task as to a preferred one.

The Student as Teacher

Educational research and years of experience show the value to both student and teacher in having older children teach younger ones. In home schools it is also a matter of efficient use of resources. We have found it best when the age difference between teacher and student is at least two or three years, but we know of cases where it has been very successful with children closer together in age. The high school student who has a good mastery of mathematics can learn much about organization and presentation of material when asked to teach his younger brother or sister about multiplication of fractions. The younger sibling can be given an adequate lesson while the parent utilizes that time for lesson planning or other activities.

The interactions between siblings can increase the appreciation of each child for the other. The older one frequently finds that his younger brother or sister is smarter than he thought and the younger child gets to know his older sibling as more than a hormone-driven, telephone-answering machine. Also, the teenager, having experienced the role of teacher, can appreciate his own teachers more. We have found peer tutoring to be a wonderful tool for counteracting sibling rivalry (but that's another story).

Co-op teaching

If academic excellence is a part of the reason why you home school, then plan on co-op teaching in high school. By co-op teaching we mean having people other than yourself teach selected courses in the high school curriculum. These other people could be parents of other home school children or simply people who have expertise in an area. It may even be necessary, on occasion, to hire a tutor to work within a particular discipline. In any event, it would be the truly unusual parent, or couple, who could do an adequate job teaching all the courses required for a reasonable, comprehensive high school curriculum.

Co-op teaching usually takes one of two forms. ✓ In the most likely case, parents from one home schooling family recognize their deficiency in one or more content areas which the parents of another home schooling family happen to possess. An arrangement is worked out such that the first couple teaches children from both families subject A, and the second couple teaches the children from both families subject B. Care must be taken any time co-op arrangements are developed to insure that all parties are in agreement about such things as absences, homework, planned or unplanned vacations, grading scales, and other questionable matters. Any books or supplies should be provided by each student's parents.

✓ The other typical form co-op teaching takes involves asking a person with a known expertise to teach his specialty. This can be individual tutoring, or several families may join together and request that a small class be formed.

You may hesitate to ask an expert with no obviously vested interest in your children. However, we know of several cases where the knowledgeable person considered it a compliment to be thought of and enthusiastically agreed to teach their specialty. In one case from our personal experience a member of the community was asked to teach the lab of a science course. He responded to the request somewhat hesitantly, but with some curiosity. After looking over the book and lab material and meeting the three youngsters in question, he agreed to the "experiment." Before the first semester was over he was asking what would be necessary for him and his wife to home school their young daughters.

As noted in the previous paragraph, co-op teaching need not be for the entire course. The co-op teacher might teach only the lab portion of the course, or a course for a part of a semester or year. Or two or three different co-op teachers could each cover a portion of a course. In fact, we think of ourselves more as "education brokers" than home teachers. We make a thorough search of the best teaching circumstances for a given course. Although we often decide that one of us would be the best teacher, we do not hesitate to arrange for co-op teachers when that plan would be better.

Apprenticeship

Whether or not your youth intends to pursue academic studies after high school, consider the possibility of one or more apprenticeships during the high school years. In spite of evidence confirming the extraordinary usefulness of mentors, few high school students have the opportunity to serve as an apprentice to a journeyman.

Apprenticeships are especially important for the youth who does not expect to attend college. If he has interests along a certain vocational line, try to arrange for him to volunteer his services with someone in that field. He may have to start off by doing janitorial work or simple tasks, but if he applies himself he may very well work himself into a paying job while in high school. Be sure to be aware of the relevant child labor laws in your area as you contemplate such a possibility.

Our son, Chris, has had a lifelong interest in electronics. While still in high school he worked with a man who repaired electronic appliances, primarily videotape machines. During his association with this gentleman he received a great deal of information about how to read schematic diagrams, how to diagnose electrical problems, how to work with customers, etc. He was also given a lot of used equipment which he cannibalized to make his own creations. Subsequently he started doing some work as a consultant for people who had personal computers but did not know how to use them very well. He even started his own computer sales business while still in high school.

Our daughter, Julie, had the opportunity to volunteer one morning a week in a school for handicapped children. She had often thought she might like to work in this area after she became an adult. From this experience she learned something of the nature of the work. During that time she learned American Sign Language and many other useful skills. A job making eyeglasses for an optician provided another learning opportunity. It is a relatively small shop, and the owner does most of the optical lab work himself. When he became aware of her interest he trained her and used her primarily through the summer as his assistant in the lab. Over time, he came to depend on her to the point that she ran the lab on several occasions when he was absent from the community. All this while still in high school (and after she had completed the work on her core subjects).

Apprenticeships are important even for those youngsters who will likely go on to college. It teaches them necessary work skills and gives them a special ability which they can use to earn money while attending college. There is nothing wrong with working in a fast food place, but a more specific skill may allow them to earn more money or have better working conditions.

Apprenticeships also allow children to be exposed to other competent adult role models. Although we all know that one of the main reasons for home schooling is to allow the parents to exercise greater supervision over the socialization of their children, by the time the youngsters are in high school they should be encouraged to form good relationships with other adults. The apprenticeship association is an excellent one. It provides an opportunity for children to develop friendships and respect for people who demonstrate vocational integrity. As a parent, you should investigate the employer's character and integrity well before making plans.

Finally, the apprenticeship experience can provide a letter of reference. Such letters are valuable when applying for work, college admission, admission military service, etc. They also help the youth sense the value of a good reputation.

College prep

Parents of college-bound youth should consider several matters when planning the curriculum. In the unusual case where they know at the beginning of high school what college the child will attend, they need to find out what curriculum that college requires. Since most parents do not know that early where their child will be going to college, they must work from a more generic listing of college prep recommendations. Some states publish a list of classes required for admission to any state school.

For general purposes, however, see the side bar for a list of courses typically required for admissions to four-year colleges:

Please note that this suggestion is for a *minimum* curriculum for a college prep course of study.

Be sure to maintain accurate, professional records of your students' progress through high school. Blank transcript forms may be obtained from commercial publishers, or you may make your own. In any case, make sure courses are listed according to the year in which they are taken and be explicit about the grade received for each course. Also include the grading scale used and the weight of each course, if they are weighted differently. Most colleges we have spoken to require that the transcript be submitted during the application process. However, they do not pay a great deal of attention to it since they have no quick way to determine how much faith they should put into the document. That means home schooled youth often have to prove themselves through the use of standardized tests.

Probably the most frequently used standardized test is the exam given for granting the General Equivalency Diploma (GED). Some home schoolers take the GED exam upon completing their course of high school study and then use the GED as their "credential" for the purposes of college or vocational application. Be sure to investigate the rules governing GED examinations in your state before deciding to use this option. Some states allow the young person to take the GED after a certain age, while others delay participation until he is old enough to have graduated from high school.

An option favored by home schoolers is the use of college entrance exams, notably the Scholastic Assessment Test (SAT) and the American College Testing (ACT) program test. Be sure to inquire about the preferences of any college you may be considering.

Typical College Entrance Requirements

Grammar/composition: four years.
English/literature: three years, including at least one year of American literature.
History: three years, including world history, American history, and civics.
Math: three years, including algebra I & II and geometry.
Science: two years minimum, including general science and biology or chemistry.
Computer: many colleges now strongly recommend that all entering freshmen be "computer literate."
Foreign language: most colleges "strongly recommend" two years of a foreign language.
Other requirements, such as physical education, art, typing, etc. vary from state to state.

Standardized testing is highly controversial among home schoolers and we do not wish to argue the case at this point. Most colleges do require these tests, however, so what you think of them may not matter. So you should help prepare him for them. One way to prepare for either the ACT or the SAT, is to take the Preliminary ACT and/or the Preliminary SAT. The PACT is given once a year, in the fall, to sophomores. The PSAT (which also serves as the National Merit Scholarship qualifying test) is given once a year, in the fall, to juniors. These tests are normally administered in the local high school. Call the guidance counselor's office to make appropriate arrangements for taking the tests. Both the SAT and ACT are given about six times a year, usually three times before Christmas and three or four times after Christmas. In order to register for these tests you must have a preregistration packet, normally provided free at local high school guidance counseling offices, or directly from the test publishers. These tests can be taken as many times as a youngster wishes to register and take them. A fee is charged.

In our own home school we routinely tested our children with conventional achievement tests through the ninth grade. From that point forward we no longer used achievement tests but let the Scholastic Aptitude Tests serve in their stead. We do think it is important for college-bound youngsters to have some practice taking such monitored tests because the skill will be important by the time they reach college. (The Scholastic Aptitude Test is now called the Scholastic Assessment Test.)

Conclusion

We believe that home schooled children of today will be the leaders of tomorrow. Teaching teenagers at home is not for everyone, but many reluctant parents could succeed at this higher level. We made our commitment to home schooling on a year-by-year basis. With each successive year we found ourselves liking it more, and our children wanted to continue. With the help of some pioneers, and as a result of some of our own trial and error, our high school home teaching years have been among the most gratifying experiences in our life. We trust you will give it your thoughtful consideration.

45

Preparing for College

Virginia Birt Baker

Choosing the right college is one of the most important decisions in life. Impressions from college or university days remain with us for life, both personally and educationally. The student's goal is not to find a "good" college, or the "best" college, but the college that is "just right" for him. The key is to plan purposefully, prepare prayerfully, proceed positively, and pursue persistently!

Demonstrating academic preparation

During the high school years keep a grade book and record every homework and test grade, with a final letter grade at the end of each year. If your child plans to attend a college or university, you will need this yearly record from the ninth grade on in order to prepare his high school transcript. Transcripts generally list the subjects, the letter grades made in each subject, the number of credits required for graduation in your state (usually about eighteen: one credit per subject at each grade level), and the date of graduation. College admissions officers say that the difficulty of high school courses and the grades earned there have the greatest influence on a student's acceptance. These grades count even more for borderline students and for those with generally bright records which slacked off in the senior year.

During the tenth grade make inquiries about taking the SAT (Scholastic Assessment test) or the ACT (American College Test). These tests are offered at many public high schools several times during the year for anyone who has applied. The admissions office of any college will give you full information. You can also buy old tests at college bookstores so your child can practice and become familiar with their layout. A test may be taken in the eleventh grade and definitely again in the twelfth. Your college will accept the best score. All colleges and universities accept the SAT but not all of them accept the ACT. You must check your college catalogs for these details.

Some colleges require home educated students to take the GED (General Education Development) test. Most will for those who are under age seventeen when they apply. To measure general high school knowledge, achievement tests may also be required in subjects such as English, math, history, science and/or a foreign language. These are specific tests offered by the College Board of the Educational Testing Service,[1] and it is the responsibility of the student applicant, not the college, to take and produce the results of these tests. In our area, for example, Southern Methodist University specifically requires six such tests as part of the home schooler's transcript.

__Virginia Baker__ and her husband, Charles ("Ginny and Chet") live on a small farm in Texas. Ginny taught their four children at home for fifteen years.

All four of their children attended or graduated from college. Julie took a phonics course for teachers, at Xavier University. She and her husband, Louie, live on their own ranch in Montana where she teaches their eight children. Chris received his MS. He and his wife Leah live in San Marcos, Texas. Nancy has a degree in accounting and business management. She and Sammy have two daughters. And Matthew, who was entirely home schooled through the twelfth grade, graduated from Texas A&M and works in Austin as an agricultural engineer.

Other tests, known as CLEP (College Level Examination Program) tests, may be taken to show proficiency in a subject or for exemption from certain courses. These tests measure knowledge at the college level and are not required for admission. However, home schooled students' transcripts are too often viewed with suspicion or doubt of "Mom's grading system." Since the transcript is the first and most important piece of paper the admissions counselor sees, it wouldn't hurt to bolster its claims with reports from some professionally administered achievement or CLEP tests.

Prepare for college year by year

High school students should start looking ahead to college early, rather than waiting until their senior year.

GRADE 9 Since some selective colleges look for leadership skills, high school students are encouraged to get involved in extra-curricular activities already in their freshman year. Home educated students have other ways to exercise leadership. The fact that they are not peer grouped helps them relate effective to older and younger people.

Students and parents may inquire about college grade and admissions requirements as well as about curriculum options. Academic excellence should be a goal from the beginning.

GRADE 10 Concentrate on schoolwork and grades. Study challenging and difficult course areas.

GRADE 11 Begin looking more seriously into schooling beyond high school. Narrow your focus on just a few (6-10) colleges that offer what you are looking for in terms of spiritual goals, location, cost, academics and extra curricular activities. Public libraries are a good source of information about colleges and many have the actual college directories. Investigate each college's requirements for admissions and grades. Ask about financial aid options including loans, grants, scholarships, plus any aid that is available that is not strictly based on need. Write to your state legislator about state scholarships, and look into other scholarship options such as service clubs. This is also a good time to take the SAT or ACT tests. In the summer months, begin to narrow the list down further and even go to some of the colleges and speak with the administration officials. Check out the facilities.

GRADE 12 This is the busiest time, and final decisions will be made here. Take the SAT and/or ACT over again. The higher score of the two years will be considered. Begin writing to the colleges that have been selected and get their application and financial aid materials. Get recommendations from people who know your academic and character qualities. Before Christmas, mail all applications, recommendations, financial aid requests, and transcripts to the various colleges. Follow up by calling administration offices at the colleges to see if you have sent them everything and to confirm that they received your information.

T.W

What the admissions officer wants to see

I think it is important that the student and his parents visit an admissions officer as soon as you have decided which university to attend, even if it is as early as the ninth or tenth grade. It is equally important to visit an assistant dean of the college of choice within that university. This holds true for small colleges too. Share with these officers your plans and goals, and discuss with them their school's admission requirements. Remember, admissions officers are used to evaluating students in relation to their academic rank in large classes in "established" schools and are not always sure how to appraise the "top student out of a class of one!" Personal interviews are a necessity for the university personnel to measure your child's maturity and interest and must be done before the time of admission.

What do admissions officers look for? High SAT (or ACT) scores, although this is increasingly becoming a small percentage of the overall evaluation, according to most universities. They look for good grades and the degree of difficulty in the courses. A "B" in an honors English course is better than and "A" in a regular course. Many colleges require letters of recommendation, a letter from the student describing why he picked that college, and a written essay.

The trustees of the College Board in Princeton, New Jersey, sponsors of the SAT test, have changed it. The older version, called the "Scholastic Aptitude Test," was a "reasoning" test, with emphasis on critical reading performance and depended somewhat on the student's IQ. It was used from 1926 to 1994. The new "Scholastic Assessment Test" (SAT II) is called a "subject" test and does not tend so much to measure IQ. It emphasizes critical reading and writing and has more problem-solving math questions. Calculators may now be used.

Colleges require evidence of the student's interaction with "the outside world." Some examples are, a part-time job during the school months and/or a full-time job during the summer months; and/or some sort of outside-the-home instruction (musical instrument, sports, foreign language, etc.); local community involvement (church activities, Fellowship of Christian Athletes, hospital volunteer, etc.); and some public speaking skills (debate, teaching Sunday School class, etc.). The colleges are impressed with kids who cram their days full of extracurricular activities, volunteer work, sports, and who hold positions of leadership in various organizations. They are more interested in a student who shows persistence in the same kind of activity than one who hops around from job to job. Community service is certainly commendable, but some groups and schools place more emphasis on "volunteerism" and less on a student's academic and intellectual acquisitions, hence the dwindling emphasis on SAT scores.

Be sure to ask about any other special requirements. For example, some land grant universities here in Texas require a year of high school Texas history. Our oldest son was home schooled during his high school years in Missouri, yet he was required by Texas A&M to take a Texas history course in order to receive his undergraduate degree. Some colleges require a foreign language or additional math courses, depending on your child's proposed major. Each school is different.

Financial aid

All college applicants may apply for scholarships, student loans, and grants. Scholarships and grants are outright gifts. Loans must be repaid after the student graduates or is no longer a student anywhere. Visit with the college financial aid officer for suggestions and details. The reference department of your library will likely list many scholarships given by companies or foundations in your own community. Top grades are not always necessary to qualify for a scholarship. Your son or daughter may be the only one who has applied for a little-known scholarship. Persistence is important here too. We know one young man whose family speaks Spanish in the home, yet his mother taught him in the English language during his last five years at home. He scored extremely high on his SAT and is proficient in four languages. But he was refused admittance to one of the largest schools in the state by the director of admissions, who had the ultimate say, solely because he was home schooled by his mother ("Your school is not on our list.") After a year of personal visits to the university, phone calls from friends, and even letters and calls from his Congressman, the young man was not only accepted to begin his studies in aerospace engineering, but he was awarded a $10,000 Presidential scholarship!

Two kinds of colleges

Which college should your student choose? The most flexible entrance requirements but not necessarily the lowest standards are found in the small private schools. The most rigid requirements are found in the large state universities. It is not impossible for the home educated student to enter a state university, but it is easier to start in a small private or community college. He could take the basic freshman courses, establish the best grade point average (GPA) possible, then transfer as soon as it's practical. It is important to confirm from the final degree-granting institution, even before taking the courses, that all course credits from the smaller institution are transferable.

There are generally two kinds of colleges. One is the large, prestigious, world-class university where research is given high priority. These schools have large numbers of graduate student teaching assistants (TAs) who are understandably completing their own education. While many of the professors are preoccupied with their research, the teaching role of graduate students is far larger than many people – especially parents and high school students – realize, often at a cost to the undergraduate program. Our son was taught a science course by a TA from Pakistan whose English was hard to understand. Many of the students failed this course because of the poor communication. In the large university it can be difficult to take the basic courses in the right sequence because of the large freshman enrollment. Our son's roommate had to wait three semesters to get into freshman English for this reason.

The other type of college is the small liberal arts college. Professors who enjoy teaching more than research are more likely to seek employment here. The learning process can be more manageable, and the student is less likely to get lost in the crowd. There is more of the "college community" atmosphere, simply because most students live on campus. Schools emphasizing Christian principles are a community of staff and students who live, study, play and pray together, bound not only through the pursuit of education, but through their common commitment to Christ. There are pockets of such support groups in the larger schools, too, but also there are more distractions. The smaller colleges offer a limited choice of academic courses and majors, yet a greater percentage of their graduates go on through graduate school to complete Ph.D. degrees. For graduate school, your child might understandably choose the world class university with its renowned professors. Undergraduate education is what matters when you are first choosing a college.

The importance of the college years cannot be overestimated. Education is more than learning from the books. Some of your child's closest friendships and many cherished moments and formative experiences will occur during this period of his life.

Information for making a choice

I recommend two books for the home educated student who is preparing for college. *College Admissions: A Guide for Homeschoolers*,[2] by Judy Gelner, is a delightful story of her experiences helping her son "work his way through the college admissions tests, forms, and deadlines all without a high school guidance office, accredited diploma or a lot of the `objective measurements' that most high school students present to a college."[3] Her son entered the highly esteemed Rice University in Houston, and received a considerable amount of financial aid.

Choosing a College: A Guide for Parents & Students[4] by Thomas Sowell, is especially helpful (if you can locate a copy). This book starts you "at square one, before you even know what questions to ask, what colleges to read about, or what statistics to look up. . . It is designed to help parents and students find the kind of college that will fit their own particular goals, ability, pocketbook, and way of life. . . . It tells you what to look for during a campus visit, how to read a college brochure regardless of what message the college itself is trying to send, the nuts and bolts of the admissions process, how to evaluate the admissions and financial aid offers, and sources of advice that can be helpful or could lead you right into a catastrophe. This book hopes to put some backbone into parents who might otherwise be intimidated by `experts.'"[5]

Mr. Sowell explains some aspects of evaluating a college that we parents may not be aware of, or that we cannot always discern from the catalog. To some, college means a place to develop one's mind. To others, college means a place to prepare for a career. And there are those for whom college means fraternities, football, parties, and a world-renowned campus. Some colleges (and he names Pepperdine as one example) have campuses which continue to maintain the strict control over dorm visits by the opposite sex that was widespread when my generation went to college. Other campuses (and he names some) have "intervisitation unlimited," which means a man can spend the night in the women's dorm.

Tuition can cost as much as $10,000 a year or as little as $300. Many colleges are politically left or even socialist, while others are solidly conservative. We parents don't always realize the vast range of diversity in these schools. Such things as values, cultural activities, and even regulations about dress and manners are important in matching student and college. "The right college can be an exhilarating experience; many alumni are grateful for life for what their colleges did for them. The wrong college can be a tiresome chore without meaning – a burden that many cannot endure for four long years."[6] A college you have never heard of may be just the perfect one you are looking for, and *Choosing a College* will help you find it.

Keeping in touch

After being accepted to a college, tell your freshman to keep in close touch with his assigned academic adviser, who is there to guide him through the complexities and problems of the early years. Occasionally some academic advising consists of a weary tutor's hasty suggestions, but in most cases the adviser is one of the professors. Our son stopped by at least every other week to say "Hi" even when things were going well, and his adviser also became his friend. If problems should arise or future recommendations are required, it's nice to be personally acquainted with some of the teaching staff on campus.

Endnotes

1. College Board ATP, P.O. Box 6200, Princeton, NJ 08541-6200.
2. Judy Gelner, *College Admissions: A Guide for Homeschoolers*, 1995. Poppyseed Press, 7490 W. Apache, Sedalia, CO 80135. See Appendix J.
3. *Ibid.*, p. 1.
4. Thomas Sowell, *Choosing a College: A Guide for Parents & Students*. 1989. Unfortunately, this book is now out of print, but I urge parents to get a copy from their library, or through the interlibrary loan program if necessary. It is well worth the trouble. (What a shame that it is no longer available for sale.)
5. *Ibid.*, Introduction.
6. *Ibid.*, p. 4.

Comments on Entrance Tests

✔ Fewer colleges and university systems require the SAT — nearly 200.

✔ More are accepting the ACT.

✔ Coaching helps and they expect you to prepare.

From an Oct. 17, 1994 report in *U.S. News and World Report.*

T.W.

46

Teaching Special Needs Children

David and Laurie Lanier

In this chapter we review the history and range of conditions referred to by the term "special needs," and we consider implications for home schoolers.[1] We hope you will understand these children and their families better; if you have a special needs child, we hope you will find particular information you can use right away.

There have always been children who have not fit into the common mold. In the past, they have been labeled "simple," "slow," or " 'teched." As culture, and particularly education, have become more "scientific," these children have acquired new names. And new conditions have been identified as well:

✓ Babies still *in utero* have been damaged by new drugs, both pharmaceutical and illicit.

✓ Learning problems often surface in children saved from premature birth by new technology.

✓ More children are now *labeled* as "handicapped" or "children with special needs" as government funding for educational opportunities has brought them into special programs.

Parents, the single best resource

⌘ The first step in working with your special needs child is to recognize that you are, in all likelihood, the single best resource. You should not expect anyone to care for the child the *way* you do, or to the *extent* you do. You must learn as much as possible about your child's problem. Draw information from medical journals, experts, popular books, support groups and any other good resource. Become knowledgeable about competing points of view to avoid placing too much weight on a false idea.

⌘ Second, set goals for home schooling your special child. For Christian parents, the first step will always be to pray for wisdom and the leading of the Holy Spirit. This should guide your understanding as you develop plans and list desired outcomes.

⌘ Be willing to try new approaches. Don't reject an idea just because it is new. If it seems reasonable, give it a try, especially if your current program is not working well. On the other hand, the old maxim "if it ain't broke, don't fix it" reminds us to maintain some consistency. Don't tinker indefinitely, hoping to find the perfect program.

⌘ Identify the natural learning style of your child.[2] Having a special need does not eliminate learning-styles considerations. While recommendations for particular learning styles may have to be adapted for your child, they still will be helpful.

⌘ Be realistic but don't let it hem you in. Although you should not believe every "magic cure" that comes along, neither should you forget that miracles still happen. It is crucial to maintain a balance between reasonable expectations and a willingness to hope in the unexpected. This also applies to interpreting what the experts say about your child. Extract the professional's "grain" while leaving the "chaff" behind.

⌘ Maintain structure and good order but be flexible in how you do it. All children need structure, and special needs children often need more than others. But too much structure can be stifle your special learning environment.

A special kind of structure may be

needed. For instance, the order of the daily lessons may not be nearly as important for a child suffering from attention deficit hyperactivity disorder (ADHD) as having the furniture in the room set up the same way every day.

The home as a refuge

The outside world may reject your child, depending on his (or her) handicap. Our homes should be shelters as well as training grounds for all our children. A secure home depends first on the marriage of the parents. If you allow the needs of your child to deplete your emotional resources for each other, it will ultimately hurt him.

Strain from the birth of a handicapped child may interfere with nurturing your marriage. Mothers tend to feel indispensable in the care of the special child. Remember, Mom, that your strong marriage is the best situation you can give him. Dads, remember to encourage and support your wife. Even as the birth of this child was a joint effort, the journey of raising him should also be. It may sound strange, but a date for dinner every other weekend would be a good element in the educational strategy for your child.

Next, remember your other children. A special needs child, of necessity, requires extra attention. In an attempt to "make up the difference" you can emotionally shortchange the others. Set aside time for them individually and together. Pay attention to their special projects. And involve them in caring for the handicapped one. Thus they may see how the body of Christ ministers to the weaker members and how even the "weakest" person can also contribute.

Appropriate discipline is a critical factor in the education of special needs children. You can never allow "feeling sorry" for your child to keep you from adequately disciplining him. Learning is hampered for any child, handicapped or normal, who has not been taught to respond to authority. Even if your child cannot reach high academic success, relating appropriately to people will more likely bring him acceptance.

Handicaps, even profound ones, should not prevent you from attending to the spiritual needs of your youngster. While he may not respond to spiritual instruction in the "normal" way, Bible stories, spiritual question and answers, and godly character development are as important for him as for anyone else. Remember, Christ will meet us all wherever we are. Often special needs children are exceptionally receptive to spiritual matters.

Choosing standards

The terms *idiographic* and *nomothetic* are probably unfamiliar to you, but you use the principles every day. Idiographic measurement compares a person with himself. Marks on the door frame which record a child's height each successive year show idiographic measurement. He is not compared with a norm, just with himself at different times.

Nomothetic measurement compares a child with a standard or norm. A child's height at the age of ten compared to the height of other ten year olds would show him to be taller, shorter, or about the same height as the others. Nomothetic measures are used when you wish to compare your child to other children.

Neither of these kinds of measurement is inherently good or bad. Both have uses. For instance, when preparing a child for competition, nomothetic measurements may be used. Applications for a college scholarship are judged by performance on nomothetic ACT or SAT exams, not on good idiographic effort. On the other hand, in areas where a child is not especially gifted, pointing out how much better he did this time is encouraging.

Your can see the value of idiographic measurement when working with special needs children. You would not want to compare their performance with that of other children.

Involvement with professionals

The frantic plant manager called a retired engineer and said his plant's production was paralyzed. The consultant flew in, walked around the plant for a couple of hours, and eventually stopped underneath a large pipe. After a sharp rap with a hammer, operation was immediately restored. Upon receiving a $10,000 bill the manager asked the consultant why he should pay him that much money for walking around a couple of hours and hitting a pipe with a hammer. The consultant replied, "I didn't charge you to hit a pipe; I charged you to know where to hit."

Working with professionals may remind you of the consultant and his hammer. Their charges may seem high for doing what appear to be simple things. The fee is for the experience and training they bring to help you understand and assist your child do his best. Professionals will never love or care for your child as you do, but they probably know things you do not know. Learn as much as you can from them.

Some professionals have a condescending attitude toward parents and are unwilling, once they have made diagnoses or treatment plans, to turn responsibility back to the parent. Most parents, however, can be trained and are very effective therapists for their own children. A fine line separates relying on professional help and remembering that you are still the child's best resource.

We might add one other observation in this section: the American landscape is dotted with freestanding institutes and associations which advertise unique or revolutionary services for handicapped children. We find the quality of these non-mainstream groups to be very uneven. Some appear to provide useful services under eccentric names while others are frauds. We are concerned that such a group or individual may make unsubstantiated claims of success and thereby unrealistically raise the parents' expectations. On the other hand, it may be at such a place that the next big advance in the treatment of handicapped individuals is made. It is usually the hope of just such a breakthrough that sends parents of special needs children to the open arms of noncredentialed groups.

We are not, here, recommending or condemning any particular non-mainstream group or individual; rather, we suggest that you prayerfully and soberly consider the claims of such groups and obtain wise counsel when making a decision. Desperate people have been victims of con artists for centuries.

How we got here

Before we discuss the subject of cooperation with local public schools, a bit of history is in order. The story of "special needs" and the resulting phenomenon known as "special education" began with the public school system. So even though this is a *Home School* manual, please bear with a little public school history in order to understand the background of the subject.

A virtual explosion in the number and varieties of special needs children and special education classrooms have occurred in the U.S. public schools since the passage in 1975 of the federal Education of All Handicapped Children Act (Public Law 94-142). The law was revised in 1990 as Public Law 101-457 and titled Individuals with Disabilities Education Act (IDEA). This law guarantees the right of every child, regardless of handicap, to be educated in the public school system for twelve years or until the age of twenty-one. The federal government placed many requirements on the schools but also offered financial assistance to aid states and local districts in compliance.

Since the passage of this federal mandate, many more children than before have been diagnosed with some sort of problem. And diagnoses have become more specific: from the general term "dyslexia," for example, to the more specific "developmental reading disorders" to the very specific "neurologically-based motor planning disorder." In addition, new sources of disabilities have been found, such as Fetal Alcohol Syndrome, low birth weight and "crack" cocaine addiction in newborns. The new sources of learning problems have not been restricted to physical causes, however. New psychological culprits were discovered or named, including attention deficit hyperactivity disorder (ADHD), various kinds of "behavioral disorders," and many problems thought to be related to "low self esteem."

In addition to identifying more legitimate cases of special needs, many school districts seemed to discover a large group of students who had previously been "overlooked" as persons with disabilities. Several incentives prompted these discoveries:

1. School districts had a financial reason to identify special needs children because they received more federal and state money for them.

2. A higher percentage of such children helped deflect criticism in school districts where student performance was subpar. School administrators then had an explanation.

3. Parents often liked the designation of "special needs" for the same reason as the administrators did. It provided a reason for their otherwise poorly-performing children.

Hence, the term "special needs" has lost much of its original specificity and usefulness, and has often identified a controversial topic in the debates surrounding public education.

The home schooling community is by no means isolated from the issue of special education. Disagreements of parents with the public schools about how their special needs children are being treated motivates new families to teach them at home. Parents already home schooling often mention "special needs" to explain a child's lack of progress or his idiosyncratic behavior. Periodic articles recounting inappropriate diagnoses by experts are routinely distributed in home schooling circles. Such articles perpetuate the notion that experts are incompetent at best, and malicious at worst, and that parents can dispense with or ignore them because the parents "know their children best." At the same time, the do-it-yourself ethos of home schooling allows many parents to perpetuate their view that their child has "special needs" without any credible confirming evidence.

Special needs children do exist, of course, but a proper understanding of the field in general, or a child in particular, requires maturity, discernment, and a willingness to appreciate God's creativity.

Involvement with the Public Schools

Your state may have special laws on home schooling special needs children. Check with local state authorities, the state home school association, or Home School Legal Defense Association for more information.

There are pros and cons on participation with the public school system. One advantage is for the respite it provides. Many parents of young special needs children find the emotional and financial toll of home schooling over many years to be too great. Some of them ultimately divorce or have other serious problems from the stress. Time away from the child can help parents cope.

Involvement with the public school could also provide access to services of professionals you might not otherwise be able to afford. Public school special education programs routinely offer occupational therapy, speech therapy, psychological evaluations, etc.

Even partial involvement with the public school system will probably involve cooperation with the IEP process. IEP stands for "individualized education plan." and one is developed for each handicapped child by a committee made up of the parents, professionals, and educators. The IEP team normally meets once yearly and sets up a series of goals which are reviewed and updated as necessary.

This leads to some of the objections to involvement with the public school system. You will quickly lose much of the control over your child's education. Obtaining necessary services or respite may be worth this loss of control, but approach the decision with caution.

Involvement with the public school system could heighten your family's chances of scrutiny by social service agencies. Many people in the educational and social work establishment view home schooling as a "fringe," or even abusive, activity. They are likely to have even greater suspicion for the home education of a special needs child. Involvement with the school system piques official curiosity. You would not necessarily be found guilty of child abuse, but you would probably be checked more closely.

Kinds of Special Needs Children

Before we conclude we would like to introduce you to a very brief overview of the breadth of conditions sometimes labeled "special needs." Some children manifest more than one category of disability, and no two stories are exactly alike.

Mental Retardation Mental retardation is sub-average intellectual capacity and adaptive functioning ability. A psychologist normally makes the diagnosis using I.Q. and other tests. Categories of mental retardation range from "mild" to "severe and profound." Children with mild mental retardation were previously referred to as "educable" while those with moderate and greater degrees were often referred to as "trainable" in public school special education classes. Mental retardation is a permanent condition.

Learning Disabilities This very broad category refers to children who are otherwise capable of learning at an average level but who have specific problems in one or more content areas. Among the most common areas of learning disability (LD) are reading, mathematics, writing, and expressive language. They usually require special assistance only in their LD area.[3]

Emotional Disabilities Emotionally disabled children have conditions ranging from severe chronic disorders (such as childhood schizophrenia or autism) or acute serious disturbances (such as depression or overanxious disorder) to conditions such as hyperactivity or attention deficit disorder. We categorize them as emotional disorders because it is the emotional aspect of the problem which seems to interfere with their capacity to learn in a normal fashion.[4]

Neurological Impairments Included in this category are learning problems caused by congenital or traumatic injury to the whole or part of the brain. The impairments may be permanent or temporary, treatable or not. This general category also includes other disorders such as seizure/convulsion disorders, Tourette's syndrome, and is likely the cause of attention deficit hyperactivity disorder (ADHD) symptoms.

Speaking of ADHD, no one knows for sure what causes it. ADHD used to be called minimal brain dysfunction. Then it was called hyperactivity. Now it is called attention deficit hyperactivity disorder. Most professionals believe that these children suffer a neurological problem of some kind, but no hard evidence has yet been found to confirm this belief. The issue is complicated by the difficulty in distinguishing a true ADHD child from a rebellious, ill-behaved one. Both children tend to have a low attention span and to get in trouble often. As a result, many children seen by one professional as an ADHD child are identified by someone else as simply ill-behaved. This difficulty with diagnostic clarity has resulted in much misunderstanding.

Physical Impairments This category includes youngsters with any kind of physical problem that impairs learning capacity. It ranges from single problems such as blindness or deafness, to multiple problems such as cerebral palsy or spina bifida. Environmentally-induced problems such as lead poisoning or accident are also considered physical impairments. The problems can range from mild to severe and are typically diagnosed by a physician or other professional specializing in that particular form of disability. Youngsters with physical problems often have normal intellectual capacities but are impaired in their ability to either receive instruction or communicate with others.

Behavioral Disabilities

Some children, particularly in the public school setting, behave in a peculiar fashion not identified as any of the forego-ing conditions. They often receive the diagnosis of "behavioral disorder," Their behavior can range from violent acting out to extreme social withdrawal to preco-cious sexual activity. Such children are often remanded to "behavior disorder" special classrooms, and their public school course is guided by a combination of educational and behavioral goals.

We hope you have found this article useful. If you have a special needs child, remember that there are lots of us on the adventure with you. Let's support and encourage each other along the way. If you are not the parents of a special needs child, we hope you understand us and our children better.

Endnotes

1. The Laniers write this term as one word (homeschooling), which is also a common spelling. It appears here as two words to be consistent with the rest of the book.
2. The topic of learning styles is also discussed in the chapter, "Techniques for Teaching."
3. Dyslexia, a reading disability, is in this category.
4. Emotional disabilities are conditions normally treated by psychologists and/or psychiatrists. If the same symptoms were exhibited in adults, they would be considered mentally ill. In children, the conditions may be only temporary. The causes may be genetic, psychological, or spiritual.

Organizations relating to disabilities are listed in Appendix C.

Publications on learning problems are listed in Appendix J.

47

Teaching Gifted Children

John Wesley Taylor V

"Jessica is a real problem! She is so argumentative, so stubborn. When I tell her something, she can never seem to just accept it. It's always 'Why?' or 'Why not?' When she's with other kids, she invariably tries to dominate. Things *must* go her way. At home, it seems that she can never sit still. In fact, she is forever talking – mostly about weird, impractical ideas. Funny thing, though, some of them actually work, amazingly well in fact. I really don't know what to do with her. One thing for sure, she is driving all of us nearly crazy!"

Have you met Jessica? Or a child who is a dreamer, a know-it-all, a risk-taker, a bookworm, or a clown? Perhaps in your own home? If so, this chapter just might be written with you in mind. You see, Jessica is most likely a gifted child.

If an educator trained in the area of giftedness were to write up a report, it might read something like this: "Jessica is a talented young lady. She is goal-directed and evidences high levels of task-commitment. Furthermore, she is a critical thinker and is curious about many things, with many interests and passions. When she is with other children, Jessica demonstrates leadership ability. She is proactive, impelled forward by a high energy level. She is also verbally fluent and often comes up with creative and highly innovative ideas. Jessica is a *treasure*!"

Same child. Different perspectives. So, what *do* you do with her?

Well, many parents home school their gifted child. One study (Kearney, 1991; see also Weinig, 1993) reported that nearly half of the highly gifted children surveyed had been home schooled at some point during grades K-12. Indeed, the number of parents choosing to home school gifted children seems to be on the rise.

By its very nature, the home school can be an ideal setting for nurturing a gifted child. In the traditional classroom – often geared to the lowest common denominator of the "average student", pupils move lock step through a standardized curriculum in which a gifted child is rarely stretched academically or challenged to grow in the areas of talent. This child is consequently at considerable risk for losing interest in school activities

For a long time I have been gently encouraging my friend, Wesley Taylor, to write this chapter. Now you see it. Or, I should say you see part of it. The well-written manuscript he sent would have thickened this book by some 45 pages! If you are serious about home teaching your gifted child, look for the full version as a book which I expect will soon find its way to press.

John Wesley Taylor V is well acquainted with home schooling, both through personal experience and by profession. Until entering college, he was educated primarily at home. In his professional life, he conducted the first national study on the self-concept and socialization of home schooled children and has written a number of articles on the topic. He holds an Ed.D. in Educational Psychology-Gifted from the University of Virginia and a Ph.D. in Curriculum and Instruction from Andrews University. Among other positions, he has served as dean of graduate studies at Montemorelos University and research associate at the National Research Center on the Gifted and Talented. Presently he chairs the Education Department at the Adventist International Institute of Advanced Studies in Manila, Philippines. He and his wife have two children, who are also learning at home.

and developing severe underachievement patterns which often continue throughout life. For a highly gifted student, school becomes a twelve-year sentence.

By contrast – and in harmony with the strongest research base we have in gifted education, the home school readily yields itself to a flexible, one-on-one learning environment and a rich, individually tailored curriculum, much better suited to meeting the gifted student's needs. Parents themselves soon discover that they can readily foster interest-specific learning experiences that will captivate, motivate, nurture, enrich, and accelerate their child's talents.

What is giftedness?

With the possible exception of "love," no other word in the English language seems to have garnered such a far-flung range of meaning as the term "gifted." One of the most influential definitions, however, continues to be that contained in a 1972 report to Congress by the then-Commissioner of Education, Sidney Marland. It states that "gifted and talented children are those identified by professionally qualified persons who, by virtue of outstanding abilities, are capable of high performance." It then delineates a number of broad areas in which such talents may be evidenced. These include

✓ General intellectual ability (often pegged to some measure of intelligence)

✓ Specific academic aptitude (in a particular discipline such as mathematics or language)

✓ Creative thinking (evidenced through inventions and innovative forms of expression)

✓ Leadership ability (seen in an extraordinary sense of mission coupled with personal charisma)

✓ Ability in the visual or performing arts (such as music, drama, sculpture, or caricature)

The Marland Definition also notes that these gifted children require "differentiated educational programs and/or services beyond those normally provided by the regular school program in order to realize their contributions to self and society."

More recently, the Federal definition of 1993 has reiterated many of these same concepts, adding that "outstanding talents are present in children and youth from all cultural groups, across all economic strata, and in all areas of human endeavor."

As a result, many educational systems have operationalized these ideas into more specific criteria. To be gifted in general intellectual ability, for example, a child must obtain a minimum score on a standardized IQ test such as the Stanford-Binet or the WISC-R. One of the most common IQ rankings is to define "mildly gifted" as 115-129, "moderately gifted" as 130-144, "highly gifted" as 145-159, and "profoundly gifted" as an IQ of 160 or above. To be gifted in a specific academic area, the child must score at or above a certain percentile (often the 90th or 95th percentile) on a standardized achievement test such as the Iowa Tests of Basic Skills or the California Achievement Tests.

Some educators and researchers, however, have taken a different approach to the concept of giftedness. (Joseph Renzulli, 1978), one of the leading advocates for an enriched educational experience for bright students, has defined giftedness as an above-average ability linked with creativity and task commitment. In this approach, high levels of motivation are seen as a vital component of giftedness. Others, such as Robert Sternberg of Yale and Howard Gardner of Harvard, have questioned the notion that there is such a thing as a "general intelligence." Gardner (1983), in fact, proposed the concept of multiple intelligences, including verbal/linguistic, logical/mathematical, visual/spatial, bodily/kinesthetic, musical/rhythmic, interpersonal, and intrapersonal facets.

How does all of this sort out? One implication is that giftedness is not only demonstrated ability at the upper end of the talent continuum; it is also the *potential* for the exceptional development of specific abilities. Simply stated, you don't have to be an achiever to be gifted. A child, in fact, could be receiving average or even failing grades in school and still be gifted. This is often the case when a gifted child is underachieving or handicapped. Another implication is that giftedness is not all-encompassing. A gifted child is not good in everything, but in a particular way. Finally, because a gifted child is developmentally advanced in one or more areas, he/she requires a special approach to education in order to function at a level appropriate to his/her potential.

Is my child gifted?

The most widely accepted estimate of the incidence of gifted students is 5% of the total population (Culross, 1989). So how might one go about identifying a gifted child? First of all, don't limit your criteria to the level of a prodigy. (Although all prodigies are, in fact, "severely and profoundly" gifted!) A prodigy – there are rather few around – is a child who, before the age of ten, performs at the level of an adult professional in an intellectually demanding field such as math, chess, music, or languages. On the other hand, don't simply look for a bright child – one who makes good grades in school. While some bright children may be gifted, not all gifted children will look "bright." In many ways, in fact, a gifted child will seem quite different from the typical "bright child."

So what do you look for? Outstanding talent – whether achieved or potential. I'll admit, that was a little too easy. Perhaps we should be a bit more specific. To begin, let's take a look at the five areas we noted in the Marland Definition. For each domain, I will present a brief, somewhat generic description of a gifted child in that area, followed by some more concrete examples and a set of twenty questions that you can ask yourself as you think about your own child.

While all of these characteristics do not need to be present for your child to be gifted in a particular area, the more of them you are able to see in your child, the more likely your child is to be talented in that domain. That likelihood is furthermore increased as the characteristics appear earlier, more intensely, and more frequently.

<u>General intellectual ability</u>

A child who is gifted in general intellectual ability tends to learn rapidly in most, if not all, subject areas. He/she is excited about new ideas, is inquisitive and observant, and enjoys hypothesizing and delving into abstractions. Self-initiative, complex thinking patterns, and an extensive vocabulary are often evident as well.

<u>Specific academic aptitude</u>

This form of giftedness is subject- or discipline-specific, and parallels an area of special interest to the child. A child who is gifted in a specific academic area learns new information in that interest area quite readily, pursuing the learning experience with intensity and enthusiasm. He/she is well read in that area and displays an advanced understanding of its core concepts and principles. Grades are usually high in the subject(s) related to the special interest area.

<u>Creative thinking</u> When creatively gifted, a child tends to be an independent thinker and thrive on tasks that give opportunity for creative expression. There is considerable resistance to doing things "the same old way," with the child quite comfortable in marching to a different drummer from the rest of the crowd. He/she likes to invent things and may demonstrate humor and originality when speaking or writing. When confronted with a problem, the child will tend to think of quite a number of different ways that it might be

solved, often improvising on the spur of the moment.

Leadership ability A child who is gifted in the area of leadership has an unusual ability to inspire, influence, direct, and guide others. He/she is self-confident, with high expectations for self and for others. Self-expression is fluent and concise. Decision-making evidences good judgment, particularly in foreseeing implications and consequences. The child likes structure, is organized, and assumes responsibility well. He/she is well liked by peers.

Ability in the visual or performing arts Giftedness in the visual or performing arts is evidenced by an unusual ability for communicating moods, feelings, ideas, and self through expressive media such as music, painting, and drama. The gifted child often displays superb motor coordination and an outstanding sense of spatial relationships. He/she is observant and attempts to make the art form uniquely personal and original.

How will I teach my gifted child?

Let's suppose you have noticed characteristics in your child which lead you to think that he/she may be gifted in a particular way. There is talent to be nurtured, outstanding potential to be cultivated. What do you do?

First of all, I suppose we should address a question which often begs an answer: Is it even possible for an "ordinary" parent to teach a gifted child? In the conventional school setting, teachers of the gifted are not always gifted individuals themselves, at least not in the strict sense of the term. The rationale goes something like this: In order to teach a learning disabled child, one does not have to be handicapped. Similarly, in order to foster growth and talent development in a gifted child, you do not have to be gifted. Certain conditions, however, are essential. You need a good understanding of giftedness, and you need to care very much about the gifted child.

Given that these basic criteria are in place, how does one go about educating a gifted child at home? As a starting point, you should be aware that you can squash your child's talents and/or intense desire to learn by shifting the worst of conven-

tional schooling to the kitchen table. In fact, the more highly gifted the child, the greater the need for a radically different educational program. In essence, all aspects of the educational experience – goals and content, instructional strategies and resources, setting and evaluative procedures – must be tailored to create the best possible match with the characteristics and needs of your child.

While the ideas we will discuss in this section may be of value for educating any child at home, they are particularly appropriate in the case of a gifted child. Specifically, we will take a look at the curriculum, instructional approach, learning environment, and evaluative procedures, as these directly pertain to home schooling your gifted child.

The Curriculum

Instead of the traditional curriculum based on a preplanned body of knowledge, your emphasis should be on the student. Learning would not be bound to textbooks, workbooks, and printed examinations. Nor would it be prescribed by you as the teacher.

Rather than asking "What am I going to teach today?" or "What is in this next chapter?", ask yourself "What should my child learn today?" And answer that question in terms of his/her goals, abilities, interests, and learning style.

Children learn best when stretched and challenged. They must move beyond their comfort zone and into the realm of intentional growth. At the same time, however, they must believe they can succeed in these learning tasks. If success does not seem attainable, the child moves out of the learning zone and into the frustration zone, bringing negative repercussions for both motivation and achievement.

Consequently, the curriculum for a gifted student must place that child in his/her personal learning zone. To accomplish this, the curriculum should be one which quickens, broadens, deepens, and connects.

✓ *Quickening* happens when certain content is covered more rapidly than might normally be the case. In some instances, it may even be skipped entirely if the child shows mastery of concepts and skills.

✓ *Broadening* occurs when the student explores a greater variety of topics than those usually prescribed. Many of these topics may be, in fact, beyond the scope of any packaged curriculum.

✓ *Deepening* takes place when the gifted student delves into a particular topic more fully than would normally be the case. During this process, high-level thinking skills are promoted.

✓ *Connecting* transpires when interrelationships across the disciplines are ferreted out and examined more closely. In other words, a gifted curriculum must include (1) compacted and accelerated content, (2) enrichment activities, (3) advanced processes and products, and (4) interdisciplinary themes.

Compacted and accelerated content. While buying a set of standard commercial curriculum materials and just stepping up the pace will likely not provide the educational experience your gifted child needs, much content can, in fact, be compacted and accelerated. This is so because gifted students are already at an advanced developmental stage in one or more areas. Compacting the curriculum takes into account your child's substantial reservoir of knowledge and skills, and eliminates the boredom and lethargy which frequently result from unnecessary drill and practice. Compacting also provides opportunity for your child to branch out into topics of special interest or pursue an in-depth study of some aspect of the curriculum. Curriculum compacting effectively adjusts the level of required learning so that your child is continually challenged to learn. Essentially, it is a three-step process:

✓ *Assess what your child already knows about the material to be studied and what he/she still needs to master.*

✓ *Plan ways in which your child can learn the essentials that are not yet mastered and eliminate that content for which mastery has been demonstrated.*

✓ *Use the time you have gained to accelerate or enrich your child's learning.* Acceleration does not necessarily mean grade skipping, although there may be certain instances where this could be advisable. More often, it is the case of subject acceleration or an overall intensification of learning.

Enrichment activities Link enrichment to your child's interests and talents, and invite a high degree of student input and choice. More than likely, your gifted child already has the interest, curiosity, and motivation needed to pursue a special interest topic. All too often, however, he/she may not have the necessary skills such as how to collect, organize, and analyze data, for example. These skills must be taught. You should also be careful that student choice does not eat away at breadth.

Advanced processes and products While enrichment may be visualized as a horizontal expansion into new content areas, it is also important to provide your gifted child with in-depth learning experiences that focus on advanced processes and products.

This may mean casting your child in the role of a firsthand inquirer, rather than a mere learner-of-lessons. After all, problem-solving and decision-making skills are best learned, not by working through "word" problems or logic exercises, but by investigating "real world" situations.

As a result of engaging in these advanced processes, you should encourage your child to develop advanced products. These should be real attainments that require thoughtful application of learning, tangible accomplishments that require transformation and not just replication of knowledge.

Interdisciplinary themes The final component in putting together a curriculum for your gifted child is to incorporate interdisciplinary themes. Built around a core concept, basic issue, or fundamental problem, these broad-based studies endeavor to integrate the often-isolated disciplines into a more holistic fabric.

Curricular Resources Great! But where do I go about buying this kind of curriculum package? Well, wherever you bought your gifted child! You see, a gifted curriculum, like giftedness itself, cannot be purchased. The reason? Each gifted child is unique, with a special set of talents and a specific configuration of interests, needs, and learning style.

✓ As you might suspect, books themselves are an invaluable resource. I'm not particularly talking about textbooks, although some of these might be appropriate if sufficiently lucid and advanced. Rather, I am thinking about quality literature related to the area(s) of interest and talent. Periodical publications, including professional journals appropriate to the area of giftedness, are also good curricular material.

✓ Then there are specialized computer resources (such as simulations and databases, usually available on CD-ROM), on-line resources (which can be found by using the Internet search engines), and advanced hands-on materials (for which school supply stores can be a treasure trove). You will also want to include professional "tools of the trade" applicable to your child's gifted domain. And then there are cultural events, special interest clubs, and real-life experiences can become a significant part of your curricular planning.

✓ You may also want to tap into special activities and programs for the gifted at a university.

Ultimately, you and your child must work together to put into place the curriculum which will provide for optimal learning.

The Instructional Approach

A curriculum is only as good as its implementation. It is usually at the point of instruction where "the rubber meets the road." As a result, the instructional approach you take has much to do with the ultimate effectiveness of your child's educational experience.

For your gifted child, consider (1) contact with experts; (2) mentorships, apprenticeships, and internships; (3) personalized projects, (4) research experiences, (5) learning contracts, (6) high-level questions, and (7) problems, issues, and dilemmas.

You can learn more about these instructional approaches outside of this chapter. A few comments on learning contracts, however may be helpful.

Although well-suited to both personal projects and research experiences, learning contracts can be quite useful in a wide variety of learning situations. Essentially, a learning contract records an agreement between teacher and student. In this agreement, you grant certain freedoms and choices about how your child will approach a learning task, and your child will agree to use those freedoms responsibly in designing and completing work according to certain stipulated specifications. The learning contract, therefore, seeks to provide a good balance between teacher directives and student freedom of choice.

In order for a learning contract to be effective, however, certain conditions must be met. The contract should specify in writing the purpose of the learning activity, resources needed, characteristics of the intended final product, the target audience, and the dates for beginning and ending the activity and for any interim conferences.

Some do's and don'ts

As you and your child set out on the journey of learning, there are a few fundamental principles to keep in mind. While these instructional concepts may be relevant in educating any child, they are particularly applicable in the case of a gifted child.

First, let's highlight some things you will probably want to avoid.

– Don't dominate the learning experience. (This is probably the hardest!) Rather, permit your child some freedom to select topics, pursue learning activities, and create original products.

– Don't just follow a prescribed list of topics and activities. While packaged programs may have their place, you must be careful not to circumscribe learning.

– Don't make textbooks and workbooks the principal means of instruction. Rather, center your instruction on real-life experiences and high-quality literature which relate to your child's area(s) of talent.

– Don't place your major emphasis on getting things right – correct grammar, proper punctuation, neat papers, and the like. Focus, instead, on ideas, concepts, attitudes, processes, and advanced skills.

– Don't give your gifted child longer assignments for those topics related to his/her talents. On the contrary, these assignments should generally be shorter as a gifted student is able to learn with fewer repetitions. There may be times, however, when you will linger on a particular topic in order that your child may pursue some in-depth learning.

– Don't reject unusual ideas whose usefulness may not be immediately apparent. You may, inadvertently, be stifling your child's creativity. Encourage your child to explain his/her idea and the connections that prompted it.

– Don't ask your gifted child to tutor others for excessive periods of time. While there is value in the occasional experience of teaching others, you should remember that his/her school time is primarily for personal learning and growth.

Now for the positive side. Here are some things that you will most likely wish to build into your instructional approach.

+ Seek to actively develop your child's talents, particularly in areas of his/her innate intelligences.

+ Stimulate your child to construct knowledge. This may be accomplished by a progression from awareness, to exploration, understanding, utilization, and ultimately innovation.

+ Allow your child to advance at his/her own pace, providing opportunities for in-depth exploration and for going beyond grade-level material.

+ As you teach, help your child to focus on themes and patterns, structures and organizing principles, and the logic that underlies an area of study. On general principle, avoid repetitious tasks and rote memorization.

+ Encourage your child to assume leadership roles – to direct plays, chair committees, organize events, and become widely involved in planning and decision making.

+ Provide books, games, and other learning materials at more advanced cognitive levels. You may want to seek local library cooperation in providing your child with books of special interest. Do not limit him/her to the children's section of the library.

+ Finally, encourage your child to experiment and discover; don't think you must do everything yourself. Ask about things; don't just tell about them. Listen; don't just talk.

The Learning Environment

Home schooling offers a marvelous opportunity to tailor the entire learning context to match your child's needs, interests, and personal objectives. The tone of this learning environment has much to do with your child's consequent growth and achievement. So how do you go about creating a positive atmosphere for learning?

Perhaps the cardinal principle is to emphasize strengths rather than weaknesses. Spend most of your time focusing on your child's talents rather than deficiencies, on what was well done rather than what was done wrong. It is true that you cannot blissfully ignore a problem area, but don't make this the theme. It is your child's gift that will often determine the direction of his/her life. So don't allow talents to languish. Offer options that will enable your child to use his/her strengths and preferred learning style.

Another fundamental concept is to make attitude itself an important outcome of learning. The teaching/learning process is simply more effective when a student enjoys what he/she is doing. Thus, you should construct learning experiences with as much concern for enjoyment as for other goals. What type of experiences result in enjoyment? Basically, those which link up with your child's interests and goals, and which allow for self-initiated and self-directed learning and growth. Remember, a paramount goal of education is to replace passive, dependent assimilation with independence and engaged learning.

Sometimes a strong temptation crowds in for parents of gifted children to place them in competitive situations. After all, what better way to keep them on their toes (and perhaps showcase their gifts in the limelight). By and large, however, competitive environments seem to be detrimental to learning. One study of highly gifted young adolescents, for example, discovered that these students perceived greater learning, continuing motivation, and the attribution of success to effort in noncompetitive scenarios (Clinkenbeard, 1989). The study also concluded that a competitive goal structure may have negative effects even for students who consistently succeed within competition, and that these effects may be incompatible with important, long-range educational goals. Another study found that gifted students themselves tend to prefer cooperative or individualistic approaches to learning over competitive contexts (Li & Adamson, 1992). Overall, cooperation and a personal striving for excellence appear to create a more positive learning climate than does competition.

Of course, many ingredients factor into a positive learning context, but perhaps the most important are time, space, and love. Your gifted child needs to have time – uncluttered time for dreaming, for thinking, for planning. He/she needs to have space – private space for tinkering, for experimenting, for constructing. And most importantly, your child needs love – unconditional love, regardless of personality or attitude, regardless of initiative or perseverance, regardless of achievement or failure.

Evaluative Procedures

Let's suppose that you have put together a magnificent curriculum, you have formulated a conducive learning environment, and you have embarked on a carefully thought out instructional approach. All of this is wonderful. But, was it effective? Did your child change? Is he/she a different, better person than before all this happened? In essence, you must ask yourself the question, Did learning really take place? To answer that question, you must evaluate.

How do you evaluate a gifted child? First of all, don't expect too much from pencil and paper tests. On occasion, these may be useful; but as a steady fare, they probably will not adequately measure all of your objectives. This is due to the fact that test questions frequently focus on mere data recall, are often rather superficial and contrived, and provide only a small sample of what they purport to measure. Some of these problems, of course, can be minimized by relating test questions to real-life situations and by ensuring that they take into account higher-level thinking.

You have other options besides tests, quizzes, and examinations. Evaluation can happen in many different ways. In this section, however, we will limit ourselves to three main ideas: process, product, and portfolio.

Processes Evaluation is best focused on what a student can do, rather than just what he/she knows. This makes sense. Information, in and of itself, quickly becomes outdated, whereas the skills of knowledge acquisition, scrutiny, utilization, and production tend to transfer across time and space. Furthermore, if a student can perform, he/she also knows those things which are essential. So in checking performance, you have also assessed requisite knowledge.

How do you evaluate a process? As your child engages in a particular learning experience or carries out a specific learning activity, you should look for a number of things, asking yourself: Is my child striving for excellence? Is he/she functioning as much as possible with expert-like criteria? Is the process self-monitored, with my child continually critiquing and improving his/her own performance? Does he/she incorporate critical feedback from others in a productive manner? Is the process efficient? Is it creative? Is it effective?

In evaluating a learning process, your evaluative procedures should shift from quantity of information to quality of understanding, from facts and figures to concepts and relationships, from memorization and replication to inquiry and invention, from the accumulation and retrieval of knowledge to its utilization and transformation.

Products One of the most valid indicators of learning is found in the products of learning. These products can be the natural outcomes of regular curricular activities or the result of special projects, creative endeavors, or research experiences. They may take on a variety of formats – oral or written reports, stories, poems, charts, diagrams, illustrations, cartoons, models, audiovisual presentations, and the like.

How will these products be evaluated? Fundamentally, you should assess learning and document evidence of growth. This means that you will need to take a look at the product itself in terms of the criteria of excellence, innovation, high-level thinking, and originality. You should also evaluate the appropriateness of the product for its intended audience. It is a good idea to broaden the scope of assessment beyond yourself. Ask your child to do some self-appraisal, using specific and appropriate criteria. Ask for feedback, as well, from the intended audience and from experts in the particular field.

Portfolios Recording a child's growth and development is not a new phenomenon. Parents have traditionally noted milestones in baby books, recorded unusual incidents in diaries or journals, displayed artwork on the refrigerator, and snapped countless photos of first steps, birthdays, graduations, and other red-letter events. A portfolio of learning, however, takes things a step beyond.

Artists, architects, journalists, and many other professionals frequently utilize a portfolio to systematically document their accomplishments and serve as a basis for communicating these attainments to others. In a similar way, a learning portfolio is an authentic record of your child's development, a comprehensive compilation of his/her significant achievements. As such, it is an invaluable means of evaluation.

What does one include in the portfolio? Initially, while your child is still quite young, you will probably make most of the selections. You will, of course, want to document your child's abilities, perhaps through the results of standardized tests, anecdotal records, and actual samples of your child's products. You should keep tangible evidence of

- ✓ unusual ideas,
- ✓ high-level thinking
- ✓ in-depth understanding
- ✓ strong intrinsic motivation and
- ✓ exceptional maturity

These artifacts can serve to illustrate your child's talents and provide an objective validation of his/her area(s) of giftedness. Along with these talent indicators, you may also wish to compile information regarding your child's interests and preferred styles of learning, thinking, and expression.

Overall, the learning portfolio should focus on strengths rather than deficiencies. It should paint a clear picture of your child's talents and learning achievements. Furthermore, it should take the broad view. You should not limit the portfolio only to intellectual aspects, but should also include evidences from the physical, social, emotional, and spiritual domains. And within each domain, lay out your child's milestones, special interests, and patterns of development. In this way, the learning portfolio becomes a full-color portrait, a comprehensive rendition of your child.

Issues in Home Schooling a Gifted Child

We would be remiss to conclude this chapter without discussing at least some of the issues which are involved in home schooling a gifted child. These are problem areas, challenges, or opportunities, depending on your perspective. Specifically, we will address labeling, underachievement, perfectionism, and socio-emotional needs.

Labeling

It seems quite clear that your child is gifted. Talents, traits, aptitudes, and accomplishments all point in that direction. So should you tell? Should you go ahead and candidly describe your child as "gifted"? Or should you continue on as if nothing exceptional or extraordinary is happening? Furthermore, how does the "gifted" label affect siblings, friends, acquaintances, or your own gifted child for that matter? Does it help or harm?

On the down side, the label tends to include certain myths and stereotypes – odd, bookwormish, and few social interests, for example (Halpern & Luria, 1989). Furthermore, the idea of gifted carries the unfortunate connotation that these individuals did nothing to earn their abilities – unfortunate, because we tend to view with suspicion anyone who gets something for nothing, and because your child might see the gift as something apart from him/herself. By implication, it also tends to relegate all others to the perpetual category of non-gifted. Other concerns center on the fact that a "gifted" label may create undue pressures and unrealistic expectations – such as the unreasonable belief that everything that one does must be "perfect" (Anderson, 1987).

The label may also narrow horizons and limit the individual to only one dimension of life (the gift), steering him/her away from exploring and developing other important areas.

On the positive side of the matter, the "gifted" label is simply a recognition of something very special about your child, something to be cherished and nurtured, something which you do not want to merely sweep under the carpet and ignore.

Some parents and educators have tried to resolve the matter of the gifted label by looking for other terms, although this doesn't really change the situation.

Regardless of the descriptor you decide to utilize, be sure you do at least these three things: (1) Discuss the term with your child and seek to clarify what it actually means. For example, if you use the word "gifted" it should be clear that you are referring to certain aptitudes or behaviors in a specific area of human learning and expression, rather than a global state of being. (2) Don't apologize for the label you use. After all, those who are outstanding in the athletic realm – the home-run hitter, the star quarterback, and the Olympic hopeful – wear their labels quite proudly. (3) Keep priorities straight. It is all too easy for parents to misplace their pride, focusing on the gift rather than the child. Your child, however, is infinitely more important than any particular ability or talent which he/she may possess.

Underachievement

In *A Nation at Risk* (1984), the National Commission on Excellence in Education estimated that as many as half of all gifted students might be classified as underachievers. The problem, however, is that underachievement in gifted students is often difficult to spot, due mainly to the fact that a gifted underachiever may actually be receiving acceptable grades in schoolwork although performing far below his/her potential. The good news is that underachievement can often be remedied, sometimes quite readily.

Underachievement may be evidenced, for example, by exceptional results on intelligence or aptitude tests and ordinary marks on routine homework and exams. It may also be seen in uneven patterns of achievement in a given subject area, with a baseline of low scores punctuated by an outstanding attainment from time to time.

What causes underachievement? Apparently a whole host of factors contribute. These include low self-image, dependence on extrinsic motivators, learning disabilities (such as hyperactivity), and tendencies toward perfectionism (often seen in an inordinate fear of failure). Low, unrealistic, unclear, or inconsistent expectations by parents may also factor. Perhaps the most frequent cause in a home school setting, however, is simply a mismatch between the curriculum and the child's unique talents, interests, needs, and learning style. The result of this disparity is frequently a schooling experience that is either too easy, too rigid, or too boring.

What can you do if your gifted child seems to be underachieving? First of all, if you are not doing it already, try home schooling. One of the great contributors to gifted underachievement in the conventional school setting is the fear of success. Or perhaps we should say, the consequences or ramifications of success. Gifted students often become quite adept as chameleons. That is, they learn to blend in with their peer groups, hiding talents and camouflaging abilities in order to fit in with the norm and avoid rejection by their peers.

If the problem is lack of motivation, the best solution is usually to link learning activities to highly motivating areas, maybe even placing them at the center of the entire curriculum. When this happens, overall achievement usually rises and the nucleus of motivation begins to extend outward to other topics and subject areas. Underachievement is thus marginalized.

Perfectionism

In many ways, perfectionism is found at the opposite end of the effort continuum. Instead of underachieving, the perfectionist seems to have become fixated with the idea of achievement – perfect, absolute attainment. This problem is only compounded when the individual is gifted.

Especially if they have been taught in a conventional classroom, gifted children easily become accustomed to the idea of being "the best" and may soon start thinking that everything that they attempt must be exemplary. They must get all A's; their work must always receive 100%. They must please everyone; they must always finish what they start. In essence, they feel compelled to perform perfectly in everything.

Such an approach to life and learning, however, can be devastating. Unrealistic self-expectations quickly result in disappointment, distress, and depression. Eating, anxiety, or stress disorders may erupt. Furthermore, the frustration of never living up to one's standards can take a heavy toll on self-esteem and self-acceptance (Verna, 1996). Such self-defeating compulsive behavior interferes with both mental and emotional development. It is also detrimental to interpersonal social relationships, for the perfectionist's acceptance of other people is often contingent upon their ability to "measure up" to these perfect standards.

Perfectionist tendencies also confine an individual to a narrow, rigid set of options. If a gifted child finds success in one area (such as writing poems or putting together computer programs), he/she will often pursue that activity almost exclusively, rather than risk possible failure anywhere else. Performance has here been confused with the process of learning.

So what can you do if your child displays perfectionist tendencies? First of all, assess your own expectations. Are you communicating the idea that you expect your child to be perfect (or at least the next best thing!)? One of the "great gripes" of gifted kids is that they feel that "parents, teachers, and friends expect us to be perfect all the time" (Schmitz & Galbraith, 1985).

Another important measure is to create an open, supportive environment. Present your child with open-ended learning activities rather than with tasks which require a single, correct response. Help him/her understand that most situations in life do not, in fact, require *one* right answer. When you give assignments and projects, the emphasis should be on development and improvement, on the process of learning rather than merely its outcome. While you should enthusiastically communicate approval of your child's accomplishments, you must also continue to show complete acceptance of your child even when a failure occurs.

Encourage your child to be creative – to take risks, to try new things. Help him/her to understand that there are no dumb questions or a dumb answers; that it is OK to say "I don't know." Help your child see that original thinking almost always requires false starts and "wrong" answers. These are simply part of the creative endeavor. Mistakes, then, should not be viewed as defeats but as opportunities for learning. Perhaps most importantly, however, don't bemoan the mishaps of achievement. Celebrate, instead, the success of learning!

Socio-Emotional Needs

First of all, let's dispel any remnants of a lingering misconception. Gifted children generally are not emotionally unbalanced nor are they socially inept. In fact, gifted students tend to have fewer serious behavior problems or profound emotional difficulties than other students (Sayler & Brookshire, 1993). Furthermore, they do not evidence any abnormal trends toward social isolation. Gifted children do, however, have certain unique socio-emotional needs due, at least in part, to the very nature of giftedness. These include self-understanding, multipotentiality, and positive relationships with others.

Self-understanding One of the foremost needs of any gifted child is self-understanding, particularly an understanding of his/her own giftedness. What does it really mean to be gifted and talented? How is one different from and, at the same time, similar to others?

You should make it clear, first of all, that gifted people are not better people. While gifted individuals may be exceptional in particular areas of talent, there are many other valuable qualities in human beings. The whole, in this case, is greater than the sum of its parts, and individuals at all levels of ability make significant contributions to our world. What is important is what we do with what we have.

Having established this foundation, help your child to realistically assess his/her own abilities and clarify how these talents fit into the larger picture of life itself.

Multipotentiality Gifted young persons often feel overwhelmed with the number of options that are wide open before them. In terms of both education and profession, there are simply more choices to make, and these often at an earlier age. Although having too many options is preferable to having too few, such multipotentiality often makes it difficult to decide which direction one should pursue in life. As a parent, there are a number of things that you can do.

First of all, encourage your child to engage in some wide-ranging exploration, particularly in terms of career choices.

To cope with multipotentiality, it is also important for your child to develop planning and decision-making skills, to set goals and objectives, to organize and prioritize.

Relationships with others Life is a web, its interconnections yielding ultimate meaning and satisfaction. In a society, it is the network of families and communities that provide purpose, energy, and culture. Likewise in professional life, it is teamwork that often spells success in a given endeavor. These concepts are particularly important for gifted individuals, who at times perceive themselves to be autonomous and self-sufficient. Like anyone else, however, gifted students need to master social skills and build positive relationships with family, peers, authorities, and others.

An especially important relational area for gifted children concerns roles and boundaries relative to authority figures (including parents, by the way). Sometimes these factors need to be clarified. On one hand, there may be a typical adolescent reaction – the child viewing self as the final authority and attempting to do everything that parents and other authorities oppose. On the other hand, the child may become excessively preoccupied with pleasing parents or other adults, to the point of suffering severe anxiety if there is any difference of opinion. Obviously, neither of these positions is healthy. As the parent, let your child know that it is good to have a mind of one's own, but that this should be expressed within certain parameters.

Ultimately, your child's most important social relationship is with you. Value your child's individuality. Nurture his interests and talents. Love your child, not because of gifts or achievements, but for his/her own sake. Spend quality time together. Listen, talk, do things together. Let your child know you care. This makes *you* a gifted parent.

Wrapping It Up

Well, there is so much more to talk about. Recipients of great gifts have much to give. Self-centeredness is a temptation for them, as it is for everyone. So their challenge is not only developing their potential but making it shine as a blessing for the world and an honor to heaven. This is true achievement – true greatness.

Perhaps it is time to draw some thoughts from the pages of this chapter and pour them into the crucible of life. "The School" is a provocative little piece I came across by Alan Glatthorn. It seems to summarize what teaching a gifted child at home is all about

The School

What is the teacher? A guide, not a guard.
What is learning? A journey, not a destination.
What is discovery? Questioning the answer, not answering the question.
What is the process? Discovering ideas, not covering content.
What is the goal? Open minds, not closed issues.
What is the test? Being and becoming, not remembering and reviewing.
What is the school? Whatever we choose to make it.

Notes

For further information, your might wish to subscribe to journals in the area of giftedness or contact associations or publishers of books in this area. One such journal is *Gifted Child Today (G/C/T)*. This magazine is published five times a year for teachers and parents of gifted, creative, and talented children. Also *Chart Your Course*, a quarterly magazine by and for gifted, creative, and talented children. Address: G/C/T, P.O. Box 66654, Mobile, AL 36606

These are some recommended publishers:

Center for Creative Learning,. Box 13448-B, Dept. 20, Tucson, AZ 85732-3448. P.O. Box 619, Honeoye, NY 14471.

Creative Learning Press, P.O. Box 320, Mansfield Center, CT 06250

Free Spirit Publishing, 123 N. Third St., Suite 716, Minneapolis, MN 55401-9967

Torrance Center for Creative Studies, 323 Aderhold Hall, University of Georgia, Athens, GA 30602.

Zephyr Press.

References

Anderson, M. A. (1987). Facilitating parental understanding of the "gifted" label. *Techniques, 3*(3), 236–244.

Clinkenbeard, P. R. (1989). The motivation to win: Negative aspects of success at competition. *Journal for the Education of the Gifted, 12*(4), 293–305.

Culross, R. (1989). Measurement issues in the screening and selection of the gifted. *Roeper Review*, 12(2), 76–78.

Gardner, H. (1983). *Frames of mind.* New York: Basic Books.

Halpern, J. J., & Luria, Z. (1989). Labels of giftedness and gender-typicality: Effects on adults' judgments of children's traits. *Psychology in the Schools, 26*(3), 301–310.

Kearney, K. (1991). *What do highly gifted children and their families really need?* Paper presented at the 38th annual convention of the National Association for Gifted Children, Kansas City, Missouri.

Li, A. K. F., and Adamson, G. (1992). Gifted secondary students' preferred learning style: cooperative, competitive, or individualistic. *Journal for the Education of the Gifted, 16*(1), 46–54.

Renzulli, J. (1978). What makes giftedness? Reexamining a definition. *Phi Delta Kappan, 60*, 180–184, 261.

Sayler, M. F., and Brookshire, W. K. (1993). Social, emotional, and behavioral adjustment of accelerated students, students in gifted classes, and regular students in eighth grade. *Gifted Child Quarterly, 37*(4), 150–154.

Schmitz, C. C., and Galbraith, J. (1985). *Managing the social and emotional needs of the gifted.* Minneapolis: Free Spirit.

Verna, M. A. (1996). *The relationship between the home environment and academic self-concepts on achievement of gifted high school students.* Doctoral dissertation, St. John's University.

Weinig, K. M. (1993). *Parents of nonpublic elementary school students in Delaware: A demographic description, analysis of their reasons for enrolling their children in these schools, and examination of their attitudes toward public schools.* Doctoral dissertation, University of Delaware.

48

Social Success

Relatives, neighbors, school officials and sometimes even judges frequently express concern for the social development of children whose parents have made a break with tradition and are teaching them at home. It seems conceivable to these advisors that just perhaps some parents might be intelligent enough to teach their own children, but how could a child shut up at home all day away from age mates possibly develop socially? A parent's first response to such a concern may well be another question. "What do you mean by socialization? Do you think school peers should be the guides and models for my child's social development?" The answer is too obvious. And for further clarification, home schooled children, as a rule, aren't really isolated either. In fact, they generally have a better quality contact with the world and with other children than they would have in school.

Of course, whether taught at home or not, adapting to other people *is important.* Home is the best place to learn the give and take of social adjustment, but only with the right kind of parental direction and through interaction with good friends. I personally know students who have had extensive home education and who adjust very well. Parents should realize the child's need to know how to fit into a social environment.

It's not enough, however, to say that we believe "there's no place like home" assuming that social development will take care of itself. The question deserves a closer look. Avoiding the bad – removing a child from an undesirable school influence – doesn't necessarily guarantee the good.

I see two somewhat opposite character traits that need balanced development. First, we want our children to think independently. We want them to be creative and free from social pressures that violate principle. And second, we want them to get along with other people. School at home easily fosters the first trait – independent thinking. Can it also help develop abilities to become wholesome, contributing members of society? I believe it can, with concerned parents.

Characteristics of good social development

If we want our children to develop socially, it might not be a bad idea to stop and determine what characteristics we expect to see as a result of our guidance. What do we mean by social maturity? General goals like "to love sincerely," come into it but are too vague for specific planning.[1] In a side bar on the next page is a suggested list.

Home school is appropriate

From this list of objectives we can see that a good home environment must certainly be important. The primary qualification for a home that can be expected to nurture social development is a good parent-child relationship. People tend to treat others the way they were treated as children.

The parents' role changes as children mature. You are probably familiar with how children change at adolescence. What you might not have thought about is another change that usually occurs at about the same time – age ten or eleven (although I believe it happens earlier in homes with high standards and caring parents). Before this, children consider consequences more than motives in determining right and wrong. Getting caught, or even compliance with the rules, is more important than another person's getting hurt by a wrong act. With the advance in maturity, circumstances and motives begin to determine moral judgments. The *purpose* of a rule is considered instead of just dealing with the letter of the law.

Of course we want even little children to care about other people's happiness, but their young minds are still depending on us for guidance. The quality of their behavior lies directly at our doorstep. With this preadolescent change, they begin to shoulder more of the responsibility. We are talking here about maturity development, not good and evil behavior. For social development, the point is that peer influence can threaten the character development of young children who have not yet made this change. Because they do not as easily sense the reasons behind the rules, parental behavior expectations can quickly be replaced with the standards of immature peers. You knew about teen peer pressure. It's a risk for young children, too.

During preschool and early grades, a home with close guidance from parents is ideal. A substitute home environment with loving caregivers is next best. Young children learn to share toys, for example, only because you say they should and mostly when you are watching. Interacting with other little children under your supervision helps them develop patterns of sharing and some other social skills, but Mom and Dad are the most important influences.

During middle grade years social interaction with peers seems to me to become important for social development, but still it requires supervision. Instead of restricting your children to being only where you want to be, plan fun things to do together as a family. Get together with other families who have children the ages of yours. Take your children camping. Take them to church or other group activities where they can be with age mates. Send them to vacation Bible school. Enrolling them in a regular school with the kind of atmosphere you approve is satisfactory under most circumstances. So is teaching them at home.

In adolescence your children start trying their wings. You must treat them differently, but they still need you very much. School social pressures can almost overwhelm some young adolescents especially if they are trying to do right in the face of more popular lifestyles. Home study for a year or less can help them regain their self-confidence enough to face the world again.

If your high-school or junior-high youth is in home school, I suggest encouraging organized activities with peers. After the eighth grade, a suitable Christian school close to home is sometimes hard to find. From experience with my own children and from observing many others, I believe home correspondence study or a good, small day school is much better than any boarding school up through about the tenth grade. At that point the young person's value system is somewhat established, and he or she is usually ready to face peer pressure. Also classmates have become more serious, and adjustment away from home is easier.

Social skills are obviously taught differently from math or spelling. And school subjects classified as "social studies," usually make little contribution to social maturity. Here are a few ideas for helping your children grow socially:

1. *Act socially mature yourself.* This is the most important. Show courtesy to your children. Speak with kindness, never raising your voice.

2. Social grace is part of character development. *Start expecting good social behavior as soon as your child is capable of any*

social behavior. Be gentle, loving, understanding and firm.

3. When your child is old enough, *make a simple list of social skills and talk about ones that need developing.* Revise your list as appropriate with input from your boy or girl.

Evaluate progress

Think through the list once a month or so and sit down privately with your child or go for a walk together and talk over any of the skills that need improvement. Refer to occasions when poor manners or selfishness was evident and ask your child what he or she thinks about the situation. If you speak understandingly, not condemning the behavior, your boy or girl will probably see the problem rather than trying to justify the poor behavior. You might need to probe a little, asking your child how he or she would feel if the circumstances were reversed, or you might simply need to point out the problem. Then you can ask what should have been done or said instead. Talk it over. As a Christian parent, you will want your child to be familiar with the life of Jesus. You can refer to His example.

How you relate to the issues of social development and home schooling must depend on more than what you read from a book. Watching your children mature year by year should influence your guidance. Your decision to send your children to a classroom school might depend on their social development. I suggest not committing your family to home school for more than a year at a time. You might decide to teach some of your children at home and to send others to a regular school.

Evidence

As a doctoral research project, John Wesley Taylor, V, asked the question, How does the self-concept of home-schooled children compare with that of other children?[2] Surely if kids studying at home were as deprived as some people think, their self-concept would be very low. Not having the opportunity to develop a glowing personality from their school friends, they would show up in any social context like embarrassed mice running for cover.

Taylor used the Piers-Harris Children's Self-concept Scale to evaluate 224 home-schooled children. As you would expect if you know home schooling families, he found them to be anything but mousy. Half scored above the 90th percentile, and only about 10% were below the national average.

The Dating Game

I expect that most of you who read this book agree that the marriage union is a serious responsibility and a privilege, and that it should remain firm until broken by death or unfaithfulness. You no doubt regret to see so many marriages fail where love seems to mean feeling more than principle. I've become convinced that the groundwork for a good marriage is laid in the social atmosphere of childhood and youth. One of the primary elements of this groundwork is a wholesome behavior pattern for boy-girl relationships.

Jonathan Lindvall, in a newsletter to home school families under the guidance of his "Pilgrims School," has outlined dating principles that call for a rather drastic change from the routine social atmosphere of even conservative youth. I have recently come to some of the same conclusions.

Lindvall begins by describing a typical experience of two teenage couples who seek security in "going together." Then, under the pressures of envy and manipulation, they break up and form other partnerships. He makes the point that typical doesn't mean normal or right.

From a Christian standpoint he refers to Romans 12:1 and Ephesians 4:31, 32.

The pattern, as he sees it, "lends itself to disunity and distrust in present and future relationships. It creates stress as teens view their self-worth in terms of whether or not they are `going with' someone. It leaves emotional scars from the many rejections experienced by all but the most popular ones. Even these envied and wanted popular teens learn to protect their `beautiful people' status out of a dread of being left out. . . .

"Even if teens live up to the scriptural standard of sexual abstinence outside of marriage, when they are encouraged to . . . [give] themselves emotionally to one and then another, they develop social relationship patterns that are contrary to the foundation of a good marital relationship. . . ."

Lindvall makes "a distinction between the infatuation dating typical of young American teens and the serious dating, or courting, practiced by those who are seeking a spouse. . . . [The typical teenagers are] driven by their hormones and peer pressure to be `going with' someone."

He recommends first that youth unready to consider marriage, not form couples, but that mixed groups associate in a variety of activities. This is not an easy stance to maintain considering the force of natural inclination.

Then he explains that "Probably the most important issue related to teen social life is the honoring of parental authority." Counseling with understanding parents brings in more than greater wisdom. It helps place the issue of social contacts in a mature atmosphere, protected from the pressure of youth culture expectations.

I have observed youth who have set a priority sequence in meeting life goals. First, for Christian oriented individuals, is to develop a working faith relationship with God; next they achieve the basic preparation for their lifework; and finally, they form a relationship leading toward marriage. By the time major educational goals are essentially mastered, narrowing affections to one individual leads rather quickly to a well-reasoned decision for marriage.

The dating criteria set by Michael Farris and his wife Vickie are worth considering.[3] He writes, "Our older daughters have committed themselves to the idea that they will pursue a relationship with a boy only when it is consistent with these three principles:

(1) Both the young man and I are prepared for marriage.

(2) I am investigating this particular young man because he appears to meet the spiritual standards my parents and I have agreed upon for a husband.

(3) I find him to be personally interesting and attractive.

"The vast majority of people engage in dating based solely on the third criteria. I know I did. . . .

"The major difference between courtship and dating is discovered by simply following all three of the above-listed criteria rather than engaging in dating based solely on personal attraction and interest.

"Dads have a special responsibility to secure their children's commitment to following [these principles] . . . in relations with the opposite sex. Don't wait until they are sixteen or seventeen. You will have waited far too long. . . .

"From the very earliest ages, raise your children with the understanding that the whole area of boy-girl relationships is to be reserved for the time of life just prior to marriage.

"I know for a fact that I was indoctrinated into the 'religion' of secular humanism through secular education. But the damage done to me by that indoctrination was less severe and easier to correct than the damage done by the societal philosophy of early dating.

"The vast majority of parents want their

children to abstain from sexual relationships until marriage. However, we have failed to see that abstinence should include emotional abstinence as well. In other words, if we permit our children to develop boyfriend-girlfriend relationships before they are ready to get married, we are simply asking for sexual temptation, and in many cases, sexual trouble."

I have shared these concepts to help you begin to see the pitfalls of the modern dating pattern. Your conclusions may differ from mine, but you will want to prepare your children for wholesome relationships long before the pressures of the teen society begin to influence them.

A success story

Good social development of home schooled children is certainly possible, but it takes parents who care. The experience in the following letter should give you courage and ideas:

April 23, 1980
Dear Dr. Wade:

In response to your recent letter, I will try to answer some of your questions concerning our experience with home school.

In 1966 we moved to a country home that was 26 miles from the nearest church school. Our main motivation was to take our children back to the joys of nature and away from some of the pressures that are inherent in modern suburban neighborhoods. At that time our oldest son was just entering sixth grade, our second son was ready for fourth grade, our daughter was a third grader, and our youngest son was three years old.

We decided to try home school for a year, since the miles seemed very long to a Christian school. We talked to the regional education officer, who was willing to make us a part of the school system operated by our church. Both my husband and I were professional teachers — he in math and science and I in music. In order to obtain an elementary certificate, I took the required courses by correspondence.

We checked the laws of our state in regard to schools and complied with the requirements.

For the most part we followed the curriculum that the church education department recommended and obtained our books and other materials from them. Music became an important part of each day. Practice periods and lessons were built into the school schedule for each child. In addition, we spent half an hour each day playing together in a "family orchestra."

Yearly, each child was given the choice of home school or "regular" school. Always the reaction was the same — they preferred to stay at home.

In 1970 we decided to build our own schoolhouse — a 14' X 20' building in back of our house. (Up until this time we had devoted one room of the house to our school, where we had a blackboard, school desks, and the usual trappings of a schoolroom.) The children helped in the building of this structure and learned quite a lot about everything from wiring to putting on shingles.

As the older children reached high school age, they took courses from Home Study Institute in Washington, D.C. and from the Independent Study High School at the University of Nebraska. We feel that their correspondence work not only taught the subjects well, but also taught them the value of an organized study program.

For a couple of years two nephews and a niece lived with us and attended our school. On occasion we had one or two others. But our school was mainly for our own children, and we declined to take most of the other students who expressed a desire to attend.

As a person who has spent nine years teaching home school, I can testify that teaching one's own children can be the most rewarding experience available to a parent. No one else can ever understand or care so much for a child as does the parent. However, the responsibility resting on the person who assumes this task is tremendous. She holds in her hands the whole future of these children for this life and the life to come. (I use "she" because in most home schools the mother is the teacher.)

The groundwork is laid in the cradle. The well-disciplined, much-loved child responds well to a teacher-parent. Disaster awaits those who have not established a strong parent-child relationship.

I can also testify that this job is full-time, hard work. When parents go the route of teaching their children at home, they should strive to give them a better education, a closer walk with God, and a more interesting life than if they were in a regular school situation. That is a challenge that takes prayer, effort, organization, and study!

We tried to teach our children to study efficiently and well so that they could finish their assignments faster and better. With the time thus saved, they were encouraged to work on areas of interest to them such as bird-watching, building a radio, sewing, etc. We had no interest in pushing them through school faster, but we were very interested in seeing them broaden their knowledge in different fields.

We tried to emphasize the importance of courtesy and thoughtfulness within the family circle, feeling that a person who can relate to his own family will have little trouble in the wider world of people. Respect for and friendship with older people, along with activities involving others of their own age was encouraged. Camping, all-day bicycle rides, and membership in an orchestra were activities in which the whole family could take part along with friends.

Recognizing that one of the most precious gifts that God has given to the human race is the privilege of choice, we encouraged the children to make their own decisions on the level of their ability, especially in matters relating to religion. We had family worship, Bible study in school, and attended a small church regularly, but we taught the children that it was a privilege, not a requirement, to worship God and serve Him.

I certainly do not want to give the impression that everything was always perfect and that we had all the answers. Far from it. We were all too human for that!

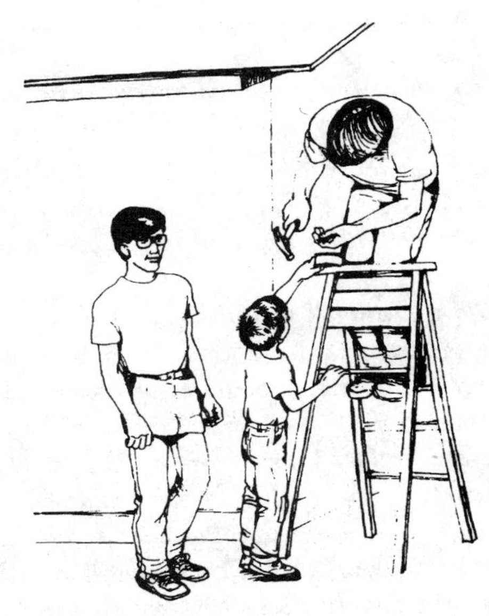

Perhaps you would be interested in how children who attended home school for so long adjust to the world. Our oldest son is a college graduate and is presently in medical school. While in college he was president of his senior class, president of the language club, and president of the biology club. He served as president of his freshman class in medical school and also plays in the orchestra there and in a string quartet. In his church he is the leader of the Young Adults' Ministries.

Our second son will graduate this year in computer science. He was principal violist in a very fine orchestra for nine years. His interests are in electronic and mechanical lines. He is active in his church. He and his lovely wife, who is a registered nurse, especially enjoy boating, water skiing, and photography.

Our daughter was concert master of the orchestra at her college, along with her special interest in biology and ornithology. Unfortunately, she became ill and had to drop out of school. She is now the wife of a minister.

Our "baby" boy, who is now 17, is a student at the Academy of Music in Vienna, Austria. He has always loved people, old or young, and has a host of friends there in Vienna. His teacher tells us that he is her best student and has invited him to appear in an international piano competition in Italy this summer.

God has blessed our efforts, and we give Him all the praise for leading us into a situation where we could get to know our children so well and in a way that we could be a major influence in their lives.

At present I teach in a Christian secondary school so still stay very busy. Consequently, I have written this letter very quickly, because I presume you want just a "peek" at our school.

Sincerely,
Velma Woodruff

As you can see, several special contributors have enriched this chapter:

To bring you up to date since ***Mrs. Woodruff's*** *letter: The children, Roger, Paula, and Douglas are professional adults, except for Gilbert who died in a drowning accident in 1982.*

Jonathan Lindvall *tells about a personal experience in his chapter, "Memorizing Scripture, a Joyous Legacy."*

Michael P. Farris *is president of Home School Legal Defense Association.*

J. Wesley Taylor, V *once sat in my classes. His doctoral research has provided insights on self-confidence, and hence social development, of home schooled children. He has contributed a chapter for this book and is described there. Yes, the V means there were four JWTs before him And in 1992 JWT VI appeared on the scene.*

Endnotes

1. Goals are listed in a side bar in the chapter, "Developing an Educational Framework."
2. J. W. Taylor, V., *Self-concept in Home-schooling Children,* (doctoral dissertation) Ann Arbor, MI; University of Michigan, 1986.
3. From "The President's Corner," *The Home School Court Report,* Jan., Feb., 1993, as adapted from *The Homeschooling Father.*

The illustration in this chapter is simplified from a photograph of the Woodruff family's schoolhouse construction project.

Theory Into Practice

SECTION THREE

49

The Lovely Game

A STORY OF PRESCHOOL YEARS AT HOME

Margaret Savage

"Mommy, I learned a new game. Come and see!" Anne-Margot, not quite two years old, tugged impatiently at my hand and led me from the kitchen to the rocky outdoor terrain of our creek-side home in the foothills of the Sierra Nevada mountains. There, beneath the great pines, she directed my attention to a row of small sticks. Warming to the occasion, her brown eyes sparkled and her little hands grasped the edges of her red dress eager to share an exciting discovery. "Families, Mommy," she explained, "stick families. See the daddy stick and the mommy stick and the baby stick? Three in a family. And look, Mom, one, two, three, four families – twelve sticks. See, Mommy? Four families of three make twelve! Isn't it a lovely game? Do you like it?"

A precious challenge

Yes, Anne-Margot, it was a lovely game. After appropriate remarks of interest I left my little daughter all hops and skips and jumps – and sticks, and returned pensively to the house. My mind seemed to spin as it began adjusting to the fact that this busy, eager child had been blessed with a keen intelligence and a self-motivated learning ability which would be an ongoing challenge to those who would carry the responsibility of her education. Through many other "lovely games" which followed, I observed, evaluated and considered. Would I regard the priceless privilege of the early years with this darting, effervescent sunbeam youngster as simply a maternal fulfillment – a time for taking snapshots and for comparing growth and development with other parents? Would it be a time for teaching meaningless rhymes, a time for plastic toys and the "electronic baby sitter"? Would these bright infant eyes be directed to the unreal and often ugly sight of cartoon-like pictures in garish colors? Would the alert ears be filled with the throbbing rock beat? Would wondering observations of the great world around her be reciprocated merely with adult laughter at her "cute" words and discoveries? And how would I relate to the wondering innocence of a tiny sister just beginning to sit up and look around at the water splashing over the rocks in the creek, the stately step of the deer in the woodlands, and all the sights and sounds of nature around her?

*I won't tell you much about **Margaret Savage** because she tells her own story in this chapter and the next. Your home situation and background probably aren't just like hers, and your home school will be a little different, too. But you'll appreciate her specific ideas on what it takes to do the job. The two girls are now married, by the way. Time passes quickly.*

No, these treasures entrusted to my care would be educated and trained to recognize the real values of life. From their earliest days their energies would be directed toward service to God and man. My years of teaching experience would develop and ripen as, with reliance upon more than human skill, I would accept the challenge of building characters fitted to stand firm and to bless others through the stresses and strains of our age. This would become my greatest priority. The golden moments would last but a short time. The opportunity was mine to grasp now.

My philosophy of education emphasizes the balanced development of the physical, mental, social and spiritual areas of life toward the formation of the whole person.

The values needed for growth are sadly warped in much of our society. To help our daughters learn good values would require new directions in our lives. I knew that accomplishments begin as concepts in the mind and, if cherished, become life goals. My little girl's "lovely game" had triggered such a goal. It was time now to lay the foundation blocks for character development. What were they to be? Obedience, self-control, respect and reverence.

The avenues of influence

We had started already. From birth I had held tiny hands in morning and evening devotions. A brief prayer of thanks mentioning the infant's name and a simple sweet song. Before ten months of age there were noticeable responses to the first notes of the song. At one year small lips were commencing a recognizable, "Happy, happy home."

How did we educate during those earliest of years? By using our wealth. Were we a moneyed family, then? Oh, no. But we were rich in the possession of delight in our children's ability to learn and in our quiet acre and a half far from town or city. The dawning of intelligence was not ushered in on harsh strains of popular rock or with a jungle of plastic ornaments and gaudy clown faces. It came quietly and naturally with consideration for the development of each of the senses.

Sight

The sense of sight promotes physical as well as practical and emotional development. An infant's visual input is a kaleidoscope of objects, movements and colors. By and by the marvelous mechanism of the brain absorbs, sorts, replays and relates these observations into sensations of pleasantness, harmony and beauty; or those of disharmony, unrest and fear. For our girls we chose loving, smiling faces; bright flowers; green grass; trees moving in the breeze; the view from Daddy's shoulders; the whiteness of winter snow with bright red berries; the comical expression of Hilda, our basset hound; funny, furry catkins hanging above the water's edge in springtime; and the heavens heavy with brilliant stars on a warm summer night.

Hearing

What about auditory input? How easily the sounds that speak to the soul are drowned out by the noise of traffic, angry voices, the power mower or the vacuum cleaner. Is there such a thing as a "still, small voice" any more? Oh, yes! "Daddy, what is the water saying when it goes all bubbly over the rocks? Oh, Mom, listen to my tinkley tune on the piano! If I'm very quiet, I can hear the bumblebee humming my name. Whatever *is* the donkey trying to say, Mom? Ooooh . . . my feet make the leaves say, 'Crunch, crunch'; they sound like cereal when my teeth bite it! Do stars crackle as they shine, Mommy, do they? Listen while I sing the new pretty song from church. Can smoke talk? Hear the grass rustle? Which birdie sings in that nice way, Mommy? Are we going to sit in the rocking chair and hear the quiet now? – are we Mom?"

Touch

The senses make the lessons of life real. Through them the physical, mental, social and spiritual can be merged into full maturity. A few of our younger daughter's early experiences illustrate learning through the sense of touch.

Little Ruth-Kyrie is coming into her own. She hasn't yet learned to talk or walk. We fix up a pup-tent of restful green and prop her just inside its shady doorway in her infant seat. Plump and content but with growing interest, she stretches out curious fingers to the many offerings brought by her faithful "big" sister. Another "lovely game" now is to "teach Ruthie." "Look, Ruthie, this is a pretty rock. Feel the big rock. Feel the little one. This is a stick. It's a rough stick. See how funny it feels on your finger? Touch it, Ruthie. It is a *rough* stick. And here is a smooth stick. See how funny it feels on your finger? Stroke them like this."

And so the "lovely game" goes on. I hang out the washing to Anne-Margot's soft crooning and I wonder. How does she know how to teach when only a year ago she was still learning to talk?

Taste

Ruth-Kyrie follows her preschool heroine's every sound and move. Small wonder that her first word is "Annie," and for the next two years a great portion of her comments will be prefaced by "Annie says." How important, then, that Anne-Margot learn to be a good example. And no better area to practice than in tasting! Here we see Ruth-Kyrie out in sunshine as usual; old enough, now, to be seated in the highchair for lunch. Her legs are pulled up high so that she can see her bare toes beyond the feeding tray, and on each toe she is carefully fitting a large, black olive. Anne-Margot gleefully trots back and forth from a tray, bringing one olive at a time. I emerge from the house with the rest of the food in time to hear, "And one more makes nine, and one more makes *ten*. Ten olives, Ruthie, and ten toes. One olive for every toe."

"See Mommy. See the olives on Ruthie's toes? How do toe olives taste? Do they taste the same as finger olives? Do they, Mom? Have you ever eaten toe olives? Have you, Mommy?" I have to admit that this is a gourmet experience which I seem to have missed. I see Anne-Margot staring pensively at my toes and glancing at the olives on the table, and I hastily change the subject. "How about the blessing?" "Oh, yes. Dear Lord, thank You for the toe olives. Amen." In my thought I'm picturing first grade workbooks teaching one-to-one relationships with such instructions as "Draw a string for each balloon." And here the lesson is learned in the freedom of childhood innocence.

Feeding Ruth-Kyrie, another "lovely game," is capably played by our busy brown-eyes standing on her toes to gently reach little sister's mouth as we talk about sweet tastes, sour tastes, red sweet tastes, yellow sour tastes, salty tastes and more.

We feed the fluffy kitten while Anne-Margot lies on her stomach and twists her head at strange angles as she stares at the lapping pink tongue. Kitty fails to reply to the stream of comments and questions about how the milk tastes, how this cat food tastes and whether he likes the taste of water.

Anne-Margot contemplates Mother's statement that we can help our sense of taste to enjoy foods that are good for us. Later we pick up a magazine to look at. Anne gleefully shows Ruthie and Kitty pictures of foods that we declare to be harmful to our bodies – hardly feeling it significant that they are both taking naps.

Smell

What does the olfactory sense have to do with the training of character? A scent is imprinted upon the memory so firmly that fifty years later when smelling a rose of the same kind, one can recall the perfume and even the occasion associated with it. Then just think about assailing the delicate nostrils and developing lung tissue with tobacco smoke, stale alcohol breath, stuffy, airless room odors or unhealthful fumes! Sometimes I have groped for tactful words in an effort to avoid these pollutants without offending the adults concerned. Frequently a humorous approach works effectively. The problem involves more than inhaling harmful substances. Years later, when confronted with a similar foul odor, will your child remember that Mother didn't allow precious little bodies to be damaged, even a very small amount, without objection? And how did Mother voice the objection? With courtesy and gentleness? With annoyance and irritation? With a frown, or with a hopeful smile?

Social development

As we have seen, physical, mental and spiritual development requires constant guidance through the right sensory inputs. What then of social development? I'm frequently asked, "In home education, how does your child get social experience?" I'll illustrate again.

Watch as Ruth-Kyrie helps to tuck the red and white checkered cloth over the crusty fresh loaf. She and Anne-Margot had helped mother pat and knead the bread. Peeping and exclaiming with delight and surprise they had watched the bread rise and eventually emerge from the oven. While we walk slowly down the road taking the bread to Mrs. Neighbor, we practice greeting her. Both little girls want to press the doorbell. We talk about taking turns. This time Anne-Margot will press it. The door opens. "Hi, Mrs. Do'bell." Whoops, let's try again! "Hi, Mrs. Neighbor." And Ruth-Kyrie adds, "Good afternoon, Mrs. Neighbor. We brought you some bread. We all *made* the bread." Both little ones sit quietly while Mrs. Neighbor and Mother visit briefly. After we have said good-by and are out on the sidewalk, Ruth-Kyrie announces, "I like Mrs. Neighbor." We talk about making others happy. Anne-Margot jumps and skips all the way home. She says she has a "happy, sharing something inside." Ruth-Kyrie say she has "happy inside, too," and Mother isn't missing a classroom full of thirty fourth-graders reciting multiplication facts at all!

"School" time

The girls were still quite young when an hour of more structured instruction was introduced each day. We had opened our home to accept developmentally disabled children. Anne-Margot and Ruth-Kyrie loved them all and learned to relate well to their special needs. A little bell heralded "school" time and the children came to sit in small chairs arranged in a semicircle. The sixty-minute program included such activities as follow:

Greeting song. (5 minutes)
"How are You Today?"
Each child's name is mentioned in the song as a mirror is held for each to see his or her face; and we shake hands.

Simple prayer. (1 minute)
Thanks for birds, flowers, trees happy day, and so on.

Color song. (4 minutes)
The children are called in turn to stand by "Teacher." For each, a color is chosen, and as we sing, I help him or her point to a garment of that color. "Who's a red bird? (Mark's) a red bird, (Mark's) a red bird,
to-o-o-day!"

Follow the leader. (5 minutes)
"This is the way we walk along,
walk along, walk along,
This is the way we walk along
On this nice, bright day."
We sing to various body movements (jump, run, tip toe, etc.) as the children follow and imitate a leader.

Drink time. (5 minutes)
Drink in small colored cups is actually poured and served by two children selected daily. We expect spills; and the children learn to clean them up.

Outdoor time. (10 minutes)
Pointing out various natural phenomena such as leaves, rocks or birds. Children help bring back objects for the nature table.

Foot-wiping procedure. (3 minutes)

Placing items on the table. (2 minutes)
An old TV tray covered with paper.

Bathroom and hand washing. (8 minutes)
A real "lesson" on proper hand washing and drying.

The nature table. (2 minutes)
Observing and discussing items.

Story time. (5 minutes)
I read or tell a short, simple story with a character-building lesson such as sharing, obedience or care for animals. We usually use a felt board, nature object, picture or other visual aid.

Activity time. (8 minutes)
For example, shoe tying, dusting chairs, raking leaves, piling blocks, learning to use a can opener, folding table napkins, brushing the dog, rhythm band, marching to music or action songs.

"School time is over" song. (2 minutes)
"We had fun. School is done.
Now we go and work and play.
Good-by, good-by,
See you all another day."

The structured hour – varied from time to time – seemed just enough to teach several needed skills and values. In the children's understanding, they were "going to school" and, by way of learning, so they were. Their minds, however, were not taxed or pushed. The remainder of their time was spent in outdoor activities, work experience (small, simple tasks in house and yard), eating, naps, walks, grocery shopping trips, play on the equipment for large muscle development (including bars of graded levels, a tire hanging from a tree, swings, slide, tether ball, balls, tricycles and seasonal equipment such as wading pools, a sand pile and snow saucers).

Preschool learning experience

During their preschool years before the girls were six and seven, they had numerous family-centered learning experiences. To give you ideas for activities you might plan, I will share some we found worthwhile:

Going for hikes and picnics; attending church programs for children; taking trips to parks, zoos, museums, historical sites.

Working with yarn, clay, scissors, finger paints, paper, crayons, paints and many other collected items. Spools were welcomed. Old wallpaper books were hailed with great rejoicing. Many happy winter hours were spent making things. Guests were sometimes rather surprised with gifts of nondescript appearance but not one failed to rise to the occasion and express warm appreciation for the effort!

Riding the pony; exploring a "dress-up box" (a large box of clothing geared to please small children); playing in the sand or water; enjoying a playhouse with table, chairs, shelves, stocked with "treasures" bought by children from local yard sales.

Helping Father in the garden, helping Mother cook and prepare food, caring for the pets, working from a pictorial job list reminder of daily responsibilities with places to check off the jobs as they are done.

Beginning piano lessons from Mother; listening to character-building stories and records; helping work on a jigsaw puzzle; purchasing, wrapping and sending socks and small gifts to an Indian reservation; buying a game and taking it to the children's ward of a local hospital; making food and gift box for and taking it to a needy family; putting on plays for senior citizens and inviting them home for a holiday meal.

Such experiences as these, the continual close family relationship and interesting, stimulating devotional periods each day, provided a start for my two little learners. "A lovely game," Anne-Margot would have said. Yes, Anne, it has all been a lovely game – the game of learning – the game of living life with eagerness and expectancy undimmed and undaunted.

A foundation to build on

An early home education with parents actively interested, working, relating and sharing life's experiences with their children builds a solid foundation for future learning. Some parents consider this preparation for life too important to entrust to any other person. Then, as the age for more formal learning approaches, home may naturally be school, and book learning is not mysterious but merely a continuation of what has gone before.

Whatever approach you choose, remember that the family educates first and most effectively. Fortunate is the child whose parents are aware of their responsibility during preschool years, and doubly fortunate are children privileged to continue home schooling into more formal learning, free from the tensions and influences which damage so many young hearts and minds.

50

The Redwooded Headpecker

A STORY OF SCHOOL YEARS AT HOME

Margaret Savage

The concept of fulfillment and reward in home teaching had not entered my conscious thinking until one day when the door burst open and wide-eyed, breathless, six-year-old Ruth-Kyrie ran in exclaiming, "Mommy, Mommy, I just saw a redwooded headpecker!" We all laughed, including Ruth-Kyrie as she became aware of her verbal mix-up.

What a golden "teachable moment"! Even through the mirth I sensed the joy and reward in being present during my child's learning experience. Had this not been my constant privilege during the early years? Why then should it cease at our state's decreed compulsory school attendance age?

Several years passed. Both daughters had learned at home until almost eight years of age and were now attending a Christian school with an enrollment of approximately ninety students. Anne-Margot was in the sixth grade and Ruth-Kyrie in the fourth. They had fine teachers whom they loved and respected. Their grades were very acceptable and, in many ways, they enjoyed school. Since the time I described in my chapter of "The Lovely Game," my husband had terminated his distant employment and was now able to stay home through the week. But, for several reasons, we began to wonder whether home education might be better for us than even desirable away-from-home learning. At last, following much thoughtful discussion, we set up a home school which, over a period of three years, included eleven other students from five to sixteen years old.

Why we chose home education

We decided on school at home (1) for the general well-being and physical health of our children, (2) to meet special learning needs, (3) for a schedule geared to family travel plans, and (4) to allow more time for many ongoing home learning projects.

*We met **Margaret Savage** in the previous chapter. Here she invites us to see her home school when her girls were older. She tells us how it worked for her and gives us lots of practical pointers.*

The girls had frequently been kept at home with bronchial ailments and illness related to the control of blood-sugar levels. They would thrive at home, but upon returning to school they would become fatigued and lethargic and before long they would be sick again. Also, frequent holiday and birthday celebrations created social pressures when rich party foods were declined. Although the girls maintained high scholastic standings, the arrangements were difficult for everyone concerned. As we studied about health, we made lifestyle changes. We began to spend far more time outdoors. Our diet improved with the elimination of almost all refined foods. We took more time for the exercise and satisfaction of practical work. I was on hand to establish habits of frequent drinks of water, deep breathing, and good posture. We took brisk midmorning walks, and the study area was moved to a spot in the sunshine by open windows or often outside. These practices obviously could not be followed in a school classroom.

During the time spent at home through bouts of illness we became well acquainted with the school curriculum. We felt that most of it was helpful and positive, but in many ways insufficiently challenging to our older daughter. We invited the county school psychologist to administer a battery of tests. He recommended that we arrange for Anne-Margot to be enrolled in the first year of a college program. We didn't agree. I believe that good home education can be an excellent alternative for gifted as well as for ordinary children.

We also found that our home "wellness" program was time consuming. We came to believe that our girls' physical health, their health education, and learning to prepare nutritious foods were more important than some of the more traditional areas of study.

The most urgent and winning factor in our decision for home education was the need to visit aging relatives overseas. A two-month stay in the United Kingdom could be arranged only by intruding on the school year.

	Mon.	Tue.	Wed.	Thur.	Fri.
8 - 12	Study	Study	Work	Study	Study
12 - 1	Lunch	. . .	. . .	. . .	. . .
1 - 3	Study	Art & Sewing	Study	Home duties	Study

How to use the advantages of home education

If you are still wondering whether a home school would be the best plan for your family, the outstanding advantages we discovered may help you decide. If you have already opted for teaching your own children, our experience may give you ideas for making the most of your opportunity.

A family-centered start to the day replaces the typical morning scramble and rush for the school bus. Your early morning program planned with consideration for the needs of each family member will bring cheerful faces to the breakfast table. Allow time for your children to begin their day with prayer. A glass of water purifies the blood stream. Outdoor chores promote deep breathing and good appetites. In our home, Father starts his meal first. He is then ready to read to the rest of us from a beloved series of books while we enjoy the main meal of the day. We frequently discuss home needs and plans. We also share family letters and check the jet plane on our family savings chart.

A home education program allows flexibility. Both our Sierra Country Home School and now Pine Acres School have had daily time schedules. But we have felt free to alter them to accommodate unexpected and nonroutine learning opportunities. For example, you may want to deviate from your schedule before a local science fair, for your daily science periods or during the arts and crafts period. Even some of the practical work periods might be used to complete an exhibit needed by a certain time deadline. We often appreciated the freedom to change our program. For instance, one day the house cleaning lady brought her guitar. During her break and ours, we all participated in a pleasurable experience in music enrichment. Another time a sick neighbor needed leaves raked.

Visits from county agency employees, interested parents, physicians, and ministers provided fine opportunities to practice social skills and to learn about the work of our visitors.

Once after an early-morning visit to the pond, Ruth-Kyrie announced that it was "tadpole-time." On only one day of the year were the pond edges that black with tadpoles. Seeing them fascinated our boys and girls. By adding our arts and crafts period to our lunch hour and packing along our sack lunches, we were able to fit the excursion into our school day even on the spur of the moment.

Another unscheduled activity occurred a little later in the year as small toads by the thousands appeared on the mud flats of the rapidly shrinking pond. A well-watered rock wall at home provided housing for as many of these interesting amphibians as eagerly cupped hands could transport. The experience gave real meaning to our study of toads from the encyclopedia in our home-school classroom! And what fun to run out to the wall, to "toad city," on our breaks to see them settling in!

At short notice our little group of students was able to respond to an invitation to participate in a "Disability Day" at a local public school. Anne-Margot and Ruth-Kyrie had been asked to share their knowledge in the area of the deaf-mute handicap. They set up a booth. We all took interest in visiting it along with other booths giving informative knowledge concerning major disabilities. Anne-Margot and Ruth-Kyrie addressed several assemblies on the subject of American Sign Language, demonstrating with their hands and delighting several hundred elementary students by teaching them a few words on their own fingers.

Local news has always been a feature in our home learning approach. When we read of a woman in our community who had been the victim of an attempted arson, the children were motivated to express their sympathy and encouragement in a letter-writing exercise. It was not the language lesson I had planned, but it presented the same skills in a far superior way. And the young writers received the unexpected surprise of an appreciative reply.

Since we spent more time on research papers than on workbooks, sudden needs for material at the public library would occur. Although the library was some miles away, no long-term scheduling was required. We took our sack lunches in the car, worked at the library and fitted in a lunch-hour at the local park with a "go" on the swings. Once we even had a great time on roller skates.

One day thirteen deer filed down through the woods across Sullivan Creek. Watching wildlife called for special breaks from the school schedule. Sometimes an extra-handsome squirrel family would perform outside our schoolroom windows, or the little hummingbird "boss" would come flashing his colorful jewels, introducing a new family to the nectar feeder. We watched new visitors come to the bird feeder and observed Mr. and Mrs. Wood Duck making their annual debut. We saw a solitary great blue heron swoop down in front of the canyon wall. Sometimes students would go to the windows for a few moments just to gaze at the rushing, splashing waters below or at the steeply wooded canyon bank beyond, or to feast their eyes on the transforming beauty of snow in winter. For these special moments of contemplation, it was in order to quietly leave one's seat. And the children understood that staying too long would abuse the privilege. One troubled child who had previously known only scholastic failure came to visit and sat for a while at our table. "I could learn here," she announced simply. She came and she did!

The art of conversation

How do children learn conversation in the traditional school setting? You can imagine. In the home school children may hear interesting and stimulating conversation in which they are naturally included. Introduce your young learners to vocabulary-building experiences. Tape recorders let them experiment with their own voices. Vocabulary building records, reading aloud, and listening to family members read, word games, singing together, family members expressing their feelings about life experiences, all aid in building skills.

Organization

Some individuals are handicapped

throughout life by poor organization and planning skills. Large school classes offer little individualized help for naturally poor organizers to master their muddled confusion. Of course, all youngsters need to learn neatness and order. Growing up aimlessly whether in a home school or in the traditional school can be devastating later in life. To teach organization to children who have a serious problem you may want to write out little lists with simple steps showing what should be done. Organizational reminders may be written at the top of work papers. Children appreciate decorations with small pictures cut from old catalogs or magazines.

Appoint a classroom monitor to assist the disorganized or younger child by helping him or her check for neat work areas, clean hands, properly wiped feet, and so on. Even for a one-child home school, take time for the several tasks required to keep up an orderly learning program.

Maintaining discipline

You will probably want to use the same discipline system for both home and school hours. We have tried several ideas: "grapetime" (actually gripe time) in family meetings, a fine/reward system, a check list, a privilege card operation and, sometimes, just "go to your room." For whatever methods you use, success demands consistency.

Peer pressure

I question whether many children below the ages of eight and nine can successfully resist peer pressure. Very small groups of both boys and girls of varying ages don't tend to produce pressure to conform to a popular behavior pattern. Certainly we would not expect it in the close and fairly constant presence of the home teacher. As peer pressure is but an aspect of cultural pressure, the answer to withstanding cultural pressure in later adult life may well be to have the young children removed, as much as possible, from *all* pressures they are too immature to control. Your child will be better fitted to gradually meet the demands of society through a wholesome home environment with much time out of doors learning that which is appropriate for his or her level of maturity. In company with experienced and, hopefully, wise parents, children learn appropriate attitudes and responses.

Personal habits

Sheer force of numbers hampers even the best-intentioned classroom teacher from helping children develop some most needed habits for good learning. The small home school can provide oral reminders from the teacher, attractive charts and notices, well-trained monitors, encouragement to cooperate, and checks to make sure that students understand reasons for requirements. Success in learning requires: good posture and breathing, ventilation, frequent movement, fresh water intake, proper rest room hygiene, avoidance of fatigue, coping with distraction, correct pen or pencil position, neat and careful work, consideration and concern for fellow students, a sense of responsibility, and consistent study habits. In the small group arrangement you can practice eye contact, clear diction, gentle tones, the close-range smile of encouragement, and the assurance of a touch on the arm or shoulder.

Balance in learning

The four main areas of learning – physical, mental, social, and spiritual – must be kept in desirable balance to meet the complete needs of each student. Maintaining constant development in all areas is an ongoing process for each child. In a large classroom it is extremely difficult to know much of the day-to-day occurrences in the life of each student. In home education with your own children and possibly a few others, you can be sensitive to this sense of balance. At certain times Peter may need more academic encouragement than Johnny. Or Mary's life at home may cause such stress that, more than anything else, she needs your counseling time.

You might be asked to teach someone like a little girl who came to our home school. She showed symptoms of a learning disability generally called dyslexia. Did she need more exposure to the printed page? We thought not. From infancy Beth had spent an average of fifty hours a week indoors in front of a television set. Her brain was overtaxed and weary. She needed an improved diet and much outdoor activity. How she enjoyed the bread-baking lessons and the dog running! Later we cautiously introduced her again to academic learning. Her problems abated. The following year she entered a larger school at only one grade behind her chronological age-level expectation.

Resource people

Many people have contributed to the total educating process in our home school. Among them have been family members, members of the community with particular skills, people suggested by the county schools office, small business owners, and those whom we have contacted through local newspaper articles featuring some particular experience or area of knowledge. So far no one has refused. A courteous note, a telephone call or a visit from one or two of our students has resulted in one interesting learning experience after another.

One usable idea from the county schools newsletter led us to contact an exchange student returned from Belgium. The young lady enthusiastically showed us her slides and answered questions about her experience living with a family in another culture.

The greatest human resource in our home school has been the input of knowledge and skill from retired people. Unanimously, those approached have warmed to the concept of home education and to the opportunity to share and teach.

Our girls' own grandmother has given careful mending and sewing lessons. A retired nurse gave skillful instruction in first aid and presented Junior Red Cross certificates at the end of the course. An elderly gentleman taught many different knots. A lady who had majored in drama imparted valuable tips on public speaking and methods of enhancing musical and vocal presentations. A retired physician conducted a special series of devotional meetings for the children, helping each one to develop a sense of security and self-respect. Visits from our church minister encouraged a sense of value in each child. Retired missionaries and others who had traveled in distant lands showed slides and shared many interesting experiences in our home.

One day a 4-H Club instructor provided a lively demonstration and practical experience in making applesauce. Another young woman came along to boost our knowledge of the American Sign Language. Authors, artists, poets, builders, fishermen and musicians have added to this group of wisdom sharers.

Field trips and travel

As a teacher, the term "field trip" brings to my mind stressful memories of bus scheduling; rest stops (especially the unscheduled ones); odors of orange peel, egg sandwiches, and wet jackets; startled sensations on counting heads and discovering that Johnny is missing – again; and the familiar frustration of pointing out the trip to the backs of students' heads, and realizing that they are riding too high on waves of group stimulation and excitement to have more than passing interest in the subject at hand. While a small proportion of children eagerly absorb knowledge in spite of distractions, many more become emotionally triggered with escape from the classroom, the presence and noise level of peers and undeveloped self-discipline. Feedback on what was learned is frequently disappointing despite careful preparation before the trip.

In contrast, the small home school venture directed by parents who can explore the learning territory with their children has a relaxed home atmosphere. The goodwill of togetherness and the subdued sense of adventure create a comfortable learning climate. In our family experience, bursts of questions and comments alternate with quiet periods of looking, listening, and considering.

Whether with only our own two daughters or with an additional half dozen of their schoolmates along, we have found field trip ventures to be most rewarding. Picture taking, postcards, giveaway brochures, maps, charts, and occasional souvenirs refresh memories for reports and letters. Our girls have several large notebooks which tell of trips taken since they were six years old.

A whole book could be written about our field trips and travels. Instead we have compiled a list of suggestions trusting that they may stimulate your own ideas.

Supplementary learning and service activities

In addition to the usual classroom activities, children learn from many experiences. Here are a few that we have tried and can recommend:

- ❑ Reading many books and periodicals each month.
- ❑ Correspondence with friends, relatives, and pen pals.
- ❑ Physical activities: gymnastics, skiing, hiking, bicycle riding, swimming, and lifesaving.
- ❑ First aid course.
- ❑ Scrapbooks, diaries, trip books.
- ❑ Crafts: leathercraft, making cards and gifts, ceramic painting, woodwork, rock tumbling.
- ❑ Art: oil painting, pastels, drawing, and water colors.
- ❑ Domestic skills: cooking and baking, needlecraft, household management.
- ❑ Music: voice and instrument lessons and practice.
- ❑ Gardening.
- ❑ Nature activities.
- ❑ Family nights.
- ❑ Projects for income.
- ❑ Planning surprises to help the unfortunate.
- ❑ Monthly contacts with elderly friends
- ❑ Jail visits accompanied by a parent.
- ❑ Helping slow learners in school.
- ❑ Collecting roadside trash.
- ❑ Gathering firewood.
- ❑ Occasional baby sitting in our own or a close friend's home (after instruction, discussion and demonstration).
- ❑ In church, assisting young mothers or sitting with the elderly.
- ❑ Helping neighbors and parents with yard work.

We feel that experiences in the real world of work give children important advantages. Academic studies take on new meaning. The young helpers begin to understand employment relationships. They observe adults busily engaged in tasks they enjoy. This kind of experience is certainly superior to an atmosphere of large scale peer pressure in a society where diligence and excellence are usually not coveted. Thus children develop a sense of the value of their small accomplishments. Here are weekly volunteer jobs our girls have done over the past school years:

❂ Employment in a local pet shop: cleaning cages, stocking aquarium tanks, bathing puppies, tidying shelves, constructing bamboo bird cages, cleaning floors and equipment, etc.

- Employment in a pet-grooming parlor: making small ribbon bows for animals ready to go home, cleaning up clippings, dusting, shampooing and brushing dogs, etc.
- Employment in a public library: organizing and replacing children's books, assisting young borrowers, dusting, replacing adult books according to code numbers, checking out books, using microfilm, answering the telephone, typing notices, making posters.
- Employment in a veterinary office: filing cards, feeding and exercising animals, pricing and labeling medicines, cleaning floors and cages, washing instruments, assisting in small ways in surgery, answering the telephone, accompanying the veterinary doctor on large-animal work at a dairy farm.

In securing work-experience situations for our children we have met with the operators of the establishments which have seemed to have suitable experiences and atmospheres. We have described our school program as well as our students' previous work experience. Employers have expressed appreciation and in some cases have given gifts to the girls.

The school and equipment

Plan and organize your physical teaching space indoors and out. Consider the work area. The teaching should occur where there is good lighting, near windows, and close to the supply area.

A name for your school means much to students who may be asked where they go to school. "Greenview" or "Parkend" is a much more satisfying reply than, "I just learn at home" or "I don't go to school." Choose the school name in advance. Let the children help decide.

Supplies should be on hand long before the first day of school. Organize and examine them and become well acquainted with teaching guides, books, and so on. Especially in the area of science, collect your equipment ahead of time. Then put most of the supplies away out of sight to provide a little element of freshness as new items are brought out to use from time to time throughout the year.

Curriculum and time planning

What to teach and when are discussed elsewhere in this book, but you might like to see a general outline showing how we divide up our week.

The actual schedule shows the specific classes beginning with Bible, each lasting 55 minutes with some variation for particular children. We also study on the weekend and add music lessons and practice. On Thursday afternoons the girls clean through the house and assist with cooking and baking for the weekend.

A monthly breakdown of the year's plan is helpful. My custom is to work by subject categories: Bible, language, math, social studies, science, health and nutrition, practical experience skills, arts and crafts, and music.

A curriculum guide or outline may be borrowed or purchased from your county schools office. You could also write to other counties or ask about the curriculum from a private school you know about. Even though you might not follow any one outline, they will give you a concept of what is generally introduced at each age level. You will also get an idea of how much is usually covered in a school year. If you are starting without experience or lack teacher training, a home-study course will be helpful.

Next make up weekly plans, and after that, daily plans – even for one student. It's not necessary to make long complicated plans. A few notes on which topics will be presented and what you want to accomplish for each is all you need.

The first two days

We have started each school year with a two-day planning session with the children. On the first day they write down all the suggestions, reminders, hopes, and desires which they can think of for the school year. They help unpack boxes, set out the reference books, arrange the schoolroom, and put up cheerful bulletin boards. On the second day they set up their own goals and aims for the year and assemble their notebooks, papers, crayons, markers, and other supplies. We do a great deal of discussing. Their input is most valuable to me as I plan the year ahead.

We work together on schedules for home and for school, considering the needs of the whole family. Father lets us know when he can teach math and science. After careful work, we put the two schedules up on the bulletin board or on the wall.

Closing the school year

Our school year does not run beyond the end of May. By then we are ready for the more informal summer learning and time out of doors. Last year we had an end-of-school program and an eighth grade graduation complete with printed programs.

Philosophy

We believe children are whole beings with development potential in physical, mental, social and spiritual areas. We teach our children broad values helping them understand the reasons for learning from the out of doors, working with their hands, service for others and making religion practical. Life in itself is education. We expose our children to its many good facets, sharing our impressions and feelings. We teach attitudes and stress that the ability to learn is a priceless resource to be developed with care. We trust that the lives of our children may be channels of helpfulness and blessing to others and an honor to the One who has lent us the gift of life.

Real education, we believe, is the balanced development of character and the grand achievement of love to God and to people.

We like home school

Three years of home education have convinced us that we are doing the right thing. We are seeing the results – two service-oriented young people, already an asset to their home and community. Although our girls are successful learners, we enrich rather than accelerate, keeping a balance among the various areas of development. Home education has helped our girls acquire individual responsibility in planning their time, both in academic and practical areas. They are truly self-motivated and love to learn.

51

A Challenge for Young Learners

When I visited the "Citadel," an old fortress not far from the north coast of Haiti, I was obliged to pay for a horse to ride up the steep hill. When people don't have much to feed their children, their animals get even less. My horse was miserable and puny. He had no real desire to carry me (although he did reward himself part way up by snatching a few bites of corn stalk planted close to the path, nearly getting me into trouble). Feeling a little tourist-trapped, I wanted to see him earn his master's money. I've since learned more about patience, but that was then.

Being more eager to get to the top than was my four-legged companion, I prodded and pleaded using the best horse language I knew. I could have walked as easily until the path got steep. Then, when I would have appreciated the ride, I could see my horse was having a really hard time. He was beginning to need me more than I needed him; so I dismounted, took the reins, and pulled to get him the rest of the way.

Children grow up to be far different from good horses which live only to serve their owners' wishes. Still, my experience illustrates a problem of immature adults who need to be pulled rather than carrying their own load and helping others.

All young learners need direction to become responsible members of society. Those of you who read this are probably already different from ordinary people your age. I'm not worried that you might end up among adults who fail to mature and who need others to pull them up the hill. I would like to set an even higher goal before you: Do more than be a cooperative student. *Begin early to feel responsible for your learning (and for all your behavior).*

Life is still a growing process. Your parents need to set guidelines and sometimes to say, no. But as you see what you need to become, begin to do what it takes without being spoon fed and watched every instant. Following are suggestions for success:

Seek excellence True greatness is more than being the fastest or smartest or most popular. It's, first of all, beauty of character. Success in life is not measured by sensual gratification or financial net worth. It's what you do to bring happiness to others who need it. So reach for the top. Do your best, and be your best for others.

Set goals Think of how you might like to use your talents in life. You will need to modify your objectives now and then, but always keep in mind your purpose for living. Besides dreaming, you need to discuss with your parents how you will use your resources of time and opportunity. Be organized. Make "to do" lists, follow a schedule, and check your progress.

Lay a good foundation Your parents and other teachers can help you establish basic strengths, spiritually, intellectually, physically, and socially. As you discover weaknesses, work on them before moving too far ahead. At the same time, judge your potential. Don't hold yourself to absolute perfection when you need to move ahead. When you have a choice, look for activities you can enjoy and still meet your goals. You interest of the moment should not be the main consideration. Learn to enjoy what, at first, seems boring if you (or your parents) see that you need the experience.

Know your limits Don't be afraid of hard work. But if, like my horse, you can't climb the mountain on your own, do something else. Try again at another time. Ask for more help. But remember that people are all different. Not everyone is able to do everything. If you have put forth reasonable effort and still aren't a shining star, this does *not* mean you are lazy and useless. No one is ever responsible in life to do what he or she can't do! Learn to enjoy what you can do while you keep gently pushing your limits. The tiny flower in the grass is as pretty as the graceful palm tree. God made them both.

Be curious Don't wait till someone starts to pull you up the mountain before you dig in and learn. Rather than guessing when you don't understand, figure out where to find what you need to know. Instead of learning the least to get by, finish your assignments and probe into related areas that interest you. Make a habit of being curious about the world around you. Ask lots of questions. Find out how things work and why people do things a certain way. Learn from your mistakes.

Use what you have As you learn, use your time, your intelligence, your strength, your influence, your financial resources, and your words of love and courage to bless others.

Sharpen your study skills Books are available to help you. Also become a faster reader.

A further note
For teens and young adults

As you get a little older, learning through curiosity means looking for better ways to do things. It means challenging the norms of our too-selfish society. Try being kind and respectful to people others pass by. Try giving without getting something in return. In all, take good care of your health as you experience the joy of service to others.

52

Developing Self-Discipline

Kathy Babbitt

So who needs this chapter?
Introduction by Ted Wade

I remember one mother who, with her husband, felt that home schooling would be best for their boys. Financial circumstances increased her incentive to avoid private school tuition and teach the boys herself, but she wasn't so sure she could make it succeed. (You have heard stories like this before.) Carrying through on long range commitments didn't seem to be easy for her. Of course I agreed that home schooling would be a good idea, and I gave her a copy of an earlier version of this book and gently suggested that the experience would be a good challenge for her to develop more self-discipline. She decided to try but the next time I saw the family, the whole idea was off. I had nothing more to say. Sending the boys to a good classroom school was better than her frequently not bothering to teach them because she had a letter to write or an interesting book to finish. I wish I had had Kathy Babbitt's chapter in that earlier edition.

So what about you? Actually, most of us need to get our self-discipline muscles in better shape. Kathy Babbitt's approach is both practical and spiritual. Even if you happen to come from a more secular background, don't give up too quickly on this chapter.

Okay, so self-discipline is a little like money. It takes it to get more. But we all do have just a little self-discipline, so let's make it grow. Here is Kathy to tell us how:

Making self-discipline a reality

To make the home schooling idea work, self-discipline is imperative. Without control of your own life, the good theory in this book will remain as only ink on paper. Good discipline is not an end in itself. It leads to desired results in our lives as well as in those of our children.

In 1 Timothy 4:7 we are urged to train ourselves to be godly. That takes *diligence.* And the writer of Hebrews says, "Make every effort to live in peace with all men and to be holy" (Heb. 12:14, NIV). That takes *work* and *perseverance.* How do we do this? By trying harder, purely through self-effort? No. We depend on God to make us able. Self-discipline is a mutual effort between the indwelling Holy Spirit and the will of one who is yielded to God's authority. It involves mastering attitudes, emotions, and actions. With the help of the Holy Spirit and the Word of God, we can develop godly motives, believing that God loves us and wants His best for us (which is sometimes very different from what we envision it to be). Then we can activate a plan to bring our desires in tune with God's plan for us. (Psalm 40:5).

Self-control is a fruit of the Spirit (Gal. 5:22, 23). It involves abstaining from what may be good in order to enjoy that which is best. It includes authentic living and breaking the cords of habit that threaten to strangle us. It focuses on restraining our actions and feelings.

Self-discipline gives direction, helps us live productive lives, and gives us the courage to stand by our convictions. We need it to meet obstacles head on. Maintaining mastery over any area of our lives requires eventual control over all the other areas.

With self-discipline we channel our efforts toward a purpose instead of stumbling through life without a grand design. Self-denial says no to our feelings and yes to what we know to be right (See Matt. 16:24).

"For the grace of God that brings salvation has appeared to all men. It teaches us to say 'No' to ungodliness and worldly passions, and to live self-controlled, upright and godly lives in this present age, while we wait for the blessed hope – the glorious appearing of our great God and Savior, Jesus Christ" (Titus 2:11–13, NIV).

Self-control is a gift. God has provided the resources and power to say no to sin, but we have to appropriate them for ourselves. The struggle between our will and God's will can be intense. But the truth of God's Word sets us free to obey the prompting of the Spirit. Self-control is Spirit control. God loves us unconditionally. We do not strengthen our self-discipline to become more worthy but rather to apply the resources He has entrusted to us. Self-discipline helps us define priorities, determine our boundaries, and develop our potential.

Sometimes we do what we do to escape what we perceive to be more threatening, demanding, or painful. We may allow mediocrity in our children's schoolwork because excellence would take more effort on our part. Or we may avoid working out conflicts because it is painful to face our weaknesses. We may thoughtlessly acquiesce to people and circumstances because we don't want to think about the inconvenience of the path God would have us follow. Some people continuously act on impulses, grabbing at whatever seems attractive at the moment. Now, some spontaneity is healthful, but when we face all of life with a senseless striving to satisfy our impulses, we defeat ourselves.

Habits, mindless life controls

Habits can help us live godly lives, or they can keep us in bondage to our sinful desires. Through self-discipline we develop good habits. Whether good or bad, habits become so ingrained in us that we often act mindlessly, giving no thought to the eventual consequences. We can form habits deliberately, but more often we form them by default – going with the flow. Repeated behavior becomes habit – an established pattern. Research has shown that it takes only about twenty-one days for an action to develop into a habit.

Developing new habits requires persevering decisions for change. We may change to avoid stress, fear, a sense of loss, or feelings of insecurity. Change can awaken old emotional responses. On the positive side change challenges our character and emboldens our thirst for life. It may stretch and try us, but it can also bring satisfaction and courage. Our perspective often determines if change will be debilitating or heartening, a pit for decay or a springboard for growth. As home schooling parents, our attitude toward change will directly affect our child's willingness to seek its positive aspects.

Are you a procrastinator?

Procrastination threatens the development of self-discipline. And in a typical home school day, it finds many opportunities to reign. Roots of procrastination sink deep. As you think through the following paragraphs, consider whether your procrastination might be feeding the habit in your child.

Think back to your childhood or teenage years. Can you remember putting off an obligation? Did you ever choose purposely not to do something you knew you should have done? Maybe it was the paper you needed to write for school. It seemed like an overwhelming task, and you didn't really understand it anyway, so you just kept pretending it wasn't there. Or maybe it was washing the dishes. Doing them right after supper might have prompted your mother to give you an additional job. But if you dawdled, she would likely feel that you had worked long enough. Or perhaps, to resist your parents' control, you would take forever doing what you knew they wanted you to do.

People procrastinate for several reasons:

Some fear failure. If they never get around to doing a thing, then nobody (including themselves) will ever see them fail. Poor self-esteem often causes this fear of failure.

Other procrastinators actually fear success. They reason, "I succeeded that time, but it was probably just luck. I'll never be able to do it again. Besides, if I were to succeed again, I would be pressured to keep it up." Or they may think, "If I am a success, then other people won't like me or be comfortable around me."

Procrastination may also be used for self-protection and control. Are you procrastinating to get attention, to hold onto someone you love by getting them to take care of you? Or even the opposite, to have an excuse for someone to not like you?

✓ Can you trace the root of your procrastination? The reason may depend on circumstances. It might be as simple as not wanting to put forth the effort of completing a project because you have developed a habit of doing what you want, when you want. You may feel that the effort expended is not going to be worth the eventual reward, so why bother?

✓ Maybe you patterned your life after a procrastinating parent; or you don't have the energy to do what you know you should; or perhaps you fear criticism even if you do your best. Maybe you just plain don't know how to do a particular task so you keep putting it off, only to face the grave consequences later.

✓ You may have gotten by all these years with someone else bailing you out – your parents because of a false concept of love, your teachers because you were the star football player, your boss because your dad was a prominent community member, your secretary because she wanted a raise, your wife because she felt it was her duty, and on it goes.

One day you will have to face your responsibility no matter how unlikely that seems. Far better to learn to do now what you don't feel like doing. And how great a lesson you could teach your children, first by example and then by training, that procrastination is an enemy of self- discipline.

Are you a perfectionist?

Perfectionism is driven by pride, by protecting self-worth. Striving to do our best or encouraging our children to do their best is not wrong. But at a certain point, working for excellence becomes compulsive, Proving ourselves as parents or as individuals has become the underlying reason for our effort. Perfection differs from excellence. It can never be attained – excellence can. Be mindful of those areas where your perfectionist tendencies threaten to go beyond healthful excellence.

Endnote

53

Organize to Survive

Marilyn Rockett

Marilyn Rockett, with the cooperation of her husband Chesley, has taught her children at home since 1982. In 1987 she developed the Time Minder *manual with forms and directions to plan and keep records for efficient home schooling. A little of her own experience appears in this chapter. What she writes here and what she says as a home schooling speaker are certainly worthy of your attention.*

Curriculum decisions to be made, books and materials to be purchased, possibly testing to be done for placement of your children, schedules to adjust, school authorities to deal with, explanations to be made to relatives – so many things to think about as you begin to home teach your children! How well I remember those frustrations during the early days of our home teaching! When I confided to a friend that I just wasn't sure where to start, I received the best advice I've ever gotten concerning home schooling.

"Clean your closets!" my friend shared jokingly. However, as I considered her statement, albeit made in jest, I realized that she was absolutely correct. If anything was out of order in my home before we began, then it would become a thorn in the flesh with all the new responsibilities we were about to face. "Organize to survive" became my motto.

What organization is

The first step was taking a new look at the true meaning of organization. After all, wasn't it among at least the top three New Year's resolutions – probably right along with diets and budgets? What was the secret to running a well organized home and a home school that functions without major catastrophe (at least most of the time)? I knew other home-teaching families that seemed to be struggling to make things work. When I questioned them about their frustrations I discovered that, in their thinking, organization meant rigidness, meticulous housekeeping, confining schedules – ideas that had a negative effect on their thinking. Soon their well-intentioned efforts were abandoned since the whole project became just too overwhelming.

Does organization involve having a perfectly neat and properly cleaned home at all times? Does it mean homes that are wonderful monuments to our decorating genius for impressing our friends? Does it mean that schedules will always be met as planned? Does it mean continually being a model family? I had to answer those questions with a resounding "no!" since I knew that wasn't real life, especially for a busy, home-teaching family.

I wanted balance in our family, so I began to ask, "What is organization, and what kind of structure will fit our situation?" We all face the problem of life being so "daily." Bringing that "dailiness" under control is our mutual struggle. I began to view organization as a tool to make life work for me and my family, rather than as an end in itself. An illustration I read brought it all into focus: When making jelly you stir pectin and sugar into fruit juice; boil it; and cool it to produce a semisoft product. That product can then be used for spreading onto bread. With reasonable preparation, the juice is transformed to meet the need. A "jelly system"; that's what I needed!

As we stepped out into this new territory, learning by trial and error, several principles began to emerge. When we followed them things went well; when we didn't we usually paid a price.

Priorities

The beginning place, and the cornerstone for all else, is knowing your priorities. I rapidly learned that time is a great deal like closets – we can fill whatever quantity we have! Without a clear picture of priorities you will lack direction, and control will be more difficult.

In choosing priorities, most would agree that people are more important than things, but things get in the way of people if not managed properly. Balance influenced by priorities is the goal to strive for. That balance can be kept best when priorities are written down.

Priorities among families change due to different seasons and stages in our lives. Families with very young children function differently from those with older children. Rural families are different from city families, small families are different from large ones, etc. Sifting out things that don't meet current needs is a continuing process that should be evaluated against written priorities. Striving to choose the best (for us that means God's best) is a changing and often convicting process.

Goals

Secondly, setting goals based on your priorities gives "legs" to the things you have determined are important. Goals enable you to live out your priorities on a daily basis.

Goal setting has undeservedly attracted a bad reputation. Proper goal setting is simply a step-by-step process for arriving at our destination, but we often fail because we confuse goals with desires. "I wish I could handle this laundry without it piling up!"; "I wish my children would clean their room!"; "I wish I had more time to read or have a quiet time!"; "I wish I could find things I need around the house!" All these are desires, not goals. We achieve them by setting goals. "I will do one load of laundry each morning, the children will fold it and put it away as soon as it is dry," or "Each child will do his or her own laundry, each on a different day," or "I will do laundry on Monday and Thursday each week and the children will fold and put it away by noon." These are goals (specific steps) to solve the laundry problem.

Goals help us stay on track. Our time is precious so we must learn to place a high value on it and on the job we do as home builders. Setting goals allows us to be in control rather than allowing circumstances to control us. Remember the laundry? It will have to be done. Will it get done when you choose or when the empty drawers choose for you?

Planning ahead oils the goal setting process. From observing many different styles of running a household, I have learned that those who look down the road beyond the present have a much smoother running home. They achieve both the necessities and the niceties. Those who have learned this make one trip to the grocery store for needed items rather than two or three trips for forgotten items. Their trips out for errands are less time consuming because they combine stops that are near each other into one trip. They keep spares of necessary or often used items like toiletries, school supplies, light bulbs, batteries, etc. Spares are replaced on the next shopping trip. These people have learned the art of heading problems off before they happen and their reward is less frustration and more time for enjoyable things.

Simplicity

Making the first two basics work well requires keeping things simple. The old KISS system (Keep It Super Simple) is still the best!

This holds true with the arrangement of your home and storage spaces, your laundry system, meal planning and preparation, cleaning, and the curriculum. If you spend as much time filing, sorting, writing, recording, etc. as you do in accomplishing your tasks, then your system is too complicated! You probably already have more to do than can be managed if being organized is difficult for you. Don't add to your frustration by adopting an idealized, complex system that eats up more time. Simplify in every area possible, and look for shortcuts that still get the job done properly.

Begin small

If at this point you feel somewhat overwhelmed, or have been defeated by frustration in the past, then the fourth basic is a necessity for you – begin small. Identify your most troublesome areas and work on them first. Learn to break large projects down into smaller pieces that can be dealt with a little at a time. Take one room at a time and tackle the problems in that room alone, or one problem area at a time (such as laundry), or damaging habits (such as leaving things out rather than putting them away when finished), and deal with that. When you have experienced some success with the problem then go on to another one. Narrow your vision to the specific problem rather than allowing yourself to become overwhelmed with the big picture. Remind yourself that the other problems will be dealt with in their turn.

Don't be bashful about enlisting help when you need it. Of course, the family should participate with regular maintenance. Teach your children to work cheerfully but don't demand perfection as they learn. Patiently teach them thoroughness as you work along with them until they have mastered a job. Older children can teach younger ones jobs they have mastered. Yes, it takes longer to teach a child how to do a job than to do it yourself, but do-it-myself parents lose the long term benefits, both to themselves and to their children. This teaching objective also means not picking up constantly after the children! Remember that you are teaching them life skills for their future homes and families. Most children respond to a cheerful, loving parent that is not just "dumping" work on them.

Write it down

The fifth basic is the glue that sticks everything together – write things down! Lists won't do the work for you but using a written "To Do Today" list will keep you on track. This should be written in one place (such as a planner, calendar) rather than on papers or notes scattered everywhere. No one's memory is so good that they won't forget something eventually, so save yourself embarrassment by cultivating the habit of planning on paper. You can relax knowing that all important information is in one place to be referred to anytime you need it. The ten to fifteen minutes per day needed to record necessary things to do is a valuable investment.

Teach your children to write things down by giving them their own small plan books or by keeping a central family calendar and allowing them to record dates and events that involve them. Make it easy for your children to be responsible for their jobs and to help you by keeping a responsibility chart (chore chart) posted. Even young children can be involved when you use pictures for the jobs they do. This habit will seem natural as they grow older and do their own planning. Written instructions on a chart are a much better motivator for responsibility than nagging!

A central family calendar, or access to a family planner, can help the husband/father also. Remember that even though he lives at home, it (probably) isn't his primary work area. He can more easily be a part of the family activities if he can refer to a central family planner.

Be flexible

Having said that you should write things down, I must follow with the sixth basic – be flexible! It would be wonderful if planning meant that nothing would ever go wrong, but, alas, that isn't true. At times I suspect that the reason God called me to stay home and teach my children is really to teach me flexibility! Distractions and unavoidable interruptions *will* happen, so expect them. Advance planning may not always work out exactly as you thought it would, but it allows you to get back on track or choose an alternate plan more easily than if you had not planned at all. Don't use a desire for flexibility as an excuse to neglect planning. Or, at the other extreme, don't be so rigid that you are full of anxiety if plans fall through.

As a Christian, I have to face the reality that at times God's plans may cancel out my own. My level of trust in Him is nakedly revealed by my response to situations He allows which change my plans. Do I get in a stew and complain or do I praise and trust Him, yielding my plans to Him, knowing that He knows what is ultimately best for my good?

I well remember what I now call "The Spaghetti Sauce Day." Our family was expecting company for a several-day visit and the grocery shopping had to be done. The day before the arrival had gone terribly and the shopping had been pushed later and later into the day. Finally in late evening I had wearily made the trip to the store and returned with a large amount of groceries. Husband and children were already in bed and I longed to join them. (Lest you think my husband is heartless, he had a very early and full work day the next day and I had urged him to go to bed. He hadn't noticed the martyred tone in my voice!)

In my hurry to finish putting everything away, I laid a large jar of spaghetti sauce on its side in the refrigerator. To this day I have no idea how the lid could have possibly come off nor how so much sauce could manage to spread to so many places! The scene resembled a major accident on the freeway! Tears began to flow as I sensed the full impact of how much time cleaning up this disaster would require. I took a deep breath, resisted the temptation to snatch my poor husband from his rest, put a praise and worship tape on the stereo, rolled up my sleeves, and began the restoration process. Little did I realize that the Lord would honor my obedience to His command to give thanks in everything by also restoring me during the cleanup. Peace began to fill my soul and by the time the cleanup neared completion, I was singing. Now, before you are blinded by the gleam of my halo, I must add that I did grab the camera and take a picture of the disaster before the cleanup with the thought that I could get just a little sympathy later. But, instead, the picture was hung on the refrigerator and became a visual reminder of God's faithfulness when we obey. It was an important lesson for me. Flexibility is vital to sanity!

Clear the clutter

The seventh basic – deal with clutter – makes all the others easier to implement. Ignoring it can create the biggest hindrance to the smooth operation of our homes. Clutter affects not only the appearance and orderliness of our environment but also our minds, heart and soul.

Remember our beginning premise that people are more important than things, but that things get in the way of people when not managed properly? This is acutely true with clutter. The things we own are only useful when they don't get in the way of people and when they help us serve and enjoy people. As Christians we also recognize their interference with our relationship with the Lord.

We live in a society that promotes accumulation, so the battle is raging all around us. Those utopian gadgets, gimmicks and gizmos find their way into our homes like metal to magnets. Soon having more can become a curse rather than a blessing. Begin to examine your reasons for adding new things to your collection. Will they benefit your family? When possible, get rid of an item each time you add a new one. Often we are blind to our own clutter and junk, and we cling tenaciously to our treasures. In order to truly be free of too much "stuff," we must get a little ruthless with ourselves.

Actually, there *is* useful clutter, but the following acid test must be applied in order to recognize it. Does the item serve a useful purpose for body, mind or spirit? Is it ministering to or serving you or the people around you? Is it being currently used and enjoyed? Is the mess temporary, and will it be cleaned up or put away later? We dub these "happy messes" in our home.

No normal home school family can live and learn without some necessary messes; but these are very different from the things we trip over, move around because they don't have a home, or constantly contend with. Creative messes still have to be cleaned up, but they are temporary. No amount of rationalization can classify anything else as useful clutter.

If clutter is a major problem for you and you are determined to deal with it, then apply basic number four: Begin small. Don't start with the garage!! Clean out a drawer, shelf or maybe a small closet. Apply the principles in the side bar to any area you plan to declutter, from your handbag right

How to Declutter

➤ Use containers as much as possible. To save money, look around for boxes, baskets, plastic jugs, coffee cans, and so on. Cut the tops off of jugs and boxes to suit your purpose. Get your children to decorate them, and putting things away will be more fun.

➤ Sort into one of these three categories: Necessary (those things that are necessary to function), Nice (those things that add niceties to life and are used at least once a year), and Never (those things that are no longer useful, are broken and won't be repaired, out of style, etc.). *Everything* will be placed in one of these categories and stored or gotten rid of accordingly.

➤ Always store things near where they are used and put them back when you are finished. Floating items that really don't have a particular home are one of the largest causes of clutter. They slow us down, keeping us from effectively cleaning and doing our jobs.

on up to the garage.

Doesn't it make sense to clear away what we *don't* use so we have room for what we *do* use? The resulting freedom to enjoy the things we have is worth the extra effort we have expended to declutter our homes and lives. Finding a balance between a *Better Homes and Gardens* environment and the local junk yard is the goal. Our families will be the beneficiaries.

Be satisfied with your best efforts

Don't compare, is the eighth basic. We can be our own worst enemy. Women especially can fall into this trap. Remember that each family and each family member is unique. Be open to learning and glean what you can from others at seminars, conventions and group meetings. We all have something to share from our experience. But remember that no one can model perfection for you. Everyone has strengths and weaknesses. Supermom, Superdad, or Superchild don't exist. Learn to major on your own (and your family's) good points, and don't worry about the minors.

Slow down and say, No

Basic number nine is, slooow down and learn to say Nooo. Our family found so many new and interesting things to do and see once we, rather than the local school system, were dictators of our time. We were tempted to pack in more than we could reasonably manage and still stay true to our priorities. When our priorities' cornerstone was firmly in place, saying no to things that did not fit in became easier. We began to relax, realizing we didn't have to do everything.

Mothers with young children must especially guard against overcommitment since there is no substitute for *time* to train, love and guide little ones. All the special attractions will still be waiting after the little ones are older. Your undistracted attention to training them will be the most far-reaching accomplishment of your life! I am certainly not advocating a hermit's life for mothers, but saying, No, now in favor of your family is an investment for rich rewards.

Your own time

As the final principle, take time for yourself and, from a Christian perspective, time with the Lord. Many frustrated mothers have said, "How? When is there time?" to which I reply, "There isn't, unless you plan it." A woman's whole being is geared to serving those around her, and burnout can easily take place when she is off balance with her time.

Consider your individual personality and plan accordingly. Possibly you function best with a break for a few minutes each day. Maybe a weekly time away, or even a weekend away every so often is the refreshment you need. Know your own pressure points and plan for them as much as possible. One mother of nine does not eat breakfast with her family in order to have a quiet time first thing in the morning. Dad and the older children prepare breakfast. Trading off with another mother for the occasional care of both families' children can give you a break for shopping or relaxing. Older children can watch younger ones for limited periods of time, but be cautious about unreasonable demands.

One mother shared that she teaches her children, beginning at very young ages, to have a quiet play time apart from each other. She sends each child to a separate room and saves special toys, games, books or music for those quiet times. As they get older and can read, she might place two trustworthy children in the same room but apart. At first, quiet time is very short, maybe only five minutes, but she gradually lengthens it according to the child's age and ability to be quietly alone. This evolves into the child's own personal time with the Lord. She might spend this time reading, planning, or, on some days, just collapsing in a chair for a few minutes. The process teaches the children that they can play alone without being entertained by Mom or someone else in the family, and that they can spend time quietly reflecting (something we all need).

Obviously, ages and number of children in the family, along with other situations, dictate how best to arrange for personal time, but remember that it usually won't happen unless you schedule it. You don't need to feel guilty about time spent in this way unless, of course, you are using excessive time as an escape from family responsibilities. We must evaluate our motives and thoughts to keep them in balance.

Organize for Success

- Determine priorities
- Set goals based on priorities
- Keep it simple
- Begin small
- Write it down
- Be flexible
- Clear the clutter
- Be satisfied with your best efforts
- Slow down and say, No
- Take time for yourself

Daniel Webster said, "He that has a `Spirit of detail' will do better in life than many who figured beyond him in the university. Such a one is minute and particular. He adjusts trifles; and these trifles compose most of the business and happiness of life. Great events happen seldom, and affect few; trifles happen every moment to everybody; and though one occurrence of them adds little to the happiness or misery of life, yet the sum total of their continual repetition is of the highest consequence." Sounds like a mother's job, doesn't it?

Running a home while being the primary educator for our children isn't easy, but sticking to the basics will greatly reduce the pressure. If our children see that we learn from our mistakes, reevaluate, and try again, they will understand that life is a learning process for the whole family. How could we better invest our time?

54

Service, Not Chores

By Jackie Wellwood

Our family has a work ethic. Children as young as one year old help with each day's tasks. It has to be that way for our home to run smoothly. In fact, it *should* be that way for optimal results in the training of our children.

Whether for pay or not, we all must work. It is as natural as taking a breath. How much better for your children to learn this principle at an early age while their attitude toward work is being shaped. Ever since the sin of Adam and Eve in the Garden of Eden, hard work has been the lot of humanity. God told Adam, "In the sweat of thy face shalt thou eat bread, till thou return unto the ground; for out of it wast thou taken: for dust thou art, and unto dust shalt thou return." (Gen. 3:19)

Have you ever been around adults who complain about having to work? Perhaps they were not required to work as children. Without responsibilities children fail to learn the rewards of strenuous effort. As adults they continue to expect others to do for them what they could do for themselves. Solomon expressed it well. "He becometh poor that dealeth with a slack hand: but the hand of the diligent maketh rich." (Prov. 10:4)

To help our children embrace work as a natural part of life, my husband and I no longer talk about "chores." The new term is "service." Typically children consider chores as something to get done quickly so they can do something else. A chore is easily thought of as unpleasant. Certainly all of us have unpleasant tasks in our routine of responsibilities but we also have joyful ones. Using the word, service, encourages cheerful, willing compliance.

Each child in my family has certain tasks to be performed as service. Now just who is that child serving? It could be a number of different people. But in serving people he or she also serves the Lord Jesus Christ. "And whatsoever ye do, do it heartily, as to the Lord, and not unto men; Knowing that of the Lord ye shall receive the reward of the inheritance: for ye serve the Lord Christ." (Col. 3:23, 24) Serving one another in the home through work is also a great model for more direct service to Christ.

> **Jackie Wellwood**
> *Teaches her six children and speaks on practical topics like the one in this chapter. Her home is north of Chicago.*
>
> *Although Scripture is quoted in this chapter, I believe even those of you with a more secular viewpoint will find the principles refreshing and useful.*

A good attitude is absolutely essential in the success of our work. We may radiate a sweet spirit in doing the most dismal job if we approach it with the right attitude. Sometimes tasks that lie in our path are difficult and stretch us beyond what we think we can do. If as children we have developed proper attitudes toward service, we will have strength to achieve true success even when our work is tough.

Service in the home is often hard for children. Some jobs take a while to master. Others are sheer drudgery. How can we help them? By our own cheerfulness under unpleasant circumstances. A grumbling parent is a bad role model. If we complain about the difficulties of home schooling, our children's complaints about their service should not surprise us. (Yes, be honest, home schooling is tough at times for most of us.) The whole family needs the advice of Paul to "do all things without murmurings and disputing," giving thanks in all things "for this is the will of God in Christ Jesus. . . ." (Phil. 2:14;1 Thess. 5:18).

If we view our work in God's perspective

we can be better stewards of the time, talents, and energy he has given us. So just how can replacing the word, chore, with the word, service, lead our children to work well? By remembering that the goal is not a perfectly executed task, but a

perfect attitude. Skills develop with instruction and practice. When applied with a cheerful attitude, true greatness of character is revealed.

Many charts are available for planning and reporting your children's service. Whether you develop your own plan or use someone else's, keep in mind the following principles.

Tell them what Make sure your children know exactly what you want them to do. I have been too vague in my directions. In asking my daughter to clean up the counter, I assumed she would wipe the stovetop, too. When I specified a countertop, she thought I meant only that. Even after explaining, the stove has been easily forgotten. For the kitchen in particular, we make standard cards for each job, listing specifically what is expected. The children can refer to them to make sure they have completed their work.

Show them how Give them a demonstration. Make the necessary tools available so they can complete the task independently. Younger children paired with older ones can learn the jobs, help their siblings, and have the needed supervision with tools, such as a broom and dustpan.

Specify when Explain when the task is to be completed. Some children need only to know to do a job on a certain day. Others may need a time specified during that day for their work to be done. Judge by the child what is needed. Establish a deadline for completion.

Inspect Follow up to be sure they have finished their service in the time frame allowed. Parents (especially me) often miss this critical step.

Praise As you commend work well done, mention attitudes, too. Courtesy words like please, thank you, and sorry reflect and actually strengthen attitudes. Although my husband and I sometimes fail as does everyone else, our work ethic with positive attitudes brings harmony to the many tasks of our busy days. And teamwork among willing helpers makes home schooling easier and better.

55

Sudden Home Schoolers

Laura Coker

Suppose you hear how home schooling does marvelous things for kids. It sounds cool so you promptly say farewell to Jenny's classroom school, buy a stack of books, and dream of adventure at home. After a few days with the new major claims on your time, reality begins to settle around you and soak in. You wonder if you have been a little like the family canine. When a dog somewhere down the street hears a strange sound he begins to warn the potential intruder and the world. Soon your dog and the rest in the neighborhood join the defense team with no idea of why they are barking. You are feeling like maybe you have barked without a good reason.

What do you need to consider for a mature decision — so you won't mis-bark? You will appreciate this chapter by Laura Coker. She is an experienced home school leader with a medical background that provides insights into parent-child interactions and school influences. Her own two children are quite different from each other. They have taught her flexibility and, I'm sure, patience.

Ted Wade

PS: Don't let all this tough talk discourage you. Not many people need it.

A generation ago, only those who held strong convictions regarding education dared to plunge into the somewhat uncharted waters of home schooling. Now the idea is much less of a counter current in society and many jump in with little or no preparation.

While I don't intend to frighten you away from home education, I'm concerned that a casual and poorly informed assumption of this responsibility could mean less than the best for your kids. I also fear that weak home schools could turn the tide of opinion and jeopardize freedom to teach at home.

Because our public education system falls further and further from the mark of meeting the needs of the individual student, more people opt to educate at home. The classroom environment is becoming a riskier place for students, especially during the middle school years. Much is at stake emotionally, socially, academically, spiritually, and some would even say physically. (More guns are taken to school by middle school students than by those of the other grade-level groups. Perhaps this is why more students are being withdrawn from middle grades.)

Home education is ideally tutorial. It allows children to learn at their own pace with the input and involvement of the teacher on a more or less one-to-one basis. Most families in the system are benefited and blessed by the experience. However, an attempt at such a big undertaking can be unsuccessful. If you risk being a "sudden" home schooler, I'd like to share with you what I consider to be the prerequisites to successful education at home.

Assuring quality

Home education flourishes where learning flows from a family's philosophy and lifestyle. Your family should be philosophically grounded. They need a common sense of direction. Perhaps this is why home schooling is the choice of so many Christian families.

A core of truth at the center of a

family's faith holds everything together. It makes family life vital and purposeful. It defines a mission for the learning process. It brings order to family life.

Success doesn't wait for perfection, however. Some families produce good learning while still struggling to find that cohesive center. So what are the essential elements for success? Your family must have (1) a vision for the result of the education process, (2) appropriate and realistic goals, and (3) accountability among family members.

Classroom teachers are different

In considering advantages of the home learning environment, keep in mind that (1) Teachers in conventional schools are generally more skillful and use better methods than some home schooling advocates realize. And (2) With a room filed with children from 8:30 to 3:30 their approaches and system for maintaining order are often different from what yours need to be.

Your advantages are:

- You more easily know your child's needs, interests, and learning styles.
- You can teach to your child's specific needs, not waiting for a whole class to understand.
- You can move between school and home responsibilities whenever you need to.
- You can take advantage of learning interests and opportunities when they arise, often blending them with your family activities, without worrying about what 29 other kids are doing.

Of course you still need a plan and a schedule. These are ways you can make modifications and exceptions.

TW

Vision

Help your family know what it wants from the educational process. Otherwise you may be writing a prescription for burnout. Without vision, you can spin you wheels processing all kinds of advice about what to do – and what to buy! Eventually you can feel overwhelmed and spread thin across an excess of approaches to instruction. You may conclude that being out of the traditional system is enough for your child. Escape, however, is not the goal of quality education.

Realistic goals

Contrary to what some might think, home education is not simply establishing the conventional classroom agenda in the home. Such a goal is neither realizable nor desirable. This is good news. It means that you do not have to jump from the frying pan to the fire. You do not have to begin imitating college–degreed classroom teachers. Explain this early in your transition process to home schooling, especially where an older student might say, "You're not teaching the way *they* do." Without considering the ultimate vision for home education in your family, you will likely despair, feeling you could never be like a "real" teacher. Remember that what they do is *not* what you are trying to emulate. You can confidently tell your child so. Home schooling is truly a lifestyle choice.

In home education you can promote a natural learning environment. You can take advantage of the practical experiences of real daily living. Your situation is more tutorial, attempting to meet your child where he is, rather than maintaining him on someone else's schedule of development. Consider the benefits of the real environment of home over the often synthetic environment of the conventional classroom. Realize the advantages of one–to–one tutoring/mentoring over the experiences of a child who is one of perhaps twenty or more in a classroom.

So, as a parent-educator, set goals which are life centered and personal for each child. With your vision in mind, these goals should move you gradually toward your vision. In my experience, the goals have become more specific as the child matures.

Accountability

Family accountability is of extreme significance to new home schoolers, especially where children are older and patterns of communication and relationship are firmly established. Home schooling requires accountability between parent and child. *Relationship* among family members must be respectful and responsible in order to enjoin the efforts of such a major lifestyle change. Can you enjoy, or learn to enjoy, being *so* involved in your older child's life? Can you, parent, forfeit many personal goals during the time while home education is a family focus?

If you are unable to be at home most of the time, can your child stay on task on his or her academic work without your inspiration and often your persistence? And *can the child be trusted to stay home* if you must work elsewhere, especially if part of the reason for withdrawal from the classroom is related to degrading peer relationships? Believe me, this is a reason for many people! These questions must be answered in the affirmative if home schooling is to be productive and worthwhile for your student.

Are you ultimately respected by your child? That is, can you expect your child to respond positively to your guidance of his or her education? If you cannot command the appropriate respect and responsibility, your home schooling experience is in danger. If cooperative relational behavior was not established during childhood years, it cannot be retrieved simply by pulling a child out of a peer-based settling. In marginal situations where you have reluctant respect, home education could succeed. Talk the whole situation over with your youth and solicit cooperation. It is imperative that parents who intend to home school their children give careful consideration to this issue. Also, seasoned home schoolers need to remember this when recommending home education as a problem solver. Much is at stake here.

Doing your homework

Here are ways to be informed for a good decision:

- Contact your local support group leader for guidance. (Ask a state or regional leadership group for information.) This person can tell you about local and general resources and how to relate to government authorities. Remember that this person is a volunteer with heavy responsibilities, so get general directions and find out what you can on your own. Then call again if you need to ask more questions.
- Read books about home education to learn what philosophical approaches are often used and what is involved. Your library or support group can help you find books.
- Visit a support group meeting.
- Subscribe to the group or state newsletter and to a few home schooling magazines. Get on your group's mailing list.
- Find a friend who has already been home schooling for a year or more. Visit her home to get a visual idea of what home schooling family is like. Of course, no two households are the same, but you will pick up good practical ideas.

Think it through

We original devotees to home education are enthusiastic about our experiences, but we would warn people who impulsively join our ranks that this decision will likely change their family's lives and that careful consideration is necessary at the outset of the transition from a traditional school or, better, *before* it. Most veteran home schoolers are eager to assist new families in this process by sharing information and by being willing listeners for those who wish to discuss their frustrations. New parent-teachers undergo a major role change from onlooker to participant and enhancer of their children's learning.

We who are experienced home schoolers must acknowledge the particular challenge other families face when they decide to home school. If the plan seems sudden or impulsive, we must help them think carefully and guide them toward success. Appropriate assistance can also preserve the reputation of home education.

So please, if you are dropping out of another system to jump into home based education, do some homework of your own and know where you will land!

56

Selecting Learning Materials

Sandra Gogel with Gayle Graham

Deciding on a curriculum for your child should be an individual matter. If you are willing to let someone else choose for you, then you may wish to join a plan where the organization sends you a set of books with a program to be completed within a prescribed length of time. In a classroom situation, the teacher survives only by having all children, or at least groups of children, learning from the same material. To my way of thinking, one of the joys of home schooling is in providing an individualized curriculum for each child.

When choosing materials, consider your child's preferred learning style. Is it visual, auditory or kinesthetic? [The topic is discussed in this book in Chapter 11, "Techniques for Teaching." Other books deal with it in greater depth.[1]]

Does your child enjoy a sense of accomplishment from finishing a written page or does he (or she) hate even to write his name at the top of the paper? A child who doesn't enjoy workbooks will do better work and learn better by listening or with hands-on materials. Keep in mind that every child over the age of eight should do some written work each day. But if it is difficult for your child to get much writing done, you may want to write some of the answers as he says them to you.

Choose books that appeal to you as well as to your child. Your enthusiasm (or lack of it) will rub off. No doubt some subjects are more interesting to you than others are. Pray for new enthusiasm for subjects you do not enjoy.

Preparation time varies considerably from one type of approach to another. Some curriculum programs, like Alpha-Omega, require very little teacher time because the workbook format includes most or all necessary instructions and explanations for the student. The weakness of this type of program is in not naturally encouraging much teacher-student interaction. Although the "who," "when," "what," and "how" are efficiently taught, the child might miss out on the "why" and on developing skill in analytical thinking. If you choose workbook type materials, be sure to plan time for discussion.

Do you enjoy research and detailed projects? Then I might recommend a unit-study program such as Weaver; Konos; or Sing, Spell, Read, and Write. As an alternative to both the workbook and the unit-type programs, you might want to consider traditional textbooks with teacher's manuals. Lesson plans would be easy to prepare following guidelines in the manuals.

When you consider materials, try to discover whether they require relatively mature learning skills. Curriculums from Rod and Staff and from A Beka would come in this category. Although they teach excellent concepts, immature students will have difficulty with them.

Some publishers label their materials for children younger than I would recommend. The Little Patriots reading program, for example, is advertised as being for a kindergarten child. Some children at that age do very well with it, but many are not ready to read this early, and could profit from it more at a later time.

If cost is a factor preventing your purchase of everything you need at once, get materials for reading and math first. You can supplement from the library for social studies and science using the *Typical Course of Study*[2] as a guide until you can afford more. But do purchase regular learning materials for these subjects as soon as possible. This is especially important by the time your child is in the fourth grade.

Since programs for teaching Bible differ widely in scope and sequence, you can feel more at liberty to organize your own plan, choosing topics as well as methods of presentation. You may find it easier to maintain consistent quality in your Bible program, however, by choosing one of the many fine sets of materials which are available.

Books are not the only items that help children learn. You may use games, puzzles, flash cards, art media, music, globes, microscopes, science equipment, and even toys. You might suggest to relatives and friends that some of these items would make appropriate gifts. The cost burden for supplying your school could thus be lightened a little.

Finally, remember that your program is a tool. You are the one in charge. If you find too much practice prescribed on a concept your child has already mastered, feel free to delete part of it. Do a project for one of your social studies units instead of going lock step through the book. In short, use the curricular materials as tools to achieve your desired end – the education of your child.

Endnotes

1. See the review of *The Way They Learn* in Appendix J.
2. Appendix G.

Cruising the Curriculum Fairs

by Gayle Gaham

You enter the curriculum hall. Beads of perspiration line your brow. Help! It's a home school curriculum fair!

For the uninitiated, a curriculum fair can be a mind-numbing experience. Hundreds of choices scream, "Buy me!" as soon as you walk in. Friends offer their expert, though often conflicting, testimony. Signs entice the budget minded: "Buy now and save!" Is it even *possible* to prepare for this experience? I believe so.

Before the big day arrives, ask yourself a few philosophical questions. Why am I home schooling? What overall goals do I see for education? And more specifically, What will I try to accomplish this particular school year?

If you feel God is speaking to you about developing Christlike characters in your children, then look for a tool that helps you achieve that goal even as you teach academic subject matter. If you see the primary goal of education as learning how to learn, you'll probably seek research-oriented materials. Is this the year you hope Suzie will learn to read? Or, do you expect to help Jamie strengthen his math skills? Prayerfully list goals (as you now see them) for each child. Then allow those goals to drive your decision making on the day of the fair. You'll naturally be eager to buy your textbooks and workbooks, but if you leave your first fair with nothing more than a few teacher help books, a grasp of what home schooling is all about, and a stack of catalogs for future curriculum purchases, your mission will have been accomplished.

If you have time to continue, focus next on the basics: reading, writing, and arithmetic. Decide what to use this year to equip your children with the skills they'll need in order to learn for a lifetime. Including sources not represented at the fair, you'll find plenty of choices. For example, I hear there are 90-plus excellent phonics programs out there! So, I suggest you select two (or a few) suppliers you like. Float back and forth, comparing and asking your hardest questions.

Once you've chosen your language arts and math materials, you're ready for what I call, "all the rest": history, science, the arts, etc.

The options you will find range from materials that are highly structured (such as correspondence courses) to moderately structured (textbooks), to highly flexible (unit study resources). Structured programs with packaged stacks of textbooks, lesson plans, and maybe even classroom videos sound secure, but there's a tradeoff. What you gain in security and efficiency, you lose in the more adaptable and motivating approach to study. Become familiar with all three levels of structure and choose what will work best for you.

So evaluate your philosophy and needs, stick to one decision at a time, and consider structure and flexibility. Enjoy your cruise!

57

What Dads Can Do

David Lanier

I would guess you're a woman; most readers of home schooling materials are. In fact, more women than men attend home school meetings. Of the men present, many have likely been urged to come by their wives. It's a little unusual to see average dads be average participants in the home schooling adventure. And that's a shame. In our culture, teaching children is often seen as "women's work," so it's easy to understand a dad's hesitancy when confronted by the home schooling enterprise. But dads often *do* make positive contributions to their home schools, and they can enjoy it to boot!

This chapter is addressed to men whose wives are interested in home schooling. Perhaps it will help them figure out what role they can play in this whole process.

Dads are important in home schools for lots of reasons, but I will confine myself to just five:

- spiritual authority
- administrative responsibility
- financial provision
- teaching
- lightening the load

I will discuss each of these in turn in the remainder of the chapter.

Spiritual authority

Scripture plainly teaches that the father is to assume the primary responsibility of spiritual leadership in his home.[1] You may say, "That's right, but what does it have to do with home schooling?" The answer is: plenty.

First of all, when parents decide to no longer delegate their children's education to others, they are accepting a greater degree of responsibility for their children's spiritual growth as well as for their academic and emotional development. Conflicts produced by misunderstanding, jealously and conviction often follow, and friendships are commonly strained. The venture should be entered into only after prayerful consideration and ongoing spiritual direction by both mother and father. If the father does not consistently encourage, protect and pray for his wife and children the enterprise will not achieve its potential.

Second, the father should routinely teach or supervise the teaching of any Bible classes included in the curriculum. Just as a cook judges the soundness of her ingredients before preparing a meal, so the father should judge the ingredients of any spiritual food served his children. Whenever possible, he should serve the spiritual meal himself.

Because mothers share the responsibility for the children's spiritual growth, parents should seek agreement on what is to be taught. Fathers who feel weak in spiritual understanding may temporarily delegate Bible teaching to the mother. They may then take the personal challenge of seeking the Lord and begin sharing the Bible knowledge they are learning.

Third, the father should be responsible for daily family devotions. Devotions, as distinct from Bible class, are designed to promote dialogue and conversation among the family, allow for the sharing of personal needs, and provide opportunities for praise and worship within the family setting. Regardless of your talents in this area, dads should assume the responsibility for leading the wife and children in regular devotional times.

Dads who feel unprepared in this area may begin their leadership by calling the family together and asking individuals to read, discuss, and pray. They can gradually increase their own participation. Gathering at the table before breakfast often works well for devotions.

Administrative responsibilities

As a dad, be prepared to "take the heat" for tough decisions. It is important that you serve as principal in your home school and fairly administer discipline, guidance and encouragement. Even though your wife may be the person who spends most of the face-to-face time working with the children, she needs your backing in all major policy decisions. Therefore, make plans together. The children need to see your support of her as wife, mother, and teacher.

Also, the dad is responsible to make sure the home school operates in a legal and organized manner. Mike Farris does a great job of discussing this area in his recent book, *The Home Schooling Father.*[2] Find out what the home schooling laws are in your state. Unless you have spiritual convictions against meeting those requirements (and these should be considered seriously and prayerfully), make sure that your school complies with them. See to it that any required records are kept in an appropriate fashion.

You should serve as the lightening rod to deflect from your wife or children any criticism that may come because of your decision to home school. That's why the Lord gave men broad shoulders; use them.

If you go ahead and faithfully assume the responsibilities mentioned in this and the previous section, you will find that your wife and children will be more congenial and peaceful. They will know they are safe and able to do the business of schooling without undue concern about criticism from outside.

Financial provision

You are aware of the importance of making appropriate financial provision for your family so that the home schooling enterprise can proceed unimpeded. Most home schooling fathers assume this responsibility readily. Adequate financial provision may involve changing jobs or schedules, modifying the family budget, or re-configuring the household responsibilities.

Without question, financial support is a major component in the success of any family school. But fathers are more than money machines. They should not become complacent simply because they provide support.

Teaching

Dads ought to actually teach something in their home school. "But," you might say, "after assuming the first three responsibilities on your list, there's no time for teaching." And, you might point out that you are already teaching a Bible class, so doesn't that count? Certainly, all those things count, and I admit that some fathers are not particularly well-suited as teachers. However, if you can fit it into a realistic schedule, I encourage you to try anyway because the benefits are so substantial. If you are unable to teach the extra class every day, consider planning it for once or twice a week. The briefer course could be something like art or auto mechanics, or it might be a topic within a larger subject area (like measurement and metric measures within math).

By actually teaching your own children (not just be in the vicinity while they are taught), you will get to know them in a way like no other. Why let your wife have all the fun? You can know for yourself what they think about various matters.

As you prepare your children, especially the older ones, to make major decisions about such things as life vocation, marriage partners, etc., it will be crucial to understand them as well as possible. Learning your children's temperaments through the discipline of teaching will be an invaluable aid as you help them grow up.

When you teach your children an actual class they get a chance to compare your way of doing things with your wife's way. Permit me to speculate: you and your wife do things differently. You have spent a good deal of your married life trying to get your wife to do things your way. Chances are, these differences will be just as apparent in home schooling as they are in other areas of your marriage.

If I'm right, I suggest you view these differences as *opportunities* rather than *problems*. Your children are probably a combination of the temperaments of you and your wife. Give them the benefit of seeing how each of your learns and teaches. Over time, they can develop a system that uses the best of both approaches.

For example, my wife routinely visits the discount store prior to each school year in order to buy thousand-card packs of 3 x 5 cards for use in her classes. She has the kids use them for language arts, science facts, math facts and just about anything else.

I have never used a note card in my life. It never occurred to me to suggest that anybody else use them. My children, after several years of home schooling, have come to appreciate the value of note cards to help them master material.

I, on the other hand, like to draw pictures. I hold that any fact or concept, properly understood, can be represented by an illustration. When I teach I draw a lot of pictures and I suggest that my students draw pictures, too. As you may have already guessed, my wife never draws pictures of anything.

Our children use note cards *and* draw pictures, according to their own inclinations. They have benefited from both our approaches to learning and teaching.

One quick hint: when you teach your children, make sure you teach different classes than your wife. In our early years of home schooling my wife and I tried to teach the same class, she on certain days and I on the others. Our different styles became obvious very quickly, to the detriment of all parties involved. We learned that things worked better if I taught my class, my way, for the whole year and she had the same independence. In spite of our mutual misgivings about how the other one was doing things, our children turned out fine.

Lightening the load

One more important factor in becoming a good home school dad involves "lightening the load" carried by your wife. You may say, "Now that you've got me teaching, in additional to all those other things, there's no time left to help her with her work!" Let me explain.

To be sure, assuming your responsibilities for spiritual authority, administration, financial provision, and teaching, will lighten your wife's load enormously. Doing your job in all those areas will give her freedom to be her best as a home schooling mom.

You can, however, help lighten your wife's load in two other ways. First, you can temper your expectations of her. If you expect the same level of housekeeping, personal attractiveness, sparkling conversation, and enthusiastic affection after a long day of home schooling as you had from her before you had children or before you started teaching them, you're asking too much. If you don't moderate your expectations in these areas, your wife will either try to live up to them (and burn out) or not try to live up to them (and feel like a failure and disappointment to you). Don't put her in that situation; clarify your expectations and discuss them to make sure they are reasonable.

If you have trouble determining reasonable expectations, take a week's vacation and be a house dad. Teach the children, do the laundry, prepare the meals, go shopping, handle car-pooling responsibilities, etc., and be uniformly charming to your wife at all times. After such a week you should be in a better position to have realistic expectations. Even thinking about this should induce a good measure of humility.

Second, help out. Every family finds their own way of dividing up the jobs. If you're just the least bit observant, and if you ask your wife, I'm sure the two of you can come up with some things you can do that are within your skill levels and which would help her. Identify those areas and do as much as you can. For starters, remember to pick up after yourself and encourage the kids to do the same. As you leave the table, take your dirty dishes to the sink and rinse them.

Third, plan for Mom to have an evening a week away from the kids. This is especially important if you are unable to share much of the teaching responsibility. She needs the refreshment of a change, time for personal growth and for cultivating friendships among her peers.

To teachers in nontraditional families

I recognize that some of you are not part of a family that includes the traditional mom, dad, and children. Some of you are single moms trying to home teach by yourself. Others of you may live in an extended family arrangement or under other unusual circumstances. While the functions carried out by dads may work best for the traditional family, they are just as important in the nontraditional situation. I encourage you to utilize other males in your extended or church family, people such as grandfathers, uncles, cousins, church youth leaders, etc., to fulfill some or all of the responsibilities normally associated with the father in the home.

Is it worth it?

You may ask, "Why should I go to all this trouble? A man's gotta watch TV and to go to ball games sometimes, doesn't he?" Two answers: first, it's the right thing to do. Second, if you help your wife in the way I'm suggesting, it is very likely that she will respond to your assistance by looking forward to seeing you when you come home, enjoying your company while you're there, and having the energy to return the affection.

So Dads, get involved. Don't let your wife have all the fun of home schooling.

Endnotes

1. Gen. 18:19; Deut. 11:18–21; Deut. 4:9; Josh 24:15; Acts 16: 31–34; Eph. 6:4.
2. *The Homeschooling Father*, Michael P. Farris, published by the author at Box 479, Hamilton, VA 22068, 1992.

58

Teaching Several Children

Meg Johnson

Teaching children of different ages naturally takes a great deal of planning and time. We become very concerned about school lessons, but children need time with their parents for more than schooling. They also deserve personal care and attention, opportunities to help Mom and Dad with projects, and so on. Meeting all these needs can be quite challenging. This chapter offers suggestions for organizing your school program to teach children at different levels without neglecting your preschoolers or other home responsibilities. Because we are deeply concerned about our responsibilities for educating our children, trying to meet all the needs at once creates most of the strain. We teach our children more than academics. Let's examine other areas of guiding and nurturing them.

Meeting individual needs

Children are all different. Even siblings may differ greatly in readiness and learning styles. Be flexible. A program or learning environment which meets the needs of one child may simply not fit the next child's abilities, interests, or aptitudes.

Because home schooling families enjoy close relationships, parents can easily capitalize on their children's individual readiness – and more importantly they can adjust to accommodate each child's differences in readiness among various learning areas. Take time to find out what your children can, should, or wants to be learning at each age or grade level. Then provide materials and an environment to help each child learn as he or she is ready.

Now let's look at a few ideas which might help in organizing activities so that you can be available to teach your older children and still have time to spend with the younger ones. Start by planning space for your "school room." You need a routine place to work and to localize the mess that results occasionally from art projects, crafts, or science experiments.

__Meg Johnson__ lives in New Hampshire. The material for her two chapters was first prepared for her Home Education Resource Center which is now inactive. Her four children, now grown, have been home taught. Of course she realizes that education is more than schooling. "It is the development of our children as total human beings," she explains, "that concerns most of us who keep our children out of school."

Using space efficiently

You need to be able to change easily from working with one child to working with another. Positioning desks or tables so that you can move around and sit between children often works well. You need to be able to work with one child while being right there to answer the questions of the others. Encourage children not directly involved with you during this time to do something they are interested in or give them something to do that will occupy them so they are not disruptive. Make a place for toddlers and young children to play adjacent to or in the working area. This may cause a certain amount of disruption, but if each person realizes that he must work and pay attention, lessons can continue and progress will occur. When a quieter atmosphere is needed for concentration, individual children can go to another room temporarily. This arrangement may not be ideal, but most of the time it works better than you might expect.

Teamwork

Younger children pick up quite a bit of basic knowledge and skills from being exposed to the learning environment of older siblings and by imitating their behavior. Far less explaining may be needed for these younger children when it comes time to learn some of the concepts already taught to their big brothers and sisters. But remember that while getting ideas across to the younger children may be faster, each child deserves quality time with his parents investigating the world, and working and doing things with them. Bonds of love and understanding formed between parent and child during early years generally hold when adolescent counseling is needed and, in fact, throughout life.

Older children, especially if they have always been home schooled, should have developed good independent study habits. Setting a goal of getting work done without being prodded can teach responsibility. Make reasonable assignments, and require that each day's work be done even if it means continuing after your regular "school" time. When a child has reached a point of independence in his own work, he can be relied on as needed to take care of very young siblings – changing diapers, keeping an eye on them, and so on. He can also learn to assist younger siblings with their learning by answering questions, explaining directions, or teaching concepts he himself has mastered. This helping can be part of the child's own school program. From the very beginning, each child should understand that he is responsible for getting his work done, and that siblings and the home teacher are there mainly to assist. Also teach your children always to give others consideration when interrupting or asking for assistance.

Being a "teacher's assistant" to younger children can be a valuable learning experience for older siblings. It reinforces their own learning and develops more of an awareness of others' needs. Younger children pick up concepts and facts by listening to discussions of older siblings, and older children understand better by teaching the younger. Because of this crossover learning, a great deal of reinforcement occurs. This strength of family cooperation and a usually calm environment lead to good learning and thinking skills.

Using time efficiently

Challenges do arise, however, when you will wish you were several people at once. For instance, older children might need to have new concepts explained or to do research or experiments which require adult assistance; infants or toddlers may need to be watched and cared for; and a six or seven year old may want to learn about some unit which requires an adult to read or help him get started. Each child needs time and attention. In such situations, just evaluate as quickly as possible how to most effectively distribute time and attention. Usually in a few moments older children can be guided in the right direction to work until you can get back to them; someone can meet the youngest child's need; and with little delay, time can be devoted to your less mature scholar. Under your organized management, your children will learn to do what they can on their own so you can meet the needs of whoever cannot go ahead alone.

To help make your teaching easier and efficient, plan as many units as feasible which involve all your students. A general topic like airplanes can have many teaching activities. Some, of course, will be too easy or too hard for part of your children. If you remember the varying abilities of your listeners and hold different expectations, they will understand and your teaching will be surprisingly successful. You may want to write your study questions in order of increasing difficulty, assigning work for a specific student up to a certain item number. In other instances you can plan team projects with roles assigned (or permitted to be chosen) according to ability.

Of course, it isn't always possible or easy to have all your students learning about the same subject at the same time with children of different ages working at different levels. Often, although not as frequently as we would like, the younger children will learn from and be interested in the activities of the older ones. Most of the time, however, your children will need to do completely different activities. Experience and trial and error will help you plan wisely and see when to change your plan. If all this sounds like it could easily lead to confusion, try it. Usually you will find that despite some confusion, activities can continue and good progress will be made.

Good planning can limit the amount of your time each child will need. On the average, a child may need one to two hours a day. Your contact time may overlap considerably if two children work together, or if you can supervise more than one at different activities. However, when home schooling involves more than one child, the entire morning or occasionally even more time may have to be devoted to directing learning activities and to meeting the school needs of your children. On many days the time you spend solely in teaching may be much less than this, but plan to commit a good portion of each day to your children. You must be available when needed and must provide guidance and supervision.

Parents don't actually have to spend as much time formally teaching their children as you might expect. Many subjects, such as science, history, geography, social studies, and religious education need discussion, practical application, experimentation, and/or outside trips. Try to provide opportunities and materials so your children can explore these areas. Take time to investigate with your children. While this demands time and energy, and housework doesn't always get done, it really can be a lot of fun. Of course, books are valuable tools too, if used carefully. They provide an efficient way of sharing accumulated knowledge and facts. At home a good balance can easily be achieved between book learning and application.

Some specific ways to teach efficiently include simple ideas such as a daily routine (which should be flexible, but fairly consistent), yearly and daily goals, written guidelines for the children to follow so they know what it is they should be doing, and a place to work which is as conducive to "school work" as possible. In order also to give older children time to be helpful, their learning should be designed to fit their needs. Limit unnecessary repetition of concepts and skills they have already mastered. Use materials with clear instructions and explanations of concepts.

Building character

Help your children develop a sense of personal responsibility for their school work and for helping around the house.

The home school learning environment lacks the classroom atmosphere with pressure from peers and teachers to enforce performance and discipline. The various demands and activities of the home environment give children a more immediate need to develop self-discipline, self-motivation, and initiative. Because these character traits are not easy to form, parents must help their children realize the need for them in their work and study tasks.

As much as possible, let the needs for responsible behavior lead to its natural development. Children may take advantage of disorder or a brother's or sister's demand for attention to fool around or disrupt the schooling. It may then be wise to discuss what each child should contribute to a more pleasant environment for everyone. Such correcting experiences help build character. As a child realizes that out of consideration for the needs of his siblings and parents, he should be responsible for tending to business, he becomes more motivated to work on his own. Self-direction takes time to develop, however, so be willing to oversee your child's work. Check regularly to see that he understands and completes his tasks.

As a teacher, be with your children during their learning activities, even if you must sit between two of them guiding their schoolwork with a younger child on each knee! Each of your children deserves time and loving attention. Even though you are only one person, if you are close by, you can give each child as much as possible.

Remember that although your home school may be less than perfect, its consistent environment, the demands it makes on each family member, and your children's achievement of self-worth from contributing to everyone's welfare, make it the best place for developing good habits of learning and helping. Leading your children to good behavior is an essential part of their education. Just as children who attend classroom schools may get up in the morning and say they don't want to go, home schooled children may refuse to do their school work cheerfully or to cooperate with chores. You can discuss with them the importance of cooperation and consideration for others. The intimacy of the home dramatically emphasizes the effects of each person's actions. Although occasionally a day of school lessons may seem to be "lost" to character building efforts, over the long term a definite maturity will evolve in the children's attitudes about working independently and assisting each other. They will gradually be able to work on their own and become valuable contributors to the household operation.

As you watch this development, your children's contributions to the family's life will balance the burdens of parenting and of home schooling. You may spend a lot of time and effort, but you will be pleased and thankful with the results. It is a most rewarding challenge!

Endnote

The illustration in this chapter was drawn from a photograph of Meg Johnson teaching three of her children some years ago.

Fitting School to Four Children

Virginia Birt Baker

The beauty of teaching your own children at home with your choice of curricula is that you can work your schedule to suit your needs. If one child needs more hours per week on arithmetic instruction, it can be arranged. If mother needs to attend to an infant at a certain hour, class can be suspended for a few minutes and the students can take their outdoor break.

We even had a "magic clock" in our school room. If something delayed the start of classwork, we reset that clock to the time designated for the beginning of school. It certainly took the pressure off, and class was always on schedule! If interrupted, we could unplug the clock and start it again.

Teaching younger and older children

When I began to home school in 1972, I had three school-age children and a toddler, but only one of me. It took several weeks to adjust and rearrange our morning school schedule to fit this situation. We worked out a schedule that allowed me to spend time with each child in each subject. Although our schedules appeared extremely structured on paper, we always were rather flexible. We remained organized, however, as organization is the key to it all.

While I worked with one child, the others did seat work. Sometimes I worked with two children at once, such as in arithmetic. I found it easy to shift mental gears from one level of math to another, so I tried to schedule all the math at the same time. This wasn't as easy in other subjects.

At times I gave a spelling lesson to one, a timed typing test to another, and instructed the third in diagramming at the chalkboard. I wasn't always that busy, though. Sometimes one child listened to phonics records with earphones, another silently read his history, and the third practiced her cursive writing. This freed me to grade papers.

Combining subjects for several levels

When the older children, who were a year apart, got into the higher grades, I scheduled many of their courses at the same time. For instance, they took the same geography, history, and vocabulary courses. All four children always shared the same Bible lesson, although assignments and homework usually were on different levels.

In essence, I often taught three levels of "school" to four children. In many subjects it really doesn't matter at what grade level the child receives his instruction. By the time he "graduates," he will have had all the required courses. Some courses should be presented sequentially for clearer understanding.

I rarely followed a publisher's manual, because I wanted flexibility. We advanced as fast as the child could handle the material and skipped some chapters entirely. If I didn't like the way one textbook presented a lesson, I used another. If an idea seemed unclear to the children after we had spent a reasonable amount of time with it, we would often study it from a different textbook. It didn't make sense to advance if the child hadn't fully understood the current lesson.

Generally our week resembled a college schedule: some subjects were taught on

Monday-Wednesday-Friday, others on Tuesday-Thursday. This provided adequate time to properly teach the subject matter, give the child time to work some problems at the board, discuss the subject and discuss the homework assignment. Exceptions to this schedule were English grammar, elementary arithmetic, phonics and reading.

The younger the child the more necessary it is to teach him a little bit every day. But the older high school children do not need to study the same subjects daily. Consequently, our college-type schedule allowed us to have longer discussion and instructional times to cover the material.

Combining two subjects sometimes facilitates teaching. Why not go over the arithmetic or geography lesson in the foreign language your children are learning? One can do all sorts of innovative things! And if you find yourself bogged down and overworked, have on older child forgo his lesson and teach a younger sibling. The younger ones love having an older child for their "teacher."

Plans and schedules

I wrote all assignments in a loose-leaf, page-a-day notebook available at office supply stores. I wrote each assignment in the space for the day it was due, and each child knew where to look for his homework assignment. They had no excuse for forgetting. This method worked smoothly. I could turn to any day and compare the assignment with the grade I recorded in a separate book.

With our magic clock, we kept close to our time schedule. I had a master schedule before me, and each child had his own schedule taped to his desk. When the time rolled around to change subjects, we did, with few exceptions. Occasionally I let one child continue with a particularly interesting reading selection or finish a math problem, while I started another child with his lesson. Before long the kids knew which subjects they must start promptly and on which ones they could take extra time.

Building men and women

Except for timed tests, I let the children take as long as was reasonably practical to finish a test. I was more interested in what they knew than in how fast they could complete tests.

Our goal in home schooling was for them to absorb the material and build a strong academic base in each subject. We believe learning should be chiefly concerned with the building of a man or woman, in which education is a means but not a goal.

So, moms, relax and be flexible. You don't have to finish every workbook. You don't have to finish the end of the year at the end of the book. Fit your school to your child, and enjoy your children. It worked for us during our fifteen years of home schooling, and it proved to be more successful than I imagined! Not only did the children love learning, but the three who went on to college entered higher education with optimism and assurance.*

God has truly blessed our family. Not only did our home schooling adequately prepare the children academically for further studies, the parent/child and child/child relationships are superb. We are the closest and greatest of friends.

Meeting Family Needs

Meg Johnson

One of the most frightening aspects of home schooling is the question of how to get everything done. The days never seem long enough even without home school. Then when the teaching responsibility is added on top of it all, how can a person adequately meet all the family needs? The ideal is no doubt impossible, but with careful planning we can do much more than we think.

Home schoolers have generally decided that personal needs of each family member are top priority. These include communication, physical care, opportunities to enjoy individual interests, and educational guidance, to name just a few. As we discuss personal needs let's consider three categories. Most demanding are the needs of the children. Second come the needs of the spouse. And last, the needs of the person responsible for the home teaching, usually the mother. The whole family should contribute to satisfying these needs, but often the major burden falls on the mother and teacher. One person can't do it all, however, so the entire family must be committed to the goals of home education. Individuals occasionally will need to forgo personal gratifications.

Meeting children's needs

Adequately caring for each child's needs can be quite a challenge, especially if two or more are under eight years of age. But even if the mother must divide her attention among several children and her other responsibilities, she still gives each child much more time and individual loving attention than could ever be received in a classroom school. Also, sharing and taking turns and waiting for attention are best learned in a family. Such goals require effort from both children and parents, but proper social behavior learned at home will be valuable to your children when they are on their own.

Planning doesn't dictate every move. Actual decisions about who needs attention minute by minute are usually obvious. The baby needs a diaper change; a young learner can't go on until a concept is explained; the telephone rings (some home schoolers ignore this); and so on. Three- to six-year-olds are probably the most easily neglected when there are several children in the family. They tend to need less guidance in learning than older children and require less physical care than the younger ones. They will often go and play quietly when you ask them to, but they still need and deserve your undivided attention for a part of each day.

Have you ever felt at the end of a long day that all you have done is run from one need to another with no time for your own interests? Remember that those who have children around all day often feel this way. Just balance these frustrating times against the days when you do see significant progress. Even though your accomplishments may not be obvious like shiny quarts of apple sauce lined up on the shelf, you have had the opportunity to provide an atmosphere of self-worth and love for each family member. As you work with each child, you can plant seeds for positive character building in a way that could not possibly be matched in a classroom. Even if you don't see much change day by day, when you look back over several months or a year, you should see significant accomplishments spiritually and emotionally as well as intellectually. Your children's real needs will be met.

Being a good spouse

Here you face another great challenge. As both mother and teacher, your children's needs often demand your first attention, but never satisfy them at the expense of your marriage relationship. You might not have as much time as you would like to be with your husband (or wife) during this period in your family's development. But allot special time for communicating. Discuss responsibilities and roles. The husband is the focal point of your family's activity and the foundation on which your home school rests. Usually he must make significant sacrifices to provide a home environment so the mother can devote large portions of time to her children instead of to him, to home making or to helping earn the family income.

Mother is usually teacher, but the roles may be reversed or not so clearly differentiated. While the father may spend little time in actual teaching, his contribution is of paramount importance to ultimate success. His participation in raising his children enhances their learning and enjoyment. His patience while the mother must devote a great deal of her energy to home schooling, considerably lessens her burden of having to meet everyone's needs while all too often no one seems to be interested in meeting hers. The father also provides a model for his children to emulate. In discussing home schools, much is often said about cooperation between parents, but all too often if they are not united, it doesn't work at all.

Dad, as I see it, the environment you help provide adds a dimension to your life. Both you and your children can certainly be enriched. Even though you may feel you are giving up personal time, you reap great rewards. When out with your children, you will have many reasons to be very pleased with them. Home schooled children tend to be calmer, more considerate, more independent, and more thoughtful than many children who spend large periods of time with their peers.

The home teacher

Mom, you are not likely to find much time for personal interests and relaxation until the children are old enough to help take care of themselves. But do set aside some time to relax. Ask the rest of the family to help out. And, just remember that this heavy schedule is temporary. The rewards will more than compensate.

Using teaching time efficiently

In addition to responsibilities for the personal needs of each family member, planning your school program and teaching demand large blocks of time. We never have all the time we would like, to do things with our children. Even letting them explore and learn on their own takes a lot of time. Take a good look at what you do, not on a daily basis, but over the long term. Set goals, of course, but avoid getting despondent when the days just aren't long enough.

If you use structured home study courses you may sometimes feel overwhelmed by what is expected. Remember that because you work closely with your children and have a sense of the learning appropriate for their level, you are the best judge of what they know and need to study. As an alternate to regular enrollment, consider using a preplanned course as a learning resource for your child, and to help you know what children in a particular grade are generally expected to learn. If you enroll your child in a course, make every effort to help him or her learn the course material. Just be sensitive to individual needs and abilities. Use tests to make sure your child is grasping the course material. Many home study courses are based on programs used in schools with children of differing abilities, and they often provide more material than may be needed for a particular individual. Try to work out a plan with the school which fits your children's needs. Good programs offer a selection of ideas and materials so that the home schooler may draw on the knowledge, experience and efforts of many people. Let your home study courses enhance your teaching rather than create pressures which might interfere with it.

For a time-efficient home school, encourage your children to develop independent study habits. Older children to a large degree must learn to teach themselves and to assist each other as well as younger children.

Household demands

Children can develop the skills and initiative to contribute a great deal to the life of their family. They can care for younger siblings, help in the kitchen or with other household chores, and work in the yard or garden. Gradually your children's attitudes about work will change from seeing chores as tedious to feeling that they are helping you and contributing to the family needs.

Teaching your children how to work thoroughly and cheerfully is worth the time and patience. Although maturing children cannot do things as well or as quickly as you can, accept their efforts in contributing to the comfort of the home, and your life together will be rewarding.

The home school routine

In our family, the days are divided informally into time blocks. Mornings belong to book learning, and Mom is available for teaching and assistance during these hours. For us, "schoolwork" must be done first. Afternoons are devoted to other activities which may include baking, household chores, sewing, home maintenance, community service, individual projects or visits with other home schoolers. Although we have found home schooling to be a full-time demanding lifestyle, it becomes easier as the children grow up. As they mature they become aware of what needs to be done and can help around the home on their own.

In addition to having flexible daily time blocks, we generally follow the regular public school vacation schedule. While home schooling really involves constant learning and growing, our normal program is limited to the school schedule of the children's peers. Vacations and weekends offer good breaks to relax and catch up on unfinished chores and projects. We all enjoy our vacations, but we also find it a relief to return to our regular routine, even though it's quite flexible.

In addition to routine and unavoidable chores, it may sometimes help to accomplish or work on one special project a day. On some days you may simply want to make learning more meaningful. On other days you could take time out to do a family or household project, go somewhere special, do extra shopping, make a doctor visit, or just get ahead in schoolwork. Each family defines, however flexibly, its own patterns and goals as home schooling is integrated into the family lifestyle.

Specific planning and record keeping makes working independently easier for the children. At the beginning of each day, we usually make an outline of what is to be done. The students can then go on and do their work even if no one is there to watch them every minute. And I can tend to other household and child care demands, as necessary, during school hours. Of course, children cannot always be left unsupervised as they may dawdle and bicker, but they become more responsible as time goes on. Eventually they realize that they must do their work. When older children work on their own, you have time to meet some of the needs of the younger ones. Then, in addition to writing out what is planned for the day, we keep a record of what has been accomplished.

Although home schooling family lifestyles tend to revolve around the children, there is more to be done than teaching. Housework and meal preparation demand attention too. Well organized home school families function efficiently but still face limitations of time and energy. In many families the first thing to slip is the housework. Until the older children can responsibly help with this, it is difficult for the mother to manage all her responsibilities. Some may have children around all day and still keep the house spotless. They are exceptions.

Our family finally had to set a few basic goals. We try to clean up before Daddy gets home to make a little room for him in our small house. We do try to keep our living room fairly neat – a challenge with a toddler. Major cleaning is done when possible but never on the weekly basis that once seemed so necessary. We seriously try to keep up only with dishes and laundry, and we make time to plan and prepare good meals. Someday we may have everything under control but, for now, housekeeping is low priority.

In our hectic struggle to do everything we think we should, let's remember that our lives have purpose. Days devoted to raising children who will have firm character and moral values are days well spent.

61

Making Home School Special

Sue Welch

School at home could seem rather ho-hum to your children when their friends are excited about beginning a new school year in the traditional classroom. In many creative ways home school can be made special. Here are some starters. You can pick up more ideas from other home schooling families.

We are not alone

Just as you need support from other teaching parents, your children need the assurance that they are not alone.

☺ Being included in your support group, even if not at every meeting, is extremely helpful. Children may not look like they are taking in as much as they really are at these times.

☺ Hearing you talk with others about home school helps them see that the idea has wide acceptance. Sometimes, when I finish a phone call, I tell Heather, "That was a mother who wants to teach her children at home, too!"

☺ Field trips with a couple of other families or a larger group help. Fifty parents and children went on our first field trip. When we got home our five year old said, "Mommy, almost everyone is teaching their kids at home!" She was impressed.

☺ When we pray during our school time opening exercises, we remember other home schooling families. Realizing that friends and relatives are beginning their home-school day the same way brings a sense of encouragement and togetherness.

Talk it up

Both what you do and the words you use to describe your school help your children realize its importance. Your child's age and whether this is your first year home schooling will determine how appropriate some of these suggestions are.

You are probably already aware that ***Sue Welch*** *manages and edits* The Teaching Home, *one of the oldest home school publications. She and her crew have developed the magazine from a home project into a quality publication. Here are some of her suggestions from one of the early issues —still great ideas.*

🔔 Name your school together. Consider just what you want your school to be, and reflect this in your name. Then make a banner with the school name on it.

🔔 Set up a schoolroom. It may be a corner of a room or an entire room. Bookshelves, globe, flags and desks make an impressive array. This will require budgeting for school expenses, although many pieces of equipment can be picked up at garage sales or secondhand stores. Procuring all of these special things will be almost as exciting as Christmas to your children. Help them understand that this is all possible because you are home schooling. Incidentally, I don't recommend substituting school supplies for gifts at regular gift-giving times.

🔔 Desks symbolize school. They make a good place to keep supplies and look important for learning even if children end up sitting close to Mother on the couch for reading or sitting at the kitchen table to do math while Mother is working.

🔔 Look forward to the first day of school. Buy school supplies, even a lunch pail for trips. Don't just buy new shoes in the fall, buy "school shoes."

🔔 For the opening day of school, plan a special "kickoff" such as a field trip a little distance from home. Let your child know that this would not be possible if your were not home schooling. To a child's perception these concrete things make home school very special.

🔔 Father may not have any teaching responsibilities – or so he and the family may think. But when you (correctly) name him the Bible teacher and identify Bible as the most important subject, things can take on a new perspective.

🔔 Have "school" pictures taken to send to grandparents.

🔔 Plan holiday parties with another home schooling family.

🔔 Have different classes in different rooms or areas in your house. Say, "Let's go into our math room now," instead of "Let's go into the kitchen."

🔔 Take clues from the public schools. If the neighbors are having a big deal wearing a different color to school each day for a week, copy the idea for your children. Tell them, "We are going to have blue day tomorrow, then red, yellow and green."

🔔 During school time, occasionally have surprises such as a lesson-related activity, an unexpected field trip for your family, a visiting home schooler to share a science experiment and anything to make and keep school exciting.

🔔 Get a school mascot, such as a fish or some gerbils.

🔔 List on a chart classroom duties such as care of the school area.

🔔 Don't just "take a break," have "recess." That's what your lower-grade child's friends are talking about.

🔔 If Father is given the title of "Science Teacher," or "Science Consultant," when questions come up at odd times, Mother can say, "Let's ask your science teacher about that. I'm sure he knows how to find that answer." This gives credibility in a child's eyes to the parent as his teacher.

🔔 When teaching a new household chore, call the time Home Ec.

🔔 Give report cards. These do not have to show letter grades, but can praise and encourage work that is being done and character that is being developed.

Making your home school special to others

Your children will view their home school, to some extent, the same way they think others view it. Peer pressure is hard to completely eradicate. Also, to help other people accept your home school, you can build bridges for communication and educate in love and patience. The following ideas might help satisfy both needs.

👍 Have an open house when your schoolroom is all ready and you have spent enough days in school to have some work and projects to display. Invite neighbors, friends and/or relatives. They are probably curious about what goes on in a home school and will be impressed when they see your school atmosphere, teaching materials, and the completed work.

👍 Invite grandparents on field trips with you. Send them schoolwork samples and brag up your children's progress. They want to be proud of their grandchildren, and their fears can be alleviated when they see that your children are achieving and not "being ruined."

👍 Ask your children's friends what they are doing in school and tell them what you are doing.

👍 Let your children hear you praising their progress in school.

👍 Put on a Christmas or school-closing program. Have your children help plan, invite guests, make refreshments and entertain. A bashful child may record a poem, a song, or a story he or she has written.

👍 The school-closing program could be a graduation, complete with formalities.

Making your home school special will take thought and a little effort, but it should amply reward you and encourage your children.

Endnote

See Appendix K for information about *The Teaching Home.*

62

Educating for Superior Achievement

One mountain-grown family seems to be sending all their children to Harvard. The story is worth taking a look at. The father, David Colfax, has a Ph.D. degree. His wife Micki is an English teacher. That sounds impressive. But it's not just a matter of genes because Reed, the third son to follow the scholarly tradition, was adopted. And the parents say it's not a matter of their own education, either.

When I was preparing the third edition of this book, a certain home schooling family was getting a lot of press since one of their four boys had just followed his two older brothers in becoming a student at Harvard University. Always eager for contributions to this book, I phoned them to inquire about getting a few pearls of wisdom on quality in home education. Dr. Colfax told me about the appearance of a new book he and his wife had written. I found the copy he sent to be enlightening.

I learned about the Archers from *Home Education Magazine*. I have appreciated communicating with the father, Jules Archer.

My own horizons have widened from considering these ideas, and I hope yours do, too.

We must also concede that the roots of success go deeper than merely learning at home. After all, the home school movement is quietly producing thousands of "graduates" that aren't catching the attention of the media for any great feats of intelligence. And people go to Harvard who haven't been home schooled.

Of course heredity does have a part in achievement, and studying at home does, too, but I'm convinced that attitudes, skills and opportunities make the greatest difference, and that these are mostly produced by the home. In this chapter I will share what I see as success factors from two families with track records. Then I'll add some thoughts of my own.

The Colfax way

In their book, *Homeschooling for Excellence,* David and Micki Colfax identify their educational goal as the development of intellect and character.[1] From their experience with the public school system, they see its educators as professing interest in individual needs of children while "in reality, their primary objective is that of moving the product – school children – on down the line with a minimum of interference from subordinates, parents, the public, or the children themselves."[2]

The Colfaxes do not expect home schooling to change the educational establishment or to "make classroom life any more meaningful for the millions of children whose parents cannot or will not take them out of the assembly-line schools." Teaching at home, they see as a response to the public system. At home, parents can control the education of their children in several ways, provide more efficient learning, and foster the development of autonomy and creativity.

The home schooled child can choose projects and invest time developing them, thus moving toward autonomy by taking responsibility for his or her own education.

"If only by virtue of the freedom it affords, homeschooling promotes creativity. It is an almost inevitable consequence of a program in which self-directed boys and girls are encouraged – and given space – to devise their own programs, to explore, and to experiment at their own pace."

Three of the chapters in the Colfaxes' book imply levels that would take the place of preschool, elementary and secondary education. The chapters are entitled: "Before Basics," "The three R's," and "Beyond Basics."

The environment recommended for the before-basics years is similar to the ideal many educators would envisage. The emphasis is on providing rather than pushing.

On the surface, the three-R's level also appears similar to other solid, individualized approaches to fundamental learning. But here we begin to see what I consider the "secret ingredient" of the whole program: keeping learning interesting so it happens at a fast pace. The Colfaxes have apparently achieved this by: (1) a challenging physical work program which provides both the diversion to make book learning a refreshing change of focus, and the physical exercise to keep the brain alert, (2) waiting for readiness, (3) using materials and methods that concentrate more on the end results of the learning than on drill and busywork, (4) encouraging independence and critical thinking, and (5) expecting achievement and providing an atmosphere for the joy of its accomplishment.

In the beyond-basics level, the young scholar is ready to explore personal interests. The doors to continued learning have been opened by a groundwork of information-processing skills and by general knowledge from wide reading. Subjects usually covered in the high school curriculum are studied – some to greater depths than others. Parents help locate resources to facilitate extensive learning in a few chosen project areas.

The Archer family, another success story

The three sons in the Archer family attended Princeton, Yale and Harvard, and have become intellectual leaders in their professions – paleontology, social psychology and medicine. In contrast to the Colfaxes, they all attended public primary and secondary schools in a small town in upstate New York.

The sons don't attribute their success to the schools, however, but to achievement-oriented parents who supported their personal goals even in childhood. The boys were allowed to establish their own ideals regardless of what peers thought, and parental expectations inspired their self-confidence.

The Archer parents emphasized character development over academic achievement. Made-up stories at bedtime and "thoughts to fall asleep by" written out and tacked to the wall were part of this emphasis. Team sports were discouraged.

"At the time," writes Jules Archer, "it did not occur to my wife and me that we were doing anything out of the ordinary in raising our sons. We believed that we were simply normal parents whose concentration was on the quality of the school curriculum and teaching. In retrospect, and only after exploring the question with my sons, I recognize the importance of the home environment in the learning process.

"All of which raises the question: Does the reputed poor scholastic achievement today reflect a failure of adequate parental support and cooperation more than a failure of the school system?"

Archer's analysis of the achievement of his sons is worth underlining: "In looking for explanations for their success and comparing their educational experiences to those of children today – a quarter of a century later – I have been led to the conclusion that the most important ingredient for improving our educational system lies in the home. Parents are the principal catalysts in their children's openness to education, fascination with learning, and spur to achievement."[3]

Ingredients for Excellence

☑ Quality sensory input: reading, watching and listening that inspire both intellectually and morally.

☑ Learning to act by principle rather than by the feeling of the moment.

☑ Emphasis on cooperation, on lifting others, rather than on competition.

☑ Balanced development. As an individual matures, more growth in some areas is appropriate, but no aspect of learning related to effective living should be neglected.

☑ Friends chosen for high ideals.

☑ Making God first and last and best.

True life success

I see success as more than intellectual achievement. In fact, adding good physical, social and emotional development wouldn't spell true success either. Only in seeking a saving relationship with the One who has created all things do we find a context for total development in every area. Talents multiply as they are wisely invested.

Most of the energies of youth in our society are spent in either worthless or harmful activities. From my own experience as a parent, I have learned the importance of helping children avoid those things that would weaken and destroy their potential. Even children with ordinary natural ability can accomplish the extraordinary when their energies are protected and channeled into wholesome directions. In the box, I have suggested six factors for assuring excellence. The final and most important one brings a dimension not mentioned by the two families highlighted in this chapter.

Endnotes

1. David and Micki Colfax, *Homeschooling for Excellence*, Warner Books, p. 95. See Appendix I.

2. *Ibid.*, pp. 33–48.

3. Jules Archer, "Educating Children, a Personal Perspective,"" *Home Education Magazine*, February, 1987, pp. 6, 7; and *The National Forum*, Fall, 1986, pp. 38–43.

Appendices — Resource Information

SECTION FOUR

A
Instructional Services

This first appendix covers organizations (or schools) that offer instruction (through parents, of course) for children who are, in some way, enrolled. High-school-only schools and those requiring Internet connection are in Appendix B. School logos were selected for convenience and do not indicate editorial preferences.

A Beka Correspondence School / A Beka Video Home School Box 18000, Pensacola, FL 32523-9160; (800) 874-3592, . A Beka offers a traditional correspondence school program where students' work is reviewed by experienced teachers at the school headquarters. A ministry of Pensacola Christian College. A Beka textbooks and materials are also available for purchase. Grades P-12. I understand that certain restrictions determine whether or not a student is considered for graduation. It might be well to inquire.

Advanced Training Institute of America Quoting from their web page, "The ATI family studies as a learning team. With the 'bus-stop approach,' sons and daughters of varying ages study the same concepts together in the *Wisdom Booklet*, then expand their learning to different levels through individual studies chosen from the *Parent Guide Planner*." A.T.I.A., Box 1, Oak Brook, IL 60522-3001; ati@iblp.org; www.iblp.org. Parents are required to attend seminars.

Academy of Home Education Services include maintaining permanent student records, validation of secondary studies, transcripts, diploma, book buy-back, optional literary club for improving writing skills. At Bob Jones University, Greenville, SC 29614. Call (888) 253-9833 or (864) 242-5100, Ext. 2047. E-mail ahe@bju.edu

Alta Vista Curriculum 12324 Rd. 37, Madera, CA 93638, (800) 544-1397. Contact person: Kelly Hollman. A fully integrated unit study program with science and social science themes. Samples cost only $5 and include lesson one of each level A, B and C of the Earth & Space Unit. They also offer a free information packet. Cross-age teaching, multiple activities for all learning styles. Studies of God's world in the light of His written word.

Bridgestone Academy A full K-8 correspondence program based on Christian values. (800) 682-7396.

Calvert School Dept. 2hsm, 105 Tuscany Rd., Baltimore, MD 21210-3098. Susan Weiss, Principal, (410) 243-6030, fax (410) 366-0674. www.calvertschool.org; inquiry@calvertschool.org. Courses include full lesson plans and all materials. Calvert offers a full K-8 curriculum including algebra. Enrichment courses cover reading, children's literature, music, art, Spanish, and French. Optional advisory teaching service (guidance and grading through the mail). Over 400,000 have enrolled since 1906.

since 1897

Christian Light Education (A division of Christian Light Publications), P.O. Box 1212, Harrisonburg, VA 22801; (540) 434-0750. Bible-based curriculum for grades 1-12. Mostly based on worktexts. Parents may opt for a full service program or only purchase the materials. Individualized approach.

Christian Liberty Academy Satellite Schools (CLASS). Home schooling families are offered individually-tailored, K-12 study programs with or without administrative guidance. The curriculum is "heavy on basics, emphasizing math, phonics, reading, writing, Biblical studies, geography, history, the Constitution, and science." Christian Liberty Academy is independent and nondenominational. They also publish some textbooks. For an information packet, write or phone: CLASS, 502 W. Euclid Ave., Arlington Heights, IL 60004; (847) 259-4444. Enrollment also at www.homeschools.org.

Clonlara School Home Based Education Program 1289 Jewett, Ann Arbor, MI 48104, (313) 769-4511, or 769-4515; clonlara@delphi.com; www.clonlara.org. Clonlara works for a close team effort among parent, student, and the Clonlara staff. Dr. Pat Montgomery, Director, writes that this school is "as different from conventional schooling as we can possibly make it. The accent is on using resources available to assure the best possible education for student and parent. Choice is practically our middle name." The school aims "to create an environment where children and parents are free to guide their own learning in a nondirective and nonpressured setting." The staff will make contacts with school or social services officials for the parents. They help keep families out of legal trouble by making sure they are in compliance.

Country Garden School P.O. Box 6, College Place, WA 99324. Gwen Hawkins, Director. (509) 525-0125. Both distance and local students in grades P-12 using mostly A Beka or Rod and Staff materials. Traditional curriculum plus practical skills. Teaching guides may be purchased with or without consultation fee (approx. $300 for elementary year or $35 for initial setup only). Testing fee $25. A system to "train a generation of men and women who can think for themselves, based on the absolutes of God's Word."

Country Garden SCHOOL

Creative Christian Education Service Box K, Angwin, CA 94508; (707) 965-3414; Fax ... 1450. CCES helps parents follow the curriculum plan they prefer (or suggests one). They help in finding them the necessary books and materials. They offer curriculum guides, phone consultation with licensed teachers, testing, and record keeping for grades K-12. This basic service costs $295 — less for each additional child. For a fee of $65 per child you receive the services of their library including textbooks, audio and video tapes, a large workbook covering typical topics for a grade, computer programs and parent help books. Ask for their brochure.

Family Christian Academy Help in designing your own curriculum along with guidance, a library, testing, record keeping and certification of credits. K-12. Optional seminars available in Tennessee and elsewhere when possible. They also offer a unit study program for girls entitled, *Far Above Rubies*. See Appendix Y. 487 Myatt Dr., Madison, TN 37115; (615) 860-3000. The school is associated with the Family Christian bookstore chain.

Family Learning Services P.O. Box 9, Junction City, OR 97448; http://www.fls-homeschool.com Crymes@rio.com. (541) 998-5735. The directors are Clayton E. Crymes, Ph.D. and Suzanne Crymes, M.S. Assistance for families in planning educational alternatives. Individual curriculum recommendations based on prior academic records, learning style, abilities, and needs of each child. FLS specializes in directing high school programs although they work with all levels. Testing, grade records, and diplomas provided.

Heritage Institute 11530 122nd St., Cologne, MN 55322, (612) 466-2414; heritage@minn.net. A K-12 service organization. They offer School of Tomorrow materials, record keeping, testing, and consultation, but no responsibility for instruction. For high school see their entry in Appendix B.

Hewitt Homeschooling Resources, provides complete home schooling services tailored to individual interests and abilities. They believe that parents are to be the first teachers, and the home the first school. Hewitt teachers coordinate and supervise the students' work providing evaluations and teaching suggestions. Programs encourage parent interaction. Hewitt also provides for special-needs students. See Appendix W for Hewitt's PASS testing plan for grades 3-8. April L. Purtell, President. Hewitt CDC, P.O. Box 9, Washougal, WA 98671; (206) 835-8708; hewitths@aol.com.

Home Study International, 12501 Old Columbia Pike, Silver Spring, MD 20904-6600; (800) 782-4769 or fax: (301) 680-6577, 74617.74@compuserve.com. HSI provides programs for kindergarten through college levels with a Christian orientation. Parents may choose from three service levels (1) the full package including testing and consultations, materials and study guides, and records under HSI's school accreditation; (2) materials and study guides if for the K-6 range; and (3) materials only. Approximately 2,500 students are enrolled.

Kathleen Sprafka, Curriculum Services. Listed under Florida in Appendix D, but serves all of the US.

Keys to Learning Institute For parents who prefer student directed learning. "Under the supervision of a resource teacher, parents and children attend school together." Scheduled meetings and resource materials are provided. They use *World Book Encyclopedia* as the basic text. Also Mortensen Math, How to Tutor, and Home Study Principles. They use an "open-ended lesson plan method," covering K-12. Although the base operation is set up for the Los Angeles area, the KTLI Private School Programs are for students living in any state. This looks like a good idea. If I wanted to use it, I would look for a little wider source of philosophical ideas. (This would be the case for any individual who promotes very specific opinions.) I would also want to add a Bible study class. Vicky Azat, Director; PO Box 3599, So. Pasadena, CA 91030-6599; (626) 799-0787; fax at same number; www.kidslearn.com.

Landmark's Freedom Baptist Curriculum for use in homes or schools. Pre-K to 12th grade. "Baptist – not just Baptistic," individualized. 2222 East Hinson Ave., Haines City, FL 33844-4902; (941) 422-0188. (800) 700-LFBC.

Laurel Springs School P.O. Box 1440, Ojai, CA; 93024-1440; (805) 646-2473;info@laurelsprings.com; www.lsurelsprings.com. A home study school with traditional requirements. High school elective credit may be earned by arranged experiences options. (A log of the activity is required.) Credits in some courses may be earned by directed study on the web as well as by using good textbooks with study guides. Recognized by the state of California.

McGuffey Academy International, Box 109, Lakemont, GA 30552; (706) 782-7709. A complete, personalized service, with choices of textbooks. Testing, phone counseling, record keeping, and high school diploma.

Midwest Christian Academy 2905 Gill St., Bloomington IL 61704; (309) 663-4477; fax (309) 662-7711. School of Tomorrow materials are used.

Moore Academy Box 1, Camas, WA 98607; (360) 835-5500; moorefnd@pacifier.com; www.pacifier.com/~moorefnd. Personalized, instructional guidance following principles they call "The Moore Formula." Materials from a variety of sources. A service of The Moore Foundation.

North Atlantic Regional Schools A K-12 service of Homeschool Associates. Consultations, support, annual portfolio reviews or testing and curriculum design. See Appendix B for high school features. Also sales by bookmobile (see Appendix Z) workshops and a periodical (see Appendix K), and workshops. 116 Third Ave., Auburn, ME 02410, (207) 777-1700, (800) 882-2828; homeschool@home schoolassociates.com.

Oak Meadow, Inc. P.O. Box 740, Putney, VT 05346; (802) 387-2021; oms@oakmeadow.com; www.oakmeadow.com "We emphasize an integrated approach to learning that presents concepts and skills in a developmentally appropriate sequence, facilitating the development of body, mind, and spirit." Application of the Waldorf philosophy. For my personal concerns, use the index to look for "Waldorf."

Old Dominion Academy P.O. Box 742, Kosciusko, MS 39090. Phone (601) 289-5703, FAX (601) 289-4224.

Pinewood School Now a part of Clonlara, listed earlier in this appendix.

Plantation Christian School, P.O. Box 53690, San Jose, CA 95123-5690; (408) 972-8211. A private, distance-education school ministering to the needs of home schooling families. Services include cumulative file maintenance, transcripts, high school diploma, work permits, student and faculty cards, curriculum counseling, HSLDA discount (membership required). Plantation has expanded to include students anywhere. Visit PCS at http://www.geocities.com/Athens/Olympus/3244, or e-mail, planting@geocities.com.

School of Tomorrow A publisher of individualized curriculum and resource materials including learning-to-read programs, academic core subjects, and electives for preschool through 12th grade. (See my review of *Readmaster* in Appendix O.) In many courses, workbook-type booklets called PACEs provide instruction for less teacher dependent learning. Video interactive computer programs are available for high school math and science. Diagnostic tests determine placement in each subject. Parents may purchase materials and manage their own program or enroll their children in Living Heritage Academy which counsels with the home teacher and otherwise administers the home school. A group of families may participate in an agreement with School of Tomorrow and receive discounts, teacher training, and conventions. (School of Tomorrow was formerly known as Accelerated Christian Education), P.O. Box 299000, Lewisville, TX 75029-9000; (800) 925-7777; (972) 315-1776 or fax ... 2862; mcook@em-schooloftomorrow .com; www.schooloftomorrow.com

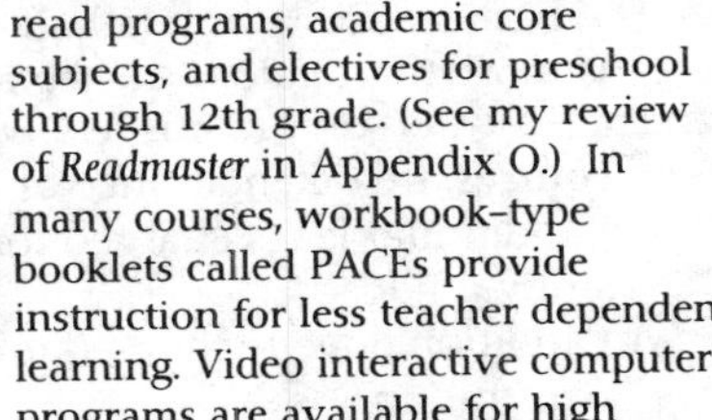

Seton Home Study School 1350 Progress Dr., Front Royal, VA 22630; (703) 636-9990. A Catholic program. (information not confirmed)

SonLight Educational Ministry P.O. Box 518, Colville, WA 99114. (627 Highland Loop Road, Kettle Falls, WA 99141); (509) 684-6843. A strongly Bible-oriented, K-8 program. You may want to change the emphasis at times. A large portion of the instructional materials are prepared by the school staff. Delayed academics is recommended (except for phonics).

Summit Christian Academy DFW Corporate Park, 2100 N. Hwy. 360, Suite 503, Grand Prairie, TX 75050; (972) 602-8050; Fax ... 8243; (800) 362-9180; sca100@aol.com. "Summit Christian Academy believes in the development of the total child, mentally, physically, spiritually, and socially." They use the Alpha-Omega, Bob Jones, or Abeka curriculua. Tuition varies with the grade, K-12. Enrollment and testing fees are extra. (Information not confirmed)

The Sycamore Tree 2179 Meyer Place, Costa Mesa, CA 92627; (714) 650-4466. 75767.1417@compuserve.com. For orders and catalog requests, call (800) 779-6750. Home education guidance service with credentialed teachers to help parents choose materials according to the individual children. For their materials catalog and other information, see Appendix Z.

The Sycamore Tree Center for Home Education

***Also see** Appendix B, for schools which include elementary courses.*

B
High School Distance Education

Schools in this appendix offer instructional services for secondary (high school) students. The information is divided between **Part 1,** *schools which do not require Internet communication (although they may use it to some extent) and,* **Part 2**, *schools depending on the Internet.*

The alphabet code at the end of most descriptions describes school characteristics. The most important factors - course quality and course availability - can't be shown in a listing as we have here. Course fees, as well as other items in the list are subject to change. Many of the organizations shown in the previous appendix also offer guidance for high school youth.

A 90% of the courses have been replaced or significantly revised during the past 4 years.
B 90% have been, during the past 10 years.
C Science course(s) with lab kit(s) are available.
D Audio cassettes are used in some courses.
E Video cassettes and/or compact disks are used in some courses.
F A computer is needed for some courses.
G An Internet site is available for student responses or interactive learning monitored by the school for some or all courses.
H Some essay-type items (or reports) are required in student work for at least 90% of the non-math courses.

I Less than 1 year is granted for completion of a course (unless special arrangements are made).
J An extension of six months or more is available (possibly for a fee).
K All failed exams (not lesson submissions) may be repeated at least once (possibly for a fee).
L At least one exam for all credit courses requires out-of-home supervision.
M A student may drop a course and apply at least part of the fee to another course.

N Many teachers are either available for phone consultation during most business hours or their direct phone numbers are usually available.
O E-mail communication with some of the teachers is available.
P Distance Education and Training Council accreditation. (University schools are usually considered accredited through the university, and many private schools do not feel it is important or appropriate.)
Q National University Continuing Education Association membership.
R A diploma is offered by the correspondence school.
S 90% of the lessons are graded and back in the mail within 2 working days of the time they are received. (unusually fast)
T 90% are back in the mail within 3 or 4 days.
U It usually takes longer than 4 days.

V The base fee for ½ unit (a half-year in one course) is more than half of the fee for 1 unit.
W The cost-per-unit rate is less when several courses are taken at once or in succession.
X An additional fee is charged for the syllabus or study guide.
Y An additional fee is charged for admission or registration.
Z Study materials may be purchased without the tuition charge (and without instructional services).

Part 1, Schools not requiring Internet access

A Beka See Appendix A.

Academy of Home Education See under Florida, Services, in Appendix D.

American Academy Southpark Centre, #314, 12651 S. Dixie Hwy., Miami, FL 33156; (305) 233-5723. Project HomeSchool is one of the programs of this institution. Stan Simmons, Contact Person. High school study programs for grades 10-12 with resources and parent services. According to AA, their programs are not "canned." Credit may be recognized for out-of-school learning.

American School, 850 E. 58th St., Chicago, IL 60637; (312) 947-3300. Standard traditional curriculum. Tuition rates depend on how many years of their program are taken. Payment plans available.

Arizona, University of, Independent Study / Correspondence, 888 N. Euclid Ave., Tucson, AZ 857721-0158. (520) 626-4222. $79 per half unit. On the high school level, they offer grades 4 to 12, special bilingual (Sp/Eng) courses, and English as a second language. ACDEGHLMOQT

Arkansas, University of, Department of Independent Study, 2 University Center, Fayetteville, AR 72701. (501) 575-3647. Study guides may be purchased. Textbooks are rented to enrolled students. Tuition $50.00 in-state, $55.00 out-of-state, per half unit.

BYU Independent Study, 206 HCEB, P.O. Box 21514, Provo, UT 84602-1514; (801) 378-2868, (801) 378-5078; indstudy@byu.edu; http://coned.byu.edu/is/indstudy.htm; Grades: 9-12; BYU offers web courses, floppy submission, grade check by web, and on-line exams. They still use pencil and paper, too. ½ unit, $79; BDEFGKLMOQRT.

California, University of, Extension Center for Media and Independent Learning, 2000 Center St., Suite 400, Berkeley, CA 94704. askcmil@uclink4.berkeley.edu; www-cmil.unex.berkeley.edu. In addition to high school correspondence courses, UC offers college and professional level courses by independent learning and online. ½ unit costs $25.50. BCHJKLMPQU.

Christian Liberty Academy See Appendix A.

Citizens' High School, P.O. Box 1929 (118 College Dr.), Orange Park, FL 32067; (904) 276-1700.

Colorado, University of, at Boulder, Division of Continuing Education, Boulder, CO 80309-0178. (800) 331-2801. Tuition $70.00 per half unit. AHHJNOQTXZ

Country Garden School See Appendix A. BEHIJKNR UXZ

Family Christian Academy See Appendix A.

Florida, University of, Division of Continuing Education, Department of Independent Study by Correspondence & Distance Education, 2209 NW 13th St., Suite D, Gainesville, FL 32609-3498. For Florida call (904) 392-1711, Outside of Florida, (800) 327-4218, ext. 200 or 201. $110 per half unit high school course.

Heritage Institute Service for K-12. See Appendix A. BCENORYZ.

Home Study International See Appendix A. Rebate for quantity of courses. See Appendix A. BCDEFJL-MOPRTVW.

ICS Newport / Pacific High School, 925 Oak St., Scranton, PA 18515-0002. (717) 342-7701. A full diploma program following the Pennsylvania Department of Education curriculum requirements. 21 Carnegie Units. Graduates qualify for a Certificate of Preliminary Education from the Pennsylvania Department of Education. International Correspondence Schools (ICS) is accredited by the National Home Study Council and licensed by the Pennsylvania State board of Private Licensed Schools.

Idaho, University of, Correspondence Study in Idaho, University of Idaho, Moscow, ID 83844-3225. (800) 422-6013, (208) 885-6641. Tuition $74.00 per half unit.

Indiana University, Independent Study Program, Owen Hall, Bloomington, IN 47405. (800) 334-1011 (national); (800) 342-5410 or (812) 855-3693 (Indiana). $53.00 per half unit.

Keystone National High School 420 West 5th St., Bloomsburg, PA 17815. Diploma program. (800) 255-4937; info@keystonehighschool.com; www.keystonehighschool .com. Regular correspondence program for grades 9-12. Grades 5-12 served as "summer school." 1 unit costs $150 plus a handling fee. Materials are included. ACDFGHIJKM NOPQRTV.

Laurel Springs School Credit options. See Appendix A.

McGuffy Academy International See Appendix A.

Missouri, University of, Center for Independent Study, 136 Clark Hall, Columbia, MO 65211. (314) 882-2491. Tuition, $89 per half unit, plus a handling fee. BCDEGILMOQST.

Nebraska, University of, at Lincoln, Independent Study High School, 269 Clifford Hardin Nebraska Center for Continuing Education, Lincoln, NE 68583-9800. (402) 472-1901, FAX (402) 472-1926. Tuition $79 resident, $83 authorized nonresident, per half unit. 125 half-unit courses are offered. Two tracks.

North Atlantic Regional Schools They direct your study and offer a high school diploma. They certify credits by properly documented work including a variety of study in and out of classrooms and by special exams. Call Steve or Carol Moitozo. (800) 882-2828 or (207) 777-1700. http://www.homeschool@homeschoolassociates.com. High school doesn't need to take four years. NORY

North Dakota, Division of Independent Study, Box 5036, Fargo, ND 58105-5036. (701) 231-6000; Fax (701) 231-6052; e-mail stone@sendit.nodak.edu. Tuition $42 resident, $53 nonresident per half unit. $10 handling fee. Junior high courses available. www.dis.dpi.state.nd.us ACDEFGHMNOQRTWXYZ

Oklahoma, University of, Independent Study Department, 1700 Asp, Ave., B-1, Norman, OK 73072. (800) 942-5702. Tuition $70.00 per half unit. BCDEJLMPQU.

PA Homeschoolers Advanced placement courses. See Appendix Y.

Phoenix Special Programs & Academies 3132 W. Clarendon Ave., Phoenix, AZ 85017-4589. (602) 263-5601; (800) 426-4952; e-mail@phoenixacademies.org; www.phoenixacademies.org; Grades 7-12. ½ unit $85. ACDFGHIJKLNORT.

Seaton Home Study School A Catholic program. See Appendix A.

South Carolina, University of Distance Education and Instructional Support (DEIS). High school enrollment: Independent Study, Div. of Distance Educ., University of Alabama, Box 870388, Tuscloosa, AL 35487-0388. (803) 777-7210. http://ua1ix.ua.edu/~disted/info or www.sc.edu/deis/

Summit Christian Academy. See Appendix A for more information. ACDEJMRVXYZ.

Tennessee, University of, Dept. of Independent Study, Knoxville, TN 37996-0300. (800) 670-8657(national and Tennessee), (423) 974-5134. $72 per half unit plus $10.75 postage. BDEHILMNQU.

Texas Tech Address: Guided Study, TTU, Box 42191, Lubbock, TX 79409-2191; (800) 692-6877. Cooperaton with local high schools or a diploma program directly through TTU. Dual enrollment in some courses allows both college and high school credit. They also offer several middle school courses.

Texas, University of, at Austin, Correspondence Division, P.O. Box 7700, Austin, TX 78713-7700, (800) 252-3461; or (512) 471-2910. Computer grading allows a one-day lesson return time for many courses. Also Internet use, www.utexas.edu/dce/eimc/. Tuition (not including books) is $79 for a half unit. BCDGHIKLMOQUYZ.

Walkersville Christian Family Schools 4 West Main St., Thurmont, MD 21788-1824; http://www.wcfs.edu; info@wcfs.edu; (301) 271-0123; fax: (301) 845-7254. The WCFS Distance Program is now open for enrollment nationally and internationally for families who are missionaries, pastors and church leaders, and all members of the body of Jesus Christ. ACDEFGHIJNO.

Wisconsin, University of Independent Study, Univ. of Wisc. Extension, 432 North Lake St. 104, Madison, WI 53706. General information, (608) 263-2055. Tuition $55 per half unit.

Wyoming, University of, Correspondence Study Department, Box 3294, Laramie, WY 82071. (800) 448-7801. Tuition for a half unit is $76.

Independent Study Catalog See Appendix J.

Canadian universities, See Association of Universities and Colleges of Canada, Appendix E.

Part 2, Schools with a mostly Internet base

Alyeska Central School, Free to Alaskans. 3141 Channel Dr., #100, Juneau, AK 99801. Traditional curriculum. (907) 465-2835; ascmail@educ.state.ak.us; www.educ.state.ak.us/alaskan-study/ACS/Home.html. BCDEHJNOPRT

Christa McAuliffe Academy A wide scope of resources is applied to teach core subjects plus physical education, music, art, computer applications, and occupational education; 3601 W. Washington Avenue, Yakima, WA 98903, (509) 575-4989; glen@cmacademy.org; www.cmacademy.org. For K-12. A flat fee is charged for all courses. Named for the teacher who lost her life in the US space launch accident. ACDEFGHKMNORY

Compuhigh High school by Internet. See Clonlara ... in Appendix A.

CyberSchool A project of Eugene, Oregon School District 4J. Also available for students elsewhere. cybersch@oregon.uoregon.edu; 1277 University of Oregon, Eugene, OR 97403-1277; (541) 346-3537. http://CyberSchool.4j.lane.edu/Registration

Dennison On-Line Internet School www.dennisononline.com; dennison@mail.com (P.O. Box 29781, Los Angeles, CA 90029).

Electronic High School, The Traditional high school curriculum on the Internet. One purpose of the school is "to grant credit to home-school students or others who are unable or unwilling to attend the local high school." Jolene M. Morris morris@tech.grand.k12.ut.us, Technology Director, Grand County School District, 264 South 400 East, Moab, Utah 84532. (1997 information but not reconfirmed)

Outreach and Technical Assistance Network (OTAN) A GED preparation program using audio and visual Internet communication and cable. From Sacramento's San Juan school district. www.sanjuan.edu/studioe3

Willoway School, The, http://204.186.19.24/Willoway. jbhale@postoffice.ptd.net; (610) 678-0214 A Private Video-conferencing CyberSchool 267 Mountaintop Road, Reinholds, PA 17569; Offering programs for grades 5 to 12. Tracks with empahsis in literature, math, or science. Tuition up to $2500.

C
Other Organizations Serving Home Schools

This appendix is divided into the following sections:
*(**1**) National general organizations,*
*(**2**) National legal organizations,*
*(**3**) Support for special category parents,*
*(**4**) Organizations involving children with learning or physical challenges. And*
*(**5**) Other organizations.*

Part 1, US National Organizations Promoting Home Education

The American Homeschool Association, A networking and services organization for home schooling families, sponsored by the publishers of *Home Education Magazine* and by generous donations. Its purpose is "to advocate and promote home education, and to support those providing materials, programs, and services for home schooling families."

The association's monthly Internet publication, AHA Online Newsletter is sent free upon request to anyone with an e-mail address. It contains news and information from home schooling individuals and families, and others interested in home schooling including writers, media reporters, authors, and school and government leaders.

The AHA website offers downloadable information files for all fifty states, featuring home schooling support groups and legal information. You will also find downloadable lists of home schooling websites, educational websites, e-mail networking lists and newsgroups for home schoolers, a resources file with information updated by the companies listed, and much more.

www.home-ed-press.com/AHA/aha.html; AHAonline@aol.com; P.O. Box 3142, Palmer, Alaska 99645; (907) 746-1323; fax: (907) 746-1335.

National Center for Home Education, P.O. Box 159, Paeonian Springs, VA 22129, (17333 Pickwick Dr., Purcellville, VA 22132); (540) 338-7600; Fax (540) 338-2733. Michael Farris, President/Director; Douglas Phillips, Director of Government Affairs. The Center was founded by the Home School Legal Defense Association to serve state leaders by disseminating pertinent government and legislative information related to home schooling information. HSLDA fully funds the Center as a subsidiary ministry. NCHE's services are available to any state organization upon request and without charge.

In addition to monitoring legislation on the state and federal levels, the Center works on special public relations projects involving home schoolers such as: clarifying the viability of this education choice to concerned officials, promoting proper understanding of methodology and standardized test scores, communicating with the media to avoid misunderstandings, and holding regional meetings for support group leaders.

National Homeschool Association P.O. Box 290, Hartland, MI 48353-0290; Voice mail (513) 772-9580. Contact: Susan Evans. NHA exists to advocate individual choice and freedom in education, to support those who choose to homeschool, and to inform the general public about home education. Membership is open to all. Servic[e]s and resources include: conferences (meeting and sharing), networking (referrals to support groups and individuals); and communication (keeping in touch and mailings). Sen[d] $4 for an information pack and $15 for family membershi[p].

NHA also publishes *The Homeschool Travel Directory*.Described in Appendix

---

Part 2, US Legal Assistance Organizations

Home School Legal Defense Association. For a yearly membership fee of $100, the association guarantee[s] legal defense and sends a bi-monthly magazine. HSLDA was established in 1983 for the sole purpose of defending the rights of parents to home school through state and federal courts and legislatures. Its attorneys have handle[d] over 10,000 legal conflicts, hundreds of cases, and dozens of legislative initiatives on behalf of home schoolers. For free information on HSLDA, a summary of your state law, and a how-to-home school packet, write or phone: HSLD[A] at P.O. Box 159, Paeonian Springs, VA 22129, (540) 338-560[0]

National Assn. for the Legal Support of Alt. Schools P.O. Box 2823, Santa Fe, NM 87504. I know little about this organization.

Rutherford Institute, P.O. Box 7482, Charlottesville, VA 22906, (804) 978-3888. tristaff@rutherford.org; www.rutherford.org. John W. Whitehead, President and founder. A nationwide legal defense organization providing educational and legal services for the protection of God-given liberties through national and international offices. This organization provides legal services and information without charge. It deals with various constitution[al] issues, including the right of parents to direct the educatio[n] of their children through private and home schools. (Legi[s]lation is also monitored by most state home schooling organizations.)

Part 3, Support or Networking for Special Categories of Parents

(General parent interest groups are listed by geographical area in Appendices D, E, and F.)

Adventist Home Educator See Appendix K.

Jewish Home Educator's Network Family Learning Exchange, P.O. Box 5629, Olympia, WA 98509-5629; Phone: (360) 438-1865; E-mail: FmlyLrngEx@aol.com (not confirmed)

Catholic Home School Network of America (CHSNA), P.O. Box 6343, River Forest, IL 60305-6343; (813) 931-1639 or fax ... -1033. Also see below. Katie Moran, President, (330) 652-4923 or fax -5322; moran@nlcomm.com. Ed Gudan VicePresident, (708) 386-4884 or ... -6330 or fax ... -3380; ekgtampa@juno.com. Ginny Seuffert, Secretary, (608)-592-5899 or ... -5799 or fax ... -5893; seuff815@aol.com Also see a different Catholic organization below.

Home schoolers of Colour Cheryl Edwards, 2850 Lakeshore Blvd. W. #80068, Etobicoke, Ontario M8V 4A1, Canada; (416) 374-0661 (voice mail); Cher@sympatico.ca. Newsletter

Latter Day Saints Home Educators Association, 2770 South 1000 West, Perry, UT 84302, (435) 723-5355. Joyce Kinmont. A support organization for members of the Church of Jesus Christ of Latter-Day Saints.

Mulsim Home School Network and Resource Contact person: Cynthia Sulaiman. Newsletter, Al-Madrasah Al-Ula, Meaning "the first school" which is the home and family. E-mail MHSNR@aol. com Also two web sites: http://www.ici.net/ cust_pages/taadah/taadah.html and http://www. islamicity.org/MHSNR/default.html. (They moved 12/97 and I don't have current address and phone.)

National Association of Catholic Home Educators, P.O. Box 787, Montrose, AL 36559; www.nache.com. Membership including subscription to the quarterly newsletter is $12. Contact information for members or nonmembers.

Our Father's House Products of interest to Catholic home schooling families. Free catalog. Julia Fogussy, 5530 So. Orcas St., Seattle, WA 98118. jfogassy@aol.com; (206) 725-9026.

Resource Center for Single Parents Offers help for guiding home learning whether as a supplement to classroom education or as home schooling. 866 W. 126th St., #7, Los Angeles, CA 90044, (213) 757-7128. vicki@afewgoodwomen.com; http://www.afewgoodwomen.com

---

Part 4, Organizations Involving Children With Physical or Learning Challenges

Also part of Appendix J describes books on this topic. And several chapters relate to learning problems.

Children and Adults With Attention Deficit Disorder, 499 NW 70th Ave., Suite 101, Plantation, FL 33317; (954) 587-3700.

Hadley School for the Blind Since 1920, this school has offered, without charge, home study courses to blind and visually impaired people. Now courses are available for parents of visually impaired children and family members of adults who are blind. Instructors communicate by phone or letter to supplement the materials. Write or call the school for more information. 700 Elm, Winnetka, IL 60093; (847) 446-8111.

Learning Disabilities Association of America, 4156 Library Rd., Pittsburgh, PA 15234, (888) 300-6700; LDAnatl@usaor.net;Our Web-site is www.ldanatl.org.

National Handicapped Homeschoolers Association NATHHAN, 5383 Alpine Rd., SE, Olalla, WA 98359; (253) 857-4257; nathanews@aol.com. National support group with coordinators in 40 states and Canadian provinces. If you explain your child's "challenge" when you write, they can put you in touch with other families and with information resources. Send for more information. Services include a family directory, lending library access, and HSLDA discount.

National Information Center for Children and Youth with Disabilities, (NICHCY), P. O. Box 1492, Washington, DC 20013-1492. Phone for voice or TT (202) 884-8200 or (800) 695-0285 or Fax (202) 884-8441. Nichcy@aed.org. NICHCY's publications are available through the Internet at: http://www.nichcy.org The organization provides information to assist parents, educators, care givers, advocates and others in helping children and youth with disabilities participate as fully as possible in school, at home, and in the community. A publications catalog is available upon request. The organization provides free information to assist parents, educators, care givers, advocates and others in helping children and youth with disabilities participate as fully as possible in school, at home, and in the community.

National Organization of Parents of Blind Children, 1800 Johnson St., Baltimore, MD 21230; (410) 659-9314 or Fax (410) 685-5653; On line: NFB NET (410) 752-5011. Mrs. Barbara Cheadle, President. A national group for support and information. Family membership, including magazine, $8. State or regional divisions in all parts of the US NOPBC is a division of the National Federation of the Blind.

Orton Dyslexia Society, The The society provides information and referrals for assistance for those interested in dyslexia. It is highly recommended. National office: 8600 La Salle Rd., Chester Bldg., 382, Baltimore, MD 21286-2044; (410) 296-0232; Messages, (800) ABCD123; e-mail info@ods.org; Web site: http://ods.org

Uniqueness, Twice-Gifted, Gifted Network, (UTGNET) M Bradley-Simard, 18252 Taylors Creek Road, Montpelier, VA 23192; (804) 883-6757; UniGift@aol.com A network for parents and home educators who are concerned about appropriate education and related services for students characterized by the terms, "Uniqueness" (Special Needs), "Twice-Gifted" (Crossover), and "Gifted." Networking, consultant contact information, and special resource channels. Support by regular mail and e-mail and Internet discussion groups. The organization does not advocate any particular materials or service providers.

Part 5, Other organizations of interest to home educators

Find religious organizations mostly in Appendix N

Alternative Education Resource Organization, 417 Roslyn Rd., Roslyn Hts., NY 11577; (516) 621-2195; JerryAERO@aol.com; http://www.speakeasy.org/~aero. Jerry Mintz. Alternative education network and information. "We promote alternative education nationally and internationally, by newsletter, videos, speaking and consulting." Their *Almanac of Educational Choices* listing over 6000 "unconventional" schools is available for $23 from AERO. "Alternative," by the way, includes more than home education and implies largely secular approaches. AERO also publishes a newsletter, *Aero-Gramme* for $15/yr. and hosts a radio show. See Appendix I

Association of Universities and Colleges of Canada, An organization similar to the National University Continuing Education Association. Described in the appendix for Canada.

Christian Homesteading Movement, Turner St., Oxford, NY 13830-E, Richard & Anna Marie Fahey. Homesteading means staying at home. Through seminars you learn how to live off the land, self-employed, using horses, and following a simple lifestyle. "What our courses do," writes Mr. Fahey, "is get parents out of the book knowledge and into reality to better comprehend the whole fabric of life and open the world up to their children."

Costlands Consultants For developing relationships between home school and Christian school communities in New England. Establishing home schooling programs for Christian schools. Christopher B. Anderson is available for consultation and seminars. 43 Western Ave., Rochester, NH 03867; (603) 332-3519; fax ... -9580; INLET@ttlc.net.

Distance Education and Training Council, Washington, D.C. (202) 234-5100. Accrediting agency and professional organization for home study schools. The schools they accredit teach trades like truck driving and building yachts. Also included are military schools, artist schools, some proprietary elementary, secondary and college schools, and many more. Ask for their list which is indexed by topic.

Solutions for Integrating Church and Home Education, P.O. Box 630, Lorton, VA 22199; (703) 455-5163; fax (703) 440-9798; solution77@aol.com. Eric Wallace Director.

Holt Associates, 2269 Massachusetts Ave., Cambridge, MA 02140. Since 1970. Patrick Farenga, President, (617) 864-3100. "Holt Associates is a national clearinghouse for information about home education, John Holt's work, and how people of all ages can learn outside of school. We believe children are good at learning and that learning is not separate from the rest of life. We are interested in how teaching and learning can best be supported outside of schools, and how adults can best respond to and nurture children's growth."

Homeschool Associates A service organization currently for the East, South, and part of the Midwest. Book sales, testing, diploma program, workshops, etc. See under Maine in Appendix D, as North Atlantic Regional Schools in A, and for book sales in Z.

Homeschoolers for Peace and Justice Pam Gingold edits a newsletter for those interested in the topic. Send her $3 and several SASEs to help with expenses. P.O. Box 74, Midpines, CA 95345; (209) 742-6802; gingold@sierratel.com

National Home Education Research Institute, Brian D. Ray, Ph.D., President. P.O. Box 13939, Salem, OR 97309; (503) 364-1490; fax ... -2827; mail@nheri.org; www.nheri.org. NHERI engages in basic research in home education and keeps track of the body of related research. It also provides consulting, testimony to legislatures and courts, and public speaking. Numerous publications available. See research reported through this institution which I refer to in Chapter 2. Ray's work of keeping track of research is important in our defense of freedom to home teach. The publication, *Home School Researcher*, is described in Appendix L

National Independent Study Accreditation Council 10489 Sunland Blvd., P.O. Box 4070, Sunland, CA 91040; (818)951-9652 (800) 525-4419; Fax (818) 951-5963; aq483@lafn.org. NISAC offers accreditation for home school or independent study programs. The commission is not a rubber-stamp to help schools look good. They expect clear standards, integrity, and professional quality.

Testing and evaluation services: See under Appendix W.

D

Information by Region for the United States

In this appendix, we provide information about home schooling support and administrative organizations. We list most of the major ones along with a sampling of regional and local groups. State organizations are able to refer people to support groups in their area.

If your organization is not listed and is open to members or clients please send us information.

Also shown are other service organizations working in a specific state or states. Those with a larger scope of operation are listed in other appendices.

Information of this type changes frequently since local groups and even state groups are operated mainly by volunteers. We feel having it available offsets the risk of some expired addresses.

Information in this appendix is not intended to imply endorsement or legal advice.

Legal summary

For several reasons you need to know more than this list shows before starting a home school: Laws and regulations change, and many states have detailed requirements which are oversimplified in the summary shown here. Contact a state organization or an organization like The Home School Legal Defense Association for current information and advice. Based on HSLDA information as of January, 1998.

Key to abbreviations

HoSch Statutes or regulations specifically authorize home schools. In other states home schools operate under different rules.
PrSch Operation permitted under private school statutes
Rel Religious convictions specifically honored
Group Groups of home schoolers qualify as private or church schools
PQ Parent qualifications are specified (usually high school diploma or equivalent)
FA Filing annually with school authorities is required
TA Testing is required annually
TL Testing is required less often
AT Testing is required but an alternative is provided
LA Approval of local authorities is required
7-16 The age range for compulsory attendance at regular schools is shown as a pair of numbers.

Alabama PrSch, 7-16, Rel (Operation without teacher certification is permitted only under a church or as a church school.)
Alaska HoSch, Rel, 7-16
Arizona HoSch, 6-16
Arkansas PrSch, TL, 5-17
California PrSch, FA, 6-18
Colorado HoSch, Group, FA, AT, 7-16, Min. of 13th percentile required on tests.
Connecticut HoSch, AT, 7-16
Delaware HoSch, Group, 5-16
Distr. of Columbia Requirements suspended, 5-18
Florida HoSch, GROUP, AT, 6-16
Georgia HoSch, TL, FA, 7-16, PQ (Hi. S. diploma or GED)
Hawaii HoSch, FA, TL, 6-18
Idaho 7-16, No requirements. Home schools are classified as "otherwise comparably instructed."
Illinois PrSch, 7-16
Indiana PrSch, 7-16
Iowa HoSch, FA, AT, 6-16
Kansas PrSch, 7-18
Kentucky PrSch, 6-16
Louisiana PrSch, AT, 7-17
Maine HoSch, Group, FA, AT, LA, 7-17
Maryland HoSch, Rel, 5-15
Massachusetts AT, LA, 6-16
Michigan HoSch, 6-16
Minnesota HoSch, FA, TA, 7-16, Min. of 30th percentile required on tests.
Mississippi HoSch, FA, 6-17
Missouri HoSch, FA, 7-16
Montana HoSch, FA, 7-16
Nebraska PrSch, Rel, 7-16
Nevada HoSch, 7-17
New Hampshire HoSch, AT, 6-16
New Jersey 6-16, No requirements. Home schools qualify as "Equivalent instruction elsewhere than at school"
New Mexico HoSch, FA, TL, 5-18, PQ (Hi.S. dipl. or GED)
New York HoSch, FA, TL, 6-16
North Carolina HoSch, FA, TA, 7-16, PQ (H.S. dipl. or GED)
North Dakota HoSch, FA, TL, 7-16, PQ: Passage of "teacher's test" or college degree
Ohio HoSch, AT, 6-18, PQ (Hi.S. dipl. or GED)
Oklahoma 5-18, State constitutional provision allows home schools as "other than school."
Oregon HoSch, FA, TA, 7-18, 15th percentile required on tests
Pennsylvania HoSch, Rel, FA, TL, 8-17, PQ (Hi.S. dip. or GED)
Rhode Island HoSch, LA, 6-16
South Carolina HoSch, AT, 5-17, PQ (Hi.S. dip. or GED)
South Dakota TL, 6-16, Home schools are classified as "alternative instruction."
Tennessee HoSch, Rel, FA, TL, 6-17, Testing in gr. 2, 3, 6, 8, and 10, PQ: H.S. Diploma or GED
Texas PrSch, 6-18
Utah HoSch, GROUP, FA, LA, 6-18
Vermont HoSch, Rel, FA, AT, 7-16
Virginia HoSch, Rel, Group, FA, AT, 5-18, 23rd percentile required on tests
Washington HoSch, FA, AT, 8-18
West Virginia HoSch, FA, AT, 6-16, 40th percentile required on tests, PQ (Stay four years ahead of student)
Wisconsin HoSch, FA, 6-18
Wyoming HoSch, 7-16

ALABAMA

Statewide organization

Christian Home Education Fellowship of Alabama, P.O. Box 563, Alabaster, AL 35007; (205) 664-2232; Fax (205) 663-0287; http://www.alchef.org/. Members are directed to church schools throughout the state to meet state enrollment requirements. Information packet available.

Some of the organizations which follow also cover the whole state.

Area organizations which cover and/or support home education

Some groups are for people with specific religious beliefs. (Contact the state organization for other groups.)

Whole state Maranatha Christian Academy, 207 Pleasant Hill Rd., Ashland, AL 36251; (205) 354-5281 or ... 7842. Alabama as well as Mississippi and Georgia.

Whole state The Way Home Christian School, 2461 Lawrence Cove Rd., Eva, AL 35621; (205) 482-2801. A parent must sign a statement of cooperation including a profession of faith in the Jesus Christ as Savior and Lord. Administrators Stuart and Martha Whitney. Area coordinators are in key cities. For a local contact person or for further information, call the main office. *The way of the cross leads home.*

Alabaster HOPE Christian School, P.O. Box 563, Alabaster, AL 35007; (205) 664-2232; Fax 663-0287. Wayne and Connie Atchison, Administrators. Help offered for curriculum choices, common pitfalls, making learning aids, creation vs. evolution, unit studies, research papers, apprenticeships. Workshops may be arranged.

Anniston Vineyard Christian Academy, P.O. Box 4095 (3511 Old Alexandria Rd.), Anniston, AL 36204; (205) 238-6289.

Birmingham Heritage Academy, Reformed Heritage Presbyterian Church, 1401 Montgomery Hwy., Birmingham, AL 35216; (205) 979-9912.

DeKalb county and nearby areas Grace Presbyterian Church School, P.O. Box 681086, Fort Payne, AL 35968-1086; (205) 845-4756

Dothan Grace Bible Church Academy, Linda Cannavan, 344 Westgate Parkway, Dothan, AL 36303; (334)794-8813 or 2337; fax ... -4770.

Etowah County Grace Bible Church School, Debbie Hansen, 1229 Appalachian Rd., Gadsden, AL 35902; (205) 547-2050.

Florence Faith Tabernacle Academy, 3601 Florence Blvd., Florence, AL 35634; (205) 767-4382; faith@hiway.net.

Jefferson and Shelby counties Woodland West Christian School, P O Box 236, Adamsville, AL 35005; (205) 674-8673. Attendance at any church required,; doctrinal statement.

Leeds Ashville Road Family Christian School, 1260 Ashville Rd. NE, Leeds, AL 35094; (205) 338-1843; MTM528@aol.com; contact Mark & Teah McWhorter.

North North Alabama Christian School, P.O. Box 3328, Huntsville, AL 35810; (205) 852-2956 or res. 776-9976. For Church of Christ members.

Tuscaloosa Abundant Life School, 3423 19th St., Tuscaloosa, AL 35401; (205) 752-6082; fax ... -6082. Serving all Christians within 100 miles.

Tuscaloosa Vision Christian Academy, Joy Allison, P.O. Box 1071, Tuscaloosa, AL 35403; (205) 339-6073.

Winston County. Fellowship Christian School, Christ's Fellowship Assembly of God, P.O. Box 583, Double Springs, AL 35553; (205) 486-4372; zildjian12@juno.com

Materials sales (Also see Appendix Z.)

Chula Vista Books, 420 Chula Vista Mt. Rd., Pell City, AL 35125; (205) 338-1843. E-mail MTM528@aol.com. A variety of materials are available through the local store, by phone, and by mail.

Government office (if more information is needed after contacting home schooling organizations): Coordinator-accreditations, Gordon Persous Bldg., 50 Ripley, Montgomery, AL 36130-3901. (205) 242-8165.

ALASKA

Organizations

Alaska Private and Home Educators Association (APHEA), P.O. Box 141764, Anchorage, AK 99514, (907) 696-0641; http://www.aphea.org. Contact APHEA for support group information.

Government office (after contacting APHE)

State office information: Education Administrator, Centralized Correspondence Study, Department of Education, P.O. Box GA, Juneau, AK 99811-0544. (907) 465-2835.

ARIZONA

Statewide organization

Arizona Families for Home Education, P.O. Box 4661, Scottsdale, AZ 85261-4661; (602) 443-0612; http://www.primenet.com/~afhe. Publisher of *The Arizona Home Education Journal* and assisting with statewide and regional issues. Information is provided for making the home schooling decision. State convention.

Area groups (Contact AFHE for others.)

Apache Junction Unschoolers, P.O. Box 6341, Apache Junction, AZ 85278; http://members.aol.com/ajunschl; ajunschl@aol.com

Hualapai Hills Home-Schoolers, (no current information) Kingman, AZ

SPICE, organization of home educators, 10414 W. Mulberry Dr., Avondale, AZ 85323; Most members are in the Phoenix area. (602) 877-3642. Host to a special interest group on Freenet. E-mail azhome@aztec.asu .edu

Telao Home Educators; 4700 N. Tonalea Trl., Tucson, AZ 85749; (502) 749-4557.

Sales organization

The Salt Seller Resource Catalog P.O. Box 56701, Phoenix,

AZ 85079-6701; (602) 249-2699, Fax (602) 249-6151, SaltSeller@aol.com A resource catalog for home educators to buy and sell their used materials, find business services. You will also find area home schooling information and ideas. SS also hosts the Arizona State Used Curriculum & Book Fair. Write your name, address and phone number on an index card and include $5.00 for a full year (6 issues) for The Salt Seller Resource Catalog.

Government office (if more information is needed after contacting AFHE): Kelly Powell, Research Unit, Arizona Department of Education, 1535 W. Jefferson St., Phoenix, AZ 80078. (602) 542-3759.

ARKANSAS

Statewide organizations

Arkansas Christian Home Education Association, P.O. Box 94025, North Little Rock AR 72190-94025; (501) 758-9099; info@achea.org; http://www.achea.org.

Coalition of Arkansas Parents (CAP), P.O. Box 192455, Little Rock, AR 72219; Phone: (501) 565-6583; Fax: (501) 565-5539; http://bucket.ualr.edu/~sort/cap.html; jtgreen@athena.ualr.edu

Local and regional

Northwest Arkansas Curriculum Fair, 114 S. Country Club Rd., Siloam Springs, AR 72761; (501) 524-4094

Newton County and area around Good Shepherd Home School Fellowship, George & Cindy Alexander, 7123 Little Rock-Decatur Rd., Little Rock, MS 39337; (601) 774-5429; Email: galexand@netdoor.com

Government contact

Information is available from your local district office. (Contact home school org. first). If you need help finding it, call the student assessment office (Yvette Dillingham) at the Department of Education. (501) 682-4252.

CALIFORNIA

Most California home schooling families choose to file a private school affidavit. This is a notification to the state. It is not an application for a license to operate.

Statewide Organizations

Christian Home Educators Association of California, P.O. Box 2009, Norwalk, 90651-2009. Information line (800) 564-2432. Office (562) 864-2432; cheaofca@aol.com; http://www.cheaofca.org. Philip Troutt, Executive Director. Membership, $35/yr ($25, renewal) includes a subscription to *The Parent Educator*. State and area conventions. Their book, *Introduction to Home Education*, includes information on filing the affidavit for California and costs $30.53 (or $26.78 for members) with tax and shipping.

CHEA of CA also publishes a "learning Disabilities Resource Packet." $7.78 with tax and shipping.

California Homeschool Network, P.O. Box 44, Vineburg, CA 95487-0044, (800) 327-5339; CHNmail@aol.com; http://www.comenius.org/chn. CHN offers the *California Homeschool Information Packet* and other publications. *California News* is for individual and institutional members. Contact persons throughout the state direct people to suitable support groups. Seminars sponsored around the state.

The HomeSchool Association of California ⌂ honors the diversity of homeschoolers, ⌂ supports and promotes the entire spectrum of HomeSchooling, ⌂ provides information, ⌂ monitors and influences legislation, and ⌂ offers opportunities for families to get together. HSC also publishes the bimonthly *California Homeschooler*, holds annual conferences and other events, and works to promote the interests of homeschoolers in California. HSC welcomes anyone who has an interest in homeschooling. HSC, P.O. Box 2442, Atascadero., CA 93423, (888) HSC-4440 (toll free), info@hsc.org;http://www.hsc.org. The annual dues of $25 include subscription to their magazine.

Statewide special services

Family Protection Ministries Consultant Roy Hanson cooperates with other leaders in California in following legal developments that affect home education and he works for an environment of freedom for parents to decide, according to religious convictions, how their children will be educated. I recommend his newsletter, *Private - Home Educators of California, Legal - Legislative Update.* It is sent free to contributors ($30 or more), to various group leaders, and to pastors. He and his wife are working for you. They would appreciate your prayers and financial support. 910 Sunrise Ave., Suite A-1, Roseville, CA 95661.

The California Home-Education Conference, PO Box 231324, Sacramento, CA 95823; Barbara David, 916-391-4942; CHEC95@aol.com; http://www.chec95.com. An annual, secular event for both Northern and Southern California.

Home School Legal Defense Fund Legal defense for California parents who home school through a private school independent study program ($25/yr.) Participating schools receive administrative counsel for operating their ISP. Ask California Home Educators, 10489 Sunland Blvd., P.O. Box 4070, Sunland, CA 91040; (818)951-9652 (800) 525-4419; Fax (818) 951-5963; aq483@lafn.org. This organization is separate from HSLDA listed in Appendix C.

The Learning Tree See under Regional Groups (following) at "Newcastle."

Pilgrims School, P.O. Box 820, Springville, CA 93265; Pilgrims@BoldChristianLiving.com; http://www.BoldChristianLiving.com. Available primarily for those in the vicinity of the Southern San Joaquin Valley. Jonathan Lindvall, Superintendent. (209) 539-0500. Distinctives are: 1} prioritizing instruction according to 2 Peter 1:5-8; 2} encouraging leadership of fathers; and 3} emphasizing discipleship rather than schooling (this includes at least delaying formal academic pressure until children are more mature). Jonathan Lindvall has contributed a chapter for this book. Also see Bold Parenting in Appendix N.

Plantation Christian School Distance education no longer limited to California. See Appendix A.

Sunland Christian School home school program Enrollment, curriculum counseling, administration, accountability, record keeping, testing, and special programs. Now serving over 500 students through 17 satellite locations in Southern California. 10489 Sunland Blvd., P.O. Box 4070, Sunland, CA 91040; (818) 951-9652 (800) 525-4419; Fax (818) 951-5963; aq483@lafn.org.

Regional groups and services (Contact a state organization for other groups.)

Antelope Valley Rose Rock Homeschool Support Group of the Antelope Valley, 1752 East Avenue J, Suite 115, Lancaster, CA 93535; roserock@geocities.com, ww.geocities.com/Athens/Parthenon/8503/

Bakersfield See Kern County.

Berkeley East Bay Family Educators, 1090 Mariposa Ave., Berkeley, CA 94707; (510) 524-1224

Boulder Creek, South St. Centre, P.O. Box 227, Boulder Creek, CA 95006, (408) 338-2540; southst@cruzio.com. Betsy Herbert, Director. "is to provide a form of education which recognizes and honors all stages of children's growth, and honors and supports parents in their roles as caregivers and teachers. It's existence gives a means for families to move from home-centered learning to commnity-connected education. We offer educational counseling, programs and activities for families, and host conferences for homeschooling educators. Some of our services are contracted by the local school district's charter school.."

Butte County Butte Homeschool Network; Christina Dyer,1375 Brill Road, Paradise, CA 95969; (530) 877-3543; CedarMt@aol.com

Escondido Boston, John A., Homeschool Consultant P.O. Box 92, Escondido, CA 92033, (760) 479-1522. Mr. Boston is dedicated to assisting families using the unschooling model promoted by the late John Holt.

Humboldt Humboldt Homeschoolers Paige Smith, 688 S. Westhaven Dr., Trinidad, CA 95570; (707) 677-3290. Support group open to all who are interested in home education. E-mail PSmith@Humboldtl.com (Note that the last character, the one after "Humboldt," is the numeral, 1.)

Kern County Christian Home Educators of the County of Kern (CHECK). P.O. Box 42101, Bakersfield, CA 93384; (805) 765-7500; Sandra Cruz; Information and inspiration for all home schooling families; quarterly meetings, park days, etc.

Antelope Valley and elsewhere Rose Rock Homeschool Support Group, 1752 E Ave J, Suite 115, Lancaster, CA 93535, e-mail: roserock@geocities.com; http://www.geocities.com/Athens/Parthenon/8503/

Santa Barbara County Lompoc Valley Home Educators, Contact Christine Tykeson, 3343 Via Dona, Lompoc, CA 93436; (805) 733-2710.

San Fernando Valley Rose Rock groups. See under Antelope Valley.

Los Angeles See Keys to Learning Institute in Appendix A. There are also many support groups in the area.

Los Angeles Weekly Radio Broadcast, *Educating Our Children.* Saturdays at 10:30 a.m. on KGSG, 96.3 fm.

Los Angeles South Bay area See Rose Rock under Antelope Valley.

Marin County So. Marin Homeschoolers, 905 Tiburon Blvd., Tiburon, CA 94920, (415) 435-0768.

Modesto Valley Home Educators, PO Box 4016, Modesto CA 95352-4016; (209) 527-5471; vheleisa@aol.com.

Riverside Riverside Area Home Learners, 731 Mt. Whitney Cir, Corona, CA 91719; Charlie Miles-Prystowsky, (909) 279-4026.

Sacramento, Sacramento Council of Parent Educators (SCOPE) P.O. Box 163178, Sacramento, CA 95816. Rocky Livoni, Chairman. Phone and fax (916) 646-0401. A Christian support group. $16/yr. Monthly newsletter, group activities. Write or call for information.

Sacramento Valley Spice Homeschool Group. Variety of philosophies, P.O. Box 282, Wilton, CA 95693; (916) 687-7053. spice-sacramento@juno.com

San Francisco Homeschoolers, 3639 Webster St., San Francisco, CA 94123; Francesca Pera, (415) 673-8092. Address and phone will change in spring, 1998

San Joaquin Valley, South end. See Pilgrims School above.

San Luis Obispo County, Central California Homeschoolers. Contact Barbara Alward, 7600 Marchant Ave., Atascadero, CA 93422; (805) 462-0726.

San Luis Obispo Family Learning Cooperative. Contact person is also Barbara Alward (above); balward@aol.com.

Santa Clara County South Valley Homeschool Association. Cynthia Walker, 7233 Hanna St., Gilroy, CA 95020 or Mary Drummond, 7500 Chestnut St., Gilroy. Support group, newsletter, field trips open to all who are interested in home schooling.

Silicon Valley See Santa Clara County.

Sonoma County Sonoma County Homeschool Assn. 7851 Brookside Ave., Sebastopol, CA 95472. Everyone welcome. Contact (707) 874-2740. wrensong@monitor.net

San Fernando Valley Contact for information. The Bradbury Academy (a home school), P.O. Box 922191, Sylmar, CA 91392-2191, (818) 513-0831; tootoo@ix.netcom.com; vancamp1@juno.com

Yosemite Area Homeschoolers, Pam Gingold, P.O. Box 74, Midpines, CA 95345; gingold@sierratel.com; (209) 742-6802.

Victorville High Desert Homeschoolers, Karen Taylor , (760) 956-1588; taylors@mscomm.com; general homeschoolers/unschoolers in Victorville, Apple Valley, Hesperia & Lucerne Valley

Government office (if more information is needed after contacting home schooling organizations): Carolyn Pirillo, Deputy General Counsel, California Department of Education, P.O. Box 944272, Sacramento, CA 94244-2720. (916) 657-2453.

COLORADO

Statewide leadership and service organizations

Christian Home Educators of Colorado, 3739 E. 4th Ave., Denver, CO 80206; (303) 388-1888; http://www.chec.org

Colorado Home Education Association, 2687 S. Pagosa St., Aurora, CO 80013. Voice mail (303) 441-9938. Purposes:

(1) to promote and encourage local support groups, (2) promote quality education, and (3) promote public acceptance. Phone tree, newsletter, legislative watching, referrals to local groups.

Concerned Parents of Colorado, an information and legislative network. Treon Goossen, P.O. Box 547, Florissant, CO 80816-0547. Voice and fax line (719) 748-8360. E-mail Treonelain@aol.com.

Homeschool Support Network. One of three offices is in Colorado., P.O. Box 441646, Aurora, CO 80044; (303) 680-6316; Jill Renee Jones. Questions answered. Information pack available

Rocky Mountain Education Connection, an information and resource network for all Colorado homeschoolers. Diverse educational and religious viewpoints are welcomed. Bimonthly newsletter, beginner's workshops, phone support and low-cost information packet available. Contact RMEC at 20774 E. Buchanan Drive, Aurora, CO 80011; (303) 341-2242, or e-mail: connect@pcisys.net.

Local groups and services (Contact CHEC or CHEA for others.)

Boulder County Boulder County Home Educators, Lynn Householder, (303) 494-9543.

Colorado Springs Home School Book & Bible Store, 4742 Barnes Rd., Colorado Springs, CO 80917; (719) 574-4222.

Colorado Springs The Colorado Springs Homeschool Support Group, P.O. Box 26117, Colorado Springs, CO 80936; http://hschool.com; board@hschool.com (719) 598-2636; Information (800) 532-7011. Membership $15/yr.

Colorado Springs Secular Homeschool Support Group, 2407 Marlborough Place, Colorado Springs, CO 80909; (719) 634-4098; mkantor@iex.net. For those who prefer to keep their religious and political beliefs separate from their interest in academic excellence.

Estes Park Christian Home Educators, 6792 Hwy. 36, Estes Park, CO 80517; (970) 577-0182; slweber@juno.com

Four Corners Mesa Verde Homeschoolers, Deirere and Joe MacLaren, P.O. Box 134, Mancos, CO 81328; (970) 882-7802.

Loveland Agape Family Schools, P.O. Box 2704, Loveland, CO 80539. AFS is a forthright Christian organization providing support and activities. Monthly meetings; newsletter. Ask CHEC for current phone contact.

Northern Colorado Homeschoolers Corner, A local resource for homeschoolers in the Longmont/Northern Colorado area. Includes calendar, forum, and email directory. Contact: webmaster@longmont.com; PO Box 494, Longmont CO 80502-0494.

Southeast Colorado Barb Burson, (719) 324-5815, P.O. Box 553, Walsh, CO 81090; sonburst@ria.com The group also serves nearby Southwestern Kansas.

Delta County Christian Home Educators of the North Fork. Lynn Johnson, 4066 N. 80 Lane, Paonia, CO 81428; (970) 527-6183; bumper@fgn.net.

Eastern Plaines Prairie HOME (Homes of Meaningful Education), Box 309, Byers, CO 80103. Jackie McCauley (303) 822-5251 and co-leader Jeannie Diedrich at ... -5680.

Denver Colorado Home Schooling Network, Laurie McKay, 12651 E. Bates Cir., Aurora, CO 80014. A secular group.

Northeast Colorado Plains Home Educators, Contact Alice Skold, 70CR21, Haxtun, CO 80731; (970) 774-7542; hawskold@sosinc.net. Also serving nearby Western Nebraska.

Pueblo and SE Colorado Pueblo Home School Association, Betty McMurrey, (719) 544-6610; 2204 W 17, Pueblo, CO 81003; bmcmurrey@aol.com

Government office (after contacting home schooling organizations)

Suzie Parker, Program Assistant I, Colorado Dept. of Education, 201 E. Colfax Ave. Denver CO 80203-1799; (303) 866-6678 voice, (303) 866-6974 fax.

CONNECTICUT

Statewide organizations

Connecticut Home Educators Association, 80 Coopermine Rd., Oxford, CT 06478; (203) 781-8569; needels@home.com; http://www.connix.com/~dschroth/chea/; http://pages.prodigy.com/ct_homeschool/chea.htm. A general-interest, decentralized group open to everyone; publisher of the biomonthly newsletter, *HearthNotes*.

The Education Association of Christian Homeschoolers (TEACH), 25 Field Stone Run, Farmington, CT 06032; From within Conn. (800) 205-7844 or (860) 677-4538; fax (860) 677-4677.

Other organizations

CT's Citizens to Uphold the Right to Educate (CD's CURE), P.O. Box 597, Sherman, CT 06784; Alison Brion, (203) 355-4824; Debi Stevenson-Mincheener, 226 E. Flag Swamp Rd., Southbury, CT 06488-1122; (203) 354-3590.

Unschoolers Support, 22 Wildrose Ave., Guilford, CT 06437; Contact Luz Shosie, (203) 458-7402; guiluniv@ctl.nai.net. For CT and Southern England.

Also see Homeschool Associates, an organization offering many services including a newspaper, listed in Appendix C.

Contact a state organization for support groups.

Government office (In case you have further questions)

Contact the office of: Sheila K. Brown, Consultant, State Department of Education, P.O. Box 2219, Hartford, CT 06145, (203) 566-8263.

DELAWARE

Statewide organization

Delaware Home Education Association, 1712 Marsh Rd., #172, Wilmington, DE 19810-4611; Phone contacts for the DHEA: Newcastle county (302) 479-9611 or (302) 475-0574; Kent County (302) 492-0515; Sussex County (302) 945-1446. Legislative update line (302) 998-4559.

As I understand it, a family may either declare their home as a private school and operate under the supervision of the district superintendent or may enroll in an established private school such as one of the DHEA member schools.

DHEA member schools *(with varying philosophical, religious and lifestyle standards)*

Academy Adoni, Kathryn Stout, 408 Victoria Ave., Wilmington, DE 19804–2124; (302) 998–3889.

Acorn Christian Academy, Donald Jones, P.O. Box 458, Milford, DE 19963; (302) 422–6978.

Community Learning Institute, Inc., Bill Manning, 4639 Halltown Rd., Hartly, DE 19953; (302) 492–8224.

Family Learning Academies, Inc., Contact Lori Thrash, P.O. Box 279, Kenton, DE 19955; (302) 492–0515.

Immaculata School, Teresa Suarez, 6 Michael Ct., Dover, DE 19904; (302) 734–2678.

King's Kids Academy, Contact Vince Bianco; P.O. Box 100, Georgetown, DE 19947–0100; (302) 945–1446.

Old Capitol Trail Academy, Inc., Kay Hampson, P.O. Box 7709, Newark, DE 19714–7709; (302) 998–4559.

Southern Sussex Learning Academy, Chris Frey, Director; R.D. 2, Box 4, Clarksville, DE 19970; (302) 537–2172.

Towle Institute, Corky Feldmann, P.O. Box 146; St. Georges, DE 19733; (302) 234–4442; towlesch@aol.com.

Area group

Tri-State Home School Network, P.O. Box 7193, Newark, DE 19714. (302) 234–0516. Many families in Castle County. Also includes families in nearby Pennsylvania, Maryland, and Jersey -- some 400 in all.

For support Florida information, find your county in this list and contact the FPEA district according to its number.

Alachua 3	Hamilton 3	Okeechobee 8
Baker 4	Hardee 7	Orange 6
Bay 1	Hendry 9	Osceola 6
Bradford 4	Hernando 5	Palm Beach 10
Brevard 8	Highlands 7	Pasco 5
Broward 11	Hillsborough 5	Pinellas 5
Calhoun 1	Holmes 1	Polk 6
Charlotte 7	Indian River 8	Putnam 4
Citrus 5	Jackson 1,	Santa Rosa 1
Clay 4	Jefferson 2	Sarasota 7
Collier 9	Lafayette 3	Seminole 6
Columbia 3	Lake 6	St. Johns 4
Dade 12	Lee 9	St. Lucie 8
De Soto 7	Leon2	Sumter 6
Dixie 3	Levy 3	Suwannee 3
Duval 4	Liberty 2	Taylor 2
Escambia 1	Madison 2	Union 4
Flagler 4	Manatee 7	Volusia 8
Franklin 2	Marion 3	Wakulla 2
Gadsden 2	Martin 10	Walton 1
Gilchrist 3	Monroe 12	Washington 1
Glades 9	Nassau 4	
Gulf 1,	Okaloosa 1	

Government office (For further questions):

Department of Public Instruction, The Townsend Bldg., P.O. Box 1402, Dover, DE 19903. (302) 739–4645.

DISTRICT OF COLUMBIA

LEARN. See under Virginia.

Metro Homeschool Organization. See under Maryland.

If you need further information after contacting an organization above, call the District department of education.

FLORIDA

Statewide organizations

Florida Parent-Educators Association, Inc. (FPEA) Membership $20/yr. The group keeps in contact with the Department of Education and is active in lobbying. For a sample newsletter send $1. Officers: Chairman: Gary Regoli (352) 873–1645 Vice Chairman: Marcy Krumbine Secretary: Jan Prentice Treasurer: Colleen Finley. See listing of regional contact persons.

Florida at Home, 4644 Adanson St., Orlando, FL 32804–2024. (407) 740–8877.

Florida Parent-Educators Association, information centers (and board of directors):

District 1 Bob Demme 417 Ronda St., Pensacola FL 32534; (850) 484–3027; e-mail contact through www.fpea.com

District 2 Glenn Powell,10622 FL-GA Highway, Havana, FL 32333; (850) 539–0754 mpbci@aol.com

District 3 Bill Freeman, P.O. Box 140671, Gainesville FL 32641–0671, Home: (352) 468–2785 Office: (352) 374–1531; fax (352) 468-1813; afn17391@afn.org

District 4 Lori Fox, 1433 Parental Home Road, Jacksonville FL 32216; (904) 721–2376 fx.mail@juno.com

District 5 Nina Duffield, 6419 Simons Rd., Zephyrhills FL 33541 (813) 782–5851 duff5851@mindspring.com

District 6 Guy Coburn, 2045 Houndslake Dr., Winter Park FL 32792; Information Line: (407) 263–8220; coburn@juno.com

District 7 Martha Krebeck, 3976 Pinstar Ter., North Port FL 34287; (941) 426–8164 krebeck_b@popmail.firn.edu

District 8 Muffy Amico, 1511 53rd Ave., Vero Beach FL 32966 (561) 562–4300, muffya@hotmail.com

District 9 Marcy Krumbine, Vice Chairman, 170 12th St. NE, Naples FL 34120; (941) 455–9584; fax ... –9584; mkrumbine@juno.com

District 10 Beth Kramer, 104 NW 7 Street, Boynton Beach FL 33426; (561) 737–4807; kracln7@bellsouth.net

District 11 Renee Mason, Director, 1137 SW 5 Place, Ft Lauderdale, FL 33312; (954) 463–5983; Riverview10@juno.com

District 12 Jan Prentice, Secretary, 10335 NW 5th Ave. Miami FL 33150 (305) 756–8198; fax (305) 758–9750;

d043048c@dc.seflin.org

A few specific groups (Contact the appropriate FPEA district officer or Florida at Home for others)

Bay County, Christian Home Educators of, 6836 Davis Rd., Panama City, FL 32404. (904) 763-6640. bsdavis2@juno.com. Ron & Barbara Davis. This group subscribes to fundamental biblical ideas. They provide seminars, fellowship, educational enrichment like art shows and field trips, representations at the county fair and at the mall, etc. Send $5 for an information packet.

Key West, Christian Home Educators of the Lower Keys, Leader, Nancy Hillman, H31 Miriam St., Key West, FL 33040; (405) 294-8815. Contact person, Kathy Carter; 20A 7th Ave. (305) 294-7976, Fax (305) 295-0712; httcarter@aol.com.

Escambia and Santa Rosa Counties The West Florida Home Education Support League, P.O. Box 11720, Pensacola, FL 32524; Hotline (850) 995-9444. http://www.wfhesl.org. Meetings second Tuesday of each month at Marcus Pointe Baptist Church on W Street at 7 p.m. Cell groups meet in local communities. Convention in June.

Titusville, The Family Learning Exchange, 2020 Turpentine Rd., Mims, FL 32754; (407) 268-8833. Nonsectarian.

Services

American Academy, in Miami. They help parents in Florida meet state requirements. The also serve students across the US. See Appendix B.

Circle Christian School, 4644 Adanson St., Orlando, FL 32804. Circle offers families the accountability and structure of enrollment in a private school, while insuring parents of a home schooling format. It is an independent, nondenominational Christian ministry.

Heritage Christian School, 13241 Commerce Lakes Dr., Ft. Myers, FL 33913. (941) 561-2555. A 617 private school for home educators. Connected with Gateway Baptist Church.

Kathleen Sprafka, Curriculum Services, Consultation for grades K-12. Member NCACS and FPEA. Since 1982. 26801 Pine Ave., Bonita Springs FL 34135; (941) 992-6381; fax ... 6473; hscurric@peganet.com. Service statewide and national.

The Wise Owl, materials store for the Daytona Beach area. 5622 Ridgewood Ave., Port Orange, FL 32127; (904) 756-3371; fax. 767-3015. A second store is at 5243 Nova Rd., Port Orange, FL 32127.

Government office (Contact a state group first)

Program Specialist, Student Services, Florida Department of Education, 544 Florida Education, Center, Tallahassee, FL 32399.

GEORGIA

Statewide organizations

Georgia Home Education Association 245 Buckeye Lane, Fayetteville, GA 30214; (770) 461-3657; fax ... -9053; ghea@mindspring.com; http://www.ghea.org

Georgians for Freedom in Education - Georgia's Family Educators. "A nonprofit nonsectarian organization founded in 1983 to support parents desiring to educate their children at home." I have used their lists of goals and beliefs as an example at the end of Chapter 3. Send SASE for information. 209 Cobb St., Palmetto, GA 30277; (770) 463-1563.

Regional and local groups (Contact a state organization for other groups.)

Atlanta Alternative Education Network, 1586 Rainier Falls Drive, Atlanta, GA 30329; (404) 636-6348; azthom@aol.com Adrianne Thompson, contact person. Send name and address for complimentary newsletter. http://www.mindspring.com/~lei/aaen

Augusta area (60-mile radius) CSRA Home Education Association (no current information).

Douglas County Douglas County Home Educators, Douglasville GA (770) 949-3297.

Gwinnett County and surrounding counties. Gwinnett Christian Home Educators, Sandra Rush, Clinton Pl., Lawrenceville, GA 30043. About 325 families in Northeast Atlanta, Information packet, $2. For information and the Rush residence; (770) 963-0713; mathusee@juno.com.

Northeast Georgia Hall County Home Educators, 5315 Redwood Cir., Gainesville, GA 30506-5910. Contact person, Dawn White, (770) 718-9923; http://www.newstep.net/home_educators. For six northeast counties. A group of people who have chosen home education because of religious and academic beliefs. Open to everyone. Numerous activities provided for the children including fine arts events, a science and history fair, public speaking opportunities, physical education and sports. For the parents: meetings, Mom's night out, an annual curriculum fair and picnics.

Oakwood Free to Learn at Home, 4439 Lake Forest Dr., Oakwood, GA 30566; Contact Chris Bishop, (770) 536-8077.

Service organizations

The Homeschool Advantage, 311 S. 12th St, Griffin, GA 30224; (770) 228-9063. Seminars, bookstore, book fairs, radio programs, consulting, group activities.

Mary Hood materials supplier, P.O. Box 2524, Cartersville, GA 30120. Mary is author of *The Relaxed Home School*.

Government office

(if more information is needed after contacting home schooling organizations): Georgia Department of Education, 1662 Twin Towers E., Atlanta, GA 30334. (404) 656-2446.

HAWAII

Statewide organization

Christian Homeschoolers of Hawaii, 91-824 Oama St., Ewa Beach, HI 96706. (808) 689-6398.

Area organization (Contact the state organization for other groups.)

Hawaii Island Christian Home Educators, 1765 Wailuku Dr., Hilo, HI 96720; Open to all interested persons; newsletter; resource library. Information packet.

IDAHO

Organizations

Home Educators of Idaho, 3618 Pine Hill Dr., Coeur dAlene ID 83814; (208) 667-2778

Families of Idaho Schooling in Christian Homes (FISCH). 13191 N. Smith Rd., Chubbuck, ID 83202; fisch@ida.net

Lewiston Also Clarkston, Washington: Port Cities Home Educators. 24 Hr. Activities Hotline, Newsletter, field trips, activities, crafts, sports, graduation ceremony . . . Gary & Pat Greenfield; Directors, 1880 Old Spiral Highway, Lewiston, Idaho 83501. (208) 746-0874; HomeGreen@aol.com; http://www.hibek.net/~pche

Moscow Palouse Homelearning Alternatives, 802 White Ave., Moscow, ID 83843. For the university cities of Moscow, ID {Ph. 208 882 1593} and Pullman, WA Nonsectarian.

North Idaho North Idaho Home Education Association, P.O. Box 2885, Hayden Lake, ID 83835.

Pocatello Pocatello Regional Christian Home Educators (PRCHE), 13191 N. Smith Rd., Chubbuck, ID 83202; prche@ida.net. (208) 237-8163.

Twin Falls Magic Valley Home Educators, 2392 Grandview Dr. N., Twin Falls, ID 83301; (208) 733-8378; Contact Jody Hollander; jody@magiclink.com; http://www.diademdesign.com/mvhe.

Family Learning Organization. See listing under Washington.

ILLINOIS

Statewide organizations

Christian Home Educators Coalition, P.O. Box 470322, Chicago IL 60647. (773) 278-0673; ilchec@aol.com.

Illinois Christian Home Educators, Box 261, Zion, IL 60099; (847) 670-7150. che83@juno.com

Regional (Contact state organizations for other groups.)

Burbank and nearby coummunities Seminars and general information. Contact Robin Morrison. (708) 598-8740 or sdaken@aol.com.

Peoria area Association of Peoria Area Christian Home Educators (APACHE), P.O. Box 5203, Peoria, IL 61601-5203; (309) 589-1307; PeoHmEdu@aol.com.

Service organization

Christian Liberty Academy. See Appendix A.

Government office (after contacting home schooling organizations)

Robin Cona, Legal Department Illinois State Board of Education, 100 N. First St., Springfield, IL 62777, (217) 782-5270. The state office suggests that parents who wish to register a home school contact the regional superintendent for their county to obtain the necessary information.

INDIANA

Statewide organization

Indiana Association of Home Educators, 850 N. Madison Ave., Greenwood, IN 46142; (317) 859-1202; iahe@inhomeducators.org Free newsletter, *The IAHE Informer*. Handbook available, *Home Education in Indiana*.

Regional organizations (One of these groups or the state organization can direct you to other groups.)

Fort Wayne Fort Wayne Area Home Schools, P.O. Box 12954, Fort Wayne, IN 46866-2954; (219) 483-2807.

Indianapolis Families Learning Together, 1714 E 51st St, Indianapolis, IN 46205; Jill , (317) 255-9298; whelan.mullen@juno.com

Lake County Lake County Christian Home Educators Association. Contact Dwayla Lamb, 3122 Wirth Rd., Highland, IN 46322. DwaylaL@aol.com. (219) 923-5660.

Merrillville Lake County Christian Home Educators Assn.

Michiana Christian Home Educators (information not currently available)

North central Michiana Christian Home Educators, Inc., Representing several groups and including the south edge of Michigan. No current information.

South Bend Group formerly called Konos "Cooperative Schools," Michiana Area. Contact person, Lillian Baker, (219) 271-0099.

South Bend Konos curriculum representative, Deb Barrows, 51618 N. Myrtle Ave., South Bend, IN 46637. (219) 271-8031.

Wabash Valley Wabash Valley Homeschool Association, P.O. Box 3865, Terre Haute, IN 47803; (812) 232-2931. E-mail wvha@aol.com

Government office (Contact a home schooling organization first)

State officer responsible for home schools: Indiana Department of Education, Room 229, State House, Indianapolis, IN 46204-2798. (317) 232-6614. An information brochure with the pertinent laws is available.

IOWA

Statewide organizations

Network of Iowa Christian Home Educators, Box 158, Dexter, IA 50070; NICHE@netins.net; http://www.netins.net/showcase/niche/ (800) 723-0438 (for Iowa outside Des Moines), or (515) 830-1614. Members receive the NICHE newsletter, inserts in *The Teaching Home*, help in forming groups, sponsored events, referrals for families, information packet, etc.

Secular support contact

Rebecca Leach, 2301 S. Henry St., Sioux City, IA 51106; (712) 274-0472. Beckyleach@aol.com or Beckyleach@mcleodusa.net. Contact her for general information from a secular standpoint. I'm sure she would appreciate an SASE if you write.

Government office (contact a home schooling organization first):

Consultant: Jim Tyson Consultant, Bureau of Administration, Instruction and School Improvement, Grimes State Office Building, Des Moines, IA 50319•0146. 515-281-5001. FAX 515-281-7700. e-mail jtyson@max.state.ia.us

KANSAS

Statewide organizations

Christian Home Educators Confederation of Kansas (CHECK), (316) 945-0810; fax: (316) 685-1617; 103472.447@compuserve.com; monthly newsletter, $12/year; representing approximately four dozen local support groups; annual conventions in Wichita & Kansas City.

Teaching Parents Association, P.O. Box 3968, Wichita, KS 67201, (316) 945-0810; Fax (316) 685-1617. 103472.447@CompuServe.com Jim Farthing, President. TPA is an organization of primarily evangelical Christians, but home schoolers of all backgrounds are welcomed and assisted. TPA serves as a member of CHECK. Most support groups belong to both.

Area groups with TPA

Abilene, Heartland Home Educators, Ken & Selena Book, 1019 2000 Ave., Abilene, KS 67410, (785) 263-7545.

Altamont, Education for Qualification, Inspiration & Preparation (EQUIP), Jeffrey & Debbie Phelps, P.O. Box 56, Altamont, KS 67330, (316) 784-5433

Anthony/Harper, Harper County Area Family Educators, Jack & Janice Gates, 404 N. West Ave., Anthony, KS 67003, (316) 842-3530.

Arkansas City, Private Ark City Educators, Shelly Meek, Rt. 3, Box 340, Arkansas City, KS 67005, (316) 441-0666

Atchison, Atchison County Home Educators, Dale & Benita Royer, 1102 Laramie, Atchison, KS 66002, (913) 367-1554.

Benton, Home Educators and Really Terrific Students (H.E.A.R.T.S.), Donna Mulford, 11385 SW 50th, Towanda, KS 67144, (316) 778-1573.

Bird City, Family Association for Instructing Truth at Home, Dan & Pam Thomas, R.R. #2, Box 7, McDonald, KS 67745, (785) 538-2469.

Burlington/Westphalia, Free and Independent Teaching Homes (F.A.I.T.H.), Don & Pam Small, 816 Cumberland, Burlington, KS 66839; (316) 364-8027.

Cawker City, Northern Kansas Home Educators, Carol Cordel, R.R. #2, Box 47B, Cawker City, KS 67430, (785) 781-4939.

Colby, Christian Family Educators, Ken & Eileen Codner, P.O. Box 35, Gover, KS 67736, (785) 938-2204.

Cottonwood Falls, Families Enjoying Learning Together (F.E.L.T.), Charles & Wendi Jones, Rt. 1, Box 14, Cottonwood Falls, KS 66845, (316) 273-8214.

Dodge City, Parents Educating According to Christ's Example (P.E.A.C.E.), Jesse & Anita Carlson, P.O. Box 295, Fowler, KS 67844, (316) 646-5229.

El Dorado, El Dorado support group, Scott & Paula Stoskopf, P.O. Box 1402, El Dorado, KS 67042, (316) 321-6679.

Emporia, Flint Hills Educators, Curtis & Cheryl Repp, R.R. 1, Box 172, Neosho Rapids, KS 66864, (316) 342-9137.

Fairview/Hiawatha/Powhattan, Fairview and Surrounding Territories (F.A.S.T.), Sharilyn Pollock, Rt. 1, Powhattan, KS 66527, (785) 474-3320.

Fredonia/Toronto/Yates Center, Parent-teacher Association for Christian Kids (P.A.C.K.), Jane Henry, Rt. 1, Box 126C, Toronto, KS 66777, (316) 537-6911

Garden City, High Plains Home Educators, Jed & Shawn Purdy, R.R. 1, Box 130, Deerfield, KS 67838, (316) 426-2291.

Goessel/Moundridge, Central Kansas Private Schools, Candy Snowbarger, 2318 Comanche Rd., Galva, KS 67443, (316) 345-2536.

Great Bend, Golden Belt Home Educators, Tim & Claudia Wyatt, R.R. 1, Box 62, Albert, KS 67511, (316) 923-4216.

Hanston, Christian Homeschool Fellowship, Darren & Shannon Korf, R.R. #1, Box 62, Hanston, KS 67849, (316) 623-4020.

Hays/LaCrosse, Post Rock Home Educators, Ken & Valerie Mills, R.R. #1, Box 73, McCracken, KS 67566, (785) 394-2390.

Hesston, Christ-Centered Teaching Homes, Mark & Debbie Gilmore, 4502 W. Harvest Lane, Hesston, KS 67062, (316) 327-2568.

Hill City, Solomon Valley Home Educators, Hubert Bowen, 309 W. McFarland, Hill City, KS 67642, (785) 421-6390.

Independence, Hope Support Group, Dian Graft, 1703 Overlook Dr., Independence, KS 67301, (316) 331-3510.

Iola/Allen County, SEK Support Group , Nathan & Kandace Rather, 1280 2400 St., Iola, KS 66749, (316) 496-2332.

Kansas City, Johnson County Parent Educators, Greg & Barb Akridge, 5211 Stearns, Shawnee, KS 66203, (913) 631-8282.

Lawrence, Teaching Effective Academics in Christian Homes (T.E.A.C.H.), David & Cathy Barfield, 3416 W. 9th Ct., Lawrence, KS 66049, (785) 843-9207.

Leavenworth, Christian Home Educators of Leavenworth, Steve & Teri Maxwell, 2416 S. 15th, Leavenworth, KS 66048, (913) 651-4773.

Liberal/Hugoton, Southwest Kansas Christian Family Educators, Tom & Melanie McLain, P.O. Box 15, Sublette, KS 67877, (316) 675-2380.

Lincoln/Wells, Northcentral Kansas Home Educators, Susan Arinert, Rt. 3, Lincoln, KS 67455, (785) 524-4312

Lyndon/Melvern/Overbrook, Arrow Support Group, Stan & Debbie Friesen, 14283 S. Shawnee Heights Rd., Overbrook, KS 66524, (785) 665-7373

Manhattan, Christian Homes in Educational Fellowship (C.H.I.E.F.), Kurt Mouldrup, 1616 Colorado, Manhattan, KS 66502, (785) 539-5396.

Marion/Morris/Dickinson,Tri-County Home Educators , Angela Baseor, R.R. #1, Box 172, Lincolnville, KS 66858, (316) 924-5731.

Medicine Lodge, South Central Family Educators, Paul & Shannon DeWeese, Box 482, Bucklin, KS 67834, (316) 826-3201.

Neodesha, Studying, Exhorting and Raising Children at Home (S.E.A.R.C.H.), Brad & Mary Barrett, Rt. 2, Box 260, Neodesha, KS 66757, (316) 325-5345.

Newton, Home Education Association, Dean & Jeanne Lukenbach, 427 E. 5th, Newton, KS 67114, (316) 283-1894.

Norton, Christian Homeschoolers of Norton County , Yvonne Crow, 401 E. Main, Norton, KS 67654, (785) 283-2226.

Ottawa, People Achieving Through Homeschooling (P.A.T.H.S.), Dan & Jenny Bennett, 3955 Marshall Rd., Ottawa, KS 66067, (785) 878-3373.

Parsons, Parsons Area Local Support, Barbara Pettinger, 5525 Hwy 59, Parsons, KS 67357, (316) 421-6456.

Pittsburg, Christian Home Educators Fellowship of Pittsburg, Leon & Gerri Forsythe, 1608 S. Walnut, Pittsburg, KS 66762, (316) 231-6586.

Pratt, Pratt County Home Education Association, Doug & Melinda Enick, 411 N. Pine, Pratt, KS 67124, (316) 672-3114.

Rose Hill, Butler County Independent Christian Schools , Larry & Chris Edgington, 530 N. Highway 77 #10B, Douglass, KS 67039, (316) 747-2013.

Salina, Smoky Valley Home Educators, Chuck & Lana Heaton, 2742 Bret, Salina, KS 67401, (785) 823-1018.

Scott City/Leoti, Western Plains Home Educators, Stan & Beverly Salmans, 311 E. 5th, Scott City, KS 67871, (316) 872-5201.

Sedgwick, Family Association of Christian Teaching (F.A.C.T.), Mike & Karen Eli, P.O. Box 50, Sedgwick, KS 67135., (316) 772-5215.

Topeka, Cornerstone Family School, Jan Remboldt, 2433 Duncan Dr., Topeka, KS 66614, (785) 273-6772.

Wamego, Wamego Homes Encouraging and Teaching (W.H.E.A.T), Allyn & Lori Kaufmann, 601 Warren Circle, Wamego, KS 66547, (785) 456-2089.

Wellington, Shekinah Christian Fellowship, Dane & Anne Massey, 1306 N. Cherry, Wellington, KS 67152, (316) 326-7164.

Whitewater, Whitewater Area Activity Group , Ethan & Denise Busenitz, R.R. #1, Box 176, Whitewater, KS 67154, (316) 752-3435.

Wichita, Teaching Parents Association, Jim & Mary Farthing, P.O. Box 3968, Wichita, KS 67201, (316) 945-0810.

Winfield, Walnut Valley Family Educators, Lee & Glenda Bunch, Rt. 1, Box 209, Winfield, KS 67156, (316) 221-9242.

Other groups and service

Central Kansas Circle of Homeschoolers and Unschoolers in Central Kansas Learning Eclectically (CHUCKLE), RR 1, Box 28A, Rush Center, KS 67575; Susan Peach, (785) 372-4457.

Southwest See Walsh under Colorado.

Wichita, Mrs. Kathy L. Middleton, 100 E. 109th St. N., 67147; (316) 755-2159. *Help also offered for anyone in the state.*

Government office (If more information is needed)

State Board of Education, Topeka, KS 66612. (913) 296-3142.

KENTUCKY

Statewide organizations

Christian Home Educators of Kentucky (CHEK), 691 Howardstown Rd., Hodgenville, KY 42748; (502) 358-9270 Fax: (same), kychek@juno.com, Don Woolett, Director.

Kentucky Home Education Association, P.O. Box 81, Winchester, KY 40392-0081, phone/fax (606) 744-0639. "We defend the rights of homeschoolers in Kentucky." Networking, legislative monitoring, newsletter, etc.

Area groups (Contact a state organization for information about other groups.)

Ft. Campbell See Clarksville Area Christian Support Group under Tennessee.

Lexington Lexington Christian Homeschool Support Group, Tom & Susan Vogel, (606) 245-8287. If no answer, call Pastor Billy or Brenda Henderson at 777 Rainwater Dr., Lexington, KY 40515-6026; Res. (606) 271-3646

Russellville Christian Home Educators of Russellville (CHER), 9101 Nashville Rd., Adairville, KY. 42202-8024; (502) 539-3518; earthenvesselspottery@juno.com

Lincoln, Garrard, Boyle & Surrounding Counties Bluegrass Home Educators. Contact person: Cherie Carroll, 600 Shake Rag Rd., Waynesburg, KY 40489-9759; (606) 365-8568. cherie@mis.net; http://www.books.idsite.com/NewLArt24.htm (with Ky home school requirements and articles of interest) To provide support & socialization ... promote responsible home schooling, inform the public .... Newsletter available.

Government office (if more information is needed after contacting home schooling organizations): Contact William K. Evans, Advisor of Non-public Schools, Kentucky Department of Education, 500 Mero St., Frankfort, KY 40601-1972.

LOUISIANA

Statewide organization

Christian Home Education Fellowship of Louisiana (CHEF), Box 74292, Baton Rouge, LA 70874-4292, (888) 876-2433. Statewide book fair / convention every April.

Contact person

For people regardless of religious orientation: Alyce Morgan Wise, P.O. Box 278, Cecilia, LA 70521; (318) 984-4496. *Since she is the only one I'm listing, I suggest calling her only if you have exhausted other resources or if you are in her geographical area. (tw)*

Government office (if more information is needed after contacting home schooling organizations):

Department of Education, P.O. Box 94064, Baton Rouge, LA 70804. (504) 342-3473.

MAINE

State and regional organizations

Homeschool Support Network. P.O. Box 708, Gray, ME 04039; (207) 657-2800; hsn@outrig.com. Information available.

Homeschoolers of Maine HC 62, Box 24, Hope, ME 04847, (207) 763-4251. homeschl@midcoast.com; http://members.aol.com/spikefoss/index.html. Christian orientation. Support group referrals, legislative monitoring, conventions, newsletter.

Maine Christian Homeschool Association, RR. 1, Box 4300, Vassalboro, ME 04989; (207) 872-2015; blount@wtvl.net. Parent packet available. Donation appreciated.

Homeschool Associates. A service organization with roots in Maine and spreading to the south and midwest, 116 3rd Ave., Auburn, ME 04210, (207) 777-1700; Fax (207) 777-1776; homeschool@homeschoolassociates.com. See North Atlantic Regional Schools in appendices A and B, *At Home in America* in appendix K, and Homeschool Associates for mobile book sales in appendix Z.

Area organizations (Contact a state or regional organization for information about other groups.)

Boothbay Boothbay Area Homeschoolers, 8 Appalachee Rd., Boothbay Harbor, ME 04538; (207) 633-6319.

Burnham Burnham CHESS (Christian Home Education Support System), contact person is now Susan Davis, RR 2, Box 3180, Clinton, ME 04927; tel. or fax (207) 426-8851; jcdavis@mint.net

Rumford HomeStart, John & Christina Kroger, 63 Peru Center Road, Peru, ME 04290; (207) 562-8156.

Southern Maine Southern Maine Home Education Support Network, (no current information). Nonsectarian. Members also from across the state. "An activity oriented community for others."

Northern Maine Homeschoolers of Northern Maine, 20 Fort Hill St., Fort Fairfield, ME 04742 (207) 476-8904, Contact: Julie Tornquist jetkat@bangornews.infi.net.

Government office (after contacting home sch. org.)

Approval Consultant, Department of Education, State House Station 23, Augusta, ME 04333, (207) 287-5922. http://www.state.me.us/education/hs1.htm

MARYLAND

Statewide organization

Maryland Association of Christian Home Educators, Box 247, Point of Rocks, MD 21777; (301) 607-4284; mache@juno.com

Maryland Home Education Association, 9085 Flamepool Way, Columbia, MD 21045; (410) 730-0073.

Metropolitan area

America's Metro Area Homeschool Organization, 10602 Ordway Dr., Silver Spring, MD 20901; (301) 593-3646. 24 hour Information/fax/voice mail (301) 593-4969.

Area organizations (Contact a state organization for other groups.)

Anne Arundel County, Glen Burnie Homeschool Support Group, 6514 Dolphin Ct., Glen Burnie, MD 21061. (410) 850-4496. For $2 (to help cover costs) Susan Whetzel will send you an information packet on dealing with laws, directory, etc.

North County Home Educators, Billy or Nancy Greer, 1688 Belhaven Woods Court, Pasadena, MD 21122-3727, (410) 437-5109. E-mail 619-3098 @MCImail.com

Montgomery County Montgomery Home Learning Network, Barbetta Jones, 4033 Adams Dr., Silver Spring, MD 20902; (301) 942-2950; BJones40@aol.com.

Northeast area Tri-State Home School Network, See under Delaware.

Westminster 686 Geneva Dr., Westminster, MD 21157; (410) 857-0168 or (410) 848-3390. A small group open to people of all religions. They do all the usual good things plus they foster friendships among the member children.

Service organization

Walkersville Christian Family Schools: Main office (send all correspondence here), 4 West Main St., Thurmont, MD 21788-1824 (Frederick - Hagerstown area); http://www.wcfs.edu; info@wcfs.edu; (301) 271-0123; fax: (301) 845-7254. Maryland Eastern Shore Office, P.O. Box 459, Secretary, MD 21664; wcfs-es@ezy.net (410) 943-1538. The WCFS Distance Program is now open for enrollment nationally and internationally for families who are missionaries, pastors and church leaders, and all members of the body of Jesus Christ. They are dedicated to helping parents raise a godly offspring and provide a Christ-centered education for their children through a home schooling structure. All students learn at home, except for special events.

Government office (after contacting a home school organization)

Lynda Lowry, Chief Pupil Services & Drug Free Schools Branch, Maryland State Department of Education, 200 W. Baltimore St., Baltimore, MD 21201-2595. (410) 767-0300.

MASSACHUSETTS

Statewide organizations

Massachusetts Home Learning Association, P. O. Box 1558, Marston Mills, MA 02648-5558; Eastern Mass: Loretta Heuer (508) 429-1436. Western Mass: Kathleen Smith (508) 249-9056; Elisa Wood (lisawood@aol.com), editor, MHLA newsletter. http://northshore.shore.net/~pyghill/mhla.htm. MHLA is an information network open to everyone. Send SASE for a brochure or $5 for their information packet.

Massachusetts Homeschool Organization of Parent Educators (Mass. HOPE), 5 Atwood Rd.., Cherry Valley, MA 01611-3332; (508) 755-4467. Info@masshope.org. http://www.masshope.org Serves especially Christian oriented families. Information on home schooling, on support groups, and on laws

Support groups (Contact a state or district center for many other local groups)

Cape area Christian Home Educated Children (CHEC), John & Estella Bologna, 25 Sugar Hill Rd., Harwich, MA 02645; (508) 430-2145

Salem Family Resource Center, (The), PO Box 308, Salem, MA 01970; Tammy and Rick Rosenblatt, 508-741-7188; BigBear001@aol.com

Arlington Homeschooling Together, 24 Avon Place, Arlington, MA 02174; (781) 641-0566 ses@world.std.com Cooperatively edited newsletter, monthly parent support meetings, field trips and group activities. All families are welcome.

North Shore Massachusetts Home Educators, 22 Garland St., Lynn, MA 01902; (617) 599-6267. Field trips, gym classes, meetings.

North Shore North Shore Home School Support Group; Contact Marci Anthony MarciAnth@Juno.com; 62 Matthies Street, Beverly, MA 01915-2448.

Lowell Lowell Home Education Council, Support group and liason for the local school authorities. Contact person: Bob Alba, 27 Ostrander Ave., Lowell MA 01851 (978) 937-5726. E-mail is to either sunbear41@aol.com or Marilyn Wells, (978) 446-0114 ian@rsn.hp.com.

Services based in nearby states

Homeschool Associates, an organization offering many services including a newspaper, listed in Appendix C and under Maine.

Government office (if more information is needed after contacting home schooling organizations): Commonwealth of Massachusetts Department of Education, 350 Main St., Malden, MA 02148.

MICHIGAN

Statewide organizations

Christian Home Educators of Michigan. PO Box 530760, Livonia, MI 48153-0760. 48333; (810) 626-8431. A leadership organization with a preponderance of direct contacts in the eastern part of the state. Many contact groups in the Detroit area. Information about contacting local support groups.

Information Network for Christian Homes (INCH), 4934 Cannonsburg Rd., Belmont, MI 49306. Annual convention; newsletter; contact information for local support groups. (616) 874-5656.

Support (For other groups ask a state organization.)

Bay Area Bay Area Homeschool Association, Contact person: Judy Kehr, 1396 E Wilder Rd., Bay City, MI 48706, (517) 684-6130.

Berrien County, (central), Berrien Springs Area Home School Association. Contact person: Laurie Cooper (616) 461-3326; 5797 Shanghai Rd., Eau Claire, MI 49111.

Branch County Branch County Area Home Schoolers, Sherry Ankner (517) 278-4050; 125 E. Fenn Rd., Coldwater, MI 49036.

Charlotte Charlotte Area Christian Home Educators, Penny Martin, 23701 23½ Mile Rd., Olivet, MI 49076; (517) 543-1643

Flint (NE area), Home Education and Righteous Teaching (HEART) 5432 Wilson Rd. Columbiaville, MI 48421. (810) 793-1601. 101323.617@compuserve.com.

Delta County Sue Hoffmann, (906) 384-6941..

Detroit, south HEART support group. See Homeschool Support Network below under "service institutions."

Flint Home Organized for Meaningful Education (HOME). A Christian group. Sue Cameron (810) 695-3158; 7489 Bucks Dr., Grand Blanc MI 48439.

Flint (So. area) Heritage Home Educators, Educators, Dee Morgan, 13339 Firestone Ct., Fenton, MI 48430. Open to anyone in Michigan. Now serving mostly counties of Oakland, Livingston, Genesee and Lapeer..

Flint (NE area), Home Education and Righteous Teaching (HEART) 5432 Wilson Rd. Columbiaville, MI 48421. (810) 793-1601. 101323.617@compuserve.com.

Grand Rapids Northwest Connections, 2053 Milford NW, Grand Rapids, MI 49504; (616) 453-9600. Moms' support network for homeschoolers. (There are other groups in the area.)

Holland Holland Area Home School Assn., 121 Elm Ln., Holland, MI 49424; (616) 399-0481. Newsletter.

Howard City, Tri-County Area, Heart and Home Support Group, 6450 Bass Lake Rd., Howard City, MI 49329; (616) 937-5742; jvukin@edcen.ehhs.cmich.edu.

Ishpeming, Mrs. James Janofski, 2 Gold Dr., Ishpeming, MI 49849; JJanofski@aol.com.

Jackson J.A.H.E. (517) 784-6810.

Kalamazoo KAHSA, Central contact for groups in surrounding areas. (616) 324-1942; P.O. Box 2214, Portage, MI 49081-2214.

Lansing Covenant Home Education Support System (CHESS) Kim Winter, 2710 Darien Dr., Lansing, MI 48912; (517) 462-0944. E-mail mkjcwinter@aol.com Activities and information for parents and students.

Lansing Family Active in Studies and Teaching (FAST) Shirley McGee, 4061 Holt Rd., Holt, MI 48842; (517) 699-2728. Network, newsletter.

Lowell Lowell Area Interactive Network for Kids, Contact Judy Sterling, (616) 897-5294.

Manistee County Faith Christian Home Schoolers, Donna Williams, 466 5th St., Manistee, MI 49660; (616) 723-2200.

Marshall Families Learning and Schooling at Home, 21671 B Drive North, Marshall, MI 49068. Contact Natalie Valle, (616) 781-1069.

Montcalm County / Central Michigan Cultivators of Responsible Education (CORE), Jeanne Falzon, (517) 831-4361; mfalzon@educen.ehhs.cmich.edu

Muskegon Covenant L.I.F.E. Ron & Bari Honick (616) 744-2139.

Negaunee HELP-UP, 125 E. Lincoln, Negaunee, MI 49866; (906) 475-5508; up4hmsklrs@aol.com. *The Guidde*, Monthly newsletter $15/yr. (For your interest, the newsletter name stands for "Giving Us Ideas for Directing and Diversifying Education.")

Niles area. See former Konos group under Indiana.
Oakland County See Heritage Home Educators under "Flint."

Oceana County Homeschoolers Greg Vriesman, (616) 873-0896; malcom64@juno.com.

St. Joseph - Benton Harbor Southwest Michigan Christian Scholars. (616) 429-8090.

Sterling Heights LIFE Support, 14560 Hilsdale Dr., Stirling Heights, MI 48343; (810) 247-5981; pdrossi@interserv.com.

Thumb Area Thumb Area Christian Home Schoolers. Laura Mills, (517) 665-2406.

Upper Peninsula, Central Upper Michigan Home Educators, Jim and Lonny Janofski, 2 Gold Dr., Ishpeming, MI 49849; (906) 486-4536.

Washtenaw County Washtenaw Home Schools. A network with contact information for groups throughout the county. Pam Kittel, P.O. Box 653, Saliene, MI 48176; WHINews@aol.com. Newsletter.

Older Homeschoolers' Group, Diane Linn, 9120 Dwight Dr., Detroit, MI 48214; (313) 331-8406. Serving families with kids 11-17 in Southeast Michigan and Windsor. Educational programs and social activities.

Services

A Servant's Heart 16455 Smokey Hollow Rd., Traverse City, Michigan 49686; (616) 223-7345; aservantsheart@juno.com. Lisa Craggs sells and used curriculum materials. Used materials taken on consignment. Current list available.

Christian Art for Kids. Don West provides art classes to develop art skills (not crafts) in children ages 7 and up. All projects are based on Bible or high-family-value themes. A splendid opportunity for any support group within range. The video instructional program he offers is described in appendix T. Write to Mr. West at 14811 Eleanor, Warren, MI 48089, or phone (800) ART-0033.

Educational Accents, Nancy Welliver, 7449 Ponderosa, Swartz Creek, MI 48473, (810) 655-6807; swelliver@aol.com. Counseling; Used and books.

Homeschool Support Network, P.O. Box 2457, Riverview, MI 48192; (734) 284-1249; mom@aol.com. Jackie Beattie, Director. Clearinghouse for Michigan and surrounding states. Information packet $3.

Teaching & Learning Center (TLC). Individualized learning programs set up and seminars for parents in SW Michigan. Yolande Robertson, 3387 E. Snow Rd., Berrien Springs, MI 49103; (616) 473-5437.

Government office (if more information is needed after contacting home schooling organizations): Department of Education, P.O. Box 30008, Lansing, MI 48909. (517) 373-0796.

MINNESOTA

Statewide and area organizations

Minnesota Association of Christian Home Educators, P.O. Box 32308, Fridley, MN 55432; (612) 717-9070; mache@isd.net; http://www.mache.org.

Minnesota Homeschoolers Alliance, P.O. Box 23072, Richfield, MN 55423. (612) 288-9662. A nonpolitical organization offering a network for home schooling families, a 90-page handbook on the topic, a directory of support groups a newsletter, *The Grapevine*, and more.

Minnesota Association of Roman Catholic Home Educators, 7211 Sherwood Echo, Woodbury, MN 55125. A resource center for the unique culture and traditions of Catholic families. Newsletter. Voice mail (612) 730-8101.

Area groups

For Rochester and surrounding area: Home Educators Alliance, Sherry Hanson, P.O. Box 413, Eyota, MN 55934.

Teen group For families with teens. Lori Holtorf, 1431 20th St., NE, Byron, MN 55920; (507) 775-6622.

Government office (if more information is needed)
Government Relations, Minnesota Department of Education, Room 710, Capitol Square Building, 550 Cedar St., St. Paul, MN 55101. (612) 296-6595.

MISSISSIPPI

Organizations

Mississippi Home Educators Association, Box 945, Brookhaven, MS 39601; (601) 833-9110; mhea@juno.com; http://www.mhea.org

Home Educators of Central Mississippi, (no current information).

Government office (for more information)
State Department of Education, Office of Community and Outreach Services, Sillers Bldg., Suite 306, P.O Box 777, Jackson, MS 39205. (601) 359-3598.

MISSOURI

Statewide organizations

Families for Home Education, 6209 NW Tower Drive, Platte Woods, Missouri 64151; (417) 782-8833; fhe@microlink.net; http://www.microlink.net/~fhe/index.htm

Missouri Association of Teaching Christian Homes, 307 E. Ash St., #146, Columbia, MO 65201, (573) 443-8217; ddrechse@mail.coin.missouri.edu. MATCH offers its members: newsletters, direct-dial assistance, help with private school incorporation, etc. They sponsor an annual convention in St. Louis and a family camp retreat in the Ozarks. Annual fee $30.

Support groups (For others ask a state organization.)

Christian Home Educators Fellowship, (Jon & Candy Summers) 236 St. Louis Ave., Ferguson, MO. 63135, (314) 521-8487.

Home Schooling Network, 9121 Argyle, St. Louis, MO 63114. Accepts people of all faiths.

Southwest Home Education Ministry, 3926 W. Hialeah, Springfield, MO 65803; (417) 866-0924

Government office (if more information is needed after contacting home schooling organizations): State Office, Department of Elementary and Secondary Education, P.O. Box 480, Jefferson City, MO 65102. (314) 751-7602.

MONTANA

Statewide organization

Montana Coalition of Home Educators, P.O. Box 43, Gallatin Gateway, MT 59730, (406) 587-6163white@ gomontana.com; http://www4.gomontana.com/ white/mache.htm.

Government office (if more information is needed after contacting home schooling organizations): Chief Legal Counsel, Office of Public Instruction, 1227 Eleventh Avenue, Helena, MT 59620. (406) 444-4402.

NEBRASKA

Statewide organization

Nebraska Christian Home Educators Association, Box 57041, Lincoln, NE 68505-7041; (402) 423-4297; nchea@navix.net.

Area support groups

Columbus Area Homeschoolers, Deb & Joe Nelson, R.R. 3, Box 256, Columbus, NE 68601; (402) 564-2353; jlnelso@kdsi.net.

LEARN, 7741 E. Avon Ln., Lincoln, NE 68505, Contact Rose Yonekura (402) 488-7741.

Government office (if more information is needed after contacting NCHEA): State Department of Education, 301 Centennial Mall South, P.O. Box 94987, Lincoln, NE 68509-4987. (402) 471-2783.

NEVADA

State and area organizations

Home Education and Righteous Training, 3437 Ferrell St., No. Las Vegas, NV 89030; (702) 391-7219;linkedheart@hotmail.com. Meetings, field trips, etc. Emphasis on father's role.

Home Schools United - Vegas Valley, P.O. Box 93564, Las Vegas, NV 89193-3564; (702) 870-9566; Incorporated as: Nevada Home Schools, Inc.; HSU.vegasvalley@juno.com. Although current board members are all of the Christian faith, they do not exclude anyone from membership. The main source of "starter" home school information in the area.

Government office (if more information is needed after contacting home schooling organizations): Private Schools Consultant, Nevada State Department of Education, SCA Team, 700 E. 5th St., Carson City, NV 89701-5096 . (702) 687-9134.

NEW HAMPSHIRE

Statewide Organizations

Christian Home Educators of Hampshire, Box 961, Manchester, NH 03105-0916; (603) 569-2343; http://www.mv.com/ipusers/chenh

New Hampshire Homeschool Coalition, P.O. Box 2224, Concord, NH 03302-2224. NHHC coordinator and newsletter editor, Abbey Lawrence, P.O. Box, Tuftonboro, NH 03816; abbey@worldpath.net. Representatives throughout the state. Planned activities. Guidebook on homeschooling in Hampshire, $8.50. Membership with newsletter, $15.

Support group (There are many more. Ask a state group.)

Home Schooling Friends, 204 Brackett Rd., Durham, NH 03855; (603) 859-2347; contact person: Beverly Behr, nothome@worldpath.net

Services

New Hampshire Home Schooling Resources; nhhr@dimentech.com; http://www.dimentech.com/ homeschool/Book sales. An Amazon.com associate member selling books which they have reviewed as appropriate for home schools. Books are delivered via Amazon.com.

Government office

(if more information is needed after contacting home schooling organizations): State Department of Education: Division of Standards and Certification, 101 Pleasant St., Concord, NH 03301. (603) 271- 3453.

NEW JERSEY

Statewide Organizations

Education Network of Christian Homeschoolers of Jersey, Inc. (ENOCH), 120 Mayfair Ln., Mt. Laurel, NJ 08054-4283; (609) 222-4283; fax ... -4282; enochnji@uscom.com.

Unschoolers Network, 2 Smith St., Farmingdale, NJ 07727. Nancy Plent. (908) 938-2473. An important purpose of this group is to establish people connections. They offer a generic curriculum guide through grade 12 to help parents know what is generally taught and a special teen program.

Homeschool Connection, Inc., The. 12 Twin Oaks Ln., Annandale, NJ 08801; thc_inc@blast.net; http://frontpage .inet-images.com/hsconnection; bulletin boards at http://www.kaleidoscapes.com .

Support groups

Hunter County Hunter County Cristian Homeshoolers, P.O. Box 324, Hopewell, NJ 08525.

Ocean County Ocean County Christian Home School

Association, P.O. Box 569, Lanoka Harbor, NJ 08734; (732) 269-6524, or fax ... 1919.

Southern area Homeschoolers of South Jersey, 1239 Whitaker Ave., Millville, NJ 08332; Rose, (609) 327-1224; tutor@pulsar.net; http://www.pulsar.net~tutor

Southern area Tri-State Home School Network, P.O. Box 7193, Newark, DE 19714-7193. Christian perspective. See under Deleware.

Middlesex, Monmouth, Mercer, and Burlington Counties in NJ and Bucks County, PA. Homeschoolers Support Network, P.O. Box 56198, Trenton, NJ 08638-7198; (609) 771-8002, JoanneLee2@aol.com

Service organizations

The Tutor, 1239 Whitaker Ave., Millville, NJ 08332; (609) 327-1224. Consulting service for Home Schoolers in Southern Jersey. Contact Rose Sias. and used textbooks. tutor@pulsar.net; http://www.pulsar.net~tutor

Government office (if more information is needed after contacting home schooling organizations): John Lally, Education Program Specialist, Jersey Department of Education, 100 Riverview Plaza., CN 500, Trenton, NJ 08625-0500. (609) 984-7814.

NEW MEXICO

Statewide Organizations

Christian Association of Parent Educators of Mexico, Box 25046, Albuquerque, NM 87125; (505) 898-8548; cape-nm@juno.com; newsletter, convention, support group network, etc.

New Mexico Family Educators, P.O. Box 92276, Albuquerque, NM 87199-2276. (505) 275-7053. An inter-faith group. Membership and leadership open to all. Information packet (for members) $7. Family membership $20. Legal liaison with state agencies for academic and athletic participation in the public schools. Also a newsletter, a lending library, conferences, and workshops for children and adults.

Area organizations (Ask them for support group contacts or ask NMFE if you are not in one of these areas)

Albuquerque, Unschoolers of Albuquerque, 2905 Tahiti Ct. NE, Albuquerque NM 87112; Sandra Dodd, (505) 299-2476; SandraDodd@aol.com

Española, Chimayo, Pojaque, Abique: Española Home Educators, Box 51110, Española, NM 87532; dssmdsm@roadrunner.com.; fax (505) 747-8146

Portales Homeschooling PACT, Parents and Children Together, Barbara Klapperich Senn, PO Box 961, Portales, NM 88130; 505) 359-1618; Homeschooling-PACT@Rocketmail.com; http://members .tripod.com/~HomeschoolingPACT/index.html

Santa Fe Home Educators of Santa Fe, 21 Frasco Rd., Santa Fe, NM 87505; Darla McLeod; (505) 466-4462; fax ... -8316; McLeod@sfol.com

Service organization

Title Wave Books, 7415 Manaul Blvd., NE, Albuquerque NM 87110; (505) 837-9495. Walk-in bookstore with and used books. Cindy and Nathan Heath. (no information)

Government office (for additional information)

Department of Education, Education Building, Santa Fe, NM 87501-2786. (505) 827-6515.

NEW YORK

Statewide Organization

Loving Education At Home, Inc. (LEAH) P.O. Box 88, Cato, NY 13033; (716) 346-0939; http://www.leah.org Christian home schooling network with 130 chapters and approximately 3500 families

Area support groups *Contact LEAH for others.*

Columbia County Columbia County Homeschooling Mothers' Group, 29 Kinderhood St., Chatham, NY 12037; Katherine Houk, (518) 392-4277.

Fingerlakes area Fingerlakes Unschoolers Network, Linda Holzbaur, 249 Coddington Road, Ithaca NY 14850; (607) 277-6300; Laundress@aol.com.

New York City Suburban NYC: NY, NJ, CT Tri-County Home Schoolers, PO Box 190, Ossining, NY 10562; Chris & Andy Hofer, (914) 941-5607 or voice/fax (914) 941-3004; chofer@croton.com, http:www.croton.com/home-ed/

Rochester Greater Rochester LEAH, 4 Elmwood Cir., Scottsville, NY 14546; grleahhuff@juno.com.

Southern Tier Home Education Exchange of the Southern Tier, P.O. Box 85, Southview Station, Binghamton, NY 13903-0085; http://members.tripod.com/~hee/ A nonsectarian activity and support group for homeschoolers and for those exploring educaitonal alternatives. Contact Barbara Pochily, (607) 775-2632.

Service organizations

Christian Homesteading Movement, Turner St., Oxford, NY 13830-E, Richard & Anna Marie Fahey. See Appendix C, Part 5

Ulster County Home Ed Resource Person, 94 Plains Rd, ,Paltz NY 12561; (914) 256-0464; KimSquared@aol.com

Government office (if more information is needed after contacting home schooling organizations): Contact person for home education, State Education Department, Room 481-EBA, Albany, NY 12234. (518) 474-3879.

NORTH CAROLINA

Statewide organization

North Carolinians for Home Education, 419 N. Boylan Ave., Raleigh, NC 27603-1211, (919) 834-6243; fax ... -6241; nche@mindspring.com. They "protect the freedom to educate children at home," provide encouragement, and promote home education. I'm sure they would appreciate your support. Annual conference and book fair in May. Newsletter, *The Greenhouse Report*.

Regional (For other local groups ask NCHE.)

Onslow Home Educators (OAHE), Jacksonville, NC; Contact Julia Friant; (910) 346-3082; oahenc@geocities.com http://www.geocities.com/Athens/Acropolis/9534

Durham Triangle Christian Home Educators, Lori Hoffman, Coordinator, 2901 Fawn Ave., Durham, NC 27705 (919) 477-8815; lor&jo@gloryroad.net.

Service organizations

North Carolina School of Science and Mathematics High school courses through a state network. http://www.ncssm.edu/outreach/distlearn.html

Government office

(If more information is needed): Division of Non-Public Education, 530 N. Wilmington St., Raleigh, NC 27603-1198; (919) 733-4276; (919) 733-4276. http://www.gov.state.nc.us/dnpppe.

NORTH DAKOTA

Statewide organization

North Dakota Home School Association, P.O. Box 7400, Bismarck, ND 58507-7400; (701) 223-4080; e-mail: ndhsa@wdata.com. Contact Gail Biby.

Government office

(If more information is needed after contacting NDHSA): Joan Estes, Assistant Director, Elementary Education, Department of Public Instruction, State Capitol, 600 East Boulevard Ave., Bismark, ND 58505-0440; (701) 328-2295. Jeste@c01as400.state.nd.us.

OHIO

Statewide organizations

Christian Home Educators of Ohio, 430 N. Court St., Circleville, OH 43113; (614) 464-3177. Their newsletter, *The Ohio Home School Companion*, is distributed regularly to over 2300 families. Special issues go to 15,000 families. Cheohome@bright.net; http://www.cheohome.org

Home Education Action Council of Ohio A government watchdog organization. No current information.

Ohio Educators of Catholic Homes Network 174 Morningside, Niles, OH 44446; Katie Moran, President, (330) 652-4923 or fax -5322; moran@nlcomm.com.

Regional groups

Cincinnati Christian Home Educators of Cincinnati, a network of 16 support groups in the Greater Cincinnati area. Contacts: Beth Hill/Debbie Herron 513-398-5795/513-242-9226. Address: 4320 Tower Ave., Cincinnati, OH 45217. e-mail: Blue.herron@goodnews.net; http://w3.goodnews.net/~herronrj/

Cincinnati Homeschool Network of Greater Cincinnati, 2115 Harcourt Dr., Cincinnati, OH 45244; Contact Susan M. Duncan, 3470 Greenfield Court, Maineville, OH 45039; (513) 683-1279

Northeast Ohio Ohio Home Educators Network, P.O. Box 23054; Barbara (330) 274-0542; or Debra (216) 278-2540. All are welcome. Interest-based learning supported.

Central Ohio HELP, 3636 Paris Blvd., Westerville, OH. 43081; (614) 470-2219; HomeEdCols@aol.com

Medina County HEART, 7979 Greenwich Rd., Lodi, OH 44254; Naome Carter; (330) 948-2941; zcarter@apk.net.

Northern Ohio HELP Northern Ohio, 10915 Pyle-S Amherst Rd., Oberlin, OH 44074; Gina McKay Lodge, (216) 774-2720

Northeast Older Homeschoolers' Group (for parents of teens). See under Michigan.

Norwalk Home Education Resource Organization, 170 W. Main St., Norwalk, OH 44857; Rob & Donna King (419) 663-1064

Toledo Christian Home Educators Support System -- of Toledo, Ohio. "Our desire is to support, encourage, and equip parents who are educating their children in a Christ centered way." Child care at meetings by reservation. Newsletter. c/o Brian and Delores Carter, 5117 Chatsworth, Toledo, OH 43614; (419) 385-1678; chess@glasscity.net

Westerville Westerville Families Unschooling in the Neighborhood of Ohio Homeschoolers, (FUN), 3636 Paris Blvd, Westerville, OH 43081; roy@qn.net

Government office

(after contacting home schooling organizations) Department of Education, Rich Fairchild or Abdi Mohamud, 65 S. Front St., Rm. 408, Columbus, OH 43215; (614) 466-2937.

OKLAHOMA

Statewide organizations

Christian Home Educators Fellowship of Oklahoma, Box 471363, Tulsa, 74147; (918) 583-7323.

Home Educators Resource Organization (HERO) of Oklahoma A network of homeschooling support groups and families. 4401 Quail Run Ave, Skiatook, 74070; Leslie Moyer, (918) 396-0108; moyerles@wiltel.net; http://www.geocities.com/Athens/Forum/3236 (The site includes law information). Open membership; telephone help, quarterly newsletter, directory of groups and families, *Oklahoma Homeschooling Handbook* (available free online), e-mail discussion group, annual conference.

Regional and local organizations

Miami Homeschoolers United Group Support (HUGS), 64500 E. 100 Rd., Miami, 74354; (918) 540-2066.

Oklahoma City, Oklahoma Central Home Educators' Consociation, P.O. Box 270601, 73137. (405) 521-8439 (voice box 2). Mike Jestes, Advisor.

Tulsa Home Education Coalition Newsletter, *THE News* is available through support groups or by subscription, 20 pages, 6 issues, only $10. THEC is a leadership organization, not a support group; P.O. Box 813, Glenpool, 74033. Linda Duntley, (918) 322-3984.

Government office (for more information)
Department of Education, Oklahoma City, 73105. (405) 521-3333.

OREGON

Statewide administrative organizations
Homeschool Information & Services Network (HISNet), 1044 Bismark, Klamath Falls, OR 97601; (541) 782-2466 (information line, weekdays, 9-5); hisnet@efn.org; http://www.efn.org/~hisnet. A nonmembership organization with Christian leadership. All are welcome. Support group referrals. Complimentary magazine subscriptions for leaders. On-line or hard copy *Newcomers Booklet* and *Older Homeschooler Booklet*; HSLDA group discount; Political and legislative information.

Oregon Christian Home Education Association Network, 17985 Falls City Road, Dallas, OR 97338. Automated phone line (503) 288-1285. oceanet@teleport.com; http://www.teleport.com/~chesso/ocean/; Distinctly Christian, membership organization; newsletter and local group assistance; beginner's packets; Oregon Home Education Week; annual conference; and legislative watch.

Oregon Home Education Network, 4470 SW Hall Blvd. #286, Beaverton, OR 97005; (503) 321-5166 (voice-mail), sassenak@msn.com; http://www.teleport.com/~ohen. A membership organization that welcomes everyone. Family & student activities; legislative information; quarterly newsletter; biannual conference; co-publisher of *Oregon Homeschool Support Group Directory*; county contacts for encouragement & help; homeschooler resource packets.

Parents Education Association Pac (PEA PAC), c/o Dennis Tuuri, P.O. Box 5428, Beaverton, OR 97006, 503 693-0724. Eldert@aol.com; URL: http://www.lyonscom.com/peapac. A political action group in the interest of home schooling.

Resources for guidance and materials
Family Learning Organization See under Washington.

Homeschooling in Oregon by Ann Lahrson. A very good resource for Oregon parents. It lists resources for various communities in the state. It deals with Oregon law and lists education service districts, testing sources, and various organizations in the state. Also curriculum resources and simple approaches to teaching. The 1998 edition is to have 350+ pages, including chapters on multimedia use, special needs, product reviews, much more. $14.95 plus $3 shipping. PO Box 80214, Portland, OR 97280 (503) 284-6741, Fax:(503) 284-8638 http://www.outoftheboxpublishing.com; ann@outoftheboxpublishing.com

A Heart for Home 1350 Elgarose Rd., Roseburg, OR 97470; (541) 440-0431, (888) 440-0431, heart4home@mcsi.net. A variety of learning materials from some 50 different publishers. Used curriculum materials bought and sold. Owners Sue Ellis also offer consultation, testing, book fairs, tutoring and accountability services in our southern OR area.

Area and local groups (For other groups ask a state organization.)

Ashland Families Intelligently Schooling at Home, (FISH) P.O. Box 93, Ashland, Ohio 44805; somefish@usa.net. Contacts are Jeannie Leisure: (419) 945-2319, Johnnetta Crabtree: (419) 747-7286, or Linda Studer: (330) 262-4489.

Findlay Christian Parents' Educational Fellowship, 310 Blue Bonnet Drive, Findlay, OH 45840; (419) 422-9371 or ... 422-9009 Fax ... 425-5209; rwiseman @bright.net; http://www.bright.net/~rwiseman/

Lane County Inter-Christian Guild of Home Teachers (LIGHT), P.O.Box 70498, Eugene, Oregon 97401; light@efn.org; http://www.efn.org/~light; 200+ families; Christian leadership/all welcome. Monthly meetings; newsletter; children's activities; discounts in the county, liability insurance; lending library; annual Education Exposition.

Salem Salem Area Chrisian Home School Network (SACHSN) 715 Ventura St., N., Keizer, OR 97303; (503) 390-5865 only after 2 p.m.; kacclark@open.org. Christian leaders. All are welcome.

Southern Oregon Jackson County Home Educators 4733 Hillcrest Rd., Medford, OR 97405; (541) 734-3243 afternoons; rwarrick@cdsnet.net; home.cdsnet.net/~normrowe/jche/. Many services.

Government office (if more information is needed)
Leon Fuhrman, Specialist, State Department of Education, Public Service Bldg., 225 Capitol St., NE, Salem, OR 97310-0203. (503) 378-5585 ext.682. FAX: 503-373-7968. Internet: leon.fuhrman@state.or.us.

PENNSYLVANIA

Statewide organizations
Christian Homeschool Association of Pennsylvania (CHAP), P.O. Box 3603, York, PA 17402-0603; (717) 661-2185 or ... -2428. "We are available to assist homeschoolers and support groups on how Christians can work with the law and local superintendents." Curriculum fair each spring. To learn more, send long SASE.

Pennsylvania Home Education Network (P.H.E.N.)
285 Allegheny Street, Meadville, PA 16335, (412)-561-5288; PANetwk@aol.com, "Freedom and simplicity in home education." Information packet $3 to cover costs.

Area and local organizations (There are others.)
Bucks County See Middlesex under Pennsylvania.

Chester County Chester County Homeschoolers, 226 Llandovery Dr., Exton, PA 19341; (610) 524-0296.

Langhorne Diversity United in Homeschooling. Mail enquires: D. Scott, 233 Bluebell Ave., Langhorne, PA 19047; paris204@juno.com; Phone help: Pat Porter, (215) 428-2865. A non-religious, non-discriminatory, and apolitical support network.

McKeesport The McKeesport Area Homeschoolers, c/o Barbara Page, 205 W. Virginia Ave., Munhall, PA 15120-3149; (412) 461-6788; pageclan@classic.msn.com; http://www.ontv.com/school.cgi/schoolHook.BAT?DOIT=activity&ID1=656&ID2=4 A Christ-centered group, but open to all. Activities, newsletter. Membership $8 per year.

Meadville Lakeland Home Educators, 285 Allegheny St., Meadville 16335; (814) 333-2852 or (814) 337-3630.

Pittsburgh People Always Learning Something (PALS), 105 Marie Dr., Pittsburgh, PA 15237; Christiana Barry, (412) 3677-6240.

Southeast area Tri-State Home School Network, P.O. Box 7193, Newark, DE 19714-7193. Christian perspective. See under Deleware.

Service organizations

PA Homeschoolers RD 2, Box 117, Kittanning PA 16201; (412) 783-6512; richmans@pahomeschoolers.com; http://www.pahomeschoolers.com (not a membership organization.) Services include newsletter with about 2,000 subscribers, a guide to the Pennsylvania home education law, and accreditation under Pennsylvania law to issue home education diplomas.

Rolling Green Home Ed Resource Room, 2725 Aquetong Road, Hope, PA 18938; (215) 862-2968 ph or fax; e-mail rptoy@bellatlantic.net. An art learning center. Contact information for home schooling in the area.

Government office

(if more information is needed after contacting home schooling organizations): Office of School Services, 333 Market St., 5th Fl., Harrisburg, PA 17126-0333. (717) 783-3750, or TDD ... -8445.

RHODE ISLAND

Statewide organization

Rhode Island Guild of Home Teachers, Box 11, Hope, RI 02831; (401) 821-7700; right_right@mailexcite.com; http://www.angelfire.com/ri/RIGHT

Parent Educators of Rhode Island P.O. Box 782, Glendale, RI 02826; (401) 568-8789

Also see Homeschool Associates, an organization active in this state which offers many services including a newspaper. Look in Appendix C, Part 1.

Government office

(if more information is needed after contacting home schooling organizations): Commissioner of Education, Department of Education, 22 Hayes St., Providence, RI 02908. (401) 277-2031.

SOUTH CAROLINA

Statewide organizations

South Carolina Home Educators Association , P.O. Box 3231, Columbia SC 29230-3231; phone/fax: (803) 754-6425; SCHEA1@aol.com; http://members.aol.com/SCHEA1. Referrals to local support groups, annual convention, publication of *SCHEA's IDEAS* newsletter, and other services. Information not confirmed.

South Carolina Homeschool Alliance (SCHA) is an Internet information, communication, and support network for SC homeschoolers. SCHA sponsors the South Carolina Homeschooling Website and a state mailing list. To contact SCHA, please email ConnectSC@aol.com or visit the website at: http://members.aol.com/connectsc/index.htm

Catholic Home Educators of S.C. Mary E. Jackson, trjack@group2.net (not confirmed).

Home School Supervisory Organizations (State approved) *The first organization listed below operates much the same as the others. It was established earlier.*

The South Carolina Association of Independent Home Schools, P.O. Box 2104, Irmo, SC 29063-7104; (803) 551-1003; Fax ...-5746. This organization provides guidance for home teaching and is recognized by the state as an alternate source of approval for home schooling parents. Members are required to maintain certain instructional standards. Services include counseling, resource room, newsletter, workshops, book fair, and graduation.

Christian Homeschoolers Association of South Eastern SC (CHASE SC), PO Box 366, Ladson, 29456; voice & fax, (803) 873-5942; e-mail ChaseSC1@aol.com; website: http://members.aol.com/chasesc1. Also has a Resource Center open to the public.

Greenwood Christian School Home Educators Association, Jill Leinbach, 525 Grace Street, Greenwood, SC 29649; (864) 229-6572; JLeinbach@hspower.com

Palmetto Independent Educators (PIE), PO Box 2475, Aiken, 29802; (803) 643-0807.

Palmetto Homeschool Association. (PHA), PO Box 486, Lancaster, 29721; (803) 285-3916; e-mail PalmettoHA@aol.com; website:http://members.aol.com/palmettoha/phaindex.htm

Piedmont Home Educators Association (PHEA) c/o Ann Smith, 6709 State Park Rd., Travelers Rest, SC 29690; (864) 834-1719. Rate is lower for subscribers to the *PHEA Homeschool Digest*.

Teachers, Ink. PO Box 13386, Charleston, 29422; (803) 795-9982; fax: (803) 795-2683; e-mail PFMSuper@worldnet.att.net; http://www.awod.com/gallery/probono/teachersink/

The Upstate Association of Homeschools, PO Box 15262, Spartanburg, 29302-0262; (864) 598-9996; e-mail UAH@aol.com. members.aol.com/uah Serves the 864 telephone area code only.

Services

Website of interest
http://members.aol.com/connectsc/index.htm

Area groups

Aiken Aiken Area Home Educators, 901 Hayne Ave., Aiken, SC 29801; (803) 648-6081; 76612.2454@compuserve.com

Camden Christian Home Educators of Camden (CHEC), Contact person, Carol Wilkins, 603 Holland Ln., Camden, SC 29020-8316; (803) 432-8193.

Charleston, Berkeley and Dorchester Counties Lowcountry Christian Home Educators Association, Sandra Reeder,

(803) 553-7661; wreeder@charleston.net

Cherokee County Christian Home Educators of Cherokee County (CHECC). Support group of 40+ families. Christian in philosophy & governing board; membership open to anyone interested in hsling. Covers Cherokee County & surrounding rural areas. For info: CHECC c/o Susan Moore 113 Calton Drive, Gaffney, SC 29341 or weRblessed@juno.com.

Columbia, The Northeast Educators Division. Active in the northeast section of Richland Co., near Columbia. Claudette Horn, 1125 Pine Grove Rd., Blythewood, SC 29016; (803) 754-6897; chorn@dev.admin.sc.edu (Chris Horn)

Greenville Home Education Links for Parent Support (HELPS), C/O Donna Edwards, 53 Cobblestone Rd., Greenville, SC 29615; (864) 233-2450; E-mail for HELPS "Chair-mom," Pamela: wifeonc@aol.com. http://members.aol.com/helinks/indix.html

Greenville Piedmont Home Educators (PHEA) c/o Rich and Evie Nichols, 106 Westcreek Way, Greenville, SC 29607. (864) 676-1151 (3 - 9 p.m.). MemoryKeep@aol.com

Easley Easley Home Educators, Gale & Gregg Farrier, 310 Green Tree Dr., Liberty, SC 29657; (864) 843-1034. Also includes areas of: Pickens, Liberty, and Piedmont. http://www.geocities.com/Colosseum/Field/7939 /homeskool.html; galefarrier@juno.com or tapeprod@mindspring.com; t4clerbf@mindspring.com

Hilton Head Island Home School Association of the Low Country, P.O. Box 2257, Bluffton, SC 29910; contact Vicki Nix (803) 757-2377.

Laurens, George & Marlynn Powell, Rt. 1, Box 750, Laurens, SC 29360; 682-7306.

York County and more, York Education at Home York Educators at Home, Julie Brashear, 1476 Greenwood Lane, Rock Hill, SC 29732; (803) 325-8425; julesb2@cetlink.net A Christian group with many educational philosophies represented.

Government office

Department of Education, 1429 Senate St., Columbia, SC 29201. Public information (803) 734-8815; Office of General Counsel, (803) 734-8783.

SOUTH DAKOTA

State organizations

South Dakota Home School Assn., P.O. Box 822, Sioux Falls, SD 57101

Western Dakota Christian Home Schools, P.O. Box 528, Black Hawk, SD 57718-0528, (605) 923-1893. Newsletter, conference, and activities.

Government office (Contact one of the above first.)

State contact: State Division of Education, Kneip Office Building - 700 Governors Dr., Pierre, SD 57501. (605) 773-4770.

TENNESSEE

Statewide organizations

Tennessee Home Education Assn., 3677 Richbriar Ct., Nashville, TN 37211; (615) 834-3529.

Tennessee Homeschooling Families. Providing support, sponsoring activities, and publishing a newsletter. Lin Kemper, 214 Park Ln., Oliver Springs, TN 37840; (423) 435-9644. Newsletter information, Jennifer Liverly, 1356 Cove Ln., Oliver Springs, TN 37840

Regional groups and services (For other groups ask a state organization.)

Chattanooga Southeast Tennessee Home Education Association, P. O. Box 23374, Chattanooga, TN 37422; Hotline: (423) 266-4663 (423-266-HOME); Fax (anytime): (423) 344-4753; garycarole@aol.com

Memphis Home Education Assn., P.O. Box 240402, Memphis, TN 38124-0402; Covering about 20 support groups. Charles Maddox, President. (901) 681-9938. Voice mail & fax. mhea@MemphisHomeEd.org; http://www.MemphisHomeEd.org.

Mid-East Tennessee Education Association, 385 County Road 783, Etowah, TN 37331; (423) 263-7026; mideastthea@cococo.net; Newsletter, *Community Cupboard*, currently 5 issues/yr. for $8; 5th convention, May, 1998.

Ooltawaw - Collegedale Collegedale Area Homeschoolers Contact Rosemary Dibben. The group's focus is primarily for kids in grades K-3 or 4. Special events planned. http://www.southern.edu/english/home.html. (incomplete information

Service organization

Family Christian Academy, a nonprofit satellite school with four locations in the state: Madison (Nashville Metroplex), Knoxville, Chattanooga, and Bristol. Bookstores, workshops, newsletters, speakers, video library, computer products, annual camp out. Newsletter, speakers, workshops, video library, testing, camp out, etc. 487 Myatt Dr., Madison, TN 37115; (Phone (615) 860-3000, Fax ... -9788. (not confirmed).

Government office (Contact a state group first.)

Tennessee Department of Education Office of Accountability and Assessment, 710 James Robertson Pkwy., 7th Floor, Andrew Johnson Tower, Nashville, TN 37243; (615) 532-4703.

TEXAS

Statewide organizations

Texas Home School Coalition, P.O. Box 6982, Lubbock, TX 79493-6982. (806) 797-4927 or fax ... 4629. staff@thsc.org; http://www.thsc.org. Their free magazine, *THSReview*, is published 2 or 3 times a year. "THSC is dedicated to the preservation of all parents' rights to educate their children at home free from government intervention." Christian home educators comprise the board. $25/yr.

Home-Oriented Private Education for Texas, P.O. Box

59876, Dallas, TX 75229; (214) 358-2221; E-mail: hope4tx@gte.net; http://www.hopefortexas.org.

Service organizations

The Homeschool Store, 3703 Piney Woods, Houston, TX 77018-5846 (713) 683-8894; rswircpa@ix.netcom.com; located in Near-Northwest Houston.

The Teachers Store 1001 S. Allen Genoa, South Houston, TX 77587. (713) 944-2306; teachstor@aol.com.

Regional organizations

Family Educators' Alliance of South Texas, 4719 Blanco, San Antonio, TX 78212; (210) 342-4674; fax (210) 342-7339; office@homeschoolfeast.com; homeschoolfeast.com.

North Texas Home Educators' Network (NTHEN), P.O. Box 1071, Allen, TX 75013; (214) 804-8516; lambco@mymail.net

Southeast Texas Home School Association, 4950 FM 1960 W. PO Box 692075-297 (box not confirmed); Houston, TX 77069; (281) 370-8787; fax (281) 655-0963; sethsa@mailman.ghgcorp.com

Supporting Home Educators of Lower Texas Educational Region (SHELTER), 2424 Holden Rd., Aransas Pass, TX 78336; (512) 758-2777; fax (512) 758-8698.

West Texas Regional Home Schoolers, P.O. Box 717, Brookesmith, TX 76827-0717; (915) 646-3414; texsota@web-access.net

Area and local organizations (For other support groups ask a regional organization above.)

Abilene Big Country Home Educators, P.O. Box 6861, Abilene, TX 79608; (915) 676-1749.

Austin Austin Area Homeschoolers, c/o Julie Hart, 1419 Briarcliff Blvd., Austin, Texas 78723-1808; http://members.aol.com/Jdh4words/aah-index.html

Austin Christian Home Educators Association of Central Texas, P.O. Box 141998, Austin, TX 78714-1998; 512) 450-0070.

Austin http://members.aol.com/Jdh4words/aah-index.html

Double Oak / Lewisville North Texas Self-Educators, 150 Forest Ln., Double Oak / Lewisville, TX 75067. Also Homeschool Workshop for Beginners; Sarah Jordan (817) 430-4835; source@flash.net; tdfsystem@flash.net; http://www.flash.net/~lisadahl. Unschooling emphasis; beginner packet for SASE with 2 stamps; annual conference in the D/FW area.

Houston Bay Area Christian Home Educators Network, (Ba'Chen). P.O. Box 2524, Baytown, Texas 77522-2524; Phone/Fax: (281) 843-3200; BaChen01@aol.com http://members.aol.com/bachen01/index.htm. A service-oriented network of support groups around southeast Houston and the Galveston Bay.

Central Texas Heart of Texas Home Educators. A support group with contacts spread over counties of San Saba, Mills, Comanche, Coleman, and Brown. Contact Teresa Pavlicek, 1623 Broadmoor, Brownwood, TX 76801; (915) 643-3510; gpavlice@gte.ne

El Paso Southwest Homeschooling Network, Contact Rachel Lozano, P.O. Box. 371703, El Passo, TX 79937-1703; (915) 855-6399. A primarily Christian support group, open to anyone.

Fort Worth South Fort Worth Christian Home Educators, (SFWCHE), PO Box 16573, Fort Worth, TX 76133, (817) 249-1975, (817) 923-3451; robbjh@flash.net

Fort Worth Tarrant Home Education Assn., 6080 S. Hulen St., #360-109, Fort Worth, TX 76132; (817) 292-8879; http://www.flashnet/~cmoxley/index.html. The purpose of THEA is "to encourage study, interpretation, and improvement of home education, respecting the autonomy of each individual family and its right to educate at home. . . ."

Lubbock South Plains Christian Home Educators, P.O. Box 64904, Lubbock, TX 79464; (806) 795-1260.

Magnolia P.A.T.C.H. Work Magnolia area including Hempstead, Decker Prairie, Hockey, Todd Mission, and Plantersville. Contact Bill & Martha Renfro, 502 Kelly, Magnolia, Texas 77354; brenfro@ix.netcom.com; http://pw1.netcom.com/~brenfro/patchwork.html; The Renfros also publish the area newsletter.

Government office

(If more information is needed after contacting home schooling organizations): Texas Education Agency office: 1701 N. Congress, Austin, TX 78701-1494. (512) 463-9354; FAX: 512-463-9838.

UTAH

Statewide organizations

Utah Christian Home School Association, Box 3942, Salt Lake City, UT 84110-3942. Voice mail (801) 296-7198. The association operates UTCH (pronounced U-Teach) to provide support, education, and fellowship. Members may also enroll in the group's private extension school, Utah Christian Educational Institute. http://www.ogden-ut.com/utch/utch.html; WinderJR@aol.com

Utah Home Education Association, P.O. Box 167, Roy, UT 84067, (888) 887-UHEA; uhea@itsnet.com http://www.itsnet.com/~uhea/

Utah hs, an e-mail discussion group operated by Salt Lake Home Educators. Contact bluesky@utw.com if you are interested on signing on.

Support group

Salt Lake Home Educators, Contact Holly Godard. E-mail to shark@xmission.com or look up her phone number. SLHE is a support group created to offer support and information to all home educators. They operate on a volunteer basis. Visitors are welcome at meetings. Membership with newsletter, lending library, directory, and phone tree, only $8/yr. http://ourworld.compuserve.com/homepages/Bonehead/slhe.htm.

Service organization

Electronic High School, The Traditional high school

curriculum on the Internet. Jolene M. Morris; morris@tech.grand.k12.ut.us, Technology Director, Grand County School District, 264 South 400 East, Moab, Utah 84532. They serve only 15 students living in the district. If you can't or don't want to attend a school, you might inquire. If you live elsewhere (still in Utah helps a little) your chances of being accepted are slim indeed. See http://www.grand.k12.ut.us for information.

Government office (Contact a state h.s. organization first)
State Office of Education, 250 E. 500 S., Salt Lake City, UT 84111. (801) 538-7743.

VERMONT

Statewide organizations
Christian Home Educators of Vermont, 214 N. Prospect #105, Burlington, VT 05401-1613; (802) 658-4561. Newsletter: *CHEV Notes.*
Vermont Home Schoolers Association, Current information unavialable at time of publication.
Also see Homeschool Associates, an organization active in this state which offers many services including a newspaper. See under Maine.

Service
Resource Center for Homeschooling Deb Shell, consultant for older home school children. RD 2, Box 289-C, St. Albans, VT 05478; (802) 524-9645; shell@together.net. Newsletter ($10/yr.), annual conference. If you teach teens, you might want to be on her list.

Government office (if more information is needed)
Natalie Casco, Home Study Consultant, Vermont Department of Education, 120 State St., Montpelier, VT 05620. (802) 235-2424; Fax. (802) 828-5406. e-mail: ncasco@doe.state.vt.us

VIRGINIA

Statewide organizations
Virginia Home Education Association, P.O. Box 5131, Charlottesville, VA 22905; (540) 832-3578, E-mail vhea@virginia.edu Statewide organization for individuals, families, and groups. http://poe.acc.virginia.edu/~pm6f/vhea.html Membership is $15/yr ($50/yr for groups) and includes the informative bimonthly *VHEA Newsletter.* VHEA reports news, views, events, reviews, resources, issues, etc. Government contacts at all levels.
Home Educators Association of Virginia, Box 6745, Richmond, VA 23230; (804) 288-1608. Convention in June, graduation ceremony, etc.

Area organizations (For other groups ask the state organization.)
Charlottesville, Blue Ridge Area Network for Congenial Homeschooling (BRANCH), 255 Ipswich Pl., Charlottesville, VA 22901, (804) 974-7149. ABirdwell@aol.com
Learning in a Family Environment, (L.I.F.E.), 40672 Tankerville Road, Lovettsville, VA 20180; ebarkan@aol.com
Northern Virginia and Washington DC metro LEARN/Northern VA Homeschoolers. (xx Information packet, newsletter, group directory editor: Cindy Madsen, 6906 Brisbane St., Springfield, VA 22152 For information: Sue Compton, 12310 Streamvale Circle, Herndon, VA 22070.
REACH (Richmond Educational Alternatives for Children at Home) Box 36174, Richmond, VA 23235; reach_org@geocities.com
Virginia Beach: Beach Educators Association for Creative Homeschooling (BEACH); PO Box 64516, Virginia Beach, VA, 23467-4516; (757) 479-0311; fax (757) 479-0318; 70774.114@compuserve.com; Web page: http://wwwp.exis.net/~dplast/beach.htm; regional support group; annual curriculum fair in May; local homeschool hotline (757) 479-3139.

Service organizations
Educator's Exchange 1,000's of popular home school titles. (804) 794-6994 or write Educator's Exchange, 10755 Midlothian Tpk, Richmond, VA 23236.
The Virginia Satellite Educational Network VSEN courses are broadcast daily on C-band satellite Galaxy 6. Satellite system required if you are unable to go to where the course is shown in your area. For a registration package, call (800) 246-8736 or leave your name and address with Greg Weisiger at gweisige@pen.k12.va.us Web site: pen1.pen.k12.va.us/go/VDOE/Technology/VSEN/ Current high school courses include advanced placement and foreign languages

Government office
(if more information is needed after contacting home schooling organizations): State contact person: Charles W. Finley, Virginia Department of Education, Division of Compliance Coordination, P.O. Box 2120, Richmond, VA 23216-2120; (804) 225-2747; e-mail: cfinley@pen.k12.va.us. Ask for information packet which includes regulations, list of approved home study schools, and forms.

WASHINGTON

Statewide organizations
Washington Association of Teaching Christian Homes, Mike & Laurel Carey, 2904 N. Dora, Spokane, WA 99212; (509) 922-4811.
Washington Homeschool Organization, 18130 Midvale Ave., N., Ste. C, Shoreline, WA 98133; (206) 546-9483; WHOoffice@juno.com; http://www.washhomeschool.org . WHO assists all homeschoolers regardless of their reasons, philosophy of instruction, or methods. Annual convention (usually in June) includes high school graduation ceremony. Student Expo in the spring.

Regional and local organizations
Clark County Christian Home Educators, P.O. Box 5941; Vancouver, WA 98668; Voice mail: (360) 576-5357;

cchome.ed@juno.com; Chairman: Margaret L. Zysk.

Clarkston Also Lewiston, Idaho: Port Cities Home Educators. 24 Hr. Activities Hotline, Newsletter, field trips, activities, crafts, sports, graduation ceremony . . . Gary & Pat Greenfield; Directors, 1880 Old Spiral Highway, Lewiston, Idaho 83501. (208) 746-0874; HomeGreen@aol.com;http://www.hibek.net/~pche

Edmonds Trestle Homeschool Association, 14116 52nd Ave. W., Edmonds, WA 98026; Contact: Cindy Easter; (425) 742-3367; E-mail: TrestleHSA@aol.com

King County (south) and North Pierce County Homeschoolers Support Association, P.O. Box 413, Maple Valley, WA 98038; (206) 432-9805. Janice Hedin. Well over five hundred families. Everyone is welcome. Membership $25, Newsletter.

Lower Valley Home School Support Group, Tami J. Whitmore, 750 East Rd., Bickleton, WA 99322; (509) 896-2912.

Olympia Homeschool Support Group, Contact: Kae Schmidt (President), 7325 49th Ave. SE, Olympia, WA 98513; (360) 491-0499; Dandyfam@aol.com. A Christian group with about 90 families.

Palouse Homelearning Alternatives, 405 SE Hill St., Pullman, WA 99163. (509) 332-8127. Spans the area into Idaho. Nonsectarian.

Pierce County (south) See King County (north)

Puget Sound area Homeschoolers' Support Assn. A network of six groups (around 500 families) in the. Here are phone numbers for contact volunteers: Burien 878-4633; Enumclaw (360) 823-2795; Federal Way 952-1088 Issaquah 222-6265, Kent 631-9461; Pierce Co. 770-3554. Everyone is welcome. $25 membership includes many benefits. P.O. Box 413, Maple Valley, WA 98038.

Seattle Homeschool Group 6549 42nd Ave., NE, Seattle, WA 98115-7533. Contact Julie Scandora at (206) 525-8359 or pstielstra@aol.com.

Vancouver area Network of Vancouver Area Homeschoolers (NOVA) including Clark, Skamania, and Cowlitz counties. 162 Krogstad Rd., Washougal WA 98671; Lori Loranger, 71230.66@compuserve.com or (360) 837-3760.

Whatcom County and surrounding areas Whatcom Homeschool Association, 3851 Britton Rd., Bellingham, WA 98226; (360) 671-3689 or Fax (360) 647-6052; garym@dis-corp.com. Gary and Bobbe McGill. A support network of around 500 families, open to all. Meetings, fitness opportunities, mobile library, workshops.

Service organizations

Inland Empire Home School Center, P.O. Box 1750, Airway Heights, WA 99001, (509) 299-3766. Michael T. Smith. IEHSC facilitates home educators in Washington (and surrounding states) in a number of ways. Free newsletter upon request. They also provide testing and a computer based curriculum. mts50@juno.

Family Learning Organization, PO Box 7247, Spokane, WA 99207-0247; (509) 924-3760 or 467-2552 or check them at: www.familylearning.org Order tests by calling (800) 405-TEST. Newsletter. "We believe the most successful learning experiences tend in the direction of the natural learning style of the child. Having options in the law is the best way to ensure the most freedom for all." Their testing service is world wide; their newsletter focuses on the Northwest.

Materials sales

Family Books, 6701 180th Ave., SW, Lynnwood,WA 98037; (425) 787-2714.

The Homeschool Potpourri. and used curriculum materials. Kirkland, WA. See Appendix Z.

Government office (if more information is needed)

Melinda Dyer, Home-Based Instruction Program Supervisor, Office of Superintendent of Public Instruction, Old Capitol Building, P.O. Box 47200, Olympia WA 98504-7200; (360) 664-3574; TDD number, (360) 664-3631.

WEST VIRGINIA

Statewide organizations

Christian Home Educators of West Virginia, P.O. Box 8770, S. Charleston, WV 25303-8770, (304) 776-4664; chewvadm@aol.com.

West Virginia Home Educators Association, P.O. Box 3707, Charleston, WV 25337-3707; (800) 736-WVHE (9843). dustbunny@citynet.net (Include WVHEA in the subject line of messages). WVHEA is a state-wide homeschooling group, open to all homeschoolers in the state. Membership, currently $15.00 per year, includes a monthly newsletter; discounts on conference, picnic & testing fees; and legislative information and action alerts. We have an annual fall conference, and spring picnic, both located centrally in the state. We also organize an annual "Homeschooler's Day at the Legislature" with activities including meeting representatives, tours, and serving as pages. Testing services, tester training workshops, information on portfolio assessment and "alternative assessment."

Local support groups

Jackson County Homeschoolers, P.O. Box 333, Cottageville, WV 25239; Contact: Karen Weaver; (304) 372-4333; weaver@cheerful.com

Panhandle Family Schools, Cindy Biedler, P.O. Box 252, Gerrardstown, WV 25420; biedler@intrepid.net

Service organization

Consultant Cathy Michael / HSC Workshops Personal consultations and workshops on the following topics: Basics for beginners, Graduation, Learning styles, Portfolios, and Burnout. Cathy currently is not charging fees but appreciates donations. People like her deserve a serious amount depending on the learner's financial ability. Rt. 3, Box 229; (304) 258-2301.

Government office

(if more information is needed after contacting home schooling organizations): The state coordinator of home schooling is: Coordinator, West Virginia Department of Education, Office of Accreditation and Recognition, Room

346, Bldg. 6, Capitol complex, Charleston WV 25305-0330.

WISCONSIN

Statewide organizations

Wisconsin Christian Home Educators Association, 2307 Carmel Ave., Racine, WI 53405, (414) 637-5127; Fax (414) 638-8127; jang@execpc.com; http://www.execpc.com/~jang

Wisconsin Parents Association, P.O. Box 2502, Madison, WI 53701; Voice mail (608) 283-3131. An inclusive organization – individual religious and philosophical ideas are respected. Legislation and policies are monitored at all levels. Members are kept informed by quarterly newsletters and special bulletins so that they can decide how to relate to changing situations. Valuable information book, *Home Education in Wisconsin*. Monograms on other topics are also available. Annual conferences every April or May. Currently over a thousand members.

Local groups (There are many more.)

Sheboygan County Home Scholars of Sheboygan County, c/o Darcy Zwier, W5607 Hwy. W., Adell, WI 53001; (920) 528-7057; dmz@mail.tcbi.com

East Central Wisconsin. Unschooling Families, Peter & Sarah Gilbert, 1908 N. Clark St., Appleton, WI 54911; (920) 735-9832.

Madison HOME, 5745 Bittersweet Pl, Madison, WI 53705; Alison McKee, (608) 238-3302; amckee73@hotmail.com; http://www.geocities.com/Athens/Forum/4831.

Milwaukee Milwaukee Area Christian Home Educators, an association of over 100 home school families in the metropolitan area. Large and small group support meetings, special events, sports activities, field trips, legislative information and a newsletter published eight times a year. Membership in MACHE is currently $15 per year. (414) 299-0985; MACHE, P.O. Box 428, Sussex, WI 53089; http://www.execpc.com/~djq/mache

Milwaukee Milwaukee Area Home Learners, W260 N7751 Jay Ln, Sussex, WI 53089; Erich Moraine, (414) 246-3604; emoraine@execpc.com.

Government office (if more information is needed after contacting home schooling organizations): Director, Consultative Services Team, State of Wisconsin Department of Public Instruction, 125 S. Webster St., P.O. Box 7841, Madison, WI 53707-7841. (608) 266-5761.

WYOMING

Statewide Organizations

Homeschoolers of Wyoming, P.O. Box 907, Evansville, WY 82636; (307) 237-4383; Fax ... 3080.

Unschoolers of Wyoming, Chris Anderson-Sprecher, 4512 Mockingbird Ln., Laramie, WY 82070.

Government office (if more information is needed)

State contact: Consultant; Wyoming State Department of Education, Hathaway Building, 2nd Fl., 2300 Capitol Ave., Cheyenne, WY 82002. (307) 777-6268.

E

Information for Canada

This appendix identifies national companies and institutions serving home educators. It also provides starting points for finding information specific to particular provinces and territories. In the smaller organisations, leadership (and addresses) naturally change. We invite you to keep us informed for future editions of this book.. Gazelle Publications, www.hoofprint.com.

National Information

Association of Universities and Colleges of Canada AUCC represents Canada's universities, at home and abroad. Its mandate is to foster and promote the interests of higher education. Through advocacy, policy analysis, research, communicatins, information sharing and international cooperation, AUCC strives to assure the contribution of the nation's universities. Publications available from AUCC include *The Directory of Canadian Universities.* http://www.aucc.ca; 350 Albert St., Suite 600, Ottawa K1R 1B1. (613) 563-3961, ext. 205; Fax (613) 563-9745

Canadian Home Educators Digest, The. {Formerly *Quest*} Articles from regular contributors and ones selected from other sources with a variety of opinions. Christian editorial policy. Editor, Joanne Barendregt sees the magazine as an open forum. It includes practical tips, biblical truths, encouragement from those who have been there, and bold challenges. It tackles issues which are somewhat controversial. In addition to several articles, you will find a "youth page," a "family profile," places for letters and a readers forum, and updates from several provinces. The publisher is Dick Barendregt. Subscription $20/yr. 12128-95A Street NW, Edmonton, Alberta, T5G 1R9. Phone (403) 674-3002' fax 674-3702; E-mail plough@teusplanet.net; http://www.telusplanet.net/public/plough /quest1.htm (This URL contains the numberal 1 near the end).

Canadian Home School Information Guide Author Gayle Crouser covers the important points. She begins with why parents would want to teach their children, talks about teaching principles including styles of education, planning, preparing a portfolio, high school, and the use of the web. Section 10 is "Provincial Information." Resources for getting materials are also listed. Although her book has only 63 pages, they are large and she has used them well. 1997 (with more editions to come). Eagle's Nest Home School Support Services, Box 984, Okotoks, AB T0L 1T0; 102635.266@compuserve.com

Association of Canadian Home-Based Education Canadian home schooling information including contacts for area groups. http://www.flora.ottawa .on.ca/homeschool-ca This collection of information is worth checking. If you can, please examine the web page before contacting writing. Marion F. Homer, RR #1, Rose Bay, N.S. B0J 2X0; (902) 766-4355; marion.f.homer @ns.sympatico.ca

Excel Christian Educator's Resources, (604) 857-5535, BC V4W 3H8.

Home Education News, Lael Whitehead, 3586 Creery Ave., West Vancouver, B.C., V7V 2M1 (604) 922-1835; lael@direct.ca; $18/yr. (6 issues). Free sample copy.

Home School Legal Defense Association of Canada, #2 3295 Dunmore Rd. SE, Medicine Hat, AB T1B 3R2. (403) 528-2704. Services similar to HSLDA in the US. They offer legal services to members.

Home schoolers of Colour See Appendix C, Part 3.

Home Works The Home Works 1760 Groves Rd., P.O. Box 340, Russell, ON K4R 1E1; (613) 445-3142; Fax ... 0587; toll-free order number available; homework@magma.ca. Suppliers of teaching materials specifically selected for Canadian families. Includes Usborne, curriculum packages, unit studies like Alta Vista, an extensive collection of materials for Canadian studies, as well as several books for French Second Language studies. Website: http://www.home-school.com/mall/how/how.html

Image Extension School Full curriculum including Biblical character development. 15 - 13th St. East, Prince Albert, Sask. S6V 1C7; (306) 763-4206, (800) 268-8867. (current information not received)

Lifetime Canada, Carol Singleton, RR#6 Markdale ON N0C 1H0; (519) 986-2686. Materials suppliers.

More Than Books ... All general subject areas with as many Canadian publications as possible, especially in social studies. Write or phone for free catalog. 146 McClintock Way, Kanata, ON K2L 2A4; (613) 592-5338.

Natural Life "Deschooling" shares the pages of this periodical with other topics of resourceful living. Editor Wendy Priesnitz is a veteran leader of Canadian home schooling. $24/yr. (6 issues), including GST; (or for US, US$24). The Alternate Press, RR #1, St. George, Ont., N0E 1N0; phone/fax (519) 488-4001. E-mail natural@life.ca Web site http://www.life.ca

Regional Information

If your group or service is not listed (and you would like it to be), please send information to Gazelle Publications for the next edition of this book.

ALBERTA

Alberta Home Education Association, Box 3451, Leduc, AB T9E 6M2. (403) 548-2398; gdbert@ telusplanet.net.

Home-based Learning Society of Alberta. Ask for current information.

WT Educational Services. Rudi Krause offers workshops and consulting, and he publishes for home schools. Publications of interest to Canadians. 12563 Carrs Landing Rd., Winfield, BC V4V 1A1; (604) 766-0568, Fax (604) 766-4051.

BRITISH COLUMBIA

Provincial leadership

Canadian Home Educators' Association of B.C., 6980 Marble Hill Rd., Chilliwack, BC V2P 6H3 (250) 493-0338; fax (604) 794-3940; cheabc@imag.net; President, Colleen Erzinger. Newsletter; informtaion packed.

Service organization

Fraser Valley Distance Education School, 49520 Prairie Central Road, Chilliwack, B.C. Canada V2P 6H3 (604) 794-7310; (800) 663-3381, Fax: (604)795-8480; Contact Peter Brown at pbrown@rainbow.fvrcs .gov.bc.ca A large school service for the province serving some 8,000 elementary and secondary students. (Recent information, but confirmation not received before press time.)

Support groups

Cowichan Valley Christian Homeschool Support Group. Information unavailable.

Fraser Delta Homelearners ..., Contact Cynthia Hamilton, Cynthia_Hamilton@bc.sympatico.ca; 18222-29A Avenue Surrey BC V4P 1M6; (604) 538-8163

Greater Vancouver Homelearners Network Informal and non-religious meetings. Newcomers welcome. Call Diana at (604) 298-7710 or e-mail dsandberg@lightspeed.bc.ca. 24-hour information line: (604) 873-5170.

Mid-Island Home Learners, Nanaimo B.C. on Vancouver Island. All are welcome to attend our meeting regardless of religious background, teaching philosophies or methods. Tracy Lim (250) 751-0337.; 5776 Kerry Ln., Nanaimo, BC V9T 5N5; tlim@mail.sd91.bc.ca (notice nine-one, not nine-ell)

North Shore Homelearner's Group, Annette MacKay, 212 West Windsor Rd., North Vancouver, BC, V7N 2N1. Phone: (604) 990-0948, e-mail: mackay @axionet.com Alternate contact: Heather Korsa (604) 988 7464. Open meeting 3rd Monday, 7 pm at Annette's. Call to confirm the time.

Oliver/Osoyoos Home Learners. Call Laurel Pinske, (604) 498-0244; lpinske@mail.sd56.bc.ca

White Rock Christian Home Educators Contact Phillipa Bayliss, 2076 Bower Dr., So. Surrey, B.C. V4A 6S6; (604) 535-2772.

MANITOBA

Manitoba Association for Schooling at Home. Ask for current contact information.

Manitoba Association of Christian Home Schools, P.O. Box 283, St. Vital, MB R2M 5C8; (204) 376-5423; (204) 367-5423; ghuebner@freenet.mb.ca.

For further information after contacting the Association office: Home Schooling Office, Independent Study Program, Box 7000 (555 Main St.), Winkler, MB R6W 1C4. Contact Art Rempel. (800) 668-9910 or (204) 325-2306.

NEW BRUNSWICK

Home Educators of Brunswick 9 Garrison Dr., Rothefay, NB E2H 2V1; (506) 847-4663; 104302.1060@compuserve.com

Brunswick Support Group. Ask for current contact information.

NORTHWEST TERRITORIES

Hay River Homeschoolers (current contact information unavailable at press time).

Inuvik Homeschooling Group, Box 2285, Inuvik, NT X0E 0T0

Ft. Smith Homeschooling Group, Box 1117, Ft. Smith, NT X0E 0P0 (not confirmed)

NOVA SCOTIA

Nova Scotia Home Education Assn., (902) 422-7928. Contact: Marion Homer, RR #1, Rose Bay, N.S. B0J 2X0, (902) 766-4355, marion.f.homer@ns.sympatico.ca (not confirmed)

Nova Scotia Christian Home Schooling Assn., Lynda McLaughlin, RR#3, Lunenburg, NS B0J 2C0, mclaugh@cast.navnet.net.

The two provincial groups work in cooperation, NSHEA taking more responsibility for government relations and general information. Government regulations (8/97) require annual reporting to the Department of Education reporting the child's progress. Ask a provincial group or HSLDA for more information.

ONTARIO

Ontario Federation of Teaching Parents Albert Lubberts, President Contact: Herb Jones, Administration. 145 Taylor Road, RR 1, Gananoque, ON K7G 2V3. 613) 382-4947 OFTP offers support, newsletters, a directory, information meetings, and help for homeschooling families. Membership is $25 per year per family and is money well-spent. OFTP keeps on top of the political situation of home-based education in Ontario.

Ontario Christian Home Educator's Connection, 35 King St., Branchton, Ont. N0B 1L0; President, Jim van't Voort, Box 2, Iona Station, Ont., N0L 1P0; jimvv@execulink.com. Conferences, workshops, support group connections, newsletters.

Orilla Orillia Homeschooler's Network, Marge Black, jblack@odacl.org.

Rideau Valley Homeschooling Association (contact information not confirmed) For the Ottawa Valley area and for the city of Ottawa. Field trips, meetings. Families with many perspectives including committed Christians. All believe that parents are responsible to direct education.

Windsor Older Homeschoolers Group; See under Michigan in Appendix D.

Supplier

Forever Family, 2631 Washburn Rd., RR #2, Invary, Ont., K0H 1X0; (613) 353-7390; tran@adan.kingston .net (not confirmed)

QUEBEC

Organizations

Quebec Home Schooling Advisory / Conseil pour l'Education à Domicile au Québec, 1002 Rosemarie Val David, Quebec, J0T 2N0; (819) 322-6495. Now operated by Elizabeth Edwards and Leslie Titcombe. Please send a self-addressed stamped envelope for information. A bilingual quarterly newsletter is available for $15/yr.

Vaudreuil-Dorion Homeschooling Support Group. Current contact information not available at press time. Try , Suzanne Barberini or/ Angie Blackman 42 Prevost, RR#7, Vaudreuil, Quebec J7V 8P5; vsnewltr@axess.com; No fees, non-denominational. *The Vaudreuil-Soulanges Homeschooling Newsletter*.

Western Quebec Home School Association, Jeff Schultz, RR #1, Shawville, Quebec, J0X 2Y0. Telephone: (819) 647-3665.

N.B. La loi de l'instruction publique permet certaines exemptions à l'assistance à l'école publique.

SASKATCHEWAN

Saskatchewan Government Correspondence School.

1500-4th Avenue, Regina, Sask. S4P 3V7. (306) 787-6024 or (800) 667-7166 in Saskatchewan. Internet address: http://www.sasked.gov.sk.ca/sgcs/ (1996 information)

High school courses for grades 9 - 12 are available for Saskatchewan residents including those temporarily absent from the province. Correspondence School courses follow the prescribed Saskatchewan curricula. Students may register for full service which includes instruction and evaluation. Reference materials are available as well. For further information contact the Correspondence School directly.

Provincial organizations

Saskatchewan Christian Home Schoolers Association, (current information not received)

Saskatchewan Home-Based Educators, 403 - 22nd Street West, Suite 13, Saskatoon, SK, S7M 5T3; (888) 233-7423 or (306) 545-3532 (Phone/FAX line); alramsey@sask.maple.net

Area organizations and services

Fellowship Book Center, at Yellowhead Centre, 1715 Idylwyld Dr. N., Saskatoon, SK S7L 1B4; (800) 667-6371; (306) 653-6370. Also at Grosvenor Park Centre; (306) 653-6372.

Prince Albert and Shellbrook areas: Helen Zacharias, contact person, Box 2124, Prince Albert, Sask. S6V 6V4; (306) 747-3950.

Saskatoon Home Works Educational Consulting, Lynn Peters, 1631 Vickies Ave., Saskatoon, Sask. S7N 2P2; Fax: (306) 249-0673; lpeters@webster.sk.ca

Note: We understand that registration with a local board is required for "home-based education programmes." For ages 7-15. Contact one of the organizations above.

YUKON TERRITORY

Yukon Home Educators Society, POB 4993, Whitehorse, Yukon Y1A 4S2.

Call (403) 667-5607 for information.

NEWFOUNDLAND and LABRADOR and PRINCE EDWARD ISLAND

See the *National Information* section of this appendix for listings of national organizations. Some of them may be aware of support groups in your area. Also check the Canadian Homeschooling web site.

F

Information for Countries Outside North America

In this appendix, we provide information about organisations of specific interest to home schooling families in several countries outside of the US and Canada. Our listing here (or elsewhere) does not imply endorsement. We do not know very many of the people or the histories of these groups.

For legal information, ask a support organisation.

Prices and availability for services or publications assume they are sent within the country and in its currency. Unless instructed otherwise, send a self-addressed envelope with appropriate stamps when requesting information.

Phone numbers generally assume you are calling from within the country. Otherwise you would need to use your international access prefix in addition to the numbers shown.

***Please do not copy** this information for publication without confirming with each of the original sources.*

AUSTRALIA

Information for Australia and Zealand is practically all provided as a courtesy of Kingsley Educational.

Legal provisions for homeschooling vary among the different states and territories, the Angelicos of Kingsley Educational Pty. Ltd. (KEPL) recommend seeking independent guidance on establishing a home school. Parents should contact one of the voluntary organisations and if necessary obtain independent legal advice. For those with conscientious objections to the whole process of registration and subservience to government regulations, it is essential to obtain sound advice before approaching government officials.

Expatriates on temporary assignment to Australia should make early contact with either KEPL or Light Educational Ministries who can refer enquirers to qualified legal practitioners for specialist assistance.

A.C.E. Australia, Ltd., P.O. Box 5470, Brendale, M.D.C., Queensland 4500. The organisation, also known as School of Tomorrow, supplies Christian worktext materials (Paces) and operates a membership/enrollment system of distance education. ACE schools are in various locations. Tel (07) 3205 7444 Fax (07) 3205 7331.

Alternative Education Resource Group c/– 7 Bartlett St., Moorabbin, Vic. 3189. +613 9553 4720 (answering service). Support for people wanting to find or create alternatives to mainstream forms of education. Legal and other information on home education and alternative schools, networks and like-minded families. Quarterly newsletter, resource list, and group activities.

Australian Home Education Web site of general interest. http://homeschool.3dproductions.com.au/content.html.

Canberra Home Education Network A group of some 50 families in Australian Capital Territory. Activities sponsored include science, music, sports, and excursions. Their bimonthly newsletter, *Homework*, is also available outside of the A.C.T. $10/yr. within Australia. For a free sample send a stamped self-addressed 9x4 envelope. Contact Drew or Vanessa Corrigan, 23 Bardolph St., Bonython, A.C.T. 2905; +616 293 1760 Fax +616 293 1314 E-mail: homework@cs.anu.edu.au Corrigans also publish privately *Education At Home* $26/yr., four issues.

Christian Home Education Canberra Contact: Drew & Chris Andison +616 242 9452. Newsletter address: CHEC Newsletter P O Box 189 Mitchell ACT 2911. Quarterly newsletter, fellowship meetings, excursions & camps, resource reviews and legal information. Subscription/ membership fee $A5 per half year. Excellent discipline policy & procedure for meetings. (It's worth getting the newsletter just to see how they do it!)

Families Honouring Christ, An all-volunteer Christian group based in Melbourne Victoria but serving members all over Australia. Benefits include legal news, free (at present) qualified legal assistance (the lawyers homeschool too!), second hand books sold by mail (when available), seminars, suggestions for Australian studies, Bible research studies, excursions, children's clubs, library by mail, contact information for special groups, reviews, etc. $A12/yr, for newsletters issued approximately monthly. See Kingsley Educational for contact details.

The Home Schooler Barry & Cecil Harker, 20 Long St. Point Vernon Hervey Bay, Qld 4655. Editor phone/fax +6171 24 4306. High quality magazine for parents in the South Pacific region. A$10/yr. (2 issues). Information sheets on how to get started at primary or secondary levels available. Adventist flavour but naturally open to all.

Homeschoolers Australia, Pty. Ltd., P.O. Box 420, Kelleyville, NSW 2153. A broad-based organisation concerned tc ensure the right of all parents to home educate. Referral point to groups that meet specific needs: religious, educational, and social. Mr. Greg, Mrs. Jo-Anne Beirne, co-ordinators. +612 629 3727, Fax +612 629 3278. Information package, $15. Australian Homeschool Journal, 48 pages, $30/yr. (6 issues). Agent for John Holt Book & Music Store and the books of the Moores.

Homeschooling Association 640 Caboolture River Rd., Upper Caboolture, QLD., 4510. Robert Osmak. +6174 967 884. They provide contacts for homeschoolers.

Kingsley Educational pty. ltd. Serves Australia, Zealand, South East Asia, Pacific region and Africa by supplying quality Christian materials from Alpha Omega Publications, Saxon Maths, Educators Publishing Service, Providence Project, Christian Life Workshops, Audio Memory, Ruth Beechick and local Australian sources. Authors include Wade, Fugate, Pride, Aslett, Spaulding, Harris, Blumenfeld, Rodd, McIntyre and others. Phonics program for Australia & Zealand, Group buying services, information on other Australian sources, phone advice, extra help for special families (in isolated areas, missionaries, and expatriates on assignment. Box 310 MDC, Mount Waverley, VIC 3149, Australia. Phone +(613) 9544-8792; Fax +(613) 9544 2328. E-mail: talldad@pobox.com.au

Light Educational Ministries PO Box 966 Dickson ACT 2602 ph +616 241 9201 fax +616 241 9460. Quarterly newsletter Light of Life. Suppliers of a wide range of Christian materials: Rod & Staff, A Beka, Spalding Phonics etc. Home Education Assistance Scheme (fee-based). Seminars on phonics, Christian Education topics.

Sunshine Coast Homeschooling Group, #40 Browns Rd., Belli Park, via Edmundi, 4562 Qld; Contact Maggy Purcell, +646 357 470227.

Telematics and the Electric Lyrebird Distance Education in the Dandenong Ranges. The Open Learning Network system is described on this site: www.schnet.edu.au/Docs/Home/DROLN/eleclyre.html

FRANCE

Grandir Sans Ecole B.P. 5, F-68480 Ferrette, Tel. (+33) 389 40 48 34; huub.haesen@wanadoo.fr. Quarterly newsletter with practical ideas.

GREDNA

Mike and Phyllis Harder Contact persons for the Eastern Carribean islands. Mike & Phyllis Harder; haderfam@caribsurf.com

JAPAN

Clonlara branch Contact: Mihoko Wakabayashi, Clonlara Japan Office, 8 Shokaku-cho, Fukakusa, Fushimi-ku, Kyoto-city 612, JAPAN (075) 531-0477. See Clonlara in Appendix A.

MEXICO

El Hogar Educador Mike Richardson, Fresno 931, Hacienda de los Morales, 3er Sector, 66495 San Nicolás de los Graza, N.L. México. Tel. 83-34-9405. Or 1001 So. 10th St., G-529, McAllen, TX 78501.

NEW ZEALAND

Christian Home Schoolers of Zealand, 4 Tawa St., Palmerston North. Craig S. Smith, Director, Ph./Fax +646 357 4399. CHomeS is a voluntary husband/wife ministry providing advice, support group information, government contacts, seminars, etc. A seven-booklet series is available from the organisation entitled An Introduction to Home Schooling. Post-paid for NZ$12.00 (These funds help support the ministry.) keystone.teach@xtra.co.nz

Ezra Group, 35d Salisbury Road, Birkdale, Auckland 10, Zealand; Phone + 64 9 483 6083; Fax + 64 9 483 6083; Email Denise Walmsley;Walmsley@compuserve.com

The Home Schooler Described under Australia. Available from Mrs. Marilyn Kemp, NZ editor, The Home Schooler, 146 Albany Heights Rd., RD 2, Albany, Auckland. +649 415 9782 NZ$10/yr. (2 issues). Australian-produced magazine with relevance for Zealand including a NZ feature in each issue.

Kingsley Educational See under Australia. Payment facilities by Bank of Zealand plus major bank credit cards (Visa, Mastercard, Bankcard)

Zealand Home Schooling Association 5 Thanet Ave., Mt. Albert, Auckland. Supporting a responsible choice. "We act on a political level to promote an awareness and understanding of homeschooling in all its diversity. . ." Newsletter and comprehensive starter kit available.

NZ Home Education Web site with general information including local support groups. http://ourworld.compuserve .com/homepages/astley/homeeduc.htm

PUERTO RICO

Christian Home Educators of the Caribbean, Box 7888, Suite 87, Guaynabo, PR 00970; (787) 740-6227; (787) 852-5672.

Western Home Education Association A Variety Enriched Resource (WEAVER) A nonsectarian group meeting in Mayaguez. Lisa Rodriguez, Urb. La Monserrate #418, Calle Guadalupe, Moca, PR 00676; Phone 877-1592.

SOUTH AFRICA

Association for Home Schooling, PO Box 31264, Totiusdal, Pretoria, 0134. Telephone and fax: +27 12 331 1018 (international) 012 331 1018 (national) e-mail curamus1@lantic.co.za; www.lantic.co.za/~curamus Contact persons: Leendert and Karin van Oostrum?

Theocentric Christian Education, Grams Shortridge, P.O. Box 594, Brackenfell, 7560. Voice phone: 981-0475. Fax: 21-685-5884. (1998 confirmation of this information not received)

SPAIN

Crecer sin Escuela c/o Norberg - Szil, Apdo. 45, 03580 Alfaz del Pi, (Alicante) Spain. Newsletter: "Crecer sin Escuela", biannual. Péter Szil. szil@ctv.es. Because resources are limited, please contact Crecer sin Escuela only if you are considering teaching your children as a resident of Spain.

SWITZERLAND

Vereinigung Freier Schulen der Schweiz/Association Suisse des Ecoles Nouvelles (VFSS/ASEN), Davidsbodenstrasse 63, CH-4056 Basel, Tel. (+41) 61 322 50 30, Fax (+41) 61 383 25 72. This association of alternative (free) schools also has contacts among home school families.

Unterwegs auf Neuen Lern & Erziehungswegen A magazine for people who live with kids or work with them. Hanna Marti Verlag, editor. Phone and address as above although under separate administration. E-mail unterwegs@email.ch

THE UNITED KINGDOM

British Technology Online Education and Training. www.campus.bt.com/

Educate Online Web site. Select "home education." http://www.educate.co.uk/welcome.htm

Education Otherwise, P.O. Box 7420, London, N9 9SG, UK; e_o@netlink.co.uk; http://www.education-otherwise.org. For emergency contact, phone 0891 518303 Membership is open to anyone. A national network with local co-ordinators who are willing to give personal help to the membership, and are backed by people with specialised experience in various aspects of education "otherwise." Support offered includes advice for dealing with the Local Education Authorities (LEAs). The co-ordinators are voluntary with limited time. So, after the initial questions, they need to give support preference to those signed up as members.

The Home Service, 48 Heaton Moor Road, Heaton Moor, Stockport, SK4 4NX, Tel 0161-432-3782, s.richards@zetnet.co.uk, www.alphainfo.co.uk/homeservice/ A support organisation for Christian home educators. Home service produces a growing range of guidance papers on subjects such as GCSE examinations, Resources, and Home Education. Home Service organises local workshops, in association with CARE Trust and also hosts a national two day conference every two years. One is planned for September 1998.

Newsletter for Home Educators in Sussex, Lyndon Pugh, 37 Nevill Rd., The Barn, Mongers Farm, Barcombe, LEWES, Rottingdean, Brighton, East Sussex BN2 7HH (0273) 307503.

Taking Children Seriously A journal, web site and related internet discussion lists, whose focus is upon non-coercive education and parenting. Issues addressed have included: Problems of the curriculum mentality; the implications of our fallibility for parenting, etc. Write for current subscription prices or see the information on the TCS web site at www.eeng.dcu.ie/~tcs/index.html. E-mail: sl@enterprise.net Snail mail address: 46 Latimer Grange, Latimer Road, Oxford OX3 7PH, England, UK. Telephone: (+44) (1865) 761817.

World-wide Education Service Distance learning courses enabling parents to teach their children aged 3 to 12 in the UK or abroad. Studies follow the National Curriculum for England and Wales and encourage learning from the local area, too. WES grew out of an organisation founded by educationalist, Charlotte Mason. Contact Director, Dorrie Wheldall, WES Home School, Blagrave House, 17 Blagrave Street, Reading. Berkshire RG1 1QA; Phone: 0118 958 9993; Fax: 0118 958 9994; office@weshome.demon.co.uk

G

A Typical K-12 Curriculum

The outline which follows shows topics and objectives for elementary and secondary studies. No school system would follow it exactly.

I have not included this listing to show you specifically what to teach but as a reference for comparison. Home teaching is naturally in danger of achieving a narrow range of objectives even (or especially) with some of the packaged programs. And success on standardized tests is not sufficient evidence that your child is learning the most important material. Such exams measure only the bare essentials – the common elements all children need. Compare this list with what you plan to teach, and consider expanding in selected areas you feel are important.

The items on these lists are not of equal importance. Some can be dealt with in a ten-minute discussion. Others need a long time. Some items are mentioned at one level that should be dealt with during more than one school year. They are generally arranged from simple to complex, so during the first of the three years spanned by the grouping, you would expect to cover topics earlier in the list. Some topics are appropriate at another time, and some may not be of importance at all for your child. The math section, for example, seems to me to be a little ambitious, at least at the higher levels.

You would not normally cover all the subject areas on this list. For example, the advanced math classes are taken (and needed) by only a few. Many do not study a language and few would study more than one. Not that all these things are useless, but in a typical program of eight years for elementary education and four for secondary, there simply is not enough time. Also children who have difficulties with learning need not be pressured. For example, if your child needs to spend a long time on the important math concepts in high school should you expect him or her to be taking two years of a modern language? Not usually, but to learn just a little Spanish could be fun and would provide a basis for later development. Some students would want to spend more time in a technology area and less in the more academic courses.

The topics were composed by studying the list available from World Book Educational Products, a state department of education list, a Christian school system list, and a few additions of my own. Although the topics are typical for US schools, many or most elements are common to what children and youth learn in other countries. You may want to select areas to cover and check them off when adequately learned.

If you would like a copy of the World Book list, contact Educational Services Department, World Book Educational Products, 101 Northwest Point Blvd., Elk Grove Village, IL 60007.

The material is basically divided into three elementary school levels and high school. It roughly corresponds to grade levels as follows:

Early Elementary	Grades K to 2
Later Elementary	Grades 3 to 5
Middle School	Grades 6 to 8
High School	Grades 9 to 12

EARLY ELEMENTARY

With items suggested for each level K, 1, and 2.

Early Elementary , Character Development – Bible

_
_ **K** God who made all things
_ **K** Basic Bible stories
_ **1** Story of Jesus; parables
_ **1** Worship, reverence
_ **1** Respect for God's book
_ **1** Protection of Bible characters and today
_ **1** Bible verses memorized
_ **2** Mission and character stories
_ **2** God's power in the Exodus story

Early Elementary, Art and Music

_ **K** Colors, shapes, textures
_ **K** Making pictures
_ **2** Enjoying art objects

_ **K** Songs and spiritual praise
_ **1** Rhythm
_ **1** Singing to pitch
_ **1** Various instruments
_ **1** Learning songs (and hymns)
_ **2** The ways musical pieces differ
_ **2** Simple reading of musical notes

Early Elementary, Language Arts

Reading
_ **K** Pre-reading activities for skill preparation
_ **K** Letter and simple phoneme sounds.
_ **1** Integrated decoding strategies
_ **2** Book format understood (title page, left to right, etc.)
_ **2** Questions and conclusions about stories
_ **2** Listening to develop vocabulary and usage patterns
_ **2** Developing sight word recognition
_ **2** Understanding from phrases, sentences, and story flow

Writing
_ **1** Storytelling
_ **1** Handwriting, manuscript to cursive
_ **2** Spelling gradually more important
_ **2** Write and illustrate pieces to share with others

Listening
_ **K** Attitude developed for listening
_ **K** Oral instructions followed
_ **K** Visualize what is heard
_ **2** Recognize main idea
_ **2** Listening to answer questions (comprehension)
_ **2** Learning not to be deceived

Speech
_ **1** Practice speaking and see how it is different from writing
_ **1** Courtesy in communication
_ **1** Courtesy in conversation
_ **2** Introductions and greetings

Early Elementary, Mathematics, Thinking, and Computer Skills

Mathematics
_ **K** Counting to 10
_ **K** More than, less than
_ **K** Equality, inequality
_ **1** Number concepts
_ **1** Data collection by counting, measuring, and surveying
_ **1** Exploring number relationships with manipulatives
_ **1** Simple addition and subtraction facts
_ **1** Addition and subtraction of two-digit numbers
_ **1** Counting backwards
_ **2** Number patterns
_ **2** Meaning of zero
_ **2** Number line, symbols + and -
_ **2** Place value
_ **2** Cardinal and ordinal number concepts
_ **2** Counting money
_ **2** Telling time (analog and digital)
_ **2** Simple line and bar graphs
_ **2** Concept of odd and even
_ **2** Halves, quarters and, by grade 3, thirds
_ **2** Area concept using graph paper
_ **2** Perimeter, volume
_ **2** Whole numbers
_ **2** Seeing how changing one number in a relationship makes others change

Computer skills
_ **K** Handling a mouse
_ **1** Using a keyboard for basic keys
_ **1** Menus

Early Elementary, Social Studies

In the chapter on social studies you will find a list of what has been traditionally studied in each grade.

_
_ **K** Family history
_ **K** Fairness
_ **K** Safety rules and symbols
_ **K** Participating in projects to help the community
_ **K** Stories of people in the past
_ **1** Use of clocks and calendars
_ **1** What makes geographical places different
_ **1** Economic exchanges by children
_ **1** Environmental changes by people
_ **1** Surveying other students about community life
_ **2** Goods and services produced for the community by the government
_ **2** Government authority in the community
_ **2** Discovering reasons for rules
_ **2** Markets, producers, consumers, and investors
_ **2** How coins and currency facilitate exchange
_ **2** Exploring information sources
_ **2** Discussion of an issue; comparison of viewpoints
_ **2** How people and resources from other places interact with the local community
_ **2** Writing about a home or community decision or issue
_ **2** Preparation of a statement advocating a certain action in home, church, or community
_ **2** Differentiate between historical facts and historical interpretations
_ **2** Characteristics of regions in the local area
_ **2** Family income and financial planning

Early Elementary, Science

_ **K** Safety and severe weather
_ **K** Sun, moon, planets, and their motions
_ **K** Magnetic materials and interactions
_ **K** Safety with electricity
_ **K** Develop a sensitivity to nature
_ **K** Shadows
_ **K** Seasons
_ **1** Use simple mechanical devices and explain them
_ **1** Simple "machines"
_ **1** Characteristics that help organisms survive
_ **1** Uses for water
_ **1** Classification of objects by scientific properties
_ **2** Light and vision
_ **2** The food chain
_ **2** Materials the earth is made of
_ **2** Water cycle (rain, evaporation, etc.)
_ **2** Measuring objects

Early Elementary, Health Education

_ **K** How to avoid dangerous circumstances and how to get help (for example, for child molestation dangers)
_ **K** Parts of the body
_ **K** Personal hygiene
_ **K** Dental health
_ **1** Relationship between health and lifestyle
_ **1** Habits of eating, exercise, and rest
_ **1** Diseases that threaten children including the common cold
_ **1** Dressing to care for the body
_ **2** Awareness of media influence
_ **2** Basic food groups
_ **2** Care of eyes and ears

Early Elementary, Physical Education

_ **K** Motor skill development with bean bags, jumping rope, running
_ **K** Balance, fitness
_ **K** Safety rules
_ **1** Physical activity for interpersonal development

LATER ELEMENTARY

Grades 3 to 5

Later Elementary, Character Development – Bible

_ Interpersonal and intrapersonal happiness in the divine expectations
_ The plan of salvation
_ Guidance of God's people today
_ Meaning behind Bible stories
_ Basic Bible teachings
_ Trust in God
_ Bible passages memorized

Later Elementary , Art and Music

_ Color blends
_ Texture
_ Techniques such as collage and prints

_ Group singing
_ Rhythm patterns , time signatures
_ Treble and base clefs
_ Instrument types: strings, keyboard, brass, woodwinds, percussion, electronic
_ Composers

Later Elementary, Language Arts

Reading
_ Summary and analysis skills
_ Capitalization, punctuation, and spelling awareness
_ Editing of spelling
_ Dictionary used for more details
_ Synonyms and antonyms
_ Parts of speech
_ Vowels, plurals, possessives, and pronouns
_ Figurative language
_ Story writing (simple)
_ Reference book use begins
_ Story sense understood
_ Comparison of other sources on the topic
_ Story character behavior judged
_ Skimming and scanning
_ Story writing, extending stories heard

Writing
_ Grammar
_ Sentence types
_ Appropriate details included
_ Choosing content (adding or deleting)
_ Prewriting skills such as reading, interviewing, and brainstorming
_ Audience identified
_ Forms for writing depending on purpose
_ Revision after review or critique from others
_ Beginning to write for publication
_ Spelling rules

Listening
_ Key ideas distinguished
_ Supporting information recognized
_ Paraphrasing oral information
_ New information recognized in listening
_ Evaluation of oral statements
_ Nonverbal clues

Speech
_ Basic components (introduction, body, conclusion)
_ Clear presentation with support
_ Gestures
_ Eye contact
_ Expression control

Literature
_ Text defined as author's thoughts interpreted by each reader
_ Genre defined as classifications of major types of literature
_ Informational text elements
_ Selection of literature
_ Literature as a model for writing
_ Poetic text characteristics

Study skills
_ Outlining
_ Use of reference materials: concordance, dictionary, atlas
_ Library skill
_ Keeping track of requirements and achievements

Later Elementary, Mathematics, Thinking, and Computer Skills

Mathematics

_ Making change
_ Ratio concept
_ Decimals
_ Properties of one
_ Estimation of answers in common operations
_ Word problems strategies
_ Estimation of results in word problems
_ Roman numerals
_ Numeration systems
_ Multiplication and division facts
_ Multiplication and division concepts as repeated addition and subtraction
_ Full multiplication and division processes
_ Solid figures
_ Prime numbers
_ Factoring
_ Sets and subsets
_ Equivalent fractions and decimals
_ Geometric congruence
_ Changes keeping area or volume equal
_ Making number sentences to represent problems
_ Units for measurement of various quantities
_ Metric measurement
_ Mixed numbers
_ Common and decimal fractions
_ Exponents
_ Percents
_ Estimation by sampling
_ Estimation of distance and other values
_ Use of computer software in problem solving and in making graphs
_ Making up word problems
_ Concepts of angels, diameter, radius, circumference
_ Visualizing spatial shapes in illustrations
_ Simple use of formulas for area problems
_ Simple number sequence patterns
_ Concept of average

Thinking

_ Cause and effect
_ Inference
_ Fact vs. opinion
_ Suspending judgment until all evidence is considered

Computer Skills

_ Keyboard ability
_ Word processors

Later Elementary, Social Studies

_ Experience of helping others in response to a social problem
_ Major events in the country's history in order
_ Natural resources, human capital, and capital equipment in producing goods and services
_ Differences among individual ownerships, partnerships and corporations
_ Experience in discussing social science issues
_ Experience in supporting the law
_ Purposes for local, regional, and national governments
_ Prices in a market economy
_ Community differences
_ Ecosystems and how people use and adapt to them
_ Business venture risks
_ Differences among making, enforcing, and interpreting laws
_ Methods of finding information about other people around the world
_ Constitutional rights (religious liberty, free expression, due process of law, etc.)
_ Gathering and processing information on a question involving more than the local area
_ Public policy issues
_ Maps of the local and regional areas (ability to sketch from memory)
_ Essay writing about a political issue
_ Gathering social science information for maps, graphs, and tables
_ Organization of government at various levels
_ Cost of making personal choices
_ Election campaigns
_ Interactions among nations
_ Activities advancing views on a social science issue
_ Cultural regions nearby and in the country
_ Appreciating and relating to people of other cultures

Later Elementary, Science

_ Classify familiar organisms by observable characteristics
_ Vertebrates
_ Life cycles
_ Electrical charges and interactions
_ Functions of seed plants
_ Learn stories about scientists
_ Physical changes in matter related to heat energy changes
_ Experimenting with mixtures
_ Construction of objects that show technology
_ Speed and direction of objects
_ Interaction among force, mass, and motion
_ Fossils provide evidence about ancient life
_ Describe cells as systems that combine to make plants and animals
_ Sound pitch and loudness
_ Production of sound
_ Properties of light
_ Ask good questions based on observation
_ Interrelationships among living things
_ Human effects on the environment
_ Features of the earth's surface
_ Fossils and the past
_ Natural changes in the earth's surface
_ Recycling methods and purposes
_ Water in three states
_ Atmosphere, weather, and climates

Later Elementary, Health Education

_ Interactions of the human body systems (physiology)
_ Environment influences health
_ Health problems of children
_ Interdependence of physical, intellectual, emotional and social health
_ How to get health information
_ Analyzing specific media influence
_ Nutrition
_ Simple first aid
_ Bones and muscles
_ Digestion
_ Water supply
_ Pests that carry germs
_ Bicycle and water safety
_ Divine providence in how the body heals

_ Responsibility to care for bodies and minds
_ Birth and responsibility

Later Elementary, Physical Education

_ Leadership, cooperation, and respect in playing with others
_ Hiking, camping and outdoor activities
_ Physical fitness

MIDDLE SCHOOL

Grades 6 to 8

Middle School , Character Development, Bible

_ The life of Christ
_ The fall into sin and God's plan to eliminate it; His fairness
_ Justification and sanctification
_ Other topics considered important as the child is ready to understand
_ God's leading in the past
_ Memorize the books of the Bible in order

Middle School, Art and Music

_ Art and music appreciation (observation of the arts)
_ Composition; use of space
_ Abstraction and realism
_ Proportion and perspective
_ Balance in design
_ Sculpture and other graphic art forms
_ Complimentary colors; warm and cool colors
_ Practice with still life and landscapes
_ Architecture
_ Computer graphics

_ More on reading music
_ Experimenting with musical instruments
_ Major and minor scales
_ Simple cord progressions
_ Music and culture
_ What makes music good or bad to experience

Middle School, Language Arts

Reading
_ Following directions
_ Persuasive terms noticed in reading
_ Research for writing
_ Summarizing text and developing study questions
_ Word origins from other languages
_ Propaganda techniques
_ Author bias noticed
_ Personal enjoyment reading
_ Vocabulary expansion
_ Story structure
_ Reading quickly with understanding
_ Skimming and scanning

Writing
_ Note taking skills
_ Literature as models for writing
_ Form chosen depending on purpose
_ Proofreading for basic correctness
_ Rewriting strategies used
_ Multiple drafts used
_ Paragraphs and transitions
_ Diction/tone controlled depending on audience
_ Reports written using more than one source
_ Writing style personalized

Listening
_ Guess about missing segments in an oral message
_ Summarizing an oral message
_ Purpose chosen when listening
_ Infer character of speakers
_ Effectiveness of a speaker's methods judged
_ Attention span increased
_ Distinguish among sound sources

Speech
_ Formats of public address, interpersonal
_ Purposes of oral (or other) communication group discussion, debate
_ Development of clear ideas
_ Patterns of organization (chronological, topical, etc.)
_ Unique characteristics of oral communication (immediate, irreversible, dynamic) and interviewing
_ Impromptu speech skills
_ Skill in directing a discussion
_ Resolution of differences or arguments

Literature
_ Exposure to a variety of good literature
_ Point of view
_ Poetry analysis
_ Literature interpretation improved
_ Purpose seen for choosing a particular form for a literary work
_ Author's organizational pattern
_ Genre and form
_ Evaluation criteria
_ Identification of author's techniques

Foreign Language
_ For advanced students or those whose family culture or circumstances make it a good idea.

Middle School, Mathematics, Thinking, and Computer Skills

Mathematics
_ Factoring
_ Mental solving of simple word problems
_ Identification of pertinent data for solving a problem
_ Ordering of fractions (by value)
_ Conversion to common denominators
_ Mixed and improper fractions
_ Reducing fractions
_ Fundamental operations with fractions (addition, subtraction, etc.)
_ Comparing numbers in various forms by computer
_ Use of compass and protractor
_ Metric units
_ Properties of geometric figures
_ Measurement of angels
_ Congruence, similarity, and symmetry
_ Sampling and averages
_ Problem solving with geometric shapes spatial visualization
_ Simple formulas analyzed
_ Introduction to "unknowns" in equations
_ Simple equations used to represent problems

_ Exponents
_ Scientific notation
_ Concept of variables and constants
_ Rational and irrational numbers
_ Effect of moving the decimal point
_ Ratio and proportion
_ Probability related to ratio
_ Percentage problems
_ Solid geometric figures identified
_ Terms: "mean," "average," and "median range"
_ Probability of simple events
_ Comparison of graphs
_ Data from graphs and charts extracted for solving problems
_ Order of operation and signs in algebraic expressions
_ Absolute values
_ Inequalities
_ Properties of non-negative integers
_ Sets: finite, infinite, and empty
_ Business math (checks, borrowing money, etc.)
_ Congruence of geometric figures checked
_ Sets and simple sentences
_ Numeration systems
_ Graphing of equations
_ Powers and roots of numbers
_ Polynomials
_ Pythagorean Theorem
_ Tax calculations
_ Mental addition and subtraction
_ Mental division by powers of ten
_ Estimates fractional part of a geometric figure
_ Number systems in other than base 10
_ Deductive and inductive reasoning
_ Metric and nonmetric values compared
_ Probability values of "certain' and "impossible"
_ Ranking by quartile
_ Tendency line estimated for scatter plots
_ Interpolation and extrapolation
_ Frequency charts and graphs
_ Distributive property (and other properties)
_ Square root and cube root estimates
_ Algebraic expressions evaluated
_ Open sentences solved
_ Function represented in a table or graph
_ Degree of accuracy in estimates
_ Inverse operations (shown by manipulatives and diagrams)
_ Use of mathematics in society

Thinking skills
_ Solving logic problems of relationships between items
_ Spatial perception
_ Interpretations influenced by author's perspective

Computers
_ The Internet and responsible browsing
_ Simple programming
_ Use of various computer components
_ Handling files
_ Use of databases

Middle School, Social Studies

_ Social science survey with chosen procedures, analysis of results, and report
_ Analysis of early history of the student's country
_ Stories of people in the past in early history of the country
_ Individual constitutional rights and the common good
_ Roles in the economic system by government, businesses, unions, banks, and homes
_ Why territory is divided into political units
_ Time lines for national and world history
_ Transportation and communication among communities
_ Information through electronic devices
_ Taxation impact on various groups in society
_ World ecosystems and how humans interact with them
_ Comparison of price and quality
_ Cultural, economic, political and environmental features of the continents
_ Career opportunities in light of economic trends
_ Constitutional authority in federal governments
_ International government organizations
_ Major periods in one's country
_ Market economy advantages and disadvantages
_ Freedom and limits to government control
_ Essay writing about international policies
_ Means for limiting constitutional powers of government
_ World map memorized
_ Population patterns around the world
_ Using laws or ethical rules to evaluate behavior
_ Economy control by government
_ Community history
Disparities between American ideals and realities
Religious history of the time of Christ to the Reformation
God's hand in governments

Middle School, Science

_ Use measurement devices in investigations
_ Theories of the formation of the solar system
_ Choice of measures for best describing objects
_ Atmosphere
_ Elements, compounds and mixtures
_ Use information sources
_ Conditions on a planet for supporting life
_ Planetary motion, comets, and moons
_ Energy and its forms (mechanical, heat, nuclear, etc.)
_ Air pollution
_ Follow instructions for procedures involving science
_ Organisms classified into major groups according to structure
_ Electron flow in simple circuits
_ Current and magnetic fields
_ Life cycle of flowering plants
_ Food production and storage in plants
_ System interactions in plants and animals
_ Watching the sky
_ Recognize limitations of data
_ Evaporation, condensation, and thermal expansion
_ Chemical changes; reactants and products
_ Pollution from waste products
_ Recognize risks in some technologies
_ Physical changes in terms of atomic and molecular motion

_ Formation of rocks, minerals, and soils
_ Organisms influenced by heredity and environment
_ Describe motion in three dimensions
_ Changes in speed and direction from two-dimensional forces
_ Forces of gravity, electrical charges, and magnetic fields
_ Origin of life; evolutionary and creationist viewpoints and motivation for belief
_ Single and multicellular organisms
_ Design and conduct simple investigations
_ How sound travels
_ Specialized cells
_ Light transmission (reflection, refraction, absorption, and transmission)
_ Pendulums, frequency, and amplitude
_ Energy transmission by waves
_ Changes in organism populations and the food chain
_ Sun as the energy source for living things
_ Changes over time in ecosystems
_ Cycles occurring in the environment
_ Maps and the earth's surface
_ Environmental changes by humans
_ Pollution in the hydrosphere
_ Weather patterns, changes, and measures

Middle School, Health Education

_ Body systems: nervous, circulatory, respiratory, digestive, etc.
_ Viruses and bacteria
_ Cultural patterns and health
_ Adolescent health problems
_ Stress management
_ Health and prevention of premature death
_ Coping with bad family habits and attitudes
_ Sexually transmitted diseases
_ Stimulants and narcotics
_ Circulation and respiration
_ Personal appearance
_ Antibiotics and immunization
_ Incurable diseases
_ Genetic disorders
_ Exercise and posture (also for physical ed.)
_ Poisons and what to do if in trouble

Middle School, Physical Education

_ Exercise and posture
_ Team physical activities
_ Development by physical work
_ Place of activity in total health

HIGH SCHOOL

High School , Character Development — Bible

You will want to structure this area following your own beliefs. I suggest concluding with a study of biblical principles for courtship and establishing a home. Below are a few topics to include.

_ Origin of the Bible
_ Grouping of Bible books
_ Literature in the Bible; different writing styles
_ Christ in all the Scriptures

High School, Art and Music

_ God as the source of beauty
_ Drawing and sketching
_ Landscape and architecture
_ Photography
_ Pottery
_ Sculpture
_ Design principles of printed pieces
_ Understanding what brings visual appeal

_ Opportunity to develop basic skill in playing an instrument
_ Singing
_ Listening to music
_ Changes in styles of music over the centuries
_ Danger of harsh and heavy-beat music

High School, Business Education

Areas include
_ Accounting
_ Business management
_ Computer technology and literacy
_ Keyboard skills
_ Word processing and desktop publishing

High School, English (Language)

Ninth grade English
_ Vocabulary development
_ Grammar review
_ Enjoying various types of literature
_ Composition: punctuation, paragraphs
_ Library skills
_ Evaluation of media programs
_ Reading skill improvement (if needed)

Tenth grade English
_ Note taking skill
_ Etymology, Dialects
_ Selected literature analyzed
_ How word meanings and grammar change
_ Writing a research paper
_ Writing poems, plays, etc.
_ Genres
_ Persuasion and argument in listening and speaking
_ National folklore

Eleventh grade English
_ Knowing what is significant from lectures and reading
_ Process of writing; expository and fictional writing
_ Critical analysis of what is heard and read
_ American (or national) and cross-cultural literature
_ Empathy in listening
_ Analyzing techniques and purposes of speakers
_ Determining motive in communication

Twelfth grade English
_ Various types of practical writing from memos and letters to ad copy and business reports
_ Writing with purpose, clarity, and interest

_ Speaking with purpose, clarity. and interest
_ Nonverbal communication
_ English literature
_ World literature
_ Publishing
_ The Internet

High School, Mathematics

Math courses are usually consistently defined so are not described much here.

Grade 9, Algebra 1
Basic aspects of the topic through sets, quadratic equations and probability.

Grade 9, General mathematics
Usually for those who do not take algebra

Grade 9, Consumer math
_ May be part of general math or a brief additional course if not learned well in middle school.

Grade 10, Geometry
_ Including logic, postulates, theorems, mensuration, and transformational geometry

Grade 11, Algebra 2
_ Including vectors and probability

Grade 11 or 12 (electives)
_ Trigonometry
_ Calculus
_ Computer programming
_ Accounting
_ Statistics
_ Number theory

High School, Thinking skills

_ Propaganda and nationalism
_ Techniques of persuasion
_ Role of feelings in decisions
_ Accountability for decisions
_ Inductive and deductive reasoning
_ Ethical and moral standards
_ Logic (learned partly in geometry)
_ Bias in using statistics

High School, Social Studies

Areas commonly covered in US high schools are
✓World history,
✓US history and government,
✓World and US culture (including geography)
✓Economics

Significant items within these areas follow:
_ World geography; map and globe skills
_ US Constitution; risks and purposes for amendments
_ Labor and management
_ Ethnic groups and minorities
_ Timelines for US history from the colonial period through the Civil War
_ Timelines for US history after reconstruction (after the Civil War)
_ Rationale for why historical events occurred
_ Societal solutions for health care, housing, energy, etc.
_ Decisions that influenced history
_ Changes in world regions and factors that influence them
_ Stories of people in the more recent history of the country
_ World economy and markets; influence of the US
_ Economic indicators
_ Monetary and fiscal policy influence on problems such as unemployment and inflation
_ Economic growth and government in developing countries
_ Social science issues discussed intelligently
_ Cultural influences on perceptions
_ International exchange
_ Federal form of government, advantages and disadvantages
_ Relative merits of American presidential and parliamentary systems
_ Social science survey with chosen procedures and analysis
_ Alternatives to public issue decisions
_ Cultural diversity, benefits and challenges
_ Analysis of personal resistance to application of democratic values
_ Issues and events of major periods after the Civil War
_ Analysis of later history of the country
_ Service activity experience in the community or abroad
_ Political reform
_ Influence of events in one place on other parts of the world
_ Branches of government, balance and tension
_ Human rights and American democracy
_ Foreign policy in light of national interests
_ Planning of personal financial and other resources

High School, Science

Typical science courses are
✓Earth science and astronomy
✓Biology
✓Chemistry
✓Physics

Possible topics
_ Ecological relationships among species
_ Wave properties, wave interaction, and Doppler effect
_ Energy and the formation of stars
_ Reproduction of multicelluar organisms
_ Air movements in the atmosphere
_ Assemble or investigate mechanical and electrical devices
_ Energy changes in heat transfer
_ Production of electrical current by magnetic fields
_ The sun and other stars
_ Plate tectonics theory
_ Disease diagnosis and prevention
_ Disease organisms
_ Stability maintenance in organisms
_ Cells specialized to carry out particular functions
_ Agriculture and ecosystems
_ Energy changes from physical, chemical, and nuclear changes
_ History of certain scientific concepts
_ Glaciation (past ice effects)
_ Force on an object produces an opposing force
_ Energy conversions in simple machines
_ Atoms described by parts and charge
_ Discuss evolution and natural selection
_ How cells function
_ Understand measurement limitations

_ Energy conservation during transformations
_ Types of cells
_ Comparisons of objects by mass, volume and density
_ Climate changes over a long time
_ Observing the universe; technology
_ Gather and synthesize information from books, etc.
_ Genetic transfer in reproduction
_ Discuss scientific topics being able to summarize what others have said and develop ideas by asking appropriate questions
_ Form hypotheses and suggest tests for them
_ Conservation of mass in physical and chemical changes
_ Chemical changes from rearrangement and motion of atoms and molecules
_ Design and conduct science investigations
_ Experiments to compare speed and direction
_ Elements studied by families
_ Sound waves and sound properties
_ Weather prediction
_ Chemistry and cells
_ Water below the earth's surface
_ Changes from changes in DNA
_ Organisms classified by the five-kingdom system
_ Nuclear changes
_ Discuss waste disposal and the environment
_ Sound reproduction systems
_ Colors, wavelength, and vision
_ Ecosystems and events that change them
_ Our solar system in the universe
_ Climate and the hydrosphere
_ Seasons and astronomy

High School, Industrial technology

Development of knowledge and skills one or more areas including
_ Construction
_ Medical or biological technology
_ Graphic arts
_ Electronics
_ Photography
_ Agribusiness
_ Auto repair
_ Clothing design
_ Culinary arts
_ Computer aided design
_ Computer programming and management
_ Sales
_ Bible instruction

High School, Modern or Biblical Language

Usually two years are needed for practical ability. Goals are proficiency in Listening, Speaking, Reading, and Writing

High School, Physical Education

_ Physical fitness and health
_ Aerobics
_ Sportsmanship
_ Competitive sports (optional)
_ Water safety
_ First Aid
_ Outdoor, noncompetitive, sports: Acquatics, Cycling, Hiking, back packing, Jogging.

H
Ideas That Work

In the area of human behavior, research results are often elusive. Human circumstances are much more complex than those of fish or wheat or stars. The principles for teaching and learning shown in this appendix, however, are some of the most certain and most practical. They have been sifted and checked and clarified. They represent the heart of a book published by the U.S. Department of Education under the title What Works, Research About Teaching and Learning.* *I believe you will find the majority of this material very valuable if you consider it in relation to your goals and apply it appropriately.*

The book, What Works, *contains 57 findings along with explanations. All the findings are represented, but we quote selectively from the explanations, choosing portions that would seem to be the most important for home school parents. Ellipsis points indicate only material cut from within the sentences we have included.*

To find specific principles in this section, refer to the general index.

1. Parents are their children's first and most influential teachers. What parents do to help their children learn is more important to academic success than how well-off the family is. Parents can do many things at home to help their children succeed in school. . . .

They can create a "curriculum of the home" that teaches their children what matters. They do this through their daily conversations, household routines, attention to school matters, and affectionate concern for their children's progress.

Conversation is important. Children learn to read, reason, and understand things better when their parents: ♦ read, talk, and listen to them, ♦ tell them stories, play games, share hobbies, and ♦ discuss news, TV programs, and special events.

In order to enrich the "curriculum of the home," some parents: ♦ provide books, supplies, and a special place for studying, ♦ observe routine for meals, bedtime, and homework, and ♦ monitor the amount of time spent watching TV and doing after-school jobs.

2. The best way for parents to help their children become better readers is to read to them – even when they are very young. Children benefit most from reading aloud when they discuss stories, learn to identify letters and words, and talk about the meaning of words.

. . . children whose parents simply read to them perform as well as those whose parents use workbooks or have had training in teaching.

The conversation that goes with reading aloud to children is as important as the reading itself. When parents ask children only superficial questions about stories, or don't discuss the stories at all, their children do not achieve as well in reading as the children of parents who ask questions that require thinking and who relate the stories to everyday events. Kindergarten children who know a lot about written language usually have parents who believe that reading is important and who seize every opportunity to act on that conviction by reading to their children.

3. Children improve their reading ability by reading a lot. Reading achievement is directly related to the amount of reading children do in school and outside.

Independent reading increases both vocabulary and reading fluency. Unlike using workbooks and performing computer drills, reading books gives children practice in the "whole act" of reading, that is, both in discovering the meanings of individual words and in grasping the meaning of an entire story. But American children do not spend much time reading independently at school or at home. In the average elementary school, for example, children spend just 7 to 8 minutes a day reading silently. At home, half of all fifth graders spend only 4 minutes a day reading. These same children spend an average of 130 minutes a day watching television.

Research shows that the amount of leisure time spent reading is directly related to children's reading comprehension, the size of their vocabularies, and gains in their reading ability. Clearly, reading at home can be a powerful supplement to classwork. Parents can encourage leisure reading by making books an important part of the home, by giving books or magazines as presents, and by encouraging visits to the local library.

4. Children who are encouraged to draw and scribble "stories" at an early age will later learn to compose more easily, more effectively, and with greater confidence than children who do not have this encouragement.

Studies of very young children show that their carefully formed scrawls have meaning to them, and that this writing actually helps them develop language skills. Research suggests that the best way to help children at this stage of their development as writers is to respond to the ideas they are trying to express.

Very young children take the first steps toward writing by drawing and scribbling or, if they cannot use a pencil, they may use plastic or metal letters on a felt or magnetic board. Some preschoolers may write on toy typewriters; others may dictate stories into a tape recorder or to an adult, who writes them down and reads them back. For this reason, it is best to focus on the intended meaning of what very young children write, rather than on the appearance of the writing.

Children become more effective writers when parents and teachers encourage them to choose the topics they write about, then leave them alone to exercise their own creativity.

5. A good way to teach children simple arithmetic is to build on their informal knowledge. This is why learning to count everyday objects is an effective basis for early arithmetic lessons.

A good foundation in speaking and listening helps children become better readers.

When children learn to read, they are making a transition from spoken to written language. Reading instruction builds on conversational skills: the better children are at using spoken language, the more successfully they will learn to read written language. To succeed at reading, children need a basic vocabulary, some knowledge of the world around them, and the ability to talk about what they know. These skills enable children to understand written material more readily.

Research shows a strong connection between reading and listening. A child who is listening well shows it by being able to retell stories and repeat instructions. . . .

Parents and teachers need to engage children in thoughtful discussions on all subjects. . . .

6. Excessive television viewing is associated with low academic achievement. Moderate viewing, especially when supervised by parents, can help children learn.

Watching television more than 2–3 hours a day often hurts children's achievement in reading, writing, and mathematics, especially if it disrupts homework and leisure reading. . . .

Moderate TV viewing can, however, actually help students from backgrounds in which books, magazines, and other mind-enriching resources are in short supply.

7. Many highly successful individuals have above-average but not extraordinary intelligence. Accomplishment in a particular activity is often more dependent upon hard work and self-discipline than on innate ability.

High academic achievers are not necessarily born "smarter" than others, nor do people born with extraordinary abilities necessarily become highly accomplished individuals. Parents, teachers, coaches, and the individuals themselves can influence how much a mind or talent develops by fostering self-discipline and encouraging hard work. . . .

Studies of accomplished musicians, athletes, and historical figures show that when they were children, they were competent, had good social and communication skills, and showed versatility as well as perseverance in practicing their skills over long periods.

8. Belief in the value of hard work, the importance of personal responsibility, and the importance of education itself contributes to greater success in school.

Parental involvement helps children learn more effectively. Teachers who are successful at involving parents in their children's schoolwork are successful because they work at it.

9. Children get a better start in reading if they are taught phonics. Learning phonics helps them to understand the relationship between letters and sounds and to "break the code" that links the words they hear with the words they see in print.

Because phonics is a reading tool, it is best taught in the context of reading instruction, not as a separate subject to be mastered. Good phonics strategies include teaching children the sounds of letters in isolation and in words (s/i/t), and how to blend the sounds together (s-s-i-i-t). . . .

If phonics instruction extends for too many years, it can defeat the spirit and excitement of learning to read.

[See the chapter "More Than Phonics" which reports on newer research."]

10. Children get more out of a reading assignment when the teacher precedes the lesson with background information and follows it with discussion.

Good teachers begin the day's reading lesson by preparing children for the story to be read – introducing the new words and concepts they will encounter. Many teachers develop their own introductions or adapt those offered in teachers' manuals. . . .

In the discussion after the reading lesson, good teachers ask questions that probe the major elements of the story's plot, characters, theme, or moral. . . . When children take part in a thought-provoking discussion of a story, they understand more clearly that the purpose of reading is to get information and insight, not just to decode the words on a page.

11. Students in cooperative learning teams learn to work toward a common goal, help one another learn, gain self-esteem, take more responsibility for their own learning, and come to respect and like their classmates.

12. Telling young children stories can motivate them to read. Storytelling also introduces them to cultural values and literary traditions before they can read, write, and talk about stories by themselves.

13. Children learn science best when they are able to do experiments, so they can witness "science in action."

14. Although students need to learn how to find exact answers to arithmetic problems, good math students also learn the helpful skill of estimating answers. This skill can be taught.

Research has identified three key steps used by good estimators; these can be taught to all students: ♦ Good estimators begin by altering numbers to more manageable forms – by rounding, for example. ♦ They change parts of a problem into forms they can handle more easily. In a problem with several steps, they may rearrange the steps to make estimation easier. ♦ They also adjust two numbers at a time when making their estimates. Rounding one number higher and one number lower is an example of this technique.

Before students can become good at estimating, they need to have quick, accurate recall of basic facts. They also need a good grasp of the place value system (ones, tens, hundreds, etc.).

15. Children in early grades learn mathematics more effectively when they use physical objects in their lessons.

The type or design of the objects used is not particularly important; they can be blocks, marbles, poker chips, cardboard cutouts – almost anything.

16. Students will become more adept at solving math problems if teachers encourage them to think through a problem before they begin working on it, guide them through the thinking process, and give them regular and frequent practice in solving problems.

Good mathematical problem solvers usually analyze the challenges they face and explore alternative strategies before starting work. Unsuccessful problem solvers often act impulsively when given a problem and follow the first idea that occurs to them. Too often, school instruction emphasizes and rewards the rapid solving of problems and fails to recognize and reinforce thoughtful behavior. . . .

After different strategies are identified, students can begin to solve the problem. If a plan does not work, the teacher can ask additional questions or provide hints to help students formulate other approaches. After the problem is solved, the teacher can have students analyze their strategies and consider alternatives.

Frequent practice in solving problems is most effective when teachers ask students questions about their thinking, give them hints when they are stumped, and help them see how some problems are related. These practices help students learn how to think problems through for themselves. They can also be taught other techniques to help them correctly solve problems, such as adding a diagram, removing extraneous information, and reorganizing data.

17. The most effective way to teach writing is to teach it as a process of brainstorming, composing, revising, and editing.

Students learn to write well through frequent practice. Good writing assignments are often an extension of class reading, discussion, and activities, not isolated exercises.

An effective writing lesson contains these elements:

♦ Brainstorming: Students think and talk about their topics. They collect information and ideas, frequently much more than they will finally use. They sort through their ideas to organize and clarify what they want to say.

♦ Composing: Students compose a first draft. This part is typically time-consuming and hard, even for very good writers.

♦ Revising: Students re-read what they have written, sometimes soliciting reactions from teachers, classmates, parents, and others. The most useful teacher response to an early draft focuses on what students are trying to say, not the mechanics of writing. Teachers can help most by asking for clarification, commenting on vivid expressions or fresh ideas, and suggesting ways to support the main thrust of the writing. Students can then consider the feedback and decide how to use it to improve. On the next draft, teachers may want to focus on chosen aspects of good writing such as combining sentences to improve structure and add variety. Through such exercises, teachers can help students realize that varying sentence length and structure within a paragraph yields more interesting prose. Discussing these alternatives while working on a draft emphasizes to students the importance of writing clear, interesting, and concise sentences that are appropriate for the writer's audience and goals.

♦ Editing: Students then need to check their final version for spelling, grammar, punctuation and other writing mechanics, and legibility.

Prompt feedback from teachers on written assignments is important. Students are most likely to write competently when schools routinely require writing in all subject areas, not just in English class.

18. Children learn vocabulary better when the words they study are related to familiar experiences and to knowledge they already possess.

Teachers can use students' personal experiences and prior knowledge to build vocabulary. Instruction in which children establish relationships among words is more effective than instruction that focuses only on word definitions. . . .

Teachers can foster connections between words by having students group them into categories such that relationships among the words become clear. Children can use their own experiences to create a cluster of synonyms, such as neat, tidy, clean, and spotless. They can consider similarities and differences in related words, such as examine and scrutinize. They can also group words according to certain features, such as suffixes or prefixes. Encouraging students to talk about personal experiences associated with particular words helps them grasp meanings and relationships among new words and ideas.

Using analogies is another way to help children see the relationship between old and new words. For example, when children are learning the word "province," the analogy "state is to the United States what province is to Canada" relates prior knowledge to a new concept.

19. Well-chosen diagrams, graphs, photos and illustrations can enhance students' learning.

20. Teachers who set and communicate high expectations to all their students obtain greater academic performance from those students than teachers who set low expectations.

21. Hearing good readers read and encouraging students repeatedly to read a passage aloud helps them become good readers.

Helping students learn to read aloud smoothly and easily is an important – but often overlooked – goal of reading instruction. Some authorities have called it the "missing ingredient" in early reading instruction. Teachers can help students become fluent readers by including supported and repeated readings as part of individualized, small group, or classroom instruction.

In supported reading, a child listens to – and reads along with – a good reader. The model can be an adult reader, another student able to read the passage fluently, or a rendition that has been tape recorded. Initially, the student follows along silently or in a soft voice. In subsequent readings of the same passage, the student becomes more fluent and the model gradually fades into the background. In repeated readings, students read a passage over and over until they can read it with ease.

Students may balk at having to read a passage more than once. Teachers can overcome this by providing instructional activities in which repeated readings are a natural component. For example, teachers can have students practice and perform dramatic readings, emphasizing the meaning and emotion of the passage. Teachers can also have students practice reading short stories and poems in unison, and practice singing popular songs together. These types of activities require repeated readings for proficient performance.

22. Children's understanding of the relationship between being smart and hard work changes as they grow.

When children start school, they think that ability and effort are the same thing; in other words, they believe that if they work hard they will become smart. Thus, younger children who fail believe this is because they didn't try hard enough, not because they have less ability.

Because teachers tend to reward effort in earlier grades, children frequently concentrate on working hard rather than on the quality of their work. As a result, they may not learn how to judge how well they are performing.

In later elementary grades, students slowly learn that ability and effort are not the same. They come to believe that lower ability requires harder work to keep up and that students with higher ability need not work so hard. At this stage, speed at completing tasks replaces effort as the sign of ability; high levels of effort may even carry the stigma of low ability.

Consequently, many secondary school students, despite their ability, will not expend the effort needed to achieve their potential. Underachievement can become a way of life.

Once students begin believing they have failed because they lack ability, they tend to lose hope for future success. They develop a pattern of academic hopelessness and stop trying. They see academic obstacles as insurmountable and devote less effort to learning.

Teachers who are alert to these beliefs in youngsters will keep their students motivated and on task. They will also slowly nudge their students toward the realism of judging themselves by performance. For example, teachers will set high expectations and insist that students put forth the effort required to meet the school's academic standards. They will make sure slower learners are rewarded for their progress and abler students are challenged according to their abilities.

23. As students acquire knowledge and skill, their thinking and reasoning take on distinct characteristics. Teachers who are alert to these changes can determine how well their students are progressing toward becoming competent thinkers and problem solvers.

Students ordinarily go through four changes as they master skills and acquire knowledge.

- The isolated ideas and initial explanations with which students begin to learn a new topic become integrated and more widely applicable. For example, children just beginning to learn about dinosaurs tend to classify them in terms of visible characteristics, such as size and skin texture. Children who are more familiar with dinosaurs make more elaborate classifications in which sensory features become less important than more abstract features such as dietary habits.
- When confronting problems, competent learners identify fundamental principles that allow them to reach

solutions smoothly, instead of wrestling with details. Where beginning physics students tend to classify problems in terms of surface features, more accomplished learners classify the same problems in terms of underlying physical principles. For example, beginning students view problems in mechanics as involving inclined planes and pulleys; more competent learners see the same problems as involving mechanical principles such as conservation of energy.

♦ Besides grasping rules and principles, competent learners are aware of the range of conditions under which these principles apply. In the example mentioned above, accomplished learners not only understand the principle of conservation of energy, but are also aware of problems that can be solved using such principles.

♦ Tasks that beginning students carry out with concentration are performed automatically by students with more expertise. This frees them to direct their attention to analysis, critical thinking, and other demanding aspects of performance. For example, when children first learn to read, they must devote much attention to the process of translating printed letters into pronounceable words. As their expertise increases, children more quickly and accurately recognize printed words. This frees them to devote more attention to grasping the meanings conveyed by the text.

By monitoring these changes, students and teachers can assess progress toward competence.

24. How much time students are actively engaged in learning contributes strongly to their achievement. The amount of time available for learning is determined by the instructional and management skills of the teacher and the priorities set by the school administration.

Teachers must not only know the subjects they teach, they must also be effective classroom managers. . . .

Effective time managers in the classroom do not waste valuable minutes on unimportant activities; they keep their students continuously and actively engaged. Good managers perform the following time-conserving functions:

♦ Planning Class Work: choosing the content to be studied, scheduling time for presentation and study, and choosing those instructional activities (such as grouping, seatwork, or recitation) best suited to learning the material at hand;

♦ Communicating Goals: setting and conveying expectations so students know what they are to do, what it will take to get a passing grade, and what the consequences of failure will be;

♦ Regulating Learning Activities: sequencing course content so knowledge builds on itself, pacing instruction so students are prepared for the next step, monitoring success rates so all students stay productively engaged regardless of how quickly they learn, and running an orderly, academically focused classroom that keeps wasted time and misbehavior to a minimum.

25. Good classroom management is essential for teachers to deal with students who chronically misbehave, but such students also benefit from specific suggestions from teachers on how to cope with their conflicts and frustrations. This also helps them gain insights about their behavior.

26. When teachers explain exactly what students are expected to learn, and demonstrate the steps needed to accomplish a particular academic task, students learn more.

The procedure stated above is called "direct instruction." It is based on the assumption that knowing how to learn may not come naturally to all students, especially to beginning and low-ability learners. Direct instruction takes children through learning steps systematically, helping them see both the purpose and the result of each step. In this way, children learn not only a lesson's content but also a method for learning that content.

The basic components of direct instruction are: ♦ setting clear goals for students and making sure they understand those goals, ♦ presenting a sequence of well-organized assignments, ♦ giving students clear, concise explanations and illustrations of the subject matter, ♦ asking frequent questions to see if children understand the work, and ♦ giving students frequent opportunities to practice what they have learned.

Direct instruction does not mean repetition. It does mean leading students through a process and teaching them to use that process as a skill to master other academic tasks. Direct instruction has been particularly effective in teaching basic skills to young and disadvantaged children, as well as in helping older and higher ability students to master more complex materials and to develop independent study skills.

27. Students become more interested in writing and the quality of their writing improves when there are significant learning goals for writing assignments and a clear sense of purpose for writing.

Teachers often assign writing tasks to encourage specific types of learning. For example, a teacher may assign a summary if she wants students to identify all the important concepts of a particular topic. Another teacher may assign an analytic essay if he wants students to narrow their focus and examine one aspect in greater depth.

What students learn by writing depends on what they do when they write. Those who simply paraphrase when the assignment calls for analysis may learn facts, but may not be able to draw connections or make inferences about the content. Good teachers identify what they want their writing assignments to accomplish and tell students what those goals are.

Also, students feel the keenest sense of purpose when the audience for their writing extends beyond the teacher. Publishing student writing in school literary magazines and newspapers is one effective way to do this. Students can also write books for the elementary school library, guides to high school life for entering junior high school students, letters, or scripts for school-produced audio and video programs.

Teachers can encourage their students to write for audiences outside of school by having them enter writing contests, write letters to the editors of local newspapers, and correspond with students in other states and countries.

Teachers of all subjects can use writing to help students analyze and understand content. Science teachers, for example, can have students record and organize their ideas about complex concepts in learning logs. History teachers can have students study the life of a turn-of-the-century American immigrant and then interview a present-day immigrant; an article comparing the two experiences can be written for the school or local newspaper. A health teacher can have students write about the causes and effects of morphine addiction during the Civil War and relate that information to present-day drug problems. Such exercises help students and teachers see more clearly what the student understands – or doesn't yet understand.

Good teachers help students understand that the choices they make in writing affect the quality of their learning in ways that go well beyond the writing itself.

28. Constructive feedback from teachers, including deserved praise and specific suggestions, helps students learn, as well as develop positive self-esteem.

Teachers should not underestimate the impact of constructive feedback on their students. Providing positive and timely comments is a practice that teachers at all levels can use. These comments help students correct errors and give them recognition when deserved. Helpful feedback praises successful aspects of a student's work and points out those areas that need improvement.

Useful feedback, whether positive or negative, is prompt, germane, and includes specific observations and recommendations. It tells students what they are doing, how they are doing it, and how they can improve. Whether written or spoken, effective feedback is initiated by the teacher and is given privately rather than in front of the class. An example of effective feedback: "Your book report is well written, Paul. The content is clear because the ideas are presented in a logical order and the details support your main idea. Your use of some clever examples makes your book report enjoyable to read. Next time, let's work harder to organize your time so that you will meet the assigned deadline." An example of ineffective feedback is: "Your book report is well written, Paul. But it is late and I'm upset about that."

Students who are accustomed to failure and who have difficulty mastering skills react more positively to encouragement and praise from teachers than to criticism. Effective teachers successfully use praise to motivate their low-achieving students. On the other hand, higher-achieving students respond more to specific comments and suggestions about their work.

Through constructive, timely feedback, teachers can reinforce and help develop positive self-esteem in their students. Students who believe they can succeed are usually more successful than those with low self-esteem when it comes to participating in activities, working independently, getting along with others, and achieving academically.

29. Students tutoring other students can lead to improved academic achievement for both student and tutor, and to positive attitudes toward coursework.

Tutoring programs consistently raise the achievement of both the students receiving instruction and those providing it. Peer tutoring, when used as a supplement to regular classroom teaching, helps slow and underachieving students master their lessons and succeed in school. Preparing and giving the lessons also benefits the tutors themselves because they learn more about the material they are teaching.

Of the tutoring programs that have been studied, the most effective include the following elements: ♦ highly structured and well-planned curricula and instructional methods, ♦ instruction in basic content and skills (grades 1–3), especially in arithmetic, and ♦ a relatively short duration of instruction (a few weeks or months).

30. Memorizing can help students absorb and retain the factual information on which understanding and critical thought are based.

Most children at some time memorize multiplication tables, the correct spelling of words, historical dates, and passages of literature such as the poetry of Robert Frost or the sonnets of Shakespeare. Memorizing simplifies the process of recalling information and allows its use to become automatic. Understanding and critical thought can then build on this base of knowledge and fact. Indeed, the more sophisticated mental operations of analysis, synthesis, and evaluation are impossible without rapid and accurate recall of bodies of specific knowledge.

Teachers can encourage students to develop memory skills by teaching highly structured and carefully sequenced lessons, with frequent reinforcement for correct answers. Young students, slow students, and students who lack background knowledge can benefit from such instruction.

In addition, teachers can teach "mnemonics," that is, devices and techniques for improving memory. For example, the mnemonic "Every Good Boy Does Fine" has reminded generations of music students that E, G, B, D, and F are the notes to which the lines on a treble staff correspond. Mnemonics helps students remember more information faster and retain it longer. Comprehension and retention are even greater when teachers and students connect the new information being memorized with previous knowledge.

31. Student achievement rises when teachers ask questions that require students to apply, analyze, synthesize, and evaluate information in addition to simply recalling facts.

Even before Socrates, questioning was one of teaching's most common and most effective techniques. Some teachers ask hundreds of questions, especially when teaching science, geography, history, or literature.

But questions take different forms and place different demands on students. Some questions require only factual recall and do not provoke analysis. For example, of more than 61,000 questions found in the teacher guides, student workbooks, and tests for 9 history textbooks, more than 95 percent were devoted to factual recall. This is not to say that questions meant to elicit facts are unimportant. Students need basic information to engage higher level thinking processes and discussions. Such questions also promote class participation and provide a high success rate in answering questions correctly.

The difference between factual and thought-provoking questions is the difference between asking: "When did Lincoln deliver the Gettysburg Address?" and asking: "Why was Lincoln's Gettysburg Address an important speech?" Each kind of question has its place, but the second one intends that the student analyze the speech in terms of the issues of the Civil War.

Although both kinds of questions are important, students achieve more when teachers ask thought-provoking questions and insist on thoughtful answers. Students' answers may also improve if teachers wait longer for a response, giving students more time to think.

32. The ways in which children study influence strongly how much they learn. Teachers can often help children develop better study skills.

Research has identified several study skills used by good students that can be taught to other students. Average students can learn how to use these skills. Low-ability students may need to be taught when, as well as how, to use them.

Here are some examples of sound study practices:

- Good students adjust the way they study according to several factors: (1) the demand of the material, (2) the time available for studying, (3) what they already know about the topic, (4) the purpose and importance of the assignment, and (5) the standards they must meet.
- Good students space learning sessions on a topic over time and do not cram or study the same topic continuously.
- Good students identify the main idea in new information, connect new material to what they already know, and draw inferences about its significance.
- Good students make sure their study methods are working properly by frequently appraising their own progress.

33. Student achievement rises significantly when teachers regularly assign homework and students conscientiously do it.

Extra studying helps children at all levels of ability. One research study reveals that when low-ability students do just 1 to 3 hours of homework a week, their grades are usually as high as those of average-ability students who do not do homework. Similarly, when average-ability students do 3 to 5 hours of homework a week, their grades usually equal those of high-ability students who do no homework.

Homework boosts achievement because the total time spent studying influences how much is learned. Low-achieving high school students study less than high achievers and do less homework. Time is not the only ingredient of learning, but without it little can be achieved.

Teachers, parents, and students determine how much, how useful, and how good the homework is. On average, American teachers say they assign about 10 hours of homework each week– about 2 hours per school day. But high school seniors report they spend only 4 to 5 hours a week doing homework, and 10 percent say they do none at all or have none assigned.

34. Well-designed homework assignments relate directly to classwork and extend students' learning beyond the classroom. Homework is most useful when teachers carefully prepare the assignment, thoroughly explain it, and give prompt comments and criticism when the work is completed.

To make the most of what students learn from doing homework, teachers need to give the same care to preparing homework assignments as they give to classroom instruction. When teachers prepare written instruction and discuss homework assignments with students, they find their students take the homework more seriously than if the assignments are simply announced. Students are more willing to do homework when they believe it is useful, when teachers treat it as an integral part of instruction, when it is evaluated by teacher, and when it counts as a part of the grade.

Assignments that require students to think, and are therefore more interesting, foster their desire to learn both in and out of school. Such activities include explaining what is seen or read in class; comparing, relating, and experimenting with ideas; and analyzing principles.

Effective homework assignments do not just supplement the classroom lesson; they also teach students to be independent learners. Homework gives students experience in following directions, making judgments and comparisons, raising additional questions for study, and developing responsibility and self-discipline.

35. Frequent and systematic monitoring of students' progress helps students, parents, teachers, administrators, and policymakers identify strengths and weaknesses in learning and instruction.

Teachers find out what students already know and what they still need to learn by assessing student work. They use various means, including essays, quizzes and tests, homework, classroom questions, standardized tests, and parents' comments. Teachers can use student errors on tests and in class as early warning signals to point out and correct learning problems before they worsen. Student motivation and achievement improve when teachers provide prompt feedback on assignments.

Students generally take two kinds of tests; classroom tests and standardized tests. Classroom tests help teachers find out if what they are teaching is being learned; thus, these tests serve to evaluate both student and teacher. Standardized tests apply similar gauges to everyone in a specific grade level. By giving standardized tests, school districts can see how achievement progresses over time. Such tests also help schools find out how much of the curriculum is actually being learned. Standardized tests can also reveal problems in the curriculum itself.

36. When teachers introduce new subject matter, they need to help students grasp its relationship to facts and concepts they have previously learned.

The more students already know about a particular subject, the easier it is for them to acquire new information about it. Teachers can help students learn new information by organizing courses and units of study so that topics build on one another and by helping students focus on relevant background knowledge.

Teachers can also help students grasp relationships between new information and old. Not all students spontaneously relate prior knowledge to new information. . . .

By identifying central and recurrent patterns in content areas, teachers can help students focus on important information and not get overwhelmed by minor details.

37. The most important characteristics of effective schools are strong instructional leadership, a safe and orderly climate, school-wide emphasis on basic skills, high teacher expectations for student achievement, and continuous assessment of pupil progress.

38. Schools that encourage academic achievement focus on the importance of scholastic success and on maintaining order and discipline.

39. Good character is encouraged by surrounding students with good adult examples and by building upon natural occasions for learning and practicing good character. Skillful educators know how to organize their schools, classrooms, and lessons to foster such examples.

Educators become good role models through their professionalism, courtesy, cooperation, and by demanding top performance from their students. They maintain fair and consistent discipline policies, including matters of attendance, punctuality, and meeting assignment deadlines.

40. The use of libraries enhances reading skills and encourages independent learning.

Research has shown that participating in library programs reinforces children's skills and interest in reading. Summer reading programs offered by public libraries, for example, reinforce reading skills learned during the school year. Library programs for preschool children encourage children's interest in learning to read. Both types of programs provide many opportunities for reading, listening and viewing materials.

Public and school libraries can enhance reading instruction by offering literature-based activities that stress the enjoyment of reading as well as reading skills. Hearing stories and participating in such activities help young children want to learn to read. . . .

Use of both public and school libraries encourages students to go beyond their textbooks to locate, explore, evaluate and use ideas and information that enhance classroom instruction.

41. Schools contribute to their student's academic achievement by establishing, communicating, and enforcing fair and consistent discipline policies.

For 16 of the last 17 years, the public has identified discipline as the most serious problem facing its schools. Effective discipline policies contribute to the academic atmosphere by emphasizing the importance of regular attendance, promptness, respect for teachers and academic work, and good conduct.

42. A school staff that provides encouragement and personalized attention, and monitors daily attendance can reduce unexcused absences and class-cutting.

43. Successful principals establish policies that create an orderly environment and support effective instruction.

44. When schools provide comprehensive orientation programs for students transferring from one school to another, they ease the special stresses and adjustment difficulties those students face. The result is apt to be improved student performance.

45. Underachieving or mildly handicapped students can benefit most from remedial education when the lessons in those classes are closely coordinated with those in their regular classes.

46. Students benefit academically when their teachers share ideas, cooperate in activities, and assist one another's intellectual growth.

47. Teachers welcome professional suggestions about improving their work, but they rarely receive them.

48. Many children who are physically handicapped or have emotional or learning problems can be given an appropriate education in well-supported regular classes and schools.

49. Students read more fluently and with greater understanding if they have knowledge of the world and their culture, past and present. Such knowledge and understanding is called cultural literacy.

In addition to their knowledge of the physical world, students' knowledge of their culture determines how they will grasp the meaning of what they read. Students read and understand passages better when the passages refer to events, people and places – real or fictional – with which the students are familiar.

Students' understanding of the subtleties and complexities of written information depends on how well they understand cultural traditions, attitudes, values, conventions, and connotations. The more literate students are in these ways, the better prepared they will be to read and understand serious books, magazines, and other challenging material.

Most school teachers, college professors, journalists, and social commentators agree that the general knowledge of American students is too low, and getting lower. . . .

In the United States, the national community comprises diverse groups and traditions; together they have created a rich cultural heritage. Cultural literacy not only enables students to read better and gain new knowledge; it enables them to understand the shared heritage, institutions, and values that draw Americans together.

50. The best way to learn a foreign language in school is to start early and to study it intensively over many years.

Most students who take a foreign language study it for 2 years or less in high school and do not learn to communicate with it effectively.

51. The stronger the emphasis on academic courses, the more advanced the subject matter, and the more rigorous the textbooks, the more high school students learn. Subjects that are learned mainly in school rather than at home, such as science and math, are most influenced by the number and kind of courses taken.

Students often handicap their intellectual growth by avoiding difficult courses.

52. Handicapped high school students who seek them are more likely to find jobs after graduation when schools prepare them for careers and private sector businesses provide on-the-job training.

53. Skimpy requirements and declining enrollments in history classes are contributing to a decline in students' knowledge of the past.

The decline in the study of history may hinder students from gaining an historical perspective on contemporary life.

54. Advancing gifted students at a faster pace results in their achieving more than similarly gifted students who are taught at a normal rate.

55. High school students who complement their academic studies with extracurricular activities gain experience that contributes to their success in college.

56. When students work more than 15 to 20 hours per week, their grades may suffer. They can benefit, however, from limited out-of-school work.

Students can benefit from jobs, however, if work hours are limited, the experience is well-selected, and the job does not interfere with their school work. Such jobs help improve knowledge about the workplace, foster positive attitudes and habits, and open up possibilities for careers.

57. Business leaders report that students with solid basic skills and positive work attitudes are more likely to find and keep jobs than students with vocational skills alone.

As new technologies make old job skills obsolete, the best vocational education will be solid preparation in reading, writing, mathematics, and reasoning. In the future, American workers will acquire many of their job skills in the workplace, not in school. They will need to be able to master new technologies and upgrade their skills to meet specialized job demands. Men and women who have weak basic skills, or who cannot readily master new skills, to keep pace with change, may be only marginally employed over their lifetimes.

Business leaders recommend that schools raise academic standards. They point to the need for remedial programs to help low-achieving students and to reduce dropping out.

Business leaders stress that the school curriculum should emphasize literacy, mathematics, and problem-solving skills. They believe schools should emphasize such personal qualities as self-discipline, reliability, perseverance, teamwork, accepting responsibility, and respect for the rights of others. These characteristics will serve all secondary students well, whether they go on to college or directly into the world of work.

Endnote

* United States Department of Education, What Works, Research About Teaching and Learning., 1987. 86 pp., paper. For ordering information, write to What Works, Pueblo, CO 81009.

I

Operating the Home School

Sources described in this appendix:

(**1**) *general how-to books,*
(**2**) *principles influencing home school methodology,*
(**3**) *various aspects of home schooling including collections of articles,*
(**4**) *Internet and broadcast information sources,*
(**5**) *general principles of learning,*
(**6**) *home schooling success stories,*
(**7**) *research on home schooling,*
(**8**) *legal considerations.*

Part 1, General How-to Sources

Basic Steps to Successful Homeschooling, The Vicki Brady's personal experiences make her book captivating. The "basic steps" she takes you through may need some modification for your situation, but you will know where you are going and how to get there. Recommended resources are listed. A revision is in the works as I write, so ask for information. Vital Issues Press, P.O. Box 53788, Lafayette, LA 70505; (800) 749-4009. The book is also available through the ministry directed by the Bradys, Home Education Radio Network. See Part 4.

Christian Home Educators Curriculum Manual Described in Appendix X.

Field Guide to Home Schooling Christine M. Field begins her book by describing the immoral peer influence that prompted her and her husband to withdraw their daughter from kindergarten. She proceeds to systematically discuss the advantages and approaches to home schooling often using popular authors to confirm her ideas. She then prepares her readers to get started and to deal with natural concerns of home schoolers. Her appendix lists resource publishers by subject, one leadership group for each state, and the pertinent laws for each state. Although others have said most of what she covers, her well-organized "field guide" will give any parent a solid perspective for home teaching. I feel she could have leaned less on the thoughts of some conservative critics. They make some good points about public schools. There are, indeed, lions to avoid, but we must not imagine one behind every tree in the dark before we have used our flashlight. Approx. 215 pp; spring of 1998 by Fleming H. Revell.

Home School Manual, The Print Version, People often call us asking how they can get their own copy after borrowing one from the library. The price is $30. For U.S. ground mail, add $3. Surface to Canada add $4 plus GST; Elsewhere add $4.50. Remember tax if delivered to Michigan. See the copyright page for the address. Check our web site for current information: http://www.hoofprint.com.

Home School Manual, The Electronic version for Windows on 2 diskettes. It includes chapters and forms printable with a major word processor. 1996. reduced to $12. A CD is planned for fall-1998 or 1999. Expected price, $20 plus $2 for postage.

Home School: Taking the First Step Borg Hendrickson, a former teacher, helps you understand what teachers do to teach. Her book begins by considering a number of questions that generally interest first-step home schoolers. These include: socialization, teaching qualifications, exceptional children, and what happens after home schooling years are over. And she prepares you to meet guidelines established in various states. She also includes state-by-state legal information, lists of support groups, books, curriculum suppliers, and descriptions of a number of teaching approaches. 1994 edition, 337 pp. $18.95 plus $2.80 postage. Mountain Meadow Press, P.O. Box 447, Kooskia, ID 83589; (208) 926-7875; mtmeadow@camasnet.com

Home Schooling, Answers to Questions Parents Most Often Ask. This book offers the perspective of two professional educators who have worked with home schoolers through the Orange County school system and who lecture on the topic, Deborah McIntire and Robert Windham. Chapter titles are the questions: "Why would I want to teach my children at home?" and 31 others. The appendix offers basic information. The book has good advice and a pleasant format. It would be appreciated by someone who does not want a Christian approach, although one of the questions is "How do I integrate my values and beliefs?" Three teaching approaches are recognized: textbook-driven, theme-driven, and interest-driven. 1995, $17.98 plus 15% shipping and tax if sent to GA, IN, MD, MN, NJ, or TX. Creative Teaching Press, P.O. Box 6017, Cypress, CA 90630-0017. (800) 444-4CTP, Fax (714) 995-3548. http://www.creativeteaching.com.

Homeschooling Information and Resource Guide. Free from Home Eduction Press, P.O. Box 1083, Tonasket, WA 98855

Home Educating With Confidence With fifteen years experience and a dozen children to home teach, you may expect Rick and Marilyn Boyer to know what they are writing about. Their books three main sections give an idea of its scope: (1) Thinking It Over, (2) Curriculum, and (3) Other Things. Home schooling leader Peggy Flint, introduced me to the book so I'm letting her tell you about it in the words which follow:

In one of the best chapters, Starting Right, Staying Right, Rick suggests, Clarify Your Motives. He points out how important it is to know why you are homeschooling. Then he suggests Get Your Children Under Control. Teaching is hard when your children aren't cooperative.

I especially like his third topic on assembling a basic curriculum. He describes video home school and urges against it because the essence of home education is the parent-child relationship. He is leery of correspondence schools because you have to follow a program which, he feels, keeps you from individualizing your approach. . . . .

In case you are actually looking for personal experiences and insights into child rearing and the dangers which influence the home today, you will find them in this book. Even if you aren't, and can get beyond the extraneous material the issues not directly relating to natural learning you will probably enjoy it. You'll appreciate the Boyers insights into natural learning and the need to make learning fun and applicable to the students life.

Published in 1995 by the Boyers. 241 pages, $9.95. PF, The Learning Parent, Rt. 3, Box 543, Rustburg, VA 24258.

How to Home School This book's subtitle is: "A Practical Approach." It really is. I guess I wouldn't make a very good politician, applauding the competition. Here are the chapters in Gayle Graham's book: "Why Home School?," "Planning for Success," Reading – De-mystified," "Learning and Exploring Together," and "Math – The Home School Advantage." The appendices are: "Choosing Curriculum," "Understanding Standardized Testing," and "Reproducible Forms." The book is briefer than you might expect but deals with the most important topics. For an idea see Gayle's discussion of curriculum fairs in Chapter 15. 196 pp., $20 plus $3 shipping. Available from Common Sense Press. See *Great Editing* . . . in Appendix P, Part 2.

How to Tutor Samuel L. Blumenfeld, 1986, 1993. Around 300 pages, $24.95 + $3.00 S&H + tax if ID. From its description, the book seems good. The idea was to help parents help their children achieve well in school, but it serves well for home schooling, too. 117 lessons on reading, 73 on writing and 67 on arithmetic. The Paradigm Co., P.O. Box 45161, Boise, ID 83711. (208) 322-4440.

Math workbooks with all the exercises in *How to Tutor* save writing out the numbers of the exercises. Also available are workbooks for phonics, and writing. The Blumenfeld reading course on CD presents more than 3,500 words in thousands of interactive screens and sound pronunciations. $85.

I Am a Home Schooler My name is Teigen. Im nine years old, and I am a home schooler. That means I do my schoolwork right here at home. My mom does most of the teaching. . . . And the book makes it clear that her dad is actively involved, too. Tinted photographs show games with other home educated kids on Co-op day, field trips, and other scenes of interest. Its a realistic picture of a home schooling family. This book is apparently pitched toward other children with the final page explaining what interested parents need to know. I applaud this window on a way of learning that is easily misunderstood. Author Julie Voetberg. 32 pp., $6.95 paper, 1995, Albert Whitman & Company.

Original Home Schooling Series, The Reprint of a set of six books by Charlotte Mason.

School at Home, Kendall, Ingeborg U.V. Maranto, ICER Press, P.O. Box 877, Claremont, CA 91711. 1982. $6.95 + $1 shipping + tax if CA. Ingeborg Kendall discusses reasons why home schooling meets educational needs of various families. The second half of the book explains how to devise a strategy for meeting academic, social, religious, and physical needs. She discusses advantages offered in correspondence school programs and also how to plan the whole program yourself. This is an older book but principles don't change.

Should I HOME SCHOOL? How to Decide What's Right for You & Your Child ELIZABETH & DAN HAMILTON

Should I Home School? Elizabeth and Dan Hamilton begin by discussing various learning options and asking you to think of what you want education to mean for your children. You will also get an idea of a typical home school day, what general legal requirements you might expect depending on the state you are in, your preparation, how to get started, etc. You will even find a chart of pros and cons of the various factors such as time, social needs, and quality of learning. In the back are lists of resources. The viewpoint is clearly Christian. 170 pp., 1997. From InterVarsity Press, P.O. Box 1400, Downers Grove, IL 60515.

Successful Homeschool Family Handbook, The, Raymond and Dorothy Moore. This is the Moore's basic book. It and *Minding Your Own Business* outline the principles which they call "the Moore foumula." They discuss low stress and high achievement. Address with *Better Late Than Early* in this Appendix.

Ultimate Guide to Homeschooling By Debra Bell. I have not examined this book but the description looks good. Around $20.

Part 2, Principles Influencing Instructional Methods

Child's Work, *Taking Children's Choices Seriously* Nancy Wallace, author; Holt Associates, publisher, 1990, 156 pp. $12.95. In her earlier book, *Better Than School* (1983), Nancy Wallace told about the learning experiences of her young children, Ishmael and Vita. Her thesis was reflected in the book's title. Now the story continues. Although I disagree with certain philosophical points (such as the idea that nothing true should be withheld from children), the book has an important message. Nancy Wallace would teach us to respect children's uniqueness, not expecting them to be carbon copies of ourselves. She would remind us to give them time, space, and raw materials for developing their thinking and doing abilities. Taking children's "work" seriously leads them to view themselves seriously and to make giant early strides which pay compound interest in later years.

Countdown to Consistency Mary Hood writes about how educational choices depend on philosophy. She points out that we all have a philosophy, then discuses essentialism, perennialism, progressivism, and existentialism. I found myself not fitting into any of those categories. Worksheets are provided to help readers figure out what they believe. 1992; $8.95 plus $1 shipping from Mary Hood, P.O. Box 2524, Cartersville, GA 30120.

Going Home to School In her book, LLewellyn B. Davis develops a rationale for home education. She begins by showing that everyone has a world view which includes an understanding of the nature of God, of truth, and so on. "Education not only teaches information *about* life but also teaches a way of *looking at and living* life. . . . Because an education teaches a world view as well as information about the world, there can be no such thing as value-free instruction." (pp. 7, 8). She traces aspects of the history of schooling and rejects the concept of "institutionalized education." "Can a private Christian school be Biblically sound?" (p. 108) She says "usually not," because she feels private Christian schools tend to adopt the same methods, materials, techniques, and assumptions about education as their secular counterparts. Christian schools I know get a higher score in my grade book, but her concern should be considered. The book's price is $12.95 plus $5.95 (min.) shipping from The Elijah Company. See Appendix Z.

Help, I'm Homeschooling. If you were to visit authors Deborah Castaneda and Pam Geib and ask them how to get started teaching your kids at home, what they would tell you and show you is in this book. Here are comments from the introduction: "Homeschooling does not always 'fit' neatly into your day or your life. It is not easy keeping a house clean with fourteen children underfoot. (All right, so there are only three. . . it *seems* like fourteen.) . . . Chapter 5 is about conflicts you may encounter. The table of contents shows 8 appendix sections plus blank forms. The book shows how two moms put handles on some very down-to-earth and common problems and have taken a responsible approach to teaching their children. 127 pp. 2nd ed., published 1990 by CHEA of California. $13.23 with tax and shipping. For information, see CHEA of California in appendix D. (Discount for CHEA of CA members.)

Home Schools, An Alternative, Third Edition, 1990. The title of Cheryl Gorder's book reflects its major emphasis. She helps her readers take a close look at the alternative of home education. She discusses the following aspects: psychological and emotional, social, religious and moral, and legal. She presents a historical perspective, and she discusses lesson planning and choosing materials and schooling services organizations. An appendix gives primary addresses for resources and support groups. 176 pp. $11.95. Blue Bird Publishing, 1739 E. Broadway, #306, Tempe, AZ 85282, (602) 968-4088; Fax (602) 831-1829.

I Learn Better By Teaching Myself and ***Still Teaching Ourselves*** Two books under one cover. Anges Leistico writes about her experience with her children letting them learn their own way ("interest initiated") and their experience integrating into the traditional school system. (not reviewed, see review of *Learning all the Time*. $19.95 from Holt Associates, 2269 Massachusetts Ave., Cambridge, MA 02140; (617) 864-3100.

Learning All the Time By John Holt. When I asked the Holt Associates people to check my description of their periodical, *Growing Without Schooling,* in anticipation of an earlier edition of *The Home School Manual,* I got a polite letter from Holt Associates president, Patrick Farenga. He felt that my evaluation of Holt's philosophy was inaccurate. I had described it as having "the idea that kids do best when left alone (since good comes from within)." With his letter he sent a copy of *Learning All the Time* so I could see for myself. I appreciate that approach. Too often we tend to stand back and throw stones when we disagree. I'm not really converted, but I see that I had not given an accurate picture, and I'm changing the statement.

Learning All the Time was in the mill in 1985 when Holt died. Several people who understand his ideas, drew from his earlier writings to fill in a few gaps and then polished the manuscript for publication. The work reveals a concise picture of Holt's philosophy of learning, which is foundational to his other ideas.

In describing the book he was preparing, Holt wrote, "Learning, to me, means making more sense of the world around us, and being able to do more things in it. Success in school means remembering the answers to teachers' questions, getting clever about guessing what questions they will ask, and about how to fool them when you don't know the answers." (p. xvi.) I agree with his description of learning (although there is a vertical dimension Holt never chose to know). I don't agree, however, with his conclusions about success in school.

My statement about kids being left alone distorted (unintentionally) the larger picture Holt draws. He would not have left them to learn in a vacuum. And Holt's statement about schools could have resulted from a little unintentional myopia on his part, too. Good classroom teachers encourage the kind of learning he described. The difference in what Holt advocated is that he would have basically expected the children to decide what, when, and how they wanted to learn. He would have guided them as he felt appropriate. Some of the rest of us would gently offer more guidance and set more constraints.

Good teachers design and use exercises that require certain understandings and offer grades to encourage the attainment of goals. Here Holt would have strongly objected, pointing out that learning is best when chosen by the learner. But good teachers don't stop with predetermined expectations. They also provide options and encourage exploration of independently chosen topics.

Okay Mr. Holt, maybe I should say they *ought* to provide more of this independence. I can remember looking forward to high school science labs. I had in mind some since-forgotten experiment with house flies. I wanted to learn – to explore! As you can guess, I was disappointed with lab exercises set up only for finding out what everyone else already knew. I did learn, however, and enjoyed it. I'll try my statement again. *Good teachers would like to provide more independence than they do.* The number of kids they are responsible for limits them. Here home schoolers, with a class of only one or a few children, have the advantage. So, Mr. Holt, at this point we agree.

Holt taught that children should not be expected to learn what their parents decide they should learn but what they themselves want to learn. It would be okay for us to know what we want them to learn, but we should not help them when they don't want help. "There's nothing wrong with offering a suggestion," Holt wrote, "but there are several things you have to be careful about. First of all, both parent and child must know that it *is* a suggestion, which the child is free to refuse. . . . Adults can learn to take "no" for an answer" (p. 146).

Unfortunately, this method helps children learn to be self-centered, which does not help restore society to respect for the rights of our neighbors and to know the joy of harmony with heaven. A home schooled boy, about 12 years old, demonstrated this to me during a lecture. While his mother was addressing the audience, he was talking back to her, disputing what she was saying. He had learned to tell her when he didn't want help, and she had learned to accept his "no"! One case, of course does not *prove* a method good or bad. Here it only illustrates my point. My kids weren't always like little angels but, overall, different methods do produce different results.

Please remember that real freedom comes in choosing natural constraints. We can trust the One who created us. The plan He has set for our behavior results in our ultimate happiness. The more I read His book and experience the joy of closeness to Him, the more excited I become (and the more I know my own weakness). I just wish the whole world could understand. I know some of you do. This is not salvation by works, by the way. Only the good works of Christ can stand in the place of my sin. It's just that He is faithful and just, not only to forgive but to cleanse, lifting us into the holiness of His presence. (See 1 John 1:9.) He cleanses *from* sin, not in it (Matt 1:21). Oops, I'm getting preachy again. Can't help it.

Chapters in the book include "Young Children as Research Scientists," "Loving Music," and "The Nature of Learning." I've already taken too much time on my soap box with this book, but I got a nice protest from Patrick Farenga in response to the draft of this review. And I have clarified a couple spots. I think you would like to hear some of his defense: "John liked to point out that he is not against teaching at all; indeed, he claimed that his books were all arguments for allowing the teacher to be the ultimate boss in his or her classroom. Teaching, like medicine, does indeed work. But only if the timing and dosage are correct."

I expound on the topic of learning in my chapter on structure. Here I would simply re-emphasize that we may and should have both structure and freedom. Holt's *Learning All the Time* is published by Addison Wesley, 1989, and is available from John Holt's Book Store catalog. See Appendix Z.

Relaxed Home School, The Mary Hood feels parents should think through what they believe about education, form expectations for family relationships, respect their children's ideas, set overall goals, and create a pleasant, flexible atmosphere for learning. She advises, "Take control of your children's education! And then . . . RELAX!!"

Her goals are in the areas of values, habits, skills, development of individual interests, and (in last place) knowledge. In time planning, she sees four areas of attention: academics, work, free play, and creative pursuits. "In most schools," she writes, "academics takes the upper hand and the rest of these needs are shortchanged."

I found myself agreeing with nearly everything Mary said. She presents an excellent balance of responsible management and natural learning processes against a backdrop of Christian principles. 1994, 106 pp., $10.95 plus shipping at 10% with minimum of $2. From Mary Hood, P.O. Box 2524, Cartersville, GA 30120.

School Free (rev. 1991) Wendy Priesnitz. Described as a "definitive profile of deschooling in Canada . . . from the experience of . . . Canadian deschooling families." Simple information for getting started and discussion of issues such as socialization and the variety of philosophies. Available for Cn$20 (including postage and GST) from Canadian Alliance of Home Schoolers, 195 Markville Rd., Unionville, Ontario L3R 4V8.

Simplicity of Homeschooling, The *Discover the Freedom of Learning through Living*. This title reveal's the book's "flavor." With her husband Jack, Vicky Goodchild began the venture into home education back in 1983. Since then she has been helping others know how to succeed. She recommends a blend of various methods and a "learning lifestyle" – good advice, in my opinion. The book comes with a valuable audio cassette by Jack. He gives dads a perspective on home schooling and shares the concept that the ABCs are the easy part while developing character is the hard and important part. 1997, 230-page book plus 30-minute cassette for $20. HIS Publishing Co., 1732 NE 3 Ave., Ft., Lauderdale, FL 33305. (954) 7764-4567; Fax (954) 768-9313. 282 pp., 1994, $14.95 plus $2 shipping. Out of the Box Publishing, P.O. Box 80214-R, Portland, OR 97280-1214.

Teaching Children A curriculum guide for grades K-6 by Diane Lopez. $12.99. (not examined)

Wisdom's Way Marilyn Howshall's book is for families who are seeking God for their home education adventure. She challenges us to consider our home schooling endeavor as a byproduct of our lifestyle and to develop a lifestyle of learning. As you read you will find yourself becoming excited at the possibility of validating some of your current lifestyle activities and upgrading the quality of others so that you can personalize your lifestyle with meaningful, God-ordained and, Spirit-led learning opportunities. Marilyn takes the best of all the approaches to education with which most of us are familiar, and uses them to create this lifestyle of learning. So as you read you will notice hints of Charlotte Mason's living books approach, classical education, and the Principle Approach's use of notebooks for researching, recording, relating, and reasoning. *Wisdom's Way of Learning* is a whopping 300 pages, and is expensive ($39). However, everyone should read it, whether only thinking about home schooling or having had seasoned experience. *This review has been adapted from the Lifetime Books & Gifts catalog.*

Part 3, Various Aspects, Including Collections of Articles

A to Z Guide to Educational Field Trips Gregg Harris, 208 pp., $14.95. See address for Noble Publishing in Appendix N. About finding resources in your community. Not examined.

Best of The Home School Digest Check Appendix K for the description of the magazine. A large portion of the articles from the first five years have been published in two volumes of about 200 pages each. They provide a broad resource of good reading on topics from "How to Make Your Children God's Children," and "The Heaven-Sent Gift" to "Writing the Lead Sentence," "Techniques for Disciplining the Gifted Child," and "Vacations: A Learning Extension." A total of 175 articles. Postpaid prices are $19.95 for each volume or $35 for both from Wisdom's Gate, P.O. Box 374, Covert, MI 49043.

Field Trips & Extra-Curricular Activities In this book of practical ideas, author Barbara Edtl Shelton seems more to be suggesting activities for supplementing or expanding the curriculum rather than "things outside of the scope of planned learning" as is technically indicated by the Latin term, "extra-curricular." The book contains specific ideas for field trips and how to make them successful, planning a home school presentation night, forms for support groups, etc. Christian orientation. $14.95 plus $2.85 postage. from Barbara Edtl Shelton, 182 No. Columbia Hts. Rd., Longview, WA 98632.

Home School Decisions 2770 South 1000 West, Perry, UT 84302. $7.95 + $1.25 for postage. Add tax if in Utah. The book deals with 22 educational issues including socialization, impatient parents, and how much time should be spent at desk work. Mrs. Kinmont is in charge of the Latter Day Saints Home Educator's Association. The family also distributes Brite Music books and cassettes. *Standin' Tall*, for example, is a series on 12 character traits like courage, gratitude and honesty. The booklet-cassette set for each trait costs $9.95.

Home Style Teaching, Raymond and Dorothy Moore, 1984. Topics include: Confidence as a teacher, Starting home schooling, Organizing time, Students as teachers, Making reading instruction easy, Teaching creative thinking and writing, Tests, Studying, Remotivating a burned-out child, Curriculum, Consistent reasoning, Readiness and "super baby," Grandparents, Transition to regular school, Submission to state control, etc. $10.00. (See *Better Late Than Early.*)

Home School Reader, The A collection of more than significant articles through 1994. From Home Education Press, P.O. Box 1083, Tonasket, WA 98855.

How and Why of Home Schooling, The Pastor Raymond Ballmann makes a good case for Christian home schooling. The book seems to be stronger on "why" than on "how." Crossway Books. $10.99.

How to Write a Low Cost / No Cost Curriculum For Your Home-School Child Borg Hendrickson shows you how to do what her book title says. We cover some of this in *The Home School Manual*, but her book may be better on this specific task. It leads you through the process in more of a 1-2-3 and for-example way. Included are forms to copy and work with and lists of subject matter typically taught in various grades. If you are uncertain about how to do this and live in a state where you might be expected to produce such a document, get this book. And if you are not, you might want it anyway. It helps you decide what and how to teach according to your child and your goals. 1995 ed., 180 pp., $14.95 plus $2.80 shipping. Mountain Meadow Press, P.O. Box 447, Kooskia, ID 83539; (208) 926-7875; mtmeadow@camasnet.com.

Joyful Home Schooler, The Have you ever felt depressed, eager to get away from the stress, ready to quit teaching your kids? Many moms have and so has Mary Hood. Her book helps you get right with God and remember He is in control. She discusses transforming your home for an upbeat learning center, dealing with kids at various ages, and overcoming problems. You will enjoy this burst of sunshine. 1997. $12.95 plus shipping from Ambleside Educational Press, P.O. Box 2524, Cartersville, GA 30120; (770) 917-9141.

Right Choice . . . Home Schooling, The 1998 revised edition. The whole title is *"The Right Choice, The Incredible Failure of Public Education and the Rising Hope of Home Schooling."* Subtitle: "An Academic, Historical, Practical, and Legal Perspective." After painting a solemn picture of public education, Klicka makes a good case for "the right choice." Gregg Harris contributes two chapters to explain how to begin home teaching from a biblical view. Then the reader learns about threats to home education and about getting involved in conserving freedom. At the end are appendices including an explanation of a significant court case. I agree with conclusions Klicka draws from historical information although one must always be on guard against biased sources for the reasons. The book is good and has earned its popularity. From Noble Publishing Association, P.O. Box 2250, Gresham, OR 97030; (503) 677-3942.

Survivor's Guide to Home Schooling, A If home teaching seems like stuffy theory or someone else's idea, this book will help you see how it might look, sound, feel, taste, and smell. Chapters include "Do Real People Do This?" and "Climbing Mount Never-Rest." Crossway Books, 1988, 177 pp. $10.99; order line fax (630) 682-4785; or order by e-mail sales@goodnews-crossway.org.

Part 4, Internet and broadcast sources

On line services like CompuServe, Prodigy, and America Online have forums for discussion and questions. You will find them on the web, too.

Education Revolution Weekly show about alternative education on the Talk America Network. The sponsor, Alternative Education Resource Organization (See Appendix C), deals with more than home schooling.

Homeschooling Live Radio From Home Education Radio Network, P.O. Box 3338, Idaho Springs, CO 80452. (303) 567-4092. E-mail HENRadio@aol.com. Weekly talk and information. Write for a station list. I'm sure they would appreciate your self-addressed stamped envelope. Or call or send e-mail. The broadcast is also on 3 short wave frequencies and on satellite.

Keystone high school A web site soliciting exchange of links from home school sites. With their aggressive campaign, they will probably get a good number and, I expect, will offer advertising to companies that would like to sell to you. There are a number of sites with home schooling links, and Gazelle has decided not to compete although we do have a few links and list many more in this book, usually in the descriptions of organizations they represent. For now, our "link" to keystone is this announcement. http://www.keystonehighschool.com.

wwwboard A site with a bulletin board and links to many sites of interest. http://www.vegsource.com /wwwboard/hschool/wwwboard.html/

Part 5, General Principles of Learning

Home-Grown Kids Raymond and Dorothy Moore, 1981. Chapter titles include: "The hand that rocks the cradle," "Parents in charge," "Setting the stage for birth," "Getting a good start. . . ." "The winsome ones and twos," "The exploring threes and fours," "The . . . fives and sixes," "The . . . sevens, eights and nines," and "Sources of . . . materials." $9 plus shipping and, if Washington, tax.

How Do You Know They Know What They Know? Described by the subtitle, "A Handbook of Helps for Grading nd Evaluating Student Progress." Evaluation is easy to neglect in home teaching and Teresa Moon has done a good job explaining how to do it. Forms and examples are provided for various types of learning. Being sensitive to it is essential. Should you evaluate as much as this book suggests? I'm not sure. If you are teaching from scratch, you need more help here than if you are following a good packaged program. Of course, the same time constraint applies information in some of the chapters in this book. You don't have to know it all to get started, and kids learn even if we don't quite know what they know. On the positive side, understanding characteristics of good learning will make you a better teacher. 1997. $14.95 from Grove Publishing. 16172 Huxley Cir., Westminster, CA 92683.

How to Study Subtitle: *A Practical Guide From a Christian Perspective*. The book might better have been titled "Skills for Success in School." A person could study at home and learn quite a bit without mastering all the skills outlined by author Edward J. Shewan but continuing serious study in the academic world (and often out of it) demands them. They include time management and skills in reading, writing, research, taking notes, and taking tests. On a few points, I have a little different opinion. Some of the advice seems stilted. In writing, for example, an outline is usually in order for themes and speeches but it doesn't need to come before writing begins and often it doesn't even need to be put down on paper. Also I doubt that many writers develop paragraphs by thinking up a topic sentence and trying to make proper supporting sentences. I do agree that these ideas emphasize the importance of logical thought development and hence are good learning tools. For taking notes, I'm not sure why keeping eye contact is advised – unless to impress the teacher.

The book is small (116 pages) but gives specific instruction for skill building in key areas crucial for success in learning. Your high school or upper grade youth needs it, especially in a home school where some skills might get taken for granted. 1993. $4.95 plus $1.50 shipping (and tax if Illinois) it's an excellent investment. Christian Liberty Press, 502 W. Euclid Ave., Arlington, Heights, IL 60004.

How to Study From Ron Fry's series. See Appendix J.

Infusing Critical and Creative Thinking into Content Instruction, *A lesson design handbook for the elementary grades.* Robert J. Swartz and Sandra Parks., 1994, Critical Thinking Press & Software, P.O. Box 448, Pacific Grove, CA 93950 (800) 458-4849. (Publisher's logo shown)

This large book shows you how to help kids avoid twisted thinking. It includes careful explanations and suggestions for teaching. It might not be on the top of your reading priorities unless you are particularly interested or unless you see a need for your own children. Charts and diagrams guide the thinking process. See my chapter on thinking skills to get an idea.s

Natural Learning Rhythms Understanding the right times to teach. Written from careful observation and a secular point of view. Celestial Arts, 1993, 275 pp. $21 shipping & tax included, from Josette & Ba Luvmour, P.O. Box 445, No. San Juan, CA 95960; (530) 292-3858; josette@wfv.com or ba@wfv.com.

Overnight Student, The Michael Jones is enthusiastic about his book, and that is part of the secret of success. He advises taking notes in outline form, asking questions, and reading the notes back to yourself. I'll let you read the book to find a little more about how it works. Jones' dim view of how good teachers use homework is more negative than mine, but he is definitely right that it does not necessarily produce learning. I disagree with his general assertion that university-level courses are essentially information channeled through the teacher's mouth (although this is often the case). The topic of learning to learn is definitely important, and this book is worth reading. I recommend reading other books on the topic, too. Louis Publishing, 4016 NW 68, Oklahoma City, 73116; (405) 840-1284 and tax if Okla., 63 brief pages, $4.95.

Teaching Children to Love, *80 Games & Fun Activities for Raising Balanced Children in Unbalanced Times* This book immediately caught my interest because, as you may have noticed, the first of eight goals I propose for education is learning to love. Author Doc Lew Childre sees the physical heart as the center of the feelings and as a lens that gives value to the various aspects of intelligence. Feelings of anger, frustration, worry, or depression block learning and the formation of good responses to life situations, while love enhances them. This book helps your children and youth conquer the negative feelings and enhance love. The 80 games and activities mentioned in the subtitle are arranged by aspects of nurturing love for others and self-esteem. They are also age rated.

Childre offers excellent concepts but does not relate them to the divine author of love (1 John 4:8). The love principle of the universe is the reason God calls us to loving behavior (Deut. 28; Rev. 22:14). When Jesus was asked to identify the greatest commandment, He said it was to love God with heart, mind and soul. Then He said that

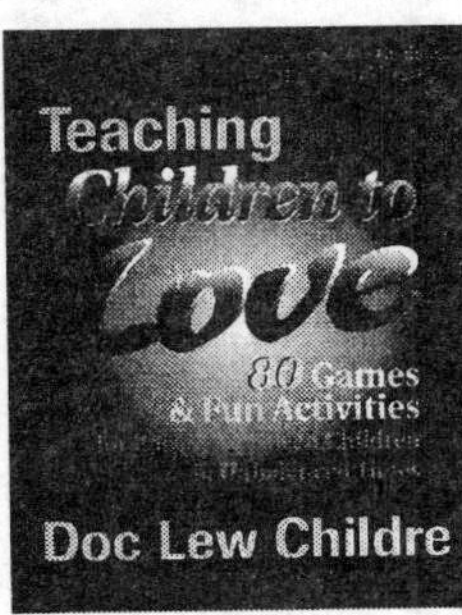

the next greatest was to love our neighbors as ourselves. (Matt. 23:36-40). This second responsibility is the focus of Childre's book. One activity acknowledges that we traditionally say grace before a meal, then suggests that we use the time to briefly turn our love to family members or to express appreciation for something in the family environment. I would use the activity but not as a replacement for the prayer seeking God's blessing. Many activities will need to be adapted a little if used with a single child. 800-372-3100

1996. $16.95 plus $5.25 priority mail or UPS Ground s&h to US addresses. Ordered from Planetary, P.O. Box 66, Boulder Creek, CA 95006. (800) 372-3100 fax (408) 338-9861; http://www.planetarypub.com, email: ecarroll@planetarypub.com

Teaching With Love & Logic The book's subtitle, Taking Control of the Classroom, would lead you to pass it by. Actually you can learn more from it than how fortunate you are to be teaching your own kids. Other good books help you know how to manage discipline in the home. This one can give you ideas for guiding the teaching-learning situation. And many of the concepts translate into managing nonscholastic interactions, too. The book is described in its preface as "an approach to working with students that: * Puts teachers in control, * Teaches kids to think for themselves, * Raises the level of student responsibility, * Prepares kids to function effectively in a society filled with temptations, decisions, and consequences."

The four key principles described are: the enhancement of self-concept, shared control, consequences with empathy, and shared thinking. This book is packed with practical ideas you can put to work and examples to help explain them. I highly recommend it. If you can't afford the $30 price tag, try your library or a university library. By Jim Fay & David Funk. 400 pages, 1995. (800) 338-4065. The Love and Logic Press, 2207 Jackson St., Golden, CO 80401

Way They Learn, The, Subtitle: *How to Discover and Teach to Your Child's Strengths.* Author Cynthia Tobias draws practical guidance for how to teach depending on your child's (and your own) learning styles. She begins with an analysis developed by Anthony F. Gregorc. In this model, people are classified according to which of two ways they perceive their environment (concrete and abstract). Each of these groups is further divided by the two ways they tend to process the information they perceive (random and sequential). So we have four combinations: concrete sequential (CS), abstract sequential (AS), abstract random (AR), and concrete random (CR). Tobias offers a simple test to help identify the group you or your child is in. Although each of us tends to think mostly in one of the four patterns, we all, to some degree, have characteristics of the other three.

For each of the groups Tobias then suggests things they do best, what makes most sense to them, what's hard for them, and the questions they ask when learning. In the chapters which follow, interesting examples describe these learners and tell how to deal with them. Then she discusses preferred learning environments followed by the familiar classification: auditory, visual, and kinesthetic.

In the system described next, learners are identified as global (those who experience the learning in a general way) and analytic (those who see all the details and know how they fit together). This personality difference, I believe, tends to divide home schoolers. In *The Home School Manual*, chapter, "Learning Structure," we discussed the importance of keeping a balance in what kind of structure (or unstructure) is important for learning.

The last classification to be discussed divides intelligence into seven areas: linguistic, logical-mathematical, spatial, musical, bodily-kinesthetic, interpersonal, and intrapersonal.

As Tobias discusses in her final chapter, learning failure may not be so much a matter of disability as of an inappropriate learning environment. In my chapter "Techniques for Teaching" I share my opinions about how to relate to leaning styles.

For you global learners, please don't be discouraged by all these categories (and my analytical description). The book is written in an interesting way and full of practical suggestions based on tendencies toward the various classifications. Tobias has put flesh on several theory skeletons. It's a great book. If you are seeking ways to help your child learn, it will provide pointers.

168 pp., 1994, $10.99, from Focus on the Family Publishing. Available at Christian bookstores or by calling (800) A FAMILY.

Part 6, Home Schooling Success Stories

Famous Home Schoolers 1998, from Unschoolers Network, 2 Smith St., Farmingdale, NJ 07727; (908) 938-2473.**n**

Hard Times in Paradise The Colfaxes tell their experience raising and educating three sons as they stood for their secular beliefs, and often had the boys learn by doing. This and their 1988 book on the topic, *Homeschooling for Excellence*, are available from John Holt's Bookstore (Appendix Z) $20 and $11. I describe their ideas in my chapter "Educating for Superior Achievement."**n**

Home Spun Schools, Raymond and Dorothy Moore, Word Books. 1982. Success stories of people who have done it. Available from The Moore Foundation for $8 plus shipping (See under *Better Late Than Early* described in this appendix).

HotHouse Transplants *Moving From Homeschool Into the "Real World."* Matthew Duffy collected stories from sixteen Christian young people who have graduated from home schooling programs and are continuing to pursue their life goals. Their experiences and viewpoints are interesting. If you have been wondering what might lie ahead when ordinary people teach their own kids, read this book. It also offers your children courage and determination. $11.95 plus $2.50 shipping (and tax if to Calif.). 1997. Grove Publishing, 16172 Huxley Cir., Westminster, CA 92683; (714) 841-1220.

Part 7, Research in Home Schooling

Home Education Across the United States A 12-page report on a large research study looking at a large study of home school families. The areas studied, were family characteristics, student achievement, and longitudinal traits. Discussed in chapter 2.

School Can Wait, Raymond and Dorothy Moore, 1979. A defense of delayed formal education backed by references to numerous research studies. $15.00 plus shipping. (See *Better Late Than Early.)*

Strengths of Their Own – *Home Schoolers Across America: Academic Achievement, Family Characteristics, and Longitudinal Traits.* An engaging comprehensive report by Brian Ray, Ph.D. on his nationwide study. It includes statistics, analyses – convincing evidence for serious parents to teach their children at home. 1997. (I have not reviewed this publication but have discussed a report summarizing the results of the study much of the book is based on. See *Home Education Across the United States.)* $12.95 plus $3 shipping, from National Home Education Research Institute, P. O. Box 13939, Salem, OR 97309. (503) 364-1490. Make check payable to NHERI.

Part 8, Legal Considerations

America 2000 / Goals 2000 Moving the Nation Educationally to a World Order. Editor and author James R. Patrick has compiled and written a weighty tome (4 pounds, 728 pp. plus chart) to convince us that our families and freedoms are in jeopardy. The nice-sounding educational goals in the United States (See my Chapter 9), according to Patrick, are designed to facilitate a takeover of the minds and liberties of our nation through the federal (and international) control of education. The curriculum and the testing of all schools (including home schools) are to be under central control. Eventually the government will determine even entrance into and continuation in the work force, and will come into our homes to be sure our toddlers are getting federally approved training.

I believe that final events in the drama – the last part of Patrick's "prophecy" – will take a different turn than he expects. But overall the signs are not a product of imagination. Freedom of education is fast slipping away – and that means freedom to train up our children in the nurture and admonition of the Lord according to our understanding of His Word. No matter who is right about the future, it's time to stand up for our convictions, and to be sure our hearts are true before our God. 1993. $15. He also publishes a periodical, *Foundations of Liberty*. $20/yr. Foundations of Liberty, East Moline Christian School, 900 46th Ave., East Moline, IL 61244.

Government Nannies, The Cradle to Grave Agenda of Goals 2000 and Outcome Based Education. This book traces through the eight national goals, showing what each of them actually mean for our children, education, health care, the job market, and the future of our country. The current edition adds an extra chapter to trace the growth of Goals 2000 programs over the year since this book was first published. 1995. Available from Grove Publishing, 16172 Huxley Circle Westminster, CA 92683 (714) 841-1220 http://www.jatec.com/grove

Home Education, Rights and Reasons Authors John W. Whitehead and Alexis Irene Crow do their best to make you into a home school lawyer. Subtitle: A Complete Handbook for Practicing and Preserving Your Home Education Rights. They start out as most home schooling books with the "badness" of public schools and the goodness of home education. Then they deal with rights, constitutional issues, legislative factors, practical issues and freedom. The listing of laws is, of course, no longer accurate since the book was published in 1992. The book is well organized and nicely written with discussions of court cases. 557 pp. $16.99 from Crossway Books.

Home Schooling Laws, In All Fifty States. This reference work by Steve Deckard, Ed.D. Shows the specific legal and regulatory requirements. It is sometimes nice to see this information even when you have been told what you need to do. In using this book you will need to verify that the laws haven't changed since the information was compiled. A state department of education will usually will provide you with information, too. See Chapter 5 for my thoughts on finding out about legal requirements. I have a copy of the book's sixth edition. It also contains some other reference information. Earlier editions which I saw seemed a bit expensive. Ask about the current edition. 9081 Inverness Rd., Santee, CA 92071.

Right to Home School, The Christopher Klicka enlarges on the topic of his chapter here in The Home School Manual. He clarifies that it is a fundamental right according to the US constitution. It is a book to help law makers understand. $10.00 from Home School Legal Defense Association. See them in Appendix C. 1995. Revision 1998 or 1999.

J
Teaching Various Types of Students

Categories:

(1) *early childhood methods,*
(2) *early childhood materials,*
(3) *elementary school methods,*
(4) *high school methods,*
(5) *high school materials,*
(6) *students with learning problems, and*
(7) *the gifted.*

Part 1, Early Education Methods and Resources

Better Late Than Early Published by McGraw-Hill and Reader's Digest. 1975. This was the book that opened the door into home education for Raymond Moore. It sets the basis of the reasons for delaying formal education and explains what to do for various age levels. $10.00. Add 10% shipping, minimum $2.50. Available from The Moore Foundation, Box 1, Camas, WA 98607.

Early Education at Home Activities for Preschool and Kindergarten. A manual of specific plans introduced with the concept of home teaching for young children when the family situation permits. Author M. Jean Soyke's list of characteristics of the young child adds some significant points to those I mentioned in the chapter, "Planning for the Early Years." She says that the child: (1) learns by imitation, (2) is fearful, lacks security; is easily upset and confused; (3) needs adult approval and love; (4) is self-centered, and (5) enjoys talking and (6) learns by asking questions. The list is offered for consideration when deciding between home and professional preschool programs. Convincing, isn't it?

Another list shows early home factors associated with high academic achievement: (1) children read (or are read to) frequently, (2) television viewing is given low priority, (3) the family travels to interesting places, (4) everyone has at least one household responsibility, (5) children are praised for doing well and are encouraged, (6) a regular family schedule is followed for sleeping, eating, working, etc., and (7) participation is encouraged in conversations, especially with adults. I agree. These points are well worth remembering. I don't agree, though that a formal program emphasizing such things as letter shapes and sounds is necessary before the young mind can pick them up quickly and naturally.

Specific curriculum suggestions are offered for 36 weeks. They emphasize such things as a number, letter and color; science and health principles; stories to read; a Bible story, character qualities; trips to take; and snack ideas. I would find these suggestions very helpful even though I would hold back on the abstract things for younger children. Also, I wouldn't stop with a 36-week school year. The principles are good for summer, too, or could be spread with weeks off. And I would stress physical activity and exploring, especially during the summer. Contact M. Jean Soyke, 2826 Roselawn Ave., Baltimore, MD 21214. $22.95 postpaid.

Early Years at Home By Ted Wade and seven contributors. What and how to teach your preschooler. How to guide heart, mind, and body during the tender years. Practical suggestions for laying foundations in reading, math, science, art, and other areas; plus a discussion of the early academics issue. Most of the material is also in this book, *The Home School Manual.* $4.95. Add $1.50 for US airmail. Address on back of title page. If you mention this listing, we will send you a copy for $3.50 postage paid anywhere.

Gryphon House, Inc. Int Web site http://www.ghbooks.com, "Early Childhood Headquarters on the Inernet. Welcome to hundreds of free learning activities!" Looks interesting.

Kindergarten programs I expect all the school service providers listed in Appendix A have kindergarten programs. Calvert School has two, neither of which I have seen. One was written by the former headmaster and is not academic (which sounds good to me). A new one to be released in the fall of 1998 is somewhat academic providing a bridge for kids not yet read for first grade.

Learning fun for preschoolers Int For more than 40 years, Jodi VanBibber has been helping young children learn. She has a lot to offer on her web site. You can (a) read several key articles, (b) read her excellent thoughts on how to tell children Bible stories, (c) share your ideas and ask questions, (d) follow directions to make hands-on learning games to play with your kids, and (e) even take an on-line workshop which Jodi presents. Of course, you can also buy teaching materials she has prepared and published through Sunny Hollow Press.

The full catalog is on the site. If you would like a brochure, write to Sunny Hallow Press, P.O. Box 518, Paulden, AZ 86334; (520) 636-0046; http://www.yavapai .com/sunny; sunnyhollow@lankaster.com

Never Too Early Never too early for what? The title is apparently a counter for Raymond Moore's book, *Better Late Than Early.* My answer to my question, in previous reviews, was "For nurturing academic development." Her own answer on the book's new cover is "Never too early to 'pass on the faith'. . . . And it all begins with our walk with the Lord, then with our husbands,' and finally through educating our children in God's truths – spiritually, morally, and academically." Her philosophy about early education and mine are very slightly different. She would teach spiritually and morally first, then academically when the child is able, not pushing. I would do the same, but just hold back a little in order to leave more effort on the physical and spiritual. Mrs. Claggett's book sets forth a serious Christian philosophy of education, it defends early phonetic reading instruction along with teaching other subjects, and it explains just how the Rocky Bayou Christian School Kindergarten program integrates the teaching of academics with biblical character development. Christian parents (and others, too) with preschoolers and kindergarteners could profit from reading this book. 191 pp. Christ Centered Publications, P.O. Box 968, Tullahoma, TN 37388-0568 (800) 778-4318.

Part 2, Early Education, Leaning Materials

More materials are in the various subject appendices

Christ Centered Curriculum for Early Childhood. A curriculum package for teaching early academics along with character development for ages 3 to 7. Illustrations and activities are based on Scripture with application of principles. The program is piloted at the Rocky Bayou Christian School. The materials cost for one year is around $200. Succeeding years are much less. From my review of the book, *Never Too Early*, above, you can see my concerns about preschool academics, but these materials could be used as well for older children.

Booklet Building Book, The Barbara Edtl Shelton shows you how to direct learning activities on any appropriate subject. Children make books on specific topics from template pages you photocopy from her book or ones you make up yourself. For example, the page to copy for "Days of Creation Book" has printed near the top, "On Day ___ of creation, God created" after which there's a long line to be filled in. A square frame is provided for drawing a picture of the "day." She suggests making eight copies of the sheet to include the earth "without form and void"before Day 1. Also you will find "Pressed Flower Book," "Wise Sayings Book," "Around My Town Book," and 22 more. For preschoolers, many of these themes would need to be adapted or just saved for a year or so.

I don't too often get excited about products I review, but this idea is a winner in my opinion. Young hands need to be active but they are often given only busywork. This idea combines activity with creativity for meaningful directed learning. $8.50 plus $2.50 shipping to Barbara Edtl Shelton, 182 No. Columbia Hts. Rd., Longview, WA 98632.

Lessons from the Farmyard Stories for children ages 4 to 6 based on adventures of farm animals and children. Teacher's guide included for bringing out biblical principles. (Not reviewed) 1992, $3.50 from Christian Liberty Press (Address in Appendix Y).

Math instruction All in Appendix Q.

My Bible Friends Etta B. Degering, Review and Herald, 55 W. Oak Ridge Dr., Hagerstown, MD 21740. 1964. The nicest Bible story books for young children I have seen; for preschool and primary grades.

One, Two, and Three: What Does Each One See? As children grow out of the toddler age, they learn that other people see things differently. The concept is important in developing abstract thinking and in relating to other people. In the story, mother, daughter, and dog visit the park. Pictures show what each of them sees in the course of the simple narrative. For example here are words and <illustrations> for a few pages: "At the playground," <general scene worth a minute or two study by young eyes>. "Lindsey hung upside-down," <the upside-down view as she sees the dog, Chaos, looking at her>. "Chaos worried that Lindsey might fall," <Lindsey's face upside-down with the dog's nose at the bottom>. "but Mama held Lindsey tight." <view of back of Lindsey's jeans with Mama's hands holding her.>

I don't ordinarily review books in this category, but this one got me excited and I had to share it with you. Be sure to look for it in your library or get your own copy. Author, Addie Lacoe. 10" x 8", 32 pp., 1995. (800) 462-4703. The Millbrook Press, 2 Old New Milford Rd., Brookfield, CT 06804-0335.

Beginning reading materials There are many materials for this area. They would properly come in this section but are in Appendix O.

Preschool Activity Books Collection of seven, including activities such as identifying shapes and numbers, listening to stories, and thinking. $17.65 postpaid. May be ordered separately. Write for more information. Rod and Staff Publishers, Inc., Crockett, KY 41413-0003.

Stories Jesus Told This is an absolutely favorite book of my two grandsons who are old enough for it (Stephen is 2 and Adrien is 3 as of 3/97). The copy in front of me got left here by serious mistake. It's a set of seven stories drawn from the parables. The first is "The Lost Sheep." It begins, "Here is a farmer. He has a hundred sheep. He is counting them." A calculator displays a sad sheep and the number 99. On the facing page we see the farmer counting the sheep crowded around him. The stories teach the basic lessons for children from 2 to 8 (and grandpas). The illustrations are excellent. The last story, "The Rich Farmer," is about the man who built bigger barns. It concludes, "Jesus says, 'How silly it is for a man to spend his whole life storing up riches for himself. To God, he is really a poor man.'"

My only complaint is about the title. These are not "stories Jesus told." They are stories following the parables with simplified themes. This doesn't stop me from recommending the book, however. Finer points of theology can be learned later. The copy I'm reviewing is imperfectly bound – probably a slip of quality control in Hong Kong. 213 pp. From Questar Publishers, Inc., P.O. Box 1720, Sisters, OR 97759.

Part 3, General Elementary Methods

Elementary Materials are found in the various subject appendices.

How to Study Although more of a high school book, it is helpful for upper elementary students, too, especially if they are transferring to a classroom school. See the title under High School Methods in this appendix.

Three R's, The by Ruth Beechick. Three booklets that tell you simply what to teach to build a foundation for the first three grades. See my review of Dr. Beechick's book which deals with the middle and upper grades, *You Can Teach Your Child Successfully*. It is also in this appendix. The package of three books with a chart is sold postpaid for $14 (money well spent).

Three R's At Home, The From the description in the Sycamore Tree catalog: "This book is about how the Richman children and other homeschooled children have learned reading, writing and arithmetic at home. Chapter titles include 'Reading to Children,' 'First Steps Toward Reading,' 'Learning Phonics,' . . . 'Tests and Records.'. . ." $7.95.

What Your Child Needs to Know When From the title, you might expect this book to be a check list of learning objectives for each grade. Indeed, it offers such a list, like the "Typical Course of Study" appendix in this book, but in more detail and for fewer grades (K–8). Also, in the first part of the book, author Robin Scarlata discusses philosophies of education and explains her views. In Section II she discusses standard achievement tests. Character is an important part of learning. I like her list of character traits with Bible verses. Then comes the detailed list of secular learning objectives which I expected. I would use the check boxes she provides for only one child if at all because it's too easy for children to compare with each other. Expanded edition, 1996, from http://www.heartofwisdom.com (800) BOOKLOG or e-mail Lifeinam@AOL.com

You Can Teach Your Child Successfully by Ruth Beechick. This may be the most practical book you will find on the job of teaching. Ruth tells you just how to get the learning across for kids in grades 4 to 8. For earlier grades, she has a set of smaller books that accomplish the same job. Here, taken almost at random, is a taste: "I cannot stress strongly enough that progress toward more mature writing happens within the child's total thinking abilities. It does not happen in any easy manner by simply learning techniques, forms, or tricks of writing. It is all right at times to learn techniques, but they, alone do not do the job." She then gives an example using a subordinating conjunction and goes on to explain: "If you want to raise your primary child's writing to this level, you can't do it simply by saying, 'Now write some sentences that begin with *although*.' That's only the technique. What the child really needs is the kind of thinking that can relate two ideas in this way." She goes on to describe life experiences that help the child develop the necessary thinking ability.#The book's first chapter is titled, "What Do You Do After Your Child Can Read?" The answers continue on through three more chapters. Part II is on writing. Then comes arithmetic and chapters on other subjects including Bible.#Get it from a home schooling supplier, a bookstore, or directly from Education Services, 8825 Blue Mountain Dr., Golden, CO 80403; (800) 421-6645; fax (303) 642-1288. Postpaid prices are $16 paper, or $21 hardcover. Add tax if in Colorado.

Part 4, High School Methods and Study Skills

College Admissions Subtitle: A Guide for Homeschoolers, Judy Gelner. A book worth reading. For parents and secondary-level students anticipating college admission. It discusses admissions tests, applications and financial aid. And you learn how one unschooling family passed the hurdles.

(We do not have current information). Poppyseed Press, P.O. Box 85, Sedalia, CO 80135.

From Homeschool to College and Work *Turning Your Homeschooled Experiences into College and Job Portfolios.* Alison McKee helped her son enter college based on a portfolio instead of a typical high school diploma or GED. He read extensively, studied algebra, foreign languages, and music, then entered college. His specialty learning was in the area of tying trout fishing flies. I believe his four years could have been better spent in a little more structured program, but that's debatable. Also, not every child can succeed this way. Mrs. McKee tells you how to document the learning and how to prepare a portfolio. 61 pp., 1997, $12.50 postpaid (plus 50¢ tax in Wisc.). 1997 from Bittersweet House, P.O. Box 5211, Madison, WI 53705-5211. (608) 238-3302.

High School Handbook, The *Junior and Senior High School at Home.* Practical information on how to know what to teach, set graduation requirements, assemble your courses, plan your school year, and be ready for post-secondary education. Mary Schofield's own approach sets the Bible as the basis of her school philosophy. Various knowledge and skills goals are seen in its light. She discusses standard expectations in the US and even gives sample course descriptions. Her planning allows flexibility rather than watching the clock yet emphasizes serious and specific scholastic expectations. I would use this book. 1997 edition, $19.97 (Maybe it will go up a penny each year; no, just kidding.) From Christian Home Educators Press (CHEP), 12440 E. Firestone, Blvd, Suite 1008, Norwalk, CA 90650, (562) 864-2432

Home School, High School, and Beyond, *3rd Edition* A clear explanation of how to plan a program to achieve learning typically required by American high schools. Because ultimate career goals are considered in this sort of planning, the book is designed to be studied like a textbook to satisfy credit. It is divided into nine sections including "Establishing Goals and Setting Priorities," "Planning Individual Courses," "Keeping Records of Your Accomplishments," and "Paying for College." Four appendices include topics in typical courses, testing information, resource addresses and a multitude of forms.

The tone of the book assumes Christian commitment and its focus promotes self-directed learning. By Beverly L. Adams-Gordon, 1996, 160 pages. $17.75, plus $3 shipping, from Castlemoyle Books, 6701 180th St SW, Lynnwood WA 98037; (888) 773-5586, (425) 787-2714, Fax ... 0631 E-mail, beverly@castlemoyle .com; http://www.castlemoyle.com

How to Study The main book in Ron Fry's How to Study Program. Major ideas from some of the other books such as *Take Notes* below are included. Fry writes well and convincingly. After an introduction relating the book to various people including parents, he gives advice about choosing the best learning environment, organizing, reading comprehension, quality work, the library, writing good papers, and taking tests. Home taught kids don't always have an opportunity to practice these skills. They need this book or a good competitor (which Fry thinks doesn't exist). I object to his use of words like "heck" which are modified profanity. They occur infrequently. I didn't see any in some of the other Fry books I browsed through. $9.99 plus shipping. Career Press, P.O. Box 687, Franklin Lakes, NJ 07417; (800) 227-3371. Or in Canada, (201) 848-0310.

Improve Your Memory Deals with remembering important things from your studies. Various types of information are discussed. $6.99, 1996. In the same set of books as *How to Study* above.

Independent Study Catalog See Appendix Y.

Record Keeping for High School By the author of *Listen My Son* unit study materials. See Appendix Y. This is a notebook with instructions for how to plan the high school program and especially for keeping careful records. It looks like it would work well for any high school program although, as with most planning helps, you could do some of this by yourself and collect from various sources. $19.95 plus $3 shipping.

Take Notes Part of the How to Study series by Ron Fry. This topic is very important for home schooled kids who have had little or no experience learning from lectures, much less in taking notes. I have made some suggestions on the topic in the book you are reading, but Fry tells you much more of what you need after home school. Even if you don't plan formal education after home schooling, you need listening and note-taking skills to learn from what people tell you. Fry deals with taking notes from books as well as from lectures. By learning to sort and digest the information from books you will be better prepared for lectures. Comments about ADD kids is included. This book or one like it should be read by students in the 6th grade or higher. 1994. $6.95 + shipping from Career Press. Contact information under *How to Study*.

Senior High: A Home Designed Form+U+la The front-cover description sums up what you may expect from this manual: "For those seeking a God-centered real-life-enriched, not-so traditional (but some!) Senior High Homeschool Education!" The book promises to help you "structure *all* your students learning experiences into 'classes'" and translate them into credits. You can also learn how to plan and document your program for keeping track of what you are doing, and, perhaps, to convince the rest of the world. Courses in math and science, for example, may be required for certain majors, and lab courses at home without a parent trained in the area and with minimal equipment would seem questionable. However, the college may offer tests to assess the knowledge or it may provide basic-level classes to teach it. In your favor would be the careful record keeping that author Barbara Edtl Shelton suggests. Discuss your plan with admissions officers of colleges your youth might want to attend.

Specific learning activities are outlined in the book (as they are in good textbooks). Of course your youth may learn from other sources, too, including textbooks and teachers, any of which you choose to include in your framework. Barb Shelton's book offers good courage, counsel, and ideas. Although my view of textbooks is less negative than hers, you will enjoy her book and your child will be better for it.

1996 edition, some 350 pages, $24.95 + $5 postage (+ tax if to Wash.). Order from: Barbara Edtl Shelton, 182 N. Columbia Hts. Rd., Longview, WA 98632.

Senior High Homeschooling Options & Resources A six-hour video seminar by Barbara Edtl Shelton including interviews and special clips. You borrow the video tapes and keep a large information packet, a syllabus, and four audio tapes. Although I have not reviewed the actual products, the cost seems reasonable. It depends on the number of people that take part. Write to Mrs. Shelton. Address above.

Part 5, High School Learning Materials

More suitable materials are described in the various subject appendices

Applications of Grammar A series for grades 7 to 12. I have reviewed the 8th grade book, *Structure for Communicating Effectively*. Vocabulary, some spelling, sentence diagramming, and even some writing skills are included in this thorough textbook/workbook series. I would ask my child to go through it all but perhaps skip exercises on areas already understood or ones which seemed unnecessary. Good explanations with the convenience offered by the workbook format. This particular book is priced at a reasonable $7.95. Answers and tests are also available. 1996 revision from Christian Liberty Press. See Appendix Y.

Christian Charm Course A guide to personal development into adult womanhood. Harvest House Publishers, 1075 Arrowsmith, Eugene, OR 97402. (800) 547-8979 or (503) 343-0123.

Christian Home Educators Curriculum Manual Volume 2 is for junior and senior high school. See Appendix X.

High School Grammar CD Basically a set of multiple-choice questions organized according to the traditional categories. The video clips are practically useless – only a rehearsal of topics to be covered! Learning grammar requires using it in writing and speaking so you need more than this CD-ROM. Pro One Software, P.O. Box 16317, Las Cruces, NM 88004. (505) 523-6200, 9-5 ET.

Nature of Music, The See Appendix T.

***Sense of History**, A* This 848-page, hard cover, selection of articles from American Heritage magazine is an excellent resource for exploring and digging into specific episodes and concepts of American history. An introductory chapter, "I wish I'd Been There," sets the stage with brief glimpses at various points in time. At the end is a summary chapter, "How Have We Changed? 1954-1994. Between are 54 chosen articles. They are pitched to mature readers but can provide good information to include younger students in a family unit study. For example, "Prairie Schooner," deals with the westward movement using the covered wagon as a connecting thread to for discussing motives, hardships, animals that pulled the wagons, wagon maintenance, the overfictionalized risk from Indians, and more. Other articles are on topics like Columbus' sighting of land, the arrogant Woolworth who invented the "five-and-dime" chain of stores, homesteading, villains of the frontier, the financial collapse of the 20s, cities, issues with the world wars, and revisionist history, a topic that provides a lesson to help us judge what we hear as the political and religious winds blow today.

I'm not generally in favor of tossing out the systematic and efficient study that, at least to some degree, leans on textbooks; but for upper grades and beyond, this book, plus a time line, some pictures, and a few other resources, would be an exception. It has been reprinted by Smithmark at $14.98 – half the original price. Ask your bookstore.

***Term Paper* CD** A simple word processor which automatically sets up sections for the paper in outline form, handling footnotes and including a spell checker. It might be helpful to some, but I found it frustrating. I prefer direct control. The tab key isn't so hard to use. Major word processors have similar features, leaving you with more control, if you want to use them. This may come bundled with other high school CDs from Pro One Software.

Us and Them A book about understanding group hatred and how to relate to it. See Appendix R, Part, 3.

Part 6, Students With Learning Problems

Descriptions followed by the initials, RB, are reviewed by Ruth Beechick. Also see Appendix C, Part 4 for organizations involving special children.

Attention Deficit Disorder, Hyperactivity Revisited H. Moghadam. Many otherwise intelligent children learn poorly because they are unable to focus their attention on the learning task. Erratic and inappropriate behavior leads also to poor social relationships. This book will help you understand and identify the condition. There is no known cure, but the situation may be improved. 2nd editioin, 1994. $12.95. Order from Temeron Books, Inc., Suite 210, 1220 Kensington Rd., NW, Calgary, Alberta T2N 3P5; (403) 283-0900, Fax (403) 283-6947.

Choosing and Using Curriculum For Your Special Child Sound advice from Joyce Herzog, author of *Learning Without Labels*. For each general area of the curriculum she suggests how to approach the subject, then lists programs generally available and judges them for use with special needs children. 1996. Greenleaf Press, 1570 Old LaGuardo Rd., Lebanon TN 37087; (615) 449-1617; E-mail greenleafp@aol.com. Also available from the author at Simplified Learning Products, P.O. Box 45387, Rio Rancho, NM 87174-5387; (800) 745-8212.

Dyslexia: A Reading & Writing Correction Method Author Dr. George Manilla, a pathologist, tried to teach his children the method he had long used for speed reading, but they thought it was dumb. Through that experience he realized that the children were "normal" and that he was dyslexic. Since then he has taught many dyslexics (in just a couple of office visits) how to make the words clear by focusing a bit above the page of print instead of directly on it [or looking at the object as if it were farther away – looking through it. Beginning with two pennies placed an inch or more apart, the individual learns to stereoscopically fuse them so that a third penny is seen between them. The penny exercise is described in clear detail, and this one technique, for one particular dyslexic problem, is the core of the book, although additional information and success stories are added to round out a slim book of 91 pages. High Desert Publishing, Box 1417, Elko, NV 89801. *RB*

Fresh Start Movement development exercises for dyslexic children by Kenneth A. Lane. This manual would not be at the top of my list but may be just what you need. Learning Potentials Publishers, Inc., 230 W. Main St., Lewisville, TX 75057; (800) 437-7976.

Game Way to Teaching Phonics and Reading This program emphasizes how the various letter sounds are formed, a step other phonics program often take for granted. You may find it helpful. See Appendix O.

Help for the Hyperactive Child by William G. Crook. This book is for more problems than hyperactivity. Also addressed are attention deficit disorders, fatigue, depression, respiratory allergies, digestive disorders, bed wetting, and prolonged use of antibiotics. Dr. Crook points out that we did not have many of these problems in the 1950s but began to see them in epidemic proportions in the late 60s and early 70s. This timing coincides with increased use of food additives and highly processed foods. Chemical contaminants may also be a cause.

Seventy-five percent of children with these problems can be helped by diet, and the book is packed with nutritional information and directions for an "elimination diet" to help families do their own detective work in locating the culprit or culprits causing their problems. The format is easy to read and easy to use. In addition to special diets, Dr. Crook believes these children need discipline and consistent management of rules and limits. $14.95. Professional Books, Inc.. *RB* (Current address unknown.)

Helping Children Overcome Learning Difficulties A step-by-step guide for parents and teachers, by Jerome Rosner, Walker Publishing Co., NY. $18.95, Available through Bob Jones University Press.

Learning in Spite of Labels Joyce Herzog has been helping mentally challenged kids learn for 25 years. In this book she shares practical ideas and information for success. Her perspective is Christian, but even people without that emphasis will relate very well to her advice.

"This book," she writes, "is to help you meet the needs of children who struggle with learning no matter what label someone is trying to put on them. It may appear on the surface that they are failing to learn. In reality, they are learning to fail! . . .

"I believe we have created the problems faced by many children who develop learning problems by forcing them into structured, fine-motor, and close-up vision tasks which involve symbols and abstract concepts, before they are developmentally ready. This is further complicated by the tension and pressure to succeed and the frustration and failure experienced by the many children who truly try to do what they are not yet capable of doing. . . .

"Others get praise and approval from the adults in their lives. And they don't understand. They know only that they want desperately to be like their more successful friends, but don't know how." (pp. vii, ix) "Let's just concentrate on our ables, instead of our labels.!" (p. viii).

The book offers a realistic and hopeful perspective. It helps you decide what is important – what education should really mean. It also outlines an approach to teaching and gives lots of practical tips and other information you need to know. *Learning in Spite of Labels* is a virtual gold mine for anyone with the challenge of helping a child who has difficulty learning. 1994, 205 pp., $9.95 plus $3.50 shipping (and tax if Tenn.) Greenleaf Press, 1570 Old LaGuardo Rd., Lebanon, TN 37087. (615) 449-1617.

Learning Disabilities Resource Packet $8.49 plus $1.50 shipping plus tax if CA. From CHEA of California, P.O. Box 2009, Norwalk, CA 90651-2009.

New Start for the Child With Reading Problems, A By Carl Delacato. The book fulfills the promise of its subtitle, *A Manual for Parents.* The first half tells clearly how to evaluate a child according to Dr. Delacato's theory. Can the child crawl in a cross pattern? Can he do cross pattern walking, pointing to each front toe with the opposite hand? What about his eyes? Do they follow an object smoothly when he holds it at arm's length and moves it in a full circle, up and down, sideways, and in other patterns? Or do the eyes exhibit a jerky start-and-stop motion? The second half of the book explains how to provide therapy, which consists of the same exercises used for diagnosing. This lets out the secret that you don't need a specialist to diagnose first and tell you what therapy to use. Diagnose and treat with the same exercises. Some school districts now are using this system, and parents may obtain the book by sending $10.95 to The Chestnut Hill Reading Clinic, Plymouth Plaza, Suite 107, Plymouth Meeting, PA 19462. *RB*

Scardy Cat Reading System See Appendix O

World Geography and You Description from Sycamore Tree: This series is written especially for older students who ahave reading difficulties but any student could use it. The reading level is grade 3 to 4. You will find a comprehensive surfey of the world's major regions. Book 1 surveys the physical, cultural, and econnomic characteristics of the Western world. The units are. . . . Book 2 surfeys the physical and cultural, and economis characteristics of the Eastern world. . . . $14.25. Teacher's guide for both books together, $9.95.

Part 7, Gifted Children

Guiding Your Gifted Child Subtitle: Resources, Options and Opportunities for Bright Kids. Janice Baker and Maggie Hogan tell you much more than how to teach. A few of the fourteen chapters are: "How Do I Know if My Child's Gifted? Parenting the Academically Gifted Learner, Acceleration and Skipping, Schooling the Whole Child ..., Apprenticeship ...," and "Preparing for High School and College." The book is balanced and briefly covers what appears to me as all the important considerations from a Christian perspective. Non-Christians will be comfortable with the book as well. The book deserves a more professional appearance and binding, but then it might look too serious for some. 1998, $15 plus $4 shipping, from Bright Ideas! Educational Resources, 116 Baltusrol Rd., Dover, DE 19904; (302) 678-3895; Hogan@inet.net.

Westbridge Academy Described as a "Unique...Inovative...Challenging...Umbrella School specially designed for the college bound, academically accelerated, gifted, talented, serious, or motivated home educated student." The school works with parents who may choose to use traditional methods, unit studies, or self-directed learning. The school provides counseling, test results reviews, and curriculum recommendations for parents and an 800 number for students. Youth are classified by three general levels of advancement in learning. The Westbridge Academy, 1610 West Highland Ave. #228, Chicago, IL 60660; (773) 743-3312. WestbrgA@aol.com

K
Periodicals About or For Home Schooling

In addition to the periodicals described here, many others are published for local areas. Periodicals especially for countries outside of the United States are described in Appendices E and F. Others not directly about home schooling are in Appendix L.

Adventist Home Educator For Seventh-day Adventists. P.O. Box 836, Camino, CA 95709. Judy Shewmake, Ed., (530) 647-2110. tjshewmake@juno.com. $10/yr, 12 issues; Sample copy, postage for 2 ounces; Canada & Mexico, US$12; Foreign, US$25. A yearly handbook is also available at $12.95 postpaid.

At Home in America From Homeschool Associates, 116 Third Ave., Auburn, ME 04210; (207) 777-1700; homeschool@homeschoolassociated.com; 3 issues/yr. Free. Homeschool Associates serves the Eastern US and the edge of the Midwest.

Christian Home Business Journal P.O. Box 402, Belgrade, MT 59714; (406) 388-4429. $16/yr. (11 issues). Not reviewed.

Christian Home Education News, P.O. Box 388, Brook, IN 47922-0388; (219) 275-6553; parsonage@juno.com. Editor Deborah Marsh. $10 for the next 12 issues (not published on a regular basis right now). The issue I'm looking at has five articles plus classified and space ads and regular features.

An electronic version is produced by HIS Publishing **Int.**, hispub@aol.com and is available through their web site, www.upnadam.com/Chen (why didn't I think of that one?). It took me more than 15 min. to download. The articles are easily readable. The space ads are not, but you can get the idea. Larger print in them can be read. These problems may be taken care of by the time you read this book.

Coming Home P.O. Box 1282, Bowling Green, KY 42102. 60 pp., bi-monthly magazine emphasizing practical Christianity and skills for simple living, homeschooling, etc. $20/yr.

EasyHomeschooling Tips & Topics P.O. Box 95, Dept. HSM, Rockville, NE 68871, EZschool@aol.com, (308) 372-3408. Quarterly for $12/yr; $20/2 yrs. 8 pp. Sample $2. EasyHomeschooling focuses on low cost, time saving, and high quality techniques. They also sell antique books of educational interest. Editor, Lorraine Curry

Family Learning Exchange This is now **Int** Internet only (and free, so far). I'll copy the description from editor, Kathleen McCurdy.

FLExOnline - The Electronic Journal of Family Learning Family Learning Exchange (FLEx) is now FLExOnline, published electronically and available to anyone with access to e-mail or the Internet. Each monthly issue is full of letters, news, resources, book and resource reviews, and networking information, as well as suggested Internet sites for families. FLExOnline advocates education for individual needs. Articles promote strong familles and positive character traits. The diversity within the homeschool community is reflected. Based on Judeo-Christian values. For more information or to subscribe, visit the FLExOnline website at: http://www.flexonline.org or write to us at: editor@flexonline.org Published byFamily Learning Exchange, PO Box 5629, Lacey, WA 98509-5629; (360) 491-5193.

Growing Without Schooling This was the first serious newsletter of the home schooling movement. John Holt was its first editor and publisher. It contained mostly letters from readers, book reviews, and Holt's comments. It appeared whenever an issue was ready. Now it's a regular and professional journal, and it has a special topic for each issue, still including letters and comments. Since John Holt's death, the work has been carried on by the faithful team he left it to. (See "Holt Associates" in Appendix C.) In Appendix J, I review the book compiled from Holt's writings, *Learning All the Time*, and discuss my understanding of his philosophy (Appendix J). Subscription price is $25/yr. (6 issues) Sample issue, $4.50. GWS, 2269 Massachusetts Ave., Cambridge, MA 02140.

Home Educator's Family Times Jane Boswell, Editor. Published 5 times a year. Large readership. Free, but a $15 donation is suggested. Annual conferences sponsored in Massachusetts and Michigan. P.O. Box 708, Gray, ME 04039; (207) 657-2800; Fax ... 2402; familytimes@outrig.com. http://www.chfweb.com/familytimes/ Also see Homeschool Support Network listed in Appendix D under Colorado, Maine, and Michigan.

Home Education Magazine A very good home schooling periodical with an often "natural" approach. $24 for six, 68-page, bimonthly issues, or $20 for those committed to home schooling. (US$33.75 for Canada). Sample issue, free. Phone (voice or fax): (509) 486-1351 or (800) 236-3278. HEM, P.O. Box 1083, Tonasket, WA 98855. HomeEdMag@aol.com; www.home-ed-press.com.

Ask for their free 24-page booklet, *HEM Homeschoolers Information and Resource Guide*. It includes information about home schooling, sources of information and support groups.

HEM Online News A free publication sent by

e-mail. A service of *Home Education Magazine* (also in this appendix). Ask editor Sandra Dodd at HEMnewsltr@aol.com to put you on her list. If you are on America Online, you might want to enter the keyword, HEM and join their active news group.

Home School Digest If you like the ideas of learning with simple living as well as serious, joyful Christianity, you will find plenty of good reading in each issue of *Home School Digest.* 96 pp. with ads all in the back, which I like. $18/yr. (4 issues). Sample $5, $36 foreign. By the way, the journal is still expanding its already-large subscriber list. Everyone who signs up may request a free gift subscription for a friend. HSD, Wisdom's Gate P.O. Box 374, Covert, MI 49043.

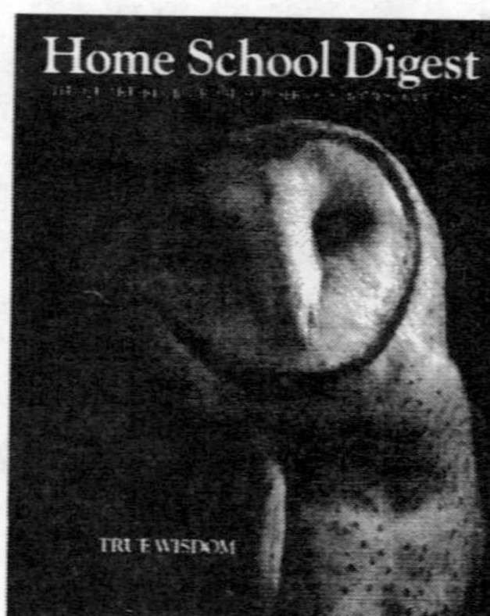

Home School Researcher Brian D. Ray, Ph.D., Editor. Scholarly journal of research related to home education since 1985. $25/yr. for individuals, $40/yr. for institutions. Other publications also available. P.O. Box 13939, Salem, OR 973309; (503) 364-1490, fax ... -2827; mail@nheri.org.

Homeschooling Today Subtitled "Practical Help for Christian Families." With an emphasis on teaching ideas. Regular features include the areas of confidence to teach, unit study, preschool, the arts, science, teens, and product reviews. Phone (954) 962-1930. $17.95/yr. (6 issues). Add $8 for outside the US. E-mail: HSTodayMag@aol.com; www.homeschooltoday.com. Homeschooling Today, P.O. Box 1425, Melrose, FL 32666.

Homeschool Seller P.O. Box 19-gp, Cherry Valley, MA 01611-3148; (508) 791-8332; HSSeller@aol.com $12 for 10 issues. Free sample issue.

Moore Report International Raymond and Dorothy Moore share their ideas and highlight activities of home schooling families. Also worthwhile articles by other home schooling writers. US $12 for one year; Canada US$20; foreign, US$25. If you ask, they will send a sample copy when the next issue comes out. From The Moore Foundation. *Moore Report International,* Box 1, Camas, WA 98607. E-mail: moorefnd@pacifier.com; www.caflink.com/morefoundation

MOORE REPORT INTERNATIONAL

Ideal Home Base for the Moore Foundation

The Miracle Part

Patriarch P.O. Box 725, Rolla, MO 65402; mail@patriarch.com A magazine for men, for developing godly leaders. $25/yr. donation suggested, (bi-monthly). Not reviewed.

Practical Homeschooling Published by Mary Pride. I'll describe the Jan./Feb., 1998 issue to give you an idea of what the magazine is like. 72 pp. The departments include contests, selected art work on envelopes, letters, classifieds, and "Day at Our House." This last section tells about three families including an expatriate family in Turkey whose picture is on the cover. Under "columns" we find the Charlotte Mason method, classical education, math, myths about Columbus, unit studies and a youth column. You will also find a number of product reviews. Feature articles are on the health care system", scheming to possible loss of availability of vitamins and herbs, safeguarding children's health, unschooling community service, and the principle approach. $19.95 (1 yr./6 issues). Check to Home Life P.O. Box 1250 Fenton, MO 63026-1850; (800) 346-6322; PHSCustSvc@aol.com; http://www.home-school.com

Relaxed Home Schooler Newsletter from Mary Hood, author of *The Relaxed Home School.* Christian perspective. The periodical is brief (several large pages). $6/yr. (4 issues). Sample issue free. Mary Hood, P.O. Box 2524, Cartersville, GA 30120.

Salt Seller P.O. Box 56701, Phoenix AZ 85079-6701; (602) 249-2699. A network for people buying and selling. Send 6 first class stamps for a year to a US address. Not reviewed.

Teachers of Good Things A newsletter based on high standards for Christian women, set in Titus 2:3-5. Melissa Adkinson, P.O. Box 499, Willamina, OR 97396; (503) 876-7002. Not reviewed.

The Teaching Home A quality magazine with a Christian perspective. Special editions include state newsletters. Each issue features teaching tips, news, book reviews, In each issue you will find teaching tips, news, and a block of practical articles on a specific topic. $15/yr. (6 issues); US$20 for Canada; $30 foreign by air. Overseas missionaries, subtract $10. Back issues on certain topics are available. Box 20219, Portland OR 97294; (503) 253-9633; fax ... -7345; tth@teaching home.com For subscriptions, call (800) 395-7760. P.O. Box 469069, Escondido CA 92046-9069.

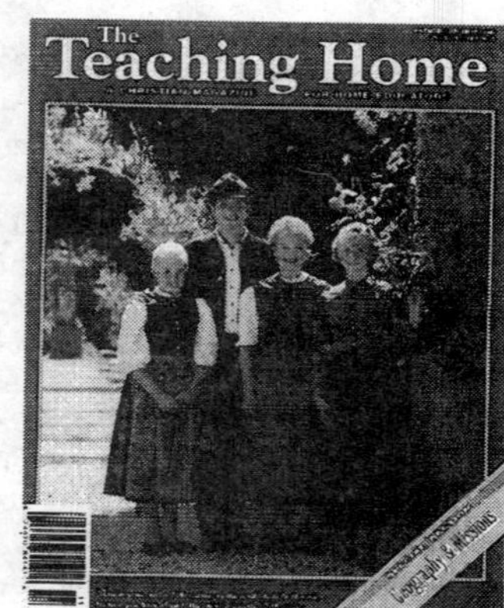

L
General Periodicals

This resource section does not list magazines relating to specific subject areas. They are listed in the corresponding appendices. Neither does it include those directly for home schooling. They are shown in the preceding appendix.

Boy's Quest 48 pages packed with interest for boys aged 6 to 13. The variety of activities, stories, and information is also commendable. The June/July '97 issue features music with a lead article on playing the harmonica. Another tells the origin of the words to *Yankee Doodle*. A cartoon story tells about Frederick the Great. The other 30 or so items are about knots, boomerangs, water drops, juggling bowling balls, poems, jokes and riddles. The cover shows a night scene under city streetlights. Four cats in dark glasses play in a jazz band. The drum is a trash can turned upside down with trash spilled out. This is not the kind of motivation I would place in my child's hands. A poem describes a boy's reluctantly going to a music lesson taught by a stupid Professor Blatt who is distracted from teaching. At the end, the boy tells his mother a half truth so she will believe he had a good lesson.

The magazine's objective, in part, is to promote early reading by emphasizing wholesome interests. I also received the December/January '98 issue and examined it carefully. It fulfills the "wholesome" objective, as did much of the other issue. I have no significant complaints about it. $15 for 1 yr. of 6 issues. Boy's Quest, P.O. Box 227, Bluffton, OH 45817-0227.

Discovery "Scripture & Science For Kids." This full-color, eight-page magazine would be most suitable for grades K-6. Older and younger ones would appreciate it, too. The March, 1998 issue is on the topic of food in the Bible. It includes articles on how olive oil was made and what it was used for, fishing on Galilee, and Jesus as the bread of life. A recipe is given for unleavened bread (looks good). There are word search and crossword puzzles and other items of interest. Questions test learning from the articles.

The magazine is interesting and avoids the trite, comic approach often used to attract kids. Bible explanations are simple and significant.

1998 subscription rates: U.S. individual $11/yr. less 10% for home schools. Canada US$13; overseas airmail US$18. Club and bulk subscriptions are also available. Apologetics Press, Inc., 230 Landmark Dr., Montgomery, AL 36117. Or phone (800) 234-8558.

Freebies, Each 32-page issue is packed with descriptions of things you can get for free or up to $2 or so. Here are a few items from the copy I'm looking at (May, June, July, 1993): a toothbrush with self-contained toothpaste dispenser, a computer disk suggesting U.S. travel routes, a pet grooming brush, a Paddington Bear rolling stamper, a 3¼-inch violin, a sea sponge, an herb seed packet, etc. Check current prices. *Freebies Magazine*, 1135 Eugenia Pl., Carpinteria, CA 93013. Also see the book, *Freebies for Teachers*, in Appendix M.

Now you can get *Family Freebies*. Lots of things to send for. The issue I'm looking at (in May, 1994) lists a jigsaw puzzle service (your photo laminated and die-cut), shareware, comet stickers, apricot recipes, crochet instructions for slippers, a fishing guide, etc. I found a 1998 special price of $5.96 for 5 issues at http://www.shopsite.com/magazine-mecca/ (without the hyphen). Freebies does not have a web site.

God's World Publications P.O. Box 2330, Asheville, NC 28802-2330. (800) 951-KIDS (5437). Excellent weekly current events periodicals which deliver just what the firm's name implies: reports and commentary about the world we live in from the viewpoint of people who know it real owner. Since they cover many of the same topics, children from different grades can discuss them together. The *Teacher's Helper* comes with each of these editions. The papers have news, puzzles, activities, Bible insights to develop children's interests, and resources for understanding how God is at work. 26 issues September to May. The 1997-'98 price for a one-copy subscription to the PreK to 3rd grade level magazine is $17.95 for the 26 issues. For the 4th to 9th magazine, it is $19.95. If more than two go to an address (even for different grade levels) the price drops significantly. *World Magazine*, for senior high youth and adults is also available for the school year. You can call to ask for more specific information and even subscribe by phone. Satisfaction guaranteed.

The illustration is fuzzy because I scanned it from a small image. It does not represent the quality of the magazine.

Good Apple Newspaper Part of a family of publications for and about children. The *Good Apple Newspaper* is for teachers of children in grades 2 to 5. It offers activities and stories ranging from geography and endangered animals, to cooking and holiday parties. $18.95/yr. (5 issues). (800) 264-9873. http://www.frankschaffer .com/

In *Lollipops*, I found several nice activities, one on making a pinwheel to turn in the wind, another on finding O's in illustrations. Some of us might object to things like the Easter bunny. I'm sure many parents appreciate these magazines, although I would find others more suitable for my family (if my kids were still young).

Oasis is for middle grades. $21.95 for 5 issues. (800) 264-9873.

Highlights for Children Subtitle: *Fun with a Purpose*. And that's true. They emphasize learning and values. The March 1998 issue (shown) has regular 16 regular features including riddles, "For Wee Folks," thinking, nature watch, you can make it, etc. Among the 15 special features are cartoons for which kids have submitted captions (quite good), nature article about insects that farm, an article about wild ponies, how to tell stories, and poems. The only story which bothers me was published with good intentions. It's about two witches. My objection is to the tendency to make the occult appealing. 1 yr. (12 issues) 29.64. Canada 1 yr. US$42.35 includes GST. Foreign 39.64. Call (888) 876-3809 or write to: Highlights, P.O. Box 182167, Columbus, OH 43218-2167. This is one of the best magazines.

Hopscotch for Girls Similar to *Boy's Quest* reviewed in this appendix. The August/September '97 issue features sports and has several good stories. Winning stories from a contest are published, and a regular feature, "Potsy's Post Office," shows lots of activity. One girl protested about articles in a previous issue about brothers. Instead of hating her brothers as the articles described, she likes hers very much. A small poster with the magazine's name shows creatures that live in the sea. See *Boy's Quest* for information.

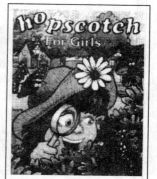

Scholastic Classroom Magazines This publisher offers a wide variety of topics for all school levels. There are 27 choices for students and 4 for teachers! They focus on news, math, art, language arts, science, Spanish, French, etc. The topics are those which interest many children with a heavy emphasis on sports. Their Baby Sitter Club has been viewed by some as pushing young kids into the romantic lifestyle pursued by some mature adults.

To give you an idea of 1998 prices a single-copy subscription the first grade *Scholastic News* comes in monthly packets of 4 weekly issues. $4 per school year for the student edition and $6.50 combined with teacher directions. *Math* for grades 7-9 costs $30 with or without the teacher part. *Junior Scholastic* $11.45 for student and $21 with teacher helps. *Update* (about current events) $12.25 or $23 with teacher helps. Credit cards accepted. P.O. Box 3710, Jefferson City, MO 65102. http://www.scholastic.com.

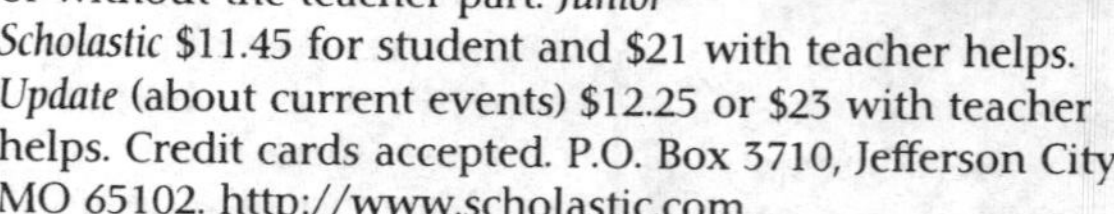

Weekly Reader This quality publication has been around for a long time. The issue illustrated is the general periodical for grade 4. This grade's periodical costs $24.95 for a single subscription, but $6.70, ea. for 2 to 9 copies. Weekly Reader Corp., 245 Long Hill Rd., Middletown, CT 06457. http:/www.weeklyreader.com; (800) 445-3355.

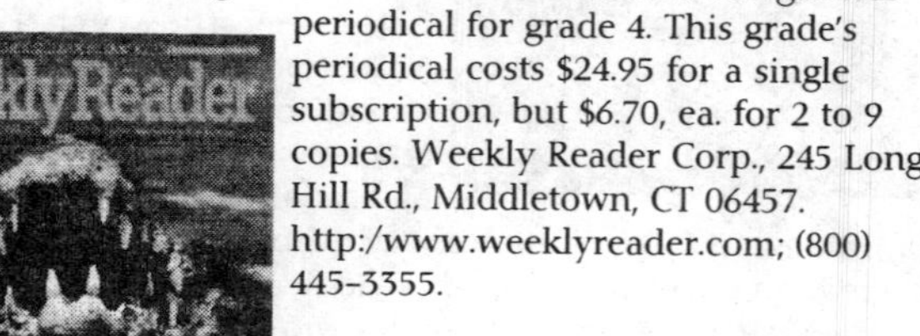

M
Teaching Aids

Part 1, Keeping Organized

Abundant Blessings Homeschool Planner. In a loose-leaf format and specifically designed for large homeschooling families. Tracks several children (not reviewed.) From Homeschool Publishing House, under the same ownership as Homeschool Seller. See them in Appendix Z.

Choreganizer, The Tasks are illustrated on 48 cards, plus blank cards for adding your own. Instructions are printed on the backs. For incentives, pretend money is awarded. Children spend it at the Chore Store – a box you stock with desirable items, some of which may be "tickets" for special places to go. $16.95 plus shipping from Steward Ship (see Appendix Y). From Noble Publishing.

CLASS Lesson Planner This book of forms is practical. I like it. 120 pp. $7.95. Christian Liberty Press. See Appendix Y for address.

Educational Support Foundation This organization provides printed personalized forms for a professional appearance. Documents include diplomas, transcripts, and stationery. Workshops may be arranged. 1523 Moritz, Houston, TX 77055; (281) 870-9194.

ELAN Publishing Co. P.O. Box 683, Meredith, NH 03253. Planning and record-keeping books for schools. For example, you may buy a weekly plan book divided into boxes for six classes per day (Their W202) for $3.25. You might also want their student plan book (for upper grades and high school) (HS-90) for $4.95. Shipping is $4.95 for up to $10.

Home School Helper Organizer for record keeping, household management, and things you wouldn't have thought of. $25. Or if you want the forms only without binder and tabs, you pay $11.85. Shipping in either case is $3.75. (Not reviewed). K.T. Productions, P.O. Box 1203, Menomonee Falls WI 53051.

Home School Lesson Planner, The Each sheet in this record book is a 10" X 12" envelope. On the front is a grid for simple lesson planning for a week. On the back is space for an attendance record and comments. A nice idea – $22.90 from Soteria (By the way, this word means "salvation" in Greek). They also publish a record book without the envelopes, $9.95; U.S.A. map masters, $19.95 and they distribute *Discover Intensive Phonics,* $90.00. Shipping is $2.50 for one item. Soteria, 1116 Independence Dr., Bartlett, IL 60103; (800) 642-3674.

My Homeschool Year A book for collecting information and photographs to remember the school year. Attractive cover and stiff pages. $8.95. For information, see under "Sycamore Tree forms" in this appendix.

Planner Plus, The Large sheets allow ample space for daily teaching plans, assignments, and results for two students in seven subject areas. Special boxes are for grades and time spent. Space for a daily plan and a weekly plan are also provided. In the back of the book are forms for a report card and a certificate of promotion.

108 pp. 8½ X 14. All for a modest $6.95 plus $2.90 shipping. Fine Line also publishes other record books and wipe-off Day.Maps™ that stick by magnets to your fridge. Fine Line Publishing, 128 N. Lincoln St., Westmont, IL 60559.

Sycamore Tree forms *Reproducible School Forms Set:* Twelve scheduling and grade report forms (Y029) $4.95. Also a *Reproducible Assignment Sheet Set* which includes planning calendar forms. 12 forms in all (Y028) $4.95. Completion certificates with gold lettering on fancy paper (Y042), $1.00 each. Add $4.95 for shipping (on up to $25 or $5.95 up to $50; more outside the US) and 7.75% tax if sent to California. The Sycamore Tree, 2179 Meyer Pl., Costa Mesa, CA 92627. Information at (714) 650-4466; www.sycamoretree .com

Training Manuals by Gregg Harris and son Josh. Statements of principles for good behavior for Christian homes. Illustrations are by Josh. Each comes with a set of sheets with the individual rules presented in the book and one laminated sheet with a list of all of them. The principles are excellent and their suggested use would make sense to children. If you feel unable to afford these sets, you and your children could make your own lists and posters. Or you could buy a set for ideas. The 21 Rules of This House. Rules are like "In this house we speak quietly and respectfully with one another." Rules for Young Friends. These rules involve circumstances for leaving the house, getting approval from parents, and so on. Uncommon Courtesy for Kids. Christian Life Workshops, P.O. Box 2250, Gresham, OR 97030. Or call (800) 225-5259.

21 Rules of This House, The Original A 57 p. book that may be colored. Suggested rules for a well disciplined home. $12.95 from Noble Publishing Associates

Part 2, Teaching Supplies

You will likely find helpful items in school supply stores which are found in most areas. Also you may want to visit an office supply store and stores selling items for art and music.

Creative Changes Charts, stickers, and related items for organizing and operating families and home schools. They will send information if you ask. 368 South 850 West, Orem, UT 84058; (801) 226-5533; Fax (801) 226-3975; info@creativechanges.com.

DIDAX Educational Resources, Inc., 395 Main St., Rowley, MA 01969; (800) 458-0024, (978) 948-2340, Fax (978) 948-2813. Teaching aids and learning resource materials for mathematics, science, readiness skills, reading, language development and social studies at preschool and elementary school levels. Reproducible resource books for phonics, math, social studies and other subjects. Originators of the Unifix Structural Mathematical Materials.

Fearon Teacher Aids, At teacher stores or http://www.frankschaffer.com/fearon.html

Freebies for Teachers By the editors of *Freebies* magazine. More than 150 offers of things that are available for a self-addressed stamped envelope or for a small handling charge. Here are a few examples: a brochure promoting careers in astronomy, a puppy coloring book, instructions for playing a harmonica, sample issue of a periodical about kindness to animals, a 15-page booklet of grammar rules, a turtles booklet, personalized award certificates, bookmark and stickers featuring dinosaurs, an Arbor Day celebration kit, a guide to U.S. museums. 79 pp. Freebies Publishings Company, 1135 Eugenia Pl., Carpinteria, CA 93013.

Also available are *Freebies for Families*, and *Freebies for Kids*, including a free puzzle, plans for a sun-powered cooker, etc.

Hayes School Publishing Co., 321 Penwood Ave., Wilkinsburg, PA 15221-3398, (800) 245-6234; info@hayespub.com; www.hayespub.com. Interesting supplementary materials including workbooks, activity books, puzzles, and black-line masters that may be photocopied to share with others.

Make Your Own A+ Electronic Flashcards A simple program on diskette for creating and presenting sets of simple questions. The person responding does not key in the answer, but when unsure he or she can ask to see it. Once he knows it, the question may be marked to omit temporarily from future appearance in the "deck," thus reducing the length of the drill. No scores are kept but sets of cards may be arranged according to individual students. New sets may be created and "cards" may be added, deleted, edited, imported and exported. Only the Mac version allows the clues/questions to be either graphic images as well as text. Both versions allow shuffling the cards for a different order. I like the program although I wish it were more affordable. A+ flash cards can be used all through school and even through college.), and more flexible allowing file management, perhaps with a word processor. Specify Mac or Windows. $24.95 plus $5.00 shipping if you are a home school parent and you refer to this book as your source of information. Otherwise, $39.95 plus shipping. Visa/MC or check. Breakthrough Productions, 15903 Shannon Way, Nevada City, CA 95959. (530) 477-8685. E-mail mktmaster@aol.com.

Trend Enterprises P.O. Box 64073, St. Paul, MN 55164-0073; (800) 328-5540. You can get along without any of the items in the Trend catalog, but you probably won't want to. Activity booklets, stickers, drawing stencils, posters and things to brighten your schoolroom. Also wipe-off maps, charts and even activity books for skill practice.

N

Religious Instruction and Ministry

In this appendix find
*(**1**) materials for teachers and parents,*
*(**2**) materials for students,*
*(**3**) religious ministries, and*
*(**4**) religious publishers*

Logos and other images are trademarks or copyrighted material from the publications they respresent.

Part 1, Material for Teachers and Parents

Biblical Discipline A seminar on audio tapes by Karl Reed. He first sets the stage by discussing responsibilities of parents and children. He counters misinformation from professional people who teach such things as that attitudes are solely a product of environment (making the parent responsible for all misbehavior of the child), or that good is within the child, or that correction would crush a child's special ability. He outlines what he calls "Instant, joyous obedience through biblical discipline." The plan includes what to teach, how to request, what to allow and not allow, and practical advice. He says it works, and I believe it. (I do not have current information on this ministry at press time.)

Christian Parenting Today Very worthwhile. $16.97 per year, 6 issues. Add US$5.40 outside the U.S. P.O. Box 36630, Colorado Springs, CO 80936-3663. For information or to subscribe, (719) 531-7776.

Easy Obedience This readable handbook on discipline emphasizes self-discipline as the overall goal. Kay Kuzma looks at parenting styles and attitudes that influence success in discipline. Then she discusses the types of problems children have offering very practical solutions. The "love cup principle" solves problems children have who misbehave to get attention. The "string strategy" teaches parents to pull instead of pushing in response to a child's desire to have control. Under "Revenge and Iceberg Psychology" you will learn how to defuse anger. Other advice in the book's 21 chapters deal with being positive, preparing for confrontation, breaking through with an unexpected response, playing with your children, negotiation, age related problems, and parenting prodigal children. Kay takes a biblical approach which you will appreciate. See her chapter in this book. 1997. The book costs around $12 and is available from Family Matters. See Part 3.

Family Educator Vocabulary Studies From the Bible If you believe that the Authorized Version (King James Version) of the Bible is *the* Bible, then it's reasonable for your children to become familiar with the older vocabulary and grammar. Louise Luthi has prepared two little books to help you. One focuses on words from selected Psalms (for ages 7 and 8; 31 pp.) and the other looks at words in "The Gospel According to St. Matthew" (for ages 9 and 10; 39 pp). Good discussion questions are included. This way of studying the Bible is a much better than doing puzzles and filling in blanks. Of course you can pick your own passages (or have your child pick them) and discuss and learn together as they unfold. These little books can get you going. $4.95 each plus $3.25 for mailing (or $2 for one). The Family Educator, P.O. Box 309, Templeton, CA 93465; (805) 434-0249.

A Family Guide to the Biblical Holidays From personal Bible study Robin Scarlata has learned how the special holidays celebrated by God's people of the Old Testament can bring beauty and understanding to our Christian experience. She and co-author Linda Pierce explain in their book how looking into what the holidays meant and following the celebrations can enrich a home learning experience much better than our cultural gift-giving times. I agree although I see some of the meanings a little differently. You can read what they wrote and study for yourself. This 581-page book provides resource information, activities, and a unit-study guide – plenty of good things to choose from. 1997, http://www.heartofwisdom.com Order: 800-BOOKLOG or e-mail Lifeinam@AOL.com.

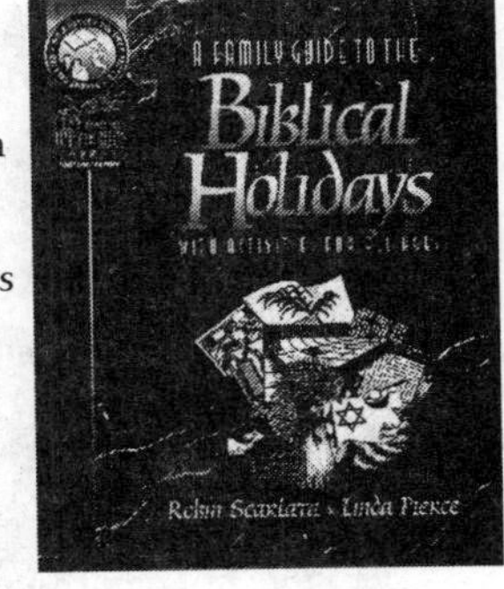

Family Times The Family Matters newspaper. See Part 3.

Home Built Discipline By Raymond & Dorothy Moore A basic book of child development advocating and illustrating a consistent style of discipline, with the parents clearly in charge. It promotes "discipling" more than "disciplining," with correction appropriate to the occasion, and never administered in the heat of anger. Discipline is seen not only as correction, but as the total spectrum of child training, including health, dress, courtesy, service to others, and fiscal responsibility. Includes a section on the development and needs of the child at different ages. $10.00 plus $2.50 shipping from The Moore Foundation, Box 1, Camas, WA 98607. *Reviewed by Karen Wade.*

Instilling Self-discipline in Children An excellent, brief guideline for home discipline. Author Gary Maldaner bases his ideas solidly on Scripture. The booklet is brief and packed with good methods. And you can't complain about the price. It's free (single copy) along with a free catalog. Just ask Plain Path Publishers, P.O. Box 830, Columbus, SC 28722. Plain@juno.com.

Parent Life 127 Ninth Ave., N., Nashville, TN 37234, A Baptist magazine with a variety of interesting topics for parents. (800) 458-2772.

Pathway Publishing An Amish firm with good books, reasonably priced. See Appendix P.

Preparing Children for School and Life Twelve writers share their Christian convictions and wisdom on the topic. The 19 chapters include: "Whose are the Children?" "Teaching Our Children to Face Life," ". . . to Think Scripturally About Himself," "Characteristics of a Well-Disciplined Child," ". . . Responsible Decision Making," and "Healthy Independence." My only objection is to the concept that a child's will must be broken. I definitely believe that obedience is to be required, but that can be done gently and firmly, leading him or her to a love relationship with the Lord. Parents are to help their children *yield* their wills to the Lord. One sentence doesn't keep me from recommending the book, however. Its counsels often refer to Scripture and are worth reading. I'm glad Keith White suggested that I check it out. 1988. $4.80 plus $1 shipping. Rod and Staff Publishers, Crockett, KY 41413; (606) 522-4348.

Part 2, Material for Students

For curriculum packages, see Appendix Y.

Adventures in Odyssey Audio/video series from Focus on the Family, P.O. Box 35500, Colorado Springs, CO 80935-3550.

The Bible in Living Sound 450 Bible stories are available on 75 cassette tapes. Each story is created with voices, music and sound-effects. Bible events come alive for listeners of all ages. Cassettes are available in sets or by monthly subscription. For example, a set entitled, *Jesus' Birth and Youth*, 2 tapes in an album, costs $10.95. You may sign up to receive one tape a month at $5.95 each including shipping costs. In fact, your first two tapes are only $2.99 ($1.49½ ea.). Write to BLS at Box 234, Nordland, WA 98358-0234, or phone (800) 634-0234, 9-5 Pacific Time.

Bible Story, The Arthur S. Maxwell, Review and Herald, 55 W. Oak Ridge Dr., Hagerstown, MD 21740. A ten-volume set running through the whole Bible. Well written and well illustrated, with attention to authenticity. 1995.

Big Book of Books and Activities, Religious Supplement Color-cut-and-paste activities in two volumes, one each for Old and New Testaments. "Jewish schools" are one of the suggested users of the Old Testament book. Each has 70 pages on paper that is a little heavier than usual. For most of the projects, you may first read and discuss the passages involved.

The New Testament volume includes a diorama to be constructed like a pyramid with a scene in each of the four sides. The story of the two debtors is made from one page folded in the form of a greeting card with a little door cut to open on each of the inside panels. On each little door is a question about how much was owed. The least interesting is a card-like object with pictures of Mary and Joseph. The pictures can be lifted from the bottom to show something your child writes behind them. The 17 projects in the Old Testament book include a mobile of Noah's Ark (which, by

the way, we might better call God's ark). On a construction-paper folder (not supplied) are attached little pictures (supplied) of Moses, Pharaoh and each of the ten plagues.

In general the activities are interesting and adaptable for older or younger kids. Making a fiery furnace fold-out doesn't substitute for discussing the lesson of faithfulness from Daniel 3, but the object would help young minds remember the lesson. Published by Dinah-Might Activities (the author is Dinah Zike). You can get them for $13 each from Common Sense Press, P.O. Box 1365, Melrose, FL 32666; For the nearest dealer call (904) 475-5757.

Child's Steps to Jesus, A A set of four books to read to your children (ages 4 to 7) and to discuss with them. Each is on a topic involving a relationship with God: God's love, salvation, forgiveness, and obedience. The girl in the first book found a kitten beside the road and rescued it from that dangerous place. 'Papa says that's like what God did. God came to save me from the sinful and dangerous world. Someday. . . .' She learns about her relationship with God in understanding the cat's relationship to her. At the end of the book is a parent's guide: 'Ways to Share God's Love With Your Child.'"

Larger print would have made them nicer for beginning readers. Some may not like to see the girls illustrated in pants. Two other sets cover other relationship topics. Overall, the books are very nice. They are multiethnic, durably hard bound, and reasonably priced (US$25.95 or Cdn$32.45 for each set), from Pacific Press (800) 765-6955.

Create-a-Notebook Bible and History The first title in this series is *Remembering God's Awesome Acts.* For an easier handle, I trimmed the series title a bit. It begins with "Susan Mortimer's" and ends with "Series." Now that we have the book's pedigree straight, let me tell you why I like it. In my opinion, real history cannot be separated from real knowledge about God. Susan has achieved her goal of presenting the Bible as "both an accurate historical document and as a handbook for daily living." The interesting study topics provide enough activity for the early grades (although words like "promiscuous" would need substitutes) and enough interest for the middle grades. It includes learning a little about ancient languages, anthropology, art, ancient religions, and the contrast between the true God and counterfeits. It relates to ancient history through the time of Moses although it doesn't teach much of the flow of events, even from a perspective in harmony with the Bible.

This casual approach to history is not necessarily bad, however. Let me tell you how I would use the series. For middle or upper grades, I would find other materials to get into more serious history. The significant points of what we really know about ancient history (the era for this first volume) are relatively few. I would bring them in later. And I would add more Bible for all the grades. This book would be good for a year's study. Also you could teach all your kids at the same time by adapting assignments for different ones. Even your high school kids would enjoy this book along with their deeper study. They could learn while teaching.

The price of $20 for the student's book and $10 for the teacher's is reasonable enough. The activities require writing in the book so not permitting photocopies makes it a little more costly for several kids (although copying all of it would not be cheaper). You can get along without the teacher's book, but I recommend it because Susan tells you just what to say. You can read explanations to your kids, (or not read them, of course). You may order from Susan Mortimer, 731 W. Camp Wisdom, Ducanville, TX 75116; (972) 780-1683. Add $3 for shipping.

Doorposts This home business produces character development charts and manuals. The chart they sent me for review is the *Brother-Offended Checklist*, with the subtitle: *What To Tell a Tattletale.* I was on guard as I looked at it since I feel our society has overemphasized the no-tattletale counsel. I need not have been concerned. The chart (with more explanations in the accpmpanying book) gives steps to take for resolution: {1} Don't be in a hurry to tell someone else. . . . {3} Be a peacemaker. . . . and so on. Steps are also shown for the offender. I feel that author/illustrator Pam Forster might have emphasized that our forgiveness should not wait for confession from the offender - that it is, first of all, a heart attitude. Even small children who can't read can understand the clear illustrations. Bible principles are used extensively. The chart is black and white on a 16 X 22 inch sheet of paper shipped in a mailing tube. The book is 28 pp., comb-plastic bound. $7.50 plus $2 postage ($4 for Canada). There are around 20 other Doorposts items. 5905 SW Lookingglass Dr., Gaston, OR 97119 (as of 1998). Phone and fax (503) 357-4749; http://www.lyonscom.com/doorposts.

Instruction in Righteousness A Topical Reference Guide for Biblical Child Training, by Pam Forster. A coil-bound book chock full of biblically-oriented ideas for child training. Chapter titles include "Pride," "Selfishness/Greed," "Anger," "Haste," "Laziness," "Dishonesty," "Gossip," "Revenge," "Poor Manners," and more than 40 more. A parent at his/her wit's end to know how to handle a character defect in the child will find not only Bible references dealing with the problem and illustrating the consequences of the defect but references dealing with and illustrating the opposite, positive trait. Along with the references are activities and object lessons which can be used to illustrate to the child what you are trying to teach and Bible verses for the child to memorize. This is not a book to read from cover to cover, but a binder of reference material from which you can draw ideas for your own situation. Every idea won't work for everyone, and you may feel some are inappropriate. But with over 300 pages, you should find something to fit your need! Address above. *–Karen Wade.*

Plants Grown Up Projects for character development in boys, based on Scripture. Character traits are arranged in project groups loosely following the list in 2 Peter 1. The suggested projects in each group are arranged by maturity from kindergarten through high school (although grades aren't mentioned). For example, one group in a set of leadership projects is "faithfulness in family worship." You aren't expected to cover them all,

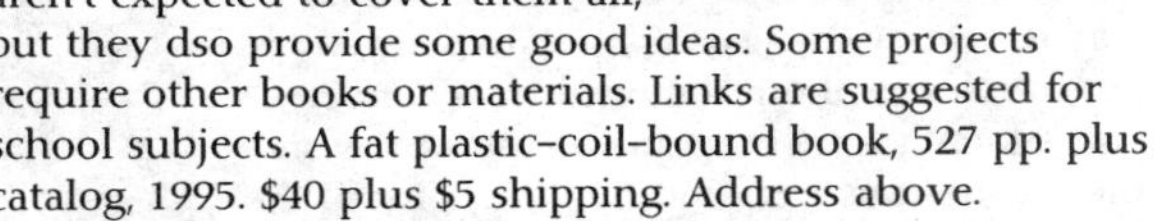

but they dso provide some good ideas. Some projects require other books or materials. Links are suggested for school subjects. A fat plastic-coil-bound book, 527 pp. plus catalog, 1995. $40 plus $5 shipping. Address above.

Polished Cornerstones A book for girls with the same general characteristics as the volume above, 566 pp. plus catalog. Charts for record keeping are included in both books. A table in the back shows the lessons for which each resource on a recommended list may be applied. You can teach character from circumstances and Bible references as they come up in study, but these materials help you keep it systematic and provide fresh ideas. 1997. Same price as *Plants Grown Up.*

Forever Stories A set of five superbly illustrated and manufactured, 64-page books explaining God's plan of redemption for humanity. They trace significant events of the drama based on the Bible accounts. The first book describes Satan's desire to be better than God's son and tells of his part in the deception in Eden. The second book, *God Makes a Promise,* picks up from the time of God's promise (Gen. 3:15) and carries through to the promise to Abraham. The third is *Getting Ready for Jesus,* and the forth is a powerful description of the life of Christ including His victory in temptation and on the cross. The last book, *Jesus Takes Us Home,* begins with the resurrection, tells a little of the

apostles' witness and describes a conception Jesus' return to take us to heaven and the final end of sin when everyone will know that the plan God gave for our happiness is right.

Written for preschoolers to hear and first graders to read, although children a little older will like them, too. Notes on the back of each book summarize the four concepts it unfolds. Going through these books and discussing them with your children will help you point young minds to Christ. *Forever Stories* make sense out of the whole scope of the Scriptures. A set of activity books, *Forever Stories Funpak*, are also available. From Review & Hearld Publishing Association, 55 West Oak Ridge Dr., Hagerstown, MD 21740; (301) 791-7000.

Jews in the Time of Jesus, The, A History A slice of secular Jewish history for a hundred years ending with the destruction of Jerusalem and Masada. This profusely illustrated book describes various aspects of family, religious, political and military life, housing and clothing. Inclusion of a royal family tree, maps, notes on geography, and many other topics makes history come alive. This is a good book, but some readers will want to use it with caution because, from author Peter Connolly's discussion of the dating of the gospels, we see that he does not agree with the biblical account. 1996. Paper, 96 pp., $9.95, Oxford University Press. KW.

MEMLOK Bible Memory System Drake Mariani publishes MEMLOK which uses an illustration to help you remember the first few words of each of some 700 verses (48 topics). A way to review the texts is included. Although I'm convinced about the need for a convenient system for memorizing scripture, I wish the illustrations were more in the spirit of the sacredness of the Bible verses since they will be remembered in connection with them. The system (cards and organizational items that go with them) costs $49 plus shipping. Or for $59 you can get it for your PC computer with all 550 cards printable for coloring. You may specify one of four popular Bible translations. Mariani also offers a 96-page book for remembering the books of the Bible, a computer game for the same purpose, and *Devotional Tools* to help make prayer more meaningful. 420 E. Montwood Ave., La Habra, CA 90631-7411; (800) 373-1947. Or order from the web: http://www.memlok.com; memlok@bigfoot.com.

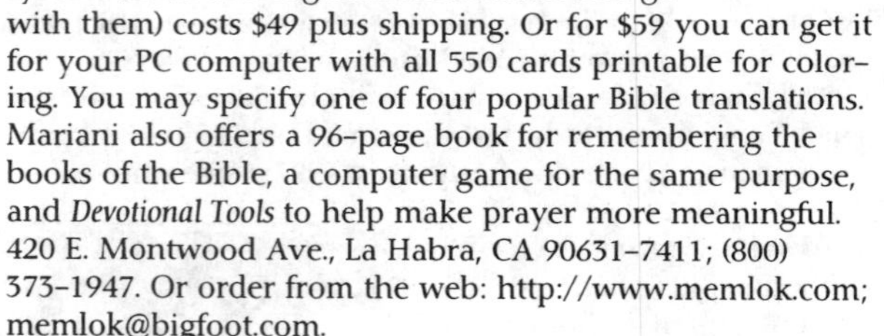

Online Bible An excellent computer concordance published by people who encourage it to be copied! You pay a fee for the diskettes and the postage if you order it direct. See my description under References in Appendix X.

Quizzes and Puzzles Three 48-page books planned for ages 10 or 12 and older. *Proverbs Puzzles, Messages with Meaning* has cryptograms, word searches and scrambled squares, based on the book of Proverbs. In *Promises of the Bible Puzzle Book* are similar puzzles. To solve the "Bible Promisegrams," for example, you write words, following clues. Letters from them are copied by number to fill out Bible promises. In *Dozens of Bible Quizzles,* crossword puzzle clues are words from a story like the one about the widow's oil. The quiz about Gideon would require reading the story.

If you want more than silly entertainment to interest your kids, get these small books. They may be photocopied. $2.50 each plus shipping of $1.20 for the first book and 30¢ for each additional one. Or ask for all three (to one address) for $8.50 postpaid. From the author, Fannie Houck, Five Star Publications, P.O. Box 1777, Port Townsend, WA 98368-1777.

Remembering God's Awesome Acts Subtitle: Create-a-notebook Bible and History Series. For grades 7-12. From Susan Mortimer, author of Considering God's Creation. A blended study of geography, anthropology, linguistics, etc. as they relate to biblical history. Although I have not reviewed this book, the description is impressive. The focus is on issues more than facts. For example, knowing something about the gods of the Egyptians helps us understand their challenge to the true God.

A teacher's manual and one student book cost $35. Other student books cost $20 each. (They may not be copied). Add $3 per item for shipping. Susan Mortimer, 731 W. Camp Wisdom, Duncanville, TX 75116.

Shining Star One of several Frank Schaffer magazines for or about children. The others are secular. In an older issue, I saw activities about Jacob bringing him down to the level of a cartoon character. One is a song to the tune of "Yankee Doodle." One is a recipe of a juice blend called "Jacob's Juicy Drink." I do like the rebus story of the Egyptian princess finding Moses in the basket. Overall, the magazine misses the opportunity to charm young children with a sense of holiness – of the spiritual depth they may be led to appreciate.

Although I have not examined a current issue, I did copy two *Shining Star* reproducible activity sheets from the web. One is quite good. It calls for classifying Bible passages into four categories, facts to be believed, warnings to be heeded, commands to be obeyed, and promises to be claimed. (800) 264-9873;

Sowers Series Biographies of famous Christians. 5th to 8th grade level (not reviewed.) From Mott Media, 100 E Huron St., Milford, MI 48381; (248) 685-8773; (800) 421-6645.

Wordy Bible memory software. Not examined. P.O. Box 9143, Wichita, KS 67277; ruepub@compuserve.com; http://ourworld.compuserve.com/homepages/ruepub

Part 3, Christian Ministries

Association of Christian Schools International, Colorado Springs, CO; (800) 367-0798; http://www.asci.org. Curriculum and administration guides and ethics materials.

Association of Christian Teachers and Schools, 8855 Dunn Rd.., Hazelwood, MO 63042-2299; (314) 837-7300; fax ... -4503; DIVofEDUPCI@juno.com. Serving Pentecostal home schools, Christian schools, and Bible schools. Dan Batchelor, Exec. Dir., phone ext 440.

Bold Parenting Seminars conducted by Jonathan Lindvall on scriptural strategies for training godly sons and daughters. Jonathan Lindvall is superintendent of Pilgrims School and has contributed a chapter for this book. Tapes available. P.O. Box 820, Springsville, CA 93265; (209) 539-0500. lindvall@ BoldChristianLiving.com; http://www .BoldChristianLiving.com

Christian Homesteading Movement A New York based parent training program. See Appendix D.

Christian Life Workshops, P.O. Box 2250, Gresham, OR 97030. Gregg Harris; (800) 225-5259. CLW conducts three types of conferences: "The Home Schooling Workshop," The Advanced Home Schooling Workshop," and regional conferences. These are hosted by state and other organizations. Host information and catalogs are available.

Christian Schools International P.O. Box 8709 Grand Rapids, MI 49512; (616) 957-1070. csi@gospelcom.net; http://www.christianschoolsint.org. Curriculum materials for Christian schools. This organization is different from Association of Christian Schools International.

Family Matters This organization provides information on child development issues and parenting skills through radio, TV, seminars (available in person or on video and audio recordings), books, and an excellent quarterly newspaper which is called, *Family Times*. I suggest you try the newspaper. It's free (although contributions are appreciated). Dr. Kay Kuzma, Family Matters president, has contributed the chapter, "Character Development" for this book. P.O. Box 7000, Cleveland, TN 37320; (423) 339-1144. 74532.333@CompuServe.com

Focus on the Family A popular ministry with many facets. "Dedicated to the preservation of the home." 8605 Explorer Dr., Colorado Springs, CO 80920; (719) 531-3400; http://www.fotf.org.

Home Schooling Live Radio See Appendix I.

Peter Marshall Ministries, 81 Finlay Rd., Orleans, MA 02653. The organization promotes the preaching and teaching ministry of Peter Marshall throughout America, and distributes materials on America's Christian heritage. See on *The Light and the Glory* in Part 1.

Part 4, Religious Publishers

Most publishers are mentioned only with their products. Secular or partly secular publishers are in Appendix Y.

Accelerated Christian Education, School of Tomorrow See Appendix A.

Alpha Omega Publications P.O. Box 3153, Tempe, AZ 85280. Robert J. Campbell, Jr., President. (800) 622-3070, Alpha Omega sells "LIFEPACs" (independent study worktexts) for grades 1-12. See Part 1. They also have a kindergarten program and sell a variety of materials.

Baker Book House P.O. Box 6287, Grand Rapids, MI 49516; (616) 676-9185. Religious books.

Bob Jones University Press, Greenville, SC 29614. (800) 845-5731 or (803) 242-5100, Ext. 4300. Quality curriculum materials for conventional Christian schools and home educators. Textbooks and teacher's editions in all subjects and grade levels. Also material available for special areas such as computer science, and speech. Testing services are offered using the Iowa Test of Basic Skills. Complete catalog available.

Christian Liberty Press The publishing division of Christinan Liberty Academy (Appendix A). A full line of curriculum materials. Some have been reviewed in appendices R and S. Shipping is 10% with $1.50 min. Add tax if Ill. Quantity discounts. Christian Liberty Press, 502 W. Euclid Ave., Arlington Heights, IL 60004; Order by mail or by fax with credit card (847) 259-2941. Call (800) 832-2741 for a catalog, or visit www.homeschools.org.

Crossway Books 1300 Crescent St., Wheaton, IL 60187. (630) 682-4300; fax ... -4785; goodnews2@aol.com. Crossway is a division of Good News Publishers and has published several books of interest to home educators.

Gazelle Publications See Appendix Y.

Noble Publishing Associates 710 NE Cleveland, #170, Gresham, OR 97030; noblebooks@aol.com; (800) 225-5259; fax (503) 618-8866.

Pacific Press Publishing Assn. P. O. Box 7000, Boise, ID 83707, (208) 465-2512. In addition to the series of books listed in this appendix, PPPA publishes *Listen*, a magazine on temperance and other Bible related materials.

Rod and Staff Publishers Highway 172, Crockett, KY 41413. Duane E. Miller and James Boll, (606) 522-4348. Rod and Staff publications have been used by many home schools over the years. Materials for the whole curriculum. Mr. Miller tells me that they take care to make and keep their materials true to the Bible and that people generally express appreciation for that. Request a free catalog and/or a sample periodical issue.

Your Story Hour P.O. Box 15, Berrien Springs, MI 49103. (616) 471-3701. Probably the largest and finest library of Bible and character-building stories available on cassette. One set the company feels is especially good is, "Life of Jesus," an album of 13 cassettes. In addition to Bible stories, they have biographies of people like Mueller, Nightingale, Pasteur, and Moody. And there are many other stories on topics like shoplifting and God's protection.

Zondervan Publishing House 5300 Patterson Ave. SE, Grand Rapids, MI 49530. Bibles and religious books.

O

Reading

This appendix is divided into

1 beginning instructional materials,

2 beginning practice and special materials, and

3 advancing in reading.

The letters LL at the end of certain reviews stand for "Lorinda Lasher" who wrote them. You will see my initials, too. For other areas of language arts and English, see Appendix P.

Part 1, Reading instructional materials / Phonics

Adventures in Phonics (Review of Level B, for first grade.) This well-designed book has perforated pages to be used as worksheets. Its tendency is toward general reading instruction, including spelling and penmanship, more than phonics. If you have chosen a way of learning phonics which is more natural than the traditional intensive way, this book would reinforce it and provide lots of handwriting (ball and stick) practice. The book assumes you have already taught a good deal of reading and basic phonics in kindergarten (not always best in my opinion). If your kindergarten and first grade are more relaxed and less academic, this book would be better for a higher level (if used at all).

1996, $8 plus shipping, from Christian Liberty Academy Press, 502 W. Euclid Ave., Arlington Heights, IL 60004. Teachers manual (which you may not need) $7.

Academic Advantage American Phonics A clear introduction to reading according to phonetic rules. Program developer, Cliff Ponder, an experienced educator, points out that, of the 26 alphabet letters, 16 nearly always have unique pronunciations. His program proceeds to teach the phonetic rules in a straightforward, simple-to-apply manner. Flash cards with the rules on them are presented and reviewed step-by-step. The whole course requires only nine lessons, with individual study in between. These are demonstrated for the parent or teacher on video tapes with words often displayed on the screen.

The rule cards are effective in that a question on one side prompts a memorized response. For example, card #8 asks, "What are the W rules"? On the other side are three rules. "W is at the beginning of a word usually makes its own sound: wet win won." The other two rules are for W at the end and W before R.

I think I would view the lesson demonstrations with my child, stopping the tape now and then to go through the learning activities shown. Or they could be reviewed after a lesson for reinforcement. The instructions are also in the manual showing you just what to say. The video tapes are nice for the pronunciations (although audio tapes could have served that purpose).

In addition to the phonetic rules, students learn terms such as "syllables" and "antonyms." At the end, Ponder demonstrates a simple way to strengthen comprehension.

The distinguishing feature of this program is its suitability for older children who have had a hard time getting a start in reading or who have been kept out of school until they are a little older. Considering younger children, we should note that uncommon words like "yak, chaos, whoa, fate, mace" and "mete" are used. (Other phonics programs also use such words, by the way. They are needed to demonstrate the rules. Our problem may be more in starting kids too young than in how the programs are designed.) Also, for the younger children, the print on the cards is smaller than the ideal; explanations are often, of necessity, complex; and there are no nice graphic illustrations and games to soften the abstract concepts. On the other hand, all these points are advantages for older students.

The program is clear and effective and would, of course, work for younger children, too. In the package you get a loose-leaf manual, three sets of laminated rule cards (for three students), and two reasonably long video tapes. The price is $129.95 plus $6 shipping. And remember tax if you are in California. Write to Catalog Sales, Weimar Institute, Box 486, Weimar, CA 95736; (916) 637-4111.

Alphabet Island Phonics Offered at two academic levels. *Alphabet Island Phonics 1* is for kindergarten. "Each 15 minute lesson has a story, a song, a poem, a game, and a blackboard or workbook activity, all geared toward optimum learning." Cards with pictures remind children of the letter sounds and the vowels. *Alphabet Island Phonics 2*, according to the descriptive brochure, "is all you need to cover spelling and phonics from 1st grade through 9th grade."

For *Alphabet Island Phonics 1* and free copy of *Kinder-Math*, send $75.40 including shipping to Eagle's Wings Educational Materials, P.O. Box 502, Duncan, 73534; (405) 252-1555; For the advanced program, *Alphabet Island Phonics*

2 with *Phonics Handbook*, $90.40. For both phonics programs, $125.95.

Alpha-Phonics, Samuel L. Blumenfeld. Subtitle, *A Primer for Beginning Readers*, Described as "an effective, step-by-step intensive phonics program. . . ." The Paradigm Co. P.O. Box 45161, Boise, ID 83711. (208) 322-4440. $29.95 + $3 shipping Add tax if Idaho.

Beginning Reading at Home A basic phonics approach for young children. It includes nine story books and a simple reading readiness test. $35 postpaid. Individualized Education Systems, Poppy Lane Publishing Co., P.O. Box 5136, Fresno, CA 93755; (209) 299-4639; bette1234@aol.com.

Dr. Christman's Learn to Read Book By Ernest Christman. A consistent, well-arranged plan for teaching phonics in the usual way. Large print words help the beginning reader. $15.95 (postpaid). Blue Bird Publishing, 1739 E. Broadway #306, Tempe, AZ 85282. (602) 968-4088; Fax (602) 831-1829.

Game Way to Phonics and Reading This approach includes two features other phonics programs may be weak in. One, implied by the title, is the games. The other is an emphasis on encoding before expecting decoding. This simply means teaching how to make the sounds for particular letters as they combine to create words, before expecting your child to look at words in order to realize what sounds they are calling for. You will learn, with pictures of mouth positions and a cassette tape, just how to demonstrate the various sounds so your child can make them. You will probably want a little more than this program for teaching reading. You could use it along with another phonics program. I think I would start with something like this and then perhaps go to the type of instruction described by Mark Thogmartin in his chapter. The program consists of a booklet with specially cut pages, a set of game cards for the Think! game using short vowel sounds, word cards (not surface protected) to cut up for the games, a card for a game board, and two short cassette tapes (one addressed to the child). 1994, By Ellen Dana. $24 plus $3.50 shipping fom Caring Communications, P.O. Box 486, Camas, WA 98607.

Gift of Reading, The Trudy Palmer believes that the greatest gift you can give your child, in addition to introducing him or her to Christ, is the gift of reading; and her goal is to give you the gift of knowing how. As a professional teacher and tutor, she studied a long-established program for phonetic-based reading and felt that it had some gaps. Her book makes the process of learning to read very clear. For example, she describes levels in reading development. These are prereading, decoding (grades 1, 2), fluency (grades 2, 3), gathering information (through junior high), multiple viewpoints (high school), and reconstruction (college and beyond). She also identifies the vowel sounds according to the tongue position.

This is a good program for the traditional phonics approach. *The Gift of Reading*, costs $14.95 (137 pp., 1996). In addition are: large phonogram cards with explanations on the back $17.95, a spelling notebook $8.95, an audio cassette for teaching the phonograms to the child $7.95, and spelling word lists in three levels $8.95 each. Her "kit" includes all of these except the two higher-level spelling lists $55. Shipping to US is $4 for up to $40 in purchases, then 10%. For elsewhere it's $5 and 15%. The physical appearance could be improved but does not hurt the end result. The tape is not as clear and crisp as would be nice. It is descriptions of the phonograms. Trudy Palmer, 423 Maplewood, San Antonio, TX 78216; (210) 828-5179.

Hooked on Phonics The program includes an advanced comprehension component. In all you get quite a few cassettes and booklets. I have not examined it. Before purchasing, I suggest you check one or more of the books of product reviews listed in Appendix X, Part 3. The price is well over $200 (800) 222-3334.

How to Teach Reading Author, Edward Fry, is known for the readability scale he developed for judging the suitability of text material for various grade levels. He has also written textbooks on teaching reading. Here he presents in a practical way the essence of the topic. His approach is suitable for illiterate adults as well as for young or older children. The six steps he describes are: (1) find present reading ability, (2) select the right reading material, (3) stress comprehension and variety, (4) teach vocabulary, (5) teach phonics, and (6) develop writing.

Although Fry doesn't discuss mental handicaps that interfere with reading, his suggestions will be helpful in dealing with poor readers. Tests in the back of the book will help you evaluate a person's reading ability. Games for strengthening the reading vocabulary are described. The specific information on the way words are put together with prefixes and suffixes will help your child recognize more word meanings. For help in teaching phonics, words with certain sounds are grouped by families. In all, Fry tells you how to teach reading and he gives you specific tools for the job. Definitely a good book. Laguna Beach Educational Books, 245 Grandview, Laguna Beach, CA 92651. 1992, 144 pp., $14.95 plus $3 shipping (not verified for this edition).

Leonardo Press This publisher was not pleased with our review of their materials several years ago, and we have granted their request not to publish it.

Learning Through Sounds A good, traditional, phonics program. It looks easy to use. You get two student workbooks (80 and 87 pages) and a 117-page teacher's manual for a grand total of $8.20 plus $2 shipping for U.S. or Canadian addresses. Add 7% for Canada or 5% if sent to Indiana. At $20, the materials would still be relatively reasonably priced. Pathway Publishing. See Appendix P for the address. By the way, the $2 for U.S. is all you pay for up to $25 in books. Then shipping is free.

Making Smiles: Helping Kids Read, *A Manual for School Volunteers* The book could as well have been called "a manual for parent teachers." It recognizes that learning to read takes a good deal of one-on-one guidance and shows you just how to be your a child's guide to reading. The first step is helping your child feel comfortable and to sense that you appreciate her learning success. Learning to recognize the letters is next. You are helped to be aware that your child understands the terms you will need for instruction, such as the difference between letters and words. You are told how to lay the groundwork for comprehension by showing, in a web diagram, how elements in the topic or story relate to the main point.

The book is organized according to the seven ways people are intelligent with the idea that using a variety of ways gives kids better opportunities to learn. Rather than traditional phonics instruction, children are taught to recognize certain letter combinations or "chunks." The fat book is full of activities and includes instruction on evaluation.

I have reviewed a special edition. The revised book, now directed to parents as well as others, is being published by Sunlight Publishers, 2226 So. Clearbrook, Arlington Heights, IL 60005. It will have about 180 pp., 1998, By Shirley Freed, with other contributors.

Phonics Pathways A well-planned multisensory approach to reading instruction that merges phonics and spelling into reading. Author Dolores Hiskes begins by teaching the short vowel sounds, then immediately adds consonants to form two-letter blends and then three-letter words. Later, whole sentences provide practice and illustration. Continuous review is designed to reinforce learning. Left-to-right patterning helps develop eye tracking which the author believes to be helpful for people with dyslexic tendencies. The ideas are clearly presented and are reinforced with sample words. Extra activities are included. I like this program better than many which explicitly teach practically all the phonics sounds, because of its concept of reading words and sentences nearly from the beginning. In order to provide a variety in practicing with the large numbers of sounds, however, words and concepts strange to young ears are used. For example, yearns, berth, tyrant, lunge, hysterical, and cynic.

1996, 8½ x 11 in., around 250 pp. $29.95 plus $3 shipping and tax if to Calif. Dorbooks, P.O. Box 2588, Livermore, CA 94551; (510) 447-6983; dorbooks@aol.com.

Pyramid, from the same author, is a book of reading exercises following the system of starting with a few words and adding a new one to make a new sentence, then another, etc. For example, Ken / Ken has. / Ken has a deck. / Ken has a back deck. / Ken has a big back deck. / Ken has a duck on his back deck., and so on. 80 pp., $17.95

Play 'n Talk, "Phonics in Action," 7105 Manzanita St. Carlsbad CA 92009 (760) 438-4330. Marie A. Le Doux, Ph.D. Basic and Advanced Course on **CDs, Cassettes**, and **CDrom**, contains Instructor Training Manual and 3 hr video. Teaches up to college level vocabulary. The package includes 4 books that go with a set of cassette tapes, designed to do the "teaching," plus reinforcement games and other materials. This is described as a beginning language arts program based on detailed phonics instruction. In my opinion it's on the expensive side, but some others are, too. You may judge. $250 for program with cassettes only, $350 with CDs and $395 with CDs and computer disks. A free sample kit with manual and cassette are available.

Reading Step-by-Step: A Winning Formula For some 25 years, Charlotte Lenzen has been teaching kids to read. She uses a simple, well-planned approach, and she tells you just what to say in explaining each step. She is sensitive to readiness. She stresses reading to your child and reading practice. In half an hour a day reviewing key rules, using flash cards, and explaining, you can teach easily. For grades K-3. The system includes a big binder with cards, explanations and two cassettes. Consonant sounds may be taught with picture cards. Price: $99.95. Chalen Edu-Systems, 412 Laurel Ave., Brielle, NJ 08730. (735) 528-6335; chalen@monmouth.com.

Scardy Cat Reading System (for special needs children) Joyce Herzog has developed a series of books and materials for teaching reading to special needs children. Tapes and additional materials accompany the teaching manuals. Contact Simplified Learning Products for more information. Simplified Learning Products, P.O. Box 45387, Rio Rancho, NM 87174-5387; (800) 745-8212.

Sing, Spell, Read, and Write A set of materials for teaching all the beginning language skills, as implied by its title. Author Sue Dixon uses a number of little devices (some would say gimmicks) to keep the child's interest and to encourage achievement. One is a race track goal chart. Cassette tapes provide the "sing" part of the program (although I have a concern about the type of music on them). The program teaches effectively. I can see that many parents would appreciate it. Some others may prefer to devise their own incentives and content themselves with a more bare bones early reading program to help avoid a bare pocket book, although some other programs are also pricy. You might like it very well. The basic, Level 1 kit costs $175 (as of 12/97). It teaches for all the language skill areas and includes 17 phonetic story books, 6 cassettes, an instructor's video, and various prizes and goal devices. For ages 5-8. Levels 2 and 3 follow, basically for grades 2 and 3 and are less expensive. You wouldn't have to use them. A preschool kit is also available. Ask for a brochure. International Learning Systems, 1000 112th Circle N., Suite 100, St. Petersburg, FL 33716. (800) 321-8322.

Teach a Child to Read Using Children's Books Home educators who are convicted that a strong, phonics-first approach is necessary for success in reading instruction may see Mark Thogmartin's book as revolutionary. But he is certainly not advocating a sink-or-swim dependence on sight-word memorization. His instructional plan is, in fact, logical and precise. It builds on the natural pattern of human language acquisition, including a good understanding of phonics.

I believe in phonics. I wish I had learned more as a child. But I have questioned what is often called "intensive phonics" including the idea that the major phonemes must be understood before reading more than the sample words used to teach them. I object more, however, to the instruction I'm afraid often comes under the title of "whole language," where kids are practically left to figure out whatever makes sense to them in how sounds are translated into print. Thogmartin sees his work as "whole language," but with methodical, individual instruction, carefully monitoring the child's learning. It's "whole" in the sense of depending on a variety of cues in interpreting the text. Reading, analysis of the words, and writing are merged to give the reader a strong set of tools for understanding what is read.

In his book, Thogmartin explains the basis for his ideas, thoroughly lays out a teaching strategy, and includes a discussion of the topic in an appendix for teachers in Christian schools and in home schools. In his method, carefully chosen books for children are used. Children begin with books after they have learned only a handful of sight words. In each lesson, books are read, words are analyzed, and writing occurs. Lessons last about half an hour and require one-on-one time with the child. In a classroom school, this is expensive, so its use must be limited. Here home schools have the advantage.

From Edinfo Press, Indiana University, P.O. Box 5953, Bloomington, IN 47407; (800) 925-7853.

Teach America to Read & Spell, P.O. Box 44093, Tacoma, WA 98444. (206) 531-0312. In preparing this and other editions of *The Home School Manual* I've seen many persuasive phonics/reading programs. So when Frank Rogers called to convince me that he had *the* way children should learn these skills, I wasn't, at first, very impressed. I still feel that other ways might work better than he thinks, but as you can see, I ended up inviting him to prepare a chapter for the book. I don't need to say much more here except that the continuation of his program is called "The Great Saltmine & Hifwip Direct Phonics Reading Program." The cost is around $38. In case you would like to have the information in this chapter on cassette and have the booklet from which the illustrations used here were taken, you may order the Penny Primer starter set for $10.95 (postpaid). Frank's program has been one of the more reasonably-priced ones. As you can see, it still costs much less than most others.

Teaching Reading at Home A Supplement to Romalda Spalding's *The Writing Road to Reading*. Author Wanda Sanseri studied the system with Mrs. Spalding and has trained teachers across the country in the techniques. Her book offers "a step-by-step overview, sample charts and recommended practice exercises." They also sell *The Writing Road to Reading*.

The ministry of Gary and Wanda Sanseri offers English instructional materials and other interesting books like *God's Priceless Woman* in which Wanda discusses various facets of the role of Christian women, and *A Banker's Confession: A Christian Guide to Getting Out of Debt*, one of Gary's contributions. Ask for their catalog. Back Home Industries, P.O. Box 22495, Milwaukie, OR 97269, (503) 654-2300.

Victory Drill Book A phonetic approach to reading with an emphasis on speed, by August C. Enderlin. Tough hardcover book, 78 pp. 1970. This appears to me as a straightforward and effective approach that would not overdo the phonics training. $12.95 + $5 handling for up to $30 orders + tax if CA. The $6.30 cassette demonstrates high-speed pronunciation and is a teaching guide keyed to the book. I think I would order the book and tape, then decide whether or not to also get the teachers' manual or the worksheets. For more information, request their brochure. Since I first started telling readers of *The Home School Manual* about the "victory" program, several other reasonably-priced programs have appeared. Victory Drill Book, P.O. Box 2935, Castro Valley, CA 94546-0935.

The Writing Road to Reading One of the earlier phonics programs. Although it has helped many people learn to read well, some who have used it have seen better ways to teach, and I tend to agree. Of course it may be the best for you. For more information, see Riggs Institute in Appendix P.

Part 2, Beginning practice and supplementary materials

Bob Books The author of this set of little books, Bobby Maslen, is not the first to think of writing stories that teach phonetic letter combinations. But her interesting little tales, each focused on a specific set of new sounds, will help you make learning fun. By showing your child how each phonetic rule applies to the story words, learning will be natural. You may not need to teach phonics much more, especially in connection with reading from children's literature. Following the page illustrated here, the story continues: "It ran in the sun. It ran up the hill and down the hill. It went from town to town. But one day a funny thing made the little train stop."

The little train ran in the rain.

Bobby's husband John created the professional illustrations. Each page has a picture and a few words. 28 booklets with simple instructions. They are packed in 3 boxes; $14.95 each, plus shipping from: Bob Books, P.O. Box 633, West Linn, OR 97068; (800) 733-5572.

Come Read With Me A video based course with phonics instruction for kids who know the alphabet. (Not examined). From Calvert School, 105 Tuscany Rd., Baltimore, MD 21210; (410) 366-0674; http://www.calvertschool.org

Butterfly Alphabet Book, The Here is a splendor of bright colors without the cartoonish distortions common to children's books. It's a feast for the eyes. When I find a new alphabet book, I'm curious to see how it handles the letter X. In this case, "X is for Xami Hairstreak. American butterfly watchers will travel a long way to see a Xami Hairstreak. It just barely comes into the United States in Texas and Arizona. This butterfly is easier to find in Mexico. Butterflies are insects. All insects have six legs. If some butterflies in this book appear to have only four legs, it is because the front two are very tiny." 1995.

Do alphabet books teach the alphabet? This one may at least reinforce the learning process. But it and the two others I've seen from the series by author Jerry Pallotta would be more successful in attracting interest to the science topics they feature. Notice the maturity level assumed by the text on the opening page of *The Victory Garden VEGETABLE Alphabet Book*. "When planting a garden, the first thing we have to do is prepare the soil. The ground needs to be turned over. Any sticks and stones should be tossed aside. We then might add compost to enrich the soil. Ultimately, we want the soil to be loose and level." The book starts the alphabet with Asparagus, Beets, and Carrots, then begins adding vegetables popular in various world cultures. D is for Daikon (a large white radish). F is for Fiddleheads (fern tips). The book is certainly worthwhile. The alphabet is simply an interesting way to organize it and an aid to remembering the names. This book's co-author is Bob Thomson and it is illustrated by Edgar Stewart. 1992.

The books in this series are available in paper bindings with 32 pages, from Charlesbridge Publishing, for $6.95 each. On direct orders, add 10% (min. $2) for shipping. Charlesbridge Publishing, 85 Main St., Watertown, MA 02172.

Christian Liberty Nature Reader, 2nd edition, 1996. A series of five readers reprinted, type reset, and edited from older books. For grades 1 to 5. I have examined the book for grade 1. (163 pp.). This is not a beginning reading book. It could well be used for 2nd grade, especially if you believe in a slower start for early academics. Interesting descriptions and discussions. "This reader is designed not only to improve a child's reading skills and comprehension, but also to increase the youngster's understanding of and delight in God's wonderful creation." Harder words in slightly bold type. Glossary in the back. Christian Liberty Press. See Appendix Y.

English Picture Word Book A nice way for children to increase their vocabulary. There are 14 double-page scenes full of objects with words printed in blue ink. The lettering is this size is a little smaller than ideal for young children. I've taken a small portion of one picture and reduced it to about 45% for the illustration which follows. As you might expect, the 500 plus words are all nouns. I would like to have seen an index showing the pages where each word appears. Also available for Spanish, German, and French. 32 pp., 8½ X 11, $2.95. (Hayward Cricker and Barbara Steadman.) Dover number 27776-3 See Appendix Y for ordering information.

First Thousand Words See Appendix U.

Jacket I Wear in the Snow, The "This is the jacket I wear in the snow." The jacket is pictured. "This is the zipper [picture of zipper] that's stuck on the [picture of jacket] that I wear in the snow." The story expands on this problem adding more clothing items and substituting illustrations for the previous ones as lines of the poem are repeated. Great fun and good reading practice. 30 giant pages (17½ inches tall). $18.95 from Mulberry Books.

Rev-Up for Reading - CD-ROM for Windows Teaches the alphabet letters and their sounds (short vowel sounds for the vowels) with pink mouse characters and mention of the Bible. Clicking on the proper letter reinforces recognition in various "games." The upper case letters are bent to form lower case letters so they are learned together. The computer keeps track of student progress. One nice feature is shutting down after finishing a lesson. This keeps kids from sitting too many hours in front of the screen and from information overload. This program will be very effective and reduce your teaching time. My four-year-old grandson loves it. and would be reading if pushed a little. $14.95 from Alpha Omega Publications. (800) 622-3070.

Other CDs in the series include *Rev-Up for Writing* and *Rev-Up for Arithmetic*

Word Rescue A shareware computer game. The "Gruzzles" have stolen all the words which are to be rescued. 98% entertainment and 2% word learning.

Part 3, Advancing in reading

In addition to what you see here, many textbook publishers include reading programs. See Appendix P, Part 1.

Blumenfeld Oral Reading Assessment Test Find out how well your child (or yourself) reads. You count words read wrong for the test and look at a chart which tells you a grade level. The test measures word pronunciation, not comprehension or speed. You get instructions and scoring sheets for the basic test, and the same for a posttest. $19.95 postpaid. For another $5 you get an optional tape of Dr. Blumenfeld reading the 380 words.

The process used for setting the test norms (determining what score range should be expected for each grade) was very simple. The words were tested on 207 students in one private school. This restricted sample affects the reliability of what the scores mean. We also have the limitation of examining only a narrow aspect of reading. One could pronounce a word by recognizing certain phonetic letter combinations and still not know what it meant. Or the word could be pronounced correctly as a sight word without understanding either its correct meaning or the phonetic rules involved. In addition to not testing word definitions, test results don't tell us whether the student is able to synthesize word relationships in the flow of text and develop the thoughts intended by the author.

By explaining how the Blumenfeld test does not measure all these reading skills, I'm not saying it's bad. I'm only pointing out that the conclusions we draw are definitely limited. Of course poor pronouncers will likely comprehend poorly, too, (as would kids poor in math). So you can get a rough grade-level idea which may be all you need.

For a better way to determine an approximate reading ability grade-level find a series of graded reading textbooks (from a school or school district office). Have your child read portions here and there. Ask questions to test comprehension. The book that presents only minor challenges will represent the appropriate level. This process bypasses specific reading skills and looks at the end result. On the other hand, if you are interested in the development of phonetic skills, the Blumenfeld test will be a more sensitive measure. The pretest and posttest capability will show the progress. In any case, be ready to adjust your strategy to meet your child's needs while keeping reading appealing.

The Paradigm Co., Box 45161, Boise, ID 83711. Day/night line (208) 322-4440 (with answering machine).

Improve Your Reading Part of the "How to Study" series by Ron Fry. Excellent advice. Fry relates his material to parents and various levels of students. His object is to help you understand and achieve your purpose for reading more than helping you read faster. My only objection is his use of veiled profanity like "darn" and "heck." 1996, $6.99 plus shipping from Career Press. (800) 227-3371.

New A+ English Vocabulary II, one module of an elementary school computer instructional series. Catalog description: "Reinforces and expands basic vocabulary and word use skills typically taught in grades 4-6. Assists in mastery of prefixes, suffixes, synonyms, antonyms, similes, metaphors and many more!" See "A+" in appendix S for comments about the features common to all the modules in this series. I reviewed a diskette version. it is now on **CDrom**.

My opinion *about this module*: In one of the lessons titled "Similes," instructions say: "Choose the two words which are being compared." This sort of exercise would lead to little learning beyond the definition of a simile, which itself is of minor practical value. In a more useful lesson called "Tricky Words," sentences are to be corrected by changing words in parentheses: "I (seen) the elephant run by," "Will you (learn) me . . . ." Typical exercise areas are covered.

The American Education Corporation, 756 N. Broadway, Oklahoma City, 73116; (800) 222-2811.

Reading Skills Discovery Series "A comprehensive reading program using real books." I have examined the study guides for the books, *Wilbur and Orville Wright, Young Fliers* (4th or 5th grade) and for *Caddie Woodlawn* (4th to 6th grades). For each chapter in the book, discussion questions and activities are suggested. Some of the discussion responses require only direct recall like "What practical jokes did they play on Annabelle?" and some ask opinions. Discussion is very important in developing comprehension skill. For part of your teaching, I suggest your child read orally and you stop to ask questions along the way, not waiting for the end of the chapter. Rereading a paragraph might be appropriate now and then. Also encourage your student to stop and express opinions or ask you questions. Some of the activities seem to be of minor importance to me. Others, however, will strengthen important skills in writing or searching for information. An index at the back lists the skill areas dealt with.

The guidebooks look good to me. They do some of what textbooks do which I don't feel is all that bad. They are priced at $9 each. You can also order the books themselves for $3.95. Common Sense Press, Call (904) 475-5757 for the nearest dealer.

Readmaster from the Accelerated Christian Education, School of Tomorrow. Reading speed and comprehension are improved by reading text from the screen before it fades away at a certain number of words per minute. Before presenting one of the 432 brief, character building stories, less-common words are defined and illustrated by sentences from the story. Then the story is read and a multiple choice test measures comprehension. The correct answers are reviewed. If the scores for a block of stories are less than 80%, the student is recycled back to read and test again. Each student has a personal diskette and the computer keeps track of his or her progress. Reading level and speed are to be customized for each student.

The user interface could stand a little improvement, but it's not bad. I had just started a second story set when the doorbell rang. I left the computer to go through the story by itself. When I returned, the screen was blank and I had to reset the computer. As the story is appearing, shifts to new screens of text are a little awkward for me. The letters on the new screens start disappearing almost immediately. Also, to avoid waiting for a new screen you can hit "escape" but this was not explained in the demo version. The text font on the demo disk was clear, and the fading method works well for keeping one reading.

The promotional material claims that the program is successful, and I believe it. I recommend *Readmaster* – that is, if the $250 price tag is no problem. You can also purchase the software in three-grade segments for about $70 each. For each grade, there are 24 character-building stories. Shipping is extra. HD diskettes, either size, for IBM compatibles. ACE School of Tomorrow, Home School Dept., P.O. Box 1438, Lewisville, TX 75067-1438. See Appendix A for the company description.

P

Other Language Arts, Elementary and Secondary

The parts of this appendix are:
  ***1** textbooks, as below*
  ***2** grammar*
  ***3** handwriting*
  ***4** using the library*
  ***5** literature, poetry*
  ***6** literature, prose or mixed*
  ***7** spelling*
  ***8** writing*
  ***9** speech/communication.*
Reviewer Lyn Gatling indicated by her initials, LG.

Part 1, Language arts textbooks and other broad-range materials

Bob Jones University Press The language program for BJUP starts in 4-year-old kindergarten with letter recognition, initial letter sounds, and simple handwriting, although you wouldn't need to start that early except in a casual way with some of it. Language arts are mostly taught from one book per year through the first grade. Beginning with grade 2, separate books are available for reading, handwriting, and spelling. Quality materials from a Christian perspective. See Appendix Y for contact information.

McGuffey Readers A classic series of reading textbooks available from several sources.

Moore McGuffey Readers Republication of the classic set of books with six objectionable stories replaced by material from the 1838 and 1843 editions and with color added to enhance illustrations. $55.00 plus shipping. Box 1, Camas, WA 98607. (360) 835-5500.

Open Court Reading and Writing According to the publishers, children with their program, "actually read literature sooner because of extremely powerful decoding strategies and skills taught in kindergarten and grade one and reviewed in grade two." These include phonics, sight-word recognition, and structural analysis. See *Open Court Real Math* in Appendix Q for the address.

Pathway Publishing Corporation The reading book samples from Pathway Publishing tell about horse-and-buggy days and earlier. I had it all figured out. Someone had revived a series of old textbooks to sell to McGuffy fans. But not so. The publisher's review of the draft of my review straightened me out (politely). The series is published for Amish parochial schools! With that understanding, I'm even more enthusiastic.

I have examined several books in the series. *Days Go By* is marked on the spine as "Grade 1, Primer." It seems more like "advanced grade 1" to me. (158 pp.) Lower grade books have lists of new words in the back. *Seeking True Values*, the 7th grade book (464 pp.), includes stories of Christian heroes. One is about hiding a Bible in a loaf of bread when the church of the middle ages wanted it kept only in monasteries. The story of Gutenberg's advance in printing and how he was shut down has a sequel that is not in the book. His workers fled to other cities, taking the new technology with them, and more Bibles were printed than Gutenberg probably ever imagined. John Bunyan is the object of another story. There are also animal stories and stories of pioneer children. (464 pp., $6 for home and classroom schools, plus $2 shipping, and tax if Indiana or Canada). Workbooks are available but probably wouldn't advance learning much more than other typical workbooks. I would bend my teaching energy toward discussion and writing exercises. For $8.20 you can get a whole phonics program: two student workbooks and a detailed instructor's manual. Shipping, $2.

Although I would want books with modern, character building stories for my kids, I would definitely want these, too. I'm not ready to drive a horse and buggy, but old-fashioned values will never go out of date. The books are reasonably priced and you can pass them on to your grandchildren. They are manufactured for survival in a classroom. Pathway Publishers, 2530N 250W, La Grange, IN 46761.

HBJ Language **-Medallion Edition**, 1993, A very flexible textbook series, incorporating the writing process, a traditional grammar approach and the reading-writing connection. Teacher's editions show daily lesson plans with the flexibility to choose one approach or a little of each. The colorful graphics are a little juvenile and include many nursery rhyme characters which may be offensive to some, yet the approach to language is creative. Lists of quality children's literature, story starters, writing portfolios, and hands-on activities are a few of the enhancements available. Grades K-8; (800) 225-5425. Request the home schooling form for discount prices, You will need a teaching certificate only for secondary-level teacher's editions. 5th grade student book $32.25 with discount, Teacher's Edition $90.78 with discount. Other subjects available. *LG*

Horizons American Language From Alpha Omega (See Appendix N). Appears to be a rigorous, well-organized series. May not be the best for those who want to go slow for the early years. Not examined.

Language Lessons *Primary Language Lessons.* Republication of a 1911 book for teaching language. Older books had less of the kind of wild fantasy we see today. For example a poem "to be memorized" in this book is about a grandma and a crippled boy who played hide-and-seek by guessing where the other was pretending to hide. But good reading material is also published today. This book would make a nice supplement to other language materials or, if you are well-prepared in this teaching area, you can find original reading material to fill out a balanced program. Your children might have a problem writing about the blacksmith's work and tools. And they might need to know that boys are no longer addressed as "Master" in formal writing or that today isn't spelled "to-day." For grades 3 and 4. Hardcover, 148 pp., $17.95 from Lost Classics Book Company, P.O. Box 3429, Lake Wales, FL 33859-3429; (888) 611-2665.

Intermediate Language Lessons. The second book (for grades 4 to 6) is similar. Modern writing goes by somewhat different rules, for example, in the use of shall and will, and in the frequency of using semicolons. Of course, most information is still appropriate. I notice that state abbreviations have been replaced with modern ones, which tended to spoil the antique flavor. It's fun to see how they wrote in the early 1900s. 316 pages and 301 "lessons." $24.95.

Riggs Institute 4185 S.W. 102nd Ave., Beaverton, OR 97005; (503) 644-5191; fax (503) 644-5191; riggs@riggsinst.org; http://www.riggsinst.org; A non-profit corporation directed by Myrna McCulloch, (503) 646-9459. They sell Spalding's *The Writing Road to Reading* (See Appendix O) and other items including a teacher's edition, a self-study course, phonogram cards and tape, daily lesson plans. For information by mail, send SASE with postage for 3 ounces. Otherwise contact them through one of the other channels mentioned above.

Part 2, Grammar

Audio Memory Publishing Tapes for memorizing rules for topics such as grammar. They are no doubt effective for rote memory. I listened to some tapes several years ago but the publisher didn't appreciate the draft of my review. I would only suggest that you listen to a friend's tape and judge for yourself.

Great Editing Adventure Series, The cover says, "Learn grammar as you discover errors in these exciting stories!" It's to help build skills for 4th to 6th grade students or for 7th or 8th grade review. A brief passage is written on the board or read by the student in the accompanying "Student Book." Then as errors are discovered the reasons for correcting them are discussed. Also new words are learned, and synonyms are found for words expected to be already in the vocabulary. The material is divided conveniently into three, thirty-lesson story units. That's enough for one a day for half of a typical school year. Assuming that other language skills are being studied, the material could be used half of the time, which would be plenty. Another set of three story units is available, but if I used it, I would probably keep it for another year.

The method is good and the stories are interesting. It's better than filling in workbook pages. In fact, it's a good balance between the typical workbook exercises and trying to learn grammar by only writing and reading. If you are using the material for more than one student and asking for their oral observations, be alert to the idea that one might be pushing while others coast, or develop a feeling of inadequacy. This is easy enough to deal with by sometimes alternating between (or among) students for responses. In instructions for both using the student book and the chalkboard, students are to write out the passage correctly. I think that at times, I would expect them to simply mark or write in corrections as one would in typical editing. This is made more difficult by the fact that the work to be corrected is printed white on black. If you copy it on the chalkboard or on paper, your child (or children) can simply mark your work. Also note that the program is designed to teach grammar. Editing could teach more advanced writing skills, too, but serious work in this area is best in high school.

Series 1 Teacher's book, $14; student's book, $9. Ditto for Series 2. Common Sense Press, P.O. Box 1365, 8786 Highway 21, Melrose, FL 32666. (904) 475-5757, or Fax ... call (904) 475-5757 for the nearest dealer. Or contact: LearnCSP@aol .com; http://www.cspress.com.

High School Grammar Basically a set of multiple-choice questions on **CDrom** organized according to the traditional categories of English grammar. Upon opening a topic, the student is confronted with questions to answer. He or she also has opportunity to read a good explanation, to see a general example, and to see the rationale for each solution. This program would work satisfactorily in print media, although you wouldn't hear the gasp or the crash for wrong choices. I'll insert here, that I'm very uncomfortable hearing a "hallelujah" from Handel's Messiah as one of the reinforcements for right answers. The same reinforcements are used for other Pro One CDs. In the videos on the grammar CDs, the instructor simply reads the list of topics in the category just opened. Not much help unless you want to know what he looks and sounds like. Learning grammar requires using it in writing and speaking, so you need more than this disk. Pro One Software, P.O. Box 16317, Las Cruces, NM 88004. (505) 523-6200 (9-5 ET).

Middle School Grammar CD-ROM for Windows. A decent drill program with explanations. Based on multiple-choice questions. It is not sufficient for stand-alone instruction. From Pro One Software, P.O Box 16317, Las Cruces, NM 88004. See the Pro One *High School Grammar* description for more information.

Simply Grammar Description by Diane Waring: Simply Grammar is the only grammar program I've ever seen that allows you to orally teach elements of grammar to your children and that allows them to narrate back to you. This is one of Charlotte Mason's books, revised and expanded by Karen Andreola. It is designed to give you and your children a delightful, peaceful journey though grammar (completely opposite to my experience with grammar in public school!). It is illustrated with 19th century drawings that will enhance your child's creative dialogue with you. Recommended for 4th grade and up. . . ." $24.95 from Lifetime Books & Gifts and other sources (See Appendix Z.)

Part 3, Handwriting

Italic Handwriting Series, 3rd edition, 1994. A set of seven work-textbooks and an instruction manual for teaching the system in schools (and home schools). Our chapter on teaching handwriting describes the system. The series may be used for grades K through 6 or higher. Earlier books teach larger characters for younger children. Students in the system advance from plain letters similar to what is seen in print, to what is called "cursive italic" in which letters are joined but without losing their recognizable simplicity. Children who switch to this system could begin with the book could begin with the book corresponding to the next earlier grade, or they may not need to since each book reviews the basics. The work-textbooks cost $5.75 each or $64 for the set with instruction manual. Portland State University, School of Extended Studies, Continuing Education Publications, P.O. Box 1394, Portland, OR 97207; (800) 547-8887, ext. 4891.

Write Now "A complete self-teaching program for better handwriting." The same system (and publisher) as described for Italic Handwriting Series. For older children and adults who want to improve their writing by learning a new method. 1991, $12.95. Also, from Portland State University.

A Reason for Writing "These penmanship books are so easy to use. . . . Each day the student practices letters or words that will, by the end of the week, complete a verse from the Living Bible. On day five the practice verse is

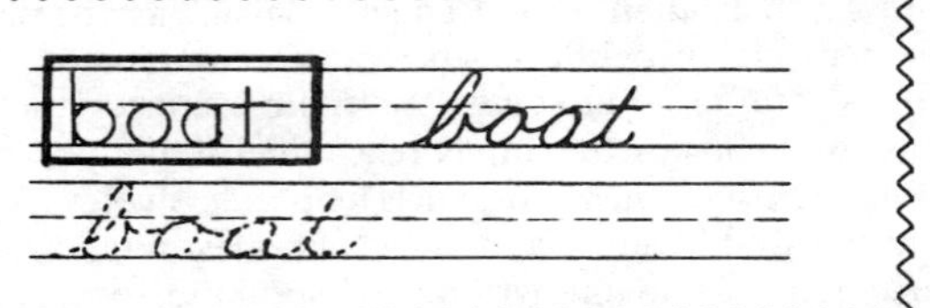

written on pretty border paper which can be displayed, framed, turned into [mats, cards, etc.]." Unless your resources are really tight, get the teacher's book, too. It provides vocabulary and spelling guidance as well as interesting notes about the lessons. The letter formations taught in this series are traditional, but the methods are fresh and practical. I've quoted the first part of this review from the C. J. Huff Books catalog (no longer in service). There are 7 books, one for each grade K-6. List price for each is $8.98. The instruction guide is $9.98. Concerned Communications, P.O. Box 1000, Siloam Springs, AR 72761.

Zaner-Bloser Educational Publishers P.O. Box 16764, Columbus, OH 43216-6764; (800) 421-3018; http://www.zaner-bloser.com. Publishers of Handwriting, spelling, writing, reading/vocabulary, critical thinking, and substance abuse prevention programs for grades K-9.

Part 4, Using the Library

How to Stock a Quality Home Library Inexpensively (3rd edition) Jane A. Williams. This is a practical book to make your home school a growing resource center. And the project sounds like fun, too. The book includes sources for discount book buying and tells how to make selections. The appendix lists other guides for selecting books. $14.95 plus $2.50 handling and tax if to Calif. Bluestocking Press, P.O. Box 1014, Placerville, CA 95667-1014.

Library Science for Christian Schools By Peggy Pickering. For a lesson each week during grades 3 through 6. Topics begin for the 3rd grade with parts of a book, the Dewey decimal system, nonfiction books and using the card or computer catalog for finding books. They finish with reference books and newspapers for the 6th grade. Biographical information on 50 Christian authors is included. There are also crossword and word-finding puzzles. Such activities may be interesting but seem to be mostly busywork. The material is well presented with teacher's guides and student books which are plastic comb bound and reproduced from typewriter-like type.

With the mass of interesting and important things to learn, I question whether this much time should be devoted to library science as a subject. Library skills will get learned when you have a purpose for using them. For example, you won't need a textbook to *teach* your child that newspapers have more current information than bound books. However, unless you are doing unit studies or are using standard language textbooks, you may have to create some of the "purpose."

You might want to get the 3rd grade student's book (fine for 4th or 5th, too). If you see the need you could go from there. Prices range from $9.00 for the 3rd grade textbook to $18.60 for the 6th grade teacher's manual. Add $2.50 per book shipping. Library Skills Curriculum For Christian Schools, 12206 Colbarn Pl., Fishers, IN 46038. (317) 595-9744.

Part 5, Literature, poetry

Only a few books are described here under "literature." Christian and secular textbook publishers often offer anthologies you might want to consider. We show two Gazelle Publications titles which are good, but do not include widely-recognized selections.

Bubbles, A great book of poetry for kids published by Gazelle. It will be back in print soon. (biased opinion).

Emily Dickinson Selected Poems This is one of a series from various literary figures. 62 pp. plus full-color cover, $1 from Dover (26466-1). See Dover in Appendix Y. From reading Emily Dickinson's poetry usually seen in anthologies, I didn't expect the morbid themes and tone of most of her work as represented in this little book.

Poem a Day, A "180 thematic poems and activities" Arranged by Helen H. Moore and mostly written by her. Activities and other books are suggested which relate to the verses. Marked as for K-3 but some older kids will enjoy them, too. 1997. $14.95 from Scholastic Professional Books, 2931 E. McCarty St., Jefferson, MO 65102.

With Joy, Poems for Children, A delightful collection of verses. Find out who the "funny, string bean face" belongs to. Listen while "roundabout, the rain patters on the pane." Here are more little samples: • *I have a cat who doesn't care / If I am here or I am there. / He's quite content to be carefree / and let me worry where is he.* (Echeles). • *At the end of the day, / When I'm tired from play, / and real dirty and all, / My mother will call, / "Bath time! . . ."* (Schaap). • *When I grow up I'd like to be, / a rope, and oh, what / things I'd see! / I'd be yellow. I'd be long. / I'd be thick and very strong. / I would live on board a ship. / And when. . . .* (Schaap).

48 pages, only $2 plus $1 for postage (and add tax if to Mich. or Canada). Gazelle Publications. Address on the back of the title page of this book.

Part 6, Literature, prose or mixed

Enjoying Christian Literature Compiler/Editor Michael J. McHugh points out that "Reading stories is still one of the best ways to develop a proper understanding of how to apply Biblical truth to everyday life." He has a nice collection. A number of the selections were taken from religious fiction prevalent a hundred years ago, literature with explicit moral objectives . Some pieces like "The Theory of Evolution: Just a Matter of Faith," is more a discussion of the topic than a "jewel" of literature. The book's introduction discusses elements of literature, particularly short stories, and it includes questions to help readers examine the stories. Although not as strong as it might be in communicating literary quality, the book is well-suited for the 7th grade, the level for which it was planned. I would prefer this book to one with selections that would draw a student away from truth and righteousness. 184 pp.

The book for Grade 8 is *Studying Christian Literature,* 248 pp., and for grade 9, *Exploring Christian Literature,* 220 pp. They use texts from other publishers for grades 11, and 12 (world, American, and English literature). Each book costs $8. Answer keys available for $1.50. Christian Liberty Press. See contact information in Appendix N.

Family Educator Reading Program, Book 1, Louise L. Luthi explains how to teach using classical children's literature. Then she discusses 10 books telling what to emphasize in each one. She feels that "children should read good books in their entirety from the start." The general teaching outline suggests discussing backgrounds of the book, preparing the student by teaching unfamiliar words that will come up in the story, reading, using questions for comprehension, then grammar, vocabulary (with word lists provided for each book), and composition. In the first story, *The Runaway Bunny,* you would discuss simple sentences and word order. In *Pelle's New Suit,* you would talk about subject and predicate, alphabetizing. In successive books you would deal with such topics as singular and plural, dictionary use, descriptions, apostrophes. Other volumes of the reading program are expected. The value in this book is in showing you how to get the best learning from storybook reading. $8.95 (57 pp.) plus $2 shipping (and tax if Calif.) from The Family Educator, P.O. Box 309, Templeton, CA 93465-0309; (805) 434-0249.

The firm also sells the recommended children's books and other items in harmony with what I would classify as a conservative, good-old-days approach. Ask for their catalog/newsletter.

The Hiding Place As described by Sycamore Tree: The classic story of hiding Jews and life in a concentration camp during World War II written by Corrie ten Boom. Any child studying [WW II] should read this book. Paper. $5.50.

Also available: *The Hiding Place Study Guide* Make your life simple. Vocabulary words and good study questions for each chapter of the book. 6th grade and up.

The Hiding Place Video The original movie filmed in Holland and other authentic European locations. Brings the book to life. 2 hours 25 min. PG. Excellent. $19.95. Add shipping costs.

King Arthur Through the Ages A well-prepared **CDrom** dealing with all aspects of the legendary character. An excellent time line pictures the flow of literature above the date line and the history and culture below. A click on each object reveals basic information about it. King Arthur has been at the heart of a great deal of legend created by many writers including Tennyson and Twain. A number of selections are available on the CD to hear while reading on the screen. A game of finding the holy grail tests what has been learned. After spending half a day or more with the program one would know a great deal about this family of literature as well as acquiring a good overview of British history.

Would I buy it for my kids (if they were still learning at home)? Because of my special concern that the imaginary can become addictive, polluting the springs of spiritual growth I would not. Some of you will feel differently. Maybe, to understand literary allusions, one could justify an overview study of common fictional literary works. This could come at the end of the teen years. Mark Twain, in one of his pieces on the CD expresses surprise that, in the King Arthur story, grown men find sport in duels, seeing who can kill the other.

You will need to reset your monitor to 640 X 480 pixels since the software does not adapt, but this is fairly easy to do in Windows. From Calvert School, 105 Tuscany Rd., Baltimore, MD 21210; (410) 243-6030; Visit http:/www.calvertschool.org; Or write to inquiry@calvertschool.org.

Little Women Description from Sycamore Tree: Louisa May Alcott's classic story based on life at home with her family. I enjoyed this book tremendously as a child, even to the point of having dolls of each of the sisters. . . . $3.99

Also available, *Little Men,* $3.99; *Louisa May Alcott, Her Girlhood Diary* $4.95; *Invincible Louisa. . . .* Find out what really happened to the sisters $5.95.

Trailblazer Books A series described as "Thrilling adventure stories introducing young readers (ages 8–12) to Christian heroes of the past." A brief explanation at the beginning of each book relates the known information to the fictional story. Three of these books, published 1966, are *The Thieves of Tyburn Square, Trial by Poison,* and *The Warrior's Challenge.* They feature respectively: Elizabeth Fry, a Quaker in nineteenth-century England; Mary Selssor, missionary to West Africa, and David Ziesberger, an eighteenth century missionary from Monrovia (now part of the Czech republic) who led to safety a group of American Indians who had accepted Christ. From Bethany House Publishers, 11300 Hampshire Ave., S., Minneapolis, MN 55438; (612) 829-2500.

Part 7, Spelling

Common Sense Spelling Book A reprint of a 1913 book. The author felt that, "Good spelling, like good grammar, is a distinct mark of culture." Exercises and poetry are used for teaching spelling. Students expand their vocabulary while mastering phonetics and spelling. They also learn writing concepts, suffixes, homonyms, synonyms, Latin and Greek prefixes, and Latin words with English derivatives. The book has been republished in two parts, one for grades 1-8 (about 100 pages), and the other for grades 9-12 (over 100 pages).

If you decide to use these books, you will want to check a modern dictionary now and then because our language changes. In fact a dictionary is required by the program. Old is not bad but, in my opinion, it does not prepare children to communicate with the modern world. For example, the word "haycock" is British (book 1, p.15). "Today" is hyphenated on page 85 (beginning of book 2). Oklahoma Indian words are interesting but of little use today. My greater concern is about the usage notes in volume 2. According to one note, "A man may be *amid* enemies but not *among* them." Now "among" is used for both similar and dissimilar things or people. "Amid" is seldom used at all. Another note (p. 149) says "It is wrong to use the word *couple* instead of *two* with days, weeks, miles, etc." The word was then used only for things that were united. Such is no longer the case. My dictionary shows it as a synonym for "several." Of course, most of the usage notes are quite appropriate. The print is small for first graders. Your kids can learn well from these books although they will take more vigilance and explaining than would modern spelling books.

Each volume is priced at $19.95. Both cost $36.95 plus shipping. 1998 from Republic Policy Institute Press, 44519 Foxton Ave. (P.O. Box 789), Lancaster, CA 93584; (800) 244-7196; http://www.rolnet.com/rpip/cssb.html.

How to Teach Any Child to Spell By Gayle Graham. Published by Common Sense Press. Address in Part 2. Not examined.

Spelling Book Subtitle: *Words Most Needed Plus Phonics for Grades 1st - 6th.* A carefully planned manual with words to be learned in larger print. Teaching methods are suggested. With the word lists are studies highlighting such features as phonograms, homonyms, sentences to read or write, origins, and so on. The book would be effective. It could have pictures or color to make it more appealing. 231 pp., $29.95 plus $3 shipping (and 8% for Californians). Laguna Beach Educational books, 245 Grandview, Laguna Beach, CA 92651.

Spelling for Christian Schools A thorough study of words. I have examined the 5th grade materials. Two-thirds of the 214 page, consumable student book is divided into 36 lessons, one for each week of a typical school year. Each lesson (except for the reviews) has a word list, various activities that require focusing on writing and spelling the words, and interesting backgrounds including notes on older words from the King James Bible. The rest of the book directs learning about the dictionary and provides for practice using it. A brief dictionary (25 pages of the book) contains the words to be looked up. The inside back cover is a form for recording scores. 1985, $7.95 plus shipping.

The home teacher's edition would not be necessary, although it would save a little time if one wanted to grade all the exercises. Just remember that a big part of spelling instruction is the list of words to be learned.

Bob Jones University Press, Greenville, SC 29614. Call (800) 845-5731 for questions and short credit card orders from the US and Canada. Local: (803) 242-5100, ext. 3300.

Spelling Power Author Beverly L. Adams-Gordon tried several spelling programs for her daughter then wrote one of her own which brought reasonable success. The book is well planned, and uses a variety of approaches. Spelling games and diagnostic tools are included.

In my opinion, children with a strong phonics preparation need little special emphasis on spelling except for becoming vigilant readers and writers. With a more natural reading program, a regular spelling program may be helpful.

Third edition, 1997. Around 400 pages. $49.95. For another $24.95 they will send you a set of "task cards" to accompany the book. Shipping extra. Castlemoyle Books, 6701 180th St. SW, Lynnwood, WA 98037, (425) 787-2714. Orders: (888) 773-5586. E-mail: beverly@castlemoyle.com; htt;://www.castlemoyle.com; (206) 439-0248.

Spelling Strategies That Work Two early grades teachers share how they made the teaching of spelling practical and sucessful. Instead of giving lists of words to be memorized by rote, they have each child create lists from his or her writing errors. Phonetic and other clues help them remember. Peers and teacher help students edit their papers. Problems are identified and the student gets help. Spelling isn't taught in isolation.

This book for teachers would be a good investment if your young child is having problems with spelling. I think I would first use a traditional spelling book with word lists (where the textbook authors have chosen a particular spelling rule as a focus for the list, adding other words). In a one-on-one situation, your child will move quickly over words easily spelled. Then I would encourage writing even without knowing how to spell all the words. I would ask him or her to make a list of misspelled words (not all at once if there are very many), and I would work with my child to learn principles for troublesome ones. The book has some nice activities. 80 pp., $10.s95 from Scholastic Professional Books, 2931 E. McCarty St., Jefferson City, MO 65102.

Spelling test Check the web site globalvillagemall.com /spelling. The free test (with answers) may convince you that spelling instruction is important. Of course, you will have a chance to buy the program offered.

Part 8, Writing

Beginning Writers Manual The largest, and perhaps most valuable part of this little book is its "spelling checker," a list organized for finding words fast, with simple notes to differentiate among homophones (such as "lode" and "load." Also included are grammar and punctuation rules and a few writing techniques. The "beginning" in the title means grades 4–8. The manual is for more mature readers. By Edward Fry and Elizabeth Sakiey. 128 pp., $14.95 plus $4 shipping. Laguna Beach Educational Books, 245 Grandview, Laguna Beach, CA 92651.

Christian Liberty Academy Composition evaluation service. Call (800) 832-2741 or visit htt;://www.homeschools.org or write Christian Liberty Academy, 502 W. Euclid Ave., Arlington Heights, IL 60004.

Gentle Steps to Writing is for kids (or adults) whose interests and abilities tend to be less academic – those who work better with specific, short assignments with forms to fill in. Suitable for children with learning disabilities. 90 brief learning sessions are outlined. You can see easily what is expected. A computer diskette entitled Fixit accompanies each book. From a menu you may select any one of 30 common writing problems and read how to avoid it. The same information is in the backs of the books. Reading it in print might be easier but the diskette could be valuable if it adds interest. the "Skill Level 1" book corresponds to *Writing Strands* level 2, and skill level 2 to WS level 3. $30 each. Tapes and a manual for judging writing skill are included.

Add $2 per book but not less than $4 for shipping. Satisfaction guaranteed. National Writing Institute, 810 Damon Court, Houston, TX 77006; (800) 688-5375.

Latin and Greek Roots On Line **Int.** http://www.imt.net/~nwwa/roots-class

Learning Vitamins Beginning writing skill building. See under Mathematics in appendix Q.

Poets and Writers Journal Publication suspended.

Rookie Reporter With this **CDrom** kids can choose a story source, gather information, and write a report including "photos" in simple layout software that comes with the program. You click on particular items or person on the screen to "ask" questions which are already written out. In the zoo story, you ask the animals. Gathering information for a real story would be more rewarding, but going through this provides ideas about deciding what information to use and how to put it together. Older kids can do this more effectively.

In the 60-page print manual which accompanies the disk, school subject areas are shown for the various story scenes (scenarios). While math problems, for example, could be created to use the baseball cards scenario, I wouldn't consider the program valuable to teach anything but reporting and writing.

Rookie News Room

1996. From Maridian Creataive Group, 5178 Station Rd. Erie, PA 16510; (800) 695-9427; http://www.home .meridiang.com

Teaching Your Child to Write Writing teacher Cheri Fuller shares her skills in this valuable book. Her goal is not only to show you how to teach writing, but how to help your child love to write. And you will love this excellent resource. Her 16 chapters include ". . . Writing in the Early Years," "How Writers Write. . . ," "Helping Young Writers break Into Print." Other chapters describe many fun activities including making a book to share, newsletters, using the Internet, and book reports. In the back are basic grammar rules, evaluation principles, and publications that accept writing from children and teens. $12, 1997, from Berkley Publishing Group.

Term Paper A simple word processor which automatically sets up sections for the paper in outline form, handling footnotes and including a spell checker. It might be helpful to some, but I would prefer to have more direct control even though it meant more use of the tab key and indent. Major word processors have similar features if you want to use them. Part of a high school package of **CDroms** (for Windows) from Pro One Software.

Writing Conference, The P.O. Box 664, Ottawa KS 66067; (785) 242-0407; jbushman@writingconference.com; http://www.writingconference.com; John H. Bushman, Director. Teaching materials and a magazine publishing student work.

Writing Strands National Writing Institute, 810 Damon Court, Houston, TX 77006; (800) 688-5375. A comprehensive program for teaching writing beginning with preschool oral activities and continuing through 7 more 90-day modules which may be used through the elementary or high school grades. Students are prepared for four types of writing: argumentative, explanatory, creative, and report. Dave Marks, a writing teacher of some 30 years experience, removed his son from elementary school language arts classes because he felt that the activities being used weren't going to add up to writing skill. Then he discovered the need for curriculum materials, too, and developed this program for home teaching.

Marks taught me a new concept. He pointed out that, since learning isolated grammar rules has never been found to improve writing skill, teaching them is impractical. He has similar ideas about spelling. As I see it, we need to know the workings behind enough grammar vocabulary to be able to discuss language conveniently. Spelling, properly taught, ties the skill with other language knowledge. And the ability to write neatly is certainly a communications asset. Still Marks has a good point. We seem to be putting the emphasis in the wrong places. Actually Writing Strands introduces necessary grammar concepts as they become important to writing skills, and it asks the student to make lists of words to learn to spell. Maybe that's enough.

I have examined the manuals for levels 4 (grade 8 or earlier) and 7 (grades 11 or 12, or earlier). The four "strands" at Level 4 are "creative, " "basic," "descriptive," and "organization." Assignment 9, as an example, works on the "descriptive" strand. It is laid out in portions for five days. In the previous lesson the student carefully observed his (or her) house and made a floor plan. This lesson begins the description process with instructions for including various aspects of the home. A model paragraph guides each step, and a conclusion ties ideas together. The home teacher is to be consulted at various points. In the following lesson, another person is shown the description and draws a floor plan from it. This reveals the need for improvements either in the writing or in the reading of the description.

The strands for Levels 6 and 7 are "Creative," "Research/Report," and "Expository." Fiction writing is an advanced program. In addition to the work-text, *Creating Fiction*, Dave Marks has prepared a book for the teacher (or the student), *Understanding Fiction*.

Book prices range from $15.95 for Level 1 (ages 3 to 8), to $22.95 for Level 7 and the fiction books. It seems to me that the numbers could have been a little less. National Writing Institute now offers help for students who might not profit from the main Writing Strands program. See *Gentle Steps To Writing* in this section.

Understanding Writing A language arts curriculum for grades 1–12. Susan Bradrick felt that none of the available programs were adequate for the type of training she wanted her children to have, so with her own educational background in teaching English, she researched what writers wrote about writing, and put together a fat (339 page) notebook of instructions. (You also get a line-drawing template and a pad of forms.) You will need a dictionary and several other reference books. Along the writing trail, you will be teaching attitudes that relate to the topics. You can start in the middle of the first grade, after a phonics program.

The course of study is thorough and well organized. It is based on a Christian perspective. Of course it is not a complete language arts program (neither are other textbooks or programs like Writing Strands). In addition to phonics, you will want to consider language growth in reading, spelling, handwriting, listening and speaking.

The curriculum is divided into levels corresponding to grades. Within the levels are suggestions for weeks and days with examples and instructions. General goals for all the lessons include "Godly communications," "giving of oneself through writing," and "serving through writing." Of course, "Content goals," where most of the study effort is focused, are also shown. If you enter after first grade, you would probably want to drop back a little to be sure the earlier concepts and skills were mastered. By the end of the 6th level the basics have been covered (and most of the pages in the manual). Levels 7 and 8 call for attention to the structure of the language. A choice of supplementary books are used with these levels. A single large block covers grades 9–12 and includes logical reasoning and more complex writing projects.

Anyone wanting to write better can profit from this program. In college, your children would not need the basic composition course and would be getting better grades because of the careful thinking skills necessary for good writing.

Cost: $65 (satisfaction guaranteed) plus $6.50 shipping (and tax for Wash. residents). Bradrick Family Enterprises, Box 2240, Port Orchard, WA 98366.

Writing to God's Glory An organized collection of teaching ideas by Jill Bond. The book is subtitled, *A comprehensive Creative Writing Course from Crayon to Quill.*. Assuming this to imply the academic level of target students, it misses the mark a bit on the crayon end. You can find useful activities for younger children, but it appears to me to e suitable beginning with middle grades although development of some of the sills demands nearly adult maturity of verbal thinking. Varying sentence length, for example, is easy enough to do, but to keep it tuned to good, reader thought flow takes maturity. The subtitle does accurately describe the material as for creative (story) writing. You would want to cover expository writing from another source.

The book's format allows good flexibility with the natural trade off of a bit more effort to know what is best to do when. Textbooks are often taboo with home schoolers, but they do have the advantage of being easier for lesson planning. They can deal with a certain writing skill at one level and cycle back later as new skills are added while the student matures. I think I would begin serious of this book for a child in about the seventh grade and expect to cover major portions of it in two years. Jill does well in avoiding too much drill without forgetting about grammar. I appreciate her emphasis on the "God's glory" part of her title especially as she emphasizes topics like sensitivity, honesty, and responsibility. Some readers, however, may find certain exercises too doctrinally specific.

The 344 pages are perforated and punched. This makes the material more flexible and usable by several children. Priced as valuable material at a penny under $40. Homeschool Press, P.O. Box 254, Elkton, MD 21922–0254; (410) 392–5554.

Part 9, Speech / Communication

Better Vocabulary in 30 Minutes a Day In part, the book's author Edie Schwager (a "she") helps you avoid solecism. I saw this word in a quiz in the back of the book. Maybe you know what it means, but I had to find it in the main list. It means "error or absurdity in usage or meaning. . . ." You can learn new words from reading the dictionary, but the words in this collection are some of the more useful ones you may not know, and they are well explained. The first part of the book is a good commentary on words. This would not be at the top of my list, but for a mature student who may be eager for more power with the English language, its a good choice. 1996, 189 pp. $9.99 plus shipping for your order plus $1.00 for each book from Career Press, P.O. Box 687, Franklin Lakes, NJ 07417. (800) 227-3371.

Communication and Interpersonal Relationships As author Dave Marks points out, his book is not about speech – that is, not speech as we normally think of public speaking. Our spoken (and written) words, however, along with our body language, are critical to our success in relating to people. This book helps us understand how we affect other people and teaches us how to be sensitive to the way *they* feel, fostering success and happiness to both sides. Marks helps young people approach specific types of situations in the right way. He has included a chapter on how to communicate effectively in a classroom situation – important skills for those who come to a large-group situation after spending a number of years under individual instruction at home. The book targets students at the sixth grade and up. Younger children can learn some of the skills, too, by coaching from their parents. This topic, if not this specific book, deserves high priority in your curriculum.

1996, $17.95 (only 73 pp.) from National Writing Institute, 810 Damon Court, Houston, TX 77006; (800) 688-5375.

From Playpen to Podium by Jeff Myers. From Nobel Publishers. Recommended by Marilyn Rockett (not reviewed).

Q

Mathematics and Critical Thinking

This sections in this appendix are:

Part 1, Complete elementary math programs (textbook series).

Part 2, Math materials, elementary

Part 3, Math materials, elementary and Jr./Sr. high

Part 4, Math materials, Jr./Sr. high

Part 5, Thinking skills materials.

Part 1, Complete Mathematics Programs, Elementary

Developmental Mathematics This is the kind of basic self-teaching mathematics workbook series a busy parent looks for. Dr. L. George Saad and his associates have spent years developing and testing this set of materials. By simplifying and adding smaller steps whenever a question or misunderstanding arose, Dr. Saad feels confident that, in most cases, his program will free the parent from the struggle of explanations. Other highlights of this program include: ‡ sixteen workbooks, representing levels, each composed of "units;" ‡ the complete basics of math beginning with counting, progressing into the beginnings of algebra – not a rehash of "new math;" ‡ concepts and mathematical ideas taught as well as factual knowledge and computational skills; ‡ each lesson moves the student from not knowing to the highest level of mastery; ‡ each book contains a record-keeping chart, plus a diagnostic test for every level past the first level; ‡ the teacher's overview includes a "scope and sequence" list, with instructions on how to place a child on the program at the appropriate level. Special instructions to parents guide in the specifics of how to use the program.

The total set of 16 workbooks and 15 teacher's editions are $140 plus $9 shipping and handling. The information brochure shows the program's scope and sequence, and it shows you how to know where to start your child. Student books cost $6. Teacher's editions cost $7. Shipping is extra. Ask for a descriptive brochure. Mathematics Programs Associates, Inc., P.O. Box 2118, Halesite, New York, 11743, (516) 549-9061.

Elementary Math From Bob Jones University Press. The *Math 4 Home School Kit* for example, costs $59 and includes the home teacher's edition, home teacher packet (worksheets, manipulatives, fact review and cards), colorful student worktext, student materials packet, and tests. (800) 845-5731; http://www.bju.edu/press.

Horizons Mathematics A series for K-3 from Alpha Omega. For each grade, you get two colorful, work-texts and a teacher's manual. (Not examined). Address in Appendix Y

Houghton Mifflin Mathematics Review by Lyn Gatling I highly recommend this textbook series. It uses a problem solving, multicultural approach with concepts introduced by hands-on applications. Traditional pencil and paper reviews test abstract skill applications. Integration with other major curriculum areas is facilitated. The layout of each lesson, with colorful graphics, promotes organizational skills, direction following, problem solving, and critical thinking. The authors believe that "Learning mathematics is more than just finding a correct answer. It is a process of exploration and investigation, of discovery and relating new ideas. It is also a process of solving problems and applying learned skills to new problems." Students are led to love mathematics.

The series is available in six languages. Supplemental materials from manipulatives to computer programs are available. To get the teachers editions, purchasers must show a current teaching certificate or ask for purchase to be requested on a school district letterhead. 1995, for K-6. The 5th grade textbook, for example, costs $38.78. The accompanying teachers edition is $71.94. For additional information call (800) 733-2828. See Appendix Y.

Textbook Rental

In some areas, books used in pubic schools are available from local school district offices for a modest rental charge.

Making Math Meaningful A K-6 program embracing the principles of analysis and inductive learning. Published as a series of seven three-ring notebooks which include parent instructions and student worksheets.

A particular objective of Making Math Meaningful is the development of reasoning using mathematics. David Quine, author and developer of the program, seeks to accomplish this by assisting the child to progress through four stages of learning. These stages are 1) using real objects, 2) using physical representations, 3) using pictorial representations, and 4) using symbolic representations. He feels that blending the real-objects stage with the physical and pictorial representations of math concepts provides "meaning" missed in traditional curriculums.

Teaching with meaning is accomplished by providing a balance of student exploration under parent direction. Mr. Quine helps maximize the verbal interaction between parent and child. Every lesson begins with a list of materials needed, what concept is to be taught, and the way to explore the concept. Learning activities are followed by exact words suggested for the parent to say.

The term "inductive teaching strategy" may be meaningless to the average homeschooling parent, yet the steps in accomplishing this provides a full explanation. First, as the student explores with objects he is led to develop a mathematical concept. Second, he learns the name for this concept. Third, he applies the concept and puts it together with other mathematical concepts he already knows. This is inductive teaching.

Each of the six levels of math is priced at one of the more expensive math texts for lower grades. This could be a possible drawback, as would also the almost over-detailed, meticulous approach to the learning of new concepts. Most average and above students can learn the same concepts with fewer worksheets, and less instruction time. For the detailed parent with a student who needs careful instruction to perceive concepts, however, Making Math Meaningful could be the most effective program. A scope and sequence chart is available. Problem solving is the major focus of each level and concepts taught roughly adhere to other mathematical sequences of learning. *Making Math Meaningful* is available from The Cornerstone Curriculum Project, 2006 Flat Creek Place, Richardson, TX 75080. The phone number is (214) 235-5149. –LL.

Mathematics for Christian Living A new series designed to "(1) to emphasize proper Biblical values; (2) to teach useful number facts and skills; (3) to give a balanced emphasis on concepts, computation, and applications; (4) to enable the pupil to do the lessons with a minimum of help from the teacher; and (4) to include reading or reasoning problems that involve a spiritual lesson, a Biblical principle, a challenge, or some usefulness in everyday life." Sample prices for grade 4 are $12.95 for the pupil book (440 pp.), $4.20 for speed drills (168 pp.), $1.10 for tests, $31.65 for two teacher books (904 pp.).

Moving With Math This K-8 curriculum uses manipulatives to help children move from concrete to abstract. To do this, the program directs learning through five modes: ✦ using manipulatives, ✦ drawing pictures, ✦ using real world simulations, ✦ talking about math, and ✦ writing math. The program levels are K-1-2, 3-4, 5-6, 7-8, although each grade materials at the first level may be purchased separately. This level also includes stories, more teacher instructions and connections to computer software.

All programs include pre- and posttests, many review quizzes, reteaching pages, a list of numbered objectives to make record keeping easy, and student books with 240 or more pages for each level. Teacher guides are available separately. Manipulatives are also additional at $38 for grades 1-8 or they may be purchased from a teachers' store. Complete basic sets for each level cost from $45 to $57 without reproducible testing and reteaching pages, teacher guides ($29 to $49) and manipulatives. A catalog and free sample are available from Math Teachers Press, (800) 852-2435. 5100 Gamble Dr., Suite 375, MN, 55416; ckpmtp@aol.com; www.movingwithmath.com.

Open Court Real Math™ According to the publisher's description, "Real Math is a complete K-8 basal mathematics program. It develops understanding while providing plenty of drill and practice in a variety of formats. Problem-solving is integrated into every activity. . . ." *Real Math* is certainly not like other major textbook programs, and it is even more certainly not like historic American school math. It is designed to meet the standards proposed by the National Council of Teachers of Mathematics which I have described in the math chapter. The publisher's representative in my area sent excerpts from two of the teacher's guides which show the student pages, too. I have not seen actual textbooks.

Concepts are developed with story situations. As the story progresses, the student is asked questions to be sure the points are understood. Answers are not provided so that the child needs to think about what is going on. Story characters often misunderstand math principles leaving the student the challenge of figuring out what went wrong (without ever leaving him or her with a false concept). In a second grade story, Mr. Sleeby is discouraged about having so much work to do. He is advised to do half a job each day, and decides to paint a room. He counts and finds it has four walls so he does two. The next day he divides again and does one wall, then half a wall, and so on. When one wall is left the student is asked how much they think Mr. Sleeby will paint. The last of seventeen questions is, "Why would it take Mr. Sleeby forever to finish"? This is a natural way to teach as you discuss the situations together.

Although topics are presented in logical order, several concepts are dealt with in one setting. For example, the concept of infinity is a minor part of the story situation just described, although the word, "infinity" is not mentioned at this point. When the idea comes up later, the student will already have a base to relate to.
Number cubes like dice are used for games. Each game exercises a particular type of calculation. Pencil and paper calculations follow concept development and manipulative practice.

Open Court has a price list for home schoolers, and they sell the teacher's guides (some publishers don't). You can get by with less than their "recommended" items. I would order the student book, the teacher's guide, the thinking story book (stories are in the textbooks after 3rd grade), and the number cubes. When you start to use it, you can add other items like workbooks if you see they are needed. For grade 3, the 1994 prices for these items (in the same order) are: $25.30, 49.70, 18.15, 2.15. Shipping (10%) and tax are extra.

The program you choose should depend partly on your child and what you feel you could teach. For me, this one would likely be first choice. Open Court Publishing Co., Order Dept., P.O. Box 599, Peru, IL 61354-9975; (800) 435-6850 Or in Illinois, (800) 892-6831.

Part 2, Other Math Materials Elementary

Audio Memory Publishing See Appendix P.

Beginning Math at Home An introductory program for young children covering shapes, counting, addition, subtraction, more or less than, tests to measure progress, a game, and a guidebook. $13.95 postpaid from Individualized Education Systems, Poppy Lane Publishing Co., P.O. Box 5136, Fresno, CA 93755; (209) 299-4639.

Brain-Boosting Math Activities Books for each grade with 50 or so fun activities. Some are for groups and will need to be adapted. 1997. $9.95 each. Scholastic Professional Books, 2931 E. McCarty St., Jefferson City, MO 65102.

Cuisenaire® Rods Cuisenaire rods don't look like anything but a bunch of little colored pieces of wood. But, oh, what fun they can be!. And that's all they should be at first. Children (and adults) should play with them, build with them, enjoy them. That's how you grow to love them. Later games can be played with them. . . . Eventually addition, subtraction, multiplication, division, and even algebra can be discovered and taught with them.

What *are* Cuisenaire rods? (pronounced KWEE-zen-air) They are a math manipulative. . . . There are ten different sizes from 1 cm. to 10 cm. in length and in ten different colors. Although the rods can be purchased in an assortment of ways, this set is the most useful for families. 155 rods are included with a sorting tray, which is very important for teaching organizational skills. With the tray you always know when you've lost one too! We have found rods invaluable in actually *feeling* math problems.

This description is from the Lifetime Books and Gifts catalog (see Appendix Z). $19.95

Grocery Cart Math Description by Tina Farewell and Joyce Herzog in the Lifetime Books & Gifts catalog (See Appendix Z). Jaye Hansen, a mom in our local homeschool group, shared her ideas with me and they sounded so tremendous I encouraged her to publish them! Congratulations, Jaye. *–TF.*

Making math relevant is the theme of this new supplementary approach. After basic addition and subtraction facts are mastered, grocery cart math would be fun and educational actually using the facts in every day life. Be prepared to spend some extra time at the grocery store as your child looks for specific information on various items. Includes some study of fats in the diet, making change, making budget-wise choices, etc. *–JH.*

Learning Vitamins Edwin Myers calls his materials "vitamins" for a reason. They are like supplements to build healthy skills. Actually, they are close to being bread and potatoes, too, in some cases. Myers' company offers 6 units in math for skills spanning the first 8 grades, and one unit each in beginning writing and in the alphabetical sequence. In writing, for example, instead of kids copying long strings of boring m's and n's, they make arches in a picture helping the frog jump from one lily pad to another across the pond. For about $17 you get a unit with 16 progressive, one-page exercises. There are 12 copies of each exercise. The child continues repeating a certain exercise until the completion time gets down to a specified level. Then he moves to the next level. The idea makes sense to me. Reproducible masters are also available. If you ask for information you will get explanations and sample exercises to try out. The Providence Project, 14566 NW 110th St., Whitewater, KS 67154; (316) 799-2112.

Mad Minute Description by Joyce Herzog in the Lifetime Books & Gifts catalog (See Appendix Z). I can't believe it! Finally one minute tests for basic skills from first grade through eighth with enough space for even a special child to write an answer or use numeral rubber stamps! . . . Buy one for all the facts you'll need, then reproduce (legally!) or slip inside a page protector and use with dry erase pens and it will last forever! Being done in a minute is part of the thrill and joy, so vary by shortening the time to ½ min. or lengthening it to 1½ min., but never longer or children won't enjoy them. Other ways to vary include doing only half the page, working from top to bottom, and working from right to left. Keep track of progress with a chart. Your kids may ask to do this every day. A wonderful book to supplement *any program! –JH.* My children keep begging me for *Mad Minute. –TF.*

Math-A-Magic This book of tricks offers fun and math exercise for kids but includes deception (trick question) and gambling. Many activities are okay, or you may find them all acceptable. Published by Albert Whitman & Company in paper for $4.95.

Math by Kids A definitely unique book. Editor/author Susan Richman, through her newsletter and as a home schooling mom, encouraged kids to write word problems. And she required them to explain the solutions. So she had a good reason for making this book. Do you have a good reason to get a copy? Can math by kids be good math for kids? In this case, I believe so. The book isn't intended as an "only" math book, but I have an idea that if your kids solve a few of these problems and start cranking out some of their own, they can skip many of the textbook exercises and learn faster as well.

Here are examples of the briefer problems. The "AM–MA" problem is by Jacob Richman, age 9. The toy problem is by Curtis Swoyer, 7.

```
  A M
x M A
M O M
```

+ = $7.00

+ = $8.00

Jenny went to the toy store. She would like to buy a toy truck and a doll house, but they had no price tags. She saw that the balloon had a price tag, which was $5. there was a sign with this picture:

Can you figure out:

How much the truck costs?

How much the doll house costs?

The total of both toys?

In my own teaching, I liked to have students make questions for others to answer. It's fun to be creative. And, by the way, the idea goes for more then math. *Math by Kids* covers a range of skill levels and includes teaching suggestions.

$6.95 postage paid. Add 6% if to Pennsylvania. PA Homeschoolers, RD 2, Box 117, Kittanning, PA 16201. ***9/97***

Math for Every Kid According to author, Janice VanCleave, "This book was written to make the learning of math skills a fun experience and thus encourage the desire to investigate topics involving math in greater depth and with less trepidation." It assumes an understanding of basic operations (addition, subtraction, multiplication, and division) and deals with concepts beyond that but still on the elementary school level. Under the section on "basics" are fractions, multiples, etc. Under "measurements" are such topics as metric lengths, areas of circles, mass, and temperature. The other areas are graphing and geometry (simple concepts). Each chapter begins with purpose and facts, then has problems, exercises (more specific applications), an activity, and solutions. The activity for the chapter on volume of rectangular prisms has you make a paper, 4 inch, cubic box and pour water in it to discover that it holds a quart (or liter). Other activities in the book seem less like busywork to me.

The book is a collection of interesting ways to present important concepts. Activities are included such as making a rough measure of how much water is displaced by putting your hand in a fish bowl.

In 215 pages, it's not enough to substitute for math through grade 7 (the approximate level I judge it to reach). It includes some of what is in math books and some of what might be in science books. I feel it would shine as a supplementary book for use when your child gets bogged down in your regular program or for review – worth the cover price of $10.95. John Wiley & Sons.

Math-It, Advanced Math-It, and ***Pre Math-It*** These programs organize the "tricks" of numbers so that children can forever do away with counting fingers and toes to arrive at addition and multiplication facts. It is not a full math program, but one of the most useful math learning tools in existence, attested by its long life – some 20 years.

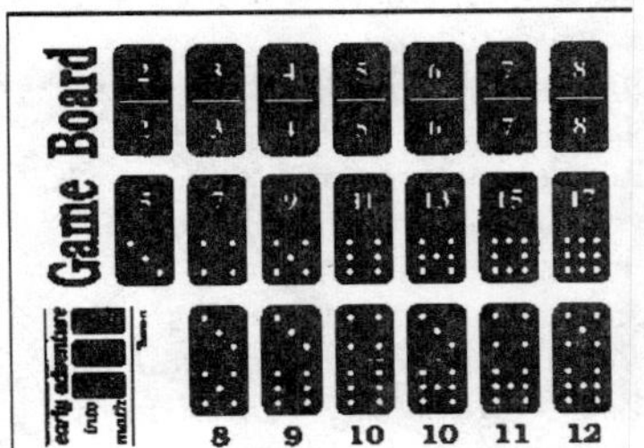

Children of 7 or 8 who can count from 20 to 1 (yes, backwards) while holding their breath and tying their shoes, according to author, Elmer Brooks, are ready for his basic course. Math-It is not a game. It is an activity done by a student alone. Non-consumable, it may be used with children from generation to generation. *Math-It* is not limited to lower grades; even adults are amazed at what they learn from it! Children who will use *Math-It* should spend plenty of time with real-life math experiences until beginning concepts and functions become clear. The first adding concept teaches that whenever you add any number to 9, you think back 1 from the number you are adding, and put "teen " in front of it. Thus your child would need a good grasp of numbers that come before and after a given number. When the student has learned this and all the other "tricks" of numbers, only 6 or 7 math facts are left to be memorized, drastically reducing possible guessing and confusion.

Basic Math-It contains three packets; *Add-It, Doublet* (another addition concept builder) and *Timez-It*. *Advanced Math-It* contains packets teaching percentages, fractions, and decimals.

Basic Math-It costs $34.95 and *Advanced Math-It* costs $19. Shipping is $4 for up to $20 in merchandise, $6 for up to $50, then $8. Order from the publisher, Weimar Institute, (P.O. Box 486, Weimar California; 800-525-9192) or from distributors. *–LL.*

Pre Math-It "For preschoolers and all who need help in basic addition facts." By arranging dominos in a playing attitude and following instructions in the small book that comes with them, you help your child become aware of numbers and how they behave. The combination patterns lead to understanding the numbers and to learning the addition facts. You get a set of quality double-nine dominos, a simple cardboard game board and a 21-page book. All fit into an attractive plastic case. $27.95.

Math-It Guidebook. Methods explained for various math tasks such as adding long columns of numbers and multiplying large numbers. 81 pp., $18.95. *–TW.*

Math Mouse Games, Elementary For $21.95 + $4.50 shipping you get a package of nine games that serve as supplements to whatever math programs you might use with children ages 6 to 11. They include simulated grocery shopping according to a budget and operating a gardening business. The games cover addition, subtraction, multiplication, division, fractions, and decimals. Parents report improvement in attitude when the games are used for practice and reinforcement of math concepts. Grove Publishing, 16172 Huxley Circle, Westminster, CA 92683. Phone: (714) 841-1220; http://www.jatec.com/grove.

Math Mouse Beginner's Games $21.95 + $4.50 shipping. Following the same idea as the Elementary level game set, Beginner's Games are suggested to kids 3 1/2 to 7 years old, although some games can be played by children even younger. Games cover colors, attributes, patterns, number recognition, counting, addition, introductory subtraction, and greater than/less than/equal to concepts.

MathSafari An interactive learning device similar in operation and price to GeoSafari. See my description in Appendix R.

Musical Math Facts **Cass.** Sue Dickson has developed a good substitute for flash cards. The plan uses spiral-bound books of plastic-laminated pages. Using an erasable marker allows doing exercises over and using the book with another child. To conceptualize adding 6 and 7, for example, little green tokens are laid out in circles printed in the book. Counting both groups reveals that there are 13. A similar process is used for multiplication. Subtraction and division are related to addition and multiplication. A few of the ideas are unnecessary crutches that don't directly build natural number concepts (like adding the digits of a teen number to see what is left after subtracting 9), but most are very good. A rap poem is used to teach a trick for multiplying by nine (which doesn't work for over 9 X 10). Singing number songs would certainly help in remembering, although more by rote. The accompaniment on the tapes is sometimes a little too jarring, but the music isn't essential. Level 1 is for addition and substraction. You get a 32 page laminated book, a teacher's book, 1 cassette, plastic tokens, marker, eraser, and sticks. Price, $36 plus shipping. Level 2 for multiplication and division has essentially the same components. Also $36. International Learning Systems, 1000–112th Cir. North, Suite 100, St. Petersburg, FL 33716; (800) 321–8322.

100 Best Ideas for Primary Math Activities for teaching K-3 math. Each activity is organized into the categories of: "outcome," "materials," "teacher prep," "group," and sometimes "group activity," or "one step further." Activity 95, for example introduces the concept of squares of numbers without calling it that. 1 set of 1, 2 sets of 2, and so on, are arranged by placing objects on the table. Students note the number in each set and how the difference between a total and the previous total increases. The "further step" for advanced students discusses how the superscript, 2, means "square" and a number by itself. The activities have "links" to other disciplines like science or language or literature.

These activities, unlike many I've seen, are more than busywork. They help build math concepts. Beyond the first grade or so, a book like this should not replace a systematic teaching plan using a textbook or similar source. Teaching & Learning Co., P.O. Box 10, Carthage, IL 62321; (800) TLC-1234. $9.95 plus $3.50 shipping. (and tax if sent to Illinois).

Providence Project See *Learning Vitamins*.

Splash! "I have a pond in my backyard. I have one turtle, two catfish. . . ." The question at the bottom of each double-spread illustration is, "How many are in my pond?" Through the book, creatures go into and come out. Good counting practice for young preschoolers and covert concepts of addition and subtraction for those a bit older. 30 pp. from Mulberry Books, an imprint of William Morrow. $4.95.

Part 3, Other Math Materials Elementary and Jr./Sr. High

A-Beka math A traditional program. Not examined. See Appendix A for contact information.

Keys To . . . is a series of workbooks, popular with homeschoolers because they start at the easiest level and build concepts with step-by-step diagrams. Parents appreciate clear directions and full explanations. Students like the large numerals and plenty of room to work problems. "Thought bubbles" accompany examples worked in the book to show a process, allowing the student to see *why* the numbers shown are correct.

Keys to Fractions allows the student to identify portions of a whole and divide shapes independently. Even first and second graders can be successful with the first book. Older children who may be struggling with fractions will want to move through the first book quickly to establish any missed concepts that may be the cause of their confusion. This is especially true also of *Keys to Geometry* that begins by asking the student to draw a line between two points, and draw two lines between three points on the page that produces an angle. By building lines, angles and shapes himself, the student is led to progress from the easiest concepts to those more difficult. The first four books in this series can be handled by a 5th or 6th grader while the last eight books would be appropriate for grades seven, eight or even high school. This is an excellent pre-geometry concept builder.

Other sets of math concept builders in this series include *Keys to Decimals* and *Keys to Percents*. The number of books in a set will vary. The decimals set, for example, contains four booklets, plus an "Answers and Notes" booklet and a "Reproducible Tests," booklet. For percents, there are three, and for fractions, four. The program is intended as reinforcement, providing additional explanation to clarify possible misunderstandings. They might be inadequate if used as complete math courses.

Books are $2 ea. Also Apple II software is available. Call (800)-338-7638 to get a catalog of these and other innovative math teaching materials. Or write to Key Curriculum Press, P.O. Box 2304, Berkeley, CA 94702. –*LL* (for "Lorinda Lasher").

The *Keys to* product line now includes a full-year algebra course in 10 books. For a total of $26.90 you get the 10 books and 3 "answers and notes" books. Add 10%, min. $3 for shipping. You could get just one book at first if uncertain. *-TW*

Math-U-See A complete K-12 math program divided into four levels: foundations, intermediate, advanced, and algebra and geometry. Author Steven P. Demme was not pleased with my evaluation opinions, and I have chosen not to publish them. For information contact *Math-U-See*, 1378 River Rd, Drumore, PA 17518-9760.

Saxon Mathematics As a basic incremental set of math materials for elementary and high school levels, the Saxon series of hardbound textbooks is a high favorite among home school parents.

Mr. Saxon [along with other math teachers] believed the key to success in math is to learn a new concept, practice a few problems using it and then review previous concepts through problem solving. Every lesson is designed according to this structure which ensues remembering old concepts while new ideas are being presented. For this reason, the preface to the book emphasizes that the student should use the book properly by working every problem in every practice set and every problem set. Problems are not to be skipped!

One reason for the popularity of the Saxon series is the clear teaching sequence introducing every new concept at the beginning of each lesson. Explanation is followed by several examples worked out in steps. Practice materials. are provided

Saxon 54 is the first of the hardbound texts, formulated for the average to high-achieving fourth grader or low-achieving fifth grader. Each subsequent volume is designed in the same way and named 65, 76, and 87.

Students use the books sequentially although a few can skip 87 going directly from 76 to Algebra 1/2 (pre-algebra) in the 8th grade. In fact, 87 was one of the last texts ready for the upper-grade market making this sequence the only option at that time. Other students move directly from 87 into Algebra I.

Algebra I, II and III include geometry, making a separate geometry course unnecessary. Trigonometry and calculus are also incorporated.

A possible drawback, is that some children become confused if given many different types of problems in one lesson. They may need more practice with only one concept in a lesson for a longer period of time before attempting multiple-concept problems. In addition, high school students who need a geometry credit when returning to a regular high school may find it difficult to establish that geometry was taken.

Home schoolers may purchase a "home school kit" which includes textbook, a full answer booklet, and tests. Examples of 1998 prices are: $47.95 (not including quizzes) for *Math 54*; $51 for the *Algebra 1 / 2* kit; $67 for calculus [These prices seem a little high but other textbooks are expensive, too. -*tw*]. –*LL*.

Part 4, Other Math Materials Jr./Sr. High

***Algebra Explorer Pre-algebra Explorer* CD** From CTC. See *The Trigonometry Explorer* in this part.

Business Math for the Numerically Challenged This book would be a good review for a student weak in simple math and interested in business. The authors explain what operations like addition and subtraction mean which is very important for someone for whom math doesn't make sense. I think they could have done a little better job, however, in getting through to the bottom of it all. First consider the vocabulary. The same students who need this book may not find words easy either. Here's a sentence on p. 65. "A fraction describes two numbers in proportion to one another." The explanation before what I quoted and the example following help, but it would all seem very austere to the target readers. Diagrams help make these things clear. In explaining addition he uses the number line. This is very good, but no time has been given to making sense out of the number line itself. No story of walking six blocks to Joe's house and then two more to the store. "Division is the inverse of multiplication." Very true but not many target readers will know what "inverse" means. A wrong word is used on p. 27. A standard elementary school textbook would be more help if the student didn't feel above taking a good look at it. Leafing through several levels with a teacher's guidance would reveal the best place to begin study. The older student will likely see it with new eyes.. 1998. $11.99 plus shipping from Career Press.

***Making Math Meaningful* (Algebra)** *Principles From Patterns*. I have examined the Algebra I manual. It comes in a binder with 301 pages. The manual is reusable for other family members, but that means making photocopies since the student writes on the pages. $45.00 from The Cornerstone Curriculum Project. (Address in the preceding review above.)

Author/publisher David Quine has designed the course to help the student reason, which he points out is important in daily decision making. He explains, "Your child will be doing more than simply memorizing principles – he will be discovering the principles that govern mathematics. Patterns derived from observations naturally lead to major principles."

Quine writes as a teacher in a class would explain, with examples, stopping now and then for students to do a few exercises to firm up the ideas. As you may remember, quadratic equations have terms with x2 but not higher powers of the variable. They are typically covered as one topic in first-year algebra with explanations and exercises. To give you an idea of how the program works, we will look at the subsection in Principles From Patterns dealing with them. The groundwork is laid carefully. A paper rectangle is cut up. A square (for x2 in a quadratic expression), strips (for the x term) and little squares (for the constant). As the understanding is developed, more rectangles are created, leading on to the idea that solutions to these equations reveal a pattern from which the quadratic formula emerges. Along the way square roots were needed and explained.

Now for my opinion. In general, it's a good program. When I taught algebra, my kids wanted simple operations like canceling this with that. I had to insist that they know why! They wanted quick rules to get them through the homework. This program really would lead students to think.

Everyone needs to work from the concrete to the abstract in understanding math. I'm not convinced, however, that older children need to cut paper in this situation. After cutting up the first rectangle and drawing a few more, the imagination could take over, confirmed by illustrations furnished in the text. I expect many students actually take this shortcut with his materials while some others would need a little more of the cutting.

The quadratic formula could be explained much more quickly, and some of the concrete ideas are as difficult to grasp as the abstract mathematical explanations would be. Although the laborious development of concepts in this course makes it different from some algebra programs, the student's time is not wasted (except for too much cutting). First, the slowly developed ideas have more time to sink in, and also, the mental process required would improve the reasoning ability.

I can see that the student could get dropped in a few places. In a classroom, questions are asked which help the teacher retrace to explain points he took for granted. A second edition will, no doubt, bring improvement. You might need to do some explaining for some children, but probably not much for most. As in any math learning process, you should encourage not going on before each point was well understood. You wouldn't need to be a math whiz since you could go back with your student to find most of the missing ideas.

One other thought, on three words at the bottom of the title page, "NOT FOR RESALE." Although, to me, selling what is mine shouldn't depend on what the original owner (manufacturer) thinks, I would hesitate in this situation, not wanting to do wrong and not wanting to be misunderstood. It's something to keep in mind when you invest.

Multimedia High School Math series **CD** From Pro One Software. I have reviewed a number of CD-ROMs from this firm. They cover the elements typically taught in the courses they cover. I found them generally adequate. But, as with many similar programs, they tend mostly to dish out facts and ask for them back. The techniques of computer multimedia have more potential for excellent teaching. While I point out a number of weaknesses, there are also many strengths that make these programs useful. After general remarks and tell you were to get this software (for Windows), then describe the high school math programs.

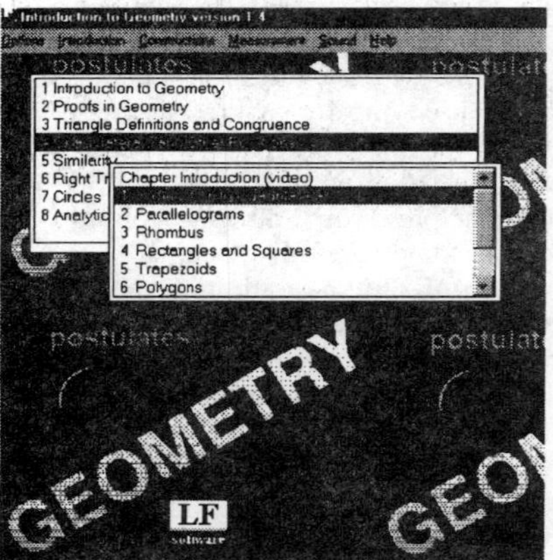

Including video clips of the teacher is a good idea. Often, however, he only reads the list of subtopics in the chapter. The audio is generally clear but poor and the writing on the cards discussed could often be easier to read. I found incidents where two different teachers did not say what they meant (although without causing serious problems).

Student activity is generally limited to answering multiple-choice questions (The typing program is an exception). A "none of these" option is included. This is good because it discourages guessing but I did not see any question where the option was actually the correct answer. The introductory screen could be improved to encourage reviewing the principles before starting to answer the questions.

The CD-ROMs are grouped with 4 to 6 in a boxed and typically street priced at around $39 per set. Individual CDs cost $19 or less. The software may be ordered at list prices from Crimson Distribution, 207 So. Villa, Suite 215, Villa Park, IL 60181; (800) 382-9409. Crimson will send a catalog if you wish. I saw the products in an office supply store and asked for review copies.

Algebra 1 and 2 (From Pro One) You could make these your whole algebra program but I recommend using them to supplement more traditional instruction. They are suitable for drill and review. I'm not totally against multiple-choice questions. Good students will still use their pencils. But the temptation is to simply guess and click. Nothing more is required or suggested. A section in algebra 1 is called "the graphing method of solving an equation" but no graph construction is required and not many are shown. (Graphing was well described earlier.) A graphing module can be opened in algebra 2 but the computer does the drawing. Graphs are flashed on the screen for numbers inserted.

Logistics and instructional quality could be significantly improved in the math programs. Whether by computer, from a book, or by lecture, students need to have a sense of why things work they way they do. Trying to answer questions by memorizing information like, "when both coordinates are positive, the point will be in quadrant I," gives kids reasons to hate math.

Geometry (From Pro One) The structure of this high school program is like the other math CDs published by Pro One. The excellent construction module shows the typical pencil and compass geometric operations step by step. Another module tries to help students know how to measure lengths and angles and fails at both. The answers given for line lengths are consistently wrong, perhaps because of my monitor dimensions.

Real Life Math **Video** A series of videos to enhance any math program being used. Not intended as the basic curriculum. Real Life Math seeks to clear up confusion, solidify concepts and make sense of numbers.

"Teachers" on the screen present math problems with clear graphics, demonstrating how answers are found. Graphs and pictures illustrate every concept. Several short skits help to point out the relevancy of math to daily life and develop interest in learning the concepts thoroughly so they may be used in work situations. The student is instructed and reminded often to put the video on pause, work the problem, and turn on the video again to check the answer. Or he or she might need to back it up and rerun a section where a difficult concept is presented. The speaker reminds the student that the series is not intended to be the main instructional source. It is meant to augment and review class lectures, or homeschooling self-teaching books.

The Video Tutorial Service which produces *Real Life Math*, offers several series of math tutorial aids. Fractions contains a total of 4 videotapes, a workbook and a teacher guide. Decimals has three videotapes, a workbook and teacher guide. For Percents here are 5 tapes with a workbook. Word Problems comes on 5 tapes and black line masters. For students needing another look at step-by-step algebraic equations and how to apply the principles, Video Tutorial Service offers Algebra in five comprehensive tapes and a workbook. This series is meant to supplement the total first year of algebra. Four exciting tapes introduce students to probability, logic, geometry and statistics in Integrated Math.

The series does not end here. For students who plan a definite math-oriented career, Pre-Calculus describes absolute values, graphs in the coordinate plane, the distance formula, circles in the plane, quadratic functions; polynomial functions and graphs, and much more in a 5 videotape series with workbook. Calculus Semesters I and II, (13 videotapes) explain the concepts of calculus with bold computer graphics that allow the student to watch curves shift before them as functions change. Moreover, the theory of calculus is lifted from the dull and boring when students see how calculus will help them reach their goals in engineering, architecture and medicine. –LL.

I viewed one of the fractions tapes. It is good. For your cost figure $39.95 per tape plus $9.95 for shipping (for orders up to $200). I wish the price were a little less. Video Tutorial Service (800) USA-MATH, or write to 205 King's Hwy., Brooklyn, NY 11223. –TW.

Ted Wade writing: Materials for K to 3 are now available. The home schooling kit (student and parent materials, including just what you should say) for kindergarten is $55 plus cost of manipulatives; and for 3rd grade you pay $90. Shipping is extra. Saxon Publishers, 2450 John Saxon Blvd., Norman, 73071. (800) 284-7019; http://www.saxonpub.com.

Secondary Math From Bob Jones University Press. *Fundamentals of Math for Christian Schools* and *Pre-Algebra*. . . . for grades 7 and 8. Also *Algebra 1*. . . , *Geometry*. . . , *Algebra 2*. . . , *Advanced Math*. . . (trigonometry, more algebra, and an introduction to calculus), and *Consumer Math*. . . . Not examined. (800) 845-5731. See Appendix Y for address.

Part 5, Thinking Skills

Critical Thinking Books & Software Materials emphasizing "thinking skills." Many would come in the math category, but science, ethics, and all significant academic areas are also represented. Thinking skills may be more important than memorized facts on college entrance exams. Two of the many games described in the book, A-1 Mathematics are as follows:

> Work with a partner. Take turns calling out a number 1 - 6. As each number is called out, add it to the previous sum. The first player to reach 50 wins. Note: this is a possible place for calculator use.
>
> A player calls out "I have 3 numbers whose sum is 10. One of them is 4 and another is 2. What is the other number?" The individual or team that is correct becomes "it."

Many challenging activity books for older students are also available. Free catalog. P.O. Box 448, Pacific Grove, CA 93950; (800) 458-4849. ct@criticalthinking.com; http://www.criticalthiking.com

Infusing Critical and Creative Thinking into Content Instruction Reviewed in Appendix I.

Private Eye, The On a summer day in 1988, Kerry Ruef was thinking about thinking. She picked up a jeweler's magnifying loupe and began to examine her hand. It immediately reminded her of another planet "dry as a desert, folded and rumpled like the land itself seen from an airplane." The experience helped her realize that the learning, creative mind naturally explores and, by analogies, relates the new to the already known.

Because the close-up views through the loupe provide an opportunity to practice fruitful thinking, Kerry believed she had discovered a way to help children develop their thinking skills. In an experimental program in Seattle public schools, her ideas were tested and refined.

Obviously great thinkers, through the ages, have sharpened their skills without jeweler's loupes, but they have applied basically the same thought processes as those outlined by Kerry Ruef. She identifies the thought steps of looking closely, thinking by analogy, changing scale, and theorizing. By following certain thinking principles while exploring, mental habits are developed that foster creativity and what I call aggressive learning. Time spent going through the program outlined in *The Private Eye Guide / Manual*, is an excellent investment for intellectual achievement in school and throughout life.

The cost is $19.95 plus $3.95 for a loupe. An 8 minute video shows how to use the program in the classroom at elementary, middle school, and high school levels. Send another $15 if you would like a copy. For shipping on a total of up to $25, add $5, otherwise 10% of total. Phone: (206) 784-8813. Fax: (206) 781-2172. Kerry Ruef & Associates Educational Consulting, 7710 31st NW, Seattle, WA 98117.

Quick Flip Questions for Critical Thinking Description from the Sycamore Tree catalog: I fear this most helpful item is lost in our big catalog, but if you can buy only one item, this ought to be it! It is a small *very esay-to-use* set of 97 open-ended questions you can ask your student of any age after reading a story to help with comprehension and critical thinking. Some questions are easy, i.e. "How did . . . happen?" Others are intermediate, such as "What facts would you select to show. . . . ?" More advanced questions include, "How would you justify. . . .?" $3.50.

Trigonometry Explorer, The An award-winning **CDrom** program covering the fundamentals of this math area. I have not examined it, but it looks very interesting. Follows good math teaching principles and includes applications to life situations. CD-ROM $29.95, home teacher's manual (optional) $25 or both for $49.95. Shipping extra.. From CTC; 5009 Cloister Dr., Rockville, MD 20852; (800) 335-0781.

Wff 'n Proof Learning Games Associates, 1490 South Boulevard, Ann Arbor, MI 48104-4699.

Zaner-Bloser Educational Publishers P.O. Box 16764, Columbus, OH 43216-6764; (800) 421-3018; http://www.zaner-bloser.com. Publishers of Handwriting, spelling, writing, reading/vocabulary, critical thinking, and substance abuse prevention programs for grades K-9.

R
Social Studies

This appendix is divided into five parts:
*(**1**) History,*
*(**2**) Geography,*
*(**3**) Culture,*
*(**4**) Government and Economics, and*
*(**5**) Textbooks and Other Topics.*

Part 1, History

Addie Series Addie Across the Prairie begins the series. It tells the story of Addie's trip from Eastern Iowa on the Mississippi River to a new pioneer life on a Dakota homestead. Author Laurie Lawlor helps you share the fears and hopes of Addie and her family as they cross the prairie and set up their new home. Readers learn why this family decided to make such a move in spite of hardships and how they coped with the result of their decision. The book provides an excellent opening for discussions of pioneers and how they lived.

Laurie Lawlor may have made up some of the story in describing the adventures of her own grandmother, but so did Laura Wilder in her "little house" books. It's nice to have an alternative. My wife, Karen (Peterson) who started this review for me, has examined her own roots in the same area of Southeast South Dakota. Geographic references are accurate and I'm sure the basic account is, too. $3.99 in paper.

Sequel books continue the story. In *Addie's Dakota Winter* readers learn how Addie finds a new friend, how the family gets acquainted with homesteaders from other countries who cope with homesickness and a new language; they see the challenges of a pioneer school; and they experience being snowbound in a blizzard. Other titles in the series are *Addie's Long Summer* and *George on his Own*. George was one of Addie's brothers. $3.50 paper. From Albert Whitman & Company.

American Pioneers and Patriots Stories about children as they may have lived in the times of various early leaders in the developing United States. Some are centered on pioneer immigrants from various countries. Good insights. Eight summary concepts and questions and activities for each of the twelve sections. 1995. Christian Liberty Press version of an older book.

Book of the Centuries The following review is by Diana Waring and copied with permission from the catalog from Lifetime Books & Gifts (See Appendix A).

This is the best create-your-own timeline we've yet seen. It is a spiral-bound book with dates at the top, empty pages for drawing pictures, lined pages for text, and pages for drawing maps. One of the special features we appreciate is the way it begins with "In the beginning, God" and goes through other undated biblical events Each of our children will have their own so that they can really personalize their study of history, but you could use one for a whole family and practice generosity and kindness! $19.95. -DW

The same author, Bonnie Dettmer, has written *History Helps*. It provides guidelines for studying history and using the timeline. $11.95. -TW.

Buck Hill Associates Perhaps out of business. The old illustration in this appendix are from the Buck Hill collection.

Calliope A Cobblestone Publishing magazine. (See "Cobblestone" in this appendix.) This one is on topics of world history. The September 1997 issue bears the theme title: *Science and Medicine in Ancient Egypt*. 48 pp. plus cover and annual index insert, and no ads except an order card. Packed with interesting information. One article is "Math and the Egyptians." The numbers system is base-10 with characters up to a million. Exercises are provided. Other article topics include boomerang aerodynamics, unwrapping and creating mummies, prescriptions, word origins, pyramid wood dating, and DNA studies. The November issue, *The Theater in Ancient Greece*, I appreciated a bit less. Some 400 back issues in print.

CLW Explorers A workbook to accompany the Usborne book, *Explorers*. See CLW Weather in Appendix S. CLW Vikings is also available.

CNN Learning CD-ROM *CNN Faces of Conflict*, published annually. A video summary of significant conflicts of the preceding year. The viewer turns a globe and clicks on stars for a report and various other information about each hot spot.

CNN Time Capsule, The defining Moments of. . . ., a quality multimedia presentation of significant world events of the year. The events or situations are classified and background information is also provided. In a special section, the viewer may read key news stories for each day of the year.

The CDs are available for around $40 each from CNN Interactive, One CNN Center, Atlanta, GA 30303. See the CNN web site for current information. http://www.cnn.com

Cobblestone Publishing Producer of a family of periodicals issued as 48-page booklets, each on a specific theme or topic. Some issues are not as helpful as others for character building, but, overall they are well-prepared and interesting. They could be springboards for short-term unit studies. Back issues on related topics are suggested. Magazines in the group are: *Cobblestone, Faces, Calliope,* and *Oddesy*. All are targeted to ages 9 to 14 and have 48 pp. plus cover with essentially no ads. There are a number of feature articles, department articles, including vocabulary notes and contests. Subscriptions, 1 yr. (9 issues), $26.95; 2 yrs., $43.95. Classroom subscriptions (to one address) only $15.95, minimum 3. Add $8/yr. outside the US. Add GST for

Canada. http://cobblestonepub.com; 7 School St., Peterborough, NH 03458-1454; (800) 821-0115.

Cobblestone A magazine covering topics in American history. The fall 1997 issues are *USS Constitution, The Battle of Antienam* (bloodiest of the Civil War), and *The Battle of the Little Bighorn*. The issue on The USS Constitution (which didn't really have iron sides) covers her history, the restoration and tour in July, 1997, and interesting information about old sailing ships. The story of The Battle of the Little Bighorn where Custer and all his men died, is an important lesson in the greed that prompted dealings with native Americans. See Cobblestone Publishing above.

Cut & Assemble Model buildings, furniture, etc. from earlier times. Although building these models won't substitute for studying the events of history, it will provide ideas of how things looked and, to some degree, how they worked. I'll have to confess: I got a little carried away when asking for samples to review. I remember what fun I had making model buildings when I was about 10. Parts for assembly are cut from cardboard pages in full color (12¼" tall). I'll describe the books I have. Those with higher prices have more pages. Dover order numbers are shown. See Dover in Appendix Y.

. . . *An Early New England Village* 12 buildings in H-O scale. A composite from various New England towns. Buildings were constructed between 1740 and 1840. Most are still standing (addresses given). 23536-X $6.95.

. . . *an Old-Fashioned Train* A steam engine, six cars, a station building, a water tower and small items typical of the latter part of the 19th century. It's nice unless you prefer the three-dimensional detail of a model train with wheels that turn. 25324-4. $6.95.

. . . *Paper Dollhouse Furniture* Replication of a boxed toy manufactured in the early 1900s by American Colortype Co. Furniture for bedroom, living room, dining room, and kitchen (with wood stove). 24150-5 $5.95.

. . . *Main Street* 9 buildings in H-O scale. From 1880 to 1930. One is a railway station. 24473-3 $6.95.

Easy-to-Make Lighthouse This and the kit which follows are like the "Cut & Assemble" series. They are a little less complex and, as appropriate (like for fences) the pieces are printed on both sides. Attached buildings and a lifeboat are included along with the lighthouse. Dover 26943-4. $3.50.

Also *Easy-to-Make Western Frontier Fort Blockhouse*, two observation towers, stockade (fence), and 17 figures (some firing their guns). 26266-9. $3.50.

Creation's Child time lines It's not bad to study history in bits and pieces, but understanding causes and effects of events requires seeing time relationships. Paula Carlson, with her husband Paul, have specialized in publishing (and selling) time lines. They sent me three for evaluation. The Simplified U.S. Time Line comes on six 8½ X 11 cards which are cut lengthwise to make twelve. It covers 1400 to 2000 A.D. in ten-year segments. Events marked are predominantly of religious interest. $3.50. The United States Activity Time Line, 1400 - 2000, comes as twelve cards and instruction sheets. The cards have no printing except ruled columns. The sheets have dates, pictures and words identifying events. Instructions suggest how to create your own time line. $7.95. The United States Time Line, Junior Version is similar but larger showing more events. $12.95. $2 shipping for each item. These products will help make history relevant and remembered. The illustrations and text could be of higher graphic quality. (However, the "junior" one has sharper images.) Several other charts are available including a simplified world chart. Creation's Child, P.O. Box 3004 #44, Corvallis, OR 97339; (541) 758-3413.

Early Settler Life Series Fascinating books with explanations and old illustrations or, in a few cases photos of reconstructed scenes. I have seen *Early Travel* (64 pp.) and *Food for the Settler* (96 pp.). Other topics in the series include stores, logging, villages, schools, and medicines. You might want to borrow some of them if you choose not to buy them. 1981-'92. The "food" book describes hunting events, growing food, preserving, fire places and brick ovens, and recipes to try out, all quite interesting. Each $8.95 from Crabtree Publishing Company, 3351 Lang Boulevard, Grand Island, NY 14072.

Earthsearch, *A Kids' Geography Museum in a Book* The books from Klutz press stretch the definition of "book." This one has an aluminum front cover. One page holds a 10-second hourglass (to impress us that, in those seconds, 45 people are born on the earth and 16 die). We also find a cutout that will make a globe when wrapped around a tennis ball, overlays to show contour lines, a paper sextant, more overlays, spinners, bags of rice to show how little many children on our planet have to eat, eight small coins, and more. The section tabs are marked: "trash"; "get lost"; "earth: a wet, dirty, bumpy rock"; "meet the humans (regrettably, including an explanation of evolution)"; and "Caesar's last breath." The book has plenty of entertaining reading, too. I'm having a hard time not being sidetracked from my writing of this review. Since I was a teenager, I have thought that making a museum would be fun. Publishing one never occurred to me.

Author John Cassidy, 1994, 109 pages. $19.95 in stores. See my review of *Explorabook* if you want to order a copy.

Explorers of the New World - CD A history teaching tool covering the era of the explorers of the New World. This program is ideal for middle grade to adult learners, although younger children can profit from it also. A set of information connected with each of three explorers, Columbus, Cortes, and Magellan, is narrated in historical sequence. Spots along a path may be clicked to learn about specific places or episodes of one of the three. Most spots offer numerous related insights. Information in an interactive database is presented about 53 other explorers plus rulers and significant documents. One branch of the program reveals how the explorations have impacted society ever since.

I have not noticed bias in glorifying historical characters or even in excusing the way religious leaders of the times exploited the native peoples. The colonists were responsible for exploiting and killing many people and for wiping out whole nations. A 54-page book comes with the program to make it easy to connect the mass of interactive audio and visual segments. In all, this is a terrific learning tool. It is fun to watch and listen to as well. Excellent educational value, excellent interactive programming.
For Windows or Mac. Future Vision Multimedia, Inc., 300 Airport Executive Park, Nanuet, NY 10954. Web site at www.fvm.com E-mail 75201.1100@compuserve.com

Exploring American History Can history textbooks be written objectively? without trying to teach particular political or religious viewpoints? Maybe not, and these influences are sometimes appropriate, if they don't leave a distorted picture. This particular book is not unique in this sense. It could be useful as its viewpoint is seen and discussed with the young learner. For example, we read about how terrible the Indians were to kill so many people (who, as we know, were so noble and brave to be taking the Indian's land by force), pp. 156, 147. The gross injustices to native Americans in those days isn't often remembered. The statement on page 7 about the maps Columbus made is probably an editorial oversight. It says: "At that time, only half of the world had been discovered." The previous chapter tells about the Vikings and correctly states that Columbus *rediscovered* the land we call America. Of course it's obvious that someone discovered it even before the Vikings since there were people here already. My complaints extend beyond the publisher. The book is an edited republication of an old book. Suggested for the 5th grade, 362, pp., $5.95. The Christian Liberty Press, (See Appendix Y)

Greenleaf Guide to Ancient Egypt Cynthia Shearer has identified half a dozen paperback books on the topic and has written a manual to suggest how to use them for a systematic study of ancient Egypt. For those with a Christian orientation, she recommends studying the Old Testament background to recognize the false religions that Moses and others were faced with. Romans 1 helps clarify the issues. I was impressed with her suggestions for handling the topic of Egyptian goddesses. In addition to the primary texts she suggests others you may want to use. Her manual is divided into ten topical lessons with discussion (or evaluation) questions. The six primary texts include the story *Tut's Mummy, Lost ... and Found,* a book on deserts, one on mummies, and a pictorial description by David Macualay of how a big pyramid was built. In all, an excellent study package, although you will want to cover more than this for social studies during the school year.

The package price of $38.50 figures a discount on the book prices. Substitutions are suggested for older children (grades 5 to 10). In other words you can teach a wide range of ages together – grade 2 and up. Add 10% for shipping. Greanleaf Press, 1570 Old LaGuardo Rd., Lebanon TN 37087; (615) 449-1617; E-mail greenleafp@aol.com e-m sene 1/23

The Greenleaf Guide to Famous Men of the Renaissance & Reformation Two geography lessons (with blank maps) as well as vocabulary and discussion questions for all 29 chapters of the Famous Men book. 1998, 64 pp. $8.95 (not examined).

Renaissance & Reformation Study Package: the "guide" and accompanying books. These are *Famous Men of the Renaissance & Reformation, The Greenleaf Guide to Famous Men of the Renaissance & Reformation, The Italian Renaissance* (from the Living History Series), *Giotto & Medieval Art* (from the Masters of Art Series), *Leonardo: Master of the Renaissance* (from the Masters of Art Series), and *The Protestant Reformation: Major Documents.* Value of $103.29. Package price $92.95. six historical novels are also available for another $135.89.

History Alive Through Music Frosting for your history cake! Listening to folk songs doesn't substitute for a more objective look at history, but the music lets us sense some of the feelings of those who have lived before us. Hear & Learn Publications offers three cassette-plus-book sets (among other items). The first is entitled, *America 1750-1890, The Heart of a New Land* (8½) X 11, 78 pp.) It covers 16 songs with a description of the historical context, illustrations from the times, and simple printed music with words. The second set covers 14 songs and is entitled, *Westward Ho! The Heart of the Old West. Songs* include, "Apple Picker's Reel," "Boll Weevil," "Missionary's Farewell, "San Juan Pig War," and "Home On the Range." Also *Musical Memories of Laura Ingalls Wilder.* The books look nice and the recordings are well done. But realizing the power of music (see my chapter on the topic), I have some special concerns. If being new and different doesn't make songs bad, old doesn't make them good. I do like many of them, though, and you may like them all. They are from popular music of the past. Each set, $19.95 plus $3 shipping. Hear & Learn Publications, 603 SE Morrison Rd., Vancouver, WA 98664; (206) 694-0034.

History In His Hands I have examined Volume II of this series covering "New Testament, early church and the middle ages." Author Joyce Herzog tells the past the way I believe every parent and every parochial school should – from the viewpoint of God's relationship to humanity. The points chosen and the opinions expressed would differ depending on the family or group. In fact, my understanding is a little different on a few points and I would add some she didn't discuss, but overall the idea is a good one. History is indeed "in His hands." (Dan. 2:21, NKJV).

The book is planned as "a read–aloud overview." It is divided into small topics covered in one or a few paragraphs each. Short sentences and clear writing will hold listeners' (and readers') attention. Chapter divisions and a table of contents would have made the book easier to use. It does have a good index. Also I would have wished for a little clearer type and pages easier to turn. It's plastic comb bound. Using this book while drawing also from a more traditional textbook and occasionally other sources would make an excellent history program. 199 pp., 1994. Price: $14.95

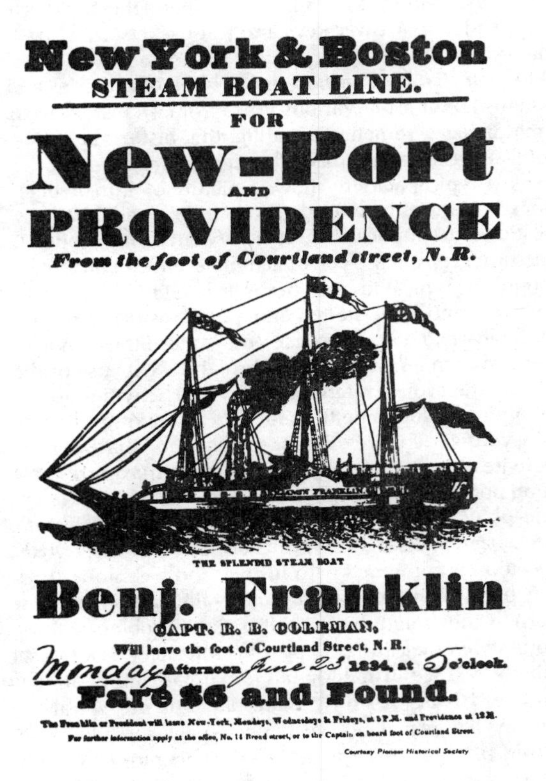

Courtesy Pioneer Historical Society

The study guide summarizes history periods by centuries, which makes up somewhat for a deficiency in the read–aloud book. It also suggests activities, and lists resources. Both books suggest how to teach. The charts to fill in which it includes would be very good for organizing the thoughts for learning. $12.95.

Volume 1 covers time up to the birth of Christ. Read aloud book $9.95. Study guide, $8.95.

Simplified Learning Products. See information at *Scardy Cat Reading System* in Appendix O.

***History Through Art* and *Art and Music* CDrom series** Available from Zane Publishing. See information in Appendix X at *Miriam Webster's Collegiate Dictionary*.

Life in the New World / Life in the Colonies Unit study materials for teaching a Christian perspective of US history for grades 3–6. From Family Christian Press, 487 Myatt Dr., Madison, TN 37115; (615) 860–3000.

The Light and the Glory, *Did God have a plan for America?* Authors Peter Marshall and David Manuel believe God did have a plan. They have researched the ideas of pioneers from Columbus onward and conclude that the plans of these leaders were generally God's plans. The first settlers "saw themselves as called into their new Promised Land in order to found a new Israel, which would be a light to the whole world" (p. 20). The authors feel that this will take relinquishing individual independence to become a covenanted people (p. 358). "In truth, this book is not intended to be a history textbook, but rather a search for the hand of God. . . . It is imperative that we Americans rediscover our spiritual moorings" (p. 22).

Although my conclusions are somewhat different, I share the goals of discovery and of leading people to commitment to God. The book is a well–documented and interesting account of religious influences in the early history of America. 384 pp., Revell, 1977. $12 (and $5 shipping up to $25) from Peter Marshall Ministries, 81, Finlay Rd., Orleans, MA 02653. (800) 879–3298.

A second book, *From Sea to Shining Sea,* covers the quest for religious principles in the expansion of the country from 1787 to 1837. 444 pp., 1986. $12.

The third in the series, *Sounding Fourth the Trumpet,* shows a February 1998 publication date. It covers events up to 1860. $19.99 (hardcover) from Baker Book House.

Lost Classics Book Company Books from the 19th and early 20th centuries described by the publishers as "wholesome historical fiction, solid programs for teaching English . . . and inspiring American history texts that enhance a child's love for his country." From Lost Classics Book Company, P.O. Box 3429, Lake Wales, FL 33859–3429; (888) 611–2665.

Hope and Have. "The fifth volume of The Woodinville Stories contains the experience of Fanny Jane Grant, who from a very naughty girl became a very good one, by the influence of a pure and beautiful example. . . ." This may have been the motive of the writer, but I think he missed his mark. The central story in the book is "The Indian Massacre." Fanny and her friend Ethan witness the murder and scalping of "Aunt Grant" then run for the barn to hide in the hay. The Indians don't find them but set the barn on fire. At the last moment the kids excape through some loose *boards*. Ethan then remembers where Mr. Grant's rifle was hidden. He grabs an Indian boy and Fannie holds and ties him threatening him with a scalping knife. With rifle and pistol the kids threatenen to kill their hostage while they negociate with the Indians. Of course the pray, too. Indians are described as willing to steal anything even from their own people, a racial characterization I would not want my child to absorb in our already hate–filled world. The feelings and behavior of both whites and Indians are probably representative of the times, but age has not made either right. 250 pp., $17.95.

A First Book in American History The purposes of author, Edward Eggleston, were to provide a brief volume for most children who would have the opportunity of little schooling and for others to provide an introduction that would help them enjoy the history they would study later. The stories are interesting, brief views of characters that made early American history. This is obviously not all the American history your elementary school children need partly because it knew nothing of nearly the last hundred years, but it is worthwhile reading. Hardcover, 240 pp. $24.95.

FRANKLIN BEGINS HIS EDUCATION

Our Christian Heritage *Christian perspectives on world and United States History*. A five-book set which I considered deficient in educational quality in 1991. I understand that revisions are being prepared (writing 12/97) no doubt for the better. Our Christian Heritage, Arvada, CO.

Rome & Romans, The Usborne Time Traveler A fascinating book showing in pictures what life was like during the glory of the Roman Empire. Scenes include "the road to Rome," "going to school," "at the baths," building in the city," and "attack!" A brief history is shown at the end. 32 pp.

Sense of History, A This book is more suitable for high school study, although mature middle-school students could learn from it. See Appendix J.

Stories of the Pilgrims The history of a group of people who escaped religious persecution in England and fled to Holland, then to New England. It continues by describing life in their early years on the North American continent. Children in the stories make them interesting reading for children. This is an old book by Margaret Pumphrey worked over by Michael J. McHugh. Although it reveals only one viewpoint of a small part of the early development of the United States, it is definitely worth reading. 244 pp., $6.00. See Christian Liberty Academy in Appendix Y.

Story of Inventions Interesting and wholesome reading about the people who participated in the explosion of technology which has impacted the prosperity of the last two centuries. Chapters on computers and rockets have been added to expand an older book on the topic. Reasonably priced. 1992. From Christian Liberty Academy, 502 W. Euclid Ave., Arlington Heights, IL 60004. Orders only by mail or, if using a credit card (MC/V), by fax to (847) 259-2941.

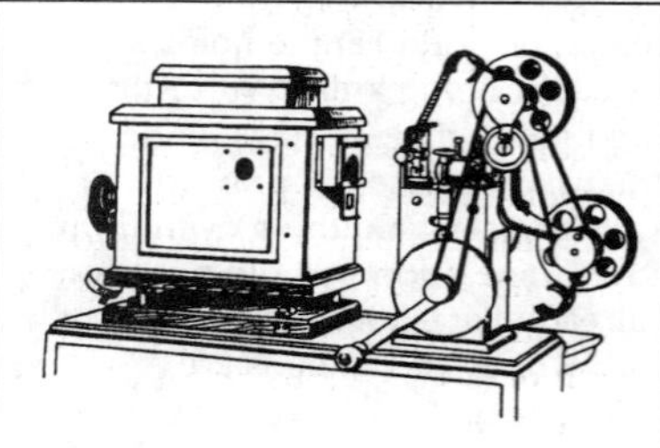

Streams of Civilization High school history textbooks written to reveal Christian influences and developments in history from a typical modern Christian worldview. This is a quality publication designed to be interesting and adequately detailed for in-depth study. It includes timelines, study questions, and suggested projects. I have reviewed Volume 2, covering time from the 1600s to 1996. 438 pp. $19.95 from Christian Liberty Press (see Appendix Y). Answer keys and test packets are also available.

Teaching History Through Art A book of activities and comments about art at various times from prehistory to the late middle ages, sometimes highlighting historic events. General suggestions are made for elementary-level art projects. A typical activity shows a picture of Stonehenge, the massive, ancient stone structures in England. The suggestion is to duplicate the structures in a clay model. Recipes are given. This type of activity seems inefficient, although it is typical in classrooms. It would help the student remember the stones, and a little history and art might be learned, too. Of course you can use the activity in connection with a history lesson, but at the expense of the extra time the project might take. Physical activities are more important for some than for others, and more important for younger children. It just seems to me that we need to evaluate what we are doing with kids to maximize their learning potential at each maturity level.

One-point perspective is introduced with a color print of *The Last Supper*. Several other prints are used similarly. Art appreciation is combined with history and technique. The book is plastic comb bound and many illustrations are not as sharp as they might be but this is not a problem if this fits your style of teaching. 55 pp. plus foil sheet. $12.95 + $3 shipping. 1997. See Visual Manna for contact information.

Time for History A sturdy, blank timeline in a spiral bound, lay-flat format. 500 years per 2-page spread in b.c. years and 100 years per spread in a.d. Spacse for children to add their own insights, pictures, drawings, etc. for each time period. From Homeschool Publishing House, under the same ownership as Homeschool Seller, listed in Appendix Z.

Veritas Press Convinced that the "classical Christian approach" is the way to teach history and not finding suitable materials for establishing an integrated time line, Marlin and Laurie Detweiler decided to fill the need. They have produced five sets of cards, each with a cassette song tape and a list of recommended additional resources. Aside from my concern about the suitability of the medieval system of education, I feel that the 5-by-8 inch cards would succeed well (as intended) in establishing a focal point for a week's history lesson. Each has a picture on one side (usually in color and classical art) and history notes on the other. The sets are numbered chronologically and include cards about biblical history. Probably the Detweilers felt that the value of medieval art in the set I reviewed justified the occasional picture of nude or partly nude figures (mostly children) which were so prevalent in art at that time. I'm sure their motives are pure. I appreciate the statement in their brochure, "After all, if God is sovereign, then He has ruled through all of history, not just that which is recorded in Scripture." Of course we would not interpret apostasy and evil in the name of God as righteousness, as in the case of Job and his friends.

Some sets are $19.95 and some $24.95. Cassettes are $6.95 each. Veritas Press, 19 Funk St., Strasburg, PA 17579; (717) 687-5122; veritasprs@aol.com.

Zane Publishing Series of CD-ROMs. Various topics in the study of history are offered by Zane Publishing which is described at Miriam Webster's Collegiate Dictionary in Appendix Y. One disk is on the US Civil War. Another is entitled 19th Century Revolutions.

Part 2, Geography

Children's Atlas series *The Children's Atlas of Exploration,* which I have examined, is a captivating learning source with two-page spreads for each of 41 areas or types of exploration. Author Antony Mason has tried to be factual. In the book's introduction, he debunks the traditional image of the heroic explorer. Many were motivated more by greed or power.

The spread on Alexander the Great is typical. It begins with a large-print historical summary and highlights significant related features. Persepoli, a city of the conquered King Darius I was burned in revenge. A photograph shows archaeological monuments. Another side bar discusses how Alexander's surveyors counted their steps and left information used for the next 1500 years. Other notes feature the terrain of central Asia which Alexander traversed, the library of Alexandria, and a map of routes taken in conquests. The two large pages have seven illustrations.

Parents who accept the biblical account of early history, however, will want to do some explaining or just leave the book off their list.

Other atlases in the series include The Children's Animal Atlas, . . . Atlas of Civilization, . . . Atlas of People and Places, . . . Space Atlas, . . . Atlas of the Human Body, . . . Atlas of Natural Wonders (1995), and . . . Atlas of the Twentieth Century (1995). 96 pp., 1993, $12.95 (paper) plus 5% shipping, from The Millbrook Press, (800) 462-4703, P.O. Box 335, Brookfield, CT 06804.

Earthsearch, *A Kids' Geography Museum in a Book* The books from Klutz press stretch the definition of "book." This one has an aluminum front cover. One page holds a 10-second hourglass (to impress us that, in those seconds, 45 people are born on the earth and 16 die). We also find a cutout that will make a globe when wrapped around a tennis ball, overlays to show contour lines, a paper sextant, more overlays, spinners, bags of rice to show how little many children on our planet have to eat, eight small coins, and more. The section tabs are marked: "trash"; "get lost"; "earth: a wet, dirty, bumpy rock"; "meet the humans (regrettably, including an explanation of evolution)"; and "Caesar's last breath." The book has plenty of entertaining reading, too. I'm having a hard time not being sidetracked from my writing of this review. Since I was a teenager, I have thought that making a museum would be fun. Publishing one never occurred to me.

Author John Cassidy, 1994, 109 pages. $19.95 in stores. See my review of *Explorabook* in Appendix S, Part 2, if you want to order a copy.

Geography for Every Kid A book covering the principles of the subject, although not much on the less-important specifics of what is where around the globe. The 20 chapters begin with "The Earth in Space." Maps continue through Chapter 12. Several of the other topics are time zones, climate, and populations. Each chapter gives a little information, asks questions, gives exercises (and answers), and describes an activity.

I like the book in general. I would not often have my kids do the activities since they are usually a lot of busywork for the amount of learning. In defense of author Janice VanCleave I should say that such activities are typical in elementary schools. As an example, the chapter on "mapping the ocean floor" would ask students to put rocks and water in a baking dish, then put a ruler across the top, measure down to the rocks at each inch, and make a graph. You probably can't take your kids out on a ship that does sonar measurements, but a video or a book on the topic might produce more learning. Or just read about the experiment and imagine. Then go on to other meaningful learning. On the other hand, young children like (and need) things that keep their hands busy. If you can't take them to see nature in action, busywork activities might be a substitute.

If you are getting your social studies from a variety of sources, this would be a good one to add and would help you cover some topics you might otherwise miss. The exercises andactivities strengthen the concepts. $10.95 postage paid, from the publisher, John Wiley & Sons, 605 3rd Ave., New York, NY 10158-0012; Or with Visa, Mastercard, or Amex, phone (800) CALL-WILEY.

GeoSafari A device like a console which essentially controls sets of matching and true/false questions. A rack holds a large card with questions on the left and right edges. Lights on the device adjacent to the questions indicate questions to be answered. Pressing a number on the keypad brings a sound from the machine indicating right or wrong answers. Two people can compete in the "game." Scores are kept. Sets have 20 or 21 games plus a blank side for you to make your own (12 cards). They are available in science, history, and other areas as well as in geography. Suggested retail price for the console with one set of cards and a DC power converter, $109.90. (not cheap).

A simpler version of the program is available for younger children, same price. And GeoSafari now comes on **CDs** for Windows 95 or Macintosh. These are not simple conversions of the older programs but take advantage of the multimedia, helping you identify bird calls, for example. At this point, early 1998, you may choose among *Animals, Geography, History*, or *Science*. Suggested price $29.95 each.

As with most electronically controlled learning programs, GeoSafari has limitations. It is good either for checking facts that happened to have been taught or for providing the simplest kind of learning (by feedback from guessing). One illustration on the inventions card in the American history set shows and describes an airplane. The student is asked to choose who built and flew it, the Wright brothers or Charles Lindbergh. Here are my opinions on a scale of 1 (worst) to 10 (best): Fun for the amount of learning achieved 7, Learning compared to that from other educational toy choices 6, Significance or depth of learning 4, Cost efficiency 2. Will I toss out the materials I tested after writing this review? Not a chance. The company produces quite a few other learning toys. From the catalog, some look more valuable than others. Call Educational Insights at (800) 933-3277 to find a dealer in your area. http://www.edin.com

Hands-on Geography Games and projects don't make a suitable curriculum — well not usually. This book is an exception. You do need good reference materials to use with it, and at least some attention to a variety of geographical places to focus on. Your kids might not learn as many state capitals (which are of trivial importance anyway) but they will have so much fun pretending they are traveling to certain places, making books, corresponding with someone in another country or having an exchange student, studying mission geography, and so on, that the information will soak in easily. Activities can be modified for maturity levels up through grades 6 or 8. Older kids don't need more geography as an isolated subject of study. If they want it, they do need a more formal program. The choice of study topics, by the way, is a matter of priority. Growing up years pass too fast to learn everything one would like to. 1994-1996. $15 plus $4 shipping from Bright Ideas! Educational Resources, 116 Baltusrol Rd., Dover, DE 19904;(302) 678-3895; Hogan@inet.net.

New A+, U.S. Geography A computer program of 34 "lessons" beginning with general terms and ideas about geography and continuing through various regions (blocks of states and U.S. territories) and landmarks (mostly national parks). It's a good supplement to a geography program. Or if you are getting your social studies from here and there, it would help fill in geography areas you might otherwise miss. A textbook with this or other supplements, in my opinion, would be the best.

The program's greatest weakness is in teaching mostly simple (although usually important) facts while not bringing out general concepts. Your kids will learn the names of states, the mountain chain that produces the most coal, the name of the tallest building, which state the marble came from for the Washington Monument, etc. The ability of these materials to relate history to geography is rather weak. One question, for example, asks the name of the first European to go to Puerto Rico. The more important geography ideas of how people relate to the earth don't seem to be present. I question the idea that pancake syrup often comes from maple trees. I know this is a little picky, but pure maple syrup is uncommon. Of course syrup often includes a little syrup from maple trees. As mentioned in my general comments, a feature allows you to write your own testing items (in the formats the publisher uses), and you can even change the items they provide.

The package advertising brags about the "extensive graphics." I didn't see any graphics in the other A+ programs to get excited about and hoped I would see more here. Some graphics are used for reinforcement, but the graphics for actually getting concepts across are very limited.

For social studies, this publisher also offers world geography and four history modules. Other modules are available for English and Science. For general comments that apply to all the modules, see my review in Appendix S.

This module (and the others) costs $35.95 plus $3 shipping (and $1.50 shipping for each for additional module) A school version has more reporting capability and costs $59.95. Available also for IBM DOS or Windows, and for Macintosh. You may ask for a demo disk. The American Education Corporation, 7506 N. Broadway Extension, Oklahoma City, 73116; (800) 222-2811.

Talking Globe, GeoSafari The globe looks like other globes except it has buttons in its base. Instead of printed questions and beeps as are used for the GeoSafari cards, the questions and feedback are voice recordings (on a memory chip). Its educational value is greater than the card program because your child can look over the globe to find what the capital of a certain country is or if British Columbia is smaller than Saskatchewan. On the negative side, the time limit for responding encourages guessing instead of hunting. Suggested price, $99.95. ($45 would have been better in my opinion) Call (800) 933-3277 to find a dealer or ask a home schooling supplier.

US Geography A series from Zane Publishing. See at Miriam Webster's Collegiate Dictionary in Appendix Y.

Part 3, Culture

Often part of geography

Faces A great periodical subtitles, People, Places, and Cultures." The issue I'm looking at is entitled "Peru, Life in a Rain Forest." The location under study is around the Curanja River, a tributary to the Amazon. A tribe in Eastern Peru is discussed along with wild creatures and conservation. Another issue covers Vietnam including people in various areas, "Hanoi Streets" ". . . Water Puppetry," the language, and a folk tale. People traveling abroad or going as missionaries would profit from back issues relating to areas they will be going to. For general information about *Faces* see Cobblestone Publishing in Part 1.

writing 12/3 *History Resource Guides* "An Integrated Multi-sensory Curriculum for Preschool through High School Students." Autumne Starr Curl and Ranell Curl outline an ungraded course of study following the theme of history from a Christian perspective. The plan is to learn from a variety of sources rather than from traditional textbooks, although the sources could supplement a textbook program. Study is divided into subject areas of: Bible/devotions (which has ties with other subject areas), history, geography, science, music, art, crafts/ projects/field trips, reading/literature, and composition. For the time period of the middle ages, I counted 472 idea items with keys to suggest the levels (preschool, elementary, etc.) for which they are appropriate. The items include: books, magazine articles, parts of encyclopedia articles, games, discussion topics, videos, craft projects, models, field trips, art and music pieces, etc. These take 15 of the 17 pages of the section on the middle ages which is part of the second book. Also covered in the book's 87 pages are general resources, renaissance / reformation, and six world areas. The other two books are *United States History*, and *The Ancient World*. The current editions (1987?) include memory verses and spelling lists.

In her response to the draft of the History Resource Guides *review, Mrs. Curl brought out some significant points. Quoting from her letter:*

In your review, you were seeking a good reason for making activities a significant part of an older student's curriculum. I believe a good reason is simply that many students do not learn best with workbooks and textbooks. You address this topic in *The Home School Manual* on page 80.

My daughter is an actual routine learner, and she thrived on structured curriculum and textbooks – "doing" books. For students such as her, we have included the page breakdowns for such textbooks as. . .. My son, however, is an actual spontaneous learner – "doing" action – who detested structured book work. In striving to keep the love of learning blazing in him, I studied learning styles and discovered that unit studies would allow me to address both my children's educational needs. Our units stretched from Creation to modern time in a chronological format. We read original source woks . . . along with exciting historic novels. . . . The historic periods came alive to my son through our reading coupled with the hands-on projects: We did not just read about frescoes, we actually made one. Many of the projects in our guides were done with my own children as middle schoolers and high schoolers.

My son is now a very well-educated young businessman with two paralegal degrees. . . . He is confident and considers himself fairly intelligent. If we had used primarily textbooks (most of which are dry listings of facts) I know he would have continued to struggle and become convinced he is not bright.

Mrs. Curl writes from professional experience in both home study schools and Christian classroom schools. I could modify what I wrote a little but will leave it and recommend her comments as a valid viewpoint to bring balance to my ideas.

Now for my opinions: The authors obviously don't expect you to cover all the items in a section. For unit studies, these books would provide resource ideas. I would spend most of my time with textbooks that bring the broader perspective to history, but I would also take time out to let my kids dig for interesting knowledge through resources like those in these guides.

For high school, such information would be helpful for writing reports, but I would want a good reason before making such activities a more significant part of the curriculum. Also, in the upper elementary grades outside of social studies, I would want a more structured plan of study.

The books are well prepared and could be useful as mentioned. Custom Curriculum Company, 76504 Poplar St., Oakridge, OR 97463-9452; ccco@efn.org.

Learning About Cultures A look at eight major cultures prominent in the US, including African American, Arabic, Chinese, and Native American. Background descriptions give some understanding of the cultures. Games, literature, celebrations and art provide activities to make the learning fun. You may not want to use activities that conflict with what you understand as truth about God, but there are plenty you won't have any problem with. The whole idea that we can understand and love people with different heritages is so important in this world seething with hatred.

The book is marked for grades 3 to 6 but much of it would be good for younger children, too. 1995, 144 pp. $13.95 plus $3.50 shipping. From Teaching & Learning Company, P.O. Box 10, Carthage, IL 62321; tandlcom@adams.net; http://www.ierc.com/tlc.

Material World An excellent program **CD**-rom showing how people in 30 countries live. The publisher has disappeared.

Towards Peace, Subtitle: Cooperative Games and Activities Selected for Conflict Resolution, Communication Enhancement, Building Self Esteem. Simple, noncompetitive, age-graded activities. For example: (1) Children standing in a circle hold the edges of a sheet and try to get a ball to go through a hole in the center; (2) Acting like an assigned animal while trying to find another person in the group acting like the same animal; (3) Lying on the floor touching the bottoms of another person's feet with the bottoms of your own feet and doing cycling movements together; (4) Telling a story with each person making up one sentence. Among 161 activities, you are bound to find several your children will enjoy. Ba and Josette Luvmour, Center for Educational Guidance, Box 445, North San Juan, CA 95960; http://www.oro.net/~pathfinder. 1989, 96 pp. $7.95 plus $1.50 postage.

Uncle Willie and the Soup Kitchen This pleasant narrative teaches sensitivity to those in need as it describes how soup kitchens operate. 30 pp. from Mulberry Books. $4.95.

Us and Them, A History of Intolerance in America This book exposes what may be the greatest weakness in the fabric of our modern society. Intolerance is not new, of course, but today it is the undoing of peace around the globe. We have seen it in Rwanda and Burundi, in the

Yugoslavia, and we may expect it in other places after this book gets into print. It arises everywhere people near each other believe or look different. Us and Them covers outbreaks of hatred through our history. Historic illustrations and numerous quotations help clarify the sad stories.

At the end of the book, author Jim Carnes expresses his forebodings: "Although this book has focused on our nation's past, it is our present and future that most concern us all." He goes on to describe the increase of hate groups and the willingness of people to support racist incidents.

When the apostle Peter was shown his prejudice by a vision and when he realized that the Holy Spirit was given to the uncircumcised Gentiles, he exclaimed, "I now realize how true it is that God does not show favoritism but accepts men from every nation who fear him and do what is right." (Acts 10:34, NIV)

Us and Them could be the best character-development component in the social studies education of your upper grade or high school child. 132 pp., quality hardcover, $22, Oxford University Press, 1996.

Part 4, Government and Economics

Oval Office: Challenge of the Presidency A multimedia, hands-on learning experience with a set of tasks to perform as US president. The tasks include signing or vetoing a stack of bills from congress, nominating one of four persons to the supreme court, adjusting the budget to send to congress, and campaigning for reelection (preparing a platform, a TV spot, etc.). A globe icon has information about a number of world cities, a set of reference books has information about past presidents, political terms in several foreign languages, etc. In a real presidency a few more variables come into play, but this program will certainly create an intelligent understanding of what the president is doing.

If you decide to purchase, or even borrow, this **CDrom**, I suggest you plan with your youth for a good chunk of learning time for it. A Teacher's Resource kit is available although you won't need it unless you are more serious about the topic than I expect. You should review the decisions and reports that your student writes for learning acquired (not so much for political wisdom). You should expect certain learning from the resources. To broaden the base of information, you might add (or substitute) opinions or hypothetical decisions about issues that face the president at the time of study. From newspapers or even from watching the congress in action on cable TV, a lot could be learned.

From Meridian Creative Group, 5178 Station Rd., Erie, PA 16510-4636; (800) 695-9427; http://www.home.meridiancg.com.

Whatever Happened to Justice? by Richard Maybury. A companion book to *Whatever Happened to Penny Candy?*, written in the same readable format of letters from "Uncle Eric" to his 9th grade nephew. [See Appendix V.] I don't totally agree with everything in the book, but he says many very important things that must be understood by everyone who values his/her freedom as well as his/her country. He tackles such questions as the difference between common law which was "discovered" by application of a Higher Law, an absolute; and political law which was "enacted" and can easily be changed at the whim of a majority of lawmakers (and the dangers of that possibility). The difference between liberty and permission. And the problems when force or fraud get mixed into the equation. Are the 100,000 new laws enacted in a year really helpful? Why? Do we need more government or less? Are we eating our seed corn? Probably best for a student a year or two older than its companion book. A very thought-provoking book that can be a springboard for discussion and research. 1992 edition, 254 pages, $14.95. Add 2.95 for shipping (and tax if Calif.) Bluestocking Press, P. O. Box 1014, Placerville, CA 95667. *–Karen Wade*

Whatever Happened to Penny Candy? by Richard Maybury. A small, readable, paperback that reduces principles of economics to logical, understandable concepts. In an interesting format it explains reasons for inflation and recession, what is meant by money velocity, the meaning of "legal tender" and much more. It's written as a series of letters from "Uncle Eric" to a 9th grade nephew. I'd say most thinking children from grade six and up could understand it. This is a much-overlooked area in most peoples' education, but it's very important to the future of any country's economy. Some concepts in the book are oversimplified but perhaps need to be for this age level. Resources are listed for those who want to dig deeper. Third Edition (1993), 125 pages, $9.95. Add 2.50 for shipping (and tax if Calif.) Bluestocking Press, P.O. Box 1014, Placerville, CA 95667. *–Karen Wade*

Two newer titles by Richard Maybury expand the concepts in the "Penny Candy" book. *The Money Mystery* discusses velocity of currency which affects stability. $8.95. Other titles by this author include *The Clipper Ship Strategy* discusses protection from government interference in the economy. $15.95. *Are You Liberal?. . .* is a book on political philosophies. $9.95. These books have not been examined.

Part 5, Textbooks and Mixed Materials

Adventures in Time and Place An innovative approach to social studies with features such as a pictorial time line and *National Geographic* inserts. Each colorful, multicultural chapter begins with "The Big Picture," and lists of words for important places and people. The series is easily integrated with other subjects. You will also find historical songs, book reviews, and map skills. I highly recommend this textbook series, Grades K–6, 1997 Call (800) 442–9685. As an example, the 5th grade student book costs $37.11, The teacher's Edition is $51.00. *Review by Lyn G. Gatling.*

National Geographic World In the 5th edition of HSM I wrote "I'm disappointed in this magazine. It tries to catch the interest of its readers by wild nonsense." When I sent the clipping back to *World* for updating, editor Susan Tejada diplomatically wrote that she hoped the "wild nonsense" was "an assessment of the magazine's lively design style, not its well-researched and well-balanced substance." She enclosed two recent issues (May and July, 1994). Article topics include the following: blue frogs with poisonous skin; reconstructing an "iceman" for the Denver museum; floating on the Dead Sea; finding hidden Indian faces in an outstanding painting; movie stunt men; kids in sports; a contest about fire prevention; nature fact cards to cut out. There is still a little of what I call nonsense, but you'll find plenty of worthwhile reading and learning. Definitely better than what I remember from before. P.O. Box 2330, Washington, DC 20013–2330; (800) 638–4077. For ages 8 and up. US. $14.95/yr (12 issues); Canada Cn$19.95 (GST incl.); Elsewhere US$22.75. Add tax if MD or DC.

S
Science

This appendix covers natural science including health. It is divided as follows:

(1) *whole curriculum, including textbook series,*
(2) *multi-topic items,*
(3) *multi-topic items for jr. and sr. high*
(4) *specific subject-areas,*
(5) *specific subject areas for jr. and sr. high*
(6) *magazines, and*
(7) *equipment.*

Part 1, Whole Curriculum Publications

Considering God's Creation An elementary school level course covering life science and earth science (but not physical science). The format for each lesson includes: preparation, vocabulary, introduction, song/poem, activity, Bible reading, notebook, "evolution stumpers," review and digging deeper. This basic information is in the first 110 pages of the book. Another reproducible 150 pages (not counting the backs which are mostly blank for ease in use) are sheets for the activities. The well-organized program is divided into 36 lessons which would make one a week for a typical school year. If you like the unit study idea, you could go through this program for the first year (not first grade), then branch into fields of interest including the physical sciences. Also, because the material is well organized, you could use it to supplement another program including a unit study. In browsing, the integrity of the information looks good. A couple of the anti-evolution items I noticed need to be checked with a scientist in the field. I'm convinced that the evolutionary theory is wrong, but simplistic arguments that fall apart with more mature study could later lead to doubt. Of course the risk depends on how you approach the whole topic.

Send $29.95 for book and a cassette, plus $3.50 postage, to Eagle's Wings, P.O. Box 502, Duncan, 73534; (580) 252-1555.

Good Science The program teaches science from a creationist viewpoint. Divided into two levels: K-3 and 4-6. Teachers (at home or school) receive a fat manual for one level or the other. Students use work/textbooks. Many pages in the back of the manual are prepared to be photocopied. Author Richard Bliss writes, "Here is a program that is not only centered around the child's natural development, with God's attributes as the central theme, but also contains significant scientific content as well as the processes of science." The manual is like a training course and teaching guide with specific instructions for more activities than you are expected to use. Cassettes are available, but you can get along without them since they cover what is in the manual.

Each level package, $59.95 and $12.95 more for the workbook. Shipping, 15%, $10 max. Institute for Creation Research, 10946 Woodside Ave., N., Santee, CA 92071; (619) 448-0900.

Science for Christian Schools A series for grades 1 to 12 from Bob Jones University Press. I reviewed materials for the 6th grade: *Science 6 for Christian Schools*, 2nd ed, 1991. The 252 page textbook covers a nice variety of topics: earthquakes, volcanoes, stars, space exploration, respiratory system, [blood] circulation, laws of motion, nuclear energy, chemistry, animal behavior, the biosphere, and balance in nature, plus glossary and index. In addition to the textbook (hard or soft cover), you may purchase the *Notebook Packet* (worksheets for recording data, etc.), the 327 page *Home Teacher's Edition* (with reduced, black and white students' pages and organized teaching instructions), and the *Home Teacher Packet* (visuals, charts, etc.). A *TestBank* (which I have not seen) is also available.

The textbook is visually and conceptually appealing. It has more "finding out" activities than I would probably use (which gives an opportunity to make choices). The discussion questions in the teacher's edition could be used for a guide in evaluation. The occasional Bible verses and comments seem appropriate. I did catch a minor mistake. The volcanic rocks pictured on page 32 are not correctly identified. Of course, you are apt to find goofs in my book, too.

You could, perhaps, get by with only the textbook. Here are the other materials I would add in descending order of importance: the teacher's edition, the notebook packet, the tests, and the home teacher's packet.

One quick idea for an approach that would depend less on the teacher's edition would be to ask your child to keep a notebook of science concepts and science definitions/descriptions seen in the textbook. You could discuss them together and refine them. Then they could be a guide in deciding what to test on.

Areas covered for higher grades are: life science, 7; earth science, 8; basic science (scientific method, measurement), 9; biology, 10; chemistry, 11; and physics, 12. Basic lab equipment for grades 1-6 is available.

BJU Press, Greenville, SC 29614. Call (800) 845-5731 for questions and orders from U.S. and Canada. Local: (803) 242-5100, ext. 3300.

Science/Health *Discover God's Creation* is the textbook in this elementary school series which I have examined. It is planned for a combined class of grades 5 or 6. (A similar book covering different topics is used with these two grades on alternate years.) Study is directed in four major science areas: Earth's Structure, The Human Body, Take Care [of your health], and Electricity and Magnetism. The book is interesting. It is clearly written and well illustrated. After discussing the evidence of movement of sections of the earth called plates, a section with the title "Biblical Perspective" explains how this corresponds with the Bible record.

"Because plates are now moving slowly, many evolutionists believe that the plates have always moved slowly. At today's speed, it would have taken 200 million years for South America and Africa to have moved so far apart. . . . Genesis 1 records that God created the dry land and seas on the third day. It is possible that He created the dry land in the form of Pangea [the connected land mass thought to have split up into today's continents]. During the Flood, however, great changes happened. . . ."

Acne and skin physiology is explained in a section of the chapter, "Integumentary System. In the next section we read, "Every year more than 8000 people in North America die from skin cancer. You can reduce your chances. . . ." On the next page (235) we begin reading about the excretory system. A simple experiment using straws and lime water demonstrates how more carbon dioxide is exhaled from the lungs after exercise.

Each section shows words to understand, the objective and review questions. Often experiments and tables are included. At the ends of chapters are suggestions for projects, questions or problems to solve and review questions. At the end of the book is a glossary and of course an index.

The series is published for the Seventh-day Adventist North American office of education. I haven't read all 487 pages, but I don't see anything that any parent who accepts the Genesis record in the Bible would object to. It's an excellent learning tool with clear, full-color illustrations. Cost is only $31.50. The teacher's edition is another $35.50, and a resource book (for experiments) is also $35.50. You could get along with only the text, or you might want only the teacher's manual. If you would like to examine the materials, ask an Adventist bookstore or school. Or call (800) 765-6955.

Science Scope All you need for teaching science is an encyclopedia or the public library (and some household items for experiments). To avoid leaving significant gaps, you should look at a list like we show in Appendix G. Or, to better organize your teaching, you could use the curriculum outline prepared by Kathryn Stout. She shows you what to cover and at what academic level. The levels are: primary, intermediate, junior high, senior high (grades 1-3, 4-6, 7-9, 10-12). Under physical science, category "energy," category "heat energy," she shows objectives for discovery, explaining, identifying, etc. and she would teach it at all levels. For primary, one line reads: "Identify many uses for heat. *(dry clothes, cook food, keep us warm)*." An item under junior-senior high school reads, "Define engine. *(A machine that changes heat energy into mechanical energy.)*" 109 pp., $15 plus $1.50 shipping. See *Design-a-Study* in Appendix Y.

Science the Search "Discovering the Principles that Govern God's Creation Through 'Hands-on' Activities." (1990) In four notebooks, The Cornerstone Curriculum Project science program proposes to teach the K-8 foundation needed for continuing study in the natural sciences. It offers directions for exploring and, through the exploration, concepts. Revisions may have been made since the time of this review.

Volumes 1 and 2 cover "property," "interaction," and "system." Volumes 3 and 4 (which I have examined) seem to be organized along the developmental sequence of subsystems, variables, concepts, and scientific models. The concepts include "energy systems" for physical science, and "ecosystems," for life science. Christianity topics appear in a few places. The four volumes cover these areas in 136 activities with the suggestion of doing one a week. (total of 250+ pp.) Now for my opinions:

On learning theory: The organizational pattern just described, follows the idea that learning should progress from particulars to complexities. (This is known as induction.) Here this transition is to take seven years. In my chapter, "Structure for Learning," I explain my concerns about this concept. Not so many years ago, science teachers were learning the wonderful idea of "inquiry." After all, don't we remember better what we find out for ourselves? As in the case of "new math" it didn't work so well in practice. If you try to invent all your own wheels, you never get around to the seats and the turn signals. It takes too long. And taking too long would soon make it tedious for the students, too. In my chapter on teaching science, I explain process versus content. An emphasis on process makes sense for the elementary years, and this course covers a lot of it. Kids also enjoy learning from books and from people just telling them how things work.

On the plan for teaching: For every activity, you are told just what to do and say as you guide the finding-out process. This is nice, but it will require lots of time. You are never asked to have the student read certain information and follow the directions. On the positive side, you can teach several grades at once. Kids at various levels can participate. You are not given instructions for this, but you can figure out what allowances to make. Older children can help the younger ones while they all learn.

On accuracy of information: I zeroed in on activities developing the concept of energy. I found some explanations which could lead to wrong ideas. Activity 94 was a case in point. It may have been corrected.

On equipment: You use mostly simple things. A kit is included for each volume with a few less common items.

In conclusion, although I would personally choose a more traditional program, this one will probably work quite well. It has many good features and learning occurs by more than one good method. If you use it, I would suggest (1) having your students read some of the instructions the author has planned for you to give, (2) discussing all the experiments, but not doing all of them, and (3) letting the kids choose additional interesting topics to explore, possibly ones related to what they are studying in the manual. They could go to the library, talk to resource people, and make some kind of report or presentation on what they learn.

The four books (with kits): *Properties* and *Interactions & Systems* (K-3) *Subsystems & Variables* (3-5); and *Scientific Models* (5-8). The Cornerstone Curriculum Project, 2006 Flat Creek Place, Richardson, TX 75080.

Part 2, Multi-topic Publications

Backyard Scientist, Jane Hoffman shares her enthusiasm through her books of well-explained science experiments. She offers five brief books of experiments. They are well illustrated. *Exploring Earthworms With Me* teaches how to handle live creatures and outlines experiments with earthworms. Backyard Scientist, P.O. Box 16966, Irvine, CA 92713.

Explorabook, *A Kid's Science Museum in a Book* A unique volume by John Cassidy introduced with these words: "First of all, please do not simply read this book. If you own the Explorabook for more than a few hours, and do not bend or smear any of its pages, nor tear open the agar packets nor attempt to lose the attached magnet, then you are probably not using it correctly. It's a tool. Please treat it that way." Although librarians might not take to that introduction, it represents the book's lighthearted approach. The activity sections are listed as: "magnetism," "light wave craziness," "illusions," "hair dryer science," "biology," and "ouchless physics."

The "book" is captivating and will teach a good deal of science. My only personal reservation is its air of carelessness. Notice the following sentence: "First off, you should know that good magic depends on good lying." The intent isn't to foster dishonesty, but such may well be the effect. Of course, not everyone will share my sensitivity.
1991, 100 stiff pages. $18.95 in retail stores; or add $5 and order from Klutz Press, 455 Portage Ave., Palo Alto, CA 94306, (415) 424-0739.

Dangerous Creatures CD-ROM. The production is generally well-designed and can't help but teach a many facts about wild animals. The various sights and sounds can be approached from several different perspectives. You can choose to follow a "tour guide." with a voice telling you, for example, about dangers in watching real nature, or how difficult it is to do nature photography. You can also learn by selecting habitats, by various world continents, or by considering various features of the animals such as their protection devices. At any screen you can click to branch off onto one of the other paths of exploration or to watch a video clip if there is one. Of course you will see some of the same scenes under different lines of discussion, but there are plenty and repetition helps learning. To find specific information, you can use the index or the table of contents. As extras, you can print out pictures form the CD, and you can even choose a screen saver. I'm not sure the animal footprint one I installed saves the screen from anything, but it does relieve boredom if you sit and stare at it.

Other titles in the *Exploration Series* include *Cinemania, Golf, Dinosaurs, Ancient Lands, Multimedia Mozart, Multimedia Beethoven, Complete NBA Basketball, Art Gallery*, and *Musical Instruments*. I'm sure more are being added. Microsoft, 1996.

Let's Explore Science A set of attractive, well-manufactured books suitable for children aged 4 to 7. I'm looking at two volumes my wife purchased through a party plan. One is *Make it Balance*. Activities are described which your kids will enjoy. The center-of-gravity concept is demonstrated in various ways ending with the old trick of toppling a row of dominos stood on end. The other book is *Building Things*. It begins with feeling to determine what something is made of and it ends with how things are changed by water, sand paper, and paint. Among other concepts explored is the difference between things as they come in nature and manufactured things. For experiments in the series, parents gather simple materials, give guidance, and let the children do the thinking. This process stimulates the intellect and is great fun.

The per-volume price marked on the books is $9.95, not unreasonable for a fancy book. My wife paid less. There are 14 sheets of quality paper between the durable covers. The books are made in Belgium. All of the information from either book, which you need to know as a parent, could have been printed on two sides of an ordinary sheet of paper in adult-readable type with a dozen small line drawings. But then we wouldn't want to pay anything to the people that would put the ideas together and those who would sell the paper. American edition 1993, Dorling Kindersley, 232 Madison Ave., New York, MN 10016. Or find a home dealer near you.

My First Science Notebook Science may be very casual for the K-3 grade level. This notebook is a good upgrade for that teaching kids to be observant and to record what they see (like drawing a dog and marking all its parts). One experiment is measuring plant growth and producing a graph – probably better for grades 2 or 3 than for K or 1. 1992, 36 pp. (36 sheets because they are blank on the back sides). The quality of production could stand some improvement, but it's okay. Castle Heights Press is listed in this appendix.

Secrets of the Forest "Shhhh. Something's moving in the bushes, and Cari and Andy can't wait to find out what it is!. . . . You'll discover all kinds of exciting things about nature and its Creator. You'll meet God's woodland builders, bankers, and garbage collectors." Leaning adventures inspired by the childhood experience of author, Colleen Reece. Easy print for young readers. For ages 6 to 10. 1997. 32 chapters in 143 pp. from Review & Herald Publishing Assn. See *Forever Stories* in Appendix N or call (800) 765-6955.

New A+ The review that follows is for a diskette version of the program. It is now on **CDrom**. I have not had opportunity to review it. From the descriptive literature, I see that the gambling game and the authoring feature are still included. Certainly the revision includes taking advantage of the better technology. Ask for information.

Science I, II, III, and IV. A software program for use with Windows (or DOS). Described as: "four programs designed for grades 1-2, 3-4, 5-6, 7-8 respectively, for facts and information on general science subjects covering earth science, life science, and biology. The scope and complexity of information increases with the level recommended for each program."

First a general description that applies to all the modules in this series (on science and on other subjects) produced by The American Education Corporation. The instructional format has four phases: (1) study one of the 36 lessons, (2) practice for the test, (3) take the test, (4) play the game. The lesson information may be read from the screen. On the bottom part of the screen are study questions. For the practice test, immediate feedback is given. Questions are true/false, multiple choice, or key in a very simple answer. In the practice phase, a "hint" button for the key-in questions gives one letter at a time to help you guess. The test itself has some of the same questions and shows which of the ten are right or wrong when you have finished. You can ask for the right answers on ones you missed. If you get 7 or more correct a hangman-type game appears. In addition to the lessons just described, are the following auxiliary features: (1) records are kept of scores by student names, (2) lesson material, tests, puzzle answers, and scores may be printed, and (3) new lessons may be created following the same format.

On educational value. This system shares the general weaknesses of workbooks. It tends to limit instruction to simple recall of objective information. With the four instructional phases, however, it does have more learning value than many software programs. And it's better than many things your kids could be doing with the computer.

On the game: It is modeled after casino slot machines. As a player, you look for letters to make a certain phrase. For example, the clue "A very, very big storm" is to lead to "Jupiter's red spot." You start with bundles of bills and click on the "pull" button to get letters which you may choose for the locations in the phrase. When you get dollar signs or choose appropriate letters in the three little windows, you are given coins which are exchanged for bills. When your total reaches $1000, the game is over. Although this is not gambling real money, I would not subject my children to its weakening influence. I would choose different software. Of course, your feeling about this may be different. Maybe the publishers will take the hint and change the game.

On the computer interface: The variety of options for learning are good (although the objectives themselves are limited as mentioned). I found using the program to be a little awkward. At the end of a study session or test, for example, you find yourself recycling through the same questions until you choose "quit" to get out of it. That option isn't at first comfortable, since "quit" often means leaving the whole system. To respond to the multiple choice items, you must click on a choice with your mouse. You don't have the option of using the keyboard to indicate the letter for your choice. On the positive side, you have the flexibility of aborting an activity and going on. The program hangs up, however, if you choose to stop the game before all the piles of your starting money are laid down. The graphics are advertised as a special feature. They do add a little interest to the software, but I have not been particularly impressed with their quality or the appropriateness of their use in particular situations.

On the lesson-writing facility: You may write a lesson (except for the study material) using the format of other lessons, or you may edit one of the lessons in the module. You write a question with explanation, choices, feedback for the wrong choices, etc. When you have completed your ten questions and save your work, it appears on the menu of lessons in that module. This is a nice feature that home teachers might use less than classroom teachers, but your kids will have fun playing with it and might learn more by writing questions than by trying to answer them.

For these modules, Science: I have taken a close look at Science I, II, and III. Some early childhood concepts relating to science are recognition of colors and shapes and the use of our senses to perceive the world around us. We tend to turn sense into nonsense, however, when we try to "teach" these fundamental concepts with truth/false, multiple choice, and fill-in-the-blank questions. Some of the items in Science I have fallen into this trap. Beyond this, I found a few other questionable questions. For example, "Practicing good safety habits is silly, T/F." and "Little robins grow up to be big robins, T/F." This latter one makes a little more sense when compared to what tadpoles become. Science III seems to teach a little more meaningful concepts.

Topics covered for Science I include plants, animals, space, simple machines, light, sound, heat, and weather. For Science II, the earth, minerals, the solar system, magnetism, electricity, machines, life cycles, etc. For Science III, weather, earthquakes, volcanoes, the solar system, cells, electricity, minerals, etc. In the lessons I have browsed in the three modules, I have not seen evolutionary theory taught. Many conservative people, however, will object to the game mentioned above.

These programs should not constitute a full science curriculum, but they could well supplement a program that was weak in making sure that basic concepts were really learned.

This module (and the others) costs $35.95 plus $3 shipping (and $1.50 shipping for each for additional module) A school version has more reporting capability and costs $59.95. Available for IBM DOS or Windows, and for Macintosh. You may ask for a demo disk. The American Education Corporation, 7506 N. Broadway, Oklahoma City, 73116; (800) 222-2811.

Science Activities for Christian Children, 3rd edition. Clifton Keller and Jeanette Appel. Gazelle Publications. Eighty-nine learning adventures using things around the house. For grades 1-6. Emphasizes process skills such as observing, measuring, and predicting. A spiritual lesson is suggested for each activity. Bible references are listed for the parent-teacher to consider discussing. A list of science topics in the back of the book classifies the various activities for use with other science programs or for study in chosen areas. Titles of a few of the activities are: Find your rock, String-and-can telephone, Find the largest, Filtering, Constellations in a box, Weather check, Floating boats, Effects of inertia, Vibrating string, Making colors, Percentage germination, etc. 127 pages. Well worth its price of only $6.50 (7¢ per activity). For U.S. shipping, add $1.50 ground, or $2.50 air. And tax if to Michigan. Address on back of title page. (Since it's hard to say negative things about my own publication, this description may not be totally objective.) Satisfaction guaranteed.

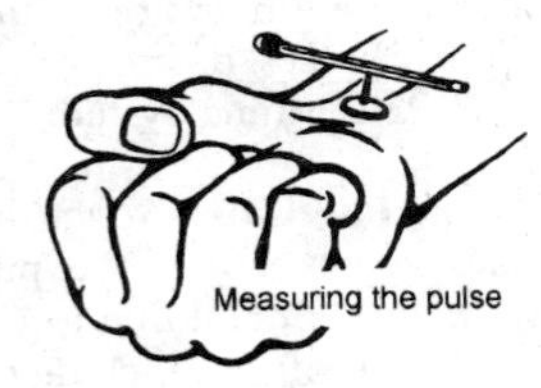
Measuring the pulse

Science Almanac for Kids, The Interesting facts of science such as how many bones there are in the human body, what black holes are, and the life cycle of a fern. The book is well written for kids 8 to 12. Each of the ten areas covered is simply and coherently developed. This 128 page book presents a good background of science for the middle grades and includes interesting illustrations of the principles. Unfortunately for those of us who accept the biblical record, the book explains that life started billions of years ago after the earth was formed. The concept of evolution, however, does not seem to color the rest of the book. Topics are the physical world, chemistry, earth, the atmosphere, water, plants, animals, ecology, the human body, and space. $7.95 plus $2.40 shipping from McClanahan Book Co., 23 W. 26th St., New York, NY 10010; Phone (212) 725-1515. Credit cards are not accepted.

Science Fair Manual A guide for the process, from choosing a topic to judging the results, with examples of projects. (not examined) $5 plus $3.75 shipping. K.T. Productions, P.O. Box 1203, Menomonee Falls WI 53051.

TOPS Simple, well-explained activities. Inexpensive for what you get, but each category has more than you may use. For example, for $11 and $4 shipping, you get 24 lessons on cohesion and adhesion, but this a narrow range. Your support group may want to order. Families could divide up the materials or borrow from a central library. It's not that the coverage includes more than you need to know, but that, in a finite amount of time, efficient science learning accepts some facts without experiment.

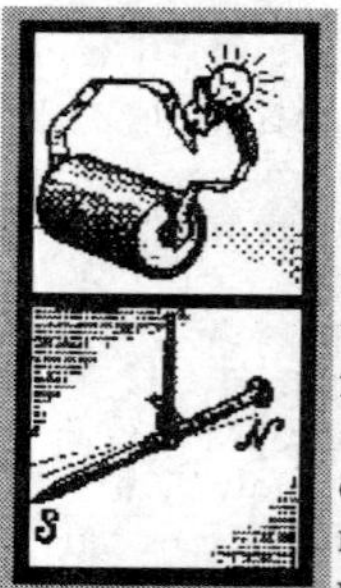

TOPS now sells lenses (50¢ or $1) so you can make your own microscope or telescope, not so slick as one you buy but it would work. In fact one experiment demonstrates the principle with only pin holes in foil and a baby-food jar.

Company president Ron Marson reminded me that home schooling allows kids to follow their own interests to greater depth. My concern is that we need a balance between depth and wide coverage for general scientific "literacy." And we need balance between learning from reading (takes less time) and learning from experimenting (often more fun and better remembered). To guide the "depth" choices, this material is very good.

TOPS Learning Systems, 10970 S. Mulino Rd., Canby, OR 97013.

Zane Publishing Series of **CDroms** Various science topics are covered by this publisher including a few interesting ones for children in lower to middle grades. Special (higher priced) sets include *Isaac Asimov's Library of the Universe* and *The Encyclopedia of US Endangered Species.* Evolutionary theories are mentioned. Contact information is given at the description of *Miriam Webster's Collegiate Dictionary* in Appendix X.

Zaner-Bloser Publishes science materials among other things. See "Critical Thinking" in Appendix Q.

Part 3, Multi-topic Publications Jr.-Sr. High School

Lab Science, The How, Why, What, Who, 'n' Where Book, 1996. Barbara Edtl Shelton has compiled useful information from various sources relating to high school level natural science. The book is intended to help you develop this area of your curriculum rather than being a complete science program itself. In one section the author highlights perspectives of traditional, field, and natural-learning approaches. In another, she helps you decide on your own approach. Planning forms are included. Throughout the book are activities you can use. $11.95 + $3.50 S&H from the author at 182 No. Columbia Heights Rd., Longview, WA 98632; (360) 423-4912.

Part 4, Specific Areas

Animal Quest An interesting game on computer **disk** for ages 5 and up. You choose to be a certain animal. Points are gained by devouring prey and avoiding predators. It's very slightly educational. You (or your child) could learn, for example, that mice are eaten by such animals as foxes and snakes and not by berries and acorns which they eat instead. You can opt to read a few basic facts about each of the animals, but success in the game doesn't depend on this knowledge.

Answers in Genesis A ministry promoting the biblical understanding of creation. For information on their seminars call (606) 727-2222; (800) 350-3232, ext. 403; P.O. Box 6330, Florence, KY 41022.

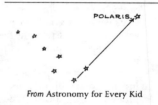

From Astronomy for Every Kid

Atoms and Molecules A clear explanation reinforced with attractive illustrations and historical notes. I suggest it for grades 6 to 9. Unless the topic is covered in other books you are using, I recommend this book or one like it. 1992, $6.95. From Usborne. See Appendix Y.

Astronomy for Every Kid Similar to *Biology for Every Kid.*

Biology for Every Kid Projects and activities to teach concepts, terminology, and (according to the author, Janice VanCleave) laboratory methods. This book and the others in the series each describe 101 experiments. For biology they are classified under plants, animals, and humans. Each is presented in a two-page spread with an illustration on the right. The order is logical. By working through the book doing some experiments and reading about the others, one would form significant concepts. An explanation is given for each activity. Growing carrots from carrot tops demonstrates that a plant can grow if it has portions of base, stem, and root, and if it receives food and water.

The explanations are oversimplified in some cases (for "finger monocle" for example). Younger students need simpler explanations, but I believe the scientific principles could be stated more accurately. Also, some of the illustrations could be improved, but basically the book is good.

For a total science program I would recommend a textbook or a number of broad topic books. Individual experiments miss some of the overall themes and some concepts are hard to demonstrate.

I have not seen evolutionary concepts in the book. It and others in the series seem best for about grades 3 through 5. Younger kids could profit from most of the activities. The explanations don't bring out the scientific principles clearly enough for older ones.

$10.95. Part of a series from John Wiley & Sons (See Appendix Y). For some free activities by this author, in the Internet: http://www.wiley.com/products/subject/children/teacher/vancleave/newsletter/

Blind Faith, Evolution Exposed, Howard Peth. Much written on this topic pleases those who already believe the Genesis story, but is insulting to people who consider themselves scientific. Peth's book is different. The secular scientific establishment won't likely put the book on their recommended reading list, but it does give responsible reasons for thinking people to believe that God was telling the truth all along, and that He is powerful enough to preserve His word. In a descriptive note, Dr. Duane Gish says, "Peth thoroughly and carefully describes the biblical and scientific evidences which provide both powerful and positive evidence for creation, and convincing evidence against the theory of evolution. Peth exposes evolution for what it really is – a religious philosophy serving as the basic dogma of secular humanism." You need this teaching reference for elementary science classes. Junior high and high school students need to read it. 188 pp., 1990. $5.95 plus $3 shipping, from Amazing Facts, Inc., P.O. Box 1058, Roseville, CA 95678-1058, (916) 624-3500.

Butterfly Book, The *A Kid's Guide to Attracting, Raising, and Keeping Butterflies.* In addition to practical information, this attractive, 40-page book has interesting science information. For example, chemical sensors on butterfly feet allow them to "taste" leaves. 21 species are described with the regions of the US and Southern Canada where they may be found. One sentence I disagree with is. "No one knows why the dinosaurs died out." 1997, $7.95 plus shipping from John Muir Publications, Box 613, Santa Fe, NM 87504; (800) 888-7504.

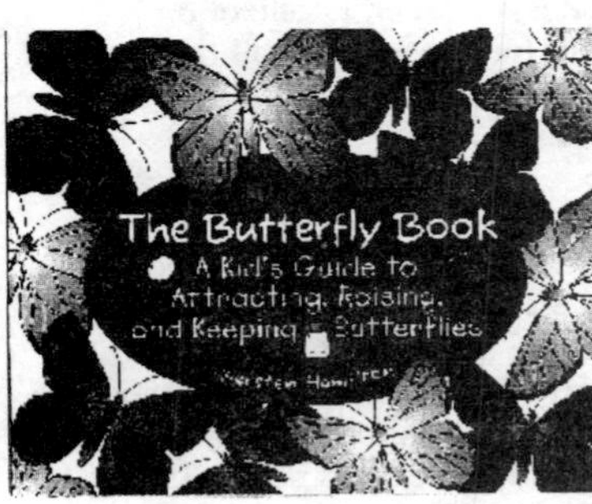

Chemistry for Every Kid See *Biology for Every Kid* For one experiment you try to fill a balloon inside a bottle with its mouth stretched open over the mouth of the bottle. I'll let you guess what that demonstrates. An activity with apples turning brown when cut open demonstrates enzyme interaction with oxygen. Acids and bases are tested with cabbage paper.

Cloud Chart A mother who had a former edition of this book wrote to tell me how her family had enjoyed learning about weather. They had made weather predictions using information from Cloud Charts. And they thought you would like to know about this product. I agree. The charts show you cloud pictures and give other information on simple weather prediction. Chart A is a big poster, maybe unnecessary for home schools. B, essentially the same, is for grades 6 and up. It has more pictures and smaller print than version C which is slated as for grades 3 to 5. Send $2 for B or C (11" X 17"). or $3 for A. Cloud Chart, Inc., P.O. Box 21298, Charleston, SC 29413-1298.; (803) 577-5268.

***CLW Weather* (and other topics)** A workbook to provide testing or exercises for the Usborne book, *Weather & Climate*. To help parents teach for comprehension, author Debby Willett has prepared workbooks with questions to answer. She puts a Christian emphasis on very secular books. A sample question: "Why is Roger Bacon a major figure in the history of science? Use complete sentences." Answer keys are provided. Other titles on science are: *CLW Seas, CLW Inventors, CLW Earthquakes* and *CLW Scientists*. CLW stands for Circle of Learning Workbooks.

Reading for what appears important, without questions to answer, is a good habit to develop. Sometimes, however, the accountability of answering questions gives reason for paying close attention to the entire selection and encourages review. The balance is between reading from internal motivation and reading for accountability. Workbooks succeed for some children more than for others. They can be part of a healthy variety of methods, especially for immature scholars. 1995, Willett Publishing, P.O. Box 1252, Canyon, TX 97015. (806) 655-4245. CLWbooks@aol.com. Also available from distributors (but currently not through discounters).

Cup and Saucer Chemistry A book introducing how chemistry works. Simple experiments, using items around the house, are described. Chemical formulas are avoided, and even the symbols designating specific substances (like H_2O for water) are not used. This keeps the chemistry from getting lost in abstractions, but it also leaves one without the handles that help show what is going on and firm it up in the memory. The book is still a good introduction to chemistry. Explanations are clear. Working, in order, through the 38 experiments and remembering what happened will give a better perspective of the natural world and will enhance achievement in high school or college chemistry. $3.95 (you would guess $8.95) Dover No. 25997-8. See Appendix Y for Dover.

Curious Creatures A series of nature books from Charlesbridge Publishing translated from French. One of the titles I have is *Animal Bandits*. "Peter daydreams in his room. He must hand in an essay tomorrow, and the page in front of him is still completely blank. Suddenly he hears a noisy commotion from the hen house. Peter rushes over to the window just in time to see a fox run by with a hen in its mouth." Peter decides to play a radio in the hen house until his mother gets the money to buy better fence wire. In bulleted columns on the next two pages is information about foxes under the following topical headings: location, description, habitat, behavior, food, reproduction, the fox and people, and threats and measures of conservation. On other four-page sections the reader learns about the magpie, the marten, the heron, the brown rat and five more creatures. Introductory pages discuss finding food and the benefits and risks to humans from various destructive animals. 1994, $14.95.

Another title in the series is *Animals in Disguise.* The focus is on animals that hide by looking like their surroundings or like a dangerous species. One orchid even attracts male insects by smelling like the female of that species (but isn't featured in the book)! The book includes the ermine, the leopard, the Alpine ptarmigan, the hedgehog, and the chameleon. I remember being impressed by chameleons when we lived in Africa. Their eyes operate independently, each looking in a different direction! 1994.

One more book is *Birds of the Night*. It is all about owls. My 5-year-old grandson likes it. As with the other titles, this one provides much more than entertainment. The categories of comparative features are: location, size/wingspan, description, feathers, natural environment, behavior/voice, reproduction, food, pellets and risks, threats, and measures of [for] conservation. 1994. The fourth book in the series is *Scary Animals.*

These are excellent books with high educational value. They are well illustrated and hardcover. I have seen no evidence of evolutionary concepts. A table of contents in each book would have made them nicer to use. Another slight disadvantage for those of us in the Western Hemisphere is that most of the species don't live here. Of course similar ones, do. Phone (617) 926-0329. Charlesbridge Publishing 85 Main St. Watertown MA 02172; http://www.charlesbridge.com; books@charlesbridge.com.

Dinosaurs for Every Kid The usual scientific dating system is mentioned placing the animals at 65 million years ago. For more on the series, see *Biology for Every Kid.*

Earth Science for Every Kid For a general description, see *Biology for Every Kid.* Activities related to this topic done in a classroom or home tend to be simulations rather than demonstrations. For example, the author wants us to know what a dike is. It's a formation caused by molten material that has hardened after being squeezed up through a crack in solid rocks. I don't think it's hard to understand the principle by discussing a good picture or drawing. In fact squeezing a closed tube of toothpaste, as the activity calls for, may serve to confuse the issue. The best way to learn earth science is to go to places where you can see the actual geological evidence. Next best is an explanation with good photographs. This book isn't bad, but I wouldn't spend my money for it.

Fowl Weather Younger kids will enjoy clicking to learn about four types of severe weather and what to do to keep the rooster safe. The program should be effective. My 2x **CDrom** player had to stop and rest a few times but it worked. (I now have a 24x player). I wanted to skip some of the options in the snow discussion (dress warmly, watch where you sled, ask before going on ice, don't overdo, etc.), but the rooster just stood there until I had clicked on all of them. Maybe this isn't such a bad idea if you want your kids to take it seriously. With perseverance I could have played the game at the end of all four storms. The others are tornadoes, floods, and lightning. From Meridian Creative Group, 5178 Station Rd., Erie PA 16510; (800) 695-9427; http://www.home.meridiancg.com

Fun Facts for Curious Kids A series of eight nature books under the Golden Book label. The actual title of the book I examined is *Mammals: Over 300 Fun Facts for Curious Kids.* Each well-illustrated pair of facing pages develops a set of facts. The first topic question is: "What does it take to be a mammal?" The dolphin, armadillo, bat and others animals are discussed as the topic is developed. The penguin looks furry but isn't an mammal. Other topic questions are "How many ants does an anteater eat?" (They eat thousands a day.) "Why are skunks so smelly?" "Why do whales squirt water?" "What is the meaning of 'monkey see, monkey do'?" "Why do beavers build dams?" and "Why does the kangaroo have a pouch?"

On the kangaroo topic, here is a sample of the text: "As soon as the joey [baby kangaroo] is born, it climbs up its mother's belly and into the pouch, where it finds a supply of milk. The fur-lined pouch keeps the little one warm and safe. After about six months, the joey is big and strong enough to leave the pouch and hop around by itself."

The book's conclusion encourages continued study and points out that animals affect each other and that they affect our lives, too. Current copyright, 1992. 32, good-sized pages in a hard laminated cover and a sown binding. Price around $5. I chose this one for a gift and am totally delighted.

Jack's Garden "This is the garden that Jack planted." The first double-spread illustration with these words shows Jack on the bare ground. Next, "This is the soil that made up the garden that Jack planted" and an underground picture of various creatures. The story repeats on each page spread adding a new line. This book is a winner. Excellent for reading practice and excellent for science with all the insects, birds, plants and so on illustrated and named. 24 pp. $4.95 from Mulberry Books

Kid Contraptions This book is a springboard for helping kids make things that work. Aims suggested by the author include: investigate the environment, recognize a need for new products, apply skill . . . to solve problems, develop logical thinking, and . . . science of why things happen.

I thought this might be descriptions of things you would find materials for kids to make. It's far more. It shows you how to get kids started letting them develop their own ideas. Of course some specifics are given, too. It teaches about "machines" invention, energy transfer, etc. Kids can make a water wheel, a cork rocket, hinges, a timer, a water xylophone, a stethoscope, etc.

It's marked for K-3, but I would say K-4. As a kid I would have had an absolute "blast" following these ideas (except we didn't use that word back then). Valuable learning experiences. 72 pp., 1995, The same author has written *Kid Creations* and *Kid Concoctions.* $8.95 plus $3.50 shipping (and tax if Illinois). Teaching & Learning Company, P.O. Box 10, Carthage IL 62321.

Nature Discoveries Hatch your own butterflies and moths. This company sells you the chrysalides and cocoons and includes instructions. What you can order depends on the time of year. The firm also sells a variety of science display sets from chemicals to tadpoles. The displays might be more practical (for financial reasons) to share among members of support groups. 389 Rock Beach Rd., Rochester, NY 14617; (716) 865-4580.

Nature's Green Umbrella Tropical Rain Forests are described and discussed in this well-illustrated book. Scholastic level around grade 5. Mentions people living in the forests for 40,000 years. 31 pp., $4.95 from Mulberry Books.

Neptune "Neptune is the eighth planet in the Solar System and takes 165 years to obit the sun." Many interesting facts about the planet are explained including new information and photos from the space probe, Voyager 2. Middle grades through high school and beyond. One of a series from Mulberry Books. 28 pp. $5.95

Pendulum This graphic computer program allows you to simulate the motion of a pendulum which you watch swinging on the screen. It is a shareware program which was a little expensive. Alternatively you can do equivalent lab experiments for learning about pendulums with a piece of string, a rock, a watch that shows seconds, and a ruler or tape measure. **disk**

Physics for Every Kid Although this book of experiments has some good activities, I'm a little disappointed. A number of them seem trivial to me, and at least a couple that I looked closely at teach error. For example, instructions are given to make a paper "helicopter" with a weighted vertical shaft and two horizontal paper "wings" at the top. The wings are given little twists in opposite directions to make the pair of them resemble the shape of a propeller. It is explained that, when the object is permitted to fall, "air rushes out from under the wings in all directions" and "hits against the body of the craft, causing it to rotate." Actually the air resists the weight of the object with an upward force which pushes partly sideways against the tilted surfaces causing the object's rotation.

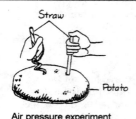

Air pressure experiment

In another activity, we are told that "a polarized lens has an endless number of parallel slits." The polarization process does *resemble* the action of a vibrating rope constrained by a slit (as a person moves one end up and down to send waves along it), but the lenses themselves don't have slits, not even microscopic ones. For other information about the series, see *Biology for Every Kid.*

The Story of Electricity A history of fascinating discoveries that helped the world understand electricity. It begins in the seventh century B.C. with Thales' description of static electricity and magnetism and continues through a description of magnetic recording tape. This is an excellent way to learn since the principles are clear in the electrical inventions. Twenty easy experiments are described. Definitely worthwhile. 91 pp. Only $4.95 from Dover (25581-6). See Appendix Y.

Weather, ... *Experiments You Can Turn Into Science Fair Projects*
Twenty experiments are laid out on topics relating to weather. They include sky color, highs and lows, wind speed, fronts, clouds, frost, hail, etc. Explanations and ideas for science fair projects are included. I got my copy of the book at an exhibit by the publisher, John Wiley & Sons. It was a pleasure to meet the author, Janice VanCleave. $9.95, 90 pp. 1995. Other books in this *Spectacular Science Projects* Series are *Animals, Earthquakes, Electricity, Gravity, Machines, Magnets, Molecules, Microscopes and Magnifying Lenses,* and *Volcanoes.*

Worms Eat My Garbage When I saw the activities book on this topic I was a little skeptical about its usefulness for science instruction. After all, science is more than worms. But I asked for a review copy anyway. Mary Appelhof sent me ▪her small book (176 pp.), *Worms Eat My Garbage,* (1997 ed.) ▪the fatter classroom activities book I had seen, ▪a video tape with teaching guide, and ▪even a couple issues of *Worm Digest.*

It did look as if she wanted to see the whole science curriculum eaten by worms. But, as I examined the materials, I saw plenty for the core of a good unit study. To breed worms you need dirt, absorbent material like shredded newspapers or manure, water, worms (Redworms are best), and something to feed them like garbage. But one additional ingredient is needed to transform this idea into action – enthusiasm – and Mary provides an ample supply. Worm breading is recycling at its best – an instructional bonus.

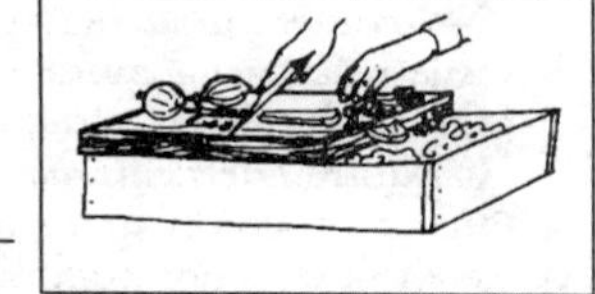

From *Worms Eat My Garbage*

Mary will sell you a number of items including a composting bin kit with book, etc, for $76 or $89 (larger) with shipping. The book itself costs $12.95 plus $2.50 S&H. The video is very well done although you don't really need it. 28 min. VHS, for $34.90 plus $3.50. The classroom activities book (works well for independent study) costs $22.95 plus $3. (616) 327-0108; Fax ... 7009. Flowerfield Enterprises, 10332 Shaver Rd., Kalamazoo, MI 49024

Part 5, Specific Areas Jr.-Sr. High School

Avaition From Castle Heights Press. See Appendix Y at *One Week Off for Unit Studies.s*

Experiences in Biology Like the chemistry manual below but with more explanations. New edition for 1998. Price same as below

Experiences in Chemistry A high school lab manual with some explanations although more should be read from a good textbook or an encyclopedia. Also, tests are important but are not provided. A student who has covered this material and has taken the time to learn what is going on, will better understand the world and will have a good base for college chemistry. 1995, 90 pp. From Castle Heights Press described in this appendix. $24.95. Accompanying, optional student activity book (for recording data) $9.95 Shipping, 15%.

Pathways in Science A 3-ring binder textbook for Jr. High physical science, also from Castle Heights.

Part 6, Magazines

Creation Illustrated (in nature, in living, in Scripture). "Our purpose is to share the wonders of God's creation. By revealing fresh insights of His infinite wisdom, gentle touch, undeniable justice, redeeming love and flawless design, pure truth shall bring renewed peace." The Spring/summer 1994 edition includes an article on maternal instincts of birds; a section featuring six health-emphasis recipes (potato waffles, Santa Fe breakfast tofu quiche, etc.); action articles on growing roses, making pottery, and rafting through the Grand Canyon; nature activities for kids; plus five more articles. People like me who love to feast on splendid nature photography will enjoy *Creation Illustrated.* 1 yr. (4 issues), $19.95. Fax (916) 637-5170; P.O. Box 7955, Auburn, CA 95604.

Creation Magazine Includes a four-page children's section. $22/yr. (4 issues). See Answers in Genesis in Part 2 of this Appendix..

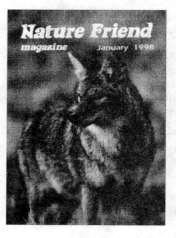

Nature Friend Magazine The January 1988 issue, as others, has simple stories, articles, puzzles, and fact lists. Here is a sentence from the lead article, "'No,' Daddy agreed. 'Birds can't sing or think the same way we can. They can praise God, though, by doing what He created them to do. . . . They help us praise Him, too. . . .'" I learned more about crows in the two-page sketch. A drawing lesson is very well explained, and shows drawings from four kids who followed the previous lesson. Bananas are featured for "Deliberate Design in Creation" and static electricity is discussed under "Learning by Doing. $22 for 12 monthly issues; US$25 for Canada; US$30 elsewhere. P.O. Box 73, Goshen, IN 46527-0073. (219) 534-2245.

Odyssey This magazine, from Cobblestone Publishers The September 1997 issue is entitled, *Imaging, From the Atom to the Cosmos.* Teaser lines on the cover: "Meet the REAL 'Visible Man,' Watch the Brain say 'Yuck'!" and "'Treasures' from Hubble's New Cameras.'" All interesting. The other issue I examines is about youth science competitions. See general information about *Oddssey* under Cobblestone Publishing in Appendix R, Part 1.

Ranger Rick's Nature Magazine An excellent magazine for youngsters 6-12. 12 monthly issues, National Wildlife Federation, 8925 Leesburg Pike, Vienna, VA 22184; http:/www.nwf.org.

Your Big Backyard Trade in Big Bird for this one. Kids learn at their level about nature the way it is. Several concepts are dealt with in each issue. In the same family as Ranger Rick's. For children 3-5. National Wildlife Federation. See *Ranger Rick's Nature Magazine.*

Part 7, Equipment

Castle Heights Press Laboratory materials for chemistry, biology, and physics at the high school level. Also some elementary. Castle Heights Press, 2578 Alexander Farms Dr. SW, Marietta, LA 30064 (770) 218-7998; or for orders (800) 763-7148; julcher@aol.com;http://www.flash .net/~wx3o/chp/ Castle Heights also sells lab manuals and unit studies materials for elementary and secondary levels. The printed materials are mostly written by Kathleen Julicher (qualified for her task) or members of her family. Plastic comb bindings. See the review of *Experiences in Chemistry.*

Home Training Tools 2827 Buffalo Horn Dr., Laurel, MT 59044; (406) 628-6614, fax ... -6454, Order and product information, (800) 860-6272. The catalog is planned for small and home schools. It has notes offering shopping guidance. "Science equipment & materials for home schools."

Microscopes A full line at discount prices from John Lind. On print catalog at this time. http://members.aol.com/gr8scopes

Nature's Workshop Christian source for children's books and supplies. Don Ruark. All kinds of books and other items from bird whistles to bat houses to microscopes to art materials.

Rainbow Collection 83 Rolling Hill Ln., Southington, CT 06489; (860) 621-7946. RAICOL@prodigy .com Nature-oriented educational materials: teacher resources, children's literature, and items related to science. Materials for younger children are included. Discounts depend on amount of purchase. Free catalog.

Tobin's Lab, P.O. Box 6503, Glendale, AZ 85312-6503; http://www.tobinlab.com; mike@tobinlab.com. Source for science teaching materials suitable for home schools.

T

Music and Art

In this appendix:

1. *Music appreciation*
2. *Music techniques*
3. *Music supplies*
4. *Art appreciation*
5. *Art techniques*
6. *Art supplies*

Music Appreciation

Music & Moments with the Masters "A five-year curriculum – introducing your children to precious moments with the masters." From Cornerstone. Address in Appendix S with review of *Science the Search.*

Music Masters A set of 40-minute cassettes, each with a vivid narration of the life of a composer and over 20 selections from his works. Also in CD format. They were recorded before the days of high-tech reproduction, but school-age children love to listen to them. They are sold in sets of six. Constructive Playthings, 1227 E. 119th St., Grandview, MO 64030-1117. (800) 832-0224; ustoy@ustoyco.com; http://www.ustoyco.com.

The Nature of Music Twelve half-hour programs aired on National Public Radio take a close look at various aspects of music to consider what it is and what it does. Programs include *Music and the Performer* on how music is formed from mechanical printed notes and individuality; *Music and the Listener* and *Music and the brain* deal with how to listen and the effects of music. In *Music and commerce* we learn how people pay for what they want to hear and what gets published. Other programs look at "time," "the creative spirit," "the human body," "tools," "words," "technology," "meaning," and "definition."

It's an excellent series for bringing meaning to music and will enrich the music experience whether in performing or in listening. Some of the examples don't lead to what I feel are good emotions, but a mature listener can use fast forward. Others are excellent. The selections are only brief excerpts. Recommended for anyone high school age and above. $44.50 plus $5.00 shipping. From Audio-Forum, 96 Broad St., Guilford, CT 06437.

Music Techniques

God Made Music Workbooks for K-7, published by Praise Hymn, Inc., P.O. Box 1325, Taylors, SC 29687. Also *Hymnplayer* piano method, *Star Series* Bible workbooks for grades 1-6. Catalog available. (800) 729-2821.

Keyboard Capers A program that teaches music theory, sight reading, and ear training with activities. A keyboard is recommended. The 100 games require manipulatives which you can make yourself (they are patterned in the book) or they may be ordered along with the book as a complete kit. Book price $18.95 plus $5.95 shipping (and tax if TN). From The Elijah Company. See Appendix Z.

Madonna Woods Piano Course for Christians A piano course by cassette tape and instructional music books with clear explanations. I have examined the materials for the "preparatory level." The amateurish appearance of the book and poorly duplicated tapes are not a real hindrance to what looks to me like material for a pleasant and successful learning experience. Six levels, in all, are available. You get the preparatory book and two cassettes for $32.75 with UPS shipping. The free catalog shows many other books by Madonna Woods and from other publishers for everything from playing by ear to playing other instruments and books of piano music. Davidsons Music 6727 Metcalf, Shawnee Mission, KS 66204; (913) 262-6533.

Mary Jo Moore Piano Course, The "A complete course for piano based on the old hymn tunes. Play hymns from the very first lesson." Five graded books with explanatory notes and more instructions on cassette tapes. For example, the preparatory book (first level) costs $6 and the cassette costs $7. Add $2 for postage. Satisfaction guaranteed. You can be your own teacher or your children's. Much modern "Christian" music is not sacred (it denies the beauty of holiness) so I appreciate this program. Of course music doesn't have to be old to be good. I recommend these materials even though I would like to have seen a few recent songs in them and the cassettes could stand a little more professional touch. Moore Publishing Co., 286 Poland Ave., Struthers, OH 44471; (216) 750-0253.

Musik Garten A program for groups of at least five young children which you may learn to conduct with minimal musical background. Children are taught the way they learn with theory postponed. Workshops available in various cities. Your support group might be interested. 409 Blandwood Ave., Greenville, NC 27401; (800) 216-6864; musgarden@aol.com.

Recorder and book set Description from Sycamore: Do you want your child to learn to lay the recorded, but don't want to spedend a lot of money! Here's the answer! The recoreder is sturdy plastic and the book has the "how-tos," note by note, with lots of easy, familiar songs to play. $11.95 plus shipping.

Your Musical Friends Focus on applied music reading ability and on using music in worship. For grades K-4. Workbooks, cassette tapes and teacher's guides available. Also books, recorders (instruments), games. Christian

Education Music Publishers, Inc., P.O. Box 388, Brook, IN 47922-0388; (219) 275-6553; (800) 573-6127.

Music Supplies

The Woodwind and the Brasswind 18990 State Line Rd., South Bend, IN 46637; (800) 348-5003. A large mail-order firm selling everything including keyboard and strings items. Tell them your interest when you call.

Art Appreciation

Adventures in Art Understanding Art's Meaning in the Flow of History. From Cornerstone. See address at *Science the Search* in Appendix S.

***Great Composers* CDrom** Eighteen composers are featured in a set of six disks. The sample I examined was excerpts from the story of Beethoven. It is quite good including excerpts from his works. Another series is entitled *The History of Music.* From Zane Publishing. See information at *Miriam Webster's Collegiate Dictionary* in Appendix X.

KidsArt Art study booklets written for kids and containing a wide variety of art activities and art culture. Also art history, drawing and painting activities, print making, cartoons, etc. with reproducible worksheets. 16 pages. $4 each. KidsArt, P.O. Box 274, Mt. Shasta, CA 96067, (530) 926-5076. http://www.kidsart.com; kidsart@macshasta.com

Masterpieces in Art A modified reprint of an old book (original copyright not shown). The book's introduction states: ". . . to render practical, the powers of pictorial expression, the mind must be saturated with the excellencies of a Raphael and an Angelo, a Rembrandt and a Millet. Picture study is in a double sense cultural and educative." The pictures are black and white. That's how they had to do it back then. Color would be nice, but this works better than you might think, and saves you money. Each picture has an introduction or background study, an appreciative and technical study, then questions. . Christian perspective. Suggested for the 8th grade. 258 pp., $, Christian Liberty Press. See Appendix Y for the address.

Celebrating Art According to information from Christian Liberty Press, "Children ages four to six will enjoy this beginning art program. . . . exposure to basic arts and crafts projects that emphasize the elements of shape, texture, proportion, and color." Complete teaching instructions. For ordering, see Appendix Y.

Art Techniques

Art Adventures at Home Level 1, a program for laying the foundation for art learning. Curriculum outlined for three school years beginning with kindergarten or first grade. Over 100 lessons, each starting with a concept like "shapes can be combined to make objects." Activities follow the concepts. All kinds of art projects compatible with Christian principles. By Patty Carlson and M. Jean Soyke. Write to M. Jean Soyke, 2826 Roselawn Ave., Baltimore, MD 21214; (410) 444-5465.

Beginning of Creativity This approach to teaching drawing is based more on the personal development of creativity than on artistic skills. Its authors consider it helpful for people with learning differences as well as for everyone else. Its design uses the right brain technique. The 35 lessons in workbook is organized according to the seven days of creation. $19.95. Shipping is $2 to US. (Add tax if to Calif.). Linda Marie, P.O. Box 2216, La Mesa, CA 91943.

How Great Thou ART Art instruction materials. (not reviewed). P.O. Box 211, Bishopville, MD 21813; (410) 352-3319.

Christian Art for Kids Don West, provides art classes to develop realistic drawing skills for children ages 7 and up. All projects are based on Bible and high family values themes (no crafts). He also offers long distance art lessons through a two-way correspondence video course. (800) ART-0033 or (810) 775-0332.

Landscapes The topic is treated nicely for beginning artists (as young as 6 or 8) or those who have had a little practice. Various techniques are illustrated referring to the work of six artists. Part of a series called, Artists' Workshop. 1996. $8.95 at bookstores. Crabtree Publishing Co.

Preschool Art by MaryAnn F. Kohl. "Over 250 process-oriented art experiences designed for children 3-6, but ideal for all ages. Uses materials commonly found in the home or school." Adult involvement is needed for many of the crafts. Some are ideas like using hair spray to slow down the smudging of chalk drawings or how to make an easy-to-store puppet stage. Many are for creating objects like "stuffed fabric" or animals made from taping cardboard boxes and mailing tubes. Both this and *Scribble Art* are excellent books. 260 pp., $19.95.

Scribble Art Author MaryAnn F. Kohl has published several successful art books for kids. I appreciated meeting her at a publisher's workshop luncheon in Chicago several years ago, and I asked to see her latest books. This one describes a variety of fun activities. For example one is called "Scribble Cookies." For it you put pieces of old crayons in the cups of a muffin tin. After melting them in the oven and letting them resolidify, they may be used for scribbles that change color as you create. Other activity involve rolling a marble over a paint spot, and driving a toy car through paint to make car tracks. You can make leaf prints, fish prints, and sculptures with nature objects. A number of activities involve stitching and weaving. 160 pp., 11 X 8½, $14.95 plus $2.50 postage. Bright Ring Publishing, P.O. Box 5768, Bellingham, WA 98227. Order line: (800) 480-4ART.

Stained glass coloring books A series of miniature books with pages of heavy tracing paper. Each has 8 pictures. They are to remove and color, then put up in the window for the sunlight to shine through. I examined *Wild Cats Stained Glass Coloring Book* by John Green. $1 from Dover (#27013-0). See Appendix Y.

Visual Manna An art curriculum for grades 1-12. Prepared by Sharon Jeffus and husband Richard. Numerous color prints of famous art masterpieces are included. A materials kit is also available. This is not just a collection of projects but an organized curriculum covering specific concepts and types of art. Instructions for many of the 55 lessons differentiate between grade ranges 1-6 and 7-12. (Kids at different levels can work at the same time on a project.) To give you a random browsing of the contents, Lesson 1 covers design, pattern, and symmetry as the children draw butterflies. In Lesson 2, colored soap bubbles make interesting images on paper. Lesson 9 is about shading, and paints are used to make a monochrome seascape. Proportions and the human figure are dealt with in Lesson 11. And in Lesson 26, knights and dragons are the subject. The last "lesson" is a collection of 55 special assignments. For example, "A new bug is found along the Amazon River. It is 2 feet long. Draw a picture of it." A test is provided for each 5 lessons and museum prints are included, too.

In my previous review, I expressed concern for the centuries-old view of art and for the drab look of the materials. The materials could still profit from better graphic design but here and there more recent art is recognized.

On the use of tests, the course authors apparently agree that an art grade should involve a lot more than responses to test questions. Even if you don't give a grade, you will want to make it clear to your child that success in art is not measured objectively.

Now that you have heard all my negative opinions, I must add that the course is not at all bad. The variety of objectives is its strong point. I'm sure many parents and teachers appreciate the materials very much, and you might, too. I just wanted you to see through my eyes. My preference for teaching art would include areas like architecture, photography, drawing or painting lessons, flower arranging, computer assisted art, using computer clip art, principles of page layout, and simply observing and discussing the beautiful things in nature. Although experiences like a visit to an art gallery are now part of the course, I would focus even more in some of these areas that are not easily quantified. And you can do just that with whatever art program you choose for your kids. Select from it but get kids to thinking and talking about good art in the real world, and imitating it. The program is similar to what is taught in schools.

$68.95 with plastic cover sheets and binder notebook or $42.95 for just the 300+ pages. Add 10% shipping for over $30. An art materials kit with a book, *The ABC's of Art*, is available for $39.95. Visual Manna also publishes a newsletter with activities, other art instructional items and a video production using art to illustration spiritual principles. P.O. Box 553, Salem, MO 65560; (573) 729-2100; arthis@rollanet.org; www.rollanet.org/~arthis/index.html.

Watercolor for the Artistically Undiscovered (Information not confirmed.) A book for practicing basic watercolor techniques (like mixing colors, applying paint in different ways, and combining with pencil), and general art principles (such as perspective, sketching first and filling in, and shading) More than half of the 72 pages are art paper with printed instructions and examples around the edges. A set of 6 basic colors and an adequate-but-not-superior brush is attached at the bottom of the book. Pages turn above it. A nice unit, although there are cheaper ways to practice with watercolors.

By Thacher Hurd and John Cassidy. Klutz Press, $18.95. Free Klutz catalog: 2121 Staunton Ct., Palo Alto, CA 94306; (650) 424-0739.

Young Masters Art Program Director, John Gordon, designed the program on the assumption that "all students with normal intelligence and sensory-motor abilities can master drawing and painting skills on a professional level. . . ." Modern thinking emphasizes creativity expressed according to the mood and feelings of the artist. Art is then an unrestricted display of what is imagined. Gordon argues that "creativity is inherent in experience – and is only secondarily realized through expression." "Unless we first learn to draw what we see, we will be unable to draw what we imagine." Thus the Young Masters courses develop hundreds of distinct techniques, each followed by application at a little greater difficulty. Success requires discipline. Although this is a serious art study program, it seems to me that other approaches could be as successful.

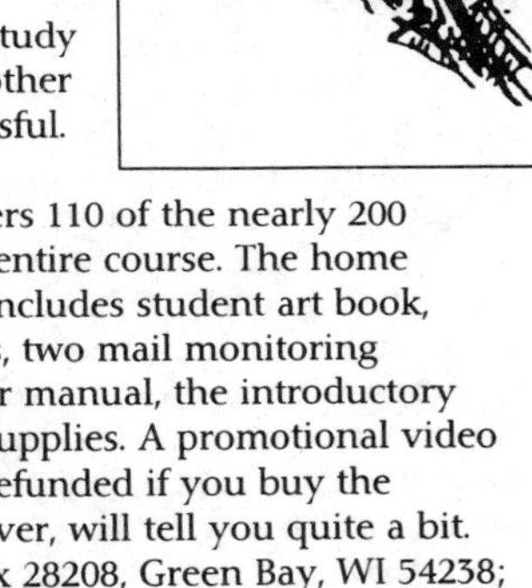

The "foundation course" (required for all students) covers 110 of the nearly 200 "technical skill groups" of the entire course. The home study version costs $200 and includes student art book, teacher guide, two video tapes, two mail monitoring sessions, a professional teacher manual, the introductory video tape and all necessary supplies. A promotional video is available for $25, with $20 refunded if you buy the program. The brochure, however, will tell you quite a bit. Gordon School of Art, P.O. Box 28208, Green Bay, WI 54238; (414) 437-6919; (800) 210-1220; gordon@netnet.net; http:/www.newmasters.com Studio instruction is available at several Wisconsin sites.

In case you were wondering, the school logo shown with this review is not a portrait of John Gordon. It's impressionist artist, Camille Pisarro as drawn by his contemporary, Paul Cezanne.

Art Supplies

KidsArt Also sells art materials, as do some program providers. See KidsArt under Art Appreciation, above. The catalog contains advice, too.

Miller Pads & Paper 2840 Neff Rd., Boscobel, WI 53805; (608) 375-2181; Fax ... -2250; (800) 475-6730. A simple catalog packed with all kinds of what you might want: materials, books, stickers, stamps, and basic kits. Discounted.

U
Foreign Languages

Because most language courses include cassette audio tapes, we do not show the **A-tapes** *key.*

In this appendix:
1. *Full language instruction programs*
2. *Supplementary or introductory items*
3. *Suppliers*

Part 1, Full instructional programs

Berlitz Interactive language programs in cooperation with The Learning Company. Not reviewed. (800) 227-5609. http://www.learningco.com. Speech recognition technology used. Also from The Learning Company, . . . *for Everyone* Inexpensive courses based on conversation interaction with the **CDrom**. Information above

Hey Andrew! Teach Me Some Greek! Instruction in Koine Greek, the common dialect at the time of Christ and after. A good language to learn for reading the New Testament in the original language. Five levels beginning with simple letter recognition. (Not reviewed.) A Latin course is also available. Greek 'n Stuff, P.O. Box 882, Moline, IL 61266-0882; (309) 797-0089; timohs@earthlink.net; http://home.earthlink.net/~timohs/

Learn Language Now I reviewed the French version of this program when it first appeared as Transparent Language. That is now the company name and they have added more features. Even then it was an innovative system using computer technology. They described it as "the easiest, most enjoyable way to learn a foreign language." I didn't agree at all. The system basically displays stories in the original languages (now 10). Highlighting words in the story in the top part of the screen, reveals in the lower part: the direct word translation, the meaning of the phrase when the word is part of one, the translation of a larger part of the text, and other notes in boxes. It's a logical way to conceptualize the original meaning.

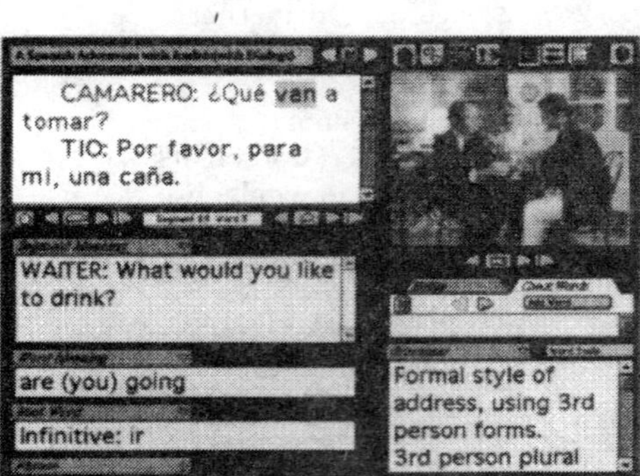

I studied basic French and spent some seven years improving it in French speaking countries. I have also studied several other languages and have edited foreign language correspondence courses. The philosophy was, and to some degree may still be, "To get a child to be a good reader, get her or him to read regularly. Everything else follows." Reading needs to be interesting so the designers use original classical literature for their stories. (Not what I recommend for character development.) It is boring, they say, to read, "The girl put the pencil on the table. What did the boy put on the table?"

They have a point, but from my experience, especially as a student in the very successful French government language school for foreigners, the program appears to me like the whole language approach would appear to a died-in-the-wool phonics teacher. In reality, we learn to read by both the phonetic details and the whole contextual reading experience. Each has a place. And in learning a foreign language, I feel both structure and contextual reading are important.

In the space of what would be a page or two in a book, I found words with the following English equivalents: hunter's game bag, strangle (in the subjunctive tense), persist, fastidious, nightmare, buttocks, and sonorous. Most of the stories are on one cassette and are read very fast. I had to strain to follow the main line of thought. The speed problem has changed, and apparently their emphasis on native literature. Their **CDrom** program now allows the audio speed to be adjusted (without changing the pitch). You now can interact directly with the computer in responding to statements you hear. You then can compare your pronunciation with that of the native speakers and enjoy a nice interface with videos. You still have grammar help and translation assistance for the text. I have not reviewed the newer versions but they look very good. Street price is around $50. Their Plus Edition, for school teaching, is more. Transparent Language, P.O. Box 575, Hollis, NH 03049; (800) 752-1767. http://www.transparent.com; (800) 332-8851; info@transparent.com.

Learn . . . the Fast and Fun Way This is one of my [*DF*] favorite courses for teens through adults. It is available for English speakers to learn German, French, Spanish, Italian, Japanese, Russian or Chinese. Another program helps Spanish speakers learn English. For Chinese, the book is available, but cassettes to go with it have not, as of this writing, been released.

I reviewed both the Spanish and the German programs. Unlike some other courses I have seen, these truly assume no previous language experience. The books are colorful and the dialogues lighthearted. The vocabulary offered is comprehensive and emphasizes colloquial usage and idiomatic phrases common to everyday speech. Grammar is introduced in a clear, forthright manner and although proper grammar terms are used, they are carefully defined first. Confusing exceptions to grammar rules are limited. Should you want to refine your grasp of the language, you could supplement this book with a more detailed grammar book in the language you are learning. Many are available. The program is divided into fifteen-minute increments.

In addition to the grammar and vocabulary introduced in the *Learn . . . the Fast and Fun Way*, the books include a pronunciation guide, phonetic transcriptions of all words as they are introduced, self-quizzes (with answers, of course), and lots of interesting cultural information. Four cassette tapes accompany the books. These include a pronunciation guide and all the dialogues. The voices on the tapes are clear and easy to follow, offering a valuable opportunity to hear the language spoken accurately. The price of each program (book and tapes) is a reasonable $39.95. Additional books (allowing several people to share the tapes) are available separately for $14.95. Published by Barrows, Hauppauge, NY. If ordering from Calliope Books, add $2.50 for shipping. *–Donna Faturos.*

Power Japanese (or Chinese) The program looks good. (Screen illustration shown.) It has audio clips. You follow the principles upon which the language is based to write and speak as well as to understand. From Transparent Language. See Learn Language Now. Not reviewed.

Power-glide Language Courses A unique and carefully planned way to learn a language making good use of cassette tapes. Instead of vocabulary lists, you begin with a few words and learn others from the context and by confirmation when the English equivalents are shown. Grammar is learned by demonstration rather than by rules. Stories begin with words you have learned interspersed with English words. New foreign words are added as the story information is rephrased where you already know what is being said. A good pronunciation guide helps you get your mouth around the often new sounds. To help you speak or think without leaning on the printed words, symbols are used. The story that continues off and on through the course is about going to an island that has been taken over by people from outer space and where the native people speak only the language you are learning. This science-fiction approach seems to foster a supernatural atmosphere which is not the flavor I would want for my children or youth.

This program will teach writing, speaking and other aspects of the language. It is designed to keep you going, by the developing stories and by ample practice. The Spanish, French and Russian courses include 6, 90-minute tapes. The Japanese and German courses have 4 tapes (at the time I reviewed them). Price for any language is $89.95. Extra workbooks are available for additional users. Teachers' materials $29.95 if you want them. Add 7% for shipping for one course. Satisfaction guaranteed. 988 Cedar Ave., Provo, UT 84604; (800) 596-0910.

A CD-ROM is available for computer interaction for the Spanish program. You get tapes, workbook and CD for $139.95.

Spanish, Say Hello Author, Louis Aarons, a foreign language dropout and later a research psychologist, figured there must be a better way to learn languages. After studying learning systems involving unconscious listening, he developed a good program. He uses recordings combined with a manual. Instead of the typical grammar-plus-vocabulary base, his primary focus is vocabulary. After thoroughly learning several lists of topically related words with practice speaking and writing, students hear dialogues that use them. Then more lists and more dialogues. Just enough grammar is presented along the way to make sense of the language. The right and left stereo channels are used to present either foreign and native words or native only words. By listening to both channels at once, each word on the lists is heard first in the two languages simultaneously (one with each ear), then in the foreign language only. Of course you can listen to only one channel if that works better for you. Dr. Aarons told me he feels that the combined way is best, but without seeing more evidence, I'm not so sure as he is.

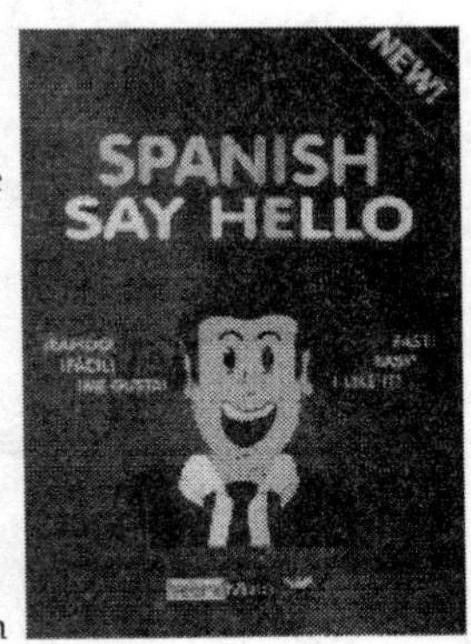

Although the program is more like ones for travel preparation than for serious scholastic study, I have an idea that those who faithfully go through the four cassettes and the manual will have a better preparation than those taking a brief high school course. The thorough grammar, needed for more complex study can come later and without oversimplifications to overcome. This program would be among my first choices except for young children and with listening to one language at a time.

Available for learning Spanish ($39.95) and Japanese ($49.95) and for native speakers of those languages to learn English. Add $4 for shipping, and add tax if you are in Illinois. WordMate, P.O. Box 992 - w, Skokie, IL 60067-0992; (888) 967-3628; Fax (847) 677-6186 ; WordMate@aol.com. For more information, see http://www.bookzone.com/bookzone/10000856.html

Part 2, Supplementary or introductory materials

All-in-one Language Fun Word games for learning a choice of five languages. **CD** format for Mac or PC. $15.00 + $5 shipping (or $10 foreign), no credit cards. Available from Timberdoodle, (360) 426-0672. Timberdoodle Co., 1510 E. Spencer Lake Rd., Shelton, WA 98584

Easy Spanish Crossword Puzzles A small book (5¾" tall, 64 pp.) of six-word puzzles. The picture clues can be colored. Word lists include articles. Answers in the back. By S. Appelbaum and N. Barbaresi. $1 from Dover (No. 27452-7). See Dover in Appendix Y.

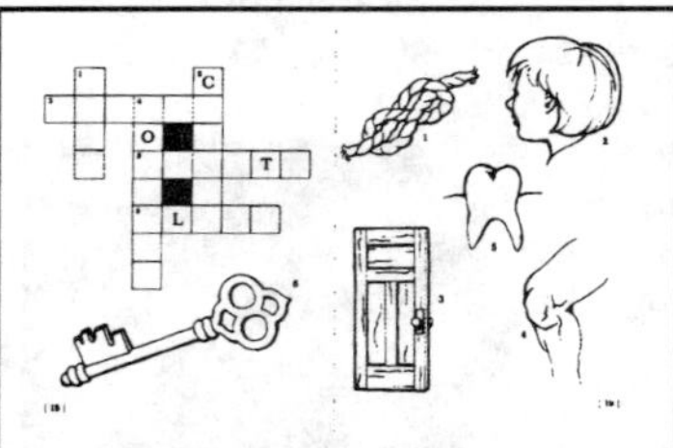

First Thousand Words, The Usborne A book of illustrations with words identifying the various objects. The "first" in the title could not mean the first words in the child's vocabulary because pictured objects are essentially limited to being concrete nouns. Usborn also publishes *First Hundred Words.* Both series are available in several foreign languages. If you don't find a local home-business, Usborn distributor, contact (in the US) EDC Publishing, P.O Box 470663, Tulsa, 74147.

French Folk Songs Listening to these songs can help tune the ear to French after having a basic start in the language. The words are a little difficult to understand in some of the songs. Folk songs tend to have repeated phrases, an obvious advantage for learning. The printed text and translation helps. The professional singing ability of the vocalists isn't the greatest, but that doesn't detract from the usefulness of the tapes. In a couple of ways, the language is different from modern spoken French: (1) Ending vowels not pronounced in speaking are generally pronounced in singing, (2) Folk songs usually have old words or usages. Two tapes (total of 72 minutes) and a 64 page booklet. $29.95 plus $4 shipping (and tax in CT). Audio-Forum (Listed in this appendix).

For other languages, the available music is different. In German, for example, you can get *Sing mit Heino*, a VHS cassette, for $39.95 plus $5 shipping.

Latin and Greek Roots On Line http://www.imt.net/~nwwa/roots-class. **Int.**

Lingua Fun A deck of cards suitable for playing go fish and other simple card games. The cards may matched sets of three. A red card is a pronoun like "I" or "you" and a verb. The gray card is an infinitive action and the blue card is an adverb or adverb phrase telling when. Thus any combination of those three colors makes a sentence. A cassette tape pronounces words on the cards. Carefully studying the cards and practicing would be very helpful in getting started with the language. From Penton Overseas, Inc. See the review of *Lyric Language* following.

Listen and Learn Travel phrases in 10 different languages. Booklet and 90-min. cassette, $8.95. From Dover. See Appendix for address Y.

Lyric Language (VHS) **v-tape** According to the back of the box, "Lyric Language® is the world's most popular bilingual music program for children of all ages . . . because it makes learning fun!" Such a superlative statement sounds impressive – until you remember that sales figures depend on a lot more than quality, and until you ask what is meant by language learning. I reviewed the French version. The tape is 35 minutes long and has a song for each of eleven topics including, visiting the zoo, birthday party, the rain, and the beach. Phrases are sung alternately in English and in French by a bilingual brother and sister while the text is shown at the bottom of the screen. Their pronunciation is very good in both languages. The foreign words would often be difficult to hear clearly because they come fast and close together. The well-planned repetition helps. No clue is offered that ending vowels which are silent in spoken French are pronounced in singing. Your children wouldn't learn much French this way but some. Except for young children, I would stop the motion on the VCR to make word lists, then get some help with pronunciation.

Similar programs are available in German, Japanese, Spanish, and Italian. $14.95 plus shipping (or $9.95 for audio versions). If you order a set of both audio and video tapes ($19.95), you will also get a list of the lyrics. A second tape for each language is also available with a slower pace. Teachers guides and CD-roms have been prepared, too. Ask for their catalog. Penton Overseas, Inc., 2470 Impala Dr., Carlsbad, CA 92008-7226; (800) 748-5804; penton@cts.com.

Spanish Lingo for the Savvy Gringo, revised Author Elizabeth Reid merges Spanish for survival communication with advice for survival in other ways when visiting Latin America. The result is a book anyone can pick up and begin learning from. Spanish words inserted into English sentences (with pronunciation guides and English equivalents) get the point across. For example: "In *la primavera* (la pree-ma-VAY-rah) (spring), many people begin to think of *un jardín* (oon har-DEEN) (a garden). Whether you enjoy *la satisfacción* (la sah-tees-fahk-see-OHN) (the satisfaction) of serving . . . *un jardín* can be a rewarding *passatiempo* (pa-sah-tee-EM-po) (hobby or pastime)." With brief dictionary. From Friendly Foreign Language Learning (See Part 3). $14.95

Multimedia French also in Spanish **CDrom** for Windows The fundamentals of what you would learn in the first year or much of the first year of study in a classroom. Video presentations provide clear explanations and the pronunciation is clear. Each lesson follows a pattern including objective, vocabulary (you click on a word to hear it), various drills, etc. A general pronunciation guide outlines the phonetic rules. On the CD case is this promise, "The tools you need to build and achieve fluency in the French language." Well, not quite. A good set of tools, yes, but to achieve fluency takes years for most of us. This CD will lead you through many hours of productive study, but it is not enough, in my opinion, to learn to the level it covers. You also need to read simple stories using the words and grammar (although you hear and read sentences). You also need to write. Point and click is not enough. And you need to speak, having someone to listen. By itself, you would learn a great deal. In connection with another French program and a live coach, this would be excellent. Pro One Software, P.O. Box 16317, Las Curces, NM 88004.

Spanish Picture Word Book 27779-8, ***German Picture Word Book*** 27778-X, ***French Picture Word Book*** 27777-1. For these, see the description of *English Picture Word Book* in Appendix O. Each $2.95.

Teach Me Series Audio tape and booklet sets pitched to children. Published for French, Spanish, German, Japanese, Hebrew, Russian, Italian, and English. A second level, *Teach Me More Series* continues the same languages except for Hebrew. Teacher's guides are available for each language for each level. I reviewed the first level for French and the second level for Spanish.

Judy Mahoney's idea is good and the material is reasonably well-produced. I don't even object to most of the music. This program (and similar ones) don't teach your children to speak and understand a language, but you may expect learning of a few words if you work with your children and later help them review. The words can then provide a little boost in serious learning later or they may be a start for picking up a travel vocabulary. Although better than many language programs for children, the materials, in my opinion, have some deficiencies.

The first level French program is good, although song words on the tape are at some points hard to understand. Also see my comment about the difference between singing and speaking French in my review of *French Folk Songs*.

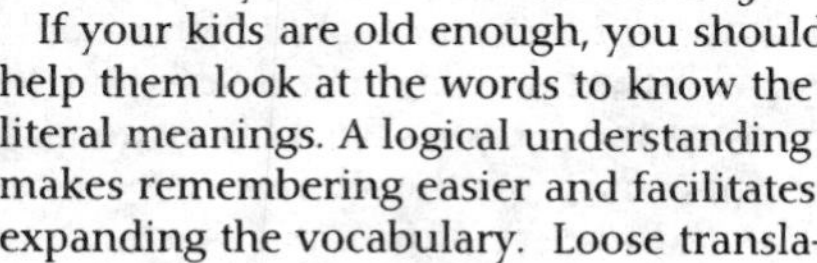

If your kids are old enough, you should help them look at the words to know the literal meanings. A logical understanding makes remembering easier and facilitates expanding the vocabulary. Loose translations are provided in the back of the 16-page booklet. You will need a dictionary. A few common words are covered including colors, days of the week, clothes, dog, cat, house, and words for riding in the car.

The second level Spanish set (the other set which I examined) could have been better. My brother and his wife have spent their professional careers (theology and music) in Latin America and know Spanish better than most nationals. A couple of things they noticed is that one of the songs is Jamaican calypso music, evidently with Spanish translation. Without the printed words, I couldn't understand even the English version. In another song on the tape, a diphthong (double vowel sound) is split into two syllables which is not generally acceptable even in singing. Of course I have looked for little flaws. Most of the material is fine. With dictionary in hand, you will find many good learning experiences for your kids.

The tapes seem short to me. People would be more reluctant to spend $26 for a single tape and brief book than they would to pay $11.95 (teach-me level) + $13.95 (teach-me-more level). Actually it's not so bad. Similar programs would be priced like this. The *Teach Me* tape lengths range from 23 to 30 min. For *Teach Me More* expect 40 to 50 min.

The program is enough for kids to get their ears tuned in a bit to a new language. Even if you're not a kid you will enjoy the tapes. Teacher's books are available but your own teaching instinct may be as good. (They show objectives, vocabulary lists and possible activities.) Add $4 for shipping (for any order). Add tax if sent to Minn. Teach Me Tapes, 9900 Bren Rd. East, #B1-100, Minnetonka, MN 55343; (800) 456-4656; teachme@wavetech.net; http://wavetech.net /~teachme

TriplePlay Plus Reading comprehension for over 1000 words. A program for Windows. Uses voice recognition with a microphone for practicing. Choice of Spanish, French, German, Hebrew, Japanese, Italian, or English. $50 plus 10% shipping (or 25% outside the US). Sold by Timberdoodle Co., 1510 E. Spencer Lake Rd., Shelton, WA 98584; (360) 426-0672.

Words for the World Description by Diane Waring and Tina Farewell from the Lifetime Books & Gifts catalog (See Appendix Z).

This full-color hardbound book covers French, Spanish, Italian, Russian, German, Norwegian, Dutch and Swedish, with 4 cassettes of beginning words and phrases and 4 cassettes of Scripture in these different languages. That alone sets it apart from any other foreign language product we know of, but the book also contains an interesting description of each country, its geography and its foods. I listened to the French and Russian tapes to see how "native"" the accents were and was very, *very* impressed. *-DW. $40.*

Part 3, Suppliers

See Appendix Z for more suppliers

Audio-Forum Publishes and markets a wide range of audio-cassette and book programs in 98 languages including ESL. They also provide tapes in music and literature. 96 Broad St., Guilford, CT 06437; (800) 243-1234; (203) 453-9794. 74537.550@compuserve.com; http://agroalang .com/audioforum.html

AUDIO·FORUM

Calliope Books Source for a wide range of materials on foreign languages. They have language programs, storybooks, comic books, workbooks, coloring books, grammar and verb guides, graded readers, imported books, and activity tapes. Languages are French, German, Hebrew, Spanish, Italian, Portuguese, Russian, and more. Owner, Donna Faturos, has prepared a chapter for this book. If you have questions, are unsure of what language materials to use, or would like a catalogue, she, invites you to call or write. See her review of *Learn the Fast and Fun Way* in this appendix. RR #3, Box 3395, Saylorsburg, PA 18353; (610) 381-2587.

Double-Pawed Software Disk The French program, public domain version, I examined has language errors.

Friendly Foreign Language Learning Books, tapes, and computer programs for learning and practicing major foreign languages. If your order amounts to $20 or more, you will receive a free subscription to *Bueno,* their newsletter (which reminds you of what they sell). Their prices look reasonable, and they sometimes offer discounts. In One EAR Publications, P.O. Box 637., Campo, CA 91906-0637.

V
Work, Business, and Home Skills

*Topic categories: (**1**) work and business, and (**2**) home skills and crafts.*

Part 1, Work Education and Business Management

Five Acres and Independence A classic book last revised in 1940 explains small scale agriculture. The topic may interest home schooling families in several ways: (1) gardening projects provide excellent work education, (2) the rural lifestyle is best for character development, and (3) family participation in growing their own food makes economic sense. This book is not the only one you would want on the topic, but it has so much basic information, from how to choose land to how to store food, that you will want it for reference. Dover No. 20974-1, $7.95. See Appendix Y for Dover.

How to Make Big Money Mowing Small Lawns How teens and others can start a small business. 138 pp., $10.95 from Noble Publishing Associates (See Appendix N). Not examined.

Minding Your Own Business The first half of this book by Raymond and Dorothy Moore philosophizes about general character qualities necessary for successful work. One of these topics is organization. The chapter title reveals the only way anyone can hope to conquer a disorderly life: "Organization: Just a Little Bit at a Time." After illustrating the problem, the authors offer a fundamentally helpful plan of attack: "*Order in my heart.* Whom do I love most, myself or others? *Order in my body.* Do I have my appetite, exercise, rest, and physique under reasonable control? *Order in my family.* Do I have the respect of my spouse and my children? *Order in my house.* Is my house reasonably well organized and my time allotted for optimum efficiency?" The second half of the book begins with the value of learning to work, then gets more specific. Examples show what other people have done as "cottage industries." More suggestions follow under various categories of businesses. The book is definitely worthwhile. 1990, 262 pp. Sold by Christian bookstores or by The Moore Foundation for $10 plus $2.50 shipping. (Box 1, Camas, WA 98607).

School of Tomorrow has high school courses in general business. From their description, their computer-driven typing course is flexible and good. I haven't seen it. See Appendix A for the address.

Small Business Advocate Talk show 6-9 AM Eastern. http://www.smallbusinessadvocate.com/

A Student's Guide to Volunteering A good book about a terrific way to learn by doing. Beyond developing marketable and useful abilities, volunteers have the opportunity to touch people showing that they care. And caring itself is something to be learned. The first part of the book covers some general principles then discusses opportunities in six major areas open to teens. The second part is a listing of resources in the six areas, then volunteer organizations by state (in the U.S.) The chapters include story examples of what volunteering in various jobs is like. One chapter discusses how to set up a youth volunteer organization.

By Theresa Digeronimo, 1995. $10.99 from Career Press, (800) 955-7373, or from bookstores.

***Typing Teacher* Cdrom** for Windows A set of exercises which would lead to keyboard skill. In the "games," words or phrases come across the screen to be typed before they disappear. Pro One Software, 16317, Las Cruces, NM 88004.

Whatever Happened to Penny Candy? See Appendix R for this basic book on economics.

Work at Home Sourcebook A popular book from Live Oak Publications.

Young Entreprneur A periodical with success stories from kids 8 to 18 and tips for small businesses kids can run. 16 pp., 6 issues/yr. $16, US$18 Canada. A catalog of helpful books is available. KidsWay, Inc., 5589 Peachtree Rd., Chamblee, GA 30341; (888) KidsWay; http:/www.kidsway.com

Part 2, Home Skills and Crafts

The Book of Wood Carving Techniques for carving wood in flat wood surfaces, not sculpting of figurines (although I expect the same principles would apply). Children can learn as soon as their fine motor skills are developed.

Author Charles Marshall Sayers writes as if he were in his workshop explaining while you listen. He tells about tools and woods, and he takes you through a series of projects for developing your skill. The "course" won't take a long time to finish although you will need more than a couple of evenings. Why not get the book and browse through it. It's a chance to develop a skill you can enjoy the rest of your life. Or even if you (or your child) do spend only an evening or two on a special project, chances are it will be a rewarding experience. $6.95 from Dover (23654-4). See Appendix Y.

The Carpenter's Son Woodcraft Kits for making small objects with precut wood pieces, "designed to be both educational and recreational." I have examined the "Cassette Crates" kit. Pieces of wood become a set of two racks. Each holds a dozen cassettes. Building them requires sanding, measuring to see where to attach the slats that run between the end blocks, gluing, and nailing. In addition to the wood pieces, you get sandpaper, nails, and paints. Instructions are clear. Price $8.95. Other kits (various prices) are a cedar chest, bookends, an apple-shaped bank with clear plastic sides, doll furniture, etc. A set of 120 blocks costs $37.95. The log building sets also look interesting. Shipping is $4.75 for purchases through $20 and $5.75 to $40. .3209 Willowbrook Circle, Waco, TX 76711; (254) 756-5261.

Easy-to-Make Old-Fashioned Toys "Often the most exciting toys for the child are those that are based upon a scientific principle. A spinning top demonstrates the idea of centrifugal force, and a picture flip-book demonstrates the phenomenon of the persistence of vision, which makes possible motion-picture films."

You may have seen a few of the thirty-nine 18th and 19th century toys described in this 271-page book, but I expect most will be totally new. Fascinating historical information and some 300 illustrations. The book is not an antique reprint, although it was adapted from an old book. Instructions require simple easy-to-use materials like tape and plastic straws. Six-year olds can make a few of the toys. Others require more maturity. $8.95 from Dover. Item 25958-7. See Dover in Appendix Y.

Fun With Kids in the Kitchen Cookbook Vegetarian ideas for healthful food kids can prepare. Some are very simple like making your own trail mix. Many, still simple, are marked "adult help needed." Food names reveal the cheerful approach of the book: "Rocket Banana Pops," "Apple Smiles," "Garden Basket Salad," and "Edible Play Dough," for example. From Review & Herald. See *Forever Stories* in Appendix N.

My First Sewing Books Each of Winky Cherry's sewing kits includes an instruction booklet and materials. Level I, *My First Sewing Book* (available also in Spanish) has the child make two felt stuffed birds about 5 inches across with hand stitching using a large needle and embroidery-type thread. At Level II, *My First Embroidery Book,* your child will make a simple name sampler. Level III is called *My First Doll Book.* Two simple felt stuffed dolls 5½ inches tall are made. Level IV is *My First Machine Sewing Book.* In introducing the use of the sewing machine it teaches making straight and curved stitch lines. Two star shapes are sewn inside-out, then turned and stuffed.

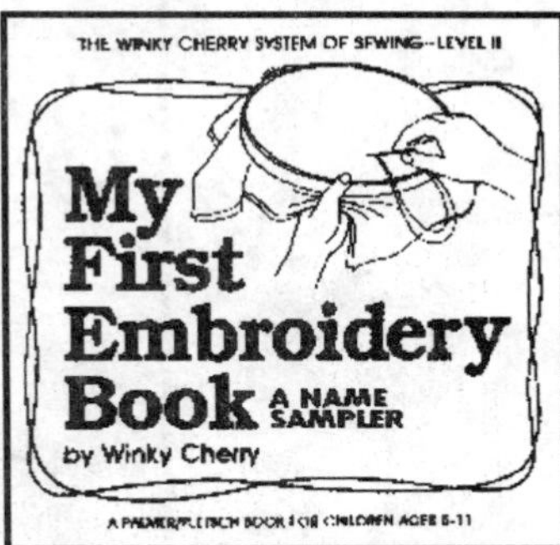

All four books are mostly written in rhyming verse. Ellipsis points show as they appear in the verses.

> Wash your hands . . .
> before you sew.
> Make a clean workspace . . .
> and you are ready to go!

Handling even a large needle and heavy thread requires a certain amount of fine motor control. So although the first three kits are advertised for ages 5-11, I wonder if children might find them easier when older than 5. But I learned to sew doll clothes with a small clamp on-the-table, hand crank sewing machine so young that I don't remember actually "learning" to sew. Maybe I'm selling the 5-year-olds-too short! Of course, it depends on the individual. At $12.95 each, there are cheaper ways to learn to sew, but these kits do look like fun. From Palmer/Pletsch Publishing, P.O. Box 12046, Portland, OR 97212-0046; (800) 728-3784; ron@palmerpletsch.com. *–Karen Wade.*

Primary Patterns Sewing patterns for kids to use to make clothes for them to wear. Heavy paper, sizes 6-16. Also a book on methods for teaching sewing. P.O. Box 19429, Detroit, MI 48219-0429; (800) 578-4201.

W

Testing Services

Testing provides the objective evaluation to help you know where and how to strengthen your teaching, and it gives you assurance in knowing how well you and your child have succeeded. Different kinds of tests are available as you can see below. Several service providers are listed on the next page. The descriptions in the box on this page are from the Bob Jones University Press booklet, Testing and Evaluation Service; Information and Order Form. *Copyright 1998 by the Bob Jones University Press Testing and Evaluation Service. Used by permission.*

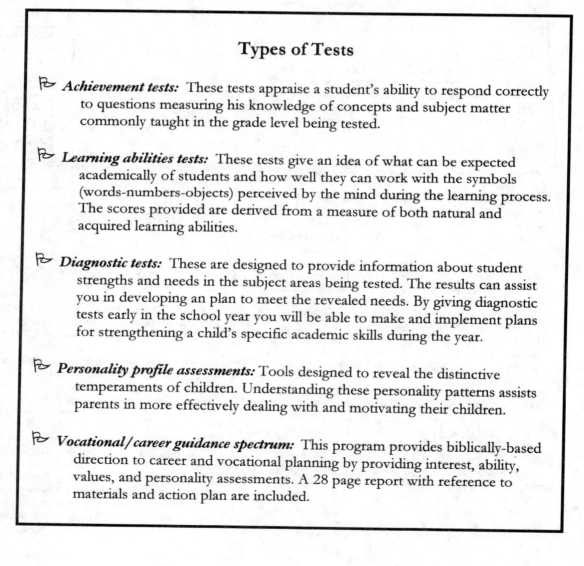

Types of Tests

- ***Achievement tests:*** These tests appraise a student's ability to respond correctly to questions measuring his knowledge of concepts and subject matter commonly taught in the grade level being tested.

- ***Learning abilities tests:*** These tests give an idea of what can be expected academically of students and how well they can work with the symbols (words-numbers-objects) perceived by the mind during the learning process. The scores provided are derived from a measure of both natural and acquired learning abilities.

- ***Diagnostic tests:*** These are designed to provide information about student strengths and needs in the subject areas being tested. The results can assist you in developing an plan to meet the revealed needs. By giving diagnostic tests early in the school year you will be able to make and implement plans for strengthening a child's specific academic skills during the year.

- ***Personality profile assessments:*** Tools designed to reveal the distinctive temperaments of children. Understanding these personality patterns assists parents in more effectively dealing with and motivating their children.

- ***Vocational/career guidance spectrum:*** This program provides biblically-based direction to career and vocational planning by providing interest, ability, values, and personality assessments. A 28 page report with reference to materials and action plan are included.

Bob Jones University Press, Testing and Evaluation Service You can have your children tested just about anywhere in the world through the BJUP service. Some tests may be administered only by an approved person. A variety of standardized tests is available including The Iowa Test of Basic Skills and The Metropolitan Diagnostic Tests. BJUP also offers a writing evaluation series, personality profiles, and career guidance. Test fees seem reasonable. Discounts on achievement tests are offered to members of Home School Legal Defense Association. You should also expect to compensate the person who administers the tests. BJU Press Testing Service, Greenville, SC 29614–0062; (800) 845–5731; fax (800) 525–9398.

Christian Liberty Academy Testing Service. Call (800) 832–2741 or visit www.homeschools.org or write Christian Liberty Academy, 502 W. Euclid Ave., Arlington Heights, IL 60004.

Diagnostic Prescriptive Assessment For a long time I have held the idea that tests could be prepared to substitute for the standardized achievement tests generally used for external evaluation. Tests from textbook publishers come into this category but I have not seen many others. Jill Dixon who has studied in areas of English education and special education has prepared a set of tests with the goals expressed by the title she has given them. She sent me a copy of her second grade test for my review.

To judge the quality of a test we must see how well it reaches its goals. Considering her first goal, to diagnose the degree of ability of a child studying at a certain grade level, let's consider what you should expect. (1) The test must measure what its creators says it does. (2) Responses (answers) must not be influenced by abilities in other areas or in basic intelligence. (3) Test items must mean to the student what they do to the one who determines what the right answers are.

For the first criterion, Mrs. Dixon based her test items on the expectations reflected by textbooks and from her knowledge, as a testing consultant, of the more traditional tests. She also analyzed lists of what is typically covered in each grade. The scope announced for her tests is reasonable, assuming she has kept her test up to date.

For our second expectation, test results must not be influenced by abilities outside of the topics being tested. A tough expectation to meet. Obviously, reading ability affects any test that requires reading the questions. For a child who is an unusually poor reader, we can take the circumstances into account. Of course a good test avoids items that may likely be answered from common sense or special knowledge other than the one being tested.

The usual measuring instruments Mrs. Dixon's tests might substitute for, go through a rigorous and expensive process. They are prepared by teams of people who hammer out the items. Then drafts of the test are tried out on large numbers of students with many different backgrounds. Feedback from these trials guides revision before publication. Then the final version is given to a wide variety of students and those scores are analyzed to determine what to expect from students at different levels of ability. Periodically the tests are revised to keep pace with the changing instructional process.

The test I saw has many good qualities, but also what I consider weaknesses. In the area of word recognition, students are asked to pronounce a list of words. The stated objective is, "The student must correctly pronounce 146 of the following 182 words in order to master 2nd grade word recognition skills." You need to be aware of this special definition for "recognition." The meanings of the words are not directly tested. The major exam publishers also test pronunciation to determine understanding. They apparently have found, or at least assume, that better pronouncers understand better, too. It seems to me that in the four seconds allotted per word, a child who has learned phonics well should be able to pronounce even invented words which have no meaning.

Some questions in the social studies section and some in the reading section may be answered by common sense. Several sections specifically measure phonics skills. Reading comprehension (the end result) is not measured here. Nor does the test say it is. The writing and handwriting test is quite good; and you are shown how to evaluate it. The math section is good in calculation skill but does not deal with concepts behind the way we manipulate numbers in math operations. In recent years, mathematics instruction standards have called for helping children understand why numbers behave as they do. This basic understanding is better measured in tests for higher grades where it is more important. I have not seen those tests. The science section may not test what you teach, but you can recognize this from the items, and judge your teaching accordingly.

Mrs. Dixon's tests begin with kindergarten. I have reservations about the validity of any printed tests (even when the test giver reads the questions) before the second or third grade because children mature slowly and differently and their ability to communicate what they know tends to make test results unreliable.

In summary, this tool can give you an idea of your child's weak or missing areas. I have judged it by quality standards I would expect from such instruments. While scores from this test series might not provide very precise measures, the tests do offer some advantages. You can use them whenever you wish. As you watch your child's performance you will still get ideas for helping him or her. I would not hesitate to use these tests although, from time to time, I would use one of the more common tests such as the Iowa Test of Basic Skills..

The second grade book has 66 pages including instructions, key, and remedial suggestions. (You don't give all the tests at one time.) Higher grades would need to be larger. Available for K through 5. Price per grade, $35 plus $3 shipping. Add tax if in Georgia. Diagnostic Prescriptive Services, P.O. Box 5098 TE, Savannah, GA 31414.

Blumenfeld Oral Reading Assessment Test Described in Appendix O.

***Hewitt PASS* (Personalized Achievement Summary System)** ". . . designed to identify your child's learning strengths and needs, and to help you select activities and materials which will further aid your child in the acquisition of knowledge." Tests are available in the areas of reading, mathematics and languages for upper and lower elementary grades. A short preliminary test is provided to assign a test form at close to the level of your child's ability. All the forms are in the booklet which you get on loan from Hewitt. Reasonable care was given to establishing the quality of the tests. Items were tried out on many students. The tests are returned to Hewitt for scoring and interpreting.

I have a few concerns about the quality of the tests, but overall I think you will find them quite helpful. In the math tests, story problems are very simple thus limiting what can be known about the ability to apply math to real situations. Also the ability to work problems in logical steps showing *how* an answer was determined is not tested in the multiple-choice format. One test item I noticed was unclear since the choices came before the question. It took me a good while to see what was happening. This is an exception to the usually clear items.

In the reading tests brief paragraphs are given followed by multiple-choice questions. Many of the questions can be answered by common sense without reading the paragraph. Here is an example of a set of choices which I have made up (since it wouldn't be fair to copy from the test). Imagine a paragraph about going shopping followed by these options: *Before selecting the breakfast cereal, Roger's mom (a) paid the clerk, (b) helped Roger carry the groceries to the car, (c) read the nutrition information on the boxes, (d) drove home.* Of course reading is tested by reading the choices, too, so you still have some idea but, in my opinion, the test may measure intelligence and experience as much as it does reading.

The PASS tests in other language areas measure the usual spelling, punctuation, etc. Hewitt Research Foundation, P.O. Box 9, Washougal, WA 98671.

Johnson O'Connor Research Foundation 347 Beacon St., Boston, MA 02116. A testing and research organization specializing in aptitude tests since 1922. This type of tests measure natural abilities – activities that an individual is apt to do well. They do not test intelligence or achievement. Eleven locations: Atlanta (404) 261-8013; Boston (as Human Engineering Laboratory) (617) 536-0409; Chicago (312) 787-9141; Dallas/FW (972) 550-9033; Denver (303) 388-5600; Houston (713) 783-3411; Los Angeles (213) 380-1947; New York (212) 838-0550; San Francisco (415) 772-9030; Seattle (206) 623-4070; Washington, DC (301) 424-9445.

School of Tomorrow (ACE) offers the California Achievement Test (to measure achievement) and the Test of Cognitive Skills (to measure potential). Diagnostic tests for their program are also available. See Appendix A.

Sylvan Children's Skills Tests Available for K-3, 4-6, and 7-9 on **CDrom** for Windows or Mac. Testing in areas of reading, math, and spelling broken into components. The tests are like games. They may be used as often as you like. You set it up to keep records for each child. Web price, $29.95 each. You might pay a different price when ordering by phone. Other tests are available, too. Their IQ test, for example costs $24.95. They have samples of some tests on their web site. I tried the creativity one. You can answer the questions to make the test come out as you would like to appear, but probably most such tests are that way. The need for shuch a test may be questioned. Sylvan, 200 Highland Ave., Needham, MA 02194; (800) 301-9545; fax (781) 449-4887; http://www.VirtualKnowledge.com/SkillsTest.htm

Writing Performance Evaluations: Produced and offered by BJU Press in addition to tests in several categories. They assist in the development of writing skills. The series permits students in grades 3 to 12 to be guided through the creation of writing samples then to have their writing performance evaluated by professionals. I have not reviewed them.

X

Reference Works

This appendix covers:
(part **1***) encyclopedias*
(part **2***) other principle reference works,*
(part **3***) product review sources,*
(part **4***) other reference materials.*

On Choosing an encyclopedia

A good encyclopedia is an asset to a home school. I have not reviewed any of the print versions.

I suggest you go to a library and look at the sets they have. You could ask the opinion of the children's librarian, too. Getting the very latest edition is less important than finding a book suitable for the level of your children. The regular editions of *Britannica* and *Americana* are probably not good choices before the senior high level (and even used ones would be quite expensive.) *The New Columbia Encyclopedia* is published in one volume, fine print. I have found my copy useful but it is not for elementary level students.

Because you buy a lot of pages in a major reference set, prices are usually enough to take a considerable bite out of a home schooling budget. You may be able to find a used set discarded from a library or in a used book store.

Something has happened recently in our exploding information age that we would not have thought of a few years ago. Encyclopedias on compact disc have become popular. They offer more than their print counterparts by including sounds and animations and they are cheaper. A few years ago Compton's came out with their CD version at $895. Now the prices of the popular ones (including Compton's) which you are apt to choose from are less than 10% of that at around $50 and the products are better. You may be able to pick up a older edition of a CD encyclopedia for $20 or even less. Read the ads carefully because you may not realize when you are getting an older version. The actual information probably won't change all that much in a year or two, but the interface of newer versions could be a bit nicer.

Selling points for CD encyclopedias are the animations, sound clips, and videos. These are fun but not as valuable as the text (except for less mature kids), and they are used with a very small percent of the articles. In other words, they may not be a good measure of the book's value.

Computers have gotten more sophisticated and cheaper too. To pinch the pennies, you can look for a used older-generation one. Just get some good advice. If you feel unable to afford a computer, your kids will learn just the same. You could put them in school and get a job to afford the computer, but no computer will replace the quality time you spend with them. Real wealth isn't measured in bank

Part 1, Encyclopedias

Collier's Encyclopedia The 1998 edition has 3 **CDroms** and boasts 45,000 articles and multimedia elements. In comparing, be careful to notice that not all the 45,000 are articles. It includes maps from De Agostini Rand-McNally and *The American Heritage Dictionary* with over 100,000 words. Simulations include visiting the Mayan ruins, creating an earthquake, doing a chemistry experiment, conducting a band, and discovering the results of health lifestyles. You may connect automatically to a large number of Internet sites (through your Internet provider). Collier's has been around for more than a century. For being short of time, I didn't ask for a copy to review. When I saw it in Sam's Club

for $55 less $50 rebate, I couldn't resist. Sorry, the $50 rebate has expired, but you might not pay as much as $55 either. List is $79.95. Apparently for Windows only. http://www.sierra .com plus sites for the UK, France, and Germany. US phone (425) 644-4343. Published by Sierra On-Line.

***Encarta* CDrom** This, I understand, is the Funk & Wagnall's encyclopedia which has been taken over by Microsoft. I have the '95 edition which will likely not change drastically in the near future. Its fundamental search tool called "find" lets you key in a word or several words. As you do, it brings the menu list to article titles at or near what you specified. Instead of using "find" you may narrow your field by one of nine general categories each with sub-topics. You may also specify a historical time frame and a geographical location and what multimedia features you want (excluding articles that don't have them).

From the article itself, you see highlighted words which hyperlink to related topics. Illustrations can be enlarged and even sent to your printer (as they may in other CD encyclopedias). Only certain articles have pictures and among them, only certain ones have sound clips. Still the encyclopedia boasts of 9.5 hours of audio and 8,000 illustrations.

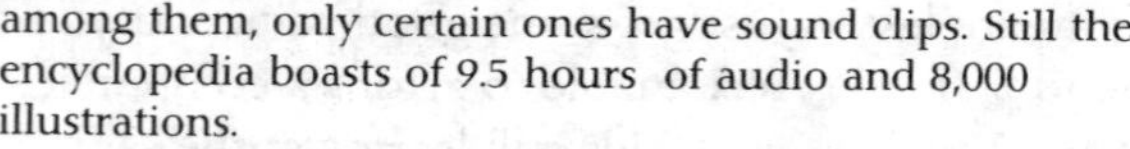

As "tools" you will find a dictionary, a thesaurus, and a note pad. The note pad is a small window you can use to record your ideas while viewing the larger window or article on your screen. You can cut and paste from the articles, as well as from the notepad. When you do, the software makes sure to add the copyright information. When you set up the encyclopedia it allows you to choose a word processor which it will open when needed, ready for you to paste into or to write in.

500 maps are available and clicking on many of the names on them brings up the pronunciations. As in other encyclopedias, bird calls and musical instrument sounds enhance the information.

The "Mind Maze" is a game that asks for information from your selection of one of the encyclopedia's nine categories. You try to work your way through doors and areas in a castle. It is not at all intuitive (a bummer for one who likes to explore without reading the directions). My real objection, however, is to the game's psychic motif although such is popular in our society. With children to influence, I would look for a different encyclopedia.

Overall, the "book" provides a pleasurable way to get information. For 1998, you may expect to pay $45 for a 1-CD version, which is the size of my older edition. Or you could pay $75 for a 2-CD version.

Encyclopedia Americana This is a **CD** version of the 25 million word "megapedia" of information. The number of articles -- 45,000 -- is not so many more than in Compton's and Encarta, but these are long and often technical articles. They are by some 6,500 contributors (a few more than we brag about for *The Home School Manual*). From what I understand you may expect good search capabilities, line art and numerous tables, but no fancy audio-visual entertainment. Published by Grolier. Suggested retail in 1997, starting at $500. You may also subscribe to on-line Internet access to this encyclopedia. Figure paying $1000.

Family Encyclopedia This single-volume print book has over 13,000 entries and 1500 color illustrations. I have not examined it. It's from Oxford University Press and is likely selections or abridgments from the publisher's Columbia Encyclopedia which I own. My 1975 edition is also a single volume which has 3,000 pages small print. The *Family Encyclopedia* has 744 pages, and I expect you will like it. 1997, $45.

Grolier Multimedia Encyclopedia The 1998 edition offers the typical number of articles (35,000). Nearly half have at least an illustration. Some have other multimedia features. I have reviewed the "deluxe 2-**CDrom**s edition" which, with the necessary nuisance of switching discs when prompted, enlarges the wealth of information to a total of, 15 hours of sound, and 15,000 images, and more movies. The most important information along with many multimedia items are on the single-disc version. As with other CD encyclopedias, you can copy text and images to your word processor and save locations to find easily for future reading.

The two-disk version offers more of the fancy things that require large portions of disk space plus a dictionary and online connections. You also have Internet access to some of Grolier's massive *Encyclopedia Americana* (21,000 links) and to their easier reading encyclopedia *The New Book of Knowledge* (16,000 links). This gives you more articles on the topic of your interest, with inevitable duplication of information. It also offers "Online Knowledge Explorer," a system of links to specific web sites which offer information on many topics you might choose. Article updates (around 500 a month) are also available on line.

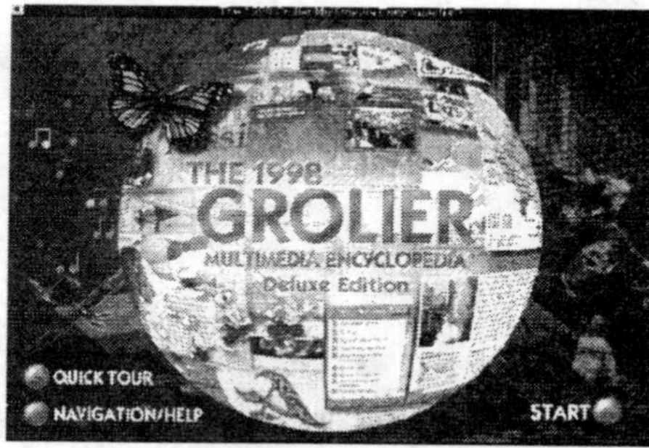

The software could be more intuitive and easier to use, but it's not bad. Official prices are $49.95 + $5.95 shipping for the single disc, and $20 more for the 2-disk version. Upgrades are $20 and $30 less. New purchasers get a software premium. I noticed a street price for the 2-CD version at $50 ($20 less than list). (800) 285-4534; http://www.grolier.com.

A DVD-ROM version, spring 1998. DVD technology increases the capacity by a factor of seven. This means more to see and hear with better sound and full motion video. For Windows and Mac.

Infopedia A **CD** reference tool with the unique feature of drawing from more than its base, *The Funk & Wagnalls New Encyclopedia*. The other sources are a thesaurus, a world atlas, an almanac, and dictionaries of words, quotations, usage, and biography. Searches show which sources cover the selected topic. For example, you can read the definition of scientific principle in the word dictionary then read more about how it works in the encyclopedia, watch a video clip or an animation (in a few cases) and then turn to biographies of key people involved in discovering it. In all, over 200,000 entries are within several clicks of your mouse. Although some of the sources are less detailed than one might wish, in all, this CD appears to offer better coverage of a topic you are likely to select than does its competitors.

The Boolean word search capability allows you to find topics that have all or any of several words and not others, and it draws on all the sources at once (encyclopedia, dictionary, etc.). The tool includes morphing maps to discus changes over time, animations (such as a demonstration of the CAT scanner), pictures, videos, and sound clips. The project tool makes it easy to write papers for school assignments and include multimedia clips. Most of these features are also offered by other CD encyclopedias.

In the next version I would like to see a few of the features more intuitive. It took a little trial and error for me to discover how to switch among the 12 major subject areas. The Boolean search results need to highlight all the words in an article that match the selected ones, and paragraphs breaks need to be clearer. These points are relative minor, however. As with similar applications, you need a not-too-old computer with Windows.™ This software is very reasonably priced and published by Softkey. Version 2.0 reviewed.

Random House Kid's Encyclopedia Multimedia with report writing feature. There are 2,000 text entries, 1,000 narrated entries, and 150 animations and movie clips. **CDrom** for Windows. Not reviewed.

World Book According to their web site, the 1998 home version has three **CDrom** disks including a "medical encyclopedia." The telephone order line announced on their site has been disconnected – a slip that will likely have been fixed long before you read this (or I made some kind of error). In a chain office supply store, I found a 1-CD version for $40 (round numbers) less $10 rebate. *World Book* has been known for the editorial policy of making the beginnings of their articles easy for children who read to understand. http://www.worldbook.com. Not examined.

On choosing a dictionary

A children's dictionary may be helpful for young scholars, but soon becomes inadequate. An adult, college-level, dictionary is suitable for children in the middle grades and up. You could explain now and then if necessary. A good dictionary is more important than other reference books.

Your CD encyclopedia will likely include a dictionary, but you will want a pint dictionary, too, if you can afford it because cranking up the computer and putting the right CD in the drive is a lot more hassle than simply pulling a book from the shelf.

Part 2, Other Principle Reference Works

Merriam Webster's Collegiate Dictionary **CD** (Windows or Macintosh). A good basic dictionary for serious study. 10th edition, 160,000 entries. The disc reviewed here I received from a friend who is an Amway distributor. The dictionary includes tables and a phonetic pronunciation guide for the marks it uses but no other frills that gobble up megabytes. In fact, 97% of the recorded space on the disc is a catalog with samples of 170 CD-ROMs published by Zane Publishing and distributed by Amway. If you can borrow a copy, it's worth spending some time browsing.

The standard edition of this electronic dictionary comes with a thesaurus and the 15,000 entry *American Concise Encyclopedia*. Price $25 (with a penny change). Zane publishes a wide range of titles (currently over 200) on the sorts of topics that make good use of multimedia. The publisher is not a part of Amway and uses other distribution channels as well. Most of the discs are priced at a penny under $15. Add $5.99 shipping for any size order. In sets, they cost less. Zane Publishing, 1950 Stemmons, Suite 4044, Dallas, TX 75207-3109; (800) 485-5947; http://www.zane.com.

Scholastic Children's Dictionary From the advertisement, this looks like a nice book for $16.95. 30,000 entries including current topics like *cyberspace* and *acid rain*. Phonetic pronunciation, they say, helps with spelling. 1000 diagrammed illustrations. 1996, For ages 8 and up. (800)-724-6527.

Thesaurus for Kids This reference book has a degree of value for choosing fresh words for writing projects. Occasional idioms add to the interest. The book is marked as for ages 8 to 12. I expect many kids in this bracket could use a regular thesaurus even though they would understand a smaller percentage of the words. 1993, 144 pp., $7.95 plus $2.50 for shipping. From McClanahan Book Company, 23 W. 26th St., New York NY 10010.

Webster's Concise Encyclopedia CD-ROM for Windows. Although this encyclopedia is indeed "concise" compared to others on CD, it has good information (as of 1994). It would not work for me before I followed instructions to adjust my screen pixels down from 1024 X 768 and to reduce my font size. It did operate on more than the minimum 640 X 480. Most Windows software is written so that it looks at your computer settings and adjusts to fit them. The interface isn't as intuitive as it might be, but it works fine when you see what to do. Over 20,000 entries. From Pro One Software (labeled as Softsource), P.. Box 16317, Las Cruces, NM 88004; (505) 523-6200. The disc may be bundled with others from this company. See on *Multimedia* High School Math Series in appendix Q.

Webster's Concise Reference Library A trio of basic reference information combining a dictionary, a world atlas, and a guide to grammar and usage. Although I would emphasize "concise" more than "library" in the book's title, it's a good investment for a home school with very limited money. The dictionary has brief definitions of the 40,000 more common English words and is in small print. The atlas, from the cartographers of *Encyclopedia Britannica,* is clear and counts 14,000 locations. The third part is a "concise guide to punctuation and style." You get a lot of information packed into 228 eleven-inch pages. Hardcover, 1996, from Smithmark Publishers. Priced at about $10. Available through bookstores.

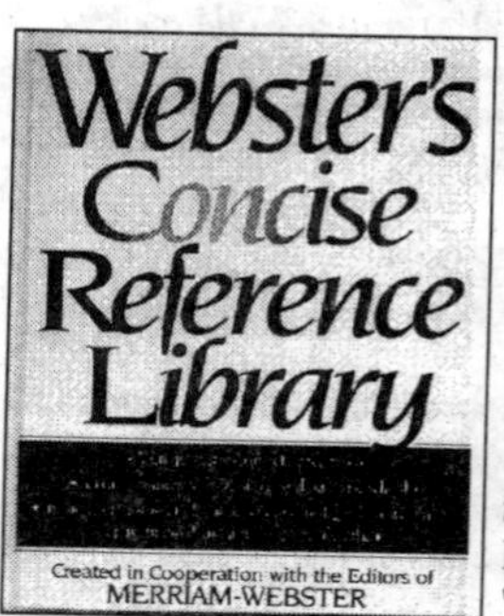

Part 3, Product Review Publications

The Big Book of Home Learning The "big book" is now three books, each covering a different type of learning materials. (1) Getting Started, (2) Preschool and Elementary, (3) Jr. high through college. They include detailed product reviews and discussions of the issues or methods involved with various categories of learning and teaching. Mary tries to look out for your best interests. 20 reviewers contributed to this set. If you can't buy all three books, you could get the first one and one of the others. By Mary Pride. 1997. $25 each. Published by Crossway Books. Available also from Home Life, Inc., P.O. Box 1250, Fenton, MO 63026-1850, (800) 346-6322; Fax (314) 343-7203.

Christian Home Educators' Curriculum Manual, in two volumes: *Elementary Grades* (K-6) and *Junior/Senior High* (7-12). By Cathy Duffy. Both volumes discuss learning styles, planning (with charts you may photocopy), materials, and methods for general teaching and for each major subject. 1997-98 editions are each close to 400 pages in length. The "recommendations" section in each book is organized by general grade level. Each block is divided into subjects, and options for various books and other materials are discussed. We expect that you will appreciate reviews in *The Home School Manual,* but a variety of viewpoints is good, and you may find Cathy's specific curriculum suggestions more practical in some ways. These reference books are updated every two years. The Duffys began teaching their three boys in 1982.

Prices: $19.95 for each book plus $2.50 shipping. For both books with shipping, send $38.90. Grove Publishing, 16172 Huxley Cir., Westminster, CA 92683. Phone: (714) 841-1220; http://www.jatec.com/grove

Good Stuff, *Learning Tools for All Ages.* Description and evaluation of a large number of materials. Author Rebecca Rupp explains that she and her husband "try to maintain an even flow of basic academics" in their home schooling program while encouraging their children's individual learning interests. "All this variety, as any parent/teacher quickly discovers, soon leads to an overwhelming feeling of too many spinning plates in the air." Then she mentions some of her sons' interests which require learning materials. "The resources listed in this book," she continues, "are intended to help parents and teachers provide a fertile learning environment for their children."

The product reviews are divided into categories: "Reading and Literature," "Creative Thinking," etc. Within each, the products appear alphabetically. Prices and other ordering information are not shown but, of course, addresses and phone numbers are so you can get current information. Materials are selected from secular sources; but many will be of interest to those who home teach from a religious motivation.

By Rebecca Rupp. 392 pp., 1997 edition, $22.95 from Holt Associates, 2269 Massachusetts Ave., Cambridge, MA 02140; (617) 864-3100.

Home School Manual, The Which you are looking at.

Home School Source Book, The Second Edition, Revised. In an earlier *Home School Manual,* I described the first edition as significant "particularly for those families who prefer an open, less-religious emphasis (different from mine)." In response to my description, author Donn Reed explained, "I don't think it's really fair or accurate to say I have *less* religion just because it's different." I can buy that. He was certainly an independent thinker, and he has made a significant contribution to the variety of ideas about home education. Donn is now deceased. His wife, Jean, is carrying the torch.

He was one of the early leaders of the home schooling movement as it came to prominence in the 70s. In fact, he was practicing it then as well as preaching about it. His book comes from combining and updating his earlier books, *The First Home-school Catalogue* (a listing and discussion of educational products) and *The Home-school Challenge* ("methods and philosophy of a common-sense, 'no-tears,' approach" including minimal structure and resistance to organized religion). Among the topics dealt with are: global awareness, cultural literacy, discipline, censorship, the teaching of fundamental school subjects, and getting legal permission to do it. The current 1994 edition has about 280 pages. $20 plus $2 postage. For more information, send a first-class stamp to: "Free Brochure" Brook Farm Books, P.O. Box 246, Bridgewater, ME 04735. In Canada, the book costs C$25.50 + $3 shipping, GST included, from Brook Farm Books, Glassville, N.B. E0J 1L0.) bfbooks@nbnet.nb.ca

A Bible concordance

This is an important reference tool for those who are studying the Bible. There is no substitute for digging to find your own information. Concordances are available for modern translations, and you may want one. Strong's is maybe the best of the old ones and because it is in the public domain, you can buy them for a very reasonable price. In the back of the standard Strong's version is a dictionary which gives you other possible meanings of words. The King James Version concordances are adequate for finding just about anything you want even if you actually look up your passage in a modern Bible. You just have to remember the what the older words mean. For example "conversation" in the KJV means behavior, "suffer" means permit, and "prevent" means precede. Nearly all the words still mean the same as they did. Also spellings have changed for a few words.

Also you might want a computer concordance. They are not only quicker, but you can limit your searches to verses that have all of several words or one of several words. Consider *On Line Bible.*

Prides' Guide to Educational Software Bill and Mary Pride share their evaluations of hundreds of educational software programs. They give the basic information about what your computer needs to run the program, the price, the publisher, etc. They grade each program on concept, usability, and educational value, and they describe it in some detail from a user point of view. To introduce their reviews, they discuss the history of educational software, types and options for computers, and how to buy them. Revised edition due fall, 1998. http://www.home-school.com

Part 4, Other Reference Sources

Home Schooling Resource Guide & Directory of Organizations From Ambleside Educational Press, P.O. Box 2524, Cartersville, GA 30120; (770) 917-9141. 1998, 42 pp. spiral bound. $15.

How to Stock a Quality Home Library Inexpensively See Appendix P.

The Authentic Jane Williams' Home School Market Guide A resource book for those dealing with the home schooling market $150 plus $8.00 shipping and 7¼% tax if to California. Bluestocking Press, P.O. Box 2030, Shingle Springs, CA 95682-2030.

On Line Bible A first-rate software product published with the purpose of sharing with friends. Because royalties have to be paid for modern Bible versions, the electronic databases for them can't be copied legally without permission, access to them costs a little more than the otherwise minimal fee. A KJV-only version may be copied. The materials and shipping cost for the (unrestricted) KJV, IBM version – **disks** and manual – is $24. They also have it on a **CDrom** with windows interface which includes KJ, KJ21, Asv, BBE, Young's and Weymouth NT. It has lexicons, topical information, a dictionary, some maps, stories, and Matthew Henry's concise commentary. The search engine is very good, too. Price $9.95 (plus their flat postage charge of $3). They have other features on more expensive versions. These include access to NIV, NRSV, RSV, and some older Bibles including foreign languages, even the McGuffy readers. Versions for windows and Mac at various prices. Ask for their catalog. Online Bible USA, P.O. Box 21, Bronson, MI 49028; (800) 243-7124; or Fax (517) 369-2518. You can even use your credit card.

Parent Educator's Ready Reference, The To be published shortly after this book appears. Described as "A quick reference guide to terms, math processes, dates, etc. in the four main subject areas (Language Arts, Math, Social Studies, and Science) for parent and student. Includes a home school glossary for everyone confused by all those acronyms like HSLDA, ISP, IEP, and words like cumulative file, branches of study, etc." 1998, from Christian Home Educators Press.

What Your Child Needs to Know When See Appendix J.

Y

Mixed Subjects, Mixed Publishers

This appendix is divided as follows:
(1) *Unit studies materials,*
(2) *Full curriculum packages,*
(3) *Other products for more than one subject area,*
(4) *Multi-topic publishers which may not be listed elsewhere in this book, and*
(5) *Other interests of home schoolers.*

We have shown most curriculum products in one of the subject appendices. Publishers offering products in several categories, but with a dominant area, are generally listed in the appendix for that area. Other multi-area publishers, however, seem best represented in this general "mixed" category.

Part 1, Unit studies materials

Unit study guides for specific subjects are included in the respective subject appendices

Everything You Need to Know About Unit Studies Jennifer Steward simplifies and explains unit studies in chapters entitled, "Choosing a Teaching Method," "Get on Your Mark . . . GO!," "The Two Key Elements of Unit Studies," "Incorporating Subjects Into Unit Studies," "Planning Unit Studies," "Books," and so on. I have not seen the book because it is in press as HSM is being prepared. Price is expected to be around $15 plus shipping. From Steward Ship, P.O. Box 164, Garden Valley, CA 95633 Phone (888) 4 R UNITS. http://www.unitstudies.com. 1998 (not examined).

STEWARD SHIP

Also from Steward Ship: (1) *Everything You Need to Build a Unit Study Notebook*, a collection of forms to fill out, section dividers, K-12 assignment ideas, and explanations. $19.95. (2) Unit study guides including the following topics: Pilgrims, nutrition, ants, colonial times, volcanoes, California History, creation science, civil war, tall tales, and Columbus. Shipping to the contiguous US is 10% with a minimum of $4.

Far Above Rubies A full high school curriculum prepared like a unit study. *Listen My Son* is similar. See Part 2.

How to Create Your Own Unit Study After spending several years developing her ideas about how best to home teach her children, Valerie Bendt wrote this manual to share the plan she developed. It covers essential ideas of how to be a home teacher using unit studies.

For a unit study, you pick a topic like "transportation" and expand it in profitable learning areas with the input of your children. Learning areas like reading, social studies, science, and art may come into it. Mrs. Bendt teaches math as a separate subject. To keep the bases covered, she recommends (and sells) the book, *Teaching Children, a Curriculum Guide to What Children Need to Know at Each Level Through Sixth Grade.* by Diane Lopez. For her home school she plans four 10-week sessions throughout a 12-month school year – not a bad idea. She generally covers two units in each session.

Here is the outline of the core section of her book: (A) Major subjects integrated into a particular topic, theme, or historical time period, (B) Studies can be approached biblically, (C) Lesson plans simplified as all ages study one topic, (D) Family unit strengthened, (E) Skills strengthened as each child works at his own level.

She makes a point that her way is better than the traditional textbook and workbook way. While good learning can occur without textbooks, I'm not convinced that she understands how good teachers use them. Even workbooks can, at times, be useful. In her opinion, "In order to partake of the excellent, we must throw out what the curriculum specialists have deemed as good." I believe we can have both.

Mrs. Bendt also despises multiple-choice questions. This, too, may be because of her particular perspective. Good multiple-choice questions take significant time to write, and they save even more time for classroom teachers. Of course, for a home school they don't make much sense except to practice for standardized tests. Professional educators do not consider them appropriate for measuring some of the most important learning.

See my comments about unit studies in Chapters on resources and structure. Although some other authors would see things slightly differently (and others likely agree with Mrs. Bendt), you are the teacher and this book will provide good help for you. 116 pp., 1990, $16 with free shipping to US addresses. Add 7% if to Florida. Write your check to Valerie Bendt, and send it to Bendt Family Ministries, 333 Rio Vista Ct., Tampa, FL 33604. (813) 238-3721. A catalog is available.

To accompany the book just described, you may wish to purchase *The Unit Study Idea Book.* You may not need this one if you think of your own ideas. 109 pp., 1990, $12. plus shipping.

In the *How to Create Your Own Unit Study, Audio Cassette Tape* you can listen to a presentation and hear responses to audience questions. $9.00. Shipping instructions are at the end of the book description.

One Week Off Unit Studies Potentially a very rewarding way to approach unit studies, from Castle Heights Press. The manual in hand is *Aviation*, 37 pp., 1993. It suggests what to do each day: Monday, planning; Tuesday, research (questions to answer from study plus notes on areodynamics, history, air traffic control, etc); Wednesday, study; Thursday, field trip (to a museum or to an airport for a flying lesson, etc.); Friday, notebook. You even make balsa and paper airplanes. For contact information, see Appendix S under "Equipment."

Steward Ship See *Everything You Need to Know About Unit Studies.*

Success With Unit Studies Another book from Valerie Bendt. From the description, it looks good. "Valerie reviews what she calls the Five-R's of Unit Studies: Research, Reading, Writing, Recording and Reporting." 1997, $15. See ordering information in this section, or ask for a brochure.

Unit Study Idea Kit for World Book Ideas and outlines for suggested unit study topics. Grade levels P-6. $12 from Sycamore Tree. For information, see Sycamore Tree in Appendix Z.

Part 2, Curriculum packages

In addition to sources here, many of the school service organizations listed in Appendix A offer curriculum packages. Some may be purchased without the guidance service. None of the materials as described here include school services, although school service providers may use some of them.

Comprehensive Curriculum of Basic Skills A series of eight books covering preschool through grade 6. I examined the second grade book. This fat book covers activities for the whole year, although you would also want to teach some things that are not in it and to encourage reading. This classifies as a workbook but could be used effectively. Topic areas are reading, English, math, spelling and writing, comprehension, thinking skills, citizenship and environmental science. Answers and teaching suggestions are in the back. It is attractive – all color – and would be easy to use. 544 pp., 1993. Beginning with grade 1, all have 544 pages. While you can do a fairly good job for 2nd grade with this size book, I expect that books for the higher grades don't cover enough territory. This is not bad as long as you plan to use them more as supplements. ($19.95, except Pr & K which cost $10.95 and have 176 pages). From American Education Publishing.

ESP Super Yearbooks Similar to the *Comprehensive Curriculum ...* above. Review copies not sent, so not examined. They have more pages for higher grades – up to 984 for 7th grade. Cost about $30 each.

Far Above Rubies A complete high school course of study for girls. *"Far Above Rubies,"* according to the teacher's guide, "is a curriculum that puts the spiritual requirements defined by God *before* the academic requirements defined by man. By allowing God's Word to discipline our daughters (instead of man's teachings, programs, and standards), our daughters will learn to die to self and seek God's will in all areas of life." The material is carefully planned and would be easy to teach and manage. With the emphasis on preparing good wives and mothers, the intellect could be somewhat neglected, although the program may be planned for college prep. You do have many options for gaining the points to make up the various high school credits. This will permit you to direct your daughter according to her personality and abilities. A number of outside books are suggested for study, and assignments are based on them. You can buy them as packages.

I like the course. However, since I am a little uneasy about committing so large a portion of teen learning to one program, I would plan some digressions. The course is sold by Family Christian Academy and they offer a diploma based on evidence of successful completion. I expect they would approve my digressions, too. Here are approximate prices: Basic textbook, 1995, 316 pp., $55. *Far Above Rubies Companion*, describes methodology, outlines the units for teaching, describes the books used and, contains forms for keeping records. 1995, 314 pp. plus ads, $26. Four lesson plan books, one for each year of study, which you might be able to do without (300+ pages), $26 each. *Preview Package*, a booklet of sample pages and explanations, $5. Testing fees also apply when used. If enrolled in Family Christian Academy, tuition fees apply. http://www.heartofwisdom.com; 800-BOOKLOG or e-mail Lifeinam@AOL.com

Konos Curriculum, P.O. Box 1534, Richardson, TX 75083. Jessica Hulcy, 1985, (214) 669-8337. The Konos Character Curriculum is coordinated around character themes. K-6. It's been around for a long time and people who use it have given good reports. Seminars and cassettes tell how to teach with it.

Lifepac Gold A full instructional program: Bible, language arts, math, science, and history and geography. A set of booklets with reference to Biblical ideas. Major revision completed in 1996. Each grade level 1-12 has a set for each subject area: The booklets contain instructional material with questions to answer requiring higher level thinking skills. A modest number of other books and materials are called for by the lifepacs. Costs for the lifepacs are around $200 per grade, although getting all the subjects is not required. A correspondence school for K-8 called Bridgstone Academy offers guidance services for parents who use the materials. Alpha Omega Publications, 300 N. McKenny Ave., Chandler, AZ 85226-2618; (800) 622-3070; Fax, (602) 940-8924.

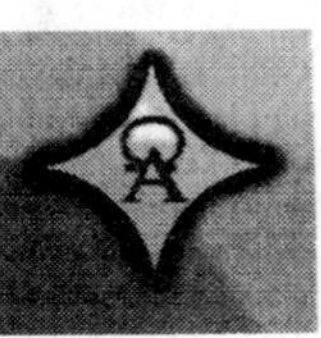

One of my reviewers has used the series. Here is her opinion: "It is thorough but very dry and VERY time consuming, not leaving much time for investigation and exploration. For the student that likes busy work it would be a good program. For the parent with little experience and not much confidence, it would be a good way to get a home schooling program started. Each LifePac Curriculum comes with 10 workbooks and a teachers edition with answer keys and workbook tests. The series covers 1st-12th grade subjects." I also spoke with someone who works with missionary families. She felt it was not their best option, alt4hough I can see how some would find it helpful being easy for the parent to use.

Lighthouse, P.O. Box 972, Fenton, MO 63026-0972; (314) 843-2811. Home school curriculum materials for grades K-4 developed by Dr. Lloyd Bellamy. Kindergarten level does not require learning to read. Lesson plans include daily teaching instructions. Books from other publishers are used.

Listen, My Son A full high school curriculum for boys. (By definition, "curriculum," is a plan for learning, not learning materials. Home schoolers have tended to define it differently. Here the curriculum includes the physical materials) This is a fine program on a character-development pattern, similar to *Far Above Rubies,* also reviewed in this part. In fact, the two may be used together, for a boy and a girl in your family. Proverbs 3 is used as the framework here. Proverbs 31 is used for the girls. Suggestions for lesson planning and record keeping are different from the other curriculum. Prices are essentially the same. This one is sold by the author. A relatively small number of books are to be purchased to be used as directed. Math is separate. Listen, My Son Unit Study $54.95. Sample unit $5 shipping paid. Planning materials and resource books cost extra. 1996. For more information, write to LindaBul@AOL.com or Listen, My Son, 444 Oriole Cir., Clarksville, TN 37043.

Plants Grown Up A curriculum for character development with projects relating to various school subjects. This one is for boy. A companion course, *Polished Cornerstones,* is for girls. Both are described under *Doorposts* in Appendix N.

Robinson Self-Teaching Home School Curriculum When Arthur Robinson's wife died he was left with six children and a mass of teaching materials to continue the home instructional program she had begun. As he considered his increased responsibilities he concluded that, with proper direction, the children could learn mostly by themselves. He decided on a set of principles and, with the children themselves, established a course of study for the elementary and high school years. After following the plan, his oldest, at age 18, entered a chemistry program in college at the third-year level.

The curriculum focuses on the three Rs beginning with phonics and more actual teaching in the first year. The 'ritmetic R uses Saxon math books and continues on through calculus. No serious science is studied until the math is finished. Topics like foreign language and geography are considered easily leaned later. Bible study is not part of the curriculum but the sacred book is read each evening. Music also is extracurricular. The school year is all year six days a week except during two months or so of vacations. School time begins early in the day and continues for five hours. Each day the kids do their math then read, mostly from old books, and write a short report for Dad to evaluate. Robinson's program forbids sugar, tobacco, alcohol, drugs, and TV.

All the needed books, other than the math books are on a set of 22 CDs. You view clear reproductions of some 120,000 actual pages. The books include old literature such as *Alice's Adventures in Wonderland,* history accounts like *Fifty Years in the Royal Navy,* a 1911 encyclopedia, a 1913 dictionary and books on advanced math and science. Self-tests and a vocabulary drill program are provided for the literature.

Although I would do some things differently, the program has potential. Old literature is better than today's, but my selections would exclude the fantasy and non-character-building excitement and would add some good modern reading and reference material. The pages are graphic images and so do not allow cut-and-paste or searching for certain words. You may print out individual pages but the cost would add up if you copied many whole books. The pages are easy to read on my 15-inch monitor. You also have the convenience of printing out whatever pages you want. I would also provide more, planned supervision. I don't believe the program would work for every child, but many would learn well. Of course you can use it for a supplement.

Arthur Robinson, Ph.D. taught at the University of California, San Diego, and now directs the Oregon Institute of Science and Medicine, a nonprofit research facility which he founded. The 1997 edition of Robinson's home school program costs $195 including shipping for enough study material (except for math) to keep your kids busy for twelve years. Send your check to the institute at 2251 Dick George Rd., Cave Junction, OR 97523. Specify the PC or Mac version. If the price is a problem for your budget, ask about their scholarship program.

School of Tomorrow has had a unit system since before Alpha Omega started a similar one. See Appendix Z.

Switched-On Schoolhouse Described as "traditional education in a computer age." The demo **CDrom** contains only the program for the 7th grade. It has a Christian viewpoint. I found it a little difficult to use. In response to my draft of this review I got a nice response from Tye Rausch who is in charge of the project development. I expect that some of my criticism is still valid, but a lot of new features make up for much of it. Unfortunately I don't have time to review the current product. First I'll tell you some of what I found, then what I learned from Tye.

The program, like most other multimedia instructional materials depends largely on giving information and asking factual questions to see if the facts have been absorbed. The quizzes are questions easy for a computer to score, but requiring little or no original thinking by the student. Information is given in small-print text stretching across the computer screen accompanied by some illustrations. (The text would be easier to read on an older monitor with 640x480 pixels.) Word lists indicate definitions to be learned. I discovered, partly by accident, that clicking on the words yields their pronunciation. A little lisp, although not a major problem, makes words like "mass" sound like "math." The teacher can set up work for the student and can check the results of the quizzes. The computer can be set to recycle questions until answered correctly. The multimedia aspect adds a little interest, but it seems to me that the material would be easier to learn from a good textbook. Switched-On Schoolhouse might be nice to use in connection with more traditional materials. Or, the other way around, you could branch out from it and add your own field trips and discovery learning.

Now, some more positive comments. First, it is an excellent tool to manage learning. The home teacher can assign and check allowing time to work personally with a child who is having a problem in an area. The lisp may have been fixed by better sound capabilities of the software on the current CDs, but I am doubtful. All types of questions are asked and thinking is encouraged in different ways. Essay questions or paragraphs which are written are, of course, not graded by the computer. You can compensate as needed. A printed manual and contextual help makes it easy to know both student and teacher can use the program. Alpha Omega Publications, 300 N. McKemy Ave., Chandler, AZ 85226; (800) 622-3070; http://www.Switched-OnSchoolhouse.com.

Weaver Curriculum Series A K-6 home study program weaving academics and Scripture into lives through direct Bible study. Care has been taken to give the home teacher the responsibility for teaching children what to believe. Emphasizes thinking ability. Coordinated for teaching children in different grades at the same time. Supplements available for grades 7-12. The K-6 Bible program is followed. What I see looks good. You get a thorough program including teaching instructions. Weaver now offers grammar, math, and phonics, (which I have not seen) so you may want to stay with them for everything. However, I would want to keep my options open considering what might work best for my kids in each subject. New publisher.

Part 3, Other products for more than one subject area

Classroom Connect **Int** A good source of instructional information relating to the Internet. Topics from finding keypals (like pen pals) to helpful instructional sites and how to help kids learn from them. 20 pp., 9 issues/yr, $39. You can learn lots just from their web site. If your newsletter editor had a subscription, the information could be shared. 1866 Colonial village Ln., Lancaster, PA 17601-6704; (800) 638-1639; connect@classroom.net; http://www.classroom.net

Design-a-Study Resource manuals for creating a custom curriculum. Kathryn Stout takes a different approach. She assumes you don't want to follow either traditional textbooks or a curriculum package with a prescribed learning track. She believes that, as long as you know what you need to cover and know where to find resources, you can make extensive use of projects on topics of interest. Her way is designed to develop your kids as independent, aggressive learners without missing important concepts and skills they should know. Kathryn is a professional educator who now teaches her own children at home. Her way might not be quite as easy for you as it is for her, but unless your own schooling is very weak, I believe you can do it. She and her husband offer manuals on composition, critical thinking, history, spelling, science (which I describe in Appendix S), and now *Maximum Math* described as "the ultimate homeschooler's guide. . . ."

These curriculum surveys cover grades 1-8 or 1-12. Even if you use other materials, her ideas will give you a better understanding of the process of good teaching. 408 Victoria Ave., Wilmington, DE 19804-2124; http://www.designastudy.com/; kathryn@designastudy.com.

Make Your Own A+ Electronic Flashcards See Appendix M.

PA Homeschoolers The "PA" stands for Pennsylvania, but many or most of their publications are for everyone. They have history textbooks, a keyboard skills book, several games, etc. The appearance of their products does not yet threaten McGraw-Hill, but then their prices won't create a budget deficit either. RD 2, Box 117, Kittanning PA 16201; (412) 783-6512; richmans@pahomeschoolers .com; http://www.pahomeschoolers.com

Ready-Set-Learn Enrichment units available from KidsArt. Titles include, *music, geography, world continents, newspapers, writing, anatomy, world wonders, and reading games.* Written for multi-age teaching emphasizing hands-on learning. Prices range from $6 to $15. Send SASE for a brochure. KidsArt, P.O. Box 274, Mt. Shasta, CA 96067.

School Mom Software for practicing a number of skills taught in elementary grades. (version 4.3 reviewed). From the general menu you select among the subjects: music, art, alphabet, math, or telling time.

The music program allows composing tunes, and recognizing notes. There are three levels of difficulty and options for accidentals and time values for notes. The art option allows selecting colors for areas on pictures, making designs, or drawing. It helps kids get used to using the computer and the mouse. Most of the programs will work without the mouse, by the way. I think pencil and paper are more efficient for learning math, but this allows a little fun. Options for math include algebra. The student is prompted in steps to solve equations and could follow the prompts without understanding much of what is going on. One of the English options requires recognizing sentence structure elements such as verbs, direct objects, etc.

In addition to the subject areas, you can read the instruction manual on screen. Also included is a utility for creating multiple choice exams, taking the exams and keeping scores. It is easy to use.

Other utilities which allow such things as creating and modifying the spelling files may be purchased. Also a simulated voice option is available. And, you also get a mail-order catalog with items of interest for home schools.

I have described only a few of the program's features. It isn't going to substitute for your personal teaching, but it can add some fun and help build understanding. It's s easy to use, and I think you'll like it. For $20 you get the basic program, the manual, and all the extra goodies besides. Dr. Motes is not currently promoting or developing his product. Free catalog includes software from several sources of interest to home school families. Motes Educational Software, P.O. Box 575, Siloam Springs, AR 72761; (501) 524-8741.

Skills Bank The purpose is to review some 300 basic skills for grades 6 to 12 which appear on standardized exams for adolescents and adults. The home edition is based on the school version. The modules deal with areas of reading, language, math, writing, and "study skills." The term "tutor" in the program's subtitle led me to look for clear explanations of the principles behind various skills – explanations such as you would expect from a tutor, or even a good textbook. I was disappointed. In my opinion, the focus in math is on how to get the answer, not on why. In other areas, it "teaches" for recall of basic facts. Under "writing", we find exercises in knowing the differences among two, too, and to.

You could use the program for grades 6 to 12 as advertised, but the material I saw seems more on the curricular level for grades 5 to 7. The program would do well for screening to find significant skill deficiencies, especially before taking standardized tests. It could also teach some, especially factual information. Reports may be generated. The "home tutor" edition has 286 lessons, 49 quizzes, and 38 tests. Skills Bank Corp.

Young Discovery Library This is a series of brief little books on a wide variety of topics for elementary-school age readers (but old graybeards like me enjoy them, too). They have excellent art and interesting descriptions. Accuracy is assured by professional consultation (although they could have been edited a bit better). I received several of them as samples. One is entitled, *Living on a Tropical Island,* and it describes how people live on a specific island off the coast of Madagascar. One page begins, "Every year, between December and February, cyclones ["typhoons" ?] may sweep across the islands. Cyclones are very violent storms. The wind rushes round, spinning in a circle. . . . But luckily, after two or three days, the weather settles down, the sun. . . ." *Music!* is the title of another book which gives bits of history and cultural background and discusses various instruments. Other titles are, *Metals: Born of Earth and Fire; The Barbarians* (a sketch of one element shaping European history); *Cathedrals: Stone upon Stone*; and *Seashore Life.* The books have 40 pages (if you count both sides of both covers). Page size is 4¼ X 7. $5.95. If you are home schooling and you order 5 or more, you may request a 15% discount. And they will pay the postage. Young Discovery Library, 217 Main St., Ossining, NY 10562.

Part 4, Publishers for More Than One Major Subject and with at least some secular publications

Addison-Wesley / Benjamin Cummings Publishing Co., 2725 Sand Hill Rd., Menlo Park, CA 94025. (800) 533-4075 or (415) 854-0300. For orders, (800) 447-2226. Subject areas: Math, science, and social studies.

Bradshaw Publishers, P.O. Box 277, Bryn Mawr, CA 92318. (909) 796-6766. Bible stories for beginning readers suitable through the second grade. Phonics based, progressive. Large print with flowing, rhythmic style and structure. Full color pictures. (Not reviewed.)

Brighter Child Books From American Education Publishing. Attractive and inexpensive supplementary books for grades P-6. For example, the Brighter Child series in math and language arts lists 32- to 48-page books with answer keys for $2.25 each. Software sets (book & disk) for the series cost $9.95. Another series is *How to Learn New Words*, one book for each grade, 2-6. $3.95. Map skills and ecology are also covered. American Education Publishing, 150 E. Wilson Bridge Rd., #145, Columbus, OH 43085-2328; (800) 542-7833. Shipping is a flat $3.50 for up to $45.

Dover Publications, 31 East 2nd St., Mineola, NY 11501. A wide variety of mostly educational and mostly republications of older books. Dover prices are still reasonable although we have seen increases in many we have listed in this edition of *The Home School Manual.* Reviews appear in various appendices. For shipping by mail to U.S. addresses, add $4 to the total invoice. For foreign orders, add 20%. No phone or credit-card orders. Satisfaction guaranteed. Their mailing list is confidential. Ask for their "complete" catalog and a fully-illustrated children's book catalog.

Family Pastimes Publisher and distributor of games of cooperation. Such games develop a mind set of helping others rather than trying to get ahead by making them lose. (not reviewed). A good choice of interesting activities, mostly board games. Graded by age. level. Older ones play with younger. All play to the end without anyone getting eliminated. Some games are licensed for manufacture in other countries. Family Pastimes, RR4, Perth, Ontario, Canada, K7H 3C6; (613) 267-4819; fp@superaje.com

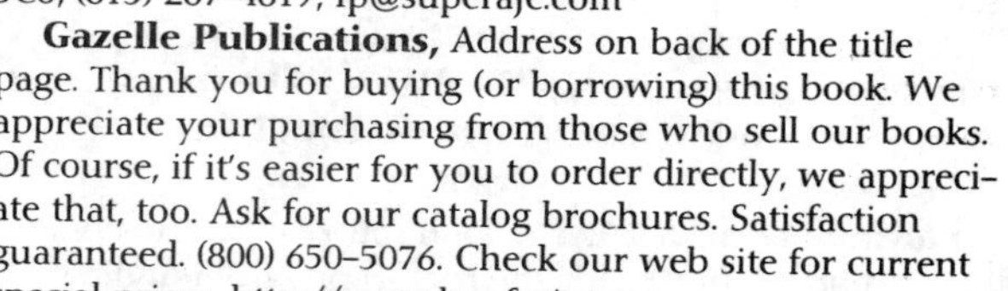

Gazelle Publications, Address on back of the title page. Thank you for buying (or borrowing) this book. We appreciate your purchasing from those who sell our books. Of course, if it's easier for you to order directly, we appreciate that, too. Ask for our catalog brochures. Satisfaction guaranteed. (800) 650-5076. Check our web site for current special prices. http://www.hoofprint.com

Our titles of most interest to home school families are: this book, *The Home School Manual,* (Appendix I) $30, *Early Years at Home,* (M) $4.95, *Home Schooling From Scratch,* about home schooling on a restricted income, $10. *Science Activities,* (S) $6.50; *Fun on the Road,* (V) $2; *With Joy,* (P) $2; and *Bubbles,* (P) *Should be back in print before the end of 1998.* Two other books on religious topics are: *Spirit Possession,* about Satanic mind control, including hypnosis, and problems in some Christian churches, $6.95; and *The Song of Songs,* An understanding of The Song of Solomon that is consistent with the rest of the Bible. A verse-by-verse commentary, $5.95. We sometimes have slightly damaged books and older editions at reduced prices. For postage to U.S. addresses by ground mail, figure 10% of price with minimum of $1.50; or 18%, w/min. $3.25 by air. If you wish to purchase for resale, please contact us for trade discounts..

Houghton Mifflin / McDougal, Littell, and Co. Publishers 1900 S. Batvia, Geneva, IL 60134; (800) 733-2828. If ordering teachers' guides, you may want to verify that your name will not be passed on to your school district.

John Wiley & Sons Order from Distribution Center, 1 Wiley Drive, Somerset, NJ 08875-1272; (732) 469-4400 or (800) 225-5945; Fax: (732) 302-2300; catalog@wiley.com or online at http://www.wiley.com In Canada call (800) 567-4797. Check the web site for overseas centers.

McGraw-Hill, School Division, 220 E. Danieldale Rd., DeSoto, TX 75115-8815. Customer Service (800) 442-9685. Their K-8 catalog shows the subject areas: reading/language arts, science, health, mathematics, social studies, and music. Also see SRA below; (800) 442-9685.

Modern Curriculum Press, 4350 Equity Dr., P.O. Cox 2649, Columbus, OH 43216; (800) 321-3106. Phonics, spelling, math (K-6), science (K-6). All consumable workbooks plus teacher's editions.; http://www.mcschool.com

Mott Media, 1000 E. Huron, Milford, MI 48381. (248) 685-8773; Fax ... -8776. This firm specializes in "classic" textbooks-revised (reprints of the ones used in the good old days: Harvey's Grammars, Spencer's Penmanship, McGuffey's Readers and Spellers, and Ray's Arithmetic). They also publish biographies and a few other titles.

Open Court Publishing Company, P.O. Box 599 (315 5th St.), Peru, IL 61354. (800) 435-6850. Major textbook publisher.

School Zone Publishing Company You may already be familiar with School Zone's brief books offering reinforcement for learning common school subjects. They appear in discount stores and elsewhere. For example, you can pick up a book of spelling puzzles, or a simple reader. 24-page books cost a little over $2 and 32-page books around $4. School Zone also sells flash cards for around $2.50 per pack and educational board games for around $7. Their *Big Get Ready* books offer head starts for levels from preschool to grades 3 and 4. They each cost nearly $12 and comprise 10 of the 32 page books.

The *Big Get Ready Book* for 2nd grade, for example has a phonics page where the student writes either "sw" or "sp" to make four words: _ _ ider, _ _ im, _ _ oon, and _ _ an. Pictures are clues. The four words are to be written at the bottom of the page. While such things may be better learned from reading and writing, workbook activities can be a pleasant break and still teach. These do not replace textbooks or creative teaching. Until age 6 or older I believe your child is better off learning from life. Children enjoy choosing books for you to buy as a special treat now and then, and these are affordable. McClanahan Book Company produces a similar line. School Zone products are usually sold through retail stores. P.O. Box 777, Grand Haven, MI 49417. (800) 253-0564.

Silver Burdett & Ginn, Customer Service Center, P.O. Box 2649, Columbus, OH 43216. Major textbook publisher.

SRA/McGraw-Hill, 220 East Danieldale Rd. Desoto, TX 75115-2490. SRA provides both supplemental and basal programs to meet the needs of students in grades K-8. Programs include, Math, Reading, Phonics, Direct Instruction, Langauge Arts, Test Preperation, ESL/Bilingual and Art. Call 1-888/SRA-4KIDS for a free Catalog, or visit http://www.sra-4kids.com.

Usborne A London based firm specializing in highly illustrated educational books with printed explanations close to the illustrations. Many have ordinary text in paragraphs, too. If you don't find a local home-business, distributor, contact (in the US) EDC Publishing, P.O Box 470663, Tulsa, 74147.

William Morrow Publications are available only through bookstores.

Zaner-Bloser Educational Publishers P.O. Box 16764, Columbus, OH 43216-6764; (800) 421-3018. Publishers of educational materials including critical thinking, science, whole language, substance abuse prevention, handwriting, spelling, and Modality Materials for K-8.

Part 5, Other Interests of Home Schooling Families

The Busy Mom's Guide to Simple Living If you enjoyed Jackie Wellwood's chapter, "Service, not Chores," you will find this book helpful, too. It covers all kinds of advice on managing the household and directing a good lifestyle. The Wellwoods teach their own children so you may expect the ideas to be helpful. From Crossway Books. (800) 543-1659.

Family Pastimes R.R. 4, Perth, Ontario K7H 3C6; (613) 267-4819, Fax (613) 264-0696; fp@superaje.com. Trade name, Co-operative Games(TM). Free catalog.

Fun on the Road By Ted Wade. This is more a vacation book than a school book, but it does teach thinking and a bit of geography. And it helps the miles pass quickly. Activities involve a bingo-type hunt for objects along the highway (with pictures in little squares), choosing words on signs and on other vehicles, guessing which boxes an opponent has marked, and so on. In one activity, you use an outline map to figure out how to get from the Atlantic Ocean to the Pacific Ocean entering each of the 48 touching states only once. 40 pp. $2. Add $1.30 for U.S. shipping (sent by air). And sales tax if you are in our state. See the back of the title page for our address.

Psychological Seduction The Failure of Modern Psychology, William Kirk Kilpatrick. Thomas Nelson Publishers, 1983. 236 pp. A look at "the disturbing results of a society seduced by the claims of psychiatry." Kilpatrick feels that "many Americans equate self-esteem and personal growth with personal salvation" and that "positive thinking often takes the place of God." He sees the thrust of modern psychology as a type of religion. Maybe this is getting away from the topic of home schooling, but religion is very much education, and you should give some careful thought to the atmosphere your children are growing up in.

In this vein, I should mention two more books: *The Seduction of Christianity*, by Dave Hunt and T. A. McMahon. This one is excellent. It touches an area close to most of us – occult influences that are changing the Christian churches. It's a well-documented and clearly explained exposition. From Harvest House Publishers, 1985, (800) 547-8979.

The other book is *Spirit Possession, The Counterfeit With Many Faces.* My father, T. E. Wade, M.D., (who has now passed to his rest) is the author. He wrote with a specific Christian orientation but with respect for people who hold different viewpoints. The book explains how hypnotism works and why it is wrong. Other topics include the dangers of the deliverance ministry, and the false holy-spirit experience. It includes stories of defeat and of victory from demons. It explains the importance of the will and that spirit possession, in various forms, counterfeits possession by the Holy Spirit. One of the book's two co-authors has come out of the new age movement and the other relates his sound approach to dealing with demon possession. 1991, 96 pp. For the US, $6.95 plus $1.50 postage by ground or $1.80 by air. Add tax as appropriate. See back of title page for our address.

Homeschool Travel Directory If you are traveling and would like to know of homes that might welcome your family as overnight guests, get a copy of this book from the National Homeschool Association. Membership in NHA is not required, and all home schooling families are welcome to participate.

If you would accept such guests in your home, just send your name, address (including country), phone, family member names and birth years, and other significant information. This is a nice idea and takes people like you to make it work. You can always say no if someone wants to visit at an inconvenient time.

To make for happy new friendships just let me add a few pointers for travelers. (1) Don't drop in without making arrangements, hopefully a week or more in advance. (2) Plan to leave a gift. Homes have laundry to do, corn flakes to buy, and taxes to pay just as motels do (even though an appropriate amount might be less than you would pay the motel). (3) Prepare your kids for a stricter disciplinary atmosphere than they might be used to. Behavior acceptable to you might not be appropriate in the home you visit. Then keep a vigilant watch on them. (4) If you are expecting meals and have dietary restrictions such as not eating meat, be sure the homes you visit are used to them, let them know you will be eating out.

Send $5 to National Homeschool Association, P.O. Box 290, Hartland, MI 48353; (513) 772-9580.

Z
Suppliers

These organizations sell materials from various publishers and, in some cases, produce their own products as well. Sellers dealing with a major subject area are generally listed in the corresponding appendix and not here. Suppliers serving specific US regions or countries outside the US are listed in the appendices for those areas. Appendix X is for general school supplies.

Back Pack (The) New and used textbooks and supplemental materials for K-12 studies at reasonable prices. For around $150 they will discuss your child's needs with you and assemble a package of materials for the whole school year. Free catalog including a dated listing of used books. P.O. Box 125, Ernul NC 28527; (919) 244-0728.

Bluestocking Press Publisher-consultant, Jane Williams provides learning materials in several general areas: economics and law; American history; and entrepreneurship for kids. She also specializes in books by and about Laura Ingalls Wilder and her daughter (Little House books). For her catalog, please send $3 for mailing expense. P.O. Box 2030-tw, Shingle Springs, CA 95682-2030. (530) 621-1123; Fax (530) 642-9222. Or for orders, (800) 959-8586.

Bright Spark Press Described as follows: "Providing inspiring and delightful educational resources at rock-bottom prices." Some of the materials are published by Bright Spark and some purchased for resale. A newsletter, *Super Learning Tools,* is also available for $5.75/yr. (6 issues). The issue I'm looking at has an article, "Principle-Centered Home Education." There are four other features/articles including recipes and materials reviews. Author/editor /publisher Alison Moore Smith. Bright Spark Press, 20887 N. Springs Trce. Boca Raton, FL 33428-1453; (407) 487-3199, Fax ... -8930. E-mail BrghtSprk@aol.com And web site: http://members.aol.com/brghtsprk

Brook Farm Books, P.O. Box 246, Bridgewater, ME 04735. (In Canada, Brook Farm Books, Glassville, N.B. E0J 1L0.) Jean Reed publishes *The Home School Sourcebook* which is the basis for what she sells. See Appendix X.

Builder Books, P.O. Box 99, Riverside, WA 98849, (509) 826-6021; Orders: (800) 260-5461. "We are concerned with quality as well as practicality and price. The materials we choose for the training of our children . . . will make a difference in building knowledge and character. . . ." Thus the name for the company. Critical thinking books are included in addition to the usual parent helps and various subject areas. Volume discount. Free catalog.

Cassidy & Nells, 421 Dodd Dr., NW, Leesburg, VA 20176; (703) 779-8240; Fax ... 8241; (800) 453-6114. A large selection of educational materials including Fischertechnik, Saxon Math, biographies and much more.

Conservative Book Club, 422 1st St., S.E., Washington, DC 20003. "We offer a very broad variety of books of interest to homeschoolers and political, religious and economic conservatives. We also offer children's books."

Custom Curriculum Company An Oregon firm that is spreading to nearby states and across the nation. See Appendix D.

Curriculum Services, 26801 Pine Ave., Bonita Springs, FL 34135; (941) 992-6381, fax (941) 992-6473. E-mail hscurric@peganet.com Material selected for home schooling, from mainstream textbook publishers. Write-in texts. Free brochure.

Education Services, 8825 Blue Mountain Dr., Golden, CO 80403; (800) 421-6645. Dr. Beechick's books help parents make better use of preplanned curriculum materials or put together their own program.

Education Source, The 3751 Bolsa Court, Sacramento, CA. 95864. http://www.edusource.com The Education Source reviews educational products and Internet sites. Their free, online newsletter has over 150,000 readers. Back issues covering science, math, distance learning, Internet safety, Web site awards and alternative education, are available at their Web site. To subscribe to the newsletter, send your email address to: editor@edusource.com

Elijah Company (The), 1053 Eldridge Loop, Crossville, TN 38558; (888) 2-Elijah (toll free); (423) 456-6284. elijahco@elijahco.com. The catalog Chris and Llewellyn Davis publish is somewhat like a Christian home schooling how-to book. They tell you not only what they think you should buy from them, but go into detail telling you why.

Excellence in Education 527 Franklin Pl., Monrovia, CA 91016; (626) 357-4443. Carolyn Forté. Perhaps the name of their operation best describes their intention.

Family Christian Bookstores A chain of home schooling bookstores: Nashville (main office) (615) 860-3000; Knoxville store 423-588-2106; Bristol (423) 968-7182; Chattanooga (423) 875-2686; Orlando (407) 671-3343; Colorado Springs (719) 574-4222; and Dallas. Their free catalog includes a special unit study and Hebraic roots section. Orders FCAPub@AOL.com; Contact Robin Scarlata Rscarlata@AOL.com; Order from (800) 788-0840 by credit card 10-5 central time or (615) 860-9788 by fax any time; or FACPub@aol.com by e-mail.

Family Learning Center According to their catalog, FLC "was created to provide high quality educational material in an easy to use format especially for home education." Prominent in the items they offer is *Learning Language Arts Through Literature,* a K-12 program. 221 Long Lake Road, Hawthorne, FL 32640; (352) 475-5869.

Family Pastimes Game publisher. See Appendix Y.

Farm Country General Store Rt. 2, Box 412, Metamora, IL 61578; (309) 367-2844; order line (800) 551-3276. General materials for home schooling plus special items like games and puzzles.

Follett Home Education Used textbooks (800) 554-5754. Their ad says they charge at 15% off the publishers' retail price. For new books, that's fine. Hopefully thier used books are cheaper.

Geode Educational Options Owner, Sarah Gerding-Oresic explains, "We search for high quality materials which facilitate ecological, ethical, responsible and stimulating teaching, parenting, and living." Secular materials. http://www.geodeopt.com.

Great Christian Books, P.O. Box 8000, (229 S. Bridge St.), Elkton, MD 21922-8000, (800) 775-5422; (410) 392-3590; Fax. (410) 392-3103. A discount book source carrying a wide selection of titles on home education.

Hands on and Beyond 4813 E. Marshall Dr., Vestal, NY 13850; (888) 20-LEARN or (607) 722-6563 Hands-on learning materials for all subjects including Bible. learn@handsonandbeyond.com; http://www.handsonandbeyond.com.

Home School, The Books & Supplies. 104 S. West Ave., Arlington, WA 98223; (360) 435-0376 or for orders only: (800) 788-1221. Bill Jury describes his operation as "more than just a bookstore. Our goal," he explains, "is to meet your particular needs through research and experience." Thousands of different books and other materials for preschool through high school.

Homeschool Associates Book sales through a 40,000 volume used textbook store (either mail-order or walk-in) and a bookmobile which visits 35 states in the East, South, and Midwest. Contact Steve or Carol Moitozo for conference design, lectures, and workshop leadership. 116 Third Ave., Auburn, ME 02410, (207) 777-1700, (800) 869-2051 for bookmobile schedule. homeschool@homeschoolassociates.com.

Homeschool Potpourri, The A unique consignment shop with used and new curriculum materials for home schools. Owner, Jenny Sockey, sells for 50 to 85% of current retail and sends half of that back to the former owner. To buy, make up your wish list and Call (425) 820-4626. To sell, call the same number and listen for instructions. Most typical Christian school material is accepted. 10:30 to 5:00 Pacific Time, M-F and Sat. 9 a.m. - 12 noon. Washington.

Homeschool Seller P.O. Box 19, Cherry Valley, MA 01611. Used curriculum material advertising paper. Send your list of items to sell. When they are sold, you pay a small percentage of the price they sold for. Ask for a free copy of the paper or see http://bravewc.com/hph. (508) 791-8332; HssHph@ibm.net

Homeschooling Book Club 1000 E. Huron, Milford, MI 48381; (810) 685-8773. A discount book sales division of Mott Media.

Hometext, 283 Nevins St., Brooklyn, NY 11217; (718) 852-6583. New and used textbooks from major publishers.

In His Steps 1618 Kendolph, Denton,TX 76205; (800) 583-1336; (940) 566-6123; inhissteps@juno.com. Lora Gleaton, Mailorder (and walk-in) supplier of materials for home schools. Also seen at book fairs.

John Holt's Book Store A lot more than the writings of John Holt. Well annotated catalog: books on education, books on learning and specific subject areas, musical instruments, etc. Holt Associates, 2269 Massachusetts Ave., Cambridge, MA 02140.

Library & Educational Services, P.O. Box 146, Berrien Springs, MI 49103. Dick Proctor, (616) 695-1800. Felts, books. Special prices.

Lifetime Books & Gifts The Always Incomplete Resource Guide and Catalog, 224 pp., $3. Bob and Tina Farewell lean toward the philosophies of Charlotte Mason using real or "living" books. Nearly 200 books for families with special needs children. Reviews and hints. 3900 Chalet Suzanne Dr., Lake Wales, FL 33853-7763; (941) 676-6311 or fax ... -2732; Web page http://www.lifetimeonline.com. For orders only, call (800) 377-0390, 8 a.m. - 5 p.m. M-F Shipping charges: 8%-10% with a minimum of $3.00 Free shipping for orders over $150.00 in the U.S. If to Florida add 6% sales tax.

M&M Software Shareware and public domain, educational software. http://www.mm-soft.com mmsoft@aol.com; (800) 642-6163; Fax, (526) 420-2955. P.O. Box 15769, Long Beach, CA 90815. Free catalog.

Once Upon a Time Family Bookstore, P.O. Box 296, Manchester, IA 52057. Operated by the Kenyon family. They sell quality used books through the mail, specializing in classics, " books you loved as a child," and educational books. They also buy books through the mail. Send them $2 or 6 one-ounce US stamps (refundable) for a list of over 2000 quality titles!

Pratte Publications, 841 Hillandale Dr., Antioch, IL 60002. (847) 395-8937. For a SASE David Pratte will send you his complete one-sheet catalog. Books for home schooling. Of special interest are his leaflets and on topics like homosexuality, Dungeons and Dragons, corrupt music, Bible teachings on suicide, gambling, and women's liberation. Discount prices.

Rainbow Resource Center ". . . a home- schooling family-operated venture. Products for home schools. Free catalog. Rt. 1, Box 159A, Toulon, IL 61483.

Shekinah Curriculum Cellar, 101 Meador Rd., Kilgore, TX 75662-9620. E-mail: to customerservice@ shekinahcc.com; www.she kinahcc.com. Their catalog contains thousands of educational items which have been selected especially for home educators. Fast service. Money back and price guarantees. As Michele Robinson explains, "the main thrust for raising and educating children should be to foster a love for their Creator and to give them a Christian perspective of the world." Send $1 for a catalog.

Sycamore Tree The catalog offered by Sandy Gogel and husband Bill (and all their helpers) is one of the oldest around, going on about 12 years now. If you mention *The Home School Manual*, there will be no catalog charge. You will enjoy the illustration by Lishi Laurance whose work also appears in this book.

Sycamore has lots of items for all the common school areas. You might want to consider the special items they publish like reproducible school forms, incentive charts, church worship sheets, etc. They chose items to offer for "academic excellence, spiritual influence, and value per dollar." Volume discounts. Sycamore also provides a guidance service (Described in Appendix A).

2179 Meyer Place, Costa Mesa, CA 92627, (714) 650-4466 for information. And for orders, (714) 642-6750 or (800) 779-6750 (voice or fax). 75767.1417@compuserve.com http://www.SycamoreTree.com

Timberdoodle, The Dan and Deb Deffinbaugh and kids and kin must have great fun selling the things they seem so sold on themselves. If you don't already have a copy of their catalog, I suggest you ask for one. You'll find chatty descriptions of everything from spelling tests and Amish, simple-life readers to map puzzles, stickers and a variety of good books. I'm impressed with The Fischertechnik kits with pieces for building all sorts of things from little tractors to computer driven devices. E. 1510 Spencer Lake Rd., Shelton, WA 98584. Or for questions, (360) 426-0672; Fax (360) 427-5625; mailbag@mail.nwrain.com - 8 a.m. to noon PST, except Sundays. www.timberdoodle.com

More suppliers are listed in the appendices for regions. Suppliers that specialize in certain curriculum areas are listed in the appendices for those areas.

Forms for Planning and Records

SECTION FIVE

The Finish Line
Forms

Make planning and record keeping easy (by Marilyn Rockett)

Record keeping can be a source of great frustration for home teaching families. Common sense, if not some external agent, tells us that it is wise to keep track of our children's progress. But which records are really necessary?

Apply the rule, "first need – future need." Do I need this information now for evaluation and planning? Will I need it in the future for reporting, encouragement or possible changes in the schooling situation? Choose forms that allow you to record information that answers these basic questions, and eliminate unnecessary forms (or portions of forms). Your individual situation will determine how many details you need. In general, somewhat less detailed information is needed for younger students than for older ones.

Forms or plan books are tools to free you for the more important tasks of living. Don't be enslaved to filling them out without knowing a purpose. Ask yourself, "Are the tools I'm using enabling me to accomplish the necessary and important things?" If not, consider whether you are diligent enough in record keeping and are using the forms in a good way.

Most of us don't have the luxury of time for everything we would like to do. Trying to get by without some reasonable planning leaves us harried and trapped in a cycle, feeling as though we are never accomplishing anything. Good planning does take some time but not as much as you might imagine. The small investment pays big dividends.

Excessive rigidity is the antithesis to little or no planning. Avoid over planning and remember to be flexible. If you have a base plan to work from, you can always expand it. Trying to micro manage too many details will leave you frustrated not being able get it all done. Make a very general plan for the school year and plan the specifics in smaller blocks. The Curriculum Calendar is a good place to lay out your general plan.

We all feel overwhelmed at times when we view the entire picture of our many responsibilities to our families and to our children as their educators. Breaking down these responsibilities into bite sized pieces by effective planning keeps our priorities on track and helps establish balance in our lives. I invite you to use the forms in this book for that greater purpose.

Using This Section in The Home School Manual (by Ted Wade)

We anticipate that having forms to copy will make this book more useful. You may still wish to purchase a book with forms bound together and in ample number. Or you may want to pick and choose from what you find available. For example, health forms are not included here. If you need them, you might look in a book of forms or check with your local school board office or health department.

You are welcome to copy these forms for your own personal use.

I appreciate Marilyn Rockett's willingness to share her experience with forms. You will notice from the copyright statements, that I have added several to provide more options.

Choosing which forms to use

As mentioned, we don't expect anyone to use all the forms. For most purposes, you have several options. Just to give you an idea to start working from, I'll show you which ones I would use for a child beyond the early years. I'm sure Marilyn's list would be different. You can look over the five forms I'm suggesting and make up your own list. As you discover other needs, you can look for forms to help you. Or you can simply get a notebook and keep records you need without prepared forms. Here are suggestions:

To get the whole household organized
✓ Master Schedule
✓ Daily Responsibilities (perhaps without the assignments)

To plan for the school year
✓ Curriculum Calendar
✓ Curriculum Sources

To manage the school program
✓ Weekly Plans and Progress (Be sure to keep grade and progress reports somewhere if not on this form.)

Form Descriptions with page numbers

Home Management

❖ Master Schedule **517**
This schedule is a framework for your week. You may block off periods of time for household jobs, school, and other family activities. It can help you maintain a proper sense of priorities by giving you an overall view of how you spend your time. You may note generalities or you may be specific. For most families this schedule will change by seasons of the year so you will need several copies.

I expect that after using this schedule for a week or so, the family program would work smoothly and writing out the activities may no longer be needed. You can judge this as you see what is happening. It might be well to start it again later.

❖ Household Responsibilities **518**
In appropriate squares under each family member name, specify responsibilities for the week. "Dust" might be for a room or an area. For "Pick up / Put up" a room or the dishwasher might be specified. "Wash/Wipe" could be for car, dishes, or windows. "Change" could be for bed sheets or oil in the car, and so on. If responsibilities change more often than weekly, days of the weeks could be marked. Extra squares can be used for tasks unique to your household; and the wider column could be divided.

❖ Weekly Home Management Plans **519**
This is a to-do list for Mom.

❖ Daily Responsibilities **520**
This schedule shows activities for the whole family for the day. Mom can post it so that several children can work independently with minimal supervision. Use initials for names and short phrases or abbreviations to show responsibilities. The Weekly Studies Log may be used jointly with this form for detailed schoolwork instructions if needed.

School Annual Planning

❖ Individual Evaluation **521**
Evaluations at the beginning and end of the year can clarify your children's and your own needs. Written evaluations bring encouragement for setting goals and for reaching them. Goal statements may be categorized as spiritual, physical, mental (or academic), and emotional. Consider your student's strengths, weaknesses, and needs in your curriculum planning. This sheet may also be used to list and evaluate family goals.

❖ Curriculum Sources 522

The explanation in the note at the top of the form itself is sufficient.

❖ Curriculum Calendar 523

Spaces in the body of the grid are for mapping your program for the year. First divide your year into periods. Elementary schools typically have 4, 9-week periods or 6, 6-week periods. The total weeks exclude vacation time, although you may wish to include the vacation days on your schedule.

Then decide what you want to teach and figure out how much to expect to cover in a given time. Also dividing your year into school weeks is a good idea. From that rough sketch, make your daily lesson plans. Of course, you may want to adjust your overall plan as you see what takes more and less time. I would use a good quality pencil.

This form can show large time blocks. Even deciding what chapters to cover when, and making notes in your book's table of contents is a plan to help you see where you are going.

You may wish to mark time periods in the six boxes across the top. Down the left edge, you could fill in the subjects – for example, Math, Reading, Soc. Stud., Science, and Home Skills. If my first line were "math," I might write in the first box, "ch. 1, 2 Number systems, Review multiplication facts."

❖ Subject or Unit Worksheet 524

An organized plan brings focus to a study unit or project. Combine this planning sheet with reports and a progress record if you need to convince the authorities that the learning is worthwhile.

School Continual Planning and Reporting

❖ Weekly Plans and Progress 525

This form allows you to plan a week's learning by subject all on a single page. Attendance may also be checked. On the line for each day (under each subject) you can write the topic or assignment. Two boxes on the line are for the work flow. One may be checked by the student when the assignment is completed, the other by the teacher either to indicate that the work has been explained or when it is approved as satisfactory. Evaluation boxes provide space to mark grades or points for the homework or the activity assigned, and for a quiz or test. An extra narrow column may be used for whatever you wish. Space is provided for comments by the teacher indicating work to redo, weaknesses, strengths, or whatever is desired.

Knowing what is to be done, the student may work ahead. If, on the other hand, the work takes more time than expected, some can be added at the beginning of the next week when the new plans are made. Or, writing in pencil, assignments can be changed during the week.

I believe you will find this form quite useful.

❖ Weekly Studies Log 526

On this sheet you may record assignments. Your student may check them off. It may also be used by the student to log work as it is completed. There are boxes to check attendance if needed and space for daily and/or weekly grades. The left hand column may be used to record subjects/units/topics and/or the assigned time of day. The far right column is for additional notes and for recording special things that require ongoing work. File these sheets for a record of all work done for the year.

❖ Grade and Attendance Record 527

Each of the six grids may be used for a week. A typical school year of 180 days would have six periods of six school weeks, not including vacations. You could modify the table for odd weeks affected by vacations or simply use more than one form for a period. If you plan overall grade boxes in the lower right for that summary.

Days without marks could indicate no school or absence. You could show why. Since you aren't likely to give an actual grade in every subject every day, you could use check marks to show that the topic was studied. You might use the boxes to record points, making more points possible for more important tasks.

For unit studies, you could show separate grades for subjects outside the unit then write across the rest of the boxes, for the unit, to make notes of progress, areas covered, or evaluations of reports. At the end you could record grades for various school subject categories. Or you could provide for evaluation of various aspects of the unit.

❖ Attendance Log and Evaluation Summary **528**

The blocks of 3 weeks may be used for keeping attendance records. The sheet also provides for recording major test and period grades.

❖ Books Read **529**

This form is for younger children. The word "Title" suggests what to write, but the line may also include a date or whatever you would like.

❖ Books Read **530**

On this sheet you may record books read. Or if you use it to list books assigned, the dates may show when they have been finished. If the form is posted or in a specific place, your children can place stars or check marks on it to indicate completed books. Space at the bottom of each rectangle, may be used to note a special thought from the reading. You might also find the form convenient for videos, TV programs, Bible reading, or memory work.

On the other "Books Read" form, younger children may write titles of books they have finished. The space at the right in each box may be used for completion dates, or as more space for the title.

❖ Field Trip Plans **531**

Adequately clear from the form itself.

❖ Standardized or Achievement Test Record **532**

Adequately clear.

Special Form

❖ Solving a Problem **533**

This form is not part of planning and record keeping. It is to be used in connection with learning the logic of careful thinking as explained in the chapter, "Thinking Precisely."

Master Schedule

Date planned ___________

	Monday	Tuesday	Wednesday	Thursday	Friday	Saturday	Sunday
5:00 5:30							
6:00 6:30							
7:00 7:30							
8:00 8:30							
9:00 9:30							
10:00 10:30							
11:00 11:30							
Noon **12:30**							
1:00 **1:30**							
2:00 **2:30**							
3:00 **3:30**							
4:00 **4:30**							
5:00 **5:30**							
6:00 **6:30**							
7:00 **7:30**							
8:00 **8:30**							
9:00 **9:30**							
10:00							

Household Responsibilities

Week of ____________

Type of chore \ Names							
Pets / animals							
Dust							
Vacuum							
Mop / scrub							
Sweep / shovel							
Pick up / put up							
Wash / wipe							
Wax / polish							
Prepare food							
Set / arrange							
Change							
Launder							
Clean out / sort							
Trash							
Mow/weed/trim							
Water							
Repair							

Weekly Home Management Plans

Week of ____________

Note: Prepare copies of this planner for one to three months in advance. Write things down! You will probably get more done if you do. The few minutes in planning are worth the effort . Mark special occasions although a specific column is not provided.

	To do:	To call:	To buy:	Meal
Monday				
Tuesday				
Wednesday				
Thursday				
Friday				
Saturday				
Sunday				

Daily Responsibilities

Day/Date______________

BREAKFAST

Responsibilities

Name					
Job					

Menu

P= Prepare, HP = Help prepare, ST = Set Table, C = Cleanup & dishes, HC = Help Cleanup & dishes

MORNING

Morning devotional: ______________________________

Household responsibilities

Name	Job

School responsibilities

Name	Assignments

LUNCH

Responsibilities

Name					
Job					

Menu

AFTERNOON

Responsibilities (schoolwork / project / service / activity)

Name	

Name	

DINNER / SUPPER

Responsibilities

Name					
Job					

Menu

EVENING

Evening devotional ______________________________

Activity

Individual Evaluation

Name ______________________________ Date ______________________

Strengths:

Weaknesses / needs:

Goals:

Goal	**Plan**
______________________	______________________
______________________	______________________
______________________	______________________
______________________	______________________
______________________	______________________
______________________	______________________

Progress / improvements:

Curriculum Sources

Student(s) ________________________ School Year ______________

Note: As you decide what materials you will use, it's not a bad idea to list them all in one place. Including specific information such as suppliers' addresses and book titles will avoid confusion when you are ready to order.

Subject / Unit	Materials and sources	Notes / How used

Curriculum Calendar

Student ____________________ School year __________

Time Blocks during the year

Subjects Or Units						

Subject or Unit Worksheet

Student (s) ______________________________ Subject / unit __________________

Grade level (approx.) __________________ School year ________________

Source of instruction:

- ❖ home instruction
- ❖ independent study
- ❖ co-op study
- ❖ tutor
- ❖ apprenticeship
- ❖ community college
- ❖ correspondence or similar
- ❖ internship
- ❖ ________________________

Goals:

Materials to be used Books, portions, reasons, etc.

Notes:

Weekly Plans and Progress

Name ______________________ Week ending ________________ Attendance: M ☐, T ☐, W ☐, Θ ☐, F ☐.

Subject / Unit

	Topics / assignments / experiences	Comments	Okay S	Okay T		Evaluation H	Evaluation Q
M							
T							
W							
Θ							
F							

S = student, T = teacher, H = homework or project, Q = test or quiz, Θ = Thursday (the Greek letter, theta – which is used for the "Th" sound)

Subject / Unit

	Topics / assignments / experiences	Comments	Okay S	Okay T		Evaluation H	Evaluation Q
M							
T							
W							
Θ							
F							

Subject / Unit

	Topics / assignments / experiences	Comments	Okay S	Okay T		Evaluation H	Evaluation Q
M							
T							
W							
Θ							
F							

Subject / Unit

	Topics / assignments / experiences	Comments	Okay S	Okay T		Evaluation H	Evaluation Q
M							
T							
W							
Θ							
F							

Subject / Unit

	Topics / assignments / experiences	Comments	Okay S	Okay T		Evaluation H	Evaluation Q
M							
T							
W							
Θ							
F							

Weekly Studies Log

Student ______________________ **Week of** ______________

Subject / Unit Topic / Time	Monday	Tuesday	Wednesday	Thursday	Friday	Weekly Grades	Other Weekly Items
	Attendance: ☐ Grade:	☐ Grade:	☐ Grade:	☐ Grade:	☐ Grade:		Goals:
	☐ Grade:	☐ Grade:	☐ Grade:	☐ Grade:	☐ Grade:		Project:
	☐ Grade:	☐ Grade:	☐ Grade:	☐ Grade:	☐ Grade:		Field trip:
	☐ Grade:	☐ Grade:	☐ Grade:	☐ Grade:	☐ Grade:		Writing: Book:
	☐ Grade:	☐ Grade:	☐ Grade:	☐ Grade:	☐ Grade:		Service:
	☐ Grade:	☐ Grade:	☐ Grade:	☐ Grade:	☐ Grade:		Spiritual:
	☐ Grade:	☐ Grade:	☐ Grade:	☐ Grade:	☐ Grade:		Notes / Comments: